Advance praise for

The Discursive-Material Knot

"*The Discursive-Material Knot* takes us to a highly significant, yet under-studied, region and provides a rich account of community based media in Cyprus. I particularly commend Nico Carpentier's fine work to bring together the discursive and the material on the basis of a well-researched case. This is a must-read for anyone who is interested in discourse theory and community media."

—*Miyase Christensen, Stockholm University, Sweden*

"Every few years a book offers great insight on the often contested relationship between citizen media and agency. *The Discursive-Material Knot is* one such remarkable contribution. Embracing both critical reflection of participation theories and analytical interpretation of empirical studies, this book articulates an original model that deepens understanding of community media and conflict transformation."

—*Tao Papaioannou, University of Nicosia, Cyprus*

"This book is a must-read! Guaranteed to make you think about the role of community media and its impact on conflict transformation. Nico Carpentier provides a detailed and sensitive analysis of the Cyprus conflict from its past to its present and offers valuable insight into to the many mechanisms at play in shaping its future."

—*Shirin Jetha, independent consultant*

"*The Discursive-Material Knot* will be an invaluable methodological toolkit for all those that will be researching community media organizations within the context of the ecological systems in which they operate. Its non-hierarchical nature and the use of a knot model for its analysis, is a very fitting tool to tackle the variety of diverse community media practices across the globe. The combination of highly theoretical work with empirical research, embedded within a mix of participatory use of qualitative research methods, promises to be a great resource for scholars and reflective practitioners alike."

—*Salvatore Scifo, Bournemouth University, United Kingdom*

More advance praise for

The Discursive-Material Knot

"Nico Carpentier's latest book on community media inspires the reader to imagine a 'non-hierarchical buffer zone' in 'triptych' form. Taking Cyprus as a case study is not only a courageous act, but also a transcending experiment for rhizomatic media creating their own agency... 'The discursive-material knot' is a creative referral throughout the book; a perpetual reminder of antagonistic interactions between conflict, community and participation."

—*Asli Telli Aydemir, Researcher and digital rights activist*

"Blending theory and collaborative research, this book presents discursive-material analyses of participation, community media organizations and conflict transformation with a case study so close to home. Nico Carpentier has been tirelessly exploring the Cypriot conflict through the lens of community media for years; this brilliant and comprehensive work comes as no surprise!"

—*Orestis Tringides and Hazal Yolga, Cyprus Community Media Centre and Cyprus Community Media Research Program researchers*

"In this inspiring and outstanding book, Nico Carpentier provides an innovative theoretical framework which allows understanding and explaining the complexity of civil society community media. This integrated interdisciplinary approach is complemented by a fascinating in-depth history and ethnography of Cypriot society and its range of—sometimes—agonistic media production and reception, thus succeeding in grounding the grand theories in discursive and material practices."

—*Ruth Wodak, Emeritus Professor, Lancaster University, United Kingdom, and University of Vienna, Austria*

This book is part of the Peter Lang Media and Communication list.
Every volume is peer reviewed and meets
the highest quality standards for content and production.

PETER LANG
New York • Bern • Frankfurt • Berlin
Brussels • Vienna • Oxford • Warsaw

The Discursive-Material

Nico Carpentier

The Discursive-Material Knot

Cyprus in Conflict and Community Media Participation

PETER LANG
New York • Bern • Frankfurt • Berlin
Brussels • Vienna • Oxford • Warsaw

Library of Congress Cataloging-in-Publication Data

Names: Carpentier, Nico, author.
Title: The discursive-material knot: Cyprus in conflict and community media participation / Nico Carpentier.
Description: New York: Peter Lang Publishing, Inc.
Includes bibliographical references and index.
Identifiers: LCCN 2017019217 | ISBN 978-1-4331-3753-2 (pbk.: alk. paper)
ISBN 978-1-4331-2885-1 (hardback: alk. paper) | ISBN 978-1-4331-3754-9 (epub)
ISBN 978-1-4331-3755-6 (epub) | ISBN 978-1-4331-3756-3 (mobi)
Subjects: LCSH: Discourse analysis—Social aspects—Cyprus.
Cyprus—History—Cyprus Crisis, 1974–
Classification: LCC P302.84.C37 2017 | DDC 401/.41—dc23
LC record available at https://lccn.loc.gov/2017019217
doi: 10.3726/978-1-4331-3754-9

Bibliographic information published by **Die Deutsche Nationalbibliothek**.
Die Deutsche Nationalbibliothek lists this publication in the "Deutsche Nationalbibliografie"; detailed bibliographic data are available on the Internet at http://dnb.d-nb.de/.

The paper in this book meets the guidelines for permanence and durability of the Committee on Production Guidelines for Book Longevity of the Council of Library Resources.

29 Broadway, 18th floor, New York, NY 10006
www.peterlang.com

Printed in the United States of America

CONTENTS

FIGURES

ACKNOWLEDGMENTS

Many people have been involved in this research project. Usually the most significant persons are kept to the end, but in this case I want to thank Vaia Doudaki first, as her help has been so indispensable. Also a number of other academics working in Cyprus and/or in Belgium have helped me a lot: Christophoros Christophorou, Tao Papaioannou, Karin Nys, Aysu Arsoy, and Tony Maslic should be mentioned here. The Cyprus University of Technology, and in particular the Department of Communication and Internet Studies has been most hospitable and supportive and I want to thank all my colleagues there, but in particular Stelios Stylianou, Angeliki Gazi, Yiannis Christidis, Yorgos Zotos, Nicolas Tsapatsoulis, Dimitra Milioni, Vasiliki Triga, and Venetia Papa. Also the old and new (PhD) researchers of the Cyprus Community Media Research Programme, Christiana Voniati, Derya Yüksek, Hazal Yolga, Orestis Tringides, and Nicolas Defteras, have helped me with my work on this project.

This project also had a group of people providing more direct support, as mappers, translators, or transcribers. Here I want to thank Christos Petrou, Ani Elmaoğlu, Charalampos Rizopoulos, Erini Avraam, Konstantina Neofytou, and Angeliki Boubouka for their work. A special thank you goes out to Nicolas (I only know his first name), who became our driver when our car broke down on a field trip in the Machairas Mountains.

At the very end of this research project, I was fortunate to be able to organize two editions of a photography exhibition, entitled '*Iconoclastic Controversies*,' reporting on a spin-off research project on nationalism. This project involved a large team of people, who did a wonderful job in putting this exhibition together, and I want to thank Helene Black, Yiannis Colakides, Eva Giannoukou, Yiannis Christidis (again), Fatma Nazli Köksal, Stella Theocharous, Nadia Kornioti, Shirin Jetha, and Christos Mais for the great job they did.

Also, staff and volunteers, former and current, at the CCMC were of great help, and I could not have completed this project without them. It is a group of people that proves on a daily basis that community media are possible. My warmest thanks to Michael Simopoulos, Orestis Tringides, Hazal Yolga, Natalie Konyalian, Larry Fergeson, Sarah Malian, Beran Djemal, Katherine Kotsireas, George Andriotis, Yiannis Ioannou, Yiorgos Kakouris, Doğukan Müezzinler, and Nicoletta Christodoulou. Also, my thanks to Seán Ó Siochrú, who briefed me on the period when CCMC was established.

Another group of people to thank are the participants of a PhD course at Helsinki University, who got to work with a first draft of this book, and who provided me with valuable feedback. They are: Jose Antonio Canada, Timo Juhani Harjuniemi, Ida Hummelstedt-Djedou, Laura Maria Huuskonen, Kamilla Mari Karhunmaa, Johanna Maria Kronstedt, Anastasia Orlova, Katarina Melica Elisabet Pettersson, Kinga Natalia Polynczuk-Alenius, Justyna Maria Pierzynska, Sehlem Sebik, Marko Tapani Stenroos, Tuure Johannes Tammi, Terhi Varonen, Satu Maarit Venäläinen, Yan Wang, and Ziyu Wang.

At the Vrije Universiteit Brussel (VUB), three people in the university administration and management, Erez Shimel, Kim Ongena, and Mieke Gijsemans, proved to be rock-solid and patient, and I am grateful to them for both characteristics. At the more institutional level, I also want to express my appreciation for the sabbatical grant provided by the VUB-OZR Research Council, for the research grant (G016114N) provided by the FWO, the Research Foundation—Flanders, and for the writing-up time provided by Uppsala University.

Finally, as always, the responsibility for any mistakes made in this book is solely mine, and not that of the people I thanked here. And, my apologies to the people I should have thanked here, but somehow, for inexplicable reasons, forgot ...

Earlier Publications

A number of texts, already published elsewhere or in the process of being published, have been used in this book, although their presence has become virtually invisible through their integration in the book's narrative. A first cluster of publications are related to discourse studies. This list includes the book chapter '*Deploying Discourse Theory*' (Carpentier, 2010), the journal article '*Discursive Structures in the Network Society*' (Carpentier, 2012), and the book chapter '*The Trinity of Decidedness, Undecidedness and Undecidability*' (Carpentier, 2016b). Forthcoming are the two following book chapters: '*Discourse*' in the *Keywords in Media Studies* book, edited by Laurie Ouellette and Jonathan Gray, and published by NYU Press; and '*Discourse-Theoretical Analysis (DTA)*' in the *Handbook of Critical Discourse Studies*, edited by John Flowerdew and John E. Richardson, and published by Routledge.

A second cluster deals with participation and community media, and includes six texts that have already been published: The book *Media and Participation* (Carpentier, 2011); the book chapters '*The Identity Constructions of Media Professionals*' (Carpentier, 2013a), '*Reality Television's Construction of Ordinary People*' (Carpentier, 2014b), '*Facing the Death of the Author*' (Carpentier, 2014f), '*Power as Participation's Master Signifier*' (Carpentier, 2016c), and the journal article '*Beyond the Ladder of Participation*' (Carpentier, 2016a).

A third and final cluster are the texts relating to Cyprus and CCMC. This list includes the book chapter '*Ethics, Killing and Dying*' (Carpentier, 2014d) and the journal articles '*Community Media for Reconciliation*,' co-authored with Vaia Doudaki (Carpentier & Doudaki, 2014); '*The Cypriot Web Radio MYCYRadio as a Participatory* Mélange' (Carpentier 2014a); '"*Fuck the Clowns From Grease!!" Fantasies of Participation and Agency in the YouTube Comments on a Cypriot Problem Documentary*' (Carpentier, 2014c), and '*Articulating Participation and Agonism*' (Carpentier, 2015a). Two book chapters are still forthcoming: '*Moulded in Bronze*' and '*Afterword: Studying Conflicts in Cyprus*,' both of which will be published in the edited volume *Cyprus and Its Conflicts: Representations, Materialities and Cultures*, edited by Vaia Doudaki and Nico Carpentier, and to be published by Berghahn. Also, the journal article '*Visual Sociology as a Tool to De-Naturalize Nationalism: A Case Study on Greek Cypriot Memorials*,' authored by Nico Carpentier, Vaia Doudaki, Yiannis Christidis, and Fatma Nazli Köksal is still forthcoming.

"I think there is a saying, anyway, that says that if you think you are very small to change things, try sleeping in the same room with a mosquito" (Focus group respondent FG10D_GNL).

THE INTRODUCTION OF A TRIPTYCH

It is unusual to refer to a book as a triptych. The concept of the triptych is often associated with the world of painting, and eras that have long since passed. It may even suggest an old-fashioned mind-set and/or an outdated perspective. Nevertheless, the allocation of such a prominent role to the concept is intentional, because it is vital for describing and understanding this book's intellectual project. A triptych consists of three panels that have a certain degree of independence but that are also part of a whole. These panels are three interdependent representations of reality, and that is exactly what this book aims to do, by creating three different platforms, bound together in one book.

This notion of the platform is equally helpful in explaining the approach that is used in this book. Inspiration has been found in Deleuze and Guattari's (1987) *A Thousand Plateaus*, although my book is a more modest version, with its ambition to offer only three platforms, and not a thousand. Still, the idea that each platform has a degree of independence, and can be accessed on its own right, remains, and the reader is invited to find her or his own way through the book. This independence is generated through the diversity of issues that are raised in the three platforms, and the different levels of abstraction that characterize them. At the same time, these platforms are still interconnected, articulated in one book, connected through the materiality of the paper on which the book is printed (or of the e-file by which it is distributed), but also by their alignment in the same research project. The three platforms came to fruition together, cross-fertilizing and affecting each other, talking to each other, and sometimes giving the author an idea of their collective agency, with one platform making demands on the other platform (luckily still requiring the author's intervention). In a slightly more down-to-earth version: The interconnection of the three platforms is generated and protected by the iterative-cyclical methodology deployed throughout the entire research project. Whatever version is preferred: The collective genesis of the three platforms binds them together, in a more intimate way than the platform metaphor, or the book's unavoidably linear way of writing, might suggest, even when the three platforms continue to claim their independence, inviting to be read in their own right.

What unifies these platforms, and characterizes this book, is a choice for a radical combination of theory and empirical research. This implies, first of all, a very strong presence of high theory, and the high levels of abstraction that coincide with high theory. Moreover, the book consistently uses the constructionist paradigm, and is deeply invested in post-structuralist theory, both of which have a tendency to come across as more abstract (even though I would contest this, as the sense of abstraction is also influenced by conceptual familiarity). In particular, the first platform, with its discussion of the ontology of the discursive-material knot, might give the reader the feeling of being catapulted into an orbit around the planet, finding herself, or himself, in the position of reading a text that is disconnected from the realities of everyday life. Again, this needs to be contested. The production of high theory in itself is of crucial importance, even if it does not immediately serve empirical research. Also, the first platform—with its ontological focus—speaks clearly about, and to, our world, in the most fundamental way possible. But Platform 1 does even more: It also prepares the ground for a series of theoretical re-readings of very different, but still very needed, theoretical concepts, from a variety of fields, namely, participatory theory, community media theory, conflict theory, conflict resolution/transformation theory (all in Platform 2), and theories of nationalism (in Platform 3).

But these theoretical reflections, as found in Platform 1, were not produced in a void. A radical combination of high theory and empirical research implies a confrontation between this high theory and a specific social reality, where the latter is entitled to talk back to the theory, to challenge, alter, and enrich it. Even if the data are always mediated through theoretical frameworks, this does *not* mean that these theoretical frameworks should be given the right to colonize a social reality, impose themselves upon it and smother it in the process. In this book, the choice was made for a particular socio-organizational reality: The Cyprus Community Media Center (CCMC) and its webradio station, MYCYradio, within the context of the Cyprus Problem—a choice that brings about the risk of simply adding to the libraries of books that have already been written about this conflict. The theoretical tools developed in Platform 1 and Platform 2 will be used (as sensitizing concepts—an analytical strategy that will be discussed at the end of Platform 1) for an analysis of the role that CCMC and MYCYradio, as a participatory community media assemblage, can play in the transformation of the Cyprus Problem, or, in other words, in the transformation of antagonism into agonism.

This third platform, with its two chapters, is extensive, as it contains a detailed analysis of the Cyprus Problem, first reverting to a factual historical narrative, providing an academic-historical anchorage point that is very necessary in a conflict where almost every historical event is contested. This historical narrative is then re-analyzed to comprehend the workings of the discursive-material knot in the Cyprus Problem. Although this extensive contextual analysis might seem superfluous at first glance, this analysis has intensively strengthened both the theoretical analyses in Platform 1 and Platform 2, and the CCMC/MYCYradio analysis in the second chapter of Platform 3. In the second chapter of Platform 3, CCMC and MYCYradio are analyzed, first as a participatory assemblage, and then as an agonist assemblage. The concluding reflection analyzes the articulation of participation and agonism.

This (finally) brings me to the main title of my book, to what provides the foundation of this entire book, with its three platforms, namely, the concept of the discursive-material knot. This concept has been chosen (and developed) to emphasize the need for bringing the discursive and the material, both theoretically and empirically, closer together. Different theoretical frameworks and traditions have identified this need, and this book is definitely not the first plea to study what Hardy and Thomas (2015: 692) have very recently called "[...] the material effects of discourse and the discursive effects of materiality [...]." I even have the luxury of being able to point to an earlier article of my own (Carpentier, 2012), where I argued for this theoretical model to be developed. This is not an easy project, though, and many of the existing reflections on the discursive and the material have ended up (implicitly or explicitly) privileging one of the two components.

The theoretical framework of the discursive-material knot that I want to introduce and support with this book does not privilege the discursive over the material, or the material over the discursive. The discursive-material knot is a non-hierarchical ontology that theorizes the knotted interactions of the discursive and the material as restless and contingent, sometimes incessantly changing shapes and sometimes deeply sedimented. But this relation of interdependence will never result in one component becoming more important than the other. In this sense, the metaphor of the knot is important to express this intense and inseparable entanglement, but we should also acknowledge the limits of this metaphor and keep in mind that the knot can never be unraveled or disentangled. What we can do, as analysts of the discursive-material knot, is follow the rope (a bit like Actor Network Theory (ANT) researchers 'follow the actor'—see Law, 1991; Ruming, 2009). Even then, we should remain realistic about what (academic) language allows us to do, and the constraints it creates. Having to work with (academic) language sometimes, for merely analytical reasons, causes the discursive and the material component to be discussed separately, in a particular order. One component always has to come first, but this is done without ever implying that their relationship is hierarchical.

Equally important to keep in mind is that the ontology of the discursive-material knot operates at all levels of the social. Here, Foucault's (1977) 'micro-physics of power' offers a good parallel to the multi-level nature of the discursive-material knot. Foucault argued in *Discipline and Punish* that the workings of power enter the micro-processes of the social, structuring all our social relations. A similar argument can be made for the discursive-material knot. The knotted interaction of the discursive and the material—in always particular and contingent ways—structures large-scale assemblages, such as state apparatuses, armies, or markets, but it also enters into the micro-processes of the everyday without these different levels ever becoming disconnected.

In order to capture the translation of the discursive-material knot into social practice, the concept of the assemblage is used. While the discursive-material knot is located at the ontological level, the assemblage is positioned in this book at the ontic level, in order to theorize how the flows that characterize the social, with their endless range of possibilities to become fixated and to fixate, are arrested and channeled into particular combinations of the discursive and the material. It is the assemblage that enables us to think of the social as a tapestry, characterized by assemblages with their increased densities, surrounded by ever-moving flows. This is very reminiscent of Laclau and Mouffe's (1985: 112) description of how a discourse functions (which is explicitly inspired by Lacan), and can be expanded to the workings of the discursive-material assemblage: "Any discourse is constituted as an attempt to dominate the field of discursivity, to arrest the flow of differences, to construct a centre."

In developing this theoretical reflection about the discursive-material knot, one has to start somewhere, and as the previous citation already suggests, Laclau and Mouffe's (1985) discourse theory will be the starting point to construct my theoretical reflections about the discursive-material knot, as their discourse theory has been my theoretical and intellectual home for a very long time (and still is). These dialogues with discourse theory will lead to a mild re-thinking of Laclau and Mouffe's work, taking some of the critiques on discourse theory into consideration,[1] oscillating between loyalty and disloyalty, in always respectful ways for their work, and for the closely related work of some of their colleagues (in particular Butler, 1990, 1993, 1997). This re-thinking is aimed at expanding discourse theory, infusing (or infecting) it with the material, and using the mutation to feed further theoretizations and empirical research. At the same time, this re-thinking remains faithful to the basic logic of discourse theory, which results in a radically consistent use of the discourse-theoretical conceptual frameworks (e.g., the distinction between discourses and signifying practices) to think through the discursive-material knot in its entirety.

As this book remains firmly grounded in discourse theory, I need to briefly explain the particularity of its approach towards discourse, which is defined (following Laclau, 1988: 254) as "[…] a structure in which meaning is constantly negotiated and constructed […]." This definition implies the preference for a macro-textual usage of the discourse concept—related to what is known as a big D discourse definition—which treats discourse as a concept closely related to (but not synonymous with) ideology (as will be explained more in Platform 1). Although discourse theory continuously emphasized the importance of the material (see, for instance, Laclau and Mouffe's (1990: 101) reference to radical materialism), there is still a need to expand the theoretical reflections on the discursive-material knot, and the ways that the discursive and the material are interconnected. Moreover, this reconciliation is also constructive from an analytical point of view, as it allows for a much richer analysis, not merely focusing on media talk, for instance, but also on the contextualized processes of discursive-ideological production and their material components.

This expanding-discourse-theory project loudly acknowledges the accomplishments of 'old' materialisms—after all, Laclau and Mouffe's discourse theory is a post-Marxist theory—but it is particularly sympathetic towards the developments in the field of new materialism,[2] which aims to rethink and revalidate the role of the material in cultural theory. In this approach (or set of approaches), the material is seen as "agential matter" (Barad, 2007: 246) or "generative matter," a concept that Dolphijn and van der Tuin (2012: 93) attributed to DeLanda (1996). Dolphijn and van der Tuin (2012: 93) immediately added to their reference to "generative matter" that the new materialist approaches are aimed at avoiding being locked in the dualism of "matter-of-opposed-to-signification." Instead, new materialism "[…] captures *mattering* as simultaneously material and representational […]" (Dolphijn and van der Tuin, 2012: 93), a crucial position that prevents either the role of the discursive in producing meaning, or the agentic role of the material, being ignored. A similar position can be found with Rahman and Witz (2003: 256), when they wrote:

> "The social constructionism being worked at here is not one that is limited by physical matter, but rather one that is able to incorporate body matters as an indivisible part of lived, gendered experience and action. Thus the scope of the social or the cultural evoked […] confronts the limits of constructionism, whether sociological or discursive, by sometimes admitting, sometimes asserting the body as a problematic yet inescapable component of a social ontology of gender and sexuality."

The new materialist agenda is translated in a focus on a "material-semiotic actor" (Haraway, 1988: 595), or the use of a "material-discursive" (Barad, 2007) approach, which is indeed closely related to the discursive-material knot approach advocated here. At the risk of engaging in a semantic play: The order of the two concepts, as the discursive-material, matters. It is important, first of all, to emphasize that the starting point of my book is discourse-theoretical, which is then combined with an effort to make the material more visible in this discourse-theoretical strand. This more developed approach towards the discursive has an additional advantage, as it enriches new materialism and enables us to think more in detail *how* the discursive and the material are entangled. Also, the label of the discursive-material knot is used here to generate distance from some of the new materialist stances that are not shared. Although I am very sympathetic towards the idea of moving away from the discursive-material dualism, and I applaud the existence of pleas to strike a balance, the alleged domination of the representational, and the need to give the representational and linguisticality "[...] its proper place, that is, a more modest one [...]" (Dolphijn and van der Tuin, 2012: 98), is sometimes hard to agree with. There are more kind versions (e.g., Kirby, 2006), but also some of the new materialist language towards post-structuralist authors, such as Butler, is slightly uncomfortable. This citation from Barad (2007: 145—my emphasis) contains some of the language that generates my discomfort:

> "[...] however, Butler's concern is limited to the production of human bodies (and only certain aspects of their production, at that), and her theorization of materialization is *parasitic* on Foucault's notions of regulatory power and discursive practices, which are limited to the domain of human social practices."

This quote also brings us to the post-humanist agenda, which is (sometimes) part of new materialism. Again, much sympathy exists here for the idea (developed within ANT) that the agency concept can be applied to the material, but I am less sympathetic towards the idea that also the notion of discourse (production)—at least in the way I use it in this book—can, and even *should*, be more than a social-human process. This opens the door for the idea that non-humans are able to produce discourses. Barad (2007: 148) formulated this post-humanist approach towards discourse as follows: "However, the common belief that discursive practices and meanings are peculiarly human phenomena won't do." Actually, for me, it will do perfectly. Or, in other words, the choice of the label of discursive-material analysis (and not for Barad's "material-discursive" approach) is also legitimated by my preference for a more anthropocentric definition of discourse, as will be used in this book.

To further support and enrich the combination of the discursive and the material, a second dimension, the structure/agency dimension, will be added. This addition is not intended to undermine the importance of the discursive-material knot, but the structure/agency dimension assists in better explaining the workings and dynamics of the discursive-material knot. Also, discursive-theoretical frameworks are sometimes perceived as structuralist, and, as such, as being at odds with human freedom and agency, while new materialist theories are seen to exaggerate the role of agency. By explicitly incorporating the structure/agency dimension into what will be visually represented as a four-component model (in Platform 1), a more nuanced perspective on the relationship between the discursive and the material, its structuring capacities, and the ways it actually allows for human freedom and agency, will be provided. Finally, the introduction of structure and agency into the analysis also enables a more nuanced perspective on the social, where the overdetermined and contingent logic of structure, which is both enabling and disabling, is combined with a plurality of subjectivations and identifications, invitations and dislocations.

The theoretical development of the discursive-theoretical knot aims to engage scholars from a number of academic fields in a constructive dialogue. One of these fields is communication and media studies, the field in which I am still very much embedded (and indebted to), which is also a field whose theoretical backbone needs further strengthening. Communication and media studies' embrace of the discourse concept has been ambiguous, even though discourse is a crucial vehicle for communicating ideas, and merits a more prominent position in communication and media studies. Although some progress has been made (e.g., Colman, 2014), it is also time for the material to become more explicitly visible in all subfields of communication and media studies. Secondly, I would like to argue that the development of the discursive-material knot is one way to take a step back from the still-existing tension (or semi-latent struggle) between cultural studies and (critical) political economy. This ontology offers another route of thinking about the relationship between the discursive-representational and the materiality of the economy. This strategy might be better than each side trying to explain to the other that the self has been misunderstood (as Garnham, 1995, did), or trying to create a new enemy to unite both (as Babe, 2010, did). By now, the reader can guess that I am not too sympathetic towards Babe's (2010: 196) proposal to solve this conflict, summarized as follows: "Reintegrating critical political economy and cultural studies also means, most fundamentally, setting aside poststructuralist cultural studies. In fact, if poststructuralist cultural studies is disregarded, political economy and cultural studies (cultural materialism) are united already." In contrast, I would like to argue that a way out of this conflict might be to organize a more fundamental reflection about the discursive and the material, as this book does in its own way, accompanied by the immediate acknowledgement that many other routes remain open. Finally, the development of the theoretical framework of the discursive-material knot might also reach out to scholars committed to discourse studies and to new materialism, calling upon them to make further progress in better theorizing entanglement and in genuinely balancing the material and the discursive, without one of these two components (and together with that one, the entire field of its academic supporters) having to win a glorious victory, not even in the last instance. A tie is just as good.

Notes

1. Some of these critiques were discussed in Carpentier and Spinoy (2008).
2. Dolphijn and van der Tuin (2012: 93) located the origins of the label 'new materialism'—with the work of Manuel DeLanda and Rosi Braidotti from the second half of the 1990s.

PLATFORM 1

· 1 ·

RECONCILING THE DISCURSIVE AND THE MATERIAL—A KNOTTED THEORETICAL FRAMEWORK

Platform 1 of this book contains the detailed development of the two dimensions that provide the theoretical backbone for the entire work. The first dimension, the discursive and the material, forms the very heart of the book's theoretical framework. Here, the main argument is that we need to understand the relationship between the discursive and the material as a knot, where both components are intrinsically, intensely, and intimately entangled (see Barad, 2007; Gamble & Hanan, 2016), without either of the components being necessarily dominant. Fraser (1997: 15), writing in a very different context, formulates this idea as follows:

> "Even the most material economic institutions have a constitutive, irreducible cultural dimension; they are shot through with significations and norms. Conversely, even the most discursive cultural practices have a constitutive, irreducible political-economic dimension; they are underpinned by material supports."

The metaphor of the Gordian knot may come to mind here, but it might not be the best one, as the simple stroke of a sword will not suffice to deal with this knot. What this theoretical discussion aims to do instead, is to provide an understanding of how the material and the discursive interact, without attempting to untie the knot, or, in other words, without segregating the material and the discursive, even though, for analytical reasons, the two concepts are used (and distinguished). In contrast, the knot is seen as constitutive for the discursive, for the material, and for the social. Instead of dissecting the knot, and in the process privileging one of its components, this part aims to develop a particular theoretical toolbox that can be used to better understand these interrelationships, and the knot as an entangled whole.

Still, one has to start somewhere, also because one is rooted in always specific theoretical traditions and ontological perspectives. In this case, Laclau and Mouffe's (1985) discourse theory provides me with the starting point of the theoretical voyage across these two dimensions. There are many reasons for this choice, and my theoretical rootedness is only one of them. This specific discourse theory has a strong potential for reaching out the material, which makes it particularly suitable for a non-hierarchical approach towards the discursive and the material. It also provides a proper counter-balance for new materialist approaches that tend to (mostly implicitly) privilege the material.[1] And, finally, discourse theory's positioning of the notion of discourse at the macro-societal level (at a similar level as ideology and knowledge) facilitates the constructive dialogue with more materialist approaches.

Even if the second dimension, structure and agency, is cast in a more supportive role, its significance for understanding the discursive-material knot cannot be overestimated, while at the same time, the structure/agency dimension remains an intrinsic part of this knot. It is no coincidence that the first platform of the book has a nested structure in which the discursive/material dimension 'embraces' the structure/agency dimension. This implies that the book's narration flows, in the first four subparts, from discourse, to structure, to agency, and then to the material (also spending a lot of attention on the material). After discussing the two dimensions, the knotted relationships between its four components are thematized in the fifth subpart, this time starting from agency. Again, this way of structuring the text illustrates the importance of the structure/agency dimension. Using this dimension (as a dimension) offers a counterweight to the (rather unfounded) critiques of structuralism launched at discourse theories, and for the (equally unfair) critiques deployed against the use of agency in (new) materialist theories. Here too, a balanced and non-hierarchical approach towards agency and structure is taken on board.

Finally, I want to repeat that this book, with its three platforms, has three entry points, which also has repercussions for how the first theoretical platform is read. One way of reading consists of articulating this first platform of the book as an autonomous theoretical reflection on the two dimensions and their knotted interactions. Another way of reading sees this platform as a starting point for the rest of this book. Even if I consider the first way of reading as just as legitimate as the second way, it is important to stress one more time that the *development* of this first platform was dependent on the second and third platforms of the book (following the iterative/cyclical logic of qualitative research), which renders the three parts interdependent, at least in the way they came into being.

1 The Discursive

Discourse is a concept that is used in a wide variety of approaches, many of which are located in the field of discourse studies. As is often the case with academic concepts, their plurality of meanings is an interesting research topic in itself, but at the same time, when the discourse concept needs to be put to work, clarity and specification remain a necessity. In the latter scenario, Foucault's (1972: 80) slightly ironizing statement about his approach to the discourse concept might not be the most helpful route in dealing with this semantic diversity, even though it nicely illustrates its existence:

> "Instead of gradually reducing the rather fluctuating meaning of the word 'discourse', I believe I have in fact added to its meanings: treating it sometimes as the general domain of all statements, sometimes as an individualizable group of statements, and sometimes as a regulated practice that accounts for a number of statements."

In order to further show this diversity of meanings attributed to the concept of discourse, and to situate my choice for a particular approach in relationship to the discourse concept—namely discourse theory—within the broader field of discourse studies, we can firstly distinguish between micro-textual and macro-textual approaches (see Carpentier & De Cleen, 2007, for an earlier version of this argument). In the micro-textual approaches of discourse, the concept's close affiliation with language is emphasized, an approach we can also label, following Philips and Jørgensen (2002: 62), discourse-as-language. Van Dijk's (1997: 3) definition provides us with a helpful illustration: "Although many discourse analysts specifically focus on spoken language or talk, it is [...] useful to include also written texts in the concept of discourse." Macro-textual approaches use a broader definition of text, much in congruence with Barthes (1975), seeing texts as materializations of meaning and/or ideology. In this macro-textual approach, where discourse becomes discourse-as-representation, or discourse-as-ideology, the focus is placed on the meanings, representations, or ideologies embedded in the text, and not so much on the language used. One related (but not entirely overlapping) strategy to distinguish between more micro-textual and more macro-textual approaches is Gee's (1990) distinction between 'big D' Discourse and 'little d' discourse, where the latter refers to "[…] connected stretches of language that make sense, like conversations, stories, reports, arguments, essays […]" (Gee, 1990: 142). Big D Discourse is "[…] always more than just language," and refers to "[…] saying (writing)-doing-being-valuing-believing combinations" (Gee, 1990: 142—emphasis removed). One could argue that 'thinking' and 'knowing' should be added to Gee's list, to describe the approaches at the very end of the macro-textual part of the micro/macro-textual spectrum, but Gee's approach remains important in mapping the diversity in the field of discourse studies.

A second distinction that enables us to map the different meanings of the discourse concept is that between micro- and macro-contextual approaches. Micro-contextual approaches confine the context to specific social settings (such as a speech act or a conversation). We can take conversation analysis as example, where—according to Heritage's (1984: 242—my emphasis) interpretation—context is defined at a micro-level: "A speaker's action is context-shaped in that its contribution to an on-going sequence of actions cannot adequately be understood except by reference to the context—including, *especially, the immediately preceding configuration of actions*—in which it participates." Heritage (1984: 242) continued: "[…] every 'current' action will itself form the immediate context for some 'next' action in a sequence […]." Another example is sociolinguistics' emphasis on the linguistic rule system, the syntactic and lexical planning strategies, and speech codes to explain discourse, as Dittmar (1976: 12) explained. But it would be unfair to claim that micro-contextual approaches remain exclusively focused on the micro-context, even if that is where they are rooted. Sociolinguistics, with its emphasis on social groupings, class positions, social relations, and sociocultural and situational rules (Dittmar, 1976: 12) is a case in point. Nevertheless, the role of context in macro-contextual is structurally different, as these approaches look at how discourses circulate within the social, paying much less attention to more localized settings (or micro-contexts). This leads to much broader analyses, for instance, how democratic discourse (Laclau and Mouffe, 1985) or gender identity (Butler, 1990) is articulated within the social. Again, the emphasis on the macro-context of the social does not imply a complete disregard of the micro-contexts of language, social settings, or social practices, although the starting point of these approaches remains embedded in the macro-levels. A more streamlined version of this debate, and the many different positions, can be found in Figure 1.

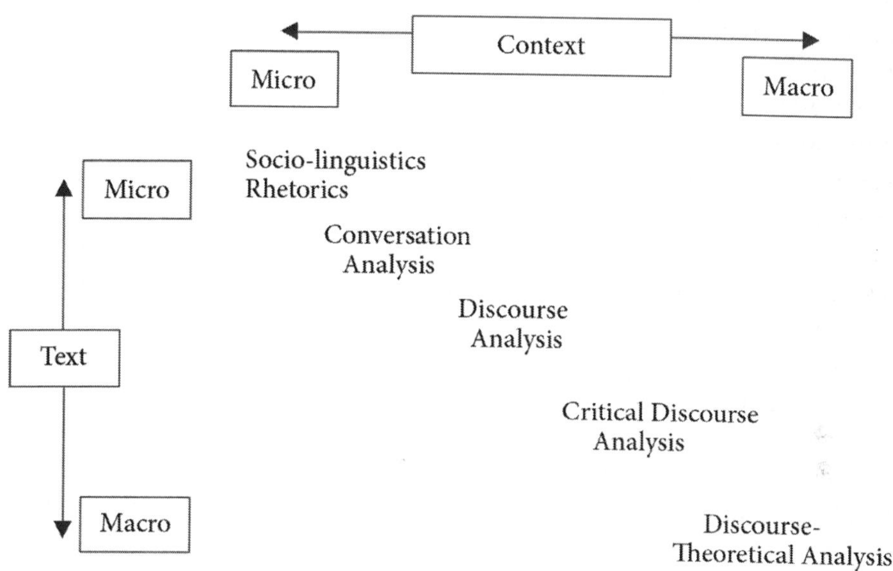

Figure 1. Approaches to discourse.
Source: Carpentier and De Cleen, 2007: 277.

In this book, the macro-textual and macro-contextual approach of discourse theory is preferred, exactly for its broad and encompassing conceptualization of discourse, which will more easily enable it to connect to a discussion on the material, and will more easily support an analysis of conflict transformation. But, as discourse theory also still has different strands, more specificity is needed. A first choice is made for what Glynos and Howarth (2007: 4) called poststructuralist discourse theory, but even in this subfield the diversity is considerable. For this reason, the choice is made to deploy Laclau and Mouffe's (1985) strand of discourse theory, as it was first fully developed in *Hegemony and Socialist Strategy* (*HSS*), and not so much the Foucauldian strand of discourse theory,[2] as, for instance, can be found in *The Archaeology of Knowledge* (1972), or any other strand, for that matter.

Laclau and Mouffe's (1985) *HSS* is a highly valuable, complex, and slightly hermetic work, which—as has been argued elsewhere (Carpentier & De

Cleen, 2007; Carpentier & Spinoy, 2008)—can be read on three interrelated levels. The first level, which we can call discourse theory in the strict sense, refers to Laclau and Mouffe's social ontology (Howarth, 2000: 17) and to the position they negotiated between materialism and idealism, between structure and agency. At this level, we can find the vocabulary and the mechanics of discourse theory. A second—and strongly related—level is what Smith (1999: 87) has called Laclau and Mouffe's political identity theory, which is tributary to conflict theory. Key concepts at this level are hegemony, antagonism, and the later-added agonism. Here, (more) attention is given to how discourses, identities, and their nodal points are constructed and obtain fixity through political processes. Laclau and Mouffe's post-Marxist approach becomes even more evident at the third level, where their plea for a radical democratic politics places them in the field of democratic theory. Laclau and Mouffe (1985: 190) still situated themselves within the "classic ideal of socialism," but at the same time pleaded for a "polyphony of voice" in which the different (radical) democratic political struggles—such as antiracism, antisexism, and anticapitalism—are allotted an equally important role (Mouffe, 1997: 18).

In this brief introduction to discourse theory, I will focus on the first two levels only, as the third level finds its main application within democratic theory, which is less relevant here. At the first (ontological) level of Laclau and Mouffe's discourse theory, their interpretation of the key notion of discourse is developed. Their theoretical starting point is that all social phenomena and objects obtain their meaning(s) through discourse, which is defined as "[…] a structure in which meaning is constantly negotiated and constructed" (Laclau, 1988: 254). Discourse thus becomes a very necessary part of our social reality, as it provides us with the frameworks of intelligibility. To use Howarth's (2000: 101) words: "The concept of discourse in Laclau and Mouffe's theory captures the idea that all objects and actions are meaningful, and that their meaning is conferred by particular systems of significant differences."

This position has a series of implications. First of all, the discursive becomes seen as a dimension of our social world that spans it in its entirety and not as a delimited part of it. Laclau and Mouffe "[…] reject the idea that ideological practices simply constitute one area or 'region' of social relations" (Howarth & Stavrakakis, 2000: 4). Later, Laclau (2014: 169) was even more clear in his reference to class and the Marxist base/superstructure model: "Articulations are not the superstructure of anything, but the primary terrain of constitution of social objectivity."

Secondly, Laclau and Mouffe's position does not imply that the existence of the material is questioned (see also later), only that they deny that extra-discursive meaning exists, very much in line with Hall's interpretation, which rejects "The idea that 'discourse produces the objects of knowledge' and that nothing which is meaningful exists *outside discourse* [...]" (Hall, 1997a: 44—emphasis in original). In Hall's statement, the presence of the words "nothing is meaningful" is crucial, as he (similar to Laclau and Mouffe) did not want to argue that "nothing exists but discourse," which is a common misunderstanding when discussing discourse theory (and constructionism in general). Also, Butler (1993: 6) referred to this misunderstanding when she wrote: "Critics making that presumption can be heard to say, 'If everything is discourse, what about the body?'" Discourse theory acknowledges the existence of the material (including the body) as structurally different from the discursive, but it also rejects the "[...] classical dichotomy between an objective field constituted outside of any discursive intervention, and a discourse consisting of the pure expression of thought" (Laclau & Mouffe, 1985: 108). Discourse is not the same as the material, but still very necessary to make sense of it. One of the examples Laclau and Mouffe (1990: 108) used to explain the indispensable role of the discursive is that of the stone, which "[...] exists independently of any system of social relation [...] it is, for instance, either a projectile or an object of aesthetic contemplation only within a specific discursive configuration."

Laclau and Mouffe (1985: 105) also defined the concept of discourse as a structured entity that is the result of articulation, which is, in turn, viewed as "[...] any practice establishing a relation among elements[3] such that their identity is modified as a result of the articulatory practice." The articulation of these elements produces discourses that gain a certain (and very necessary) degree of stability. Discursive stability is enhanced by the role of privileged signifiers, or nodal points. Torfing (1999: 88–89) pointed out that these nodal points "[...] sustain the identity of a certain discourse by constructing a knot of definite meanings." Or, to use Laclau and Mouffe's (1985: 113) words:

> "The practice of articulation consists in the construction of nodal points which partially fix meaning; and the partial character of this fixation proceeds from the openness of the social, a result, in its turn, of the constant overflowing of every discourse by the infinitude of the field of discursivity."

Hall (1996a: 141—emphasis in original) gave the following description of articulation:

> "[...] the form of the connection that *can* make a unity of two different elements, under certain conditions. It is a linkage which is not necessary, determined, absolute and essential for all time. You have to ask under what circumstances *can* a connection be forged or made? The so-called 'unity' of a discourse is really the articulation of different, distinct elements which can be re-articulated in different ways because they have no necessary 'belongingness.'"

Discourses have to be partially fixed, since the abundance of meaning would otherwise make any meaning impossible: "[...] a discourse incapable of generating any fixity of meaning is the discourse of the psychotic," as Laclau and Mouffe (1985: 112) wrote. But discursive fixations are not given; they are the result of social interventions that produce particular articulations of particular discourses. These articulations select signifying elements from the discursive reservoir that Laclau and Mouffe (1985: 111) called the field of discursivity,[4] and integrate them within a particular discourse, contributing to their particularity. By producing these particular fixations, discourses are "[...] an attempt to dominate the field of discursivity, to arrest the flow of differences, to construct a centre" (Laclau and Mouffe, 1985: 112). And this, in turn, renders articulation a political intervention, which generates meaning in always particular ways through the logic of fixation.

But this fixity is only partial, and Laclau and Mouffe emphasized the contingency of discourses at several levels (see Carpentier and Van Brussel, 2012). At their first level of discourse theory, the notion of the field of discursivity (Laclau and Mouffe, 1985: 112), which was mentioned only a few lines previously, plays an important role to think this contingency, as the field of discursivity contains an infinite number of elements that are not connected to a specific discourse at a given moment in time. Instability enters the equation through the idea that these unconnected elements can always *become* articulated within a specific discourse, sometimes replacing (or disarticulating) other elements, which affects the discourse's meaning. Due to the infinitude of the field of discursivity and the inability of a discourse to permanently keep its meaning fixated and its elements stable, discourses are liable to disintegration and re-articulation. Another way that the overdetermination of discourses (and the impossibility to reach "a final closure" (Howarth, 1998: 273)) is made explicit is through the concept of the floating signifier. This concept is defined as a signifier that is "overflowed with meaning" (Torfing, 1999: 301). Floating signifiers will, in other words, assume different meanings in different contexts/discourses, again enhancing contingency. Thirdly, and later on (mainly), Laclau referred to the Lacanian concept of lack to theorize this structural openness. For Laclau (1996: 92), the contingency of structures originates from "[...] the structure [not being] fully reconciled with itself [...]" and "[...] inhabited by an original lack, by a radical undecidability that needs to be constantly superseded by acts of decision."

At the second level of discourse theory, we can find more emphasis on political processes and discursive struggles, for whose analysis two key notions are mobilized in *HSS*: hegemony and antagonism.[5] For Laclau and Mouffe, hegemony refers to situations where particular discourses obtain social dominance. Originally, Gramsci (1999: 261) defined this notion in relation to the dominance that social actors obtained through the creation of alliances. For Gramsci, this dominance was based on the formation of consent, rather than on the (exclusive) domination of the other, without, however, excluding a certain form of pressure and repression: "The 'normal' exercise of hegemony [...] is characterized by the combination of force and consent variously balancing one another, without force exceeding consent too much." Howarth (1998: 279) described Laclau and Mouffe's interpretation of Gramsci—an interpretation that focuses more on the discursive—as follows: "[...] hegemonic practices are an exemplary form of political articulation which involves linking together different identities into a common project." The objective of hegemonic projects is to construct and stabilize nodal points that are the basis of a social order, the main aim being to become a social imaginary, or the horizon that "[...] is not one among other objects but an absolute limit which structures a field of intelligibility and is thus the condition of possibility of the emergence of any object" (Laclau, 1990a: 64).

If we turn to a more psycho-analytical vocabulary, we can say that social imaginaries are fantasies that enable an overcoming of the lack generated by the contingency of the social and the structural impossibility of attaining reality (or the Real, as Lacan would have it). In Lacanian psycho-analytic theory, fantasy is conceptualized as having (among others) a protective role (Lacan, 1979: 41). In providing the subject with discourse, which attempt to conceal and finally to overcome the lack (Lacan, 1994: 119–120), fantasy functions as "[...] the support that gives consistency to what we call 'reality'" (Žižek, 1995: 44). Subjects "[...] push away reality in fantasy" (Lacan, 1999: 107); in order to make reality consistent, social imaginaries are produced, accepted, and then taken for granted.

As Marchart (2007: 139) put it, "hegemonic success" results in what Laclau (1990a)—inspired by Husserl—labeled sedimentation. The moment of sedimentation occurs when a hegemonic order is established, resulting in the forgetting of its constructed nature and its articulation as natural and objective. In this scenario, a social imaginary is created, which pushes other meanings beyond the horizon, threatening them with oblivion. Sedimentation implies a "forgetting of the origins" where "[…] the system of possible alternatives tends to vanish and the traces of the original contingency to fade" (Laclau, 1990a: 34). For Laclau, these sedimented forms constitute what he called 'the social,' which is contrasted with 'the political.' Even when the political can become reactivated and attempt to politicize sedimented meanings (and thus de-sediment them), the social remains the backdrop of these interventions: "Any political construction takes place against the background of a range of sedimented practices" (Laclau, 1990a: 35). One significant implication of this line of reasoning is that not everything is political at a given time and space.

Laclau's emphasis on the political is related to the idea that hegemonic practices still suppose an open system, which makes articulation possible. In a closed system there would only be repetition, and nothing could be hegemonized (Laclau and Mouffe, 1985: 134). Mere articulation, however, is not sufficient to be able to speak of hegemony. According to Laclau and Mouffe (1985: 135–136), antagonisms that link elements in so-called chains of equivalence are a prerequisite: "[…] in other words, that hegemony should emerge in a field criss-crossed by antagonisms and therefore suppose phenomena of equivalence and frontier effects. But, conversely, not every antagonism supposes hegemonic practices." Antagonisms have both negative and positive aspects, as they attempt to destabilize the 'other' identity but desperately need that very 'other' as a constitutive outside to stabilize the proper identity. An example of an antagonism can be found in Howarth (2000: 106):

> "Consider the emergence of the Black Consciousness Movement in South Africa during the late 1960s and early 1970s […]. In its formative stages, leaders of this movement constructed a series of antagonistic relationships with different groups within South African society. These included white liberals, the National Party and its apartheid project, as well as other anti-apartheid organisations—the exiled African National Congress and its allies such as the Natal Indian Congress and the Inkatha Movement led by Mangosuthu Buthelezi. Their discourse emphasized that the main 'blockage' to their identity was 'white racism', which systematically denied and prevented the construction and assertion of a black identity. Their political project endeavored to link together all those who were opposed to apartheid and who identified themselves as black, rather than 'non-white' or 'non-racial', by instituting a political frontier dividing the South African society into two antagonistic camps organized around the black/'anti-black' division […]."

This logic of equivalence and the creation of chains of equivalence is, for Laclau and Mouffe, the main answer to the question of how antagonisms are discursively constructed. In these chains, different identities are aligned with each other—made equivalent—and opposed to another negative identity. To put this differently: In the logic of equivalence, a number of identities are brought into one discourse, which unites them without dissolving their specificity. Howarth (2000: 107) used as illustration the letters a, b, and c for the equivalent identities (in which a≈b≈c) and the letter d for the negative identity. The logic of the equivalence results in the formula d = −(a, b, c), of which the final result is the coming into being of two antagonistic poles. Laclau (1988: 256) gave an example of a possible chain of equivalence:

> "For instance, if I say that, from the point of view of the interests of the working class, liberals, conservatives, and radicals are all the same, I have transformed three elements that were different into substitutes within a chain of equivalence."

Laclau and Mouffe also discerned logics of difference, in which existing chains of equivalence are broken and the elements incorporated into another discursive order (Howarth, 1998: 277). As opposed to the logic of the equivalence, the logic of difference weakens existing antagonisms. Applied to Howarth's play with the four letters this would mean that d = −(a, b, c) changes into (d, a, b) = −c, in which the constitutive outside d has succeeded in disarticulating the two identities (a and b) from the chain of equivalence a≈b≈c and incorporating them into d's own discursive order.

Contingency also plays an equally important role at this second level. In other words, contingency is not only intra-discursive, but also generated through inter-discursive political struggles. Laclau and Mouffe's discourse theory, in its indebtedness to conflict theory, emphasizes the significance of the political, and the ways that discourses enter into struggles in their attempts to attain hegemonic positions over other discourses, and, thus, to stabilize, saturate, and sediment meanings. Through these struggles and through the attempts to create discursive alliances, or chains of equivalence (Howarth, 1998: 279; Howarth and Stavrakakis, 2000: 14), discourses are altered, which in turn produces contingency. This also implies that sedimentations are always temporal. As Sayyid and Zac (1998: 262) formulated it, "Hegemony is always possible but can never be total." There is always the possibility of resistance, of the resurfacing of a discursive struggle, and the re-politicization of sedimented discourses, combined with the permanent threat to every discourse of re-articulation. And, again, this generates contingency. As Mouffe (2005: 18) formulated it:

> "Every hegemonic order is susceptible of being challenged by counter-hegemonic practices, i.e. practices which will attempt to disarticulate the existing order so as to install other forms of hegemony."

2 Discursive Structures

When discussing discourse, the notion of structure seems to be difficult to avoid, also given the 'accusations' of structuralism often launched against discourse theory. At the same time, in order to understand the workings of discourses, a reflection on (discursive) structures remains instrumental and actually very necessary. Structure, as Walsh (1998: 8) remarked, is a crucial sociological concept anyway: "Of all the concepts which sociology has developed to understand and investigate society, social structure is the most important and absolutely central to the discipline." At the same time, in sociology there is a tendency to privilege more material perspectives on structure, not acknowledging (or thematizing) the presence of structure in culture, as Sewell (1992: 3) argued:

> "Sociologists typically contrast 'structure' to 'culture'. Structure, in normal sociological usage, is thought of as 'hard' or 'material' and therefore as primary and determining, whereas culture is regarded as 'soft' or 'mental' and therefore as secondary or derived. By contrast, semiotically inclined social scientists, most particularly anthropologists, regard culture as the preeminent site of structure."

If we take Giddens's structuration theory as an example, we first of all have to make the obvious point that for Giddens, structure and agency are intimately intertwined. Giddens argued against a dualism between agency and structure, and proposed instead a duality of structure, where structure is both the medium and outcome of social action. To use his words: "By this duality of structure I mean that social structures are both constituted by human agency, and yet at the same time are the very medium of this constitution" (Giddens, 1976: 121). For Giddens (1998: 76), this implies the reproduction of structures through agency-driven activities: "We should see the social life not just as 'society' out there, or just the product of 'the individual' here, but as a series of ongoing activities and practices that people carry out, which at the same time reproduce larger institutions." Secondly, Giddens moved away from the restrictive definition of structure as mere constraint, as the following quote illustrates:

> "Structure is not to be equated with constraint but is always both constraining and enabling. This, of course, does not prevent the structured properties of social systems

> from stretching away, in time and space, beyond the control of any individual actors. Nor does it compromise the possibility that actors' own theories of the social systems which they help to constitute and reconstitute in their activities may reify those systems. The reification of social relations, or the discursive 'naturalization' of the historically contingent circumstances and products of human action, is one of the main dimensions of ideology in human life." (Giddens, 1984: 25–26)

But thirdly, Giddens also tended to approach structure from a material perspective. Structure itself is defined by Giddens (1984: 25) as "Rules and resources, or sets of transformation relations, organized as properties of social systems." We should remain fair to Giddens's work, and acknowledge that the immaterial aspects are not completely ignored. As the above quote from *The Constitution of Society*, for instance, indicates, ideology plays a role in his work. Also, his definition of structure itself, as the combination of rules and resources, brings in a more culturalist dimension. Rules are seen as "[…] techniques or generalisable procedures applied in the enactment/reproduction of social practices" (Giddens, 1984: 21), and their role in the constitution of meaning is emphasized (Giddens, 1984: 20), which opens up possibilities for a more culturalist reading. Recourses are located at the level of allocation and authority, and defined as "[…] the media whereby transformative capacity is employed as power in the routine course of social interaction […]" (Giddens, 1979: 92). While allocation covers those "[…] capabilities which generate command over objects or other material phenomena," and thus has a clear materialist focus, authorization—seen as those "[…] capabilities which generate command over persons […]" (Giddens, 1979: 100—emphasis removed)—again has a potential culturalist dimension. Despite these (still rather vague) links to the more immaterial dimension of structure, Giddens's main focus is on the material, which has led authors such as Archer (1988: xi) to add a third element to the (material) structure and agency debate, namely (immaterial) culture. Archer, for instance, wrote that "[…] there is a similar task of reconciling objective knowledge […] with human activity and our capacity for generating new interpretations within our heads or for the interpersonal negotiation of new meanings."

A discourse-theoretical perspective enables radicalizing these positions and acknowledging the presence of the cultural in the structural and the existence of discursive structures. This leads us back to one of Laclau and Mouffe's definitions of discourse, as a structured entity (Laclau and Mouffe, 1985: 105). This, first of all, means that discourses themselves are *structured*, through the logic of articulation. Articulation implies the inclusion of particular signifiers, and the exclusion of others. Moreover, as discourses gain stability through nodal points, or privileged signifiers, a particular hierarchy—in other words, a structure—is created within a discourse. As Philips and Jørgensen (2002: 29) phrased this, discourse "[...] can be understood as a type of structure in a Saussurian sense—a fixation of signs in a relational net." This type of argument is similar to Hall's (1997a: 17) discussion of systems of representation as consisting "[...] not of individual concepts, but of different ways of organizing, clustering, arranging and classifying concepts, and of establishing complex relations between them." But we should immediately add to this debate—as has been argued before—the already-discussed idea that the structure of a discourse is contingent, as new signifiers can become (re)articulated and existent signifiers can become disarticulated. It is not a coincidence that when Philips and Jørgensen (2002: 29) pointed to the Saussurian connection, they immediately added that "There are always other meaning potentials which, when actualised in specific articulations, may challenge and transform the structure of the discourse."

But more important in this context is that discourses are also *structuring*. As frameworks of intelligibility that are circulating within our societies, discourses structure the conceptual and material world. As structures, they are indispensable to think about, understand, and provide meaning to that world (and ourselves, as subjects). As forms of knowledge, discourses are just as much resources as material resources are resources. Butler (1993: xi) stressed the importance of (discursive) constructions through the following rhetorical question: "Are [...] constructions [...] constitutive in this sense: that we could not operate without them, that without them there would be no 'I,' no 'we'?" Moreover, in their implicit (or sometimes explicit) claim to know a social reality, discourses also structure that very same social reality, offering particular perspectives on what matters and how it matters, excluding other elements that do not matter. In this sense, discourse is a "constitutive constraint" (Butler, 1993: xi). This brings us to the Foucauldian power/knowledge argument, which emphasizes the role discourses play in constructing the world: "There is no power relation without the correlative constitution of a field of knowledge, nor any knowledge that does not presuppose and constitute at the same time, power relations" (Foucault, 1977: 27).

From a perspective more in line with Laclau and Mouffe's language, we should in particular emphasize the structuring force of hegemony in producing a horizon of thought that is difficult to bypass (or even perceive) and that plays a major role in how we see a particular social reality. Hegemonies that are active in very different fields, such as capitalism, war-as-a-last-resort, or monogamy, offer ways of thinking that deeply structure our economic, political, and relational realities. Again, we should bring contingency into the equation, arguing that these discursive structures—even in the case of the most intense hegemonies—are always overdetermined and to be contextualized. Struggles between competing discursive structures, and in the case of hegemony, counter-hegemonic contestations, undermine the capacity of a particular discourse to provide a permanently closed structure of meaning. And hegemonies in particular spaces and times might not (have) be(en) hegemonic in others.

One of the areas Laclau and Mouffe focused on is how the identity of individual or collective agents is discursively structured. Identity is—according to Sayyid and Zac (1998: 263)—defined in two related ways. First, identity is defined as "the unity of any object or subject." This definition links up with Fuss' (1989: ix) definition of identity as "[...] the 'whatness' of a given entity." A second component of the definition of identity arises when this concept is applied to the ways in which social agents can be identified and/or identify themselves within a certain discourse. Sayyid and Zac's (1998: 263) examples of these structural positionings are "[...] workers, women, atheists, British." Laclau and Mouffe called this last component of identity a subject position, and defined it as the positioning of subjects within a discursive structure:

> "Whenever we use the category of 'subject' in this text, we will do so in the sense of 'subject positions' within a discursive structure. Subjects cannot, therefore, be the origin of social relations—not even in the limited sense of being endowed with powers that render an experience possible—as all 'experience' depends on precise discursive conditions of possibility." (Laclau & Mouffe, 1985: 115)

This last definition implies neither a structuralist position (privileging structures) nor a voluntarist position (privileging agencies). In spite of Laclau and Mouffe's unanimity with Althusser's critique on the autonomous and completely self-transparent subject[6] (which is a voluntarist position), they vehemently rejected Althusser's deterministic working of the economy in the last instance (which is a structuralist position), as they thought that this aspect of Althusser's theory leads to a "new variant of essentialism" (Laclau and Mouffe, 1985: 98):

> "Society and social agents lack any essence, and their regularities merely consist of the relative and precarious forms of fixation which accompany the establishment of a certain order. This analysis [of Althusser] seemed to open up the possibility

> of elaborating a new concept of articulation, which would start from the overdetermined character of social relations. But this did not occur." (Laclau & Mouffe, 1985: 98)

Their critical attitude towards Althusser does not alter the fact that Laclau and Mouffe borrowed the originally Freudian concept of overdetermination from Althusser (1982), though not without altering its meaning. Laclau and Mouffe saw identity as a fusion of a multiplicity of identities, where the overdetermined presence of some identities in others prevents their closure. As Torfing (1999: 150) illustrated, there are many possible points of identification:

> "A student who is expelled from the university might seek to restore the full identity she never had by becoming either a militant who rebels against the 'system', the perfect mother for her two children, or an independent artist who cares nothing for formal education."

Although even in *HSS* identities were seen as a fusion of a multiplicity of identities, where the overdetermined presence of some identities in others prevents their closure, Laclau's later work more clearly distinguishes between subject and subjectivation, and between identity and identification. The multiplicity of the discursive structures prevents their full and complete constitution, because of the inevitable distance between the obtained identity and the subject, and because of the (always possible) subversion of that identity by other identities. In Laclau's (1990a: 60) own words: "[...] the identification never reaches the point of full identity." Precisely, the contingency of identities and the failure to reach a fully constituted identity creates the space for subjectivity, agency, freedom, and the particularity of human behavior:

> "The freedom thus won in relation to the structure is therefore a traumatic fact initially: I am condemned to be free, not because I have no structural identity as the existentialists assert, but because I have a failed structural identity. This means that the subject is partially self-determined. However, as this self-determination is not the expression of what the subject already is but the result of the lack of its being instead, selfdetermination can only proceed though processes of identification." (Laclau, 1990a: 44)

As I will discuss in depth in the next part (this approach to), agency implies that subjects can identify with particular discourses and subject positions, in always particular variations and interpretations, but also that they might not identify with other discourses and subject positions. Still, even if subjects do not identify with a particular discourse, because the interpellation is unsuccessful, they might still *recognize* the discourses that do not appeal to them, and refer to them in particular signifying practices.

3 Agency

The previous citation brings us to agency, which is also the second component of the structure-agency duality. Traditionally, agency refers to the capacity of individuals for independent action and free choice, while structure is used as an overarching label for patterned social arrangements that are sometimes (too restrictively) defined as limiting individual freedom. As Gardner (2004: 1) summarized it, agency:

> "[...] concerns the nature of individual freedom in the face of social constraints, the role of socialisation in the forming of 'persons' and the place of particular ways of doing things in the reproduction of culture. In short, it is about the relationships between an individual human organism and everyone and everything that surrounds it."

Also here we can use Giddens' structuration theory as a starting point, given the importance he attributed to agency, within a context of duality: "By this duality of structure I mean that social structures are both constituted by human agency, and yet at the same time are the very medium of this constitution" (Giddens, 1976: 121). For Giddens (1998: 76), this implies that "We should see the social life not just as 'society' out there, or just the product of 'the individual' here, but as a series of ongoing activities and practices that people carry out, which at the same time reproduce larger institutions."

Although still very different, discourse theory uses a model of interconnectedness that is similar to structuration theory. The construction of discourses remains a social process, where discursive structures are created through collective social action (and the creation of other discursive structures is blocked), which in turn then enables (or disables) future social action. But this process of discursive production is not merely located at the level of the individual—here we concur with Burr's (2003) argument that constructionism is not constructivism.[7] In other words, discursive construction is not an act "[...] which happens once and whose effects are firmly fixed," as this would reduce the construction process to "[...] determinism and implies the evacuation or displacement of human agency" (Butler, 1993: 6). We should thus avoid an interpretation of discourse where

> "[...] construction is figuratively reduced to a verbal action which appears to presuppose a subject, critics working within such a presumption can be heard to say, 'If gender is constructed, then who is doing the constructing?'; though, of course, [...] the most pertinent formulation of this question is the following: 'If the subject is constructed, then who is constructing the subject?'" (Butler, 1993: 6)

This does raise questions about the position of the individual, and its (individual) agency in relation to discourse. As was argued previously, identities are never fully fixated, and agency resides in this impossibility to create a permanent discursive closure. The process of identification will never be complete and saturated by discursive positions, there will always be gaps between identity and identification, subject and subjectivation. These gaps partially originate from within the discursive itself,[8] and the instabilities the discursive generates, within a particular discourse, but also in the interactions between different discourses.

Firstly, internal discursive instability refers to the (small or more substantial) variations that discourses have, with different articulations. Even though a discourse is stabilized by its nodal points, variations do occur, not least because the practice of entextualization (see later) allows for discursive mutations. Here we can turn to Butler's (1997: 148) discussion of Derrida's (1988) approach towards iterability, where he locates the "force of the performative" with the "[...] structural feature of any sign that [it] must break with its prior contexts in order to sustain its iterability as a sign." Butler summarized Derrida's position as follows: "That break, that force of rupture, is the force of the performative, beyond all question of truth or meaning." A few lines earlier, Butler opened up for the possibility of a less necessary relationship—"Whether the mark is 'cut off' from its origin, as Derrida contends, or loosely tethered to it [...]" (Butler, 1997: 148)—which still illustrates the possibility of agency arising from discursive instability.

Secondly, it is important to return to the idea of discursive plurality, where multiple discourses enter into struggles with each other, and all offer themselves as objects of identification to individuals. The choice of identifying with one of these particular discourses is not exactly the same as a supermarket choice: The process of identification is dependent on how an individual is embedded in other discursive fields and one could also argue that individuals will tend to (try to) avoid (too heavy forms of) discursive dissonance.[9] This discursive plurality opens up spaces for agency through identificatory choices. Especially in situations where a discourse becomes dislocated, and their discursive hold is weakened, opportunities for the exercise of agency increase, as Howarth (2012: 264) explained:

> "Once their 'undecidability' [of discursive structures] becomes visible in dislocatory situations when structures no longer function to confer identity, subjects become political agents in the stronger sense of the term, as they identity with new discursive objects and act to re-constitute structures."

This discursive plurality also implies that many discourses co-exist and cohabit our social spaces without entering into struggles, as they cover different terrains of the social. Laclau (1996: 99) referred to this diversity of identities when he wrote in the introduction of a chapter that in contemporary societies "[…] social agents are becoming more and more 'multiple selves', with loosely integrated and unstable identities." One way this idea is captured is in the cultural studies discussion on multiple identities, as described by Barker (2004: 128): "Here identity does not involve an essence of the self but rather a set of continually shifting subject positions where the points of difference around which cultural identities could form are multiple and proliferating." In this type of argument, subjectivity is created by the identification with a multitude of identities and discourses, which positions the subject at the crossroads of this wide variety of identifications, rendering each individual a unique combination of interacting identifications with the discursive (and material) multitude, which again creates opportunities for agency.

The debate on agency also raises questions on the status of language, keeping Butler's (1997: 7) question in mind: "But is the agency of language the same as the agency of the subject?" She continued by saying "We do things with language, produce effects with language, and we do things to language, but language is also the thing that we do" (Butler, 1997: 8). Language has a degree of autonomy, which makes it spin out of our control and provides it with its own agency. In Laclau's (2000b: 70) words, we have to take the "autonomisation of the signifier" into account. But human agency also lies in the capacity to engage in—what I will label here as (see below)—signifying practices. Although language is embedded in structures itself (for instance, the linguistic system and the social regulation of speech), my point here is that language and its usage cannot be equated with discourse—at least not in the way that discourse is defined in this book. This means that the relationship between signifying practices and discursive production is not necessarily unilateral and direct. Language does not necessarily produce discourse. One illustration that comes to mind is Spivak's (1988) argument that the subaltern cannot speak, which should be understood as "The subaltern as female cannot be heard or read" (Spivak, 1988: 308), even though the subaltern can (of course) engage in signifying practices.

The translation of signifying practices into discourse is an act of power, highly dependent on the context of the speaker, the signifying practice itself, the medium and the audience, and not an automatism that is to be taken for granted. In other words, the construction of discourses is a social process that moves beyond language and thus escapes the control of the individual speaker. Discourses come into being through societal dialogues, often institutionalized, that privilege particular processes, events, or subjects that are worthy of discursification and de-privilege others, and that privilege particular meanings to be attributed to these processes (through the logic of articulation). For instance, Foucault's (1978: 43) analysis of the subject position of the homosexual shows how a society moved away from older articulations that focused more on practices that were not necessarily identity-defining and produced a new dominant discourse on a particular identity: "The nineteenth-century homosexual became a personage, a past, a case history, and a childhood [...]." These discursive constructions came into being through the work of particular authoritative institutions (e.g., the church—see later) that firstly coordinated, synchronized, and harmonized these still diverse signifying practices; secondly validated and authorized the more unified signifying practices; and thirdly distributed and defended them, enabling these signifying practices (or better, their signifiers and their articulations) to be transformed into discourse.

This argumentation is somewhat similar to the myth of the lone inventor (Israel, 1992; Montuori & Purser, 1995), a myth that is grounded in the idea that an individual produces technological innovations in a totally decontextualized setting, in the privacy of the study or laboratory, disconnected from societal institutions. Discursive innovation is equally institutionalized and equally contextualized, and most often is not the act of an individual. Although, this does not totally exclude the role of individuals (and their agency) as part of these institutions, neither does it exclude isolated ('lone') human beings from triggering discursive production, even if this only happens in rare cases. Individual signifying practices, for instance those originating from charismatic leaders (whether they are active in the political, intellectual, cultural, or economic realm) can still have a major societal impact and become translated into discourse, just as some inventors did produce world-changing technologies. But even in these cases, societal contexts are needed for the validation and circulation of these signifying practices and their full transformation into discourse. In most cases, though, individual subjects do not actively and consciously produce new discourses. But they do contribute—through their signifying practices that cite and invoke discourses—to the maintenance, weakening, or strengthening of particular discourses. As subjects, their agency lies in the ability to identify with particular discourses. Their signifying practices can approvingly or disapprovingly, literally or metaphorically, cite signifiers that belong to a discourse.[10] Even if subjects cannot immediately and individually change discourses, their signifying practices remain very necessary to breathe life into discourses, and the lack of signifying practice support can (and will) eventually obliterate discourses.

4 The Material

In the fourth subpart, our attention will turn to the material. This subpart is the most exhaustive, to make sure that (theoretical) justice is done to the material, given the fact that the discursive is used as the starting point of this theoretical voyage. This subpart looks at a wide variety of approaches and fields that thematize the material, incorporating reflections about machines and assemblages; technologies and architectures; bodies, signifiers, and languages; and organizations. To better ensure the integration of this subpart into the general direction of this book, I will first initiate a discussion of Laclau and Mouffe's references to the material.

Before moving in that direction, the notion of the material itself needs to be developed a bit further, which is not an easy task given the wide variety of definitions and approaches. Ingold (2007: 1) used a rather down-to-earth approach when he referred to materials as "[…] the stuff that things are made of […]." Deleuze (1993: 5) used a slightly more elaborate definition of matter as something that

> "[…] offers an infinitely porous, spongy or cavernous texture without emptiness, caverns endlessly contained in other caverns: no matter how small, each body contains a world pierced with irregular passages, surrounded and penetrated by an increasingly vaporous fluid, the totality of the universe resembling a 'pond of matter in which there exist different flows and waves.'"

As is often the case, typologies are developed to deal with this conceptual fluidity. For instance, there is Gosden's (1999: 152) suggestion: "For purely heuristic purposes we can divide the material world into two: landscape and artefacts." Ashcraft, Kuhn, and Cooren (2009) used objects, bodies, and sites, while Hardy and Thomas (2015), who built on the Ashcraft et al. (2009) article, distinguished between bodies, objects, spaces, and practices. This book will be no exception, and will gratefully use these earlier categorizations. But before initiating this more detailed discussion of the material, one more clarification—grounded in Ingold's (2007) article '*Materials Against Materiality*'—is very necessary. In this subpart (and in this book as a whole), I consciously use the notion of 'the material'—and not the notion of materiality—as the overarching notion. This choice for 'the material' is aligned with the ways that Laclau and Mouffe used 'the political' and 'the social.' But this choice (for the material) is also inspired by one of the definitions of materiality, namely as "[…] what makes things 'thingly' […]." This definition of materiality problematically connotes the existence of a "[…] generalized substrate upon which the forms of all things are said to be imposed or inscribed" (Ingold, 2007: 9), which I want to try to avoid. Still, in this book, materiality is still sometimes used, but then it only refers to being-material, moving explicitly away from an essentialist connotation of materiality, very much in line with Ingold's (2007: 9) suggestion:

> "In urging that we take a step back, from the materiality of objects to the properties of materials, I propose that we lift the carpet, to reveal beneath its surface a tangled web of meandrine complexity, in which—among a myriad other things—oaken wasp galls get caught up with old iron, acacia sap, goose feathers and calf-skins, and the residue from heated limestone mixes with emissions from pigs, cattle, hens and bees."

4.1 Discourse Theory's Relationship to the Material

Some authors have critiqued Laclau and Mouffe's position as idealist. One example is Joseph's (2003: 112) statement, commenting on Laclau and Mouffe's work: "[…] the idea that an object only acquires an identity through discourse is a clear example of the epistemic fallacy or the reduction of intrinsic being to transformative knowledge." He continued that Laclau and Mouffe's idealism "[…] reduces material things to the conceptions, not of an individual or a *geist*, but of a community" (Joseph, 2003: 112—emphasis in original). Others, in particular Geras (1987: 65), are harsher in their language, accusing Laclau and Mouffe of a "shamefaced idealism." This critique in turn provoked responses of disagreement with Geras's rather extreme position, but the idealism thesis is often maintained. For instance, Edward (2008) argued that it was appropriate "[…] to label LacLau and Mouffe as idealist because their discourse analysis concentrates on how interpretations and meanings are given to the world from humans. This is their 'constructivist idealism' […]."

In Laclau and Mouffe's (1985, 1990) work, we do find a rather clear acknowledgement of the material dimension of social reality, which is indeed combined with the position that discourses are necessary to generate meaning for the material. This—what Howarth (1998: 289) called their—"radical materialism" opposes the "[...] classical dichotomy between an objective field constituted outside of any discursive intervention, and a discourse consisting of the pure expression of thought" (Laclau & Mouffe, 1985: 108). Pre-empting the idealism critique, their position is defended through a series of examples[11] that refer to materiality:

> "An earthquake or the falling of a brick is an event that certainly exists, in the sense that it occurs here and now, independently of my will. But whether their specificity as objects is constructed in terms of 'natural phenomena' or 'expressions of the wrath of God' depends upon the structuring of a discursive field. What is denied is not that such objects exist externally to thought, but the rather different assertions that they could constitute themselves as objects outside any discursive condition of emergence." (Laclau & Mouffe, 1985: 108)

Several other authors have defended Laclau and Mouffe's claim on a non-idealist position (e.g., Glynos & Howarth, 2007: 109; Schou, 2016: 302). Also, Torfing (1999: 45–48) argued that Laclau and Mouffe's model is materialist because it questions the symmetry between the 'realist object' and the 'object of thought'. This (described by Torfing as a) non-idealist constructivism presupposes "[...] the incompleteness of both the given world and the subject that undertakes the construction of the object" (Torfing, 1999: 48). One more author that defended Laclau and Mouffe against the idealism critique is Hall (1997a: 44–45), who constructed his own language game in order to make this point:

> "Is Foucault saying [...] that nothing exists outside of discourse?' In fact, Foucault does not deny that things can have a real, material existence in the world. What he does argue is that 'nothing has any meaning outside of discourse'. As Laclau and Mouffe put it: 'we use it [the term discourse] to emphasize the fact that every social configuration is meaningful.'"

There are also more specific traces of the material in Laclau and Mouffe's discourse theory. A first trace can be found in Laclau's use of the notion of dislocation. Although this concept already featured in *HSS*, it took a more prominent role in *New Reflections on the Revolution of Our Time*, where Laclau (1990c) used it to further theorize the limits of discursive structures. In most cases, dislocation gains its meaning in relation to the discursive; for instance, when Laclau (1990a: 39) claimed that "[...] every identity is dislocated insofar as it depends on an outside which denies that identity and provides its condition of possibility at the same time." In this meaning, dislocation supports the notion of contingency, but is also seen as the "very form of possibility" (Laclau, 1990a: 42), as dislocations show that the structure (before the dislocation) is only one of the possible articulatory ensembles (Laclau, 1990a: 43). It thus becomes "[…] the very form of temporality, possibility and freedom" (Laclau, 1990a: 41–43, summarized by Torfing, 1999: 149). At the same time, there is also a more material use of the dislocation; for instance, when Laclau (1990a: 39) talked about the "[…] dislocatory effects of emerging capitalism on the lives of workers": "They are well known: the destruction of traditional communities, the brutal and exhausting discipline of the factory, low wages and insecurity of work." This connection between the dislocation and material events becomes even clearer in Torfing's (1999: 148—my emphasis) description of the dislocation, which, according to him, "[…] refers to the emergence of *an event, or a set of events*, that cannot be represented, symbolized, or in other ways domesticated by the discursive structure—which is therefore disrupted." Also Marchart (2007: 139–140—emphasis in original) referred to the dislocation as event when writing about the "constitutive outside of space" as

> "[…] something which cannot be explained from the inner logic of the system itself, or which has never had any prescribed place in the topography. Yet it occurs *within* such topography as its dislocation, disturbance, or interruption: *as event*."

It is important to clarify that in this context the notion of the event refers to a *material change* that at least has the potential to dislocate a particular discourse. An event, in its materiality, dislocates a discourse because this discourse turns out to be unable to attribute meaning to the event, while the event simultaneously invites for its incorporation into this discourse. The emphasis on change (or on novelty) and the event's dislocatory potential can be illustrated with Žižek's (2014: 11) description of "The basic feature of an event […]" as "[…] the surprising emergence of something new which undermines every stable scheme." In Deleuze's (1993: 77) reference to the event as "[…] a vibration with an infinity of harmonics or submultiples […]," support for the more material emphasis can be found. He goes on to stress the movement and articulation of the event: "[…] extensive series have intrinsic properties (for example, height, intensity, timbre of a sound, a tint, a value, a saturation of color), which enter on their own account in new infinite series […]" (Deleuze, 1993: 77). This very open and materialist approach to the event is different from how the event is often used in media studies, where the notion of the *media event* refers to the "televisional ceremonies" that are "[…] the high holidays of mass communication" (Dayan & Katz, 2009: 1). Even if these media events have clear material dimensions, the conceptual focus on the televisional representations of material changes renders them more specific than the notion of the event that is used here.

As Biglieri and Perelló (2011) have argued, it is particularly in Laclau's (2005) *On Populist Reason* that the material[12] is introduced, through the concept of social heterogeneity. Laclau defined this concept as a particular exteriority: "[…] the kind of exteriority we are referring to now presupposes not only an exteriority to something within a space of representation, but to the space of representation as such. I will call this type of exteriority social heterogeneity" (Laclau, 2005: 140). Biglieri and Perelló, (2011: 60) labeled it "a structure with a beyond." It is through the invocation of Lacan, for instance, when Laclau wrote that "[…] the field of representation is a broken and murky mirror, constantly interrupted by a heterogeneous 'Real' which it cannot symbolically master" (Laclau, 2005: 140), that the material regains more prominence.

Even if there are traces of the material (mainly) in Laclau's work, and despite Laclau and Mouffe's plea for a position that Howarth (1998: 289) termed "radical materialism" as a "tertium quid," their strong orientation towards the analysis of the discursive components of reality, and, more specifically, towards the analysis of signifiers as democracy, socialism, and populism, remains. Practically speaking, this means that in their specific analyses they will pay considerably less attention to material components of reality (as, for example, bodies, objects, organizations, technologies, or human interactions). If we return to some of the critiques on Laclau and Mouffe's alleged idealism, we can find this kind of argumentation. For instance, Edward (2008) wrote:

> "Unlike Deleuze and Guattari, Laclau and Mouffe are more concerned with discourse than they are about geology (inorganic), biology (organic), and technology (alloplastic). It is for this reason that Laclau and Mouffe are not radical constructivists and remain social constructivists. Their discourse analysis can only explain the construction of the world when there is discourses and articulation of meaning."

A stronger critique can be found in Joseph (2003: 112), who, in my opinion, overstated the argument, but is still a good representative of the critique that the material remains too much at a distance, in particular when he wrote:

> "To say that without discourse the object is meaningless is to say that its natural properties are insignificant until discursively articulated, that it is in fact discursively

rather than physically constituted. And this leads to the idealist notion that changes in description lead to changes in the object itself."

4.2 Machines as Entry Points Into the Material

These lasts quotations exemplify the need for a more developed theoritization of the material in its relationship to the discursive. At the same time, I want to maintain the discourse-theoretical starting point that all social phenomena and objects obtain their meaning(s) through discourse, and I want to avoid the trap of dichotomizing the discursive and the material (and the reduction to either an idealist or a materialist position). In this sense, the sometimes harsh idealism critiques on Laclau and Mouffe's work are not shared. A different route is chosen by increasing the theoretical visibility of the material in the interactions between the discursive and the material, whilst remaining firmly embedded in discourse theory.

The Lacanian route that Laclau used offers a very broad way to achieve this objective, as the Real also enables thinking the material. Moreover, Lacanian theory is highly compatible with discourse theory in its emphasis on the inaccessibility of the Real, as such, and the necessity of the symbolic to represent the Real without coinciding with it. Lacanian theory, then, sees the subject launched on an endless search for "[...] what was lost for him, the subject, the moment he entered into this discourse" (Lacan, 1977: 16), bridging the unbridgeable. Simultaneously, Lacanian theory also acknowledges the Real manifesting itself, sometimes creating an "encounter with the real"—as Lacan (1979: 53) put it—"[...] which stretches from the trauma to the phantasy—in so far as the phantasy is never anything more than the screen that conceals something quite primary, something determinant in the function of the repetition" (Lacan, 1979: 60). These encounters arguably also contain challenges to make discursive sense of them, even if they are always (and necessarily) "the missed encounter" (Lacan, 1979: 55).

Despite the capacity of the Lacanian perspective to provide us with tools to transcend the mere discursive (or the mere symbolic), I would like to argue that there is still a need to look at other conceptual instruments to assist in this task. Although many different materials can be distinguished, in this text there is an explicit interest in a series of particular material configurations, namely (proto-)machines, bodies, organizational structures, and spatial orderings. One way to further unpack these materials and, in a second stage, to (re-)connect them to the discursive, is to turn to Deleuze and Guattari's work, and, more specifically, their notion of the machine, an argument I have made before (Carpentier, 2011: 219). In their *Anti-Oedipus*, Deleuze and Guattari defined the machine as "a system of interruptions or breaks," whereas the breaks "[…] should in no way be considered as a separation from reality; rather, they operate along lines that vary according to whatever aspect of them we are considering. Every machine, in the first place, is related to a continual material flow […] that it cuts into" (Deleuze & Guattari, 1984: 36—emphasis removed). Here it could be added that this process of cutting into the flow can also be a very disruptive and destructive process. Also in their discussion of the war machine, Deleuze and Guattari (1987: 422) pointed to the potential of the war machine to take "[…] war for its object and [to form] a line of destruction prolongable to the limits of the universe," even if they (optimistically) also argued for the existence of a second and contrasting pole, where the war machine has the drawing of "a creative line of flight" as its object.

Deleuze and Guattari (1984: 36) also pointed to the entanglement of machines when they said that "[…] every machine is the machine of a machine […]." It is seen as the law of the production of production: "[…] every machine functions as a break in the flow in relation to the machine to which it is connected, but at the same time is also a flow itself, or the production of a flow, in relation to the machine connected to it." Deleuze and Guattari often applied their machine concept to the human body (e.g., the mouth-machine), but they also used the machine concept in a much broader way, for instance when talking about abstract machines such as capitalism. As Raunig (2007: 147) pointed out, in Guattari's (1972) first machine text ('*Machine and Structure*,' originally written in 1969) he used the machine to discuss the revolutionary organization as an institutional machine that does not become a state or party structure. Without being completely faithful to Guattari's framework, which sees the machine as unstructuralizable (see Genosko, 2002: 197), his theoretical reflections on the revolutionary machine enable me to articulate organizations, but also bodies, as machines.

4.3 Proto-Machines and Architectures

Defining organizations and bodies as machines begs the question, how to refer to technologies, which in everyday language are often referred to as 'machines'? As a starting point of this argument,[13] we should acknowledge the broadness of the technological field, as Bain's (1937: 860) definition of technology shows: "[…] technology includes all tools, machines, utensils, weapons, instruments, housing, clothing, communicating and transporting devices and the skills by which we produce and use them." In this definition, there is a strong emphasis on the material,[14] which we also find in Stiegler's (1998: 82) brief definition of technology as "organized inorganic matter." Here, too, we can return to Guattari's work on the machine. In his chapter '*Machinic Heterogenesis*,' Guattari (1993: 14) referred to the "[…] first type of machine that comes to mind […]," which is that of "material assemblages […] put together artificially by the human hand and by the intermediary of other machines, according to the diagrammatic schemas whose end is the production of effects, of products, or of particular services." In the next sentence, Guattari immediately pointed to the need to go beyond the "[…] delimitation of machines in the strict sense to include the functional ensemble that associates them with humankind to multiple components […]." This list of components is lengthy, and includes material and energy components, semiotic components that are diagrammatic and algorithmic, social components, components related to the human body, representational components, investments by what he called desiring machines, and abstract machines. Guattari (1993: 14) termed this functional ensemble the machinic assemblage, in which the basic material components are called proto-machines: "[…] the utensils, the instruments, the simplest tools and, […] the least structured pieces of a machinery will acquire the status of a proto-machine."

The arrangement (or assemblage) has many interconnecting material components, as Volti's (2006: 5) argument of proto-machines as a material system shows. Volti used the example of the invention of the light bulb to show that the isolated material object is useless unless it is (quite literally) connected to an electrical generator through a network of electrical lines, combined with metering devices, which enables its commodification. A similar argument can be made about architecture as an assemblage of walls, doors, windows, cables, pipes, … where it "[…] is impossible to understand the room, building, street, district, city or nation without considering the connections between them" (Dovey, 2013: 135). This also brings us to the (material aspects of the) notions of space and place, and the spatiality of assemblages. Assemblages find themselves located in particular spaces, integrating natural resources—with their own "physical and chemical properties" (Kaup, 2008: 1735)—that are present within these spaces, in combination with a variety of other (proto-) machines.

Still, Guattari's approach to the machinic assemblage includes more than matter. For instance, DeLanda's (2006: 12) work on assemblage theory uses this idea, as he distinguishes between the material and the expressive roles of the components of assemblages, although he is quick to add—and rightfully so—that "[…] expressivity cannot be reduced to language and symbols." If we cross-fertilize these ideas with the discourse-theoretical approach used in this book, then we can say that the discursive dimension and our sense-making practices of proto-machines should also be considered of fundamental importance in assemblages.

The individual use of technology is highly discursive; for instance, when people use proto-machines to generate distinctions or to support their identity constructions. As Du Gay, Hall, Janes, Mackay, and Negus (1997) illustrated with the case of the Sony Walkman, meanings are attributed through the production process of proto-machines, but also, the consumption process is a location of a multitude of generated meanings. Also, when talking about architecture, Dovey (2013: 134) emphasized the interconnection between the discursive and the material when she wrote that,

> "[…] the assemblage is not a thing nor a collection of things. Buildings, rooms, trees, cars, gates, people and signs all connect in certain ways and it is the connection between them that make an assemblage."

Also, some of the discussions on spatiality enable me to emphasize the discursive-material knot. Castree (1995: 13—emphasis in original) approvingly pointed to the "[…] attempts to take seriously […] the *materiality of nature*," but also argued for combining this taking-the-material-seriously with a constructionist position "[…] because we always come to understand 'natural' entities posited as ontologically real and outside us through and in terms of categories, concepts and language" (Castree, 1995: 15). In *For Space*, Massey (2005: 9) formulated three opening propositions, which also illustrate the combination of the material and the discursive in her thinking about space. The first proposition is "[…] that we recognise space as the product of interrelations; as constituted through interactions […]" (Massey, 2005: 9). Secondly, Massey emphasized the plurality of space, where "Multiplicity and space [are seen as] as co-constitutive" (Massey, 2005: 9). Finally, Massey's (2005: 9) third proposition is "[…] that we recognise space as always under construction":

> "Precisely because space on this reading is a product of relations-between, relations which are necessarily embedded material practices which have to be carried out, it is always in the process of being made. It is never finished; never closed."

When focusing on place—as a concrete "*point* in space" (Horton & Kraftl, 2014: 267—emphasis in original), or as a "type of object" (Tuan, 1977: 17)—its constructed nature is often emphasized. Here we can find the combination of material construction processes, where "[…] places are marked out by boundaries (walls, fences), and by physical features (buildings, trees, pavements, street furniture) […]" (Horton & Kraftl, 2014: 267), with social (or discursive) construction processes where "[…] norms, values and meanings […]" (Horton & Kraftl, 2014: 267) are invested in particular places. Tuan (1977: 17) explicitly mentioned the materiality of this investment, using the concept of embodiment:

> "Human beings not only discern geometric patterns in nature and create abstract spaces in the mind, they also try to embody their feelings, images, and thoughts in tangible material. The result is sculptural and architectural space, and on a large scale, the planned city."

These materials are simultaneously coded (or double-coded—see Jencks, 1977) and given meaning in a variety of ways. Even if, "Compared to space, place is a calm center of established values" (Tuan, 1977: 54), it is still the object of varying signifying practices, and of discursive struggle, in which the material, through the logic of the invitation, plays an important role. Cresswell (1996: 59) stressed both that significatory diversity, and the invitational role of the material, when he wrote:

> "[…] places are the result of tensions between different meanings and […] they are also active players in these tensions. Places have more than one meaning. Some meanings are complementary and fit neatly on top of each other. Other meanings seem to be incompatible—to be awkward and displaced—if they are located with other meanings. The incompatibility is not natural or inevitable (we need only realize that some places have different meanings at different times—meanings that may have once seemed heretical.) Rather meanings are said to be incompatible by someone whose interests lie in preserving a particular set of meanings."

This also brings us back to the discursive, and Laclau and Mouffe's discourse-theoretical position that discursive frameworks are needed to provide objects with meaning. But this last argument is only partially satisfying, as it still brings about the danger of presupposing a hierarchical relationship between the discursive and the material, where the discursive—quite literally—holds the last word. Arguably, there is a need to look at other approaches that have developed more in-depth reflections about the material, which can be used here.

One helpful concept that features in psychology and design studies (amongst other fields), is the notion of the affordance. To describe affordances, Gibson (1979: 18) referred to "[…] these offerings of nature, these possibilities or opportunities […]," whereas, for instance, "Both the air and the water do afford breathing." Later in his book, when talking about animals, Gibson (1979: 127) described the notion more, by referring to "The affordances of the environment [that] are what it *offers* the animal, what it *provides* or *furnishes*, either for good or ill […] It implies the complementarity of the animal and the environment." In this sense, an affordance "[…] points two ways, to the environment and to the observer," which enables Gibson (1979: 141) to avoid "[…] dualism in any form, either mind-matter dualism or mind-body dualism." In a later version, Norman (1988: 9—emphasis in original) introduced a broadened version of the affordance, which, in contrast to Gibson, integrates perception within the notion of the affordance, as his definition exemplifies:

> "[…] the term *affordance* refers to the perceived and actual properties of the thing, primarily those fundamental properties that determine just how the thing could possibly be used […] Affordances provide strong clues to the operations of things. Plates are for pushing. Knobs are for turning. Slots are for inserting things into. Balls are for throwing or bouncing. When affordances are taken advantage of, the user knows what to do just by looking: no picture, label, or instruction needed."

Here, the notion of the affordance also obtains a psychological dimension (which has been critiqued—see Lindberg & Lyytinen, 2013; Soegaard, 2015), shifting the exclusive attention away from the material, although both Gibson's and Norman's work can be read as an attempt to think about the materiality of objects, without isolating it from the social (or the cultural). Nevertheless, their approach—what Gibson (1979: 127) called the theory of affordances—still attributes a fairly passive role to the material.

Another theoretical field that needs to be integrated into this discussion is Actor Network Theory (ANT), which aims to attribute a more active role to the material by awarding it agency. As Latour (2005: 73) put it: "[…] objects are nowhere to be said and everywhere to be felt." ANT's claim is that objects (or, more broadly, non-humans) should be integrated into the study of the social, first of all because the material is an integrated and crucial component of the social: "When power is exerted for good, it is because it is not made of social ties; when it has to relate only on social ties, it is not exerted for long" (Latour, 2005: 66). But more importantly in this context, objects enter into co-determining relationships with humans; after all: "[…] *any thing* that does modify a state of affairs by making a difference is an actor" (Latour, 2005: 71—emphasis in original). Through the connections with humans, objects can become mediators and/or intermediaries, and thus become implicated in the social. Bennett (2010: viii) referred to the vitality of matter to describe this, which is

> "[…] the capacity of things—edibles, commodities, storms, metals—not only to impede or block the will and designs of humans but also to act as quasi agents or forces with trajectories, propensities, or tendencies of their own."

Similar arguments have been made in relation to architecture: Love (2013: 752) referred to "the materiality of architecture," which "[…] can be understood through the active position of objects that actively defines subjects and explores both the practical and socio-symbolic aspects of objects." She referred to an earlier article, written by Vellinga (2007: 763), who raised a similar point: "[…] it has become clear that it is really no longer possible to study the house and understand its cultural meaning without looking at its material, architectural aspects." For instance, how the rooms of a house (or a home) are organized plays a role in "[…] the development of intimacy and in ordering and segregating space in specific gendered ways" (Bennett, 2002: 17). This type of argument is reminiscent of Deleuze and Guattari's (1987: 208) (older) discussion on segmentarity—where "[…] the house is segmented according to its rooms' assigned purpose; streets, according to the order of the city; the factory, according to the nature of the work and operations performed in it." Also, Foucault's (1977: 30) work on the prison, with its emphasis on walls and cells, on the prison's "[…] very materiality as an instrument and vector of power […]" is important to mention here, for one because Foucault's work is an elegant illustration of the combined workings of the discursive and the material. In his work, the material prison is (part of) a "[…] *political* investment in the body […]" (Foucault, 1977: 25—my emphasis): "[…] power relations have an immediate hold upon it; they invest it, train it, torture it, force it to carry out tasks, to perform ceremonies, to emit signs" (Foucault, 1977: 26), all of which is embedded in a society's power/knowledge conjuncture.

Also, in new materialist approaches, the emphasis is placed on a broader perspective on agency, shifting it away from an exclusive connection with human activity, or with things, for that matter. Barad's (2012: 54) re-conceptualization illustrates this argument: "Agency is not held, it is not a property of persons or things; rather, agency is an enactment, a matter of possibilities for reconfiguring entanglements." As she also formulates it: "Agency is about possibilities for wordly re-configurings" (Barad, 2012: 55). This connects with an argument that was mentioned in my text before, when discussing Deleuze and Guattari's (1984: 36) definition of the machine as a system of interruptions: Machines interrupt the flow in particular ways, allowing some usages and disallowing others. Still, these processes are not outside the discursive-material knot, as human and non-humans become discursified, even when this occurs reluctantly, as Mackenzie (2002: 5) noted:

> "[Proto-machines] strongly resists reduction to discourse and signification. Rather, it tends to condition them. This is not to say that technology, or some aspect of technology, is outside discourse. Rather it is to say that we can think, signify, make sense and represent who we are in part only because of technology."

The conceptual solution that I would like to propose here, integrating the material more into the discourse-theoretical perspective, is based on the notion of the *invitation* as the positive version of the dislocation. Discourse is indeed needed to provide meaning to machines, proto-machines, and assemblages of machines, at the level of their production and their consumption (or use). Simultaneously (proto-)machines have a materiality that invites for particular meanings to be attributed to them, and that dissuades other particular meanings from becoming attributed to them. In its structure, this invitational logic is similar to the way that Buckingham (1987: 37), inspired by Iser's (1978) work, talked about television programs (in particular, the British soap opera, *EastEnders*) and the invitation that these programs extend towards the viewers to identify with, for instance, particular characters. As Turner (2005: 127) wrote, "From this perspective, texts do not produce or determine meaning, they 'invite' their readers to accept particular positions [...]." In the more material version of the invitation that I am advocating here, materials extend an invitation to be discursified, or to be integrated in discourses, in always particular ways. These invitations, originating from the material, do not fix or determine meanings, but their material characteristics still privilege and facilitate the attribution of particular meanings through the invitation.

This does not imply that the logic of the invitation functions outside the discursive-material knot. Materials like objects and technologies consist of an endless and restless combination of the material and the discursive, where the material invites for particular discourses to become part of the assemblage, frustrating other discourses, and assisting in other discourses (and materials) to be produced. But the material is also always invested with meaning.

Hegemonic orders provide contextual frameworks of intelligibility that intervene in these assemblages. This also implies that discourses impact on the production of materials, not only to give meaning to them, but also to co-determine their materiality. To use a deceivingly simple object, made famous by Heidegger (1996), as an example: A hammer is made to be a hammer, partially because of all sorts of material characteristics that facilitate hammering and that give the hammer its handiness (to use one of Heidegger's terms), but also because of a series of discourses related to construction work, manual labor and carpentry, efficiency, creation, and aesthetics. There is, in other words, an interacting combination between materials and the cultural codes engrained in them, and between the material invitation and the discursive investment. To capture this engraining of meaning into the material, the concept of *investment* is thus used. The use of this concept here is inspired by how, for instance, Marres (2012: 113) used it, even if it is rather en passant, when she discussed the deployment of empirical devices in demonstrational homes, and remarked: "[…] it facilitates the investment of material entities with normative capacities."

Furthermore, contingency remains present here also. Contingency can originate from the interaction between both components of the discursive-material knot, or from changes over time. Again, the discursive-material knot functions without necessary hierarchy between its constituent components. The introduction of more agencies, also in relationship to technologies, proto-machines and other materials, shows a richer landscape of forces that can destabilize existing sedimentations, and create more contingency. If we combine the logics of the assemblage and articulation,[15] then the constitution of an assemblage can be altered through any re-articulation or disarticulation, whether this is discursive or material. Earlier, discursive contingency was discussed, and here we can make the same argument about the material. For instance, Massey's (2005: 94) words—"[…] about the truly productive characteristics of material spatiality […]"—show the contingency brought about by the material:

> "[…] its potential for the happenstance juxtaposition of previously unrelated trajectories, that business of walking round a corner and bumping into alterity, of having (somehow, and well or badly) to get on with neighbours who have got 'here' (this block of flats, this neighbourhood, this country—this meeting-up) by different routes from you; your being here together is, in that sense, quite uncoordinated."

Moreover, the material, through its agency, can dislocate particular discursive orders (but also disrupt or destroy other materials). It can also form assemblages, and—through its affordances, agencies, and invitations—strengthen existing discursive orders. What it cannot do, is escape from the discursive-material knot, and permanently dominate the discursive (or be dominated by it). The invitation of the material is not compelling, but can be ignored by a particular discursive order, or an alternative interpretation may arise from that particular discursive order, even if the threat of dislocation always remains, which only provides further support for the presence of contingency.

4.4 Bodies

Another type of machine that Deleuze and Guattari distinguished is the body. Also here, as Bogue (2013: 64) summarized it, the body cuts into flows: "The infant's mouth-machine, for example, cuts into the flow of milk, its anus-machine cuts into the flow of excretion. Yet though we speak of machine and flow as separate entities, they actually constitute a single process." Their approach, as the body that is interconnected to its material and discursive environment, is very different from the more traditional approaches, as exemplified by this Cartesian description of the difference between the living and the dead body:

> "[…] the body of a living man differs from that of a dead man just as does a watch or other automation (i.e. a machine that moves of itself), when it is wound up […], from the same watch or other machine when it is broken." (Descartes, 1985: 329)

The approaches that emphasize the material dimension of the body as a container of the inner self, separated from the outside world, creating a universal experience of embodiment, are still commonly used. A more recent example of this disconnecting materialist approach is Johnson's (1987: 21) work in the field of cognitive semantics:

> "Our encounter with containment and boundedness is one of the most pervasive features of our bodily experience. We are intimately aware of our bodies as three-dimensional containers into which we put certain things (food, water, air) and out of which other things emerge (food and water wastes, air, blood, etc.)."

These approaches have been criticized, for instance by feminist authors such as Battersby (2013: 41), who have pointed to the reductionist nature of this approach, where "[…] cultural differences act merely as an overlay which affects the way meanings are encoded and transformed; underneath there is human sameness." This kind of critique does not aim to deny the specificity of the material body, but refuses the hierarchy created between the material and the discursive (or the cultural). Moreover, the notion of affect also becomes implicated, as affects intersect with the materiality of the body. They are "registers of experience" (Blackman, 2012: 4) that are situated within the material body and simultaneously transcend it. To use Blackman's (2012: 4) words: Affect is "[…] not a thing but rather refers to processes of life and vitality which circulate and pass between bodies […]." She, together with Seigworth and Gregg (2010: 7), reminded us of Williams's (1977: 128ff) definition of culture as "structures of feeling" (Blackman, 2012: 4–5), which captures this complex set of relations well.

This way of thinking about the body is aligned with Butler's (1990) argument in *Gender Trouble* that biological sex, and not only gender, is a social construction. Her rejection of the dichotomy between "sexed bodies" and "culturally constructed genders" (Butler, 1990: 6) shows the continuous impact of processes of meaning-making, even if this goes against our common sense:

> "For surely bodies live and die; eat and sleep; feel pain, pleasure; endure illness and violence; and these 'facts,' one might skeptically proclaim, cannot be dismissed as mere construction." (Butler, 1993: xi)

For Butler (1993), the material is embedded in, and made present through, a (cultural) process of materialization, which defines it and regulates it. For instance, "[…] 'sex' is an ideal construct that is forcibly materialized through time," and not a "[…] simple fact or static condition of a body […]" (Butler, 1993: 1–2). At the same time, this materialization requires the "forcible reiteration of those norms," which implied for Butler (1993: 2) "[…] that materialization is never quite complete, that bodies never quite comply with the norms by which their materialization is impelled." Exactly this gap opens up the space to develop the non-hierarchical approach towards the material and the materialized body, where the material *an sich* also matters.

For this argument we can find support in the writings of Merleau-Ponty (2005: 511), who emphasized the materiality of the body: "Insofar as I have hands, feet; a body, I sustain around me intentions which are not dependent on my decisions and which affect my surroundings in a way that I do not choose." Lacan (1998: 72), in his discussion of Merleau-Ponty's work, distinguished between the eye and the gaze, a split he summarized as follows: "I see only from one point, but in my existence I am looked at from all sides." Although Lacan tended to prioritize the gaze in this lecture, he also pointed out that the eye, in Merleau-Ponty's work, together with the subject's "[…] expectations, his movement, his grip, his muscular and visceral emotion—in short, his constitutive presence" (Lacan, 1998: 71) regulates and governs what Lacan called form. To illustrate the workings of these body-related powers of corporealization, one could ask the simple question, how could visual culture exist without the eye? For Merleau-Ponty (1988: 133–134), the flesh is a "primordial being" that "[...] in every respect baffles reflection," and is still distinct from both the "subject-being" and the "object-being."

At the same time, the flesh is intrinsically part of the subject: "From this primordial being to us, there is no derivation, nor any break [...]." As a part of the subject, the materiality of the flesh allows and disallows, invites and dissuades. But then again, the flesh does not escape discursification either, even if it sometimes resists and dislocates discourses, and does not allow itself to become subordinated to the discursive. Discourses remain contingent in what meanings they generate about bodies, which implies that hegemonies (about bodies) can be contested. It is, for instance, possible

> "[...] to promote an alternative imaginary to a hegemonic imaginary and to show, through that assertion, the ways in which the hegemonic imaginary constitutes itself through the naturalization of an exclusionary heterosexual morphology." (Butler, 1993: 91)

At the same time, contingency also originates from the dislocatory capacities of the material. As the material body is bound to escape discursification, and there is always a gap between the discursive and the material, the material body has the capacity to challenge the discursive, to contradict it and to dislocate it. In a more positive version, the material also has characteristics that invite for particular discursifications. In this sense, we can speak about the field of materiality (in parallel with Laclau and Mouffe's notion of the field of discursivity), with its own (material) elements that can be articulated and/or assembled. This field of materiality offers material elements to be discursified as meaningful, but also to disrupt particular discourses by creating dislocations.

So far, the argument has been based on the materiality of bodies (and objects) who have been left slightly immobile. Obviously, bodies and objects not only exist, but they also do things. The material acts bring us to notions such as practices and (inter)actions. Again, Butler's work is a useful starting point here, given her emphasis on the performance of identity, which demonstrates the role of material, bodily practices in the construction of (gendered) identities. Here, we need to distinguish between performative acts and performativity. Performative acts are linked to "individual actors," who are required in order for the (gender) script "[...] to be actualized and reproduced as reality once again," but at the same time gender is "[…] an act which has been rehearsed, much as a script survives the particular actors who make use of it" (Butler, 1988: 526). Even though performative acts are located with individuals, and "[…] there are nuanced and individual ways of *doing* one's gender, but *that* one does it, and that one does it *in accord with* certain sanctions and proscriptions, is clearly not a fully individual matter" (Butler, 1988: 525—emphasis in original). This brings us to performativity, which, for Butler (1993: 2), "[…] must be understood not as a singular or deliberate 'act,' but, rather, as the reiterative and citational practice by which discourse produces the effects that it names."

A second concept—besides acts—that is frequently used to capture acting bodies is the notion of practice. Laclau and Mouffe (1985) frequently used the practice concept in *HSS*—for instance, when referring to 'articulatory practices' and 'hegemonic practices'—but they did not provide much clarity when it comes to the meaning of the practice concept.[16] For this reason, we need to look elsewhere. One older definition of practice is Kant's statement in the 1793 essay '*On the Common Saying*,' where he distinguished between doing and practices in the following terms: "Conversely, not all activities are called *practice*, but only those realisations of a particular purpose which are considered to comply with certain generally conceived principles of procedure" (Kant, 1991: 61—emphasis in original). Commenting on Kant's definition, Svare (2006: 84) suggested two main characteristics of practice in the Kantian definition. Practices are "[…] only acts following some sort of general rules or principles for behaviour." Moreover, according to Svare (2006: 84), Kant's examples illustrate that "[…] people involved in a practice do it in order to attain an end." This more specific use of practice is not shared by more recent authors. De Certeau (1984: xi) simply referred to "'ways of operating' or doing things," although he immediately distanced himself from social atomism. Ortner (1984: 149), one of the key authors in the field of practice theory, answered her own question "What is practice?" as follows: "In principle, the answer to this question is almost unlimited: anything people do." She continued her discussion of the practice concept by stating that "[…] the most significant forms of practice are those with intentional or intentional political consequences," with the qualification that "[…] almost anything people do has such implications" (Ortner, 1984: 149). Ortner also suggested that practice theory tends to focus on individual actors (but also critiqued this), that practices are considered in relation to both long or short time frames, and that the "[…] view of action largely in terms of pragmatic choice and decision making, and/or calculating and strategizing" (Ortner, 1984: 150) prevails.

Finally, the notion of interaction should also be mentioned in this context. If we look at the work of Argentinean philosopher Bunge (1977: 259), we can find there the following treacherously simple and general definition of interaction: "[...] two different things x and y interact if each acts upon the other," combined with the following postulate: "Every thing acts on, and is acted upon by, other things." In sociological theory, where the notion of social interaction has often been used, we find definitions of interaction and interactivity that are more focused on human behavior. An example of the conceptual openness can be found in Giddens's (2006: 1034) definition of social interaction in the Glossary of *Sociology*. He defined social interaction as "Any form of social encounter between individuals." Some of the older definitions are similarly brief and open: For Gist (1950: 363), social interaction is "[...] the reciprocal influences that human beings exert on each other through interstimulation and response," while Merrill and Eldredge (1957: 32) saw social interaction as "[...] the general series of activities whereby two or more persons are in meaningful contact." But not all definitions are this brief. Garton (1995: 11) suggested the following:

> "A definition of social interaction states that at a minimum two persons exchanging information are essential. Social interaction further implies some degree of reciprocity and bidirectionality between both (although it must be acknowledged that there are degrees of both)."

An even more elaborate definition can be found from De Jaegher and Di Paolo (2007: 493), who emphasized the regulated (or social, I would add) nature of social interaction:

> "Social interaction is the regulated coupling between at least two autonomous agents, where the regulation is aimed at aspects of the coupling itself so that it constitutes an emergent autonomous organization in the domain of relational dynamics, without destroying in the process the autonomy of the agents involved (though the latter's scope can be augmented or reduced)."

Despite the differences (for instance, concerning the role of influence in defining social interaction), these definitions also have quite a lot in common, in emphasizing the social and the communicative dimensions of interaction. While the social dimension of the definition can be found in concepts such as contact, encounter, and reciprocity (but also (social) regulation), the communicative dimension is referred to by concepts such as response, meaning, and communication itself. As Sharma (1996: 359) formulated it, the "[…] two basic conditions of social interaction […]" are "[…] social contact and communication […]," which has led me to emphasize in earlier work (Carpentier, 2011) that social interaction can be defined as the establishment of socio-communicative relationships. This focus on the human and the social has triggered a response that brings us back to Bunge's approach to interaction, as defined a few paragraphs before. To stress the need to broaden the scope, but also to question the presence of autonomous agents, Barad (2007) introduced the notion of intra-action, "[…] a kind of neologism, which gets us to shift from interaction, where we start with separate entities and they interact, to intra-action, where there are interactions through which subject and object emerge" (Barad, 2012: 55).

In particular, the notions of practices and interactions tend to be rather broad concepts,[17] even in their more conventional meanings, which incorporate both the discursive and material dimensions of human activity.[18] This has triggered a series of specifications that aim to delimit the notions of practice and interaction. Svare (2006: 85), for instance, focused on embodied practices, which she distinguished from practices "[…] taking place solely at the mental level." But things are not that straightforward, as Robertson (1997: 209), in her article '*Cooperative Work and Lived Cognition: A Taxonomy of Embodied Actions*,' pointed to the close relationship between cognition and sensory experiences:

> "Embodied actions are the actions of an active and perceiving embodied subject. The consideration of embodied actions as classes of cognitive practices recognises that human cognition depends on the 'kinds of experiences that come from having a body with specific sensorimotor capacities.'" (Varela et al., 1991, pp. 172–173)

Similarly, when discussing memories, Salerno and Zarankin (2014: 94) stressed the importance of images, which are in turn fed by sensory experiences, or "[…] in other words, […] the engagement with a world that clearly has a material dimension." Other authors, such as Dourish (2001: 126), for instance, work the other way around to connect the material combination of the definition of embodiment with meaning, as in this example:

> "Embodiment is the property of our engagement with the world that allows us to make it meaningful. Similarly, then, we can say: Embodied interaction is the creation, manipulation, and sharing of meaning through engaged interaction with artifacts."

This co-presence of matter and meaning in the notion of embedded practices is both its strength and its weakness, as its capacity to capture the combination of matter and meaning also black-boxes the balance between its two constitutive components. For this reason, two types of practices are mobilized: material bodily practices and signifying practices, as shown in Figure 2.

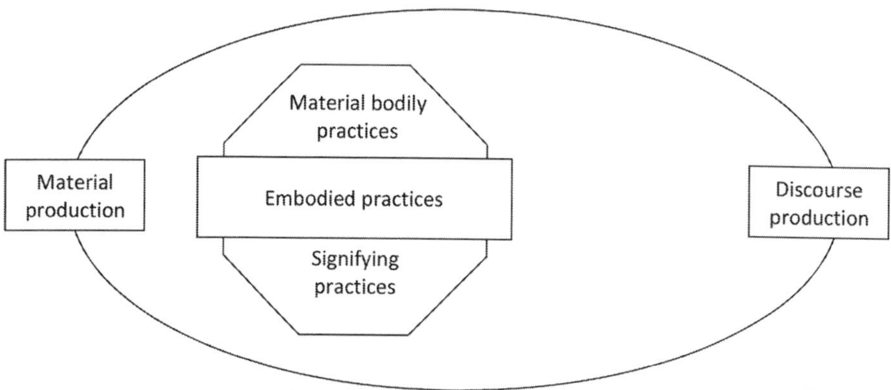

Figure 2. An elliptical model of human practices.

This model implies that material bodily practices and signifying practices are seen as embodied, but with a stronger emphasis on matter and meaning, respectively, in the intentions or outcomes of human practices. Moreover, social practices are seen as distinct from material and discursive production processes.[19] As discussed before, the production of discourses is a social process that transcends individual actions and practices, and most often remains quite out of reach.[20] As material production results more easily from embodied practices, the model takes the shape of an ellipse.

Through this articulation of these different notions of practice, material bodily practices are seen as one of the two components of embodied practices, taking Knapp and Meskell's (1997: 188—see also Shilling, 1993: 10) call for groundedness, where the body is regarded "[…] as a material, physical and biological phenomenon irreducible to immediate social processes and classifications," seriously. Or, to use de Certeau's (1984: 61) words, to deal with "[…] this non-discursive activity, […] this immense 'remainder' constituted by the part of human experience that has not been tamed and symbolized in language." Material bodily practices refer to the actions of the complex ensemble of organs, muscles, and bones that we call body, that takes a material place in the world and that can operate other materials (and bodies).

In her taxonomy, Robertson (1997: 211)—even when discussing embodied practices—still refers to material bodily practices, which are: "[...] individual embodied actions—in relation to physical objects—in relation to other bodies—in relation to the physical workspace [...]" and "[...] group activities constituted by individual embodied actions." At the same time, we should immediately point to the significance of bodily diversity, which has been particularly thematized in gender studies and feminist theory (but also in race and ethnicity studies, and in disability studies), given the political nature of these differences:

> "The very fact that women are able in general to menstruate, to develop another body unseen within their own, give birth, and to lactate is enough to suggest a potentially dangerous volatility that marks the female body as out of control, beyond, and set against, the force of reason." (Shildrick, 1999: 3)

This is one more reason why we should keep Mol's (2002: 6) words about bodily diversity in mind: "[...] no object, no body, no disease, is singular." And, moreover, as Blackman (2008: 125) stressed, the body is "[...] an open system that connects with others, human and non-human. The body is extended to include how it becomes connected up to techniques, artefacts and practices which produce particular kinds of object and entities." But most importantly, as the above-mentioned reference to the female body already indicated, material bodily practices are not outside culture and discourse, they are part of the discursive-material knot: "Ultimately, embodiment can never exist outside of culture" (Farman, 2013: 23), or, in the words of Grosz (1994: 23—emphasis in original):

> "The body must be regarded as a site of social, political, cultural, and geographic inscriptions, production or constitution. The body is not opposed to culture, a resistant throwback to a natural past; it is itself a cultural, *the* cultural product."

The second component is the signifying practice, in the ways that the concept has been used by Hall in his 1997 edited volume *Representation. Cultural Representations and Signifying Practices*. In an interview published in the same year, Hall (1997b) distinguished signifying practices from how Williams defined culture (as "a whole way of life"), where, for Williams, "[...] the practices and the signification, they're all one; the family and ideas about the family are all the same thing. For Williams, everything is dissolved into practice" (Hall, 1997b). As the example of the family illustrates, signifying practices tends to zoom in on (the generation of) ideas, although Barker (2011: 7) focused more on the role of language in defining signifying practices. His definition also uses the notion of social practice in a way that disconnects it from the concept of the signifying practice, which does not assist in producing a clear definition:

> "[…] language gives meaning to material objects and social practices that are brought into view by language and made intelligible to us in terms that language delimits. These processes of meaning production are signifying practices."

Signifying practices are seen here as the human practices that are aimed at, or result in, the attribution of meaning to humans and other living creatures; to non-human machines; to actions, events, and processes; to concepts. In this sense, signifying practices are referential, allowing for the attribution of meaning, but they are also communicative, as they allow for the exchange (and potential sharing) of meaning. Through this combination of referentiality and communicability, signifying practices can contribute to the production of discourses, although no linear relationship between them exists, and there is no guarantee that a particular signifying practice will result in the creation, strengthening, or weakening of a discourse. Signifying practices remain embodied—the concept of the signifying practice simply zooms in on the generation-of-meaning component of embodied practices—as human bodies remain crucial in the acts of meaning production, though their speaking, writing, thinking, broadcasting, publishing … which combines the body as communicational tool with the body as operator of other communicational tools.

Signifying practices can use many different media to come into existence. Without going knee-deep into the debates about the definition of media, it remains important to touch briefly upon how media are approached here. The media definition used here navigates between an "extensions of man" approach (McLuhan, 1964), which is seen as too broad, and a technical media approach (Kittler, 1990), which is deemed too narrow. Media are the assemblages, embedded in the discursive-material knot, that provide the necessary support for signifying practices and their referential and communicative dimensions. In other words, media are the assemblages needed by signifying practices in order to materially and discursively exist. Media allow subjects to allocate and share meanings. Language is an important example of a medium, quickly followed (because of the context of this book) by mass media, community media, and social media, although many other media can be added to the list.[21] We should be careful not to ignore the many differences and contingencies that characterize the media field, where each media assemblage has its specific ways (or modalities—see Elleström, 2010) of breathing life into signifying practices. To use Kittler's (1990: 369) words: The ways that the "network of technologies and institutions that allow a given culture to select, store, and process relevant data" operate shows substantial internal differences, even though these different media assemblages still—each in their own ways—support and enable the existence of signifying practices.

Again, we need to reflect on the relation of these media to the discursive, but also to the material. Language is a helpful case study here. Traditional Saussurian semiotics defines the sign as constituted through the workings of signifier and signified, in a rather closed encounter, which also ignores the materiality of the sign (Chandler, 2004: 50) and its (potential) referentiality to the material.[22] Here, we can take Butler's (1993: 68) position, which refers to the materiality of language and its referentiality: "[…] language both is and refers to that which is material, and what is material never fully escapes from the process by which it is signified." As is shown in Figure 3, The sign is defined here as M/M, Matter and Meaning (and not so much as De Saussure does, as S/S or Signifier/Signified), to bring out the materiality of language. Thomas's (2007: 2) description of the book as a material object[23] mentions not only the physicality of the book, but also of the language used.

> "Like any building, the book you have in your hands right now is a material object. But as you read it you will be unlikely to think of it this way. The materiality of the book has probably gone unnoticed: at most you might be aware of its weight, or the smell or texture of the pages—and even these immediate sensory qualities are secondary while you are concentrating on the contributors' ideas through their words and images. To shift your attention to the book as a material object would be to see that it is not only the ideas of the authors which shape it. Like any building, this book is in fact the result of a vast network of practices. There are conventions of its structure and of the English language in written form; the design of typefaces and the software in which the print is set; the manufacture of papers, glues and inks from which it is constructed."

Signifying practices are not merely self-referential—signifying practices have the objective or outcome to speak about our social world, in a more specific fashion, providing meaning to particular materials or concepts, or, in a more general way, connecting signifiers to the material and the discursive (as shown in Figure 3—with its focus on the signifier[24]). They are part of the discursive-material knot, which brings about different interactions. At the same time, their specificity matters. To capture this, Figure 3 has three different levels, with the signifier (and its interconnected meaning and matter) located at the first level. Signifiers provide meaning to particular materials and concepts (or signifieds), but—as repeatedly mentioned—individual signifying practices cannot automatically alter (or create) discourses, because social construction is an extra-individual—social—process. In other words, Level 1 and Level 3 are not automatically connected (hence the dotted arrow between the signifier, concepts, and discourses). In contrast, materials transgress the difference between Level 2 and Level 3, which implies that signifying practices can relate to particular materials, but also, discourses are seen to give meaning to materials, through the activation of signifying practices (and thus going through the loop, from right to left).

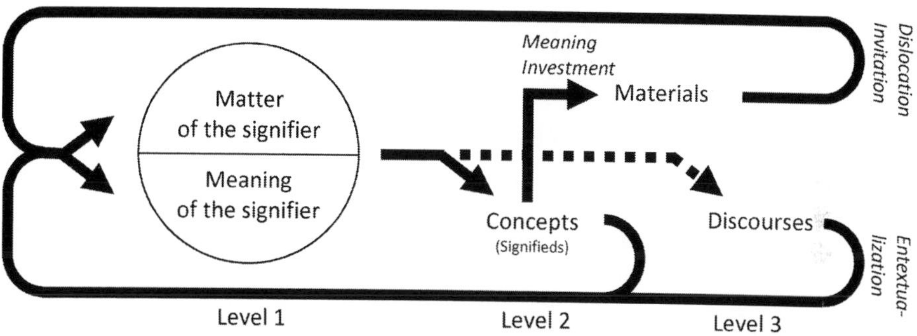

Figure 3. A model of the signifier and its relation to the material and the discursive.

The process is dynamic, as both the specific and the general levels produce contexts that impact on the meaning and the materiality of the signifier (which is captured by the two arrows curling from right to left). Particular materials and concepts can impact on the signifier that attempts to provide meaning. The material invites for particular signifying practices, and can dislocate others. Also, discourses invest materials with meaning and can accept or reject particular signifying practices. Moreover, discourses are the structures that allow (and disallow) for the interpretation of signifiers, their meanings, but also their materiality. The latter can be illustrated by Derrida's analysis of phonocentrism, the discourse that claims the superiority of the spoken word over the written word, that—for Derrida (1998: 12—emphasis in original)—"[…] merges with the historical determination of the meaning of being in general as *presence*."

If we return to the elliptical model of human practices (see Figure 2) and use the above discussion on language, we can provide another version of the elliptical model that is more focused on texts (see Figure 4). This model's

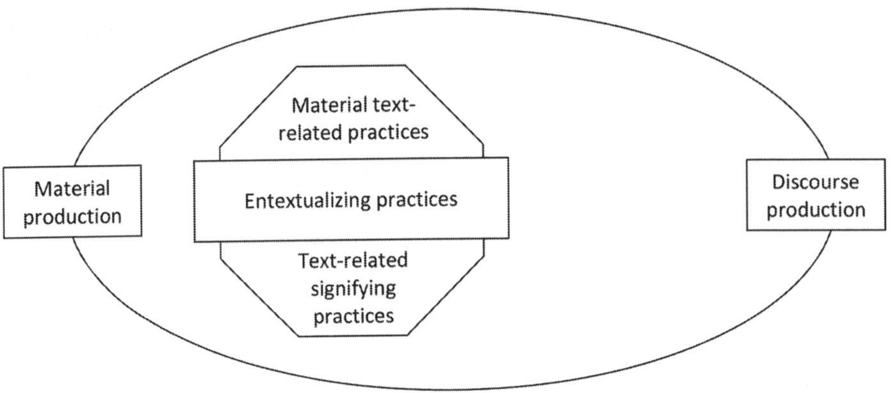

Figure 4. An elliptical model of text-related practices.

key notion—entextualization—is inspired by the work of Bauman and Briggs (1990: 73—emphasis in original), who defined entextualization as:

> "[...] the process of rendering discourse extractable, of making a stretch of linguistic production into a unit-*a text*-that can be lifted out of its interactional setting. A text, then, from this vantage point, is discourse rendered decontextualizable. Entextualization may well incorporate aspects of context, such that the resultant text carries elements of its history of use within it."

The way that entextualization is used here does not remain entirely loyal to Bauman and Briggs' article. Entextualization is seen as the practice(s) of the (linguistic) condensation of discourse into text, a process we can also label the textual representation[25] of discourse. It is a movement that takes us back from Level 3 to Level 1, as the loops indicate in Figure 3. This practice is grounded in a knotted combination of material and signifying practices, where the materiality of textual production (or what Dourish and Mazmanian, 2013, focusing on digital representation, called the "materiality of representation" and the "materiality of information") refers to the assemblage of writing, storage, and distribution technologies. Dourish and Mazmanian (2013: 95) argued that "Particular material properties might include mutability, persistence, robustness, spatiality, size, durability, flexibility, and mobility." In addition, textual production also incorporates signifying practices, where meaning is stored in these representational containers and is shared and communicated. In this sense, entextualization, or entextualizing practices, are always a combination of both material and signifying (text-related) practices, embedded in the broader fields of materiality and discursivity. In turn, entextualizing practices contribute (potentially) to material and discursive production at a broader level. In the case of material production, we can refer to media production practices, where texts become media products. Less likely, as the above-formulated reservations towards the automatic translation of signifying practices into discourse also holds here, we can still think of entextualizing practices that contribute to discursive production.

Contingency enters these different equations, as none of these different relationships are stable. At Level 1 (in Figure 3), the signifier's meaning is influenced by its materiality, and vice versa—both what is written and the surface that is written on impacts on the writing. The relationship between the signifier, on the one hand, and the concepts and/or materials it aims to provide meaning to (Level 2), on the other hand, is also contingent, as materials (and concepts) "[…] never fully [escape] from the process by which [they are] signified," and as "[…] materiality [cannot] be summarily collapsed in an identity with language" (Butler, 1993: 68). And finally, the relation between signifier (and signifying practices) and discourse (and, indirectly, materials, through the loop) (at Level 3) is also contingent. This contingency occurs through the discursive struggles that produce instability, even when meanings can be hegemonically fixated for long periods of time in considerably vast spaces. Contingency also arises from the workings of the dislocation/invitation pair, and from the logics of investment and entextualization.

4.5 Organizational Machines

One of the locations where bodies and objects, including proto-machines, become aligned and assembled is within organizational machines. The complexity of organizational machines as assemblages and the workings of the discursive and the material can, to some degree, be rendered more clear by distinguishing between an internal and external organizational dimension. *Inside* organizations, we can find the entanglements of the material and the discursive, with its contingencies, where specific people and objects are arranged and regulated within the organization. This assemblage is distinguished from an outside world through the creation of an in/out frontier. Simultaneously, organizations can also be seen as actors that establish discursive and material links with their political, economic, technological, and cultural environments. When building these interconnections with their outside worlds, an organization can be seen as an active actor in its own right, "[…] capable of behaving in a purposeful, intentional manner" (King, Felin, & Whetten,

2010: 291), although care should be taken not to reify organizations (see Fairhurst & Putnam, 2004: 13).

In order to highlight the specificity of organizational machines as a particular kind of assemblage, we can revert, as a starting point, to organizational sociology. There we can find a wide variety of definitions of the concept of the organization, but as Lammers (1987: 22) remarked, there is also (a relatively high degree of) consensus on a number of key characteristics. Lammers (1987: 29) described the organization as a social structure that has been consciously constructed and is (more or less) regularly reconstructed. Organizations have a formally defined design that is intended to be rational and is characterized by functionalization, coordination, and finalization. Within the organization, tasks are defined and grouped together (functionalization); these tasks are then combined (coordination) with the aim of achieving the general objective(s) (finalization), which can range from utilitarian to normative (Etzioni, 1961). A short definition that emphasizes this aspect can be found in Etzioni (1964: 3): "Organizations are social units (or human groupings) deliberately constructed and reconstructed to seek specific goals." Through these logics, hierarchies, and power imbalances become embedded within the organization, as described in Stinchcombe's (1967: 155) definition: "Any social arrangement in which the activities of some people are systematically planned by other people (who, therefore, have authority over them) in order to achieve some special purpose is called a formal organization."

These definitions are not meant to create the impression that all organizations are similar, and necessarily have vertical hierarchies. As in many fields of the social, there is a wide variety of organizational structures, practices, and cultures. Attempts to deal with this complexity have resulted in a series of categorizations, among which the distinction between the mechanistic, organic, and bureaucratic organization is one of the most prominent. Hatch (1997) used three characteristics—complexity, formalization, and centralization—to support this typology. Whereas organic organizations have low levels of complexity, formalization, and centralization, mechanistic and bureaucratic organizations have high levels of complexity and formalization. The distinction between mechanistic and bureaucratic organizations is that the former are characterized by high levels of centralization, while bureaucracies—though highly formalized—function in a decentralized way. This typology also serves as a reminder that state and government are also (clusters of) organizations, especially because in some research, e.g., the Esrc's Whitehall Programme, where "[…] only modest attention was given to government *qua* organization

(Rhodes, 2000)," as Jacobsson, Pierre, and Sundström (2015: 27—emphasis in original) contended.

Further complexity is generated by the process of institutionalization, or the way that organizations become "[...] infused with value beyond the technical requirements of the task at hand" (Selznick, 1957: 17). Institutions are different from organizations, as the former are "[...] systems of *rules* that apply to the future behavior of actors" (Offe, 2006: 10—emphasis in original). Rawls (2009: 55) used the following (related) definition of the institution, which he sees as "a public system of rules which defines offices and positions with their rights and duties, powers and immunities, and the like." Despite these conceptual differences, organizations and institutions are not disconnected. Organizations can still play a structuring and supportive role in relation to institutions, and, as Scott (1992) argued, institutionalization implies that the organization is embedded in an environment with specific expectations of the organization, which imposes rules in order to ensure the organization's social legitimacy. If we shift towards a more discourse-theoretical perspective, Howarth's (2000: 120) argument that "Institutions are [to be] understood as 'sedimented discourses' [...]," is helpful, as this shows the specificity of the discursive context in which institutions (and their supportive organizational machines) are embedded, their integration into an assemblage (with also a material component), and the legitimacy and authority of the signifying practices that these institutions may generate.

Returning to our discursive-material knot, first of all, *within* the organizational machinery, we can find a series of discursive and material interactions (see Figure 5). As our organizational sociology detour shows, organizations are characterized by their focus on the realization of a specific set of objectives, which is very much an internal-discursive component. Moreover, in order to achieve this aim, people and objects are constructed as internal to the organization. Through this logic, but in a variety of ways, people become members, and objects become owned, which is enabled by discourses on membership and ownership. Keeping in mind Rafaeli's (1997) argument, we should not lose sight of the complexities of membership, because membership might be based on physical or temporal relationships, production relationships, or cultural relationships, but this membership offers identificatory positions to those who move within the organizations, and they, in their turn, contribute to the construction of the organizational identity (see Albert & Whetten, 1985, for an early version) and the identities of other members. Similarly, people within the organization give meaning to particular objects and their relation to them, for instance, through the concept of ownership, and the subject position of the owner.

One concept that is used to capture the workings of this internal-discursive level is organizational culture, which is seen to develop, circulate, and be preserved within organizations. Siehl and Martin (1984: 227) described organizational culture as follows: "[…] organizational culture can be thought of as the glue that holds an organization together through a sharing of patterns of meaning. The culture focuses on the values, beliefs, and expectations that members come to share." As Martin (2002: 3) remarked, the field of organizational culture is broad, and, for instance, includes "[…] the stories people tell to newcomers to explain 'how things are done around here,' the ways in which offices are arranged and personal items are or are not displayed, jokes people tell, the working atmosphere […], the relations among people […], and so on." Organizational culture, or "the way of life in an organization" (Hatch, 1997: 204), is supported by signifying practices on (amongst many other areas) the general objectives and specific tasks of the organization; the means and decision-making procedures that need to be used to achieve them; the language and conceptual framework; the membership boundaries and criteria for inclusion (and exclusion) and the criteria for allocation of status, power, and authority; and rewards and punishments (based on Schein, 1985, see also the summary by Hatch, 1997: 213). At the same time, again, organizational culture is not homogeneous, and the above-mentioned areas provide ample opportunity for conflict, contestation, and power struggles within the organization.

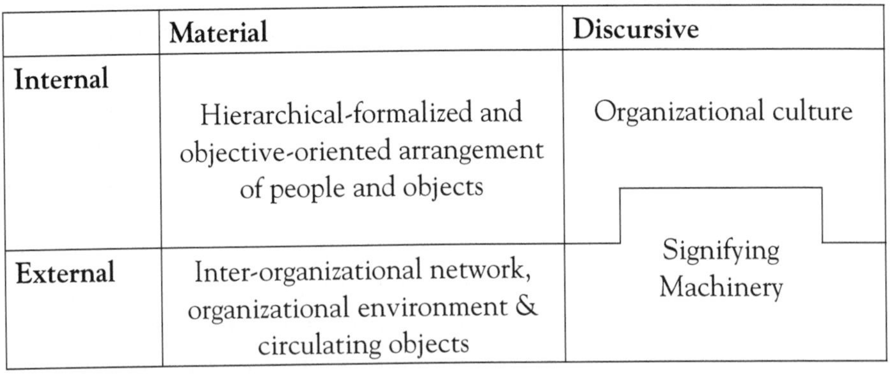

	Material	**Discursive**
Internal	Hierarchical-formalized and objective-oriented arrangement of people and objects	Organizational culture
External	Inter-organizational network, organizational environment & circulating objects	Signifying Machinery

Figure 5. Organizational characteristics.
Adapted from Carpentier, 2011: 217.

These internal-discursive characteristics are first of all complemented by a series of materialities that operate within organizations. Obviously, bodies and objects are often (but not always) grouped within delineated spaces, forming hierarchical-formalized and objective-oriented arrangements. Müller (2012: 382—emphasis in original) wrote that they are "[...] ensembles of human *and* material elements that work together toward a shared mission." From this perspective, organizations can be seen as attempts to materially delineate a unity through the mobilization of resources. Cooren, Brummans, and Charrieras (2008: 1342) used the notion of "organizational presentification": "[...] a term that refers to the ways in which an organization is made present through contributions of human and nonhuman agents engaged in ongoing processes of interaction." Cooren, Brummans, and Charrieras (2008: 1344) listed the people and materials that are used for this: "[...] it is through spokespersons, employees, a president, logos, by-laws, buildings, machines, stock certificates, and so on, that a company exists and acts." In their case study introduction, Cooren, Brummans, and Charrieras (2008: 1348) also mentioned a more abstract list: "[...] we first examine how MSF's [Médecins Sans Frontières—Doctors Without Borders] presence was coproduced through specific representatives, buildings, technologies, procedures, and even [sic] discourses." Again, these materialities are not disconnected from the discursive, as Fairhurst and Putnam (2013: 284—emphasis removed) remarked: "[...] organizations are filled with a plenum of human and nonhuman agencies, including discursive objects (such as authority), which can become text objects (e.g., a memory trace, written or recorded documents, memos, work order, checklists)."

The concept of processes returns us to the discussion on practices that was initiated when discussing human and text-related practices (and Figures 2 and 4). Organizational machines are (one of the) locations were these practices are deployed, driven by the logics of functionalization, coordination, finalization, formalization, and centralization that characterize organizations. In many cases, material production is at the very heart of organizational remits, and this is not only related to the more traditional production processes of the manufacturing industry, or to the post-industrial and post-Fordist economies. For instance, also in the service economy and the social economy, the material is abundantly present, as Pettinger's (2006) analyses of the retail industry shows. Pettinger (2006: 62) suggested taking into account "[...] the embodiment of the workers who also perform physical work to manipulate the products and aesthetic work to present themselves" in combination with "[...] the role of retail in the circulation of goods from the point of production to consumption." In the case of the media industry, we can also find this material component of the production process, with printing presses, radio, television studios, and film sets with their recording devices, data centers, archives, and warehouses, and the vast number of human bodies moving through them, using them, and operating proto-machines within them. At the same time, the media industry focuses on textual production, which brings in the combination of matter and meaning. One example that Schwanecke (2015: 275) gave deals with film:

> "Filmic technologies and materiality […] include cameras, projectors, film screens, film reels, super 8, digital production, 3D-screenings, pyrotechnics, and stunt units. Among the semiotic symbols a film typically makes use of are moving pictures, verbal language, sound […], and music."

Even when, in some cases, organizations have the explicit ambition to engage in discourse production—Althusser's ideological state apparatuses come to mind—within the discourse-theoretical approach used in this book there is no guarantee that the translation of signifying practices into discourse will be successful. They nevertheless engage in signifying practices (or can be seen as "producers of representations," as Müller, 2012: 380, formulated it). At the same time, organizations, in particular when they have discursive production as their principle objective, are privileged in their capacity to unify different voices within the organization, and support a regularity of dispersion—to use one of Foucault's (1972) formulations. These processes of coordination, synchronization, and harmonization are combined with the disciplining, policing, and silencing voices that invoke alternative discourses. One example can be found in the history of the Catholic Church, with the development of the concept of the heretic: "'Heresy', and therefore the idea of 'the heritic' and the identification of those who might qualify, is a construction of early Christian rhetoric within the process of shaping some form of self-definition or identity" (Lieu, 2015: 443). As Hunter, Laursen, and Nederman (2013: 1) argued, heresy "[…] can be found in any religion that attempts to define or codify its doctrines as orthodoxy" but "Christianity, with the universalistic pretentions of its 'catholic' church, found temporal resources to enforce its spiritual vision in a way that other religions were unable or unprepared to pursue." In addition to the processes of coordination, synchronization, and harmonization, also the organizations' capacity for validation, legitimation, and authorization contribute to their power positions. Although discussions on legitimacy often focus on institutions and the way they are legitimated (see, e.g., Berger & Luckmann,

1966: 110ff; Van Dijk, 1998: 255ff), the emphasis needs to be placed here on the capacity of organizations to legitimate and authorize particular signifying practices, which makes them more susceptible to becoming discourses. Finally, organizations have the resources to distribute their signifying practices, and to defend them when other actors launch alternative truth claims.

One particular set of practices within the organization are related to decision-making processes. These practices are crucial to the organization, as King, Felin, and Whetten (2000: 300) formulated it, when referring to "[…] the organization's unique properties as structuring elements of the decision making process." A similar argument was made by Wodak (2013: 185) when she wrote that "Decision making constitutes the life of organizations." The significatory component of decision-making practices is quite strong, as they involve what Laclau (1996: 92) called moments of (significatory) fixation, where discourses are invoked in particular ways and political struggles are waged (see also Mouffe, 2000: 130), leading to particular outcomes. Mouffe (2000: 130) added to this idea that the decision—as a moment of fixation—entails "[…] an element of force and violence […]." At the same time, decision-making also has a material dimension, with technologies for presenting, registering, and archiving regulatory documents such as statutes, embedded in legal frameworks, but also meetings, which are "[…] perceived as a necessary and pervasive characteristic of organizations—they are events that people are required to be engaged in if decisions are to be made and goals are to be accomplished" (Mumby, 1988: 68). Important in this context are the material hierarchical structures within the organization, as always embedded in discourses on leadership, membership, and organizational democracy. Although there is a tendency towards vertically organized hierarchies, more horizontally structured hierarchies remain possible.[26] The materiality of these organizational decision-making structures and the presence (or absence) of more balanced power relations play a crucial role in organizational life.

Apart from these internal components, there are also external ones that further illustrate the complex workings of the discursive-material knot. Organizations are not isolated entities, floating freely within the social; they are simultaneously exposed to centrifugal and centripetal forces. If we look at them from an external-material perspective, then, the organization is positioned within an assemblage of other organizations and within the context of the organizational environment. This assemblage can be extended to include the circulating objects that leave or enter the organization. Although the internal logics of organizations should not necessarily be articulated as stable, especially the relations of organizations, which, with their environments and the constant flux of people and objects that move across their boundaries, show the structural instability and contingency of organizations. Moreover, organizational machines, in particular those that support institutions, can produce authoritative signifying practices that affect other fields. Government, and the state itself, are here obvious examples, as policy is driven by the production of authoritative signifying practices (or political decisions) within the assemblage(s) of institutionalized politics. These authoritative signifying practices are outcomes of complex processes within and beyond institutionalized politics, and can be seen as temporal sedimentations of equally complex power plays (embedded within the discursive-material knot). Once established, authoritative signifying practices invoke (and sometimes produce) discourses and mobilize materials in a wide variety of societal fields: They can, for instance, initiate the redistribution of resources, the engagement in practices of legislation, or the deployment of an army.

Also, organizational culture does not stop at the borders of the organization—however permeable these borders might be. Organizational identities and discourses interact with the assemblages, environments, and cultures in which the organizations are embedded. These outsides offer to organizations discourses that provide the elements to construct the organizational cultures. Obviously, discourses on 'good' decision-making, leadership, and membership, and on the legitimacy of the organizational objectives, are not continuously reinvented by each individual organization, but are part of a broader cultural configuration that seeps into these organizations. At the same time, organizations are not without agency, and can, within the limits of a set of hegemonies, articulate existing elements into particular discourses. Through their practices and discourses, organizations also support, normalize, and sometimes undermine and contradict existing cultural configurations. Their voices contribute to society's discursive production, sometimes entailing the promise of social change, but often contributing to the continued fixation of society's rigidities.

5 The Two Dimensions and Their Knotted Relationships

If we combine the different components and their relationships in one model (as the 'Overview' model in Figure 6 attempts to do), we get a good hint of the complexity generated by the interactions between the different components. Even if this model fails to provide a clear overview of these many relationships (which is my reason for including it), it produces a visualization of the discursive-material knot in itself, characterized by the permanent and restless interplay between the four different components of the discursive and the material, structure and agency. None of these four components ever manages to dominate the others, but they relate to each other in a non-hierarchical and overdetermined way.

In discussing the different components, ample emphasis was placed on the contingent logics that operated within and between the components, but the model of Figure 6 shows the multitude of relationships whose

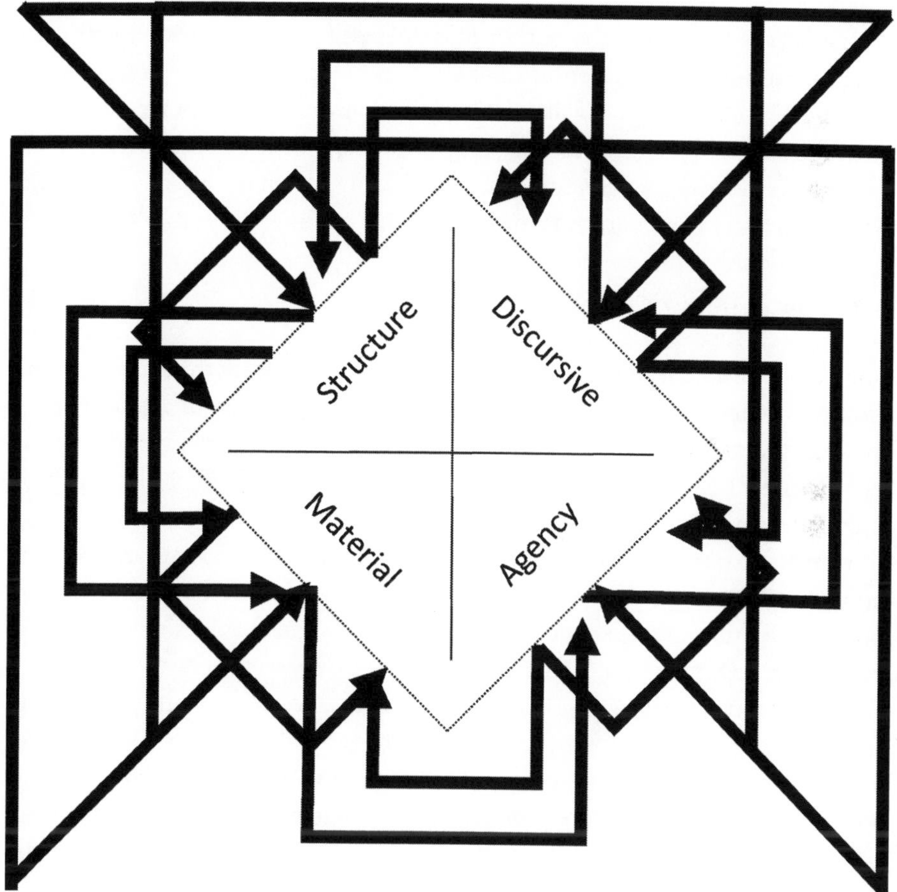

Figure 6. The 'overview' of the discursive-material knot.

incessant interactions create the breeding ground for contingency. When each component is intrinsically contingent, and contingency is enhanced by the interactions between two components, then contingency can only be seen as incrementally increased by the interplay of all components. Even if in the following (summarizing) parts the context of contingency is not always explicitly mentioned or discussed (to avoid repetition), it is always presupposed.

The 'overview' in Figure 6 not only illustrates the difficulties in visually representing these relations, but also shows how difficult it is to discuss these relations in a linear text. Obviously, the common disclaimer—that these four components are analytical categories, not to be equated with social reality—also applies here, although it might be more appropriate to refer to these four components as signifying practices, or, perhaps, discourses. As this disclaimer mostly serves to protect the author and does not assist the reader, it is combined with another representational strategy to make these overviews more accessible. This strategy consists of focusing on one of the four components at the time, and briefly sketching its relationships with the other three components[27] (in the knowledge that these relationships have already been analyzed, in a fairly thorough way, in the previous parts).

5.1 The Agency Component

The first component to have its relationship with the other three components discussed is agency (see Figure 7). Agency impacts on the discursive through the exercise of identificatory choices, where in a context of discursive plurality the subject can align herself or himself through the logic of identification with different discourses in always different ways. Moreover, even if individuals (often) do not have the capacity to engage in individual discursive production, they—as part of the social—do collectively construct discourses through their signifying practices, and become part of the many discursive struggles that define that very social. This immediately brings us to the second component, structure, as structures themselves are constructed through the workings of agencies. The constructive capabilities of agency apply to discursive structures (through the above-described mechanics of identificatory and signifying practices), but also to material structures (through machines, which consist of arrangements of bodies, proto-machines, and other objects). It is through the workings of agency that discursive closure, but arguably also material closure (or maybe better: material enclosure), is avoided.

Here too, agency plays a role, as it feeds into the diversity of material bodily practices that subjects perform on a daily basis, which consist of a combination of bodily movements, the operation of objects and proto-machines, and bodily interactions with other subjects, sometimes in more isolated settings, and on other occasions in hyper-organized locations. Through these agencies (always surrounded by discourses), subjects engage in material production, and in some cases, in material destructions (as the example of war painfully shows).

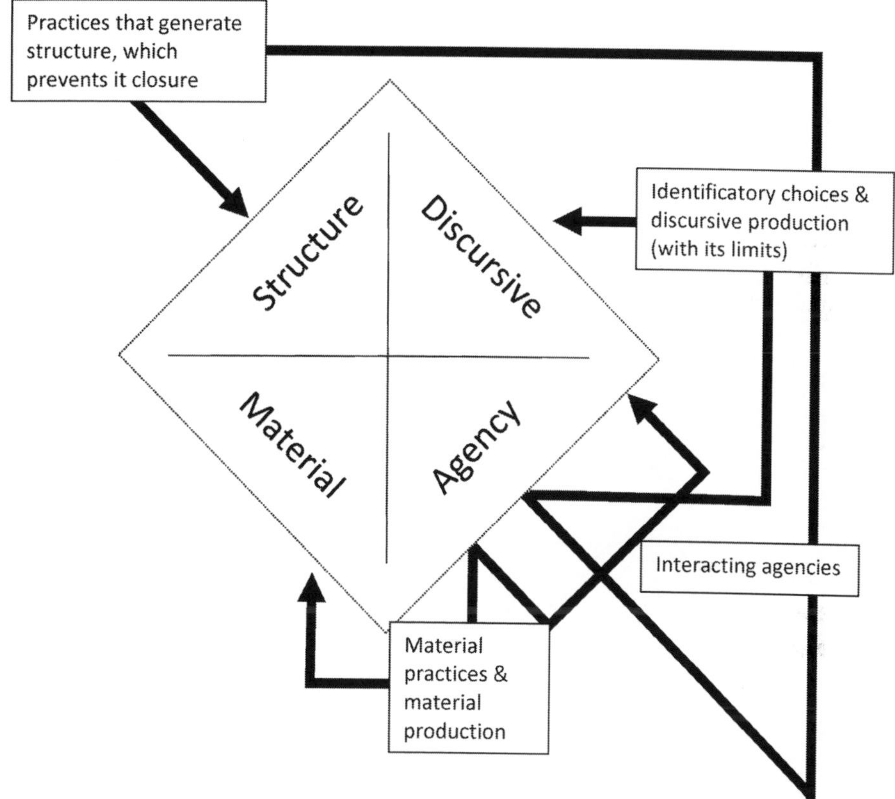

Figure 7. The agency component and its relations.

5.2 The Material Component

The material impacts on the three other components in a variety of ways (see Figure 8). Firstly, the material is structuring—it constructs the social through its very materiality. It allows and disallows bodies to move, in providing access to some spaces (and places) and impeding access to others. Objects and (proto-)machines, for instance, through their affordances, allow for particular actions to be performed, and dissuade the performance of others. The latter idea also implies that the material can be de-structuring, that it can unsettle structures or de/re-assemble assemblages. These disruptions are very much part of the workings of the material, e.g., in the case of war and collective violence, where matter destroys matter.

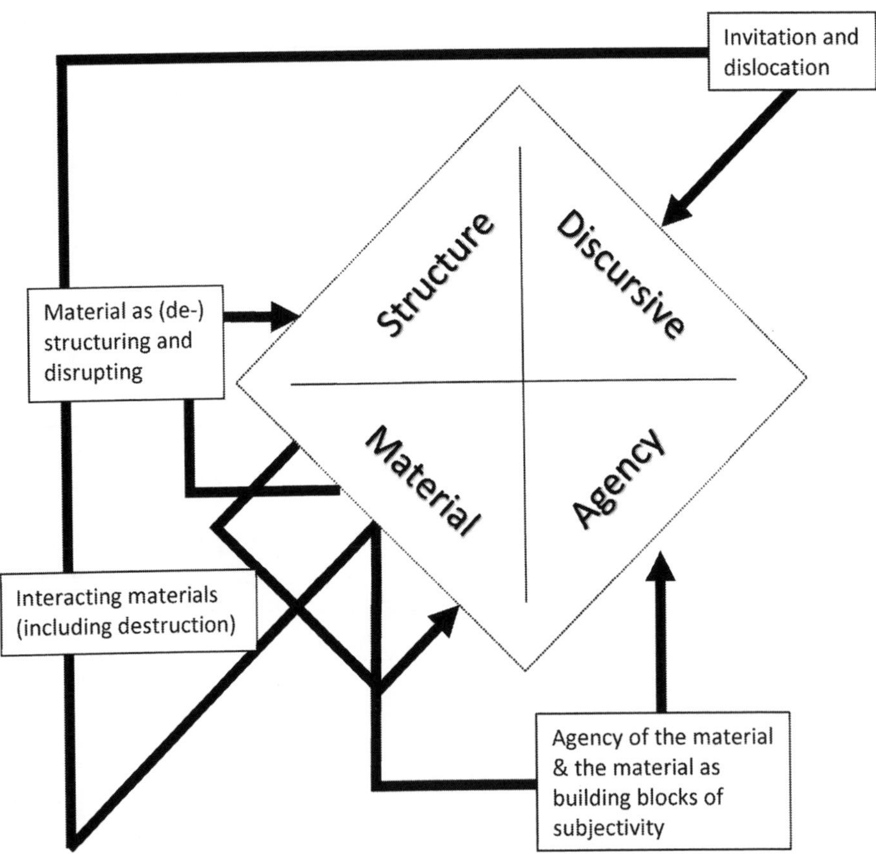

Figure 8. The material component and its relations.

One example of the material's structuring capacity comes from architecture, where living spaces structure social interactions. For this reason, Donley-Reid (1990: 119) referred to the (Swahili) house as a 'structuring structure,' where "[…] the coral house and its internal divisions provided the structuring framework for creating and maintaining power relations." The material's structuring force comes out of its agency, which brings us to the second component. As Horton and Kraftl (2014: 215—emphasis removed) remarked: "[...] things other than human beings do stuff," sometimes by breaking down, malfunctioning, or transforming: "A malfunctioning material thing (perhaps a broken phone, a lost toy, a gritty contact lens) can have an effect, prompt activity, and transform spaces too" (Horton & Kraftl, 2014: 216 & 218). Heidegger's (1996: 73ff) discussion of conspicuousness, obtrusiveness, and obstinacy, where a thing becomes un-useful because it is respectively damaged, incomplete, or a hindrance, can be understood in a similar vain. Even though it is sometimes—depending on the definition of agency—"[...] hard to see how a hammer, a basket, a door closer, a cat, a rug, a mug, a list, or a tag could act," but these objects can "[...] make a difference in the course of some other agent's action" and have agency, at least in this sense (Latour, 2005: 71). One example Latour gave is the weighted hotel door key, which inhibits hotel clients from taking the key with them: "Customers no longer leave their room keys: instead, they get rid of an unwieldy object that deforms their pockets. If they conform to the manager's wishes, it is not because they read the sign, nor because they are particularly well-mannered. It is because they cannot do otherwise" (Latour, 1991: 105).

In addition, the material can also be used as building blocks of human agency, through the meanings allocated to the material. Earlier, I referred to the role that fashion materials can play in the construction of personal subjectivity, but many objects can play significant roles, as Donley-Reid's (1990: 117) reference to the royal crown illustrates: "People use objects to define or to give social or symbolic value to people. People decide that a crown is used to define a king and the crown's value is also reinforced by the king's use of it."

This example also brings us to the role of the discursive, which cannot be removed from the equation. At the same time, we should acknowledge that the material escapes representation and discursification. As Bergson (2004: 236) wrote: "[...] matter goes in every direction beyond our representation of it." Moreover, the material can dislocate discourses by confronting them with the limits in representing a social reality and/or their internal contradictions, unless discursive repair takes place. In a more positive version, the material can also invite for the activation of particular discourses, when the material becomes aligned with a particular discourse, easily allowing for its articulation in a discursive-material assemblage.

5.3 The Structure Component

The material is not only structuring, it is also structured (see Figure 9). At the risk of descending into—at least for me—too unknown territory: the natural sciences have in many different ways focused on the structure of the material. For instance, in the preface of *The Concise Encyclopedia of the Structure of Materials*, Martin (2007: vii) described the notion of structure as follows: it "[…] may be defined on many scales, from the sub-atomic (in the case of electrical and magnetic properties), the atomic scale (in the case of crystalline materials), the molecular scale (in polymers, for example), and of course also the microscopic and macroscopic scales." This is part of a much longer intellectual history, where many philosophers have dealt with the question of how the material is structured. One example is Plato's (2000) *Timaeus*, where he referred to the traditional Empedoclesean elements of earth, fire, air, and water, but also to mathematical shapes (in particular triangles) as structuring elements.

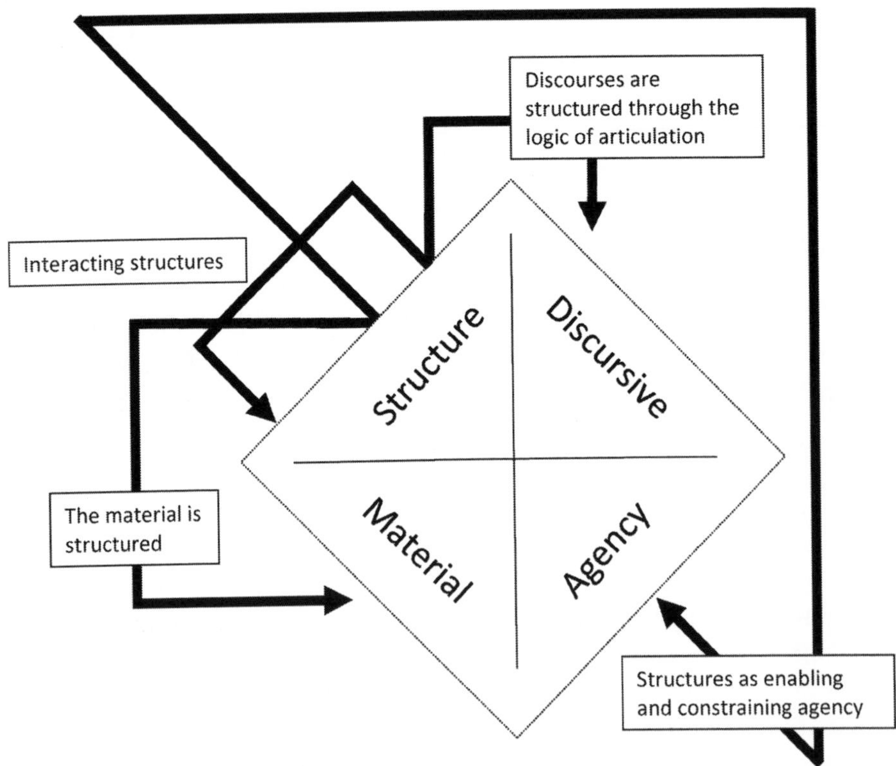

Figure 9. The structure component and its relationships.

Moving away from the intra-material structures, we can also see how assemblages of materials are structured entities. Borrowing discourse theory's way of thinking about articulation, we can furthermore argue that materials change through their incorporation into an assemblage. One rather straightforward example, at least at first sight, can be found in Lefebvre (1991: 113—emphasis in original):

> "Producing an object invariably involves the modification of a raw material by the application to it of an appropriate knowledge, a technical procedure, an effort and a repeated gesture (labour). […] The object produced bears traces of the *matériel* and time that have gone into its production—clues to the operations that have modified the raw material used."

When discussing assemblages, we should keep Müller's (2015: 28) words in mind: "[…] assemblage is a mode of ordering heterogeneous entities so that they work together for a certain time," as this notion of ordering refers to the structured dimension of assemblages (and its fluid nature), also in relation to material orderings. Simultaneously, this enables me to return to the structured nature of discourses, with the articulation of signifiers within a discourse sometimes privileging them as nodal points, functioning as structuring logics, providing order within these discourses.

Finally, we can again return to the notion of structuration, to look at how structure also impacts on agency, providing the material and discursive building blocks that enable, but also constrain, agency. To use Fararo and Skvoretz's (2002: 306) words: "Agency is structured but not fully determined by structure." Even if this citation might be seen as circular, it captures the idea that agency does not function outside the structural but that its provision of building blocks, which can be used for so many purposes, also comes with a price, as it necessarily limits human subjectivity to the use of these building blocks, with the affordances they have, both at the material and the discursive level.

5.4 The Discursive Component

This finally brings us back to the discursive, and its relationship with the three other components (see Figure 10). Despite the material's capacity to 'talk back' (or better: to 'act back') to the discursive, through the logics of invitation and dislocation, the discursive remains a very necessary component of the social to provide meaning to the material (and to the social in general), in some cases, investing meaning into the material itself. Here, we can

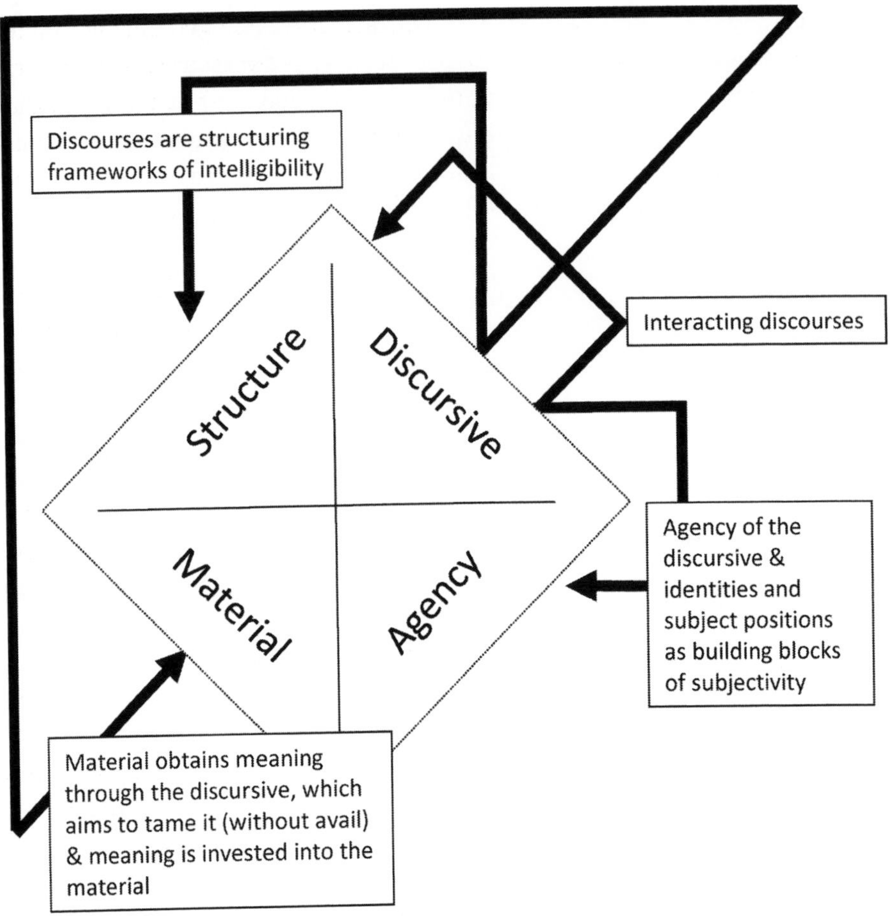

Figure 10. The discursive component and its relations.

return to Butler (1993: 9–10), and the difference she made between matter and materialization:

> "[…] matter, not as site or surface, but as a process of materialization that stabilizes over time to produce the effect of boundary, fixity, and surface we call matter. That matter is always materialized has, I think, to be thought in relation to the productive and, indeed, materializing effects of regulatory power in the Foucaultian sense."

As frameworks of intelligibility, discourses also play a structuring role.[28] Discourses structure the social by making it visible and thinkable; also, discourses have affordances that gear us towards specific interpretations and identifications. At the same time, discourses represent the social in an always incomplete way, desiring for access to the Real, potentially coming within an arm's reach but failing to coalesce with it. The gap between the discursive and the Real makes the discursive particular, even though it sometimes claims to be universal. Laclau's (2000a: 304) argument, that "[...] the only possible universality is the one constructed through an equivalential chain of particularities," not only shows the limits of universalist claims, but also the necessary particularity of the discursive.

Even if the discursive cannot perfectly capture social reality, it remains a key component of the social. In parallel with the ANT position on the agency of the material, a similar argument could be made for the agency of the discursive. Here, it is important to keep the specificity of the discursive-theoretical definition of discourse in mind, which is distinct from signifying practices. Even if discourses are social constructions, produced by interacting humans, they become detached from the individuals that might identify with them, invoke them, recognize them, or reject them. The social but non-individual nature of the discursive renders it semi-autonomous and fills it with agency, in very much the same way as the material has agency.

The discursive impacts on the agency component in one other way, namely, through the generation of subject positions, which are the building blocks of human agency. Human subjectivity requires the discursive in order to offer points of identification, for the meanings attributed to the self (and the other), and for humans to create frameworks of intelligibility that enable subjects to understand their worlds, and thus, to become human.

6 From High Theory to Research: About Sensitizing Concepts

The extensive theoretical overview in this first platform has not been written in isolation from the theoretical discussion on participation, community media, and conflict (transformation) that will follow in the next platform, and that consists of a discourse-material (theoretical) rereading of participatory, community media, and conflict (transformation) theory. Moreover, the first and second platforms of this book have not been written in isolation from the Cypriot community media case study that will be discussed in Platform 3 either. The specificity of the case study was inspirational for the development of the theoretical framework, and the theoretical framework has been illuminative for better understanding the case study. Expressed in a more methodological language: An iterative or cyclical approach was used, allowing for the cross-fertilization of theory and analysis, even if this book contains a linear narrative.

One of the frequently heard critiques on extensive theoretical frameworks, in particular when they are grounded in post-structuralist and/or post-modernist thought, is that they are self-referential and 'jargonesk' stylistic exercises with no direct relevance for (studying) social reality. I would like to argue that this theoretical framework, as it has been developed here, is indispensable for our understanding of participatory and community media theory; for our understanding of Cypriot community media's capacity to contribute to conflict transformation; for our understanding of how their voices (or signifying practices) and the discourses they invoke are combined with a series of materials; for our understanding of how people, space, objects, proto-machines are assembled in a participatory-democratic project; and for grasping the restrictions that this project faces.

Shifting from high theory to actual, hands-on research is, nevertheless, not always straightforward. Some of the key authors have high levels of reticence towards elaborating methodologies. As Derrida pleaded for the singularity of each deconstruction, and Foucault at all times wrote a specific "history of the present" (Kendall & Wickham, 1999: 4), Laclau (and Mouffe) pleaded for the articulation of theoretical concepts within each specific empirical research question (Laclau, 1990b: 208–209). It is precisely the rejection of essentialism that pushes discourse-theorists towards open-ended theoretical frameworks, which is said to hamper the methodological development and (again) the empirical application of the framework (Howarth, 1998: 288). In spite of these difficulties, Foucault's archeo-genealogical method and Derrida's deconstruction do offer often-applied methodological points of departure, and Laclau and Mouffe's discourse theory can function in a similar way. Examples of these methodological projects are what De Cleen and I have previously termed Discourse-Theoretical Analysis (Carpentier & De Cleen, 2007), but also the work of Glynos and Howarth (2007), Angermuller (2014), and Martilla (2016) is highly relevant in this context.

The strategy that is used in this book is to return to the core principles of qualitative research, as there are significant parallels between discourse theory (and its extended version, as it is developed here) and the basic principles of qualitative research. Firstly, the interpretative and '*Verstehende*' logics of qualitative research combine a strong interest in the attribution of meaning with—for instance in ethnography—a commitment to understanding material practices. Secondly, qualitative research uses a research perspective that explicitly aims to respect societal diversity and contingency. Although the categorizations that qualitative research produces are signifying practices that (aim to) fixate social realities, qualitative research simultaneously emphasizes the structural impossibility of ultimately categorizing (fixating) the social reality that is being researched. This ontological position is also translated into research procedures, which emphasize the importance of openness towards the meanings found in the communication of subjects, but also towards the theoretical frameworks that are being used to support the analysis. The iterative or cyclical character of qualitative research, where theory and empirical research permanently interact with, and impact on, each other, is one way to balance both components. In addition, the notion of the sensitizing concept has been developed in order to protect the balance between the need for theoretical foundation and the need to avoid a dominant theoretical framework that mutes the voices being analyzed.

Even though the notion of the sensitizing concept is discussed more in detail in Platform 3, it is important to briefly explain its roles here, in order to better understand what I will do in Platform 2 (and Platform 3). Sensitizing concepts are concepts that assist researchers in "[...] what to look for and where to look" (Ritzer, 1992: 365). In defining the sensitizing concept,[29] Blumer (1969: 7) contrasted it against another type of concept, the definitive concept. The definitive concept "[...] refers precisely to what is common to a class of objects, by the aid of a clear definition in terms of attributes or fixed bench marks." By contrast,

> "A sensitizing concept lacks such specification of attributes or bench marks and consequently it does not enable the use to move directly to the instance and its relevant content. Instead, it gives the use a general sense of reference and guidance in approaching empirical instances. Whereas definitive concepts provide prescriptions of what to see, sensitizing concepts merely suggest directions along which to look." (Blumer, 1969: 7)

Blumer (1969: 259) stressed that "[...] sensitizing concepts may deepen perception [...]," but that they also "[...] provide starting points for building analysis, not ending points for evading it." A similar position can be found later, when Charmaz (2003: 259—emphasis in original) explained her approach towards the sensitizing concept:

> "Sensitizing concepts offer ways of seeing, organizing, and understanding experience; they are embedded in our disciplinary emphases and perspectival proclivities. Although sensitizing concepts may deepen perception, they provide starting points

> for building analysis, not ending points for evading it. We may use sensitizing concepts *only* as points of departure from which to study the data."

In this sense, sensitizing concepts "[…] can be liked to halfway houses where data are temporarily stored and made ready for analysis" (Van den Hoonaard, 1997: 22). This openness resembles Laclau's plea for theoretical support that is specific to a set of empirical research questions. Moreover, the notion of the sensitizing concept incorporates the idea that it is structurally impossible for discursive elements (such as sensitizing concepts) to provide full closure, or to completely capture social reality. In other words, the ontological prudence in fixating theory and analysis, which is characteristic of qualitative research, aligns well with the basic premises of discourse theory (and its extension). But, at the same time, we should not see social reality as void of theory or abstraction, as Van den Hoonaard (1997: 23) remarked: "[…] we know that all data, including those that are the closes to the subject's world, are already abstracted knowledge, or theory, albeit less systematic and rigorous than the [researcher-]observer's […]."

Sensitizing concepts have yet another role to play. While some qualitative methodologies employ a completely open approach towards the selection of sensitizing concepts (which is 'merely' driven by research questions), other qualitative methodologies come with a preset of sensitizing concepts. To give just a few (rather obvious) examples: narrative analysis uses the 'narration' as a primary sensitizing concept; conversation analysis privileges the 'conversation'; and discourse analysis has 'discourse' as primary sensitizing concept. But these more directive qualitative methodologies do not restrict themselves to articulating primary sensitizing concepts. They often offer an entire toolbox of secondary sensitizing concepts, in combination with a social ontology and a normative framework. One example of the latter is Critical Discourse Analysis's (CDA) emphasis on its critical nature combined with the ontological building blocks that the social is partly linguistic-discursive and that discourse is both constitutive and constituted (see Fairclough & Wodak, 1997: 271ff).

Also, in the case of Discourse-Theoretical Analysis (DTA) (see Carpentier 2010; Carpentier & De Cleen, 2007), discourse is the primary sensitizing concept. When we turn to discursive-material analysis, which is used as a methodological label here, the discursive, the material, and the discursive-material knot are used as primary sensitizing concepts, enriched by the structure-agency dimension. The many concepts that circulate around these two dimensions, as, for instance, articulation, nodal points, hegemony, material bodily practices, signifying practices, entextualization, invitation, investment, dislocation, but also contingency and overdetermination, act as secondary sensitizing concepts (see Figure 38 and Figure 39 for a more complete overview).

Similar to DTA, and facilitated by the macro perspective of discourse theory (see Carpentier & De Cleen, 2007: 277), a second strategy to generate sensitizing concepts is deployed, apart from the list of primary and secondary sensitizing concepts that can be found in the elaborations of the discursive and the material (and structure and agency). A discursive-material analysis can also be used to generate additional sensitizing concepts by re-analyzing or rereading other theoretical frameworks and incorporating them within the logic, ontology, and language of the discursive-material knot. These sensitizing concepts, external to discourse and materialist theory, are labeled tertiary sensitizing concepts.

These re-readings are in some cases quite natural, especially when these theoretical frameworks are paradigmatically related to the discursive-material framework. The addition of, for instance, the notion of power as a tertiary sensitizing concept (using the Foucauldian approach to the analytics of power) is relatively easy, while incorporating Bourdieu's notion of the field already requires a more structural reconfiguration of field theory. But even concepts such as the Durkheimean ritual, with all its positivist-functionalist significations, can be theoretically reconfigured, as demonstrated by Couldry (2003). In the particular case of this book, three key notions are mobilized (in Platform 2 of this book) as tertiary sensitizing concepts to provide further support: Participation, community media, and conflict, combined with concepts as agonism and conflict transformation. Together, these strategies help to deliver the methodological-analytical arsenal necessary to perform a particular discursive-material analysis that can be found in Platform 3.

Notes

1. To be fair: Discourse theory also has the tendency to implicitly privilege the discursive.
2. Foucault's (1972: 38) approach to discursive formations as systems of dispersion that are characterized by regularity also remains important for this book. To quote his definition: "Whenever one can describe, between a number of statements, such a system of dispersion, whenever, between objects, types of statement, concepts, or thematic choices, one can define a regularity (an order, correlations, positions and functionings, transformations), we will say, for the sake of convenience, that we are dealing with a discursive formation [...]" (Foucault, 1972: 38).
3. Elements are seen by Laclau and Mouffe as differential positions that are not (yet) discursively articulated. Moments are differential positions, which are articulated within a discourse. This distinction is not used in my text.

4. For a conceptual critique, see Philips and Jørgensen (2002: 27).
5. For Mouffe (in Errejón and Mouffe, 2016: 19) this is where *HSS*'s theoretical specificity can be found: "[...] to have brought together Gramsci and post-structuralism."
6. As Mouffe said in Errejón and Mouffe (2016: 17): "An important part of the critique of essentialism in political theory has been a questioning of the idea of the subject as a transparent and rational identity, which, being the source of its own actions, can impose a homogeneous meaning across all of its behavioural spectrum."
7. Some authors, including Butler (1993), use inverse definitions.
8. These contingencies also originate from the material. This will be addressed more at a later stage.
9. This concept can be seen as a variation of cognitive dissonance, which—at the individual level—refers to the discomfort triggered by contradictory beliefs (see Cooper, 2007; Festinger, 1957).
10. Van Brussel (2015) used the notion of operationalization to refer to the invocation of particular discourses by signifying practices.
11. See Laclau and Mouffe (1990: 101) for another example.
12. To do justice to Biglieri and Perelló's (2011) work, they refer to the Lacanian Real.
13. See also, Carpentier (2011: 267–268) for an earlier version of this argument. The next paragraphs come from this book.
14. This definition also allows articulating architecture as a technology.
15. See, for instance, Featherstone's (2011) work. He wrote: "One of the key benefits of thinking articulation and assemblage in productive tension is the resources of accounts of the former for theorising the specificity of particular connections and political activities" (Featherstone, 2011: 141).
16. More than anything else, Schatzki's (2001: 53) discussion of Laclau and Mouffe's (1985) use of the practice concept shows the problem of Laclau and Mouffe's vagueness in using the term. He wrote: "Whereas discourses for Laclau and Mouffe are structured totalities of meaningful entities, practice—if I understand them right—is movement and change. Discourse, in other words, is being, while practice is the becoming from which discourses result and to which they eventually succumb. Conversely, discourses are the precarious fixities that precipitate from human practice and from which further practices arise." Arguably, Laclau and Mouffe (1985) often—but not always—located the notion of practice at the level of the discursive, and not so much at the level of the individual or collective, which is not helpful in the context of my discussion. One indication of this interpretation is Wenman's (2003: 589) reference to "sectors" in his discussion of practices: "[...] practices are understood as the strategic means by which competing social sectors—(feminism, anti-racism, the gay movement, for example [Laclau & Mouffe, 1985: 132])—seek to construct new collective social identities [...]."
17. See, for instance, Rouse (2001) for a discussion on the different meanings of the practice concept.
18. I prefer to keep the notion of practice linked to human activity, which implies my disagreement with the expansion of the concept to the non-human world as, for instance, suggested by Knorr Cetina (2001) when she discussed 'objectual practices.'
19. A distinction between material (and discursive) production and transformation would take me too far.

20. This is also one reason why the concept of 'discursive practice' is not used here.
21. Fashion is one interesting example, given its strong reliance on materials (clothes) for (self-)expression. Also, here, scholars have attempted to make the material more visible: see, for instance, Klepp and Bjerck's (2014) plea for wardrobe studies. Again, this does not exclude the discursive dimension, as Attfield's (2000: 128ff) discussion on textuality and textility shows.
22. Stam (2005: 218) labelled this the "bracketing of the referent" and argued (from a film studies perspective) that it "[...] occasionally went to the extreme of detaching art from all relation to social and historical context."
23. See also, for instance, Dourish and Mazmanian's (2013) chapter '*Media as Material.*'
24. Figure 3 focuses on the signifier, and its relationship with concepts, materials, and discourses. For clarity's sake, the arrows indicating the relationships between concepts, materials, and discourses, have not been included.
25. As mentioned before, Van Brussel (2015) used the term operationalization in this context.
26. See Iannello (1992) for an example from feminist practice, and my own work on the participatory organization (Carpentier, 2013b).
27. The relationship of a component with itself is included in the models, but not explicitly discussed. The structuring concept is the notion of interaction, where agencies interact with agencies, structures with structures, discourses with discourses, and materials with materials.
28. Interestingly, the discursive also produces the concepts of agency, structure, the material, and the discursive, but this is outside the realm of this book.
29. The notion of the sensitizing concept has provoked a considerable number of critiques. An overview can be found in Van den Hoonaard's book (1997: 10ff).

PLATFORM 2

·2·

PARTICIPATION, COMMUNITY MEDIA, AND CONFLICT (TRANSFORMATION)

Without desiring to claim its eternal validity, it is safe to say that the discursive-material knot is a dynamic that characterizes contemporary societies at a wide variety of levels. The discursive-material knot's all-pervasive manifestations range from the tiniest micro-level of human interaction to the macro-structures of society. The analytical implication of this omnipresence is that this conceptual apparatus can be used to analyze and comprehend an equally varied set of societal processes.

In the case of this book, I want to deploy this conceptual apparatus in relation to three focal points. My aim is to put the discursive-material knot (and its related concepts) to work, as sensitizing concepts, for the analysis of a particular type of actor, in an evenly particular setting, and in relation to a particular objective. The focus of the second and third platform of this book is on community media[1] organizations, which will be analyzed from the perspective of the discursive-material knot. As participation very much defines the particularity of this type of actor, this concept will be the starting point of Platform 2, first offering a general reflection on participation, and then moving into the realm of community media organizations.

Even though these particular types of media organizations have received considerable (academic) attention (see Atton, 2015, *The Routledge Companion to Alternative and Community Media*, as just one example), community media theory still deserves strengthening, and community media's connection to the discursive/material dimension (and to the structure/agency dimension) offers a good route to contribute to this aim. Moreover, this book wants to focus even more on an underdeveloped aspect of community media organizations, namely their role in conflict transformation. Also, this notion will be theoretically developed in this second platform of the book.

Together, these theoretizations of participation, community media organization, and conflict transformation (from the perspective of the discursive-material knot) will contribute to the second strategy for generating sensitizing concepts, which consists of the discursive-material re-analysis of existing theoretical frameworks. Together with the sensitizing concepts developed in Platform 1, they will then be used for the case study analysis in Platform 3: The particular setting of the Cyprus Problem, and the role of a particular community media organization (the Cyprus Community Media Centre—CCMC) in conflict transformation.

1 Defining Participation—A Political (Studies) Approach

One of the main problems with analyzing the concept of participation and participatory practices is the fluid nature of participation. Several decades ago, Pateman (1970: 1) wrote that "[…] the widespread use of the term […] has tended to mean that any precise, meaningful content has almost disappeared." This situation has not changed, witness Cornwall's (2008: 269) statement about the "[…] infinitely malleable concept 'participation' [that] can be used to evoke—and to signify—almost anything that involves people." In an interview with Miessen, Mouffe (in Miessen, 2010: 121) said: "Participation really depends on how you understand it. It is certainly not an innocent notion." There are many reasons for this significatory diversity, some of which are part of the 'normal' academic interplay. But I would also like to argue that the ideological nature of participation (see Carpentier, 2011) significantly contributes to the sliding of the signifier participation. Participation's meanings are very much embedded in different democratic discourses, which have turned it into a floating signifier. Academia is only one location to find the many traces of the ideological workings of participation, but it is still a good place, as the academic literature on participation, including the subfield of media and participation, has produced many different positions. Two fairly recent media-related debates, by Jenkins and Carpentier (2013) and Allen et al. (2014) exemplify this diversity quite nicely.

Even when it is important to incorporate the significatory diversity of participation in the analysis, it also remains important to provide some degree of definitional anchorage, avoiding that everything becomes labeled participation, which makes the concepts rather difficult to use for academic purposes. For this reason, this part starts with a discussion of the two main approaches towards participation, and a choice is made for one of them—labeled the political (studies) approach. This approach enables distinguishing participation from other related concepts (e.g., access and interaction), but also focuses my attention on the workings of the discursive-material knot in participatory processes.

1.1 The Two Main Approaches Towards Participation

Arguably, two main approaches to participation can be distinguished in the academic debates about participation: a sociological approach and a political (studies) approach[2] (see also Lepik, 2013). The sociological approach defines participation as taking part in particular social processes, a definition that casts a very wide net. In this approach, participation includes many (if not all) types of human interaction, in combination with interactions with texts and technologies. Power is not excluded from this approach, but remains one of the many secondary concepts to support it. One example of how participation is defined in this approach is Melucci's (1989: 174) definition, when he said that participation has a double meaning: "It means both taking part, that is, acting so as to promote the interests and the needs of an actor as well as belonging to a system, identifying with the 'general interests' of the community."

The sociological approach results, for instance, in labeling consumption as participatory, because consumers are taking part in a consumption culture and are exercising consumer choices (Lury, 2011: 12). Also, the label of participation is used for doing sports, as exemplified by Delaney and Madigan's (2009) frequent use of the participation concept in their introduction to the sociology of sports. We can find a similar approach in what is labeled cultural participation, where participation is defined as individual art (or cultural) exposure, attendance or access, in some cases complemented by individual art (or cultural) creation. As Vander Stichle and Laermans (2006: 48) described it: "In principle, cultural participation behaviour encompasses both public and private receptive practices, as well as active and interactive forms of cultural participation." In practice, this implies that the concept of participation is used for attending a concert or visiting a museum.

Within media studies, the sociological approach can, for instance, be found in how Carey (2009: 15) defined the ritual model of communication in *Communication as Culture*, as the "representation of shared beliefs," where togetherness is created and maintained, without disregarding the many contending forces that characterize the social. For Carey (2009: 15), the ritual model of communication is explicitly linked to notions of "'sharing', 'participation', 'association', 'fellowship' and the 'possession of a common faith,'" where people are (made) part of a culture through their ritualistic participation in that very same culture. (Mass) media organizations, such as newspapers (used by Carey as example), play a crucial role by inviting readers to participate in a cultural configuration, interpellating them—to use an Althusserian concept—to become part of society by offering them subject positions, or, as Carey put it, social roles, with which they can identify (or dis-identify):

> "Under a ritual view, then, news is not information but drama. It does not describe the world but portrays an arena of dramatic forces and action; it exists solely in historical time; and it invites our participation on the basis of our assuming, often vicariously, social roles within it." (Carey, 2009: 21)

This type of ritual participation[3] again defines participation as taking (and becoming) part, through a series of interactions, with—in Carey's case—media texts. Also, others have used the ritual participation concept (and the sociological approach to participation it entails), in relationship to media organizations (Dayan & Katz, 2009: 120; Real, 1996), festivals (Roemer, 2007), and the arts (Braddock, 2009).

In contrast, the political approach produces a much more restrictive definition of participation, where the situated and corrective nature of participation becomes incorporated in the definition, avoiding what Miessen (2010: 54) called romanticized versions of participation.[4] In the political approach, participation is seen to be situated in particular decision-making processes, where the power inequalities between different actors are then redressed. On the basis of this characteristic, participation becomes defined as the equalization of power relations between privileged and non-privileged actors in formal or informal decision-making processes (see Carpentier, 2011; Carpentier, Dahlgren, & Pasquali, 2014). It is this approach that will be used in this book.

In the field of democratic theory, Pateman's (1970) book *Democratic Theory and Participation* is highly instrumental in showing the significance of power in defining participation, and can be seen as a key illustration of the political approach towards participation. The two definitions of participation that she introduces are those of partial and full participation. Partial participation is defined by her as "[…] a process in which two or more parties influence each other in the making of decisions but the final power to decide rests with one party only" (Pateman, 1970: 70), while full participation is seen as "[…] a process where each individual member of a decision-making body has equal power to determine the outcome of decisions" (Pateman, 1970: 71). Also, in the field of urban planning, Arnstein (1969: 216), in her seminal article '*A Ladder of Citizen Participation*' (see below), linked participation explicitly to power, saying "[…] that citizen participation is a categorical term for citizen power."

The centrality of power in the political approach also necessitates—at least briefly—unpacking the notion of power, even if the brevity of this exposé does not do justice to the concept's complexity and the richness of the academic debates about it. Arguably, two basic models of power, namely the causal and the strategic model, can still be distinguished. The causal model goes back to Weber's (1947: 152) definition of power (and before), which he saw as "[…] the probability that one actor within a social relationship will be in a position to carry out his own will despite resistance, regardless of the basis on which this probability rests." The (traditional) Marxist model uses a similar definition of power that focuses on the dominance of the bourgeoisie, which originates from their ownership of the means of production. Different political studies scholars have enriched this model, fleshing out the role of power in relation to decisions, non-decisions, and no decisions (Bachrach & Baratz, 1970; Dahl, 1969; Lukes, 1974).

But in order to deal with the contingency, multi-layeredness, and complexity of participatory processes, preference is given here to the strategic/Foucauldian (1978) power model. In this model, we move away from power as possession, without ignoring the non-egalitarian nature of power relations. Also, resistance comes to be seen as part of the contingent exercise of power (Kendall & Wickham, 1999: 50). As no actor, however privileged, can exercise full and total control over the social, and more dominant positions will often generate resistance, the strategic/Foucauldian model enables us to see a multitude of strategies that form a complex power-game. One way of further operationalizing this power model is by using Giddens's (1979: 91) dialectics of control, in which he distinguishes between the transformative capacity of power—treating power in terms of the conduct of agents, exercising their freewill—on the one hand, and domination—treating power as a structural quality—on the other. The restrictive component aligns itself quite nicely with Foucault's recognition that power relations can be unbalanced, while the generative component refers to the objectives and achievements of the strategies on which Foucault built his analytics of power. Resistance intervenes in both the generative and the restrictive component, and thus can be considered the third component of this power model. The overall effect of restrictive, generative, and resistant strategies then becomes labeled as the productive dimension of power. All four components of power have (of course) to be taken into account when studying participatory practices.

One complexity needs to be added, as we should acknowledge the existence of trans-field participation: In some cases, a particular process in one field facilitates participation in another. For instance, an urban art project can offer little participation in the art work itself, but can offer considerable levels of participation in the urban environment, as is evidenced by Rafael Lozano-Hemmer's *Body Movies* projects.[5] Or, reader participation in the newspaper organization might be rare and limited (with some notable exceptions), but, with this mechanism, newspapers enable readers to intervene (to some degree) in the political field. To better understand these trans-field forms of participation, we can build on Wasko and Mosco's (1992: 7) distinction between democratization *in* and *through* the media, so that we can distinguish between participation *in* a particular field, and participation *through* a particular field *in* another field. There are what I would propose to call *transgressive* forms of participation (where the participatory process transgresses the boundaries of a particular field and becomes situated in several fields), and *transferred* forms of participation (where a non-participatory process in a particular field allows for participation in another field).

1.2 Access, Interaction, and the Minimalist/Maximalist Dimension of Participation

The political approach also enables emphasizing that participation is an object of struggle, and that different democratic discourses (and their proponents) defend different participatory intensities.[6] More minimalist versions of participation tend to protect the power positions of privileged (elite) actors, to the detriment of non-privileged (non-elite) actors, without totally excluding the latter. In contrast, more maximalist versions of participation strive for a full power equilibrium between all actors (which protects the non-privileged actors). This difference between minimalist and maximalist participation is not a dichotomy, but a dimension, with many in-between positions. This is where the notion of participatory intensity comes in, referring to the position(s) of the participatory process on the minimalist/maximalist dimension. Here, we should keep in mind that these participatory intensities can change over time (as they are often an object of societal struggle), but several components within one process can sometimes also yield differences (see Carpentier, 2016a). And, as argued elsewhere (Carpentier, 2014c), maximalist participation plays a significant role in contemporary Western societies as a utopian horizon but is rather difficult to achieve and even more difficult to sustain.

Keeping these complexities in mind, the minimalist/maximalist dimension is a helpful tool for analyzing participatory intensities in a wide variety of fields of inquiry. In communication and media studies, we can, for instance, distinguish between more minimalist forms of media participation, where media professionals retain strong control over process and outcome, and maximalist forms, where the power relations between the different actors that are part of the decision-making process, including (semi-)professionals and non-privileged groups, are balanced. As we shall see later on, community media tend to be geared towards participatory practices that are more maximalist.

We should also keep in mind that the more restrictive use of the notion of participation in the political approach necessitates a clearer demarcation of participation. Firstly, it is important to distinguish participation from its effects and from its conditions of possibility. Here, the basic conceptual difference with the still-related notion of empowerment is helpful in explaining this. Both participation and empowerment share a conceptual emphasis on the "process of transferring power" (Rodwell, 1996: 307). I would like to argue that different from participation, empowerment is a multi-dimensional concept (Kieffer, 2014: 9), which combines and integrates this emphasis on power equalization (the process of empowerment) with the (often deemed beneficial) consequences for the actors, rendering them empowered. This state of empowerment (or 'being empowered') implies, for instance, obtaining "[...] a positive self-esteem and recognition of the worth of self and other" (Rodwell, 1996: 307). Huesca's (2008) use of the term "personal empowerment" is quite indicative of this integration of concept and consequence. Even if some see the development of a "[...] personal or collective sense of efficacy, vitality and well-being" (Stage & Ingerslev, 2015: 126) as an integrated part of participation, I would like to argue that care needs to be taken to avoid the conflation of consequences and prerequisites of participation with the concept of participation itself.

Secondly, it is also necessary to distinguish participation from a series of other concepts that are, in the sociological approach, often used interchangeably. One key concept is engagement,[7] which Dahlgren (2013: 25) defined as the "[...] subjective disposition that motivates [the] realization [of participation] [...]" in order to distinguish it from participation. In earlier work, Dahlgren (2009) argued that the feeling of being invited, committed, and/or empowered, but also the positive inclination towards the political (and the social), are crucial components of engagement. In his civic cultures circuit, Dahlgren also emphasized (apart from more materialist elements such as practices and spaces) the importance of knowledge, trust, identities, and values for (enhancing) engagement. Engagement is thus different from participation (in the political approach), as engagement refers to the creation, or existence, of a social connection of individuals or groups with a broader political community that is aimed at protecting or improving it.

Two other related, but still distinct, concepts are access and interaction. In earlier work, when developing the AIP model,[8] I have argued that access refers to the establishment of presence, and interaction to the creation of socio-communicative relations (Carpentier, 2011: 130–131; see also Carpentier, 2015b; 2016a). As a concept, access is very much part of everyday language, which makes clear definitions rather rare. At the same time, access is used in a wide variety of (academic) fields, which we can use to deepen our understanding of this concept. One area where access is often used, is geography, when the access to specific spaces is thematized. More historical (spatial) analyses deal with access to land, and the enclosure of the common fields (Neeson, 1996), while more contemporary analyses add a focus on the access to other resources such as food (Morton et al., 2008) and water (Wegerich & Warner, 2004). The importance of presence for defining access can also be illustrated through a series of media studies examples: In the case of the digital divide discourse, the focus is, for instance, placed on the access to (online) media technologies, which in turn enables people to access media content. In both cases, access implies achieving presence (to technology or media content). Access also features in the more traditional media feedback discussions, where it has yet another meaning. Here, access implies gaining a presence within media organizations, which generates the opportunity for people to have their voices heard (in providing feedback).

A second concept that needs to be distinguished from participation is interaction. Earlier in this book, I referred to Bunge's (1977: 259) general definition of interaction as a starting point for this discussion: "[...] two different things x and y interact if each acts upon the other." The definition was combined with this postulate: "Every thing acts on, and is acted upon by, other things," which very much stresses the materiality of interaction. The approach taken here—in this book—is that (social) interaction refers to the establishment (and maintenance) of socio-communicative relationships, grounded in Sharma's (1996: 359) argument that the "two basic conditions of social interaction" are "social contact and communication." This also (again) enables pointing to the discursive-material knot, where material interactions are provided with meaning through discursive frameworks. Moreover, from a communication and media studies (and beyond) perspective on (online) technologies, the discussions about the diversity of interactions are worth mentioning here as well. In order to cope with this diversity, several categorization systems have been introduced. One group of scholars introduced a distinction between two broad types of interaction: person-to-person interaction and person-to-machine interaction (Hoffman & Novak, 1996; Lee, 2000); others used three levels of interaction. Szuprowicz's (1995) distinction between user-to-user, user-to-documents, and user-to-system is one of the more commonly used threefold systems of categorization (see also Barker & Tucker, 1990; Haeckel, 1998).

However socially and academically relevant access and interaction are, they are still different from participation, which refers—using the political approach to participation—to the rebalancing of power imbalances between privileged and non-privileged actors in decision-making processes. This firstly implies that participatory practices are radically situated: They are always located in particular fields, where these decision-making processes are located and where these processes want to have an impact. They are also always linked to particular actors, the groups they belong to, and their power positions(s) in society. And they are always connected to the enormous variety of formal and informal decisions that can be found in societal processes. Secondly, this also implies that both access and interaction matter to participatory processes, even if they are not the same as participation. Both access and interaction are actually (in the political approach) prerequisites of participation. Access is, for instance, vital as it enables the inclusion of non-privileged actors in (participatory) decision-making processes. Interaction is equally important, as a participatory process requires the interaction between the different actors in order to engage in a decision-making process (even if not all interaction is participatory). And thirdly, also, participatory processes are not outside the discursive-material knot.

1.3 Participation and the Discursive-Material Knot

Participatory processes are engulfed in an assemblage of discourses and materials, which have led some to refer explicitly to participation as "[...] a multidimensional process, where human and non-human elements assemble in ways that develop (more or less empowering) capacities" or to a "participatory assemblage" (Stage & Ingerslev, 2015: 123 & 126ff). When taking this discursive component of the discursive-material knot as a starting point—and dealing with the material component next; without desiring to create a hierarchy—we can see that participation is structured by a wide range of discourses. And as a signifier, it is, in itself, the object of discursive struggles, which, in turn, are part of the permanent and larger struggle over democracy.

1.3.1 Participation and discourse

As argued before (Carpentier, 2011), participation is an intensively political-ideological notion, which is intimately linked to the multitude of discourses on democracy that circulate in different (Western) societies. Held's (1996) *Models of Democracy* shows the co-existence of a variety of democratic models (or democratic discourses) that each articulate differently the balance between the delegation of power to political elites (or representation) and the popular exercise of power (or participation). A competitive-elitist democratic discourse (e.g., Schumpeter, 1976), which strongly privileges ruling elites and restricts popular participation to elections, articulates participation in a different manner than a participatory-democratic discourse (e.g., Macpherson, 1966, 1973, 1977; Pateman, 1970), which seeks to maximize participation and aims to do this in a variety of social settings, not restricting the reach of democracy to institutionalized politics.

Apart from the necessary, but always different, balance between representation and participation in democratic discourses, this discussion also demonstrates that different democratic models engage in a discursive struggle over the articulation of democracy, representation, and participation. This implies that different actors identify with different democratic discourses, defending different articulations of the key democratic signifiers. It is this discursive struggle that renders participation a floating signifier (see Carpentier, 2001, but also Carlbaum, 2011: 102), gaining different meanings in different and competing discursive settings. The dimension of minimalist/maximalist participation is aimed exactly at capturing this floating of the signifier participation, and how some democratic discourses articulate participation in more minimalist ways, and others articulate it in more maximalist ways. Here, it is important to stress that these different democratic discourses and the resulting articulations of participation co-exist in the very same societies, and that they engage in discursive struggles over the hegemony of 'their' articulations of democracy, representation, and participation.

It is equally important to stress that these democratic discourses reach beyond the field of institutionalized politics, even if some democratic discourses themselves try to prevent this (e.g., the competitive-elitist democratic discourse that tries to limit the reach of popular participation to the election of political representatives). Other democratic discourses (and other discourses, e.g., related to development, urban planning, health, arts, and media organizations) have managed to broaden this reach of democracy and participation, a process which Mouffe (1988: 42) has called the "deepen[ing of] the democratic revolution" and Giddens (1994: 113) the "democratisation of democracy." Mouffe's (2000: 101, see also 2005: 8) distinction between politics and the political, which she described as follows, supports this broadening of the democratic-political scope:

> "By 'the political', I refer to the dimension of antagonism that is inherent in human relations, antagonism that can take many forms and emerge in different types of social relations. 'Politics' on the other side, indicates the ensemble of practices, discourses and institutions which seek to establish a certain order and organize human coexistence in conditions that are always potentially conflictual because they are affected by the dimension of 'the political.'"

At the same time, democracy and participation can be regarded as empty signifiers. This notion is closely related to the floating signifier, but still structurally different. An empty signifier is a "signifier without signified" (Laclau, 1996: 36) that is seen as universal but at the same time points to the "limits of signification" (Laclau, 1996: 39). Gunder and Hillier (2009: 4) provided a helpful metaphor to understand the empty signifier when they wrote that the empty signifier is "[...] a word that acts just like a cup, which can contain almost anything as long as it can be poured or placed into it, for example, milk, wine, oil, blood, water or sand." Empty signifiers, such as democracy and participation, are central to a wide variety of discursive orders. From a psycho-analytical perspective, they are fantasies, impossible to capture and impossible to reach, but still key driving forces of social action. As McKinnon (2007: 779—emphasis in original) argued, they are "[…] the indeterminate something around which hegemonic struggles are formed. It is that which is struggled *for* and the ideological core of any social struggle." McKinnon's work is particularly relevant here, as she argued that development and participatory development are empty signifiers. Similarly, Sihlongonyane (2015) argued that participation is an empty signifier, supported by a wide range of African metaphors. These ideas evenly apply to Western contemporary contexts, where participation plays this role of empty signifier, what we all desire, and what cannot but be invoked by a multitude of discourses.

Other discourses, affiliated with democratic discourses, also structure the meaning of the signifier participation. This brings us to the distinction between procedural and substantive participation, which is inspired by the difference between procedural and substantive democracy, or between "rule-centered and outcome-centered conceptions of democracy" (Shapiro, 1996: 123). In the former case, procedural democracy, an outcome is "[…] acceptable as long as the relevant procedure generates it," while in the latter case, substantive democracy, a "[…] [re]distributive outcome or state of affairs (equality, lack of certain types or degrees of inequality, or some other) […]" (Shapiro, 1996: 123) is defined, which is then used to evaluate the results of the decision rules.[9] Parallel to this idea, the distinction between procedural and substantive participation can be made, where procedural participation refers to the mere redressal of power imbalances *within* the participatory process. Substantive participation then refers to how the outcomes of the participatory process relate to power imbalances *beyond* the participatory process, and other societal groups[10] (see also Cornwall & Coelho, 2007: 8–10). Extreme examples, in the case of media participation, are provided by the use of the internet by radical right-wing groups (Caiani & Parenti, 2013) that use the online to live out their nationalist and racist fantasies in ways that can only be described as formally (but not substantively) participatory, at least in relationship to the members of these groups, and to those who are ideologically aligned with them. This discussion is relevant here as substantive participation in particular shows the articulation of participation with a series of other discourses, especially those on human rights and (respect for) societal diversity. It is, for instance, no coincidence that there is a long history of attempts to have communication rights acknowledged as human rights (MacBride Commission, 1980) (see later). This articulation of participation with human rights imposes a limit on the outcomes of participatory processes, where these processes cease to be participatory when they violate the (democratic and human) rights of those who are not involved in the participatory processes. To use an extreme example: A participatory process, which results in a decision to place explosives at a particular location, in order to kill passers-by, is not a participatory process in the substantive articulation of participation.

In addition to these democratic discourses (and their affiliations with human rights), participation is structured by a set of subject positions, five of which are more generally connected to the participatory process—the citizen, the ordinary person, the expert, the owner, and the leader—and will be discussed more in detail below. These subject positions are of crucial importance, as they (may) impact on the power balance within a participatory process through the creation of more (un)privileged positions. At the same time, other subject positions, such as gender, ethnic, class, caste, rural, community, national, regional, local, and diasporic identities—to name but a few—might also play an equally crucial role in structuring the participatory process. If we look, for instance, at (participatory) prisoners' radio (Anderson, 2015) or miners' radio (O'Connor, 2004), then the identities of the prisoner or the miner, linked to their relationships with dominant cultures, and the restrictions, stigmas, and resistances these will trigger, will play a significant role in the participatory process. In all cases, it is important to note that the subject positions are structuring but not determining forces that invite subjects to identify with them—interpellating them—without being able to force subjects into acceptance. In addition, the workings of agency also makes these identifications—if they occur—always particular, as they become integrated within the subject, who is characterized by her/his many identificatory alignments.

The citizen. The first subject position that merits special attention is that of the citizen. In the more traditional approaches, citizenship is seen as the involvement of the citizenry within (institutionalized) politics. It is then seen to refer to political and civic rights. Over time, this notion has been expanded to also include social citizenship (and the encompassing social rights, see Marshall, 1992) and cultural citizenship (and "the right to know and to speak," Miller, 2011: 57—see also Hermes, 1998).

Especially Hermes's (1998: 160) interpretation of cultural citizenship, where she argued that "[…] citizenship relates not only to the directly political and social, but also to identity formation, personal identification, emotional evaluation, and so on," opens up spaces for the interpretation of citizenship as identity (or, as subject position). Later, Dahlgren's (2009: 118) civic cultures model attributes considerable attention to civic identities, or "[…] people's subjective view of themselves as members or participants of democracy." Beyond the identity of formal citizenship, Dahlgren emphasized the importance of the sense of being an empowered political agent, and the importance of membership of one or more political communities (Dahlgren, 2009: 120–121). In an earlier article, Dahlgren (2000: 338) summarized this argument as follows: "In short, in order to be able to act as a citizen, it is necessary that one can see oneself as a citizen, as subjectively encompassing the attributes this social category may involve." This emphasis on the citizen as an identity can also be found in Mouffe's (1992a: 30) work from the 1990s:

> "First, the political community should be conceived as a discursive surface and not as an empirical referent. […] The perspective that I am proposing envisages citizenship as a form of political identity that is created through identification with the political principles of modern pluralist democracy, i.e., the assertion of liberty and equality for all."

As a subject position, citizenship's contingent relationship with democracy becomes visible as different democratic discourses articulate citizenship differently, in some cases limiting it to the citizen-voter, in other cases articulating the citizen as an empowered citizen. Gaventa (2004) used the term participatory citizenship here to argue for "[…] the right to participate [which] is a prior right, necessary for making other rights real." Arguably, the differences between these articulations are based on the degree that subjects (or groups of subjects) who identify as citizens can (or cannot) exercise their agencies[11] in equal ways. An empowered citizen, one of the possible articulations of citizenship, is closely connected to, but still different from, the maximalist democratic discourses, with their emphasis on equalized power positions. Empowerment refers to the *change* in power relations, to the process where power relations become affected, where the power positions of the non-privileged become more balanced in relation to those of the privileged. Or, to use Rappaport's (1987: 122) words: Empowerment is "[…] a process, a mechanism by which people, organizations, and communities gain mastery over their affairs."

The citizen subject position impacts on the participatory processes through the degree of empoweredness[12] that is articulated with citizenship (and the ways the participants identify with these articulations). Citizen articulations with low levels of empoweredness will complicate the balancing of power imbalances (which is the core of the participatory process), as power imbalances then become more easily acceptable. In contrast, an empowered citizen identity may be more conducive towards balanced power relations, and feed resistance when these relationships are not balanced (enough). Of course, participatory processes may also impact on the material and/or discursive power base of participants, increasing the power position of non-privileged actors and affecting their citizen identities, a process we can also label empowerment; but here we are moving outside the discussion on citizen subject positions.

The ordinary person. The second subject position, the ordinary person, is related to the citizen subject position, but adds a more relationist and hierarchical perspective. This subject position is important for participatory theory (and practice) because the ordinary people subject position, despite its complexity, refers to a variety of non-privileged actors in society. If participation is about the equalization of power imbalances between privileged and non-privileged actors, then the articulation of the subject position of the ordinary intervenes in this process. Generally speaking, two approaches to ordinary people exist, as mass and (under)class, and as non-elite (see below). Both approaches enable the articulation of the ordinary as irrelevant, marginal, and not entitled to being part of a participatory process, or, inversely, as a significant location of citizenship, emancipation, and empowerment.

Its semantic complexity makes the signifier ordinary people particularly difficult to capture. De Certeau (1984: 2; see also Thumim, 2006) eloquently formulated this problem when he said that ordinary people are "Everyman & Nobody, Chacun & Personne, Jedermann & Niemand." Nevertheless, as already mentioned in the previous paragraph, two significatory strands can be distinguished, one of which sees ordinary people as mass and (under)class. The articulation of ordinary people as mass is linked to the broad definition of ordinary people as everybody, as an "undifferentiated group," where the signifier ordinary people "denies distinctiveness and difference" (Thumim, 2006: 263). This articulation carries with it the implicit threat of the mass evolving into the mob, revolting against social order, or, in a more positive version—often invoked by left-wing theorists—it signifies the potential of instigating social change as part of a class struggle. Here we find articulations of mass and class intersecting. In their introduction to *Reality Television and*

Class, Skeggs and Wood (2011: 1–2) wrote that the "[…] term 'ordinary' is one of the many euphemisms used to stand in for 'working class', because in many different nations it is no longer fashionable to speak about class identifications." Also, Hartley (1994: 173) explicitly referred to the moments when the concept of ordinary people is used as "[…] convenient 'erasures' or euphemisms for class." But the definition of ordinary people in terms of (mass and) class brings about new problems, as the question then becomes, which classes to include? An example of a broad class-based definition of ordinary people is Bennett and Watson's (2002: x) description of ordinary people as "members of the working and middle classes." In contrast, Brett's (2006) description of the use of ordinary (people) in an Australian context shows how a different ('lower') class position is connected to the notion of ordinary people:

> "In Australia, the term 'ordinary' trails with it another set of associations which are not about politics at all, but rather about class and status. 'Very ordinary' or 'rather ordinary' are class terms of disdain for people who lack manners, education and possibly intelligence. They invoke a status system based on degrees of refinement."

The ordinary-as-lower-class-articulation was also used by Ogdon (2006). But she further complicated the ordinary people subject position when she argued that the "underclass" that we get to see in reality television, for instance, is 'extraordinary' and distinct from the average (ordinary) people. She wrote that "[…] reality TV's 'real people' were consistently offered up as extraordinary, as a kind of televisual *lumpenproletariat*, a non-productive underclass, distinctly at odds with notions of the average, (exceptionally) hard-working American" (Ogdon, 2006: 30—emphasis in original).

Attempts to fixate the (meaning of the) concept of ordinary people as mass or class often lead to the use of implicit or explicit relationist strategies, where ordinary people are defined by making use of other social categories. The ordinary-people-as-mass approach, for instance, needs the constitutive outside of the extraordinary. This is exemplified by Zertal's (1998: 173) reference to the Swiss cultural historian Burckhardt and his work on greatness: "How does one define ordinary people? One way is to take Burckhardt's [1964] definition of 'great men'—'those who are all that we are not'—and turn it upside down: ordinary people are like us." As a consequence, the subject position of ordinary people becomes seen to "imply banal, dull, and mundane" (Thumim, 2006: 263). But there is also a darker version of the extraordinary, which becomes articulated with the violation of norms, and with criminal or 'fanatic' behavior. Here, the ordinary is the norm(al), and the extraordinary becomes the transgression of the norm, even if, as is emphasized in holocaust studies, ordinary people are capable of extraordinary evil (Waller, 2007, 2008). Jensen and Szejnmann's words (2008: xi)—"it is now clear, as perhaps never before, that ordinary people can be induced to be mass murderers. Ordinary has lost its ordinariness"—illustrate how the articulation of ordinary people as non-elite can be combined with the articulation of normalcy, with extraordinary evil as its constitutive outside, supporting the argument that non-elite members of society can transgress basic social norms just as much as political leaders. Also, the conceptualization of ordinary people by using the concept of class, a "[...] method of social ranking that involves money, power, culture, taste, identity, access, and exclusion" (Vitt, 2010: 65), has been approached in more relationist ways. Crucial here is the de-essentialization of class, which caused class not only to lose its privileged position as explanans but also to become articulated as more contingent and as part of a struggle to signify. Instead of the harsh (and essentialist) conceptualization of the working class on the basis of its lack of control over the means of production—potentially combined with an awareness of its exploitation, a common identity, and solidarity (where the lower class becomes a class for itself)—the necessity of the relationship between the different classes, and their contingent nature, becomes more emphasized.

This process led to the development of a second strand in defining the ordinary people subject position, which is more in line with a cultural studies agenda. Class differences became translated into an elite-versus-the-people relationship, and through this juxtaposition, ordinary people became defined as non-elite. For example, Hall (1981: 238) positioned (ordinary) people in contrast to the power bloc consisting of societal elites—that is, "[...] the side with the cultural power to decide what belongs and what does not, an alliance of social forces which constitute what is not the people." Also, Williams (1981: 226) used a people-elite approach when he referred to ordinary people as "[...] a generalised body of Others ... from the point of view of a conscious governing or administrative minority." Laclau (1977), writing from a position outside cultural studies, emphasized the conflictual and dominating nature of the relationship between ordinary people and the power bloc. He wrote that "[...] the 'people'/power bloc contradiction is an antagonism whose intelligibility depends not on the relations of production but the complex of political and ideological relations of domination constituting a determinate social formation" (Laclau, 1977: 166).

This second approach towards ordinary people, as non-elite, is also frequently used in media studies. For instance, Ytreberg (2004: 679), in his analysis of a Norwegian popular journalism show (called *Mamarrazzi*), described ordinary people as nonprofessional and nonspecialized performers. Syvertsen (2001: 319), in her analysis of dating games, defined ordinary people as people who are not media professionals, experts, celebrities, or newsworthy for any other reason. In addition, Turner (2010), in his book on the demotic turn, contrasted ordinary people with celebrities, experts, and media professionals. Also, Grindstaff (2002: 18—emphasis in original) used the distinction between ordinary, expert, and celebrity in a part of her book on television talk shows that is most definitely worth quoting in full:

> "Yet daytime talk reinforces the distinctions between the categories *ordinary*, *expert*, and *celebrity* even while seeming to challenge them, for ordinary people are expected to yield a type of dramatic performance quite different from that of professors, politicians, Hollywood stars, or other elites. Ordinary thus means something very specific in relation to daytime talk. It does not necessarily mean 'average,' 'typical,' or 'representative of the population in general.' Indeed, like the subjects of most media accounts, talk-show guests are often chosen for their unique rather than their typical qualities. Ordinary means that guests are not experts or celebrities in the conventional sense of those terms. Their claim to stardom and expertise is rooted in different criteria."

In particular, this second approach, of ordinary people as non-elite opens up articulatory possibilities within participatory processes, where the ordinary people subject position is used to label and validate people, who can be considered as non-privileged actors in relationship to the members of the diversity of only partially overlapping societal elites that characterize contemporary Western societies.

The expert. A third relevant subject position is that of the expert. Expertise is based on a combination of knowledge and skills; Sternberg (2000: 3) argued that two conceptions of expertise exist, where one conception is knowledge-based, while the other refers to the application of knowledge, which then "[…] depends on analytical, creative and practical skills." Both knowledges and skills have been attributed many different characteristics. When discussing the cognitive aspects of expertise—embedded in professional systems—Geisler (2013: 64ff), for instance, referred to the greater abstraction of expert's representations, their use of elaborate reasoning procedures, and their ability to produce case-specific adaptations. Collins and Evans' (2007: 2) work, and their emphasis on expertise that is "real and substantive," provides a good illustration of this approach and of their resistance to what they called the "relationist" perspective (captured in their use of the word "only"):

> "To treat expertise as real and substantive is to treat it as something other than *relational*. Relational approaches take expertise to be a matter of experts' relations with others. The notion that expertise is only an 'attribution'—the, often retrospective, assignment of a label—is an example of a relational theory. The realist approach adopted here is different. It starts from the view that expertise is the real and substantive possession of groups of experts and that individuals acquire real and substantive expertise through their membership of those groups. Acquiring expertise is, therefore, a social process—a matter of socialization into the practices of an expert group—and expertise can be lost if time is spent away from the group." (Collins & Evans, 2007: 2–3—emphasis in original)

This focus on particular characteristics and the defense of "real and substantive expertise" tends to distract the attention from the constructed nature of expertise, and of the subject position of the expert. Expertise is part of the political struggle over what Bourdieu (2000: 185) called legitimate knowledge, and can be seen as a way of imposing a legitimate vision on the world, while other types of knowledge (and skills), such as the situated knowledges (Haraway, 1988) circulating in communities (which can be labeled community-situated knowledges), are facing the permanent risk of being discredited. This political struggle has weakened the position of the expert over time (see e.g., Lyotard, 1984), and authors such as Collins and Evans (2007: 1–2) lamented this weakened role of scientific knowledge:

> "In today's world the scales upon which science is weighed sometimes tip to the point where ordinary people are said to have a more profound grasp of technology than do scientists. Our loss of confidence in experts and expertise seems poised to usher in an age of technological populism."

In defense of Collins and Evans, they do thematize the expertise of people without formal qualifications, such as Cumbrian sheep farmers (Collins & Evans, 2007: 48ff) and AIDS activists (Collins & Evans, 2007: 52ff). Equally relevant is the broadening of legitimate fields of expertise, as Jones, Armour, and Potrac's article (2003) on the expertise of a professional sports coach illustrates. Even if the role of the expert has been requalified over time (see also

Beck, 1996, and Hanlon, 2010, for a critique), as a subject position, it has managed to maintain a significant role in contemporary societies through its juxtaposition of expert on the one hand, and novice, ordinary person, and amateur on the other.

In the field of media production, the media professional remains a crucial location of expertise—and thus of power—endowing that very same media professional with the legitimacy to produce media content. This privileged position of the media professional has been contested by community media activists, who argued against the privileged position of the media professional, and subscribed expertise to 'ordinary' media producers. One of the clearest examples of these articulations can be found in the Introduction to Girard's (1992: 2) *A Passion for Radio*, where he formulated the following answer to the question:

> "[...] a passion for [community] radio?: The answer to that question can be found in a third type of radio—an alternative to commercial and state radio. Often referred to as community radio, its most distinguishing characteristic is its commitment to community participation at all levels. While listeners of commercial radio are able to participate in the programming in limited ways—via open line telephone shows or by requesting a favourite song, for example—community radio listeners are the producers, managers, directors and even owners of the stations."

A later contestation of the expert subject position of the media professional originated from online media discourses, and the transformation of the user into the prod-user (e.g., Bruns, 2008, or the pro-sumer—Toffler, 1980).[13] If we broaden the scope and focus more on (analyses of) participatory processes (in different societal fields) we can find a more critical emphasis on what is often called the "politics of expertise"[14] (Fischer, 2009: 300; Green & Lund, 2015), in combination with pleas and attempts to make "[...] the expert–citizen relationship more participatory [...]" (Fischer, 2009: 7). These projects and practices are grounded in re-articulations of the expert subject position (and not in its destruction), as Fischer (2009: 297) formulated it: "[...] all experts do not need to engage all of the time in participatory inquiry. But the book [*Democracy and Expertise*] has called for a reorientation back to the public and for a new specialization concerned with the policy epistemics that would inform it." Also, Green and Lund (2015: 7), in their study of participatory forestry in Tanzania, emphasized the need for expertise, but also the need to do away with its "exclusive and anti-democratic consequences," which again implies the presence of a democratic expert subject position that shies away from privilege, focusses on "redistributing expertise" (Landström et al., 2011: 1630), and "[...] entails an understanding of expertise as reproduced in local contexts rather than a property of certain actors" (Landström et al., 2011: 1618).

The owner. One more subject position that structures the participatory process is that of the owner, which negotiates the relationships between humans and objects. More specifically, ownership creates the framework for generating individuated and privileged connections between (groups of) individuals and (clusters of) objects, supported by legal and economic frameworks in a "highly commercialized and monetized society" (Kopytoff, 1986: 83–84). Renner (1949: 73) argued:

> "Whatever the social system, disposal of all goods that have been seized and assimilated must be regulated by the social order as the rights of persons over material objects. [...] The legal institutions which effect this regulation, subject the world of matter bit by bit to the will of singled-out individuals since the community exists only through its individual members. These legal institutions endow the individuals with detention so that they may dispose of the objects and possess them."

But the concept of property has more levels of complexity. As Pels (1998: 20) wrote, there are differences, for instance, between physical possession and enforceable claims, and between borders that are easily passable or relatively obstacled. Moreover, he pointed to the diversity encapsulated within the concept of the owner, which may be "individuals, kinship groups, cliques, corporations, states, or supranational bodies" (Pels, 1998: 20). The same diversity applies to the object, which may be: "[...] tangible or intangible, separable or non-separable from the person. Property can embrace the object in its entirety, or can be divided into a scatter of partial rights" (Pels, 1998: 20). Kopytoff's (1986: 65, 86) examples of slavery and the blood market in the USA illustrate this diversity even more, and the way ownership can enter into the sphere of the subject and the human body.

Here, we should acknowledge the discursive dimension of ownership (and the additional complexities this incorporates), as the relationship between the owning subject and the owned object is not fixed. Davies (2012: 174)—referring to Durkheim—pointed to the embeddedness of ownership in the social: "Ownership stems from a sense of where boundaries should or should not be recognised and depends on members of a community recognising its justice, or for Durkheim, its sacred aura (Durkheim, 1991, p. 143)." A few paragraphs earlier, Davies (2012: 174) critiqued neo-classical economics' reduction of "[…] the public to a type of technical and governmental problem […]," arguing for a sociology of ownership that does not accept the hegemony of ownership at face value. This also brings us to the constructed nature of ownership and of the subject position of the owner. Another argument to support a more discursive reading of ownership comes from Wilpert's (1991—see also Furby, 1978; Van Dyne & Pierce, 2004) work on 'psychological property' and participation, where he argued that ownership can also occur in the absence of legal ownership. Etzioni's (1991: 466) reference to property as "[…] part attitude part object, part in the mind, part 'real'" is another illustration of this more psychological approach to ownership, which creates a bridge to the discursive reading of ownership.

Moreover, ownership also gains its meaning through different political projects. There is a long tradition of critique that rejects the benevolent character of property and points to its exploitative characteristics. Not only Marxism, but also classic anarchist theory, for instance, is "[…] critical of private property to the extent that it was a source of hierarchy and privilege" (Jennings, 1999: 136), although some caution is needed: Even Proudhon's (2008) dictum—'property is theft'—was used for a specific context. Still, together with Marx and Proudhon, numerous authors, for instance in the field of political economy, have criticized the particular relationship between owner and owned, and have proposed different types of relationships. Also, in actual communist practice, private ownership was problematized and severely restricted, even if the situation was (and is) not always clear (see Martin, 2013: 69) about the Central and Eastern European Communist regimes in the 20th century). But this is not the only area where different articulations of ownership circulate. Davies (2012) also showed the differences between liberal and neoliberal projects, where the latter privileges private property rights, while traditional liberalism "[…] rests upon a moral logic of separation of economic, social and political realms," stressing the "[…] distinction between spheres of restricted ownership and spheres of unrestricted deliberation" (Davies, 2012: 179). Moreover, actual practice in capitalist societies is also characterized by diverse articulations of ownership:

> "Given that ownership is a messy, compromised and ambiguous institution, there is the opportunity to invent new forms of ownership which mediate between the public and the private, such as mutualism (in which organisations are owned by members, not shareholders), or the sharing of ownership rights between competing interests, such as the financiers and the users of assets." (Davies, 2012: 180)

In participatory processes, the articulation of ownership and the subject position of the owner can have a strong impact. Often, in discussions of participation, we can find references to a 'sense of ownership' over the process itself (see, e.g., Lachapelle, 2008), but in the approach used in this book, this type of ownership (sometimes referred to as democratic ownership) is intrinsic to the participatory process itself, as it refers to the power position of the unprivileged actors involved in the participatory process. Equally relevant here is how the subject position of the owner is defined, and how the ownership of resources is organized, whether particular participants remain in control (potentially skewing the power balance) or share or donate resources (potentially equalizing the power balance). And also relevant is how the ownership of those external to the participatory process are recognized, as examples as diverse as squatting (Fox O'Mahony, O'Mahony, & Hickey, 2014) and popular culture fan appropriation (Jenkins, 1992) show.

The leader. The fifth subject position that discursively structures participatory processes is that of the leader. Leadership refers to the privileged position of individuals in decision-making processes, entitling them to decide, and is—as a subject position—omnipresent in society, in political but also in business and other organizational settings. As Lewis (1974: 3), from an anthropological perspective, wrote: "Whether or not a society has institutionalized chiefs, rulers, or elected officials there are always, in any society, leaders who initiate action and play central roles in group-decision-making." This implies that also in less formal (and more participatory) organizations, leadership plays an important role, as research in new social movements has exemplified (Barker et al., 2001; Herda-Rapp, 1998).

Moreover, as (relatively) strong forms of leadership are dominant in Western societies, this articulation of the leader subject position impacts on participatory processes. In more traditional (19th- and first-half-of-the-20th-century) approaches, leadership was mainly seen as a unidirectional process, where the leader controlled the decision-making process, "[...] impressing the will of the leader and inducing obedience [...]" (Bass & Bass, 2008: 24). This locates the decision almost exclusively with the leader. Weber's (1947) classic distinction between charismatic, traditional, and rational legal authority can be seen as an illustration of this logic, as it takes the legitimization (strategies) of the decision-making of particular persons or institutions as a starting point (in all three cases, but mostly in the first two). Later, organizational leadership models changed and leadership became (in an organizational context) more geared towards "[...] the ability to influence, motivate and enable others to contribute to the effectiveness and success of the organizations of which they are members" (House et al., 2004: 15, quoted in Bass & Bass, 2008: 23), without fundamentally altering the leader's privilege to decide in the last instance. Also, in discussions of political leadership, the emphasis is placed more on how "[...] leaders and followers are involved in a circular process of motivation and power exchange that is often difficult to break up into a causal sequence," although leaders are still seen to "[...] mobilize a significant number of followers to accept their diagnosis of, and policy prescriptions for, collective problems or crises" (Masciulli, Molchanov, & Knight, 2013: 4).

Even when these (revised) leadership models are dominant in contemporary (Western) societies, supported by the dominance of vertically structure organizations, this does not mean that no alternative articulations of the leader subject position exist. One significant alternative articulation is labeled democratic leadership, inspired by the work of Lewin and his colleagues (Lewin & Lippitt, 1938; Lewin, Lippitt, & White, 1939; White & Lippitt, 1960). Gastil (1994) summarized the characteristics of (this early model of) democratic leadership by referring to group decision-making, active member involvement, honest praise and criticism, and a degree of comradeship. In his review of the more recent literature on democratic leadership, Gastil (1994) distinguished three primary characteristics: the distribution of responsibility within the demos, the empowerment of the membership, and aiding the demos in its deliberations. Even when the strong leadership model remains hegemonic, the contestations produced by the democratic leadership models generate contingency, undermining the taken-for-grantedness of the traditional strong leadership model. Nevertheless, the strong leadership model is still very dominant, and contestations often result in leadership replacement, which prevents more fundamental dislocations of the strong leadership model itself.

1.3.2 The material component of participation

At the same time, the participatory process also has material dimensions, which are entangled with the discursive components discussed above. The notion of process, frequently used in this book, can be used as a starting point of this analysis, as it enables an analytical difference between process-internal and process-external dimensions. Process refers here to a series of related goal-oriented practices, which is close to the ways this concept is defined in organizational (and marketing) theory. For instance, Juran (2003: 358) defined process as "[…] a systematic series of actions directed to the achievement of a goal," while Cummings and Worley (2014: 790) saw process as "[…] the way persons are relating to one another as they perform some activity." Without subscribing to the basic principles of systems theory, it should be noted that within organizational theory, systems theory is often used to define process, as, for instance, Hammer and Champy (1993: 53) did when they defined the process as a "[…] collection of activities that takes one or more kinds of input and creates an output […]."

Together with the notion of process, also the distinction between access, interaction, and participation (captured in the above-mentioned AIP model) helps in structuring the diversity of materials that, with their agencies, enter the participatory process. Further support can be gained from one of the secondary dimensions of the AIP model, notably the difference between technology, content, people, and organizations (see Carpentier, 2011). In an earlier part of this book, access has already been defined as presence, and interaction as a socio-communicative relationship. It is important to emphasize (again) that access and interaction are structurally different from participation, but that they are still necessary conditions for participation (and thus relevant in a discussion about the materiality of participation).

Two additional general points need to be raised when discussing the material dimensions of participatory processes. Firstly, the agency of the materials (that are part of these participatory processes) needs to be emphasized, as was already done in the first platform of this book. Materials are not passive components of participatory processes, but play an active role in structuring these processes through their invitations. Materials are equally important parts of participatory assemblages, and should not be placed in secondary positions. At the same time, the discursive remains important in providing meaning(s) for these materials. In her book *Material Participation*, Marres (2012: 5—emphasis in original) made a similar point when she wrote that

> "[…] material participation does *not* involve stripping participation of its informational, linguistic or discursive components. It rather makes a particular addition to, or modification of, the more usual codification of engagement as a state of informedness."

The importance of materials in participatory processes does not imply that their positions are univocal, stable, and fixed. Marres's (2012: 65) distinction between the constitutive and constituted materiality of (political) participation is helpful in illustrating the diversity and contingency that characterizes the role of material in participation processes. In the case of constitutive materiality, Marres (2012: 65) referred to a considerable number of research projects that document "[...] how material objects, technologies and settings enter into the enactment of public participation." Examples she mentioned are material techniques for generating voice, such as the opinion poll (Osborne & Rose, 1999) and the focus group (Lezaun, 2007), but also modes of demonstration (e.g., Barry's, 2001: 175ff, work on anti-road protest). Marres's own work is more related to what she called the constituted materiality of participation, where "[...] a material device of participation becomes itself the object of a 'public performance' [...]" and "[...] the device configures public participation as a form of material action [...]" (Marres, 2012: 65). The example Marres discussed on these pages is a tea light that enables people to optimize their tea-making behavior in relation to CO2 emissions. More in general, her definition of material participation—"framed as a particular kind of practice to be pursued in a particular setting, such as recycling, changing bulbs and so on" (Marres, 2012: 8)—refers to the enactment of societal engagement, which is a much broader approach towards participation (and is closer to the sociological approach discussed earlier) than the one that is used in this book.

What adds further weight to the diversity argument is the fluid role of materials in participatory processes. Again (and despite the differences in approach), one can refer to Marres's (2012: 154) *Material Participation* book, where she wrote that "Technologies of participation, like most other instruments, are under-determined in their application [...] To use a more contemporary term, these technologies are marked by performative flexibility." This is explained further as followed: "[...] a given device may be adapted to perform participation in radically different registers, form 'involvement made easy' to creative experiments in living differently" (Marres, 2012: 154). Also, here the discursive-material knot comes into play, something that Marres (2012: 21) touched upon earlier in her book: "Insofar as engaging objects are happening or 'lively' objects, their participatory capacities fluctuate—objects may become politicized (or 'issuefied') easily, but their normative charge might be lost or transformed into something less lively just as quickly."

Access. To structure (some of) this diversity and fluidity, we can return to the distinction between access, interaction, and participation (and the supportive dimension of technology, content, people, and organizations—see Carpentier, 2011: 130). Keeping in mind that access, like interaction, is a prerequisite of participation, we can argue that the access to a wide range of materials, to be brought into the participatory process, is one crucial area where the material comes to matter. The discussion on material resources, in particular capitals, brings us almost immediately to the political economy of participation, a label that groups a wide series of approaches and fields (e.g., Fuchs, 2013; Orr, 1979; Smith, 2005; Tulloss, 1995; Vujnovic et al., 2010). Within these frameworks, access to material resources is seen as an object of struggle, and the lack of access to these resources is seen as a constraint towards the participatory process. Given the capitalist contexts in which participatory processes are frequently located, material resources remain very necessary to pay salaries (if people are employed) and purchase (access to) working spaces, proto-machines, and other commodities. With the commodification of time, access to labor becomes dependent on material resources, as the remuneration of labor is important for those who provide it.[15] Conversely, being employed (or having one's own labor commodified) is often one of the few ways to enter places of production and have access to (often expensive) proto-machines. Also, the access to particular services, such as expert advice, becomes dependent upon the availability of material resources, as Smith's (2005: 36) analysis of participation and urban planning shows:

> "Both [developers and house-builders] have access to expert advice, which is necessary to engage with the complicated and legalistic procedures of the system. Rather than opening up the opportunity for a more broadly participatory approach to planning and redressing inequalities of power, in practice the UK system has created opportunities for groups that are already powerful either financially or in terms of expertise and influence."

To use Marres's (2012: 147) words: "[…] the enactment of participation and the organization of the space-times of participation must be understood as inter-related processes." Ownership, in its material dimension of controlling commodities, then becomes a significant enabling element, as it facilitates (always scarce) material resources being brought into the participatory process. Fuchs's (2013: 56) statement that "A truly participatory media democracy must also be an ownership democracy" only exemplifies the importance of ownership.

But at the same time we should acknowledge the existence of alternative practices of organization and ownership—as sometimes can be found in civil society. Different, non-commodified relationships between humans and objects continue to be practiced, however hegemonic traditional ownership is. Ownership can be suspended through the mechanics of the gift, as theorized by Mauss (1966).[16] Sahlins (1972: 168–169) described these dynamics as a shift away from the Hobbesian "war of every man against every man," which "Mauss substitutes [for] the exchange of everything between everybody [...] The gift is alliance, solidarity, communion [...]." Ownership can also be suspended through the logic of sharing, or translated into collective ownership (Curl, 2009; DeFilippis, 2004). Moreover, not all acquisition is necessarily fully embedded within the logics of monetization and commodification, as the existence of barter and do-it-yourself production illustrates (Airaghi, 2014). In other words, objects that are needed within participatory processes can be obtained by exchange or self-production, surpassing traditional ownership relations and creating alternative relations between humans and objects, not always within the letter (or even spirit) of the law. A similar argument can be raised about labor, which can also be brought into the participatory process through the logic of the gift. Voluntarism (or the donation of labor) is a significant practice within civil society (and, in particular, community media—see later) and incorporates the possibility of strengthening the collective (Eckstein, 2001; Warburton, 2006) and the circumvention of the hegemonic commodification of labor, even if this is accompanied by the risk of exploitation.

Access to material resources remains a crucial component in participatory processes. A variety of objects frequently support it, or, when production is the objective of the participatory processes, are its outcome. In the case of community media production, for instance, proto-machines (or, in other words, technology) are/is an important component of the participatory process, which relies on studio equipment, computers, transmitters, antennas, and many other objects. These objects are combined with (and, in their turn, used to gain access to) particular content—texts that are always particular combinations of material text-related practices and text-related signifying practices. Access to texts (whether it is information, people's voices and images, music ...) also has a material dimension, as books, databases, manuals, CDs, audio or video files, or people are the carriers of texts. These different objects are frequently integrated into organizational machines, with their own decision-making mechanisms and hierarchies, places and practices of access that structure and enable (or disable) different degrees of access for different people. Through their agencies, they impact on the participatory process, structuring it, favoring particular usages and hampering others. Being embedded in the discursive-material knot, materials invite support for, and identification with, particular discourses (including the discourse(s) on participation itself).

At the same time, we should not decontextualize the participatory process. Even if—sometimes—the organizational machines become counter-hegemonic islands, which do not follow (or respect) the dominant order in relation to these objects, these outside worlds still provide powerful contexts that might impose themselves upon more maximalist participatory organizational machines. There are, for instance, legal-political orders that might suppress attempts to organize alternative ownership models—the way the squatting movement had to face legal injunctions and police evictions is illustrative of (the threat of) these kind of material impositions (Fox O'Mahony, O'Mahony, & Hickey, 2014). Another example is the legal framework of copyright protection, which has—in combination with a strong lobby that articulated these infractions as piracy (De Cleen, 2008)—resulted in the prosecution of people and organizations that defended different models of intellectual ownership. A third example is the Western contemporary political constellation that is built on "[...] the separation between of domain of professional politics and that of a wider public engagement with politics" (Marres, 2012: 67). Also, economic (capitalist) orders tend to impose themselves on participatory processes, in a wide variety of ways; for instance, by rendering material resources scarce, by producing consumption market-oriented technologies that do not always rest well with participatory processes, and by transforming (labor) time into a commodity, which causes people to be "[...] too busy to perform the duties that full-fledged participation in the political community requires" (Marres, 2012: 67).[17] Lastly, also, social orders can weigh on the participatory process, in particular in relation to exclusions based on class, ethnic or gender positions, space and place, but also on the material privileges generated by expertise, ownership, and leadership. To use Gaventa's (2004: 37) words in relation to space and place as illustration: "[...] power in relationship to space and place also works to put boundaries on participation, and to exclude certain actors or views from entering the arenas for participation in the first place."

Interaction. Mere access is 'only' one of the prerequisites of participation, however important it is in itself. As argued before, interaction is also one of the conditions of possibility of participation, and can thus be used to shed light on the material dimension of participation. The idea here is that whatever impacts on interaction, as prerequisite of participation, will also impact on the participatory process itself. Proto-machines and texts can be brought into the participatory process, and access can be provided to them, but they also need to be used by people (and, in some cases, by other proto-machines and other texts). These operations are embodied practices themselves, where fingers press buttons, type on keyboards, and hold documents to read them. As Askins and Pain (2011: 816) wrote in reference to Hume-Cook et al.'s (2007) work:

> "Photography, video, and other digital technologies can be employed in participatory, 'hands on' ways, with multiple actors working on ideas, taking the camera, editing visual outputs through facilitated negotiations with each other (Hume-Cook et al, 2007)."

These usages require particular knowledge and skills that structure that interaction. Using, for instance, a video camera requires training—embodied knowledge—that enables operating this technology, familiarizing the user with the proto-machines' many functionalities (and dysfunctionalities). Moreover, quite often the operations of proto-machines are performed collectively, by different individuals that work together, interacting with each other, manipulating these proto-machines. Askins and Pain (2011) argued here that interactional (and participatory) processes are contact zones where different groups in society meet and work together, generating opportunities, tensions, and problems. Again, collaborative skills are required to structure and guide people through these interactions. Finally, these collaborations are also embedded in particular organizational structures, which are sometimes (but not always) place-based organizations, and/or that consist of different—rhizomatically connected—organizations or other structures.

Interaction plays an important role in the participatory process, as these interactions also imply decision-making processes on how to use proto-machines, how proto-machines allow themselves to be used, how to interact with textual condensations, and how these texts allow themselves to be used, how to interact with others, and how others allow to be interacted with, to give but a few examples. But it should be added that in some cases, the facilitation of interaction has a democratizing effect in itself (even if there is no participatory dimension—in the meaning used by the political approach). For instance, in discussions on museums and democratic empowerment, we can find authors that argue that being allowed to interact with particular material objects (often not even accessible to 'ordinary' visitors) increases empowerment. One example is Barry's (1998: 88) discussion of Frank Oppenheimer's Exploratorium in San Francisco, where he raised this point as follows:

> "The public would be empowered through being able to interact with objects as an experimental scientist does in the natural world of the laboratory. According to Hilde Hein, 'interactive pedagogic technique contains a key to empowerment that could transform education on a broad scale and make an avenue of general self-determination' (Hein 1990: xvi)."

Another example comes from interactive film, which is defined by Ben-Shaul (2008: 7) as "[…] audio-visual texts that strives, through the use of cinematic strategies, to offer the interactor an option to change at predetermined points the course of action by shifting to other predetermined options." It should immediately be added that interactive film is different from participatory film, as in the latter, non-professional filmmakers can co-decide on the film (production). Here, Macdougall's (1975: 282–283) description of participatory cinema, where "[…] the filmmaker acknowledges his entry upon the world of his subjects and yet asks them to imprint directly upon the film their own culture," is helpful in clarifying the difference. Nevertheless, interactive film can still have a democratizing role and touch upon (minimalist) participation, as an earlier research project into the Kinoautomat, the first interactive film, shows (Carpentier, 2011: 276ff). Particularly relevant in the Kinoautomat case is the obstinacy of the (material) film technology. With film projectors that could not be stopped in order to change film reels, the film projectionist had to cover one of the two main film projectors with a lens cap, depending on the outcome of the audience vote in order for the 'correct' part of the film to be shown.

Participation. The structuring logics of co-decision making, which is the defining component of participation, also applies to the role the material plays in participatory processes. The two previous discussions, on access and interaction, already open up many spaces of decision-making, and they produce questions about who decides on the access to particular resources, objects, people, places, etc., and about who decides on the interaction with and between them. Each of the above mentioned components can have, and most likely have, a decision-making dimension, which makes them relevant for (the analysis of) participatory processes. From a participatory perspective, the degree of shared control over material access and interactions remains a crucial component to decide over the intensity of participatory levels in these processes.

In this sense, participation has to deal with the 'administration of things,' to use one of Saint-Simon's concepts (which was also used by Engels and Foucault—see Kafka, 2012). It is about making decisions, with participants on equal footing, about how materials are deployed in these participatory processes, and what human bodies that are involved will do with them, and with each other. In the case of (participatory) media production this, for instance, relates to decisions about the use of production technologies (and by whom); the use of production spaces and places; the visibility/audibility (and its absence) of participants; the use of particular languages (or dialects), genres, and formats, etc. Participatory processes are characterized by an infinitude of micro-decisions (see Carpentier, 2016a) about materials and material practices, and structured by the attempts to equalize the power relations behind these many decisions. For instance, when it comes to the use of places, one can ask who can enter a broadcasting studio or the website back office—or, in other words, who has spatial authority (Carpignano et al., 1990: 48). Again, as repeatedly argued, in maximalist participatory processes, these authorities are evened out, and control is equally shared amongst participants.

Also, the process of participatory decision-making has a material dimension. Decision-making in itself, with its meetings and combination of voices, deploys a multitude of materials. Some of these objects are developed to serve the participatory process. They are what Marres (2012: 61) called "[…] artefacts that embody particular empirical and experimental methods of engagement." But in other cases, 'regular' materials are used to support, structure, and organize participatory processes, where again maximalist participation is characterized by the care that is taken not to create imbalances between participants through the materiality of the decision-making process. This, for instance, relates how different voices are allowed to speak, often guided by discourses of civility, or how a particular room is used to position the participants. Kaner (2014: 218), in his *Facilitator's Guide to Participatory Decision-Making*, spent some time on explaining how the materiality of a meeting room can create a challenge for a participatory process. Arguably more important is the materiality of hierarchy, where vertical decision-making structures and the related strong forms of leadership go against (maximalist) participatory practices, as they create imbalances in the degree of control participants can exert over themselves, others, and all materials implicated in the participatory process. As Pullen and Vachhani (2013: 315) argued in their Introduction to a special journal issue on the materiality of leadership, "[…] leadership is practised through and between bodies, where matter matters […]." Fisher and Robbins' (2015) analysis of embodied (military) leadership shows the importance of "doing leadership" and "leading by example," but also of relationship management—looking after each other. This "use of the body as a scene of leadership display" (Fisher & Robbins, 2015: 291) is very material, and although it may be slightly at odds with participatory processes, it nicely illustrates the importance of material practices in relation to leadership, which can again impact on the participatory processes (often through the creation of informal leaders).

Together, discourses and materials form a discursive-material knot, characterized by contingency. This contingency partially originates from participation's political nature, which renders participation the object of a discursive struggle between more minimalist and maximalist approaches. Furthermore, the many subject positions that are involved show the discursive complexity of participatory processes, where these subject positions (and how people identify with them) can become aligned with particular articulations of the democratic-participatory discourse, or can, in contrast, dislocate them. For instance, a maximalist participatory process requires the strong support of empowered citizen and ordinary person subject positions, but more counter-hegemonic re-articulations of the expert, the owner, and the leader to avoid the creation of power imbalances that would dislocate the maximalist nature of the participatory process. In the inverse, a non-participatory articulation requires strong and traditional versions of the expert, the owner, and the leader subject position, and the articulation of the citizen and the ordinary person as secondary to the expert, the owner, and the leader. Contingency arises not only from the discursive struggle over participation, but also from the difficulties in aligning the supportive articulations of the relevant subject positions with each other and with participation.

A similar argument can be made for the material components of the discursive-material knot, which can, through their agencies and invitations, support and sustain particular participatory intensities, or, on the contrary, disrupt them. Participatory processes require many different materials, each with their own agencies, to become aligned within the participatory assemblage. For instance, the lack of material (e.g., financial) resources can seriously disrupt a participatory process (and it often does, in particular the maximalist-participatory processes). But also the lack of interested people, willing and keen to participate, can (obviously) disrupt any participatory process. Participation requires human beings accessing the location of the participatory process, and interacting with each other and with (proto-) machines.[18] Technologies for the production of media content, for instance, can be sophisticated, and can resist being used by untrained hands. Even if the contemporary literature is often focused on overcoming user resistance towards technology, these publications also contain traces of user-resistant technology, for instance: "Technology must be easy and intuitive to use for the majority of the user audience—or they won't use it" (Haymes, 2008: 68). These examples show the agencies of these technologies, and the difficulties related to integrating material components into a participatory assemblage, which in turn illustrates how the lack of alignment can generate contingency.

2 Defining Community Media Organizations

One location of maximalist participation in the media field is community media organizations. Community media organizations can take many different forms and can use various technological platforms (print, radio, TV, web-based, or mixed). Even in their labeling, many differences can be found. Apart from community media, they have been described through a variety of concepts, including alternative media, citizens' media, associative media, free media, autonomous media, rhizomatic media, radical media, and civil society media. Although I am sensitive to the argument that the complete conflation of these different labels should be avoided (Howley, 2005: 4), I want to focus on what this multiplicity of community media organizations[19] have in common, seeing their diversity and hybridity as a characteristic, rather than as an analytical problem. Support for this position can be found in Atton's (2002: 209) argument that "This encourages us to approach these media from the perspective of 'mixed radicalism', once again paying attention to hybridity rather than meeting consistent adherence to a 'pure,' fixed set of criteria [...]."

Moreover, despite their differences, community media organizations share a number of key characteristics that distinguish them from other types of media organizations such as public service or market media organizations. Firstly, their close connection to civil society and their strong commitment to (maximalist forms of) participation and democracy, in both their internal decision-making practices and in their signifying practices, are important distinguishing characteristics that establish community media organizations as the third media type, distinct from public service and market media organizations. Secondly, we should keep in mind that they are community media *organizations*, which have particular formal (or semi-formal) objectives that are affiliated to participatory-democratic discourses and that align—as organizational machines—people and objects in particular ways, as will be discussed in this part of the book. This of course does not exclude the existence of community-oriented, alternative, or non-hegemonic signifying practices outside these organizational settings (see e.g., Pajnik, 2015, for this argument), but this is not the focus of my analysis.

One way to capture the diversity of community media organizations and understand what unites them is to combine the four approaches that have been used in the literature for the study of community media (discussed in Carpentier, Lie, & Servaes, 2003; see also Bailey, Cammaerts, and Carpentier, 2007; Carpentier, 2011). Taken together, these four approaches enable theorizing the complexity and rich diversity of community media, but they also facilitate showing the workings of the discursive-material knot, in particular in relation to the participatory processes that are organized in, and by, the organizational machines that community media organizations are. Each of these community media models highlights particular discourses and subject positions, and articulates them in evenly particular ways to serve community media organizations' maximalist-participatory objective, in response to hegemonic contexts that are not always supportive of community media. Moreover, each of these community media models mobilizes the material in (slightly) different ways, also in relation to the maximalist-participatory objective. In doing so, community media organizations, and the models that structure them, are counter-hegemonic interventions into the political and media landscapes—examples of articulatory agency—that aim to change the social by rendering it more democratic.

Two of the four community media models are media-centered. Built on community media (Approach 1) and alternative media (Approach 2) theory, these two models capture the more traditional ways of understanding community media. The first approach uses a more autonomist theoretical framework, stressing the importance of the media organization serving a community, while alternative media models focus on the relationship between alternative and mainstream media, putting more emphasis on the discursive relation of interdependency between two opposing sets of identities. These two traditional models for theorizing the identity of community media organizations are complemented by two more society-centered approaches.[20] The third approach defines community media as part of civil society. In order to incorporate the more relationist aspects of civil society theory—articulated, for instance, by Walzer (1992, 1998)—they are combined with Downing's (2001) and Rodríguez's (2001) critiques of alternative media, and radicalized and unified in the fourth approach, which builds on the Deleuzian metaphor of the (community media as) rhizome.

	Media-centered	**Society-centered**
Autonomous identity of CM (Autonomist)	Approach I: Serving the community	Approach III: Part of civil society
Identity of CM in relation to other identities (Relationalist)	Approach II: An alternative to mainstream	Approach IV: Rhizome

Figure 11. The four theoretical approaches towards community media.
Adjusted from Carpentier, Lie, & Servaes, 2003: 53.

The four approaches (as rendered in Figure 11) are, of course, academic-theoretical models, which together form what I would like to call the community media discourse, as it circulates in the academic field, with the aim of making sense of the discursive production and practices in the field of community media itself. This discourse is partially generated through academic signifying practices (with some models being more popular than others), but it is also fed by community media signifying (and material) practices themselves (communicated through community media publications and through academic and community media research). Seen as an integral part of the logic of the discursive-material knot, these four approaches provide us with the four nodal points of the community media (identity) discourse. This discourse structures, in always-unique ways,[21] the identifications in particular community media organizational machines. At the same time, this discourse is not completely rigid. It contains many internal and external contestations, overlaps, gaps, and contradictions. Because of this, care should be taken not to switch into a celebratory mode, reducing social reality to this community media discourse. In other words, we should be careful not to forget that these models, and the participatory practices they feed into, are characterized by contingency. It is the still unavoidable distance between academia and community media, together with the variety of identifications with these models (both in academia and community media) that creates contingency, together with the variety generated by the material components of the community media organizations. Moreover, community media, as counter-hegemonic forces, are engaged with an outside world that frequently contests its assemblages of discourses and materials, again adding to the instability and diversity that characterizes these organizations, and to the many ways they relate to the four models.

2.1 Serving the Community

In the first approach, the specific role of these media organizations in relation to the community is emphasized. Community media are seen as serving 'their' community, and thus validating and strengthening it. The nodal point of community service becomes visible in, for instance, the 2008 European Parliament's *Resolution on Community Media in Europe*,[22] which states that "[…] community media are non-profit organisations accountable to the community that they seek to serve." Access by the community and participation of the community (and its constituent subgroups) should be considered key-defining factors. An illustration can be found in Howley's (2005: 4) work, when he describes community media as "[…] locally oriented, participatory media [that facilitate the] process of collective identity construction in geographically defined communities." Another example is the 'working definition' of community radio adopted by AMARC-Europe, the European branch of the World Association of Community Radio Broadcasters,[23] an organization that encompasses a wide range of radio practices across the continents. Attempting to avoid a prescriptive definition (and focusing on radio), AMARC-Europe (1994: 4) labelled a community radio station as "[…] a 'non-profit' station, currently broadcasting, which offers a service to the community in which it is located, or to which it broadcasts, while promoting the participation of this community in the radio."

The serving-the-community model brings a cluster of subject positions into the community media discourse. These subject positions and their particular articulations structure the relationships between the community media organization and different societal actors, offering opportunities for identification. A first (and rather crucial) element of this serving-the-community model is the identity of the community itself, as they are to be empowered and given a voice. The notion of community is a rather complex concept that is often defined in relation to geography and ethnicity as structuring notions of collective identity or group relations (Leunissen, 1986). Place then becomes a significant concept, which is illustrated by Foxwell-Norton's (2015: 393) statement that "Communities do not just live in their local environment; they also 'think' their environments, bringing a host of cultural frameworks to their place […]." Also, in AMARC-Europe's (1994) definition of community radio the geographical aspect is explicitly highlighted: A community radio "[…] offers a service to the community in which it is located […]."

Nevertheless, other types of relationships[24] between media organization and community are implied in how the phrase of AMARC-Europe's definition continues, adding "to which it broadcasts" to it. This is aligned with two types of re-conceptualizations of the traditional (geography and/or ethnicity-based) approach towards community. A first set of re-conceptualizations introduces the non-geographical as a complement to the structural-geographic approach to community. In particular, the concept of the community of interest (Newman, 1980) enables emphasizing the importance of other factors in structuring a community. Although one cannot explicitly assume that a group of people has common interests (see Clark, 1973: 411), the communality of interest can form the condition of possibility for the emergence, or existence, of a community. Also, Wenger's (1999) so-called communities of practices, which are composed out of the informal arenas of family, work, and friendship networks (see also Hewson, 2005: 17) illustrate this non-geographical re-conceptualization. A second set of re-conceptualizations is based on the cultural as a complement to the structural-geographic community approach. These approaches emphasize the subjective construction of community, as illustrated by Lindlof's (1988) concept of interpretative community and Cohen's (1989) community of meaning.

But despite this significatory diversity, the notion of community is still specific, and Tönnies's (1963) old distinction—between community and society—remains helpful in describing what binds these many different approaches together. Martin-Barbero (1993: 29) summarized the way Tönnies uses community as follows: "Community is defined by the unity of thought and emotion, by the predominance of close and concrete human ties and by relations of solidarity, loyalty and collective identity." Through this logic of belonging, community also produces a subject position, namely that of the member of the community. As Lemke (1990) argued, this, for instance, means the appropriation of the community's language(s) in order to construct the community member subject position. But also, other elements matter in this construction, such as the performance of practices important to the community and the identification with the discourses on the community, about its past, for instance, Cohen, 1989) and with the discourses that are dear to the community (e.g., on particular values).

Community media organizations, with their aim to empower the community they serve, offer, use, and are defined by, particular articulations of the identity of the community, and of the community member subject position, which are grounded in ideas of community membership as active, interested, and open, but also competent and relevant, at least potentially. One example is Rennie's (2006: 37) reference to the community members obtaining particular skills:

> "Community media is sometimes pursued as a means to achieve social change. For instance, it can bring skills to a particular community, helping community members to participate in the knowledge economy."

This notion of the active and competent community, which in some cases is articulated as a community that has become activated and has gained competencies, or as a community that has the potential (and desire) of becoming activated and competent, is, in turn, embedded in democratic discourses that are related to the community's exercise of its communicational rights. Through the community media organization, the community participates in the broader society, as Fairchild (2001: 103) put it: "In short, participation in the station acts as a bridge to participation in society." One example is the 2009 *Declaration of the Committee of Ministers on the Role of Community Media in Promoting Social Cohesion and Intercultural Dialogue*, where the Council of Europe (2009) emphasized the role of community media to stimulate political (macro-)participation and enhance democratic learning:

> "Conscious that in today's radically changed media landscape, community media can play an important role, notably by promoting social cohesion, intercultural dialogue and tolerance, as well as by fostering community engagement and democratic participation at local and regional level."

Fairchild (2001: 103) took a broader-political perspective when discussing the role of community media in facilitating societal participation:

> "[...] community radio stations act as issue-based organizations devoted to counteractiving the existing distribution of power by facilitating coalitions between other issue-based organizations and giving these groups a platform for airing their views."

These articulations of the community (members) are grounded in a democratic model that validates voices coming from the community, and that assumes the societal relevance of the participation of a community at a societal level. The community is also articulated as (potentially) active and competent through its involvement in the decision-making in relation to the management of community media, as Berrigan (1979: 8) summarized it:

> "[Community media] are media to which members of the community have access, for information, education, entertainment, when they want access. They are media in which the community participates, as planners, producers, performers."

Also Tabing's (2002: 9) definition of a community radio station as "[…] one that is operated in the community, for the community, about the community and by the community" makes clear that participation in the community media organization is not only situated at the level of content production, but is also related to management and ownership. This articulates the community (members) as (becoming) active, empowered, and capable of co-managing complex organizational structures, supported by more democratic leadership practices.

A second subject position is the community media producer, which is closely related to the subject position of the community member, as community media producers are articulated as representatives of the community (and are thus seen to share their characteristics). Jenning (2015: 14), for instance, wrote, when emphasizing the importance of ensuring "[…] the provision of clear regulatory conditions and policies for the proper functioning of community radio […]," that "[…] broadcasting licences [are] issued to the stations legitimately representing the community rather than interests of a political or opportunistically commercial nature." Even if the representational logic functions more at a collective level, this logic unavoidably becomes part of the community media producer subject position. The articulation of producers and communities also renders producers emblematic for the (potentially) active communities, as those who speak on behalf of the community but also show that the community can speak. To use Berrigan's (1979: 8) words, community media (and thus community media producers) "[…] are the means of expression of the community, rather than for the community." A diversity of ordinary people is given the opportunity to have their voices heard and valued. In particular, societal groups who are misrepresented, disadvantaged, stigmatized, or even repressed are said to benefit from using the channels of communication opened by community media, strengthening their in-group identity, manifesting this identity to the outside world, and thus supporting social change and/or development.

This brings us to the third relevant subject position, which is the audience. Interestingly, the audience becomes equated with the community, and with 'its' producers. Similar to later notions (e.g., the produser in online media theory, Bruns, 2008), the audience is no longer defined in community media theory as an aggregate of individuals who share only socio-demographic or economic characteristics, but instead as a collective of people holding a series of identifying group relations. In this fashion, the situatedness of the audience, as part of a complex set of social structures, is emphasized, deepening and bridging the traditional state-citizen and medium-audience dichotomies that tend to articulate the public and the audience as an aggregate of individuals. In relation to community media theory, Howley (2005: 3) labeled this the "collapsing of distinction between media producers and media consumers":

> "[...] by collapsing the distinction between media producers and media consumers—a convenient fiction manufactured by the culture industries and legitimated over time by administrative and critical communication scholars alike—community media provide empirical evidence that local populations do indeed exercise considerable power at precisely the lasting and organizational levels Ang describes. Indeed, community media underscore the creativity, pragmatism, and resourcefulness of local populations in their struggle to control media production and distribution."

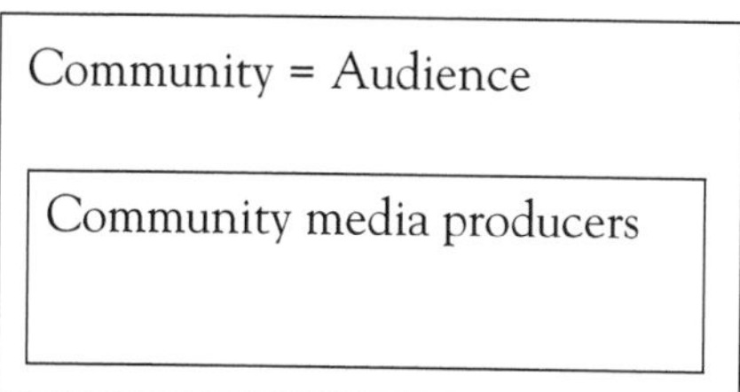

Figure 12. Serving-the-community approach key subject positions—a traditional view.

The above-rendered model (Figure 12) is treacherously simple, and hides many of the contingencies that are also part of the community media practices. Part of these contingencies are triggered by the instability of the (representation of the) community itself. As Barrett (2015: 194) put it: "Communities are contested spaces [...]," characterized by a "solidarity-exclusion dialectic." Tönnies's (1963) romantic perspective on the community should not render us blind to the many discursive and material conflicts that are a constitutive part of these very same communities, including the discursive struggles over its meanings and the material struggles over memberships, territories, and frontiers. Moreover, the use of the community concept in singular form is deceitful, as community media are a crossroads of a multiplicity of communities. Community media producers do not necessarily all identify with the very same community, but might have very different identifications with different communities (and the identities they incorporate). This is further complicated, as Rock (2005: 96) pointed out (discussing communities of practice), by the lack of unidirectional relations between an individual and a community: "[…] each individual simultaneously inhabits different communities […]." The responses to these contingencies are equally diverse: In some cases the transgressions of 'the' community are celebrated, while in other cases the community media organization withdraws into isolationism (see Mattelart & Piemme, 1983: 416).

This also implies that the articulatory relations between the community (member), the community media producer, and the audience are instable and contingent. Figure 13 shows a different set of relationships between these three subject positions, which deconstructs the taken-for-granted overlap between community and audience, and between audience and community media producers. Apart from material audience practices (see later), it is also the (still rare) audience research into community media audiences that offers a different articulation of the relationship between these subject positions. Forde, Foxwell, and Meadows (2009: 17) were explicit that this type of research remains rare: "But the 'absent issue of the virtually unknown' in community media—audience research—remains a challenge for scholars and practitioners alike." The research that does occur (Browne, 2012; Forde, Foxwell, and Meadows, 2009; King, 2015; Meadows et al., 2007) implicitly (and sometimes explicitly) undermines the equation between the audience, the community member, and the community media producer. For instance, Forde, Foxwell, and Meadows (2009: 155–156) discussed what they called the "audience-producer boundary" as a continuum:

> "[…] we have been able to identify the 'transparency' of the audience-producer boundary along a continuum—from the most intimate relationships in Indigenous community radio and television to some that are perhaps less so in the ethnic community radio sector."

Also, the idea that community media producers are necessarily representatives of the community, and that all those active in community media represent the community in similar and unproblematic ways, is sometimes countered by other ways of structuring these relationships. For instance, Hadland and Thorne (2004: 76) referred to the tendency of "board members" to interfere in the running of the community media organization, which has "lead to conflict and confusion." They continued by suggesting that "[...] boards need to be a blend of community representation and expertise," which again implicitly suggests that sometimes they are not.

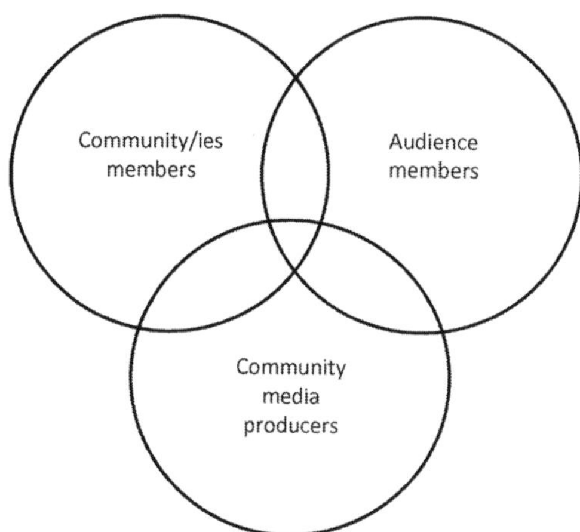

Figure 13. Serving-the-community approach key subject positions—an alternative view.

The serving-the-community model enables highlighting the significant role of the material in the community media assemblage, knotted together with the discursive. Through its agency, the material can align with the participatory objectives of community media, but the material is equally capable of disrupting its objectives. One level is the process of media production (by those who are articulated as representatives of a community), which has a strong material dimension, as people's bodies enter production facilities and gain access to use particular proto-machines (or technologies) in order to produce media content. These production facilities—places of media production—play a significant role in enabling people to collaborate, meet, and produce (or not). This is one of the reasons why Fairchild (2001: 96) claimed that:

> "Meaningful participation must include unrestricted access to production facilities and institutional resources, public involvement in management decisions and policies, and influence over the objectives and principles by which [...] broadcasters are governed."

In a brief and practice-oriented chapter entitled '*Starting a Community Radio Station*,' Tridish (2007: 273) pointed to the importance and need for a location for media production: "You may need to rent studio space—but if you are doing something positive for your neighbourhood, you should be able to get a local organisation to donate a bit of studio space." Of course, the material studio has been complemented with other locations of community media production without the material disappearing from the picture. Talking about radio and its relationship with the online, Moyo (2014: 50) made the point that it is "[…] now a virtual space, network space and mobile space while at the same time remaining a physical space when conceptualized as its studio format where citizens can participate in public debate."

The materiality of places matters for community media, as they use these places to align a variety of people and proto-machines. In the hands of community media producers, these 'technologies of freedom'—to use De Sola Pool's (1983) book title—are "[…] instruments to mobilize political resistance, articulate cultural identities, preserve popular memory, and sustain democratic movements" (Howley, 2005: 36). Access to these means of production for the community is not straightforward, and some authors, such as Feenberg (2010: 80),[25] have referred to a need for the democratization of technology. Community media contribute to this democratization of technology by making media production and distribution technologies available to the non-professional members of the community that the community media organization is serving. The materiality of these proto-machines matters, not only because they are indispensable for the core objective of community media, but also because they structure how community media producers produce content, what kind of content is produced, and how it is distributed. How a production location is constructed, what kinds of devices are present, the differences between what is called 'consumer technologies' and 'professional technologies' … impact on the interactions within a community media organization. How they allow for collaboration and sharing, how they are rhizomatically (and less arbolically) connected to (larger) machines, what kind of operating skills they require, and what levels of complexity they have, also matters. We should not forget Rennie's (2006: 5) words about broadcasting:

> "Analogue broadcasting is also a one-way technology, meaning that it goes from the broadcaster to the receiver/audience. Broadcasting has become highly regulated in most countries for reasons of cultural protection and economic stability. A nation's government controls who is allowed to broadcast and places restrictions on the type of content that is transmitted. Broadcasting is also regulated for technical reasons. When content is transmitted 'over-the-air', stations' signals can interfere with one another if they are not allocated space of their own. Community media appears to have been a marginal priority when the distribution of spectrum across all nations is tallied up."

Rennie (2006: 5) immediately added that "The new different digital media era is different." She continued, "The Internet has demonstrated that widespread participation in media technologies is both possible and desirable." Authors such as Benkler (2006) and Castells (2010a; 2010b) have argued for the democratic potential of the internet, with material structures that invite for higher levels of participation, although some critical voices have toned down these claims (see e.g., Morozov, 2011). First of all, as Howley (2005: 11) wrote: "If the history of communication technologies teaches us anything, it is this: the emancipatory potential of technology is greatly overstated." Secondly, we should keep in mind that (community) media organizations combine different technologies, each with their own materialities and invitations—turning them into what I have labeled a *mélange* in an earlier publication (Carpentier, 2014a).

Another part of the material component of the community media assemblage is the people that enter the community media places and operate the proto-machines. Their hands hold the microphones and cameras and operate the computers. Their voices are the ones that are distributed through the communication technologies that are used. Their material presence offers the opportunities for signifying the connection with the community. It is through their collaborations that media participation is enacted: "Community media involve some kind of collaboration or networking, be it face-to-face or virtual, and it is the ethos of collective engagement that these projects have in common, regardless of their medium of choice(s)" (Coyer, 2011: 168). Both the operation of technology, and the collaboration with others, requires particular embodied skills, which are then seen to strengthen the community: "Through participation, media are demystified and communities develop valuable communications skills and media literacy skills and understandings" (Fairbairn, 2009a: 9). The list of skills, and the training that enhances them, is long, and, for instance, includes communicational and interactional skills, but also maintenance skills (Ramakrishnan, 2007: 95).

The community media producers' signifying practices are always also material, through the assemblage of writing, storage, and distribution technologies. The use of language, not only the words that are chosen, but also the choice for a particular language (e.g., English, Greek, or Turkish) is very material. Each of these embodied practices structures the communication of the community media producers, but is also fed by their agency, offering them choices of identification with particular discourses (also with technological discourses) and operation of particular proto-machines.

Community media organizations—as non-profit organizations that function in a capitalist context—also need access to material resources for their continued existence, a situation that is in many cases problematic (Myers, 2011: 18). Although they often function with low-budgets, they remain dependent on collecting sufficient financial resources, which might complicate or jeopardize the realization of their participatory-democratic remit. At the same time, as Gordon (2015: 248) suggested, this is also an opportunity for the community to fund 'their' community media organization. She continued: "The local community may also support the station by giving 'in-kind' support, for example by providing labour or materials to build the fabric of the station, or professional expertise to help with legal matters or engineering." It is an argument[26] that Lewis (2015: 183) also made: "The most significant source of funding for community media is volunteer labour, an expression of community support and participation."

The interactions with (and decisions about) the material resources are structured through their ownership, which is sometimes collective, with the community media producers having legal control, but in other cases, as Fairbairn's (2009b: 30) list of options shows, ownership is linked to state or market structures:

> "[…] community media owners may be communities who own projects through community elected or appointed boards. Community media can also be owned by NGOs, educational institutions or local government structures. Our broad operational definition includes media that are run by for profit structures, so long as there is a quality community service and produced in ways that involve the communities being served."

Within these organizational structures, also, the materiality of (participatory) decision-making—and its (flattened) hierarchies—plays a significant role. The participation of community media's constituent groups and communities is often facilitated through a more horizontal power structure, where core and/or staff members (often present in community media organizations) shy away from hierarchical decision-making models and share decision-making powers with the community representatives/producers. Dealing with these particular decision-making and managerial structures again requires particular skills, e.g., "financial sustainability, organisational and management skills" (Brown & Buckley, 2011b) and "leadership, management, content production, business and technical skills, partnership building, networking and a host of others" (Fairbairn, 2009b: 31). And here too, these decision-making practices and the skills that support them are very much embodied.

Still, the existence of these more horizontal decision-making structures does not exclude the possibility that these horizontal structures are altered, that different positions, such as staff members and volunteers, affect the power balance or that strong individual (informal) power positions disrupt the horizontality of the decision-making processes, generating more contingency. In some cases, as the conflict-ridden US-based Pacifica Network shows (Dunaway, 2005), these power imbalances can be very disruptive (see also Atton, 2002: 98ff). This type of analysis is not only found in the world of community media, but is also part of a much broader debate on the workings of informal power in civil society and new social movements. One seminal article here is Freeman's (1971–1973) study of what she called the structurelessness of feminist movement groups and organizations, and how this produces power imbalances.

Also, the materiality of the community and the audience—sometimes discursively conflated (as Figure 12 symbolizes, in contrast to Figure 13)—impacts on community media. Howley (2005: 259) gave a brief hint of the materiality of the community, even if this is not the focus of his work: "Whilst my analysis foregrounds the symbolic construction of community, I do not dismiss the importance of place nor neglect material relations of power, which likewise shape, inform, and define community." As community media are articulated with a community, or with several communities, the structures of the community, and its material actions and practices, invite community media to give meaning to themselves and to the community in particular ways. Actions that originate from the community can strengthen, but also dislocate, the community media identity discourse, or can disrupt its practices, bringing in more contingency. The community remains a very necessary reservoir to provide community media with a variety of resources, including people (such as producers, managers, and technicians), places, proto-machines, and financial resources. In situations where communities are less involved, caring, or interested, community media organizations might find it hard to continue their existence. Another way of phrasing this is that the representational relationship between the community and 'its' community media organization might become dislocated.

A similar argument might be developed in relationship with the audience, which, in the traditional view of the serving-the-community model, is equated with the community members and with the community itself. This (partially) explains why there is so little audience research in relation to community media (see earlier). When actually studying material audience practices (see

Forde, Foxwell, and Meadows, 2009: 155), these practices sometimes turn out to be not entirely aligned with the community media organization (or even 'the' community). For Forde, Foxwell, and Meadows (2009: 156), this offers "[…] an insight into why particular 'repertoires of conduct' prevail and how dialogue between disparate communities of interest might be enhanced." At the same time, this also enables a more critical approach, which points to the dislocations that can be caused by an absent audience, and the contingency that the agency of audiences (preferring to be non-audiences) introduces.

2.2 Alternativity

The second approach to defining community media organizations foregrounds the nodal point of alternativity. In this model, it is emphasized that being a "third voice" (Servaes, 1999: 260), or the "third type" (Girard, 1992: 2), is still a viable option for media organizations. This concept is built on a distinction between mainstream (public and commercial) media identities on the one hand, and alternative media identities on the other, where alternative media are defined in a negative relationship to mainstream media. This relational perspective can be found in Waltz's (2005: 2) definition of alternative media as "[…] those media that provide a different point of view from that usually expressed, that cater to communities not well served by the mass media, or that expressly advocate social change […]." In this model, present-day mainstream media are articulated as large-scale and geared towards large, homogeneous (segments of) audiences; state-affiliated organizations or commercial companies; vertically structured organizations staffed by professionals; and carriers of dominant discourses and representations. Community media (as alternative) identities are then articulated through an (or several) opposite position(s) on these matters. Typically, they are seen as small-scale and oriented towards specific communities, possibly disadvantaged groups, respecting their diversity; independent from state and market; horizontally structured, allowing for the facilitation of audience access and participation within the frame of democratization and multiplicity; and carriers of non-dominant (possibly counter-hegemonic) discourses and representations, stressing the importance of self-representation.

Participation plays a crucial role in this model, on several levels. First, organizational structures are seen as a location of alternativity. Having more horizontal structures, less strong hierarchies, and democratic leadership models (in contrast to the vertically organized mainstream media) is deemed important, as these horizontal structures allow for structural participation of producers in the management of the media organizations. Prehn (1991: 259) described this as follows: "[…] participation implies a wider range of activities related to involving people directly in station programming, administration and policy activities." Second, also, the participation of non-professional producers—and in particular people affiliated to various (older and newer) social movements, minorities, and sub/counter-cultures—in the production of community media content is validated, which provides an alternative model of media production. Self-representation becomes an instrument to generate more alternative (or counter-hegemonic) content, which signifies the multiplicity and heterogeneity of societal voices. Downing (2001: v) referred to "an alternative vision to hegemonic policies, priorities, and perspectives." They provided "[…] air space to local cultural manifestations, to ethnic minority groups, to the hot political issues in the neighbourhood or locality" (Jankowski, 1994: 3). At the same time, the critical stance towards the production values of the 'professional' working in mainstream media (Atton & Hamilton, 2008) feeds into the production of a diversity of formats and genres, and creates room for experimentation with content and form.

Of course, from an analytical perspective, this dichotomized model should not be accepted at face value. In 1991 Sénécal (1991: 214–215) warned against this "dialectic of opposition: large/small media, heavy/light technology, national/local production, professional/amateur, etc." When focusing on the people involved, Downing (2002: 323) suggested "[…] to envisage a spectrum running from the non-professional to the professional […]," again warning against the dichotomization of mainstream and community media producers. And in *Alternative and Mainstream Media. The Converging Spectrum*, Kenix (2011: 17ff) referred to the "modern media continuum." Also, my own work, together with Hájek (Hájek & Carpentier, 2015), has been aimed at transgressing this dichotomy by arguing that some mainstream media identify themselves with alternativity, even if they remain mainstream media.[27] These publications, each in their own way, point to the contingencies that disrupt a dichotomized alternative media model. At the same time, the argument here is that these contingencies do not necessarily undermine the core alternative/mainstream media oppositional model (as it is represented in Figure 14), which continues to play a crucial role in the community (and alternative) media discourse. Nor does the oppositional nature of the alternative media model exclude contingency, as alternative media in themselves are disruptions of the mainstream rigidities, an argument that is thematized (even) more in the rhizomatic approach (see later). Moreover, in some cases, mainstream and community media engage in discursive struggles that only solidify the oppositions and dichotomies. Often we find the alternative marginalized, or negatively articulated, as naïve, irrelevant, or superfluous, as a result of this struggle.

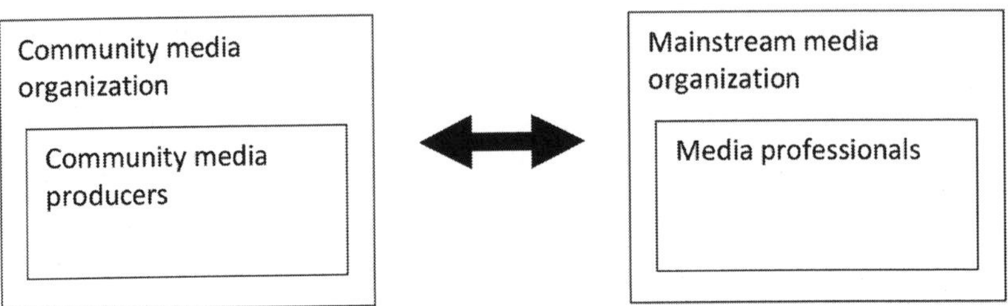

Figure 14. The key identities and subject positions of the alternative media approach.

This oppositional structure also feeds into the two main subject positions that structure this model, and again contribute to the community media discourse: the community (or alternative) media producer and the media professional (see Figure 14). Arguably, the alternative subject position questions the legitimacy of the media professional, which is deemed elitist, rejecting their social significance and central position (see Couldry's, 2003, critique on mainstream media's self-articulation as center). The traditional subject position of the media professional is articulated through a series of elements such as expertise (see earlier), public service, ethics, ontology, autonomy, institutional embeddedness, and a deployment of management and power (Bogaerts & Carpentier, 2012; Carpentier, 2005; Carpentier, 2013a; 2014f; Deuze, 2005). This identity, for instance, is articulated as grounded in expert knowledge and skills in relation to media production processes and what Downing (2002: 323) called "canonical procedure," enabling the mastery of media production technologies to perfection, combined with forms of employment that construct particular commodified connections between media professionals and 'their' organizations. This institutional embeddedness is not expected to impact on the autonomy of media professionals, as their individuality still strongly matters in the deployment of their expertise,[28] which requires the protection of these individuals against 'outside' intervention in order to come to fruition. McQuail (1994: 252) wrote about this: "Perhaps the foremost expectation about media content is that it should reflect or embody the spirit of free expression, despite the many institutional and organizational pressures

[…].” In addition, the media professional identity is also characterized by a commitment to serving the people as a public (and not so much as a community) through an ever-changing combination of information, education, and entertainment, and an ontology that combines a focus on truth, impartiality, authenticity, integrity, and honesty. But in more market-driven environments, these professional knowledges and skills are complemented, and sometimes replaced, by market-related knowledges (for instance, about audience segments and their potential behavior) and management skills. Also, other identificatory elements, such as public service, are transformed in these more market-driven environments, with entertainment increasing in significance. In both traditional public-oriented and more market-oriented versions of the media professional identity, we can nevertheless find an emphasis on the deployment of management and power. Media professionals are often placed in a hierarchically structured entity and attributed specific responsibilities for the professional production of specific cultural products. Through a combination of responsibility, (psychological) property and authorship, the articulation of the media professional as a manager of a diversity of resources, from technology via content and objects to people, is supported.

The community media producer's subject position is constructed in opposition to this media professional identity, as community media came into being in direct response to the dominance of mainstream media. To refer to Harcup's (2013: 106) interviews with what he labeled alternative media producers: “Dissatisfaction with mainstream media is, not surprisingly, frequently cited as a reason for involvement with alternative media.” Arguably, we can find two types of re-articulations. Firstly, some of the signifiers of the media professional identity are kept, but re-articulated through a mainstream media critique. In particular, societal relevance, autonomy, and ethics remain elements of the community media producer's identity, but they are re-articulated through a critique on mainstream media that argues that the mainstream media organizations (and their media professionals) fail in being *genuinely* socially relevant, autonomous, and ethical. Mainstream media are articulated as both self-centered and focused on profit, which reduces their societal relevance, but also the media professionals' capacity to remain autonomous and ethical (Albert, 1997).

As Albert (1997) argued, community media's disconnection from state and market functions as a guarantee for ‘real’ autonomy (in contrast to the situation in mainstream media). The subject position of the community media producer also remains grounded in societal relevance, because the focus on the representation of the community, simultaneously giving voice to members of these communities and being a voice of these communities, renders them relevant. This also legitimates the usages of the ethics signifier, as this participatory process is articulated as intensely ethical. This, as Harcup (2015: 320) argued, does feed into a re-articulation of the ethics signifier:

> "Journalism within alternative media tends to be less concerned with regulatory mechanisms or with following formal codes of practice on issues such as privacy, intrusion, harassment and suchlike; rather, the ethical approach of (much) alternative journalism within alternative media is more about attitude and approach towards people who may be a story's subject, source, narrator, or audience, sometimes all at the same time."

In a number of other cases, the signifiers that constitute the media professional identity are more fundamentally rejected. The notion of public service, too strongly connected to (mainstream) public service broadcasting, but also to an audience articulation that is seen as disengaging and disempowering, hardly features in community media discourse. Here, sometimes, we can find the notion of community service as an alternative signifier (see Fairbarn, 2009a: 9), articulating community media producers as providers of this community service. Also, the mainstream media's ontology of objectivity is—at least sometimes—rejected, and it becomes frequently replaced by community media work as a political activity (Atton & Hamilton, 2008: 1; Harcup, 2013: 115). At the same time, Forde's (2011) work indicates that the notion of objectivity is not always rejected, but in some cases re-articulated. As she wrote: "The rejection of objectivity was not absolute among the radical publications; and nor was the acceptance of objectivity absolute among more traditionally trained journalists working in alternative outlets" (Forde, 2011: 123).

Finally, the community media producer subject position is also characterized by a commitment to participation within, and outside, the community media organization. While a mainstream media professional identity is grounded in the deployment of management and power, legitimated by an expert-elitist position in society, community media producers articulate themselves as part of the community, positioned on equal footing with the other community members, and as 'gate-openers' (Manca, 1989) responsible for facilitating the media access of these community members. This also impacts on how the community media organization is managed, where the community media producers share managerial responsibilities and become co-manager (and co-owner) (Albert, 1997).

Also, institutional embeddedness gains a different meaning when community media producers are involved, as they are often *not* defined as employees, sometimes even in contrast to mainstream media employees. Writing about zines, Atton (2002: 23) summarized the situation of their producers as follows: "First, zine producers are amateurs […]." It should immediately be added that 'amateur' does not carry a negative connotation in the community media identity discourse. The subject position of the community media producer reconfigures the notion of the amateur in a positive way, close to what Basar (2006) called the "professional amateur" and what Said (1994: 76) meant when he was writing about amateurism as: "[…] the desire to be moved not by profit or reward but by love for and unquenchable interest in the larger picture, in making connections across lines and barriers, in refusing to be tied down to a specialty, in caring for ideas and values despite the restrictions of a profession."

Moreover, the absence of a relationship of employment does not exclude community media producers from the expert subject position. Through training, practice, and commitment, 'amateur' community media producers are seen to be capable of acquiring the expert knowledge and skills that are necessary for producing media content, strengthening the argument that one does not need to be professionally employed to work as a media producer. Still, as community media sometimes do employ staff, there is a perceived need to deal with some of the inequalities this may generate, for instance, at the levels of decision-making powers and income differences, as Albert (1997) clarified:

> "Income differentials among those working in alternative media institutions should steadily decline, and those that persist (if any) should have legitimate justification and not endow some with more power than others."

This last citation illustrates a point that was raised earlier: The dichotomy between mainstream and community media producers might serve the identity politics of community media (producers) but the material practices of these community media organizations sometimes (threatens to) dislocate the sharp juxtaposition between the two types of media organizations, showing the workings of contingency. This occurs, for instance, when in both cases particular members of staff are employed (even if many others work as volunteers in community media organizations), or when particular identifying signifiers, such as objectivity or autonomy, are shared. As these similarities might cause the community media identity to collapse, effort needs to be invested in protecting the alternativity, and, if necessary, in engaging in forms of discursive repair to emphasize the differences.

The significant role of the material, with its structuring capacities and its proper agencies, also becomes visible in the community media as alternative approach. From this perspective, community media offer alternatives to mainstream media that comfortably function in a capitalist context, producing (semi-)commodities. Community media produce different or alternative output, as Sandoval and Fuchs (2010: 145) wrote: "[…] ideal-typical alternative media differ from capitalist mass media in regard to the economic form of media products: ideal-typical alternative media provide non-commercial media products instead of commodities." Moreover, in their attempts to keep the state and market at bay, community media are located within alternative economies, with a remit that is not focused on the maximization of profit but on the maximization of participation. As community media still have to operate in capitalist contexts, they are dependent for their access to material resources on the support from community members and collaborators, including the voluntarism that has been mentioned before. Forde's (2011: 139) comment illustrates the material scarcity (and contingency) that originates from this position: "Essentially, commercial success in alternative journalism, for the most part, does not mean making a significant profit but means making enough money to pay the journalists and other staff, distribution costs, rent and facilities."

A second level where the material impacts on community media in this model, is through the material presence of alternative, non-elite voices. While mainstream media have a preference for elite voices (Pajnik, 2015: 118) (with, as always, notable exceptions), and media professionals can be considered a societal elite in their own right, community media allow other, non-elite groups in society access to the means of media production, allowing them to produce media content and have their voices heard, adding more diversity to the public spaces. Community media are locations "[…] where working people, sexual minorities, trade unions, protest groups—people of low status in terms of their relationship to elite groups of owners, managers and senior professionals—could make their own news, whether by appearing in it as significant actors or by creating news relevant to their situation" (Atton, 2002: 11; see also Girard, 1992: 2).

Thirdly, the alternative media approach also enables emphasizing the access to, and use of, alternative places and technologies. The use of places by community media is often specific, sometimes caused by a lack of material resources, but sometimes born out of subcultural or counter-cultural affiliations, and a preference for non-mainstream architectures and usages of space (see Starr, 2005: 180, for an example that combines a squat with alternative media). This alternative use of space and place is combined with alternative usages of technology, where a combination of low-tech material and a Do-It-Yourself (DIY) culture enters the community media assemblage. Community media re-assemble and re-signify proto-machines meant for 'ordinary' consumption, and integrate them in their production settings. Tridish's (2007: 273) comment shows the normality of using this 'ordinary' consumer (so-called non-professional) technology: "Consumer grade studio equipment is perfectly adequate, especially when you are starting out and short of cash." Another example, focusing on radio, is Waltz's (2005: 36) chapter entitled '*Anyone With a Cheap Transmitter Can Do Radio*,' where she discussed a variety of possibilities for radio broadcasting, including low-power and micropower radio, pirate radio, digital radio, and online radio. A similar argument was made by Coyer, Dowmunt, and Fountain (2007: 268): "But again, if all you have access to is a cassette recorder from 1970, you can still make great radio." Later, the same authors also include the following reference to a DIY approach: "[…] if you are building a radio station, consider soldering your own transmitter rather than buying one pre-built. Sometimes the more you start from scratch, the more empowered the work becomes" (Coyer, Dowmunt, & Fountain, 2007: 316). The popularization of digital technologies increased the options that were available for the low-cost production and distribution of community media content. Lievrouw (2011: 215) captured this expansion of options as follows: "Alternative, activist, oppositional, and radical media were once 'fringe' by definition." She continued:

> "Certainly, powerful interests still set much of the communications agenda today, and they protect their privileges jealously. But they must do so in a cultural and media environment where anyone with a mobile telephone or tablet computer and an internet connection has the same potential to reach listeners, viewers, and readers as a major television network or political party." (Lievrouw, 2011: 215)

I should immediately add that the more sophisticated proto-machines have become much more available for community media organizations, which, as Downing (2002: 322) argued, results in the "[…] hitherto unbridgeable chasm between aesthetically pleasing and culturally significant video is closing up […]." Also, places, and production and broadcasting technologies, whether in 'ordinary' consumer-oriented or in more 'professional' versions, also have their own agencies, which (partially) structure the ways community media can organize participatory processes and can function as alternatives to mainstream media. Places might not always be easily accessible, and their materiality might shape interactions in particular ways. At the same time, community media organizations create participatory spaces much more accessible than mainstream media production locations. Proto-machines, the functionalities they include (and not include), and the skills they require to operate them also impact on the ways they are (and can be) used to serve more maximalist participatory purposes. In particular, proto-machines have often not been conceived to serve participatory objectives, and might require technical modifications or re-configurations in their material usage. Moreover, proto-machines meant for 'ordinary' consumption resist their 'upscaled,' more intense use and frequently break-down.

The material and alternativity also intersect when it comes to the (participatory) decision-making practices in community media. As already discussed before, community media use a horizontally structured decision-making model (in combination with collective forms of ownership), which has been developed as an alternative to mainstream media practices. Also, here, the capitalist economic context, and the hegemony of strong leadership models create contingency, where community media are—out of mere necessity—being pulled into capitalist exchange models and where the lure of informal power imbalances always threatens to disrupt the material (maximalist) participatory practices. To use Pajnik's (2015: 119) words, alternative media "[…] are not immune to the political and economic constellations of society, even though their placement is usually that of 'the edge' or 'beyond' the dictates of contemporary capitalism." Things become worse when community media have to face an oppressive or violent force—in some cases a state—which can disrupt any participatory process, and the people that organize them, in very material (sometimes lethal) ways (Halleck, 2002: 216).

2.3 Part of Civil Society

In the third (society-centered) approach, community media organizations are articulated as part of civil society,[29] a societal segment considered crucial for the viability of democracy. For this reason, community media are sometimes termed citizen(s') media (Rodríguez, 2001; see also Baker & Blaagaard, 2016; Pettit, Salazar, & Dagron, 2009); or civil society media[30] (Hintz, 2007). As Rodríguez (2001: 20—emphasis in original) formulated it, citizens' media enable citizens to become a "[…] collectivity [that] is *enacting* its citizenship by actively intervening and transforming the established mediascape." Hintz

(2007: 244) referred to civil society media that encompass "[...] media organisations, groups, and projects, which fit into the basic non-state noncommercial model and share the structural and thematic tendencies of civil society." He continued, "Participation, emancipation, and empowerment represent crucial features" (Hintz, 2007: 244).

Through the nodal point of civil society, the identity of community media organizations becomes integrated within democratic discourses as an important locus for the maintenance or deepening of democracy by facilitating participation and/or increasing its intensities (Cohen & Arato, 1992: vii–viii). This articulation occurs in two distinct ways. Firstly, community media can be seen as an 'ordinary' part of civil society, as one of the many types of organizations active in the field of civil society that facilitate societal participation and allow for the enhancement of democratic life. Keane (1998: xviii) pointed to a number of reasons why civil society matters, and included civil society's capacity to enable "[...] groups and individuals freely within the law to define and express their various social identities [...]," but also its important potential to revive the democratic imagination. In this list of arguments in favor of civil society, Keane explicitly mentioned "variously seized nonstate communications media,"[31] providing support for the argument that community media are part of civil society. Howley (2010: 73) took a similar position by emphasizing the role played by community media as civil society: Community media are like other voluntary associations in their adoption of participatory decision-making structures and practices that promote a sense of belonging to, and responsibility toward, the organization, its mission, and its relationship to the wider community. Equally important for Howley is that community media encourage private individuals to work collaboratively in meaningful activities that not only promote sociability among individual participants but also serve a variety of local needs and interests. In doing so, community media cultivate a more deliberate approach to participation in public life, nurture social networks within and between communities, and, potentially at least, encourage innovative ways to think about democratic practice.

Here, community media identities are constructed through a more general, society-centered, validation of civil society as such (see Putnam, 1993; 1995). Walzer (1992: 98) formulated this as follows: "The associational life of civil society is the actual ground where all versions of the good [life] are worked out and tested [...]. What is true is that the quality of our political and economic activity and of our national culture is intimately connected to the strength and vitality of our associations." In a critical reflection on Walzer's

(1992) chapter, Foley and Edwards (1996: 38) (first) also reiterated this argument: A "[…] 'dense network of civil associations' is said to promote the stability and effectiveness of the democratic polity through both the effects of association on citizens' 'habits of the heart' and the ability of associations to mobilize citizens on behalf of public causes." Their critiques show the contingency of the civil society concept, and of its articulation with democracy, but also how material practices can disrupt the democratic role of civil society. But to be fair to Walzer (1992), I should first mention that he very explicitly shied away from romanticizing civil society. In full, the above-mentioned quote is: "The associational life of civil society is the actual ground where all versions of the good [life] are worked out and tested … and proven to be partial, incomplete, ultimately unsatisfying" (Walzer, 1992: 98). At the conceptual level, following both Walzer (1992) and Foley and Edwards (1996), it is necessary to emphasize that civil society and institutionalized politics should not be dichotomized, and that civil society is not outside political conflict. One should not gloss over "[…] the real, and often sharp, conflicts among groups in civil society. These conflicts, in the absence of specifically political settlements, may spill over into civil disruption and violence" (Foley & Edwards, 1996: 39). In this sense, the *uncivil* practices of organizations[32] that are labeled as civil society (can easily) dislocate the democratic discourse of civil society.[33] Nevertheless, in order to understand the identity of community media, its articulation (as part of civil society) with this democratic discourse remains crucial, while at the same time care needs to be taken to not overlook its potential dislocations.

A second articulation of community media as civil society emphasizes the specificity of community media within civil society. When their specificity as broadcasters, and their potential role as (one of the) major public spaces is brought into focus, and community media organizations are no longer defined as 'just' 'ordinary' parts of civil society, these media become important because they provide spaces that enable citizens to have their voices heard, and because they intervene in the mediascape. From this perspective, community media are seen again as offering different societal groups and communities the opportunity for extensive participation in public debate and for self-representation in public spaces. Although most of these arguments have been mentioned before, in particular the link between community media and communication rights is important in this context (Rodríguez, 2001: 5). This right to communicate, referred to by Jacobson (1998) as a third-generation human right (see also Dakroury, 2009; Fisher & Harms, 1982; Padovani & Calabrese, 2014;

Servaes, 1998), was originally proposed in 1969—by the French civil servant Jean d'Arcy (1969). It aimed to broaden the right to be informed, which is embedded in article 19 of the Universal Declaration of Human Rights. In the MacBride Commission report, the right to communicate implies that "[...] (a) the individual becomes an active partner and not a mere object of communication; (b) the variety of messages exchanged increases; and (c) the extent and quality of social representation or participation in communication are augmented" (MacBride Commission, 1980: 166).

The discussion on communication rights is already an indication that the citizen is the most significant subject position within this approach to community media. Citizenship (as a subject position) was already discussed earlier in this book, but it is important to mention, yet again, that citizenship is not seen "[...] as a legal status but as a form of identification, a type of political identity: something to be constructed, not empirically given" (Mouffe, 1992b: 231). In the civil society approach to community media, this subject position features dominantly, for instance (and obviously), through the use of the concept of citizens' media. In *Fissures in the Mediascape*, Rodríguez (2001: 20—emphasis in original) explained her use of the citizens' media concept by referring to:

> "[...] a collectivity [that] is *enacting* its citizenship by actively intervening and transforming the established mediascape; second that these media are contesting social codes, legitimized identities, and institutionalized social relations; and third, that these communication practices are empowering the community involved, to the point where these transformations and changes are possible."

Rodríguez (2001: 160) also referred to the notion of media citizenship[34] to capture what is most important: "[...] not what citizens do with them [community media], but how participation in these media experiments affect citizens and their communities." She continued: "[...] even if the information and communication channels are left untouched, even if the mainstream media structure is left unaltered [...], citizens' media are rupturing pre-established power structures, opening spaces that allow for new social identities and new cultural definitions, and, in a word, generating power on the side of the subordinate" (Rodríguez, 2001: 160). A similarly optimistic language can be found in Pajnik (2015: 120), who presented community media as "[...] a hope that points to possibilities for the future of citizenship, where mutual learning between the elites and the citizens, the professionals and the public might be advanced." Without taking these claims at face value, they are good indications of the role of the citizen subject position in the construction of the community media discourse.

At the same time, these discussions already provide us with additional clues on the role of the material, and its agency, in this approach.[35] Rodríguez's (2001: 20) reference to the enactment of citizenship brings us to two sets of material practices that lie at the heart of the connection between community media and citizenship. Firstly, community media enable citizens to access their production spaces, interact with others to produce media content, and to distribute these signifying practices through the use of communication technologies. This media output, whether it concerns television or radio broadcasts, printed texts, or online publications, obviously also has a material dimension, as has been argued before. Moreover, these signifying practices not only enable citizens to invoke and publicly identify with particular discourses, but also to entextualize them, which highlights their (media) productive agency. This is why, for Rennie (2006: 21), that "Community and alternative media can be seen as an articulation of citizenship, when citizenship is seen as the day-to-day endeavor to renegotiate and construct new levels of democracy and equality." Participation and civic agency matter here, not only *within* the community media organization, but also because of the consequences the increased levels of participation may have: "Newly found agency in media production may encourage a sense of political and civic agency, otherwise denied to [for instance] ethnic minorities [...]" (Couldry, 2012: 172).

Secondly, these forms of participatory media production also enable citizens to engage in material decision-making practices, both at the level of content production, and at the level of organizational management. As citizens, they become integrated in the participatory assemblage of the community media organization, with its many objects and people, often located in particular places. Citizenship is performed through the empowerment of these community media producers, who can, with a high level of autonomy, decide about the material content that they will produce, about how they will use the proto-machines and places to achieve their objectives, and about how they will collaborate with other community media producers. Citizenship is also performed through their involvement in the management of the community media organizations, by taking responsibility for, or collaborating in, particular managerial tasks or projects, or by entering in co-decision processes. Moreover, voluntary work, and the investment that it encompasses at both the levels of content production and organizational management, is another enactment of citizenship that strengthens the non-profit sector and counters the reduction of work to commodified labor.[36] The complexity of these material decision-making practices also brings in contingency. Within a capitalist context, the opportunity costs of voluntary labor are high, and community media producers and managers often struggle to find the resources to make ends meet, both personally and organizationally. Moreover, 'Making participatory democracy work,' to paraphrase the title of one of Putnam's (1993) publications, is a very difficult task, requiring constant attention, but also a wide range of particular skills (including democratic-participatory decision-making skills) and high levels of time investment. One example of the practical difficulties that this brings about is an anecdote that one of the collaborators of the Swiss community radio station Radio LoRa told during an interview in 2008: "We have our technician who calls himself some kind of anarchist and he once got so angry that he said: 'Well, I want to have a boss. I want to end these endless discussions'" (Simon Schaufelberger, 14 August 2008, interview, cited in Carpentier, 2011: 340).

2.4 Part of the Rhizome

The fourth and last approach is the rhizomatic approach, which builds on the critiques on the alternative media approach, and radicalizes the civil society approach. In discussing the notion of alternative media, Downing (2001: ix) critiqued its "oxymoronic" nature: "[...] everything, at some point, is alternative to something else," legitimizing the decision to focus on 'radical alternative media.' At the same time, he still emphasizes the diversity that characterizes these radical alternative media that are to be found in a "colossal variety of formats" (Downing, 2001: xi). A similar argument was developed by Rodríguez (2001: 20), who suggested abandoning the notion of alternative media in favor of citizens' media because 'alternative media' rests on the assumption that these media are alternative to something, and this definition will easily entrap us in binary thinking: mainstream media and their alternative, that is, alternative media. Also, the alternative media label predetermines the type of oppositional thinking that limits the potential of these media to their ability to resist the alienating power of mainstream media.

The integration of the nodal point of the rhizome in the community media discourse is inspired by Deleuze and Guattari's (1987) metaphor, in order to re-articulate approaches 2 and 3 (see Figure 11), without giving up on the concept of alternativity. These origins give the rhizomatic model a stronger materialist component than the other three models. The metaphor of the rhizome is based on the juxtaposition of rhizomatic and arbolic thinking.[37] The arbolic is a structure that is linear, hierarchic, and sedentary, and could be represented as "[...] the tree-like structure of genealogy, branches that continue to subdivide into smaller and lesser categories [...]" (Wray, 1998: 3). It is, according to Deleuze and Guattari, the philosophy of the State. The rhizomatic, on the other hand, is closely related to the alternative, as it is non-linear, anarchic, and nomadic: "Unlike trees or their roots, the rhizome connects any point to any other point" (Deleuze & Guattari, 1987: 19).

In *A Thousand Plateaus*, Deleuze and Guattari (1987) enumerated a series of characteristics of the rhizome—the principles of connection and heterogeneity, multiplicity, asignifying rupture, cartography, and decalcomania. Connection and heterogeneity imply that any point of the network can be connected to any other point, despite the different characteristics of the components. The concept of multiplicity constructs the rhizome not on the basis of elements, each operating within fixed sets of rules, but as an entity whose rules are constantly in motion because new elements are always included. The principle of the asignifying rupture means that "[...] a rhizome may be broken, shattered at a given spot, but it will start up again on one of its old lines, or on new lines" (Deleuze & Guattari, 1987: 9). Finally, the principle of the map is juxtaposed with the idea of the copy. In contrast to the copy, the map is:

> "open and connectable in all of its dimensions; it is detachable, reversible, susceptible to constant modification. It can be torn, reversed, adapted to any kind of mounting, reworked by an individual, group, or social formation. It can be drawn on a wall, conceived of as a work of art, constructed as a political action or as a meditation. Perhaps one of the most important characteristics of the rhizome is that it always has multiple entryways." (Deleuze & Guattari, 1987: 12)

It is important to add that rhizomes are not necessarily good, and arbolic structures are not necessarily evil, as Deleuze and Guattari (1987: 20) also wrote:

> "for there is no dualism, no ontological dualism between here and there, no axiological dualism between good and bad, no blend or American synthesis. There are knots of arborescence in rhizomes, and rhizomatic offshoots in roots. Moreover, there are despotic formations of immanence and channelization specific to rhizomes, just as there are anarchic deformations in transcendent systems of trees, aerial roots, and subterranean systems."

In the late 1970s and early 1980s, both authors were heavily involved in the French alternative ('free') radio scene, which they saw as an opportunity to realize their "utopie 'deleuzoguattarienne'" (Dalle, 2006). Authors such as Sakolsky (1998), Chidgey, Gunnarsson, and Zobl (2009), and Oi-Wan and Iam-Chong (2009) also used Deleuze and Guattari's metaphor to label media organizations as rhizomatic media. If we transpose the rhizomatic approach into community media theory, it thematizes three aspects: rhizomatic media's role as a crossroads of civil society, their elusiveness, and their interconnections and linkages with market and state (see Santana & Carpentier (2010) for a more elaborate argument).

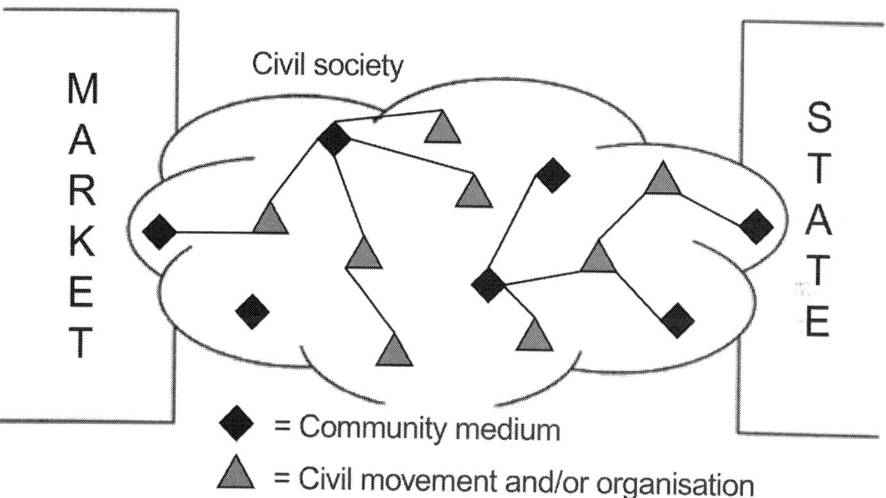

Figure 15. Civil society and community media as rhizome.
Source: Carpentier, Lie, & Servaes (2003: 62).

The rhizomatic approach articulates community media at the crossroads of a variety of civil society organizations and (new) social movements (Figure 15). Their catalytic role in functioning as the crossroads where people from different types of social movements and struggles meet and collaborate is aligned with the field of radical democratic theory, where great emphasis is put on the need to link diverse democratic struggles in order to enable, as (Mouffe, 1997: 18) put it, the "[...] common articulation of, for example, antiracism, antisexism and anticapitalism." Mouffe stressed the need to establish an equivalence between these different struggles; she considered it not sufficient to establish "a mere alliance" (Mouffe, 1997: 19): instead, "[...] the very identity of these struggles [...] [i]n order that the defence of workers' interests is not pursued at the cost of the rights of women, immigrants or consumers" (Mouffe, 1997: 19) should be modified.

In the rhizomatic approach, contingency and fluidity become articulated as signifiers in the community media discourse itself. It is community media's embeddedness in a fluid civil society (as part of a larger network) and their counter-hegemonic position towards the state and the market (as alternatives to mainstream public and commercial media organizations) that makes their identity highly elusive and fluid. In this approach, it is argued that this elusiveness and contingency, typical for a rhizome, are their main defining elements. One trace of this argument in community media theory is the emphasis on diversity within the field of community media; for instance, when Atton (2015: 8—emphasis in original) wrote in his Introduction to *The Routledge Companion to Alternative and Community Media*: "[…] the diversity of alternative media presented in this *Companion* shows how content will always be linked with social, cultural and political contexts." In an older book, Jankowski and Prehn (2002: 37) referred to "[…] the way different community media cater for different needs of community members. Differences in community media landscapes may lead to differences in community media use between communities."

At the same time, their elusiveness makes community media (as a whole) hard to control and to encapsulate in legislation, thus guaranteeing their independence. The most radical version of this idea can be found in the principle of the TAZ, the temporary autonomous zone,[38] as formulated by Bey (1985: 99–100—emphasis in original):

> "The TAZ is like an uprising which does not engage directly with the State, a guerilla operation which liberates an area (of land, of time, of imagination) and then dissolves itself to re-form elsewhere/elsewhen, *before* the State can crush it."

These translocal networks are characterized by the fluid articulation of a diversity of community media and civil society organizations, which reflects the strategy of what has been theorized by writers on contemporary resistance, such as Benasayag and Sztulwark (2002: 68—my translation):

> "[…] the counter-power affirms on the contrary the development of the multiplicity as the only road to attempt to conquer the capitalist centrality. From this perspective, each experience has to be developed, not as something isolated, 'provincial,' but in a network in the myriad of the other alternative and revolutionary experiences."

But these networks do not stop at the edge of civil society; like rhizomes, community media are articulated as cutting across borders, and build linkages between pre-existing gaps: "[…] a rhizome ceaselessly establishes connections between semiotic chains, organizations of power and circumstances relative to the arts, sciences and social struggles" (Deleuze & Guattari, 1987: 7). In the case of community media, these connections apply not only to the pivotal role community media (can) play in civil society, where they are seen to facilitate participatory networks, but also to the linkages community media (and other civil organizations) can establish with (segments of) the state and the market, without losing their proper identity and becoming incorporated and/or assimilated. This implies that the realms of the state and market are not articulated as 'no-go areas,' and that community media organizations can indeed legitimately enter these realms, even if this is with care and restraint. For instance, as Rennie (2011: 119) remarked, donorship is frequently used in the global south, where "[…] community media projects are often funded through donor agencies to build democratic media or to provide health, education, and peace information and to promote participation and community ownership." Gordon's discussion of financial models used by community media organizations also includes grants from "[…] a range of organisations, governmental, quasi-governmental and non-governmental […]" (Gordon, 2015: 252) and advertising and sponsorship. In the latter case, Gordon (2015: 251) added that "[…] local regulations may restrict a community radio station's ability to undertake this type of activity," but also the identity politics of community media organizations and the need to protect the non-profit status may lead to the imposition of self-restraint. Nevertheless, many community media organizations move into the realms of state and market, mainly because of a need for resources, which also necessitates a more complex and sophisticated discursive positioning towards state and market. In this sense, community media are not merely counter-hegemonic, but also trans-hegemonic. They can still be seen as potentially destabilizing—or deterritorializing as Deleuze and Guattari (1987) put it—the rigidities and certainties of public and market media organizations. In this argumentation, community media produce contingency, through their material existence, their signifying practices, and their discursive identifications, as they question dominant culture, also in interaction with state and market actors.

The material is very present in this rhizomatic nodal point,[39] which is not surprising, given its origins. The presence of the material can first of all be found in the role of collaborative (mostly) civil society networks, where members of different organizations and movements interact—moving beyond 'their' organizational machines. The rhizomatic model actually thematizes the collaborations that are organized between different community media organizations and between community media organizations and other civil society organizations. These collaborations can take on many forms, and the material features in them in many different ways. For instance, in some cases, community media producers and civil society representatives can travel and meet to produce community media content that fits their joint interests (Halleck, 2002: 175).

In other cases, as illustrated by the existence of the RadioSwap database (Carpentier, 2007), the encounters are not so much face-to-face, but organized through online technologies. In the case of this database, different community media producers can upload their content, enabling other community media to download and re-broadcast their material. In yet other cases, as Chidgey, Gunnarsson, and Zobl (2009: 487—emphasis in original) argued in their rhizomatic analysis of the Plotki Femzine, the community (or alternative) media organization itself becomes the meeting space:

> "However, through collaborative acts of discussion, experimental art, autobiographical essays, and critical fiction, the *Femzine* project brings together women living and working in CEE [Central and Eastern European] countries to create an emerging space for feminist discussions and an articulation of feminist identities and connections."

Of course, the rhizomatic fluidity of community media organizations can, in some cases, also work against collaboration. Different community media organizations, other civil society organizations and social movements may have very different objectives, procedures, and interests, which might not be easy to reconcile. Moreover, bringing a diversity of actors within the community media organization can potentially import conflict, which can then put a serious strain on the capacity of a community media organization to act as a civil society crossroads, and which might even jeopardize its existence (Dunaway, 2005).

Also the entries into the realm of market and state are highly material, given the often financial motivations for these initiatives. They often enable the financial survival of community media organizations, by bringing in the necessary material resources into these organizational machines. There are, nevertheless, downsides to these strategies, which also create contingency. Requests for funding, or for the continuation of this funding, might not be granted, which can jeopardize the existence of these community media organizations (see Gordon, 2015: 252, for an example). Even if the strategies are successful in providing access to material recourses, moving into the realm of market and/or state can simultaneously have material consequences. The logic of deterritorialization might not work as desired (and as the community media discourse articulates it), for instance, when subsidizing agencies require evaluations to be made, reports to be written, and sometimes even staff to be hired to comply with contractual requirements, which may exhaust the organizational energy. When discussing grant applications by community media organizations, Gordon (2015: 253) wrote: "Grant applications are time consuming to write, there are likely to be robust restrictions on the uses of any funding gained and recipients will have to service their grants with meetings and reports, which may also be time consuming." Incorporations, always threatening and often triggered by these kinds of material conditions, might fundamentally alter the community media organization, transforming it into something outside the boundaries of the community media discourse. Pavarala (2015: 15) pointed to the risk brought about by "[...] some organisations [that] are beginning to enter the arena solely to further the organisational objectives, and they take to less than participatory methods under pressure from donors to 'scale up' operations and to demonstrate 'impact' on behaviour change."

Finally, the material component of community media's elusive nature also effects their relationships with different societal actors. Community media organizations are often what Soteri-Proctor (2011) called "below the radar" organizations, which also has a clear material component. Their locations are not always easy to find and to access, and even the knowledge about their existence or functioning (e.g., by relevant community members) cannot always be taken for granted. In some cases, they might simply disappear and (sometimes) re-appear in a different form and shape, which (also) implies a re-alignment of its materials. This elusiveness also makes it hard for states to regulate and police community media organizations, as the diversity of the field is difficult to reconcile with the creation of material categorizations required for regulation attempts. In cases where community media organizations have to deal with more oppressive states (or other actors), or with states that do not have legal provisions for community media and that prosecute attempts to establish them, this elusiveness, at least partially, protects the community media organizations that have to function in these circumstances.

2.5 The Community Media Assemblage as a Discursive-Material Knot

Community media organizations are given meaning through the community media discourse that is grounded in four nodal points, as captured by the four theoretical approaches discussed in the previous part. Even though these models diverge in their emphasis on different aspects of community media, their articulations are also partially overlapping, because of community media's more general focus on the organization of participatory processes. Participation features in all four approaches, as the community that is being served through the facilitation of its participation, as the provision of a maximalist participatory alternative to non-participatory (or minimalist participatory) mainstream media, as the democratic-participatory role of civil society, or as the participatory rhizome. These discursive frameworks provide meaning to the participatory practices of the organizational machines of community media and enable them to communicate their counter-hegemonic identities to the outside worlds and to themselves, but they also provide meaning to the different actors that are involved in these communicational practices.

The subject positions that are connected to these nodal points strengthen the participatory dimension of community media organizations. Community members, and the community media producers that represent 'their' communities, are articulated as active, competent, and empowered, through their capacity to represent themselves in community media content and to co-manage the organizational structures of community media. They are seen as different from mainstream media producers and managers, as they are articulated as non-elite members of society—citizens and ordinary people—that have acquired the necessary knowledge and skills to produce media content in ways that are *genuinely* relevant, autonomous, and ethical. These citizens show the limits of state and market in connecting civil society. In this discursive process, these ordinary citizens claim the signifiers that play a key role in the participatory process—they become owners of the means of (media) production, democratic leaders embedded in equalized power structures, and amateur-experts in both content production and organizational management.

Through the logic of the discursive-material knot, the community media discourse is part of an assemblage, together with a variety of materials that are entangled with it. Figure 16 gives a structured overview of these material components of the discursive-material knot, where, first of all, the spheres of market, state, civil society, and community (plural or singular) provide access—for the community media organization—to many different materials. These bodies; places and architectures; proto-machines; services and commodities; and capitals flow from these spheres into the organizational machines of community media and sometimes back out again. Although the origins are not necessarily given and fixed (and the spheres are overlapping as well), some types of materials are more likely to come from particular spheres; for instance, services and communities are likely to flow into the community media organization from the sphere of the market, and the bodies of the community media producers flow into the organization from the spheres of community and civil society. But other materials, such as capital, can have very different origins. These materials enter into the community media assemblage, where they engage in interactions with each other, structured by the assemblage (and its hierarchies) and structuring the assemblage with their own agencies and in interaction with the agencies of others. These interactions can be described with a series of labels—Figure 16 contains several: using, producing, working, communicating, collaborating, and enhancing skills.

At the same time, these materials become part of a participatory process, where the community media producers (and community media managers and staff members) co-decide about the arrangements of these materials and how they should be deployed to serve the (participatory) objectives of the community media organization. Through these interactions, and driven by horizontally structured decision-making practices, the community media organizations produce their signifying practices, which also have their material component (namely, material text-related practices). This media content leaves the organizational machine being distributed to different audiences

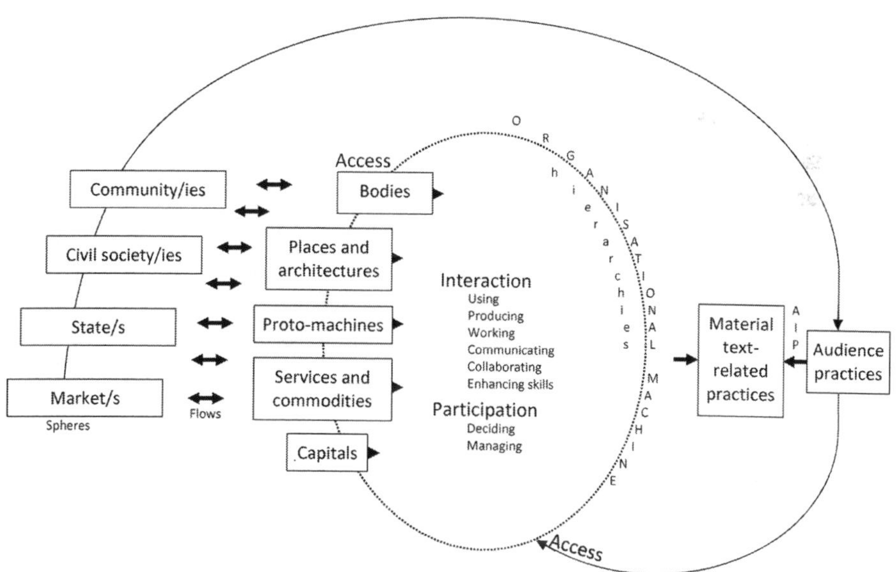

Figure 16. Community media's materiality.

using some of the community media organization's proto-machines. The audiences are not disconnected from the communities, civil societies, states, and markets, but again related to these spheres in different ways. Also, their relationship to the media content produced by the community organization, and to the community media organization, varies, with, in some cases, audience members gaining access to the community media organization and entering its assemblage.

In this community media organization's assemblage, the discursive and the material are not segregated, even though they are, for analytical reasons, discussed separately here. These materials, once they enter the community media assemblage, are invested with meaning, where, for instance, the proto-machines are redefined from consumer technologies to community media production technologies and 'technologies of democracy,' where the bodies of community members become community media producers, empowered citizens through their identification with these particular subject positions. The capitals that enter become instruments for community media maintenance or survival, even if their presence might come at a cost. These materials also bring their own agencies into the assemblage, inviting for particular meanings to be attributed to them. The spaces allocated to community media production, with their particular forms and shapes, might allow for particular kinds of signifying and material text-related practices, and disallow for others. The proto-machines have built-in affordances, with their limitations, that orient community media producers towards particular meanings and ways of operating them.

Simultaneously, this discursive-material knot is not stable, but characterized by contingency. This community media assemblage is a counter-hegemonic intervention in a political and media configuration that is characterized by a combination of non-participation and minimalist participation. One implication is that community media are almost permanently engaged in a discursive-material struggle, in trying to counter hegemonic discourses about democracy, participation, leadership, ownership, expertise, and citizenship, but also in trying to secure control over the materials needed to guarantee its continued existence. But also within the community media field, and within particular community media organizations, different identifications exist (for instance, triggered by differences in the emphasis on the four community media nodal points), which creates contingency. This intra-organizational contingency is enhanced by the agencies of the materials that enter the community media assemblage, and the disruptions and dislocations they might cause. One example here is the materiality of the community, which might not have sufficient interest to enter the community media organization to represent itself and participate in the organizational management, which might structurally unsettle the entire community media remit.

3 Conflict and Community Media

Community media's democratic contributions have often been emphasized (as the previous subpart rather extensively discussed) and even celebrated, but their (potential) role in conflict transformation has received much less academic attention. Even if there are ample community media practices that bear witness to the capacity of community media organizations to have their participatory identities contribute to conflict transformation, there is still a need for more research. This automatically also requires a theoretization of conflict (and of a series of related concepts) staying within the framework of the discursive-material knot. This leap into a discussion of conflict theory (initiated in the first subpart), which will be a substantial but necessary detour, does not overplay the hand of my discourse-theoretical starting point. In particular, Laclau and Mouffe's reflections on antagonism, and Mouffe's later work on agonism, offer the perfect foundation for a discursive-material (theoretical) analysis of conflict. As in Platform 1, the already implicit presence of the material in discourse theory only has to be enhanced.

Simultaneously, I would like to argue that there is also a more general need to enhance the theoretical backbones and paradigmatic diversity of the field of conflict studies, in particular when it comes to the discussions on conflict resolution and conflict transformation (which will be discussed in the second subpart). Here, Mouffe's work on agonism—enriched with a stronger material component—will enable strengthening these approaches that are now still dominated by a rather straightforwardly applied realist paradigm. Finally, in the last subpart, we can return to the community media organizations that are the main theme of this book and briefly discuss the rare literature on their role in conflict transformation and its theoretical articulation with participation.

3.1 Defining Conflict, Antagonism, and Agonism

Conflict itself, as a concept, has a wide variety of meanings, as Pondy (1967: 298) remarked some decades ago: "The term 'conflict' has been used at one time or another in the literature to describe: (1) antecedent conditions [...], (2) affective states [...], (3) cognitive states of individuals [...], and conflictual behaviour, ranging from passive resistance to overt aggression." Important here are the differences in the definitions of conflict as violent practices, as antagonistic positions, and as societal contradictions (Wallensteen, 1991: 130). If conflict is defined as violent behavior, it is easy to think its cessation, and the conflict's resolution is its transformation from a violent to a non-violent state. When conflict is seen as antagonistic positions between actors, as defined by Wallensteen (1991: 130), as "[...] subjectively experienced or objectively observable incompatibilities," then these antagonisms are not necessarily resolved when violent behavior disappears. For Wallensteen (1991: 131), resolution is then the "[...] transcending [of] a basic incompatibility between the parties in conflict in such a manner that they (voluntarily) express their satisfaction with the outcome [...]." Finally, if conflict is seen as societal contradictions, conflict is not resolved "[...] until more fundamental societal changes are made," and before that occurs, conflicts "[...] may shift between more latent or manifest phases [...]" (Wallensteen, 1991: 130). This idea can be further radicalized by the argument that societal contradictions do not disappear, and that a fully harmonious society is illusionary. What matters in this broad approach to conflict is the acknowledgement of the continuous presence of conflict, combined with the need to avoid violent manifestations of conflict by containing conflict within a democratic order.

The latter (broad) approach towards conflict aligns well with discourse theory. In discourse theory's perspective on the political, and through its affinity with conflict sociology, conflict is very much seen as an ontological condition that structures the social and the political. Mouffe's (1997: 3) already-mentioned definition of the concept of the political clarifies this, as she perceived the political as a "[...] dimension of antagonism that is inherent in all human society [...]," in order to argue that the political touches upon our entire world, and cannot be confined to institutionalized politics. This also implies "[...] the ineradicability of the conflictual dimension in social life [...]" (Mouffe, 2005: 4). Mouffe's reflections about conflict are very much embedded in a democratic theory of diversity, where "[...] the specificity of liberal democracy as a new political form of society consists in the legitimation of conflict and the refusal to eliminate it through the imposition of an authoritarian order" (Mouffe, 1996: 8). In this book chapter, Mouffe (1996: 8) continued by emphasizing the notion of diversity: "Its [liberal democracy's] novelty resides in its envisaging the diversity of conceptions of the good, not as something negative that should be suppressed, but as something to be valued and celebrated." The acknowledgement that conflict is central to the political (and the social) also means that a full consensus is impossible and undesirable—apart from the acceptance of "[…] the institutions that are constitutive of the democratic order" (Mouffe, 1996: 8). Mouffe's (1999a: 51) disagreement with Habermas was expressed as follows: "[…] the importance of leaving this space of contestation forever open, instead of trying to fill it through the establishment of a supposedly 'rational' consensus."

The ineradicability of conflict does not imply that, for Mouffe, social stability does not exist. Here we need to return to the earlier discussion on sedimentation (see Platform 1), a concept that Laclau used to refer to the stabilization of conflict and the generation of consensus. Also in Mouffe's (2005: 17) work we find a similar use of the sedimentation concept, for instance, when she wrote: "The social is the realm of sedimented practices, that is, practices that conceal the originary acts of their contingent political institution and which are taken for granted, as if they were self-grounded." The discourse-theoretical framework immediately brings along the argument that this sedimentation is not a given, but constructed through a political—hegemonizing—logic. After all, hegemony fixates contingency, and temporarily settles societal conflict, even if resistance to hegemony always remains possible and hegemony is never total. Also, counter-hegemonic forces can, at some stage, unsettle or even dethrone a particular hegemony. This counter-hegemonic potentiality is not necessarily translated in social reality, and despite their particularity, specific articulations can rigidly and hegemonically maintain their presence and suppress social diversity.

A theory on the ineradicability of conflict also does not imply the acceptance of oppression or violence. Laclau and Mouffe's (1985: 176) own radical democratic project is very much based on the rejection of oppression, when they, for instance, called upon democratic left-wing forces to deepen liberal democracy: "[…] the alternative of the Left should consist of locating itself fully in the field of the democratic revolution and expanding the chains of equivalents between the different struggles against oppression." And in particular, Mouffe's (2005; 2013a) agonistic democracy is aimed at democratically transforming antagonism and violence in order to limit their damaging impact. In 1993, Mouffe (153) captured this idea as follows: "Instead of shying away from the component of violence and hostility inherent in social relations, the task is to think how to create the conditions under which those aggressive forces can be defused and diverted and a pluralist democratic order made possible."

Nevertheless, Mouffe warned against the idea that violence can be eradicated: She argued that "[…] we have to realise that the social order will always be threatened by violence" (Mouffe, 2000: 131). Again, she used theories of consensus as constitutive outside, to strengthen her own argument of the permanent threat of violence and antagonism:

> "Violence and hostility are seen as an archaic phenomenon, to be eliminated thanks to the progress of exchange and the establishment, through a social contract, of a transparent communication among rational participants." (Mouffe, 2005: 3)

Despite the—arguably rather clear—positioning against oppression and violence, others have taken issue with her alleged acceptance of violence. Oksala (2012: 55), for instance, wrote: "The ineradicable character of agonism [sic] raises the crucial question whether violence is also ineradicable. Mouffe seems to accept that it is, and that it is this easy acceptance of the inevitability of violence that I find problematic in her theory." I find this reading of Mouffe's work to be rather debatable, even though there are a number of elements in her work that contribute to it. First of all, the concepts of violence and antagonism are often combined (e.g., Mouffe, 1996: 8; 2005: 3), which generates the risk of conflation. For instance, sentences such as "Rivalry and violence, far from being the exterior of exchange, are therefore its ever-present possibility. Reciprocity and hostility cannot be dissociated and we have to realize that the social order will always be threatened by violence" (Mouffe, 2000: 131), do not provide much space to distinguish between conflict, antagonism/hostility, and violence. More importantly, Mouffe used a very broad notion of violence and not that much effort is done to qualify its many different shades. Mouffe (2000: 22) mainly discussed structural violence; for instance, when referring to "[…] violence being unrecognized and hidden behind appeals to 'rationality,' […]" where "[…] liberal thinking […] disguises the necessary frontiers and forms of exclusion behind pretenses of 'neutrality.'" For Mouffe, this is connected to the democratic paradox, which creates political community through the logic of exclusion, which brings her to articulate exclusion as violence. One example is when she wrote: "I want to argue that it is very important to recognize those forms of exclusion for what they are and the violence that they signify, instead of concealing them under the veil of rationality" (Mouffe, 1993: 145). Mouffe's argumentation aligns well with Spivak's (1985) use of the notion of othering to analyze British colonial domination in its ethnicized, gendered, and class-based logics. Spivak (1985: 76) labelled "[…] the remotely orchestrated, far-flung, and heterogeneous project to constitute the colonial subject as Other," which consists of the "[...] asymmetrical obliteration of the trace of that Other in its precarious Subject-ivity" as the "[...] clearest available example of [...] epistemic violence [...]." Here, it is equally important to keep in mind that "In Spivak's explanation, othering is a dialectical process becoming the colonizing *Other* is established at the same time as its colonized *others* are produced as subjects" (Ashcroft, Griffiths, and Tiffin, 2000: 141—emphasis in original).

Reverting to our ontology of the discursive-material knot may bring more clarity in these discussions on violence. Frequently, the emphasis in conflict theory is placed on the more material dimensions of violence and conflict, and this offers a good starting point. The World Health Organization (2002: 4) defined violence in the following way, in combination with a typology that distinguishes between self-directed violence, interpersonal violence, and collective violence:

> "The intentional use of physical force or power, threatened or actual, against oneself, another person, or against a group or community, that either results in or has a high likelihood of resulting in injury, death, psychological harm, maldevelopment or deprivation."

Another example is Galtung's (1969) influential distinction between personal violence and structural violence as a way to reflect on peace research. This distinction is operationalized by reverting to concepts that signify the material, or where the material component is privileged, such as, on the one hand, bodily harm, tools, actors, organizations, and targets, and on the other, power distribution, inequality, actors, systems, structures, ranks, and levels (Galtung, 1969: 174–175). Also, the notion of conflict itself often has a strong materialist focus: Galtung's (2009) conflict triangle model connects three concepts, namely conflict, attitude, and behavior. Conflict is viewed here as incompatibilities or contradictions, as he explains in the description of his 2009 version of this model: "Conflict has been defined in terms of incompatibilities, of contradictions, and that should not be confused with the attitudinal and behavioral consequences of conflict" (Galtung, 2009: 105). Similarly, Mitchell's (1981) triadic conflict structure, which was inspired by Galtung's model (see Demmers, 2012: 5), also has three components—i.e., situation, attitudes, and behavior—and uses an equally materialist approach towards conflict, even if his core definition emphasizes the role of perception: "Any situation in which two or more 'parties' (however defined or structured) perceive that they possess mutually incompatible goals" (Mitchell, 1981: 17). Even more recent models—such as the 'hourglass' model of conflict resolution responses (Ramsbotham, Miall, & Woodhouse, 2011)—tend to emphasize the material aspect. In this 'hourglass' model, a more temporal dimension (and escalation and de-escalation phases) is added to Galtung's approach, which enables the authors to distinguish between conflict containment, conflict settlement, and conflict transformation. Interestingly, the cultural is present in this model through the notion of cultural peacebuilding, but only connected to conflict transformation (see also later).

Despite their emphasis on the material, we should not disregard the importance of the psychological, and thus, although indirectly, the cultural and the discursive, in these models. Galtung's conflict triangle model places considerable importance on the notion of attitude, which he saw as the "mental states of the actors," as distinct from the "somatic states of the actors in the action-system," a distinction that is grounded in "[…] the age-old body-soul division between the somatic and the mental states" (Galtung, 2009: 36). These attitudes become articulated with the notion of perception, both of the self and the enemy, where Galtung emphasized the structural similarities of these perceptions: "There are important symmetries in the perception, they are to some extent mirror images of each other, through imitation and projection" (Galtung, 2009: 105). These examples show how individualistic and actor-based Galtung's approach is, even if he acknowledged that actors can be collectivities, but then attitude refers "to the attitudes of the members" (Galtung, 2009: 37). Attitudes also play a significant role in Mitchell's (1981: 27) work. He defined conflict attitudes as "[…] those psychological states (both common attitudes, emotions and evaluations, as well as patterns of perception and misperception) that accompany and arise from involvement in a situation of conflict." Despite his starting point that "[…] such emotions and cognitive processes are essentially characteristic of individuals […]," he does acknowledge a societal dimension, as "[…] they can be shared by a large or small group of people" (Mitchell, 1981: 71). Also in Mitchell's case, we can find significant attention expended on perception, which brings in the representational angle, particularly because of Mitchell's (1981: 99ff) emphasis on images of the self and the enemy.[40]

Despite the presence of the more psychological aspects in some seminal works on conflict, the need to acknowledge the cultural components remains. However significant the work of authors such as Galtung and Mitchell, their focus on the psychological (more than on the cultural and the discursive) feeds into a more individualized approach, grounded in a realist paradigm.

Demmers (2012: 119) critiqued what he called "[…] both individualist and structuralist theories of violent conflict." Referring to Jabri (1996), Demmers (2012: 119) wrote that individualist approaches are "mono-causal" and "too objective regarding human rationality," while structuralist approaches are "too static." One significant consequence of this focus on either individualist or structuralist approaches is that the entangled relations between the cultural-discursive and the material (or behavioral) remain underrepresented. In particular, both the role of the discursive in providing meaning to the material (and behavioral) and the contingencies in these signifying processes, which enable space for agency and avoid the full closure of structure, are not thematized. Demmers (2012: 121) argued for a recognition of the discursive, where "The struggle over words is a power struggle. A struggle about meaning." Demmers, as his below-rendered model shows (Figure 17), saw the workings of the discursive in interaction with the material (very much in line with the argument of this book, even though a different vocabulary is used).

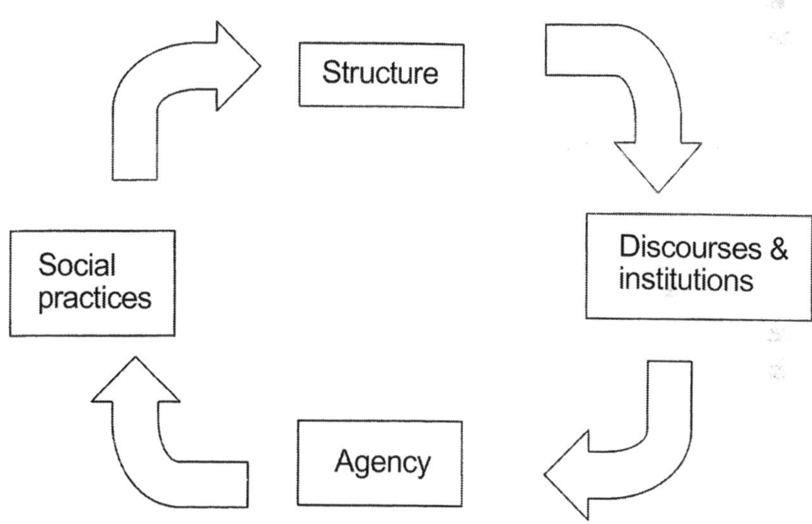

Figure 17. Discourses and practices according to Demmers.
Source: Demmers (2012: 122).

Also, other authors,[41] particularly when discussing war, have emphasized the discursive dimension of violence and war, as is illustrated by Keen (1986: 10): "In the beginning we create the enemy. Before the weapon comes the image. We think others to death and then invent the battle-axe or the ballistic missiles with which to actually kill them." Or, as Jabri (1996: 23) wrote: "[…] knowledge of human phenomena such as war is, in itself, a constitutive part of the world of meaning and practice." Mansfield (2008: 2) added to this a reflection on the political nature of the signifier war, which is "[…] not […] a simple descriptor of an unambiguous fact or a naturally occurring phenomena." Instead, "It is the recognition of a complex state of affairs in which the relationships between, and even the nature of, governments, social relationships, ideals and affects are all in play" (Mansfield, 2008: 3).

One important idea behind these discursive approaches is that discourses can incorporate violence—or, in other words, that meanings themselves can exercise violence. Bourdieu (1998) used the notion of symbolic violence[42] to capture this idea (from a gender studies perspective, in *Masculine Domination*). He referred to symbolic violence as "[…] a gentle violence, imperceptible and invisible even to its victims, exerted for the most part through the purely symbolic channels of communication and cognition (more precisely, misrecognition), recognition, or even feeling" (Bourdieu, 1998: 1–2). This "logic of domination" uses a "[…] symbolic principle known and recognized both by the dominant and by the dominated […]" (Bourdieu, 1998: 2). In a co-authored book, Bourdieu and Wacquant (1992: 168) defined symbolic violence as "[…] an act of recognition and misrecognition, which is situated beyond the control of the conscious mind and the will, in the misty regions of the schemata of the habitus." In *Masculine Domination*, Bourdieu (1998: 34) argued at length that it was not his intention to "minimize the role of physical violence," but—at the same time—that symbolic violence is also real violence.[43] For Bourdieu (1998: 34) the distinction between "'symbolic' as the opposite of 'real, actual'" and the assumption that "[…] symbolic violence is a purely 'spiritual' violence which ultimately has no real effects" are both naïve. A second misunderstanding Bourdieu (1998: 34) wished to avoid is that he was "[…] eternalizing the structure of masculine domination by describing it as unvarying and eternal." Instead, he emphasized the historical and (thus) constructed and contingent nature of the structures of domination that lie behind symbolic violence.

This brings us back to Laclau and Mouffe's work, and the discursive as a location of violence. In *HSS*, Laclau and Mouffe (1985: 126) used the notion of antagonism to theorize the "negation of a given order," where the antagonistic other becomes a constitutive outside that simultaneously produces the self and this outside. Antagonistic relations are (symbolically) violent in nature, as the self attempts to destabilize this other identity, although it ironically requires the very same other to construct its own identity. This construction of an outside, in Mouffe's (2005: 73) words, is very much part of the political: "[…] there is no consensus without exclusion, no 'we' without a 'they' and no politics is possible without the drawing of a frontier," but in the case of antagonism, the other becomes an enemy, to be excluded from the social order (see later).

In this antagonistic process, the self becomes constituted through the creation of a chain of equivalence, which has a homogenizing impact on the self. Through the workings of this chain of equivalence, a series of discourses (and materials), linked to signifying and material practices, become articulated as representative of the self, and as different from those of the constitutive other (see later). The different elements of the chain of equivalence do not naturally belong together, but they are assembled through the antagonism (which implies that the chain can be altered). Nevertheless, the particular assemblage of elements that support the identity of the self (in an antagonistic relation with an enemy) is often rather strong, and supports the idea of a homogeneous self.

These antagonistic logics are not exclusively discursive, but are grounded in assemblages that articulate the material and the discursive. In the case of violent conflict, violent practices are very present, in all their materiality. Killing the enemy remains a very material act. But signifying practices, legitimating these violent practices from within the antagonism between self and other, remain equally important. Here, we should keep in mind that "The exclusionist discourse of violent conflict is not […] confined to the battlefield […]," as Jabri (1996: 138) reminded us:

> "It is a discourse which politically legitimates and reproduces a categorisation based on those who are defined as legitimately within, against all external others, who are variously target of direct violence and/or institutionalised discrimination."

It is also important to stress that agency still plays a significant role in dealing with these discursive structures, and the interpellation of antagonism can be resisted, for instance through identifications with pacifist discourses (Jabri, 1996: 145ff). Also, the discursive component intersects with the (very) materialist dimensions of violence, where particular actors (e.g., armies, police forces, irregular soldiers, weapons manufacturers, and traders …) align themselves with a vast and sophisticated range of proto-machines to unleash deadly force.

Finally, I also want to emphasize that these assemblages remain contingent. With a vague sense of irony one could point out that the material destruction of the other is the ultimate moment of contingency, but the total destruction of the other is often more to be located at the level of the antagonistic fantasy. Actually, the unwillingness of the other to be completely destroyed generates more (or just as much) contingency, through the inability of living out the antagonistic fantasy of eliminating the other. To use Laclau and Mouffe's (1985: 125—emphasis in original) words: "Antagonism, far from being an objective relation, is a relation wherein the limits of every objectivity are *shown* [...]." They continue:

> "[...] antagonism, as a witness of the impossibility of a final suture, is the 'experience' of the limit of the social. Strictly speaking, antagonisms are not *internal* but *external* to society; or rather, they constitute the limits of society, the latter's impossibility of fully constituting itself." (Laclau & Mouffe, 1985: 125—emphasis in original)

Also, the idea of "a perfectly unified and homogenous agent" (Laclau & Mouffe, 1985: 84), constructed through a perfectly stable and eternal chain of equivalence, is open to dislocation, as the complexity of these constructions often crumbles underneath their own (discursive) weight, and have to deal with counter-discourses, in particular, in the case of long-lasting violent conflicts. Furthermore, at the material level, the antagonistic assemblages are vulnerable to contingency, ranging from military equipment not living up to the expectations (of accuracy, for instance) to military personal refusing to engage in battle, arriving too late to the battlefield, or dying of illness before they can do so.

3.2 Conflict Transformation

There is a long history of discourses that condemn the use of violence in the context of conflict, in its self-directed, interpersonal, and collective forms. If we focus on collective violence (without wishing to ignore the importance of the other forms), then we can point to the long history of pacifism, with its origins (in Europe) partly connected to religious theory and practice, and partly linked to the secular Enlightenment. Jabri (1996: 146) pointed to the role of Augustine and Thomas Aquinas, and Brock (1972: 3ff) started his overview in *Pacifism in Europe to 1914* with a discussion of antimilitarism in the early Catholic church. There are many examples of religious movements that endorsed pacifism,[44] with arguably the Quaker movement as one of its most prominent (see Brock, 1972: 255ff). The Enlightenment also produced a number of notable pacifist (or peace-oriented) texts, with, for instance, Kant's (2003) *To Perpetual Peace*. Despite the diversity of positions, these texts contain pacifist discourses that articulate the use of violence as undesirable, and provided a utopian perspective on a peaceful future, as Victor Hugo's capitalist-pacifist words spoken during his opening address of the Peace Congress in Paris, on 21 August 1849, exemplify:

> "A day will come when there will be no battlefields, but markets opening to commerce and minds opening to ideas [...]. A day will come when a cannon will be a museum-piece, as instruments of torture are today. And we will be amazed to think that these things once existed!" (Hugo, quoted by Wodiczko, 2012: 39)

At the same time, questions can be raised about the hegemony of pacifist discourse. As Jabri (1996: 146) mentioned, apart from the "[...] discourses concerned with [the] total elimination [of war]," another set of discourses focused on "[...] its rational management, only to be adopted in conditions of adversity where no other option could suffice." This discourse of war as a solution in the last instance, combined and strengthened with a just war discourse (which articulated war as legitimate in particular circumstances), has been proven to be much more persistent and dominant. Howard (2001: 6) referred to the discursive struggle between the pacifist discourse and the legitimate war discourse (arguably overestimating the strength of the pacifist discourse), when he wrote: "Throughout human history mankind has been divided between those who believe that peace must be preserved, and those who believe that it must be attained." What Howard's citation does show, is the prominence of peace as a modern ideal to be reached, even if it (according to the legitimate war discourse) has to be achieved through war.

A third discourse, which does not share this ideal and simply glorifies war, has been structurally discredited in the more contemporary European history, although it has not entirely disappeared. The glorification of war discourse articulates essentialist perspectives on human nature as intrinsically violent: "We inherit the warlike type; and for most of the capacities of heroism that the human race is full of we have to thank this cruel history" (James, 1984, quoted in Pick, 1993: 14). In this discourse, war "[...] is capable of defining precisely what it is to be human, because it involves giving up the supreme 'self-interest', life itself" (Pick, 1993: 15). Van Creveld (1991: 184) described this process of distinction as follows: "From the time of Homer on, there has always been a sense in which it is only those who risk their lives willingly, even joyfully, who can be completely themselves, completely human." Against this mechanism of distinction through heroism, valor, skills, and self-sacrifice, James (1984, quoted in Pick, 1993: 15) positioned ordinariness:

> "[War's] 'horrors' are a cheap price to pay for rescue from the only alternative supposed, of a world of clerks and teachers, of co-education and zoophily, of 'consumers' leagues' and 'associated charities,' of industrialism unlimited, and feminism unabashed. No scorn, no hardness, no valour any more! Fie upon such a cattleyard of a planet!"

The above quotation also shows the intimate connection of the glorification of war discourse with masculinity (through—in this citation—its critique of feminism). This discourse is further strengthened by reverting to what Bourke (1999: 50) called a "warrior ethic": "[…] exemplifying certain chivalric codes (or recognized formalities, ceremonies and courtesies) involving honourable exchanges, compassion and altruism at the same time as invoking reckless adventure and a high-minded disdain of death" (Bourke, 1999: 58). As Bourke's (1999: 13) work shows, the glorification of war discourse also articulates pleasure and excitement: "[…] although the act of killing another person in battle may invoke a wave of nauseous distress, it may also incite intensive feelings of pleasure."

The dominance of discourses that problematize war (and violence in general) has also led to the development of a multitude of strategies aimed at preventing, deterring, containing, regulating, or transforming violent conflict. Behind this development is an ethical-political rationale, as summarized by Väyrynen (1991: 1): "The resolution of violent conflicts is usually considered a politically desirable objective." Or, to use Galtung's (1965: 349) words: "[…] conflict is dangerous because it may in its consequences lead to a Hobbesian state of affairs where everybody uses all possible means of destruction against everybody else." The development of strategies to counter (collective) violence has a long history. Renna (1980: 61), focusing on peace education, wrote that "[…] the concept of peace education, in its broadest sense, is over 400 years old, although it did not become popular until after 1918." Of course, the study of violent conflict also has a long history, in combination with (academic) activism,[45] but the field of conflict resolution/transformation was only consolidated after the Second World War (Byrne & Senehi, 2008; Kriesberg, 2007).

3.2.1 Conflict resolution and transformation

Within this field, conflict resolution is the main signifier, giving meaning to the field of study, and demarcating it. Schellenberg (1996: 9) defined conflict resolution as "[…] a marked reduction in social conflict as a result of a conscious settlement of issues in dispute," and was quick to add an ethical dimension to this definition, by writing that "[...] we generally associate conflict resolution with what is good and desirable." He did simultaneously note that "[...] not all attempts to resolve conflict lead to justice or mutual satisfaction" (Schellenberg, 1996: 9), intrinsically not questioning his ethical stance regarding the desirability of ('good') conflict resolution. Abu-Nimer's (2012: 13) definition emphasizes the solution component even more, in combination with a reference to a "third party": Conflict resolution "[...] entails the use of collaborative problem solving in a situation where a neutral [...] third party helps the disputants engage in conciliation, facilitation, and/or mediation." This component of the definition is explicitly contested by Wallensteen (2012: 50—emphasis removed), who defined conflict resolution as

> "[...] a social situation where the armed conflicting parties in a (voluntary) agreement resolve to live peacefully with—and/or dissolve—their basic incompatibilities and hence cease to use arms against each other. This means that the conflict is transformed from violent to non-violent behaviour by the parties themselves, not by somebody else, for instance, an outsider or third party."

In the discussions on conflict resolution there is—for obvious reasons, given the field's remit—a strong focus on strategies on how to resolve conflict. Ramsbotham, Miall, and Woodhouse (2011: 175–176) focused on transformational processes, which they clustered in five fields: context transformation, structural transformation, actor transformation, issue transformation, and personal and group transformation. To give one more example, Wallensteen (2012: 53ff) discussed seven mechanisms for conflict resolution: a party shifting its priorities, dividing resources, horse-trading, sharing control, leaving control to somebody else, resorting to conflict resolution mechanisms such as arbitrage, and leaving the issues to later (or "even to oblivion"—Wallensteen, 2012: 57). These strategies immediately indicate a number of choices and preferences, which are understandable from the perspective of the conflict resolution remit, but still entail a series of reductions. Firstly, conflict resolution focuses on particular actors, namely those who are directly involved in the organization of violence. The state is prominently present, which is legitimated by Wallensteen (2012: 63) through the existence of four state monopolies: the monopoly of legitimate violence combined with fiscal, territorial, and ideological monopolies. As Wallensteen argued (2012: 64): "All these roles may make the state an actor in conflict as well as an object of conflict." There is (of course) a recognition of the role of other actors, but their unifying label as "non-state actors" again indicates the importance of the state, and the privileging of institutionalized politics. Secondly, realism[46] remains the dominant paradigm within conflict resolution. Jackson (2008: 172) acknowledged that the (related) field of international relations has opened up to constructivist/constructionist perspectives, but immediately added that constructivism/constructionism[47] "[...] has yet to make a significant impact on the study of international conflict and conflict resolution which continues to be dominated by rational choice and structurally based approaches." This implies that conflict resolution often still focuses on material processes, including the material practices of particular actors and material resources as sources of conflict, with less attention for the discursive components of conflict (resolution), or for the contingency of both the discursive and the material.

Still, conflict resolution is not a homogeneous field, and a series of authors have moved away from the exclusive focus on realist approaches towards institutionalized politics and material processes. The exclusive focus on actors within the field of politics (statist or non-statist) is complemented with attention for, for instance, the educational and cultural field. Boulding (1990: xxii) argued in favor of the development of a global civic culture, which implies the need to "develop a learning community." Ramsbotham, Miall, and Woodhouse (2011: 347) discussed the role of cultural and artistic dimensions of conflict resolution, arguing that "These creative and expressive areas of human activity provide a powerful source of peace-building energy and passion that is not always apparent in the formalized processes of political conflict resolution." In their first edition of *Contemporary Conflict Resolution*, Miall, Ramsbotham, and Woodhouse (2005: 57) pointed to a

> "[...] significant shift of emphasis away from the idea of 'top-down' peacebuilding in which powerful outsiders act as experts, importing their own conceptions and ignoring local cultures and capacities, and in favour of a cluster of practices and principles referred to collectively as 'peacebuilding from below.'"

Also, the culturalist (and more specifically, constructivist and constructionist) approaches that enable to focus on the discursive have made headway. Behind this evolution is the increased importance attributed to culture, in relation to conflict and conflict resolution. In some cases, though, culture is still defined in a fairly closed and homogeneous way, as Deutsch's (1991: 32) discussion of the sociocultural context shows, when he wrote: "Individuals, groups and nations with different cultural backgrounds must often negotiate about their conflicting interests, beliefs or values [...]." A more open perspective to culture can be found in Avruch's (1998: 12–16) book *Culture and Conflict Resolution*, in which he listed the following six "inadequate ideas" about culture: "1. Culture is homogeneous [...] 2. Culture is a thing [...] 3. Culture is uniformly distributed among members of a group [...] 4. An individual possesses but a single culture [...] 5. Culture is custom [...] 6. Culture is timeless."

The focus on culture has also enabled more explicitly discursive approaches, with Jabri's (1996) *Discourses on Violence* as an early example. Writing a decade later, Jackson (2008: 174) referred to the "constructivist turn" in international relations to legitimate a more explicit presence of constructivism in conflict resolution, discussing, amongst other things, discourses of conflict (Jackson, 2008: 180ff). His argument is based on the idea that "[...] constructivist approaches would emphasize the necessity for both structural and discursive transformation to bring about lasting conflict resolution" (Jackson, 2008: 182). Nevertheless, the critiques towards the introduction of more constructivist and post-structuralist traditions in conflict transformation (and their misinterpretation, I would like to add) remain, witness Ramsbotham, Miall, and Woodhouse's (2011: 408) comments about the post-structuralist critique on traditional conflict resolution approaches:

> "[...] there is a tendency here for post-structural thinking to ignore the fierce disruption and discontinuity of radical disagreement [...] taking the phenomenon of radical disagreement seriously, as advocated by Ramsbotham, may in some measure help to temper what is at times a somewhat didactic tendency in critical theory and a relativist tendency in post-structuralism [...]."

In addition to the reductionist problems related to the privileging actors from the field of institutionalized politics, and the underestimation of the importance of culture, also, the definition of conflict produces particular issues. The broad definition of conflict, and its ineradicability, rests uneasily with the linguistics of conflict resolution. The use of the word 'resolution' implies that a conflict can indeed be resolved and thus ended. Because of this, sometimes the concept of conflict transformation is preferred. Wallensteen (1991: 129—my emphasis) formulated this problem as a question, carefully choosing his words:[48] "Are conflicts ever resolved or are they *only* transformed?" In some cases, the severity of this ontological problem is downplayed; for instance, when Miall, Ramsbotham, and Woodhouse (2005: 60) referred to the "terminological dispute," where the choice between conflict resolution and conflict transformation, "Like all terminological issues, [...] is a matter of preference." I would like to argue that there is more at stake, as this choice is an ontological decision, dependent on the approach to conflict.

Conflict transformation enables emphasizing that "[…] conflict is normal in human relations and conflict is a motor of change" (Lederach, 2003: 5). The definition of conflict transformation used by Lederach (2003: 14), one of proponents of the conflict transformation concept, which is seen to consist of "[…] constructive change processes that reduce violence, increase justice in direct interaction and social structures," and that respond to "[…] real-life problems in human relationships," enhances this point. Lederach (2003: 29) argued that the notion of resolution is intrinsically problematic, as it "[…] implies finding a solution to a problem" and "[…] guides our thinking toward bringing some set of events or issues, usually experienced as very painful, to an end." In other words, "There is definiteness and finality created in the language [of conflict resolution]" (Lederach, 2003: 29), while conflict transformation incorporates a long-term perspective without ignoring "immediate solutions" (Lederach, 2003: 33). While the conflict resolution perspective is built around "[…] immediacy of the relationship where the symptoms of disruptions appear," the conflict transformation perspective "[…] envisions the presenting problems as an opportunity for response to symptoms and engagement of systems within which relationships are embedded" (Lederach, 2003: 33).

It should be added that proponents of the conflict resolution model do not abandon the conflict transformation concept, but still defend conflict resolution as the main concept, re-articulating conflict transformation as the "[…] longer-term and deeper structural, relational and cultural dimensions of conflict resolution" and the "[…] ultimate goal of the conflict resolution enterprise" (Miall, Ramsbotham, & Woodhouse, 2005: 60). Conflict resolution then becomes associated with the "[…] purposeful search for ways of accommodating the explicit interests of the parties in conflict" (Wallersteen, 1991: 129).

3.3.2 Bringing discourse theory into the equation

Arguably, also, this discussion can be further enriched and strengthened by making use of discourse theory, and especially Mouffe's (2005; 2013a) work on agonism, which aligns particularly well with the conflict transformation perspective. Both approaches are grounded in the idea that the issue is not to suppress conflict, but to encapsulate it in a pluralist-democratic (and peaceful) order. As argued before, Mouffe saw conflict as an ineradicable part of the social reality:

> "The specificity of modern democracy is precisely its recognition and legitimation of conflict; in democratic societies, therefore, conflict cannot and should not be eradicated. Democratic politics requires that the others be seen not as enemies to be destroyed but as adversaries whose ideas should be fought, even fiercely, but whose right to defend those ideas will never be questioned." (Mouffe, 2013b: 185)

If we look closely at Lederach's (2003: 14) definition of conflict transformation, we can identify its objective as an operationalization of agonistic conflict, which is built upon the avoidance of physical and structural violence and on the recognition of all actors as operating within the same democratic, legal, and social sphere, without ignoring the diversity of their positions. Conflict transformation itself, as a concept, can be translated as the transformation of antagonistic conflicts into agonistic conflicts.

In Mouffe's perspective, the aim of democratic politics is "[…] to transform an 'antagonism' into 'agonism'" (Mouffe, 1999b: 755), to "tame" or "sublimate" (Mouffe, 2005: 20–21) antagonisms, without eliminating passion from the political realm or relegating it to the outskirts of the private. In order to develop and theorize this model of agonistic democracy, Mouffe (2005) referred to the work of Schmitt[49] (1996), and his friend/foe distinction. As Mouffe did not provide much detail about the characteristics of agonism, and of what she later started to call antagonism proper (see Mouffe, 2013a: 109), it makes sense to return to Schmitt's work to see how he characterized antagonism and enmity. In a second step, we can then use these characteristics to further elaborate on agonism.

For Schmitt (1996: 27), the enemy is whoever is "[…] in a specially intense way, existentially something different and alien, so that in the extreme case conflicts with him are possible." A few lines later, Schmitt (1996: 28) provided a more elaborate description of the enemy, stressing its public nature:

> "The enemy is not merely any competitor or just any partner of a conflict in general. He is also not the private adversary whom one hates. An enemy exist only when, at least potentially, one fighting collectivity of people confronts a similar collectivity. The enemy is solely the public enemy, because everything that has a relationship to such a collectivity of men, particularly to a whole nation, becomes public by virtue of such a relationship."

These reflections tend to see (even if it is mostly done implicitly) antagonism as a cultural-definitional process, which brings me to define this model as an antagonistic conflict discourse,[50] which enables signifying practices that identify with this discourse (and which will be contested by other discourses).

Antagonism also has a material component—it does not escape from the discursive-material knot—which shall be discussed later. At this stage, the question is how the antagonistic discourse is articulated. Arguably, three nodal points can be distinguished in the antagonistic discourse: 1/the need for destruction of the enemy, 2/the radical difference and distance from the enemy, combined with (and supported by) a process of 3/homogenization of the self.

The definition of the Other as "an enemy to be destroyed" (Mouffe, 1999b: 755) immediately brings us to the notion of destruction (and violence). In Schmitt's (2004: 36) writings, different degrees of enmity are distinguished, with the "war of absolute enmity," which "knows no containment" as extreme form. The wish to impose destruction upon the enemy is shared by these different models of enmity, albeit with different degrees of destruction, ranging from the desire to neutralize the threat originating from the enemy, to the enemy's complete annihilation, as described by Schmitt (2004: 67):

> "In a world in which the partners push each other [...] into the abyss of total devaluation before they annihilate one another physically, new kinds of absolute enmity must come into being. Enmity will be so terrifying that one perhaps mustn't even speak any longer of the enemy or of enmity, and both words will have to be outlawed and damned fully before the work of annihilation can begin. Annihilation thus becomes entirely abstract and entirely absolute."

Secondly, the antagonistic discourse requires a radical difference between the enemy and the self, where no symbolic (or material) space is thought to be shared, and could be shared. Harle (2000: 12—emphasis in original) wrote: "The Enemy emerges if and only if 'we' and 'they' are thought to be *fundamentally* different [...]." The construction of this radical other is supported by the logic of the dichotomy, whereas the idea of the absence of a common space produces distance. In the more extreme cases, this radical othering leads to a dehumanization and demonization of the other, denying even the most basic features of humanity to that other, which makes its destruction easier and even necessary. One example here is the Nazi articulation of the Jew as parasite (Bacharach, 2002), which was one of the legitimizations of the Shoah, with its destruction of millions of lives.

Moreover, radical difference is combined with the process of hierarchization. The dichotomy that defines the enemy and the self is not considered neutral, but it supports a hierarchy that positions the enemy as inferior, and the self as superior. Delanty, Wodak, and Jones (2008: 307) pointed to the combined processes of inferiorization and superiorization when analyzing the migrations into Europe in the following terms: "The inferiorization of the 'others' and the superiorization of 'us' is a complex and often hidden process that is not easy simply to observe. It is often understood by many members of the majority society as 'normal' and 'objective.'" This citation can be seen as an illustration of how the process of hierarchization has a long history in positioning the racial and colonial other. For instance, Said (2003: 42) referred to Orientalism as the "[...] ineradicable distinction between Western superiority and Oriental inferiority." Or, as Said (2003: 7) wrote a few pages earlier: "Orientalism depends for its strategy on this flexible positional superiority, which puts the Westerner in a whole series of possible relationships with the Orient without ever losing him the relative upper hand."

The process of radical difference also has consequences for the construction of the self, which brings us to the third nodal point of antagonism: the homogenization of the self, which consists of the solidification of the chain of equivalence of the self. If we return to Schmitt's (2004: 61—emphasis in original) analysis, we can see that the self is not indifferent to the threat that the enemy-other poses to the self:

> "The enemy is our own question as *Gestalt*. If we have determined our own *Gestalt* unambiguously, where does this double enemy come from? The enemy is not something to be eliminated out of a particular reason, something to be annihilated as worthless. The enemy stands on my own plane. For this reason I must contend with him [...] in battle, in order to assure my own standard [*Maß*], my own limits, my own *Gestalt*." (Schmitt, 2004: 61—emphasis in original)

We also find this threat to the self in Laclau and Mouffe's (1985: 125) work when they wrote that: "[...] the presence of the 'Other' prevents me from being totally myself. The relation arises not from full totalities, but from the impossibility of their constitution." This also implies that "[...] the Other has an important function in establishing the identity of the Self" (Harle, 2000: 15),[51] or, to use Schmitt's (2004: 65—emphasis in original) words: "The heart of the political is not enmity *per se* but the distinction of friend and enemy; it presupposes *both* friend *and* enemy." But this relationship between self and enemy-other surpasses the process of hierarchization where "[...] the distinction is understood to reflect the struggle between good and evil, and when good is associated with 'us' but evil with 'them'" (Harle, 2000: 12—emphasis removed). The relationship with the enemy-other also homogenizes the self, through the attribution of a series of characteristics that distinguish the self from the enemy and that apply to the entire self. The self thus becomes one, united in its struggle against the enemy, rallying round the flag.[52] Laclau (1996: 40–41), in his analysis of Luxembourg's writings about the unity of the working class in its political struggle, formulated this argument as follows: "It is not, consequently, something positive that all of them share which establishes their unity, but something negative: their opposition to a common enemy." In the creation of this solidified chain of equivalence, with the enemy as its constitutive outside, little room is left for internal differences, which is evidenced by the words of the German Emperor Wilhelm, who, during the First World War, claimed that "[…] he would no longer hear of different political parties, only of Germans" (Torfing, 1999: 126). The then American president George W. Bush used an updated version during his address to the Joint Session of Congress and the American People on 20 September 2001,[53] saying: "Either you are with us, or you are with the terrorists." As a construction, the homogenization of the self becomes so hegemonic that resistance against it positions these actors as so-called enemies within, or traitors (Yiannopoulou, 2012: 127ff). Laclau and Mouffe (1985: 125) offered an important addition to this way of thinking, because they also wrote that "[…] antagonism is the failure of difference […]," which they explained as follows: "[…] antagonism constitutes the limits of every objectivity, which is revealed as partial and precarious objectification." Even when the enemy-other triggers fantasies of a homogeneous self that denies contingency and difference, or, in Laclau and Mouffe (1985: 125) words: "[…] every society [is] constituted as a repression of the consciousness of the impossibility that penetrates them," the diversity that characterizes the self is most likely to eventually dislocate the (construction of the) homogeneous self.

The construction of the self and the enemy-other is, in turn, supported by, and combined with, a series of interconnected processes: essentialization, universalization, normalization, moralization, and dehistoricization. Mouffe (2005: 30) referred to the usage of "[…] essentialist forms of identification or non-negotiable moral values." Even if "We are never confronted with 'we/they' oppositions expressing essentialist identities pre-existing the process of identification" (Mouffe, 2005: 18), the belief in these essentialisms (e.g., about the nation) feeds into the construction of the self and its homogenization. Also, the logic of universalization feeds the idea that a dominant social order is not particular, but given and universally applicable (at least within the frontiers that demarcate the self from its outside). Normalization refers to the imposition of particular social norms, which renders particular articulations as normal, neutral, and/or natural. As Foucault (1977: 184) mentioned, "[...] the power of normalisation imposes homogeneity [...]," and what moves outside the norm risks being pathologized (Foucault, 1978: 105). A fourth mechanism is moralization, where "[...] instead of being constructed in political terms, the 'we'/'they' opposition constitutive of politics is now constructed according to moral categories of 'good' versus 'evil'" (Mouffe, 2005: 75). Finally, Bourdieu pointed to the dimension of time in the normalization and legitimation of the social order. In discussing masculine domination, in his eponymous book, he referred to the "[...] dehistoricization and eternalization of the structure of the sexual division [...]" (Bourdieu, 1998: viii). Similarly, Barthes (1973: 151) referred to the dehistoricizing capacity of myth, which "[...] deprives the object of which it speaks of all History. In it, history evaporates."

One important addition to the discussion on the self and the enemy-other is the argument that often a third subject position comes into play, that of the victim, which strengthens the demonization of the enemy and opens up opportunities for glorification of the self through the saving or protecting of the enemy's victim(s) (see Carpentier, 2008). Here, too, we should keep in mind that also the victim is "a social construction that emerges in interactional and discursive practices" (Quinney, 1975; Strobl, 2004: 295). One example is Barnard-Wills's (2013: 137) analysis of discourses of surveillance. He first argued that "the terrorist" is the "[...] worst of all possible subject positions in contemporary discourses of government and security, Terrorists are always enemies rather than adversaries of positively evaluated subject positions." But he also argued that in these cases, the "honest citizen" becomes articulated as a (potential) victim—part of the chain of equivalence of the self: "[...] the honest citizen is often the victim of the malign social actors" (Barnard-Wills, 2013: 137). In other cases, the victim subject position is claimed by the entire (social) self, a phenomenon that Lomsky-Feder and Ben-Ari (2011: 123) labeled the self-as-victim. And in yet other cases, the victim itself is an other, a notion that we can label the other-victim, in contrast to the other-enemy (and the other-perpetrator).

3.2.3 Antagonism, agonism, and conflict transformation

If we use the above-discussion about antagonism to reflect about agonism and conflict transformation, when the first point to make is that not every self and other relation has to consist of a self and enemy-other relation. To use Mouffe's words for support: The political is grounded in self and other relations, but "Such a relationship is not necessarily antagonistic [in the proper sense]" (Mouffe, 2013b: 185). In *Agonistics*, Mouffe (2013a: 109) argued that "[...] this antagonistic conflict can take different forms," in order to introduce the distinction between antagonism proper and agonism. While antagonism proper is grounded in the Schmittian friend/enemy relation, agonism is not (Mouffe, in Errejón & Mouffe, 2016: 55). Agonism articulates the relationship between self and other as a "[...] we/they relation where the conflicting parties, although acknowledging that there is no rational solution to their conflict, nevertheless recognize the legitimacy of their opponents" (Mouffe, 2005: 20). Later, she also pointed to their sharing of ethico-political principles:

> "What exists between adversaries is, so to speak, a conflictual consensus—they agree about the ethico-political principles which organize their political association but disagree about the interpretation of these principles." (Mouffe, 2013a: 109)

In other words, an agonistic conflict does not hide the differences in position and interest between the involved parties; they are still "in conflict" but share "[...] a common symbolic space within which the conflict takes place" (Mouffe, 2005: 20; see also Mouffe, 2013a: 7). Still, antagonism proper[54] remains "an ever present possibility" (Mouffe, 2013b), and societies can quite easily slip into antagonistic self-other relationships, where enemies need to be destroyed.

In developing the notion of agonism further, we can return to the three nodal points of the enemy-other that were discussed before, with the argument that the agonistic model of conflict will re-articulate these characteristics in shifting from the other-enemy to the other-adversary. As one of the citations in the previous paragraph illustrates, adversaries navigate in a common symbolic space, which implies a degree of togetherness. Arendt's (1998: 175ff) writings on action produces an interesting starting point here, in particular when Arendt argues for the importance of disclosure of the actor in the act. For her, "This revelatory quality of speech and action comes to the fore where people are *with* others and neither for nor against them—that is, in sheer human togetherness" (Arendt, 1998: 180—emphasis in original). Relevant here is Arendt's (1998: 180) usage of the enemy concept to illustrate a situation without disclosure, which is connected to a situation without togetherness:

> "This [situation where action loses its specific character] happens whenever human togetherness is lost, that is, when people are only for or against other people, as for instance in modern warfare, where men go into action and use means of violence in order to achieve certain objectives for their own side and against the enemy. In these instances, which of course have always existed, speech becomes indeed 'mere talk,'

> simply one more means toward an end, whether it serves to deceive the enemy or to dazzle everybody with propaganda [...]."

For Arendt, the position of the enemy is an illustration of a situation where human togetherness is lost, which, in turn, makes this concept of togetherness highly useful to think about agonism. But this then raises questions about which togetherness, as Arendt has been critiqued for developing a too consensual model of action (and politics).[55] Breen (2009: 136—emphasis in original), for instance, problematized Arendt's "sheer human togetherness," arguing that the situation where an actor is not for or against some actor, is not possible: "Political actors are therefore never solely *with* their fellow human beings, but always *for* some and *against* others." Mouffe's (2013a: 109) argument that "[...] what exists between adversaries is, so to speak, a conflictual consensus" is useful here to see this togetherness, still important to define agonistic relations, as what I would prefer to call a conflictual togetherness. This also implies that there is a structural (power) balance between the involved actors. While the enemy model rests on hierarchization, where the enemy-other is inferiorized and the self is superiorized, the adversary model builds on a structural balance where the different actors are not hierarchically positioned.

The second nodal point of agonism is the pluralization of the self, which is to be contrasted with its homogenization. Mouffe often combined pluralism with agonism, for instance when she's referred to "agonist pluralism" (Mouffe, 1999b) and the "agonistic dynamics of pluralism" (Mouffe, 2005: 30). This combination of concepts is used to describe the need to acknowledge the ineradicability of conflict and the existence of a societal diversity that feeds this societal conflict, in combination with the need to democratically harness this conflict without suppressing it. As Mouffe (1999b: 756) formulated it: "Far from jeopardizing democracy, agonistic confrontation is in fact its very condition of existence." In the Introduction of *The Ethos of Pluralization*, Connolly (1995: xx) linked pluralism to the construction of a 'we,' arguing against the need to construct a homogeneous self, and instead pleaded for a multiple, pluralized 'we,' in the following terms:

> "You do not need a wide universal 'we' (a nation, a community, a singular practice of rationality, a particular monotheism) to foster democratic governance of a population. Numerous possibilities of intersection and collaboration between multiple, interdependent constituencies infused by a general ethos of critical responsiveness drawn from several sources suffice very nicely."

It is this idea of a pluralized self (and a pluralized other-adversary) that is seen as characteristic of agonism. In other words, agonism moves away from a dichotomization that creates impermeable and solid frontiers between the self and the other-enemy, together with hegemonic chains of equivalence of the self and the other-enemy that leave no space for internal diversity and pluralism. Or, to use Mouffe's (2005: 82) words again: "[…] the absence of an effective pluralism entails the impossibility for antagonisms to find agonistic, i.e. legitimate, forms of expression." Agonism recognizes difference and conflict, but also positions the adversary in the same symbolic space, which means that in the agonistic model, differences are no longer absolute and all-encompassing. Difference and conflict co-exist in an agonistic model with the acceptance of the other as legitimate: "Adversaries do fight—even fiercely—but according to a shared set of rules[56], and their positions, despite being ultimately irreconcilable, are accepted as legitimate perspectives" (Mouffe, 2005: 52). This acceptance of the other creates linkages with the other, acknowledging the democratic rights and humanity of the other, but it also renders the frontier between the equivalential chain of the self and its constitutive outside less solid and more permeable, allowing for transgressions of that frontier and for the creation of chains of difference.[57] Here we should keep in mind that "[…] the logic of equivalence is a logic of the simplification of political space, while the logic of difference is a logic of its expansion and increasing complexity" (Laclau & Mouffe, 1985: 130). Using linguistics as example, Laclau and Mouffe (1985: 130) argued that:

> "[…] the logic of difference tends to expand […] the number of positions that can enter into a relation of combination and hence of continuity with one another; while the logic of equivalence expends the […] elements that can be substituted for one another—thereby reducing the number of positions which can possibly be combined."

Laclau and Mouffe then connected the occurrence of several co-existing antagonisms with a "[…] situation described by Gramsci under the term 'organic crisis'" (Laclau & Mouffe, 1985: 131), and with social instability:

> "[…] the more unstable the social relations, the less successful will be any definite system of differences and the more the points of antagonism will proliferate. This proliferation will make more difficult the construction of any centrality and, consequently, the establishment of unified chains of equivalence." (Laclau & Mouffe, 1985: 131)

Arguably, the pluralization nodal point of agonism implies a much less negative reading of this situation, as the co-existence of chains of equivalence and difference allows, on the one hand, for selves and other-adversaries (in plural) to be constructed, and on the other hand, for the avoidance of a hegemonic self that homogenizes itself as a united center and transforms the other into an disconnected enemy. Pluralization, consisting of a combination of chains of equivalence and difference, enables connections between selves and other-adversaries, for changing alliances and border-crossings between them, and for the creation of affectious spaces of sharing.

Thirdly, while the antagonistic enemy discourse is characterized by the need for destruction, the agonistic adversary discourse has the need for peaceful and non-violent interaction as a nodal point. If adversaries belong to the same political space, and do not attempt to destroy (or annihilate) each other, then a reflection on the nature of that interaction becomes unavoidable. Although peaceful interaction would be an obvious choice to describe this type of interaction, we again need to emphasize the context of conflictuality that structures this peaceful interaction. For this reason, peaceful and non-violent interaction is preferred as a label. Peace and non-violence, of course, have many dimensions that can also be approached from the perspective of the discursive-material knot. Peace and non-violence, first of all, refer to the absence of collective material violence (combined with the absence of interpersonal material violence motivated by an other-enemy logic), and the absence of death and destruction that this brings. It also refers to the absence of structural violence, with inequality as "the general formula behind structural violence" (Galtung, 1969: 175). In other parts of his article, Galtung also mentioned social injustice as a defining element of structural violence (Galtung, 1969: 171). As Galtung pointed out, the combination of the absence of personal and structural violence necessitates an expansion of the definition of peace. For this reason, he introduced the concepts of negative peace (the absence of personal violence) and positive peace (the absence of structural violence) (Galtung, 1969: 183). Peaceful and non-violent interaction also implies the absence of what Bourdieu called symbolic violence, which we can define here as discourses that violate the other (or part of the self), or signifying practices that identify with these antagonistic discourses. This not only concerns discourses that call for the destruction of the other, but also discourses that are characterized by the logic of antagonism (proper) in their creation of radical differences and hierarchies, and in their constructions of homogenized and solidified—one could also say stereotyped—selves and others. Finally, there is also a temporal component to peaceful and non-violent interaction, as an agonistic discourse is fed by the trust that the other will not engage in future violent acts, or that violent acts from the past will not be repeated. Bloomfield (2003: 11) captured this idea when he wrote: "One of the biggest obstacles to [the] cooperation [between former enemies] is that, because of the violence of the past, their relations are based on antagonism, distrust, disrespect and, quite possibly, hurt and hatred."

But equally important in the discussion of this third nodal point of agonism is the focus on peaceful and non-violent *interaction*, which again has many dimensions and variations. Interaction could be minimal, in the sense that it is based on mutual but distant toleration. Williams (1996: 19), although not discussing agonism explicitly, described the necessity of toleration by contrasting it to antagonism and armed conflict:

> "It is necessary where different groups have conflicting beliefs—moral, political, or religious—and realize that there is no alternative to their living together, that is to say, no alternative except armed conflict, which will not resolve their disagreements and will impose continuous suffering."

The breakdown of agonism, and the evolution towards antagonism occurs when "[…] people find others' beliefs or ways of life deeply unacceptable" (Williams, 1996: 19). Williams (1996: 19) illustrated this with religious toleration as example: "In matters of religion, for instance […], the need for toleration arises because one of the groups, at least, thinks that the other is blasphemously, disastrously, obscenely wrong." Toleration, which implies the acceptance of the other as legitimate, is the basic level of peaceful and non-violent interaction, but more intense forms of (peaceful and non-violent) interaction, such as coordination, cooperation, and collaboration remain also possible. This then, in turn, raises questions about when the other-adversary becomes an ally, friend, or neighbor, but this will be discussed in the next part.

First, Figure 18 provides us with an overview of the nodal points of antagonism and agonism:

Antagonism	**Agonism**
Radical difference	Conflictual togetherness
Homogenization of the self	Pluralization of the self
Enemy destruction	Peaceful and non-violent interaction

Figure 18. Nodal points of antagonism and agonism.

3.2.4 Antagonism, agonism, and the discursive-material knot

Mouffe's reflections on the democratically necessary transformation of antagonism into agonism can, and arguably needs to, be integrated in the ontology of the discursive-material knot. In Mouffe's work, the discursive dimension of the agonization of conflict is clearly present, through the emphasis on the construction of the subject position of the other-enemy, and the need to re-articulate this subject position as an other-adversary. The mere fact that this re-articulation is deemed possible—however difficult it may be—illustrates the emphasis that is placed on the contingency of social reality, and the role of the political in intervening in these constructions, in this case to serve a democratic-pluralist and peace-oriented discourse. This does not mean that this re-articulation is to be taken for granted. On the contrary, hegemonic forces frequently seem to find new enemies, and the agonistic position often finds itself in the counter-hegemonic corner. Also, this shows the workings of political agency, as actors can identify with hegemonic discourses that articulate an enemy subject position, or with counter-hegemonic discourses that transform these enemy subject positions into adversaries.

Apart from the straightforward agonistic and antagonistic positions, we can distinguish several other positions and combinations (see Figure 19—labelled the palm tree model of antagonism and agonism), which enables avoiding becoming trapped in a mere dichotomy between antagonism and agonism. Firstly, both agonism and antagonism suppose the relevance of the other, either as adversary or as enemy. It is equally conceivable that actors are articulated as irrelevant non-self *and* non-other, or are not articulated at all. In some cases, as has been analyzed through the lens of symbolic annihilation (Tuchman, 1978), or the subaltern (Spivak, 1988), this is part of an antagonistic logic, but in other cases, an actor can be met with indifference, or be articulated as part of another symbolic space. This scenario is not so much a situation of a discourse of indifference (which still signifies relevance) but rather, a situation of indifference to discourse. A situation of irrelevance is not necessarily stable, and irrelevance can always be transformed in relevance (and the other way around).

Secondly, we should incorporate the co-existence of antagonisms and agonisms. When Laclau and Mouffe (1985: 131) wrote: "[…] there are a variety of possible antagonisms in the social, many of them in opposition to each other," it is a clear acknowledgment of a multitude of antagonisms (proper or in agonistic form). But dominant situations of agonism and antagonism can be combined with upsurges of antagonism and agonism, respectively. In other words, they can co-exist, temporally or more structurally. A chain of equivalence that is sustained by an antagonistic other can (and often will) be characterized by agonism within the chain itself. Inversely, in a situation of dominant agonism, antagonism can still occur, as Mouffe's (2005: 64ff) discussion of the responses of Western democracies to right-wing populism shows.

Thirdly, as already briefly indicated before, there are more others than the other-enemy and the other-adversary. One of the problems of Schmitt's (1996) friend/foe distinction is that he does not develop the friend part of the dichotomy that much in *The Concept of the Political*, although there is more attention to the friend in *The Theory of the Partisan* (2004). This is worsened by interpretations of his work that implicitly conflate the friend with the self, which tends to hide some of the complexities in relation to the subject position of the self. The equivalential chain is itself a construction that articulates a diversity of elements under the common denominator of the self, without, however, totally eliminating their differences: They "[...] can weaken, but not domesticate differences" (Laclau, 2005: 79).

As discussed earlier, the subject position of the self can become pluralized, which is considered characteristic for the agonistic model, but the self can also disintegrate, for instance, due to internal differences. More importantly, the subject position of the self can itself be articulated (or become part of a larger chain of equivalence) with other actors, who are considered allies or friends. In a book on political friendship, King and Smith (2013: 1–2) raised the question "[...] whether any community ('us') is necessarily defined in opposition to some other and also whether any such opponent ('them') is necessarily to be construed as an enemy." Their introductory chapter, and edited volume, argues for the importance of political amity, which provides a negative answer to their own question. Slomp's (2013: 85—emphasis in original) chapter in this same book returns to Schmitt's work to argue that "Two types of friends populate the world of *Theorie des Partisanen*: on the one hand there is the friend who is external to one's own group or party, whom we can call the ally, and on the other hand there is the friend who belongs to one's own group or party." Slomp's reading of Schmitt (2004) opens up space to distinguish more other-related subject positions than the enemy and the adversary. To echo's Slump's (2013: 86) words: "The presence of external allies is as important to Schmitt as the existence of enemies." We can find other references to this other-ally, for instance, in Billig's (1995: 87) work. Still, going back to Schmitt, I would like to question whether the friend is necessarily part of the "own group or party," and I would like to suggest that the other-friend is also a possible subject position. Inspiration for this argument can be found in Derrida's (2005) attempt to shift from fraternity to friendship in his *Politics of Friendship*, but also in Mehta's (1999: 41) reading of Mahatma Gandhi's use of the friendship signifier in structuring relations between Hindus and Muslims. What Chacko (2012: 74) called a "politics of friendship" within Gandhi's framework was "[…] based on equality, and when equality existed, friendship was to be cultivated through the willingness to unconditionally and disinterestedly share in the suffering of the neighbour."

This brought Bryant (2004: 250) to suggest yet another option, namely the other-neighbor, when she wrote:

> "Neighbours […] are those persons to whom one is historically connected through place and with whom one must live. […] Affection, indeed, is not the point. Even the best neighbours may be noisy, may cause trouble, may know too much about one's comings and goings. Neighbours form a moral community and a tribunal."

As is the case with the other-friend, the other-neighbor has also been addressed in philosophical texts, such as the work of Levinas (1978). For Levinas (1978: 159), the neighbor remains an other, but this other-neighbor takes a crucial place, because "[…] my relationship with the Other as neighbor gives meaning to my relations with all the others." The subject position of other-neighbor, at least in Levinas's articulation,[58] produces an obligation that cannot be escaped, and that proceeds experience: "[…] the face of a neighbor signifies for me an unexceptionable responsibility, preceding every free consent, every pact, every contract" (Levinas, 1978: 159).

These reflections enable distinguishing different articulations of the other subject positions, namely, the other-ally, the other-friend, and the other-neighbor. Arguably, this distinction of more other-related subject positions does not push the political outside the context of conflictuality, as also the other-neighbor, the other-friend, and the other-ally are not in a symbiotic relationship with the self, and this difference still has the capacity to generate conflict.

Finally, we should emphasize contingency even more, and stress changes over time, where the relationship of particular others with the self changes over time. Alliances can turn into enmities, but sometimes also enmities can evolve over time, where the other as former enemy can shift to a position that approximates the other as friend. Wallensteen's (2012: 33) brief analysis of

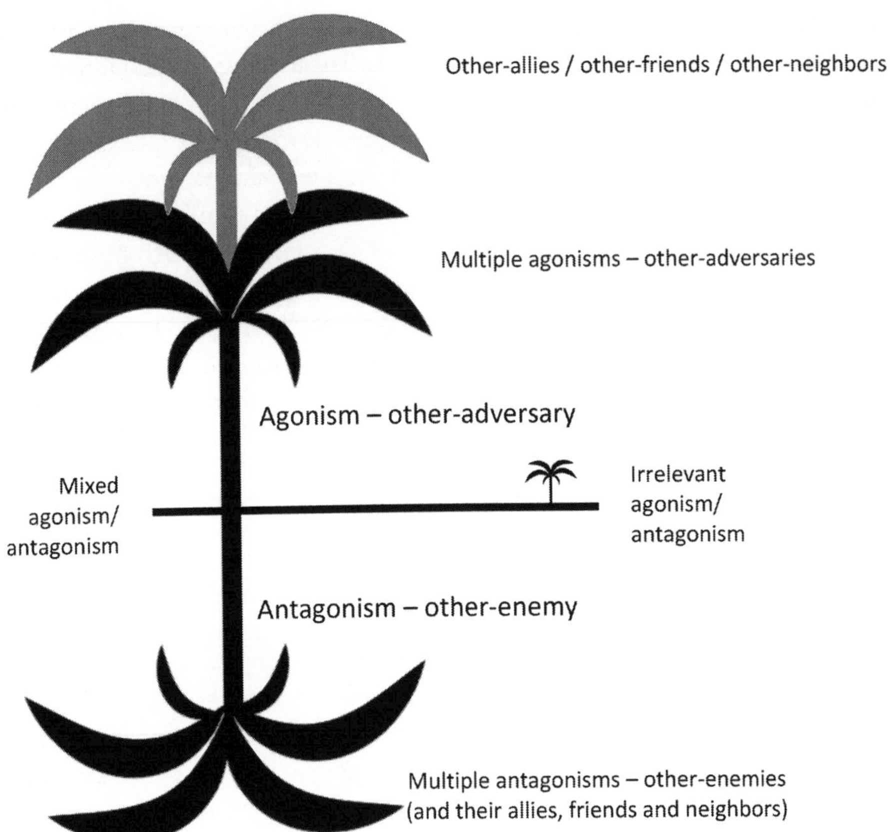

Figure 19. The palm tree model of antagonism and agonism.

the changing French/German relations in the 20th century illustrates this logic of difference, re-articulating the antagonistic chain of equivalence: "[…] the integration of the two former enemies, Germany and France, illustrated the potential of reversing dynamics. It showed it was possible to move from being enemies to allies, in a relationship that was closer than traditional alliances of convenience."

In addition to this conceptual discussion, it is equally important to integrate the material in the analysis of antagonism and agonism, in particular, because it is more absent—without it being totally excluded—in Mouffe's work on agonism. Agonistic material practices are equally important in understanding agonism, in particular, keeping the agency-driven nature of the material in mind. Here, the more traditional work on conflict resolution and a detour via antagonism offer a series of starting points. Earlier discussions on violent (collective) conflict enable us to see the many material aspects of antagonism, although a comprehensive discussion is practically unfeasible within the scope of this book, and I will only touch upon those components that enable me to illustrate the role of the material for agonism in its interaction with agonistic discourses within the discursive-material knot.

One element is the key institution of antagonism—or for dealing with antagonism: the military, which is a range of assemblages that groups sophisticated (and sometimes not so sophisticated) proto-machines, soldier-bodies, and militarized places and spaces (on the latter, see Woodward, 2011). Cockerham (2003: 491) described these military assemblages as follows: "Armed combat, however, is the military's raison d'être, and those whose role it is to fight are supported by extensive administrative and logistical systems designed to expedite that aim." The bodily practices of armies have very material outcomes, generating the material destruction of, in many, but certainly not all, cases, other-enemies. Obviously, these military assemblages contain discursive components, where the material is given meaning through particular discourses that articulate signifiers as security, protection, justice, hierarchy, efficiency, professionalism, heroism, etc. Military assemblages are also connected with other societal fields, including politics, industry, media, and education. In democracies, the sphere of institutionalized politics exerts control over these military assemblages, but sometimes, also, concepts such as the military-industrial complex—but also the military-industrial-media-entertainment complex (Der Derian, 2001) and the military-industrial-academic complex (Giroux, 2007)—are used to signify the close connection between the military and these other societal fields, although many different levels of endorsement can exist (e.g., regular armies endorsed by states, versus irregular fighters, partisans, insurgents, terrorists ...).

These complexes, or assemblages in their own right, support the construction of a radical difference with the other and the homogenization of the self, through their material articulation. Also their place-based politics are relevant here, with particular territories rendered beyond access, as they are patrolled by enemy-soldiers or made inaccessible through fortified frontiers (the Atlantik wall and fortifications as the Maginot, Sigfried, Metaxis, Rupnik, and Benesh Lines come to mind). The construction of 'own' military bases in strategic locations, the maneuvers and counter-maneuvers of troops, and the focus on strategic targets[59] further illustrates the segregative workings of these place-based politics, further strengthening how particular proto-machines (distinct uniforms, weapons systems, communicational networks for command and control, logistics ...) are used to dichotomize between the self and the other.

Also, at a more micro-level, military practices (labeled 'operations') have many material aspects, given the destructive and deadly objectives and consequences of combat, the mobilization of human (and animal) bodies and proto-machines, the (non-)care for these bodies afterwards (Reznick, 2004), the occupation and transformation of places and spaces (see, for instance, Carden-Coyne, 2014; Wilson, 2012), but also the many decision-making practices and material text-related practices (e.g., propaganda), and their (material) memorializations afterwards (Beurier, 2004; Black, 2004). The military, through its material existence, has its own agency, which can sometimes generate difficulties in not intending to deploy them—at macro-level and at micro-level, with the 'accidental discharge' as an example of the latter—and in difficulties in deploying them, given the complexity of these assemblages, with the concept of 'friendly fire' as a ghastly reminder of what can go wrong.

The relation of the military with agonism is not as straightforward as can be assumed at first sight, as it is mediated through discourses on the desirability of violent collective conflict. Obviously, the non-deployment—or even non-existence—of armies supports agonism as a form of conflictual togetherness, while the use of military violence is a materialization of antagonistic conflict. But when confronted with actors using an antagonistic model, we are thrown back to Howard's (2001: 6) dilemma—which I have already mentioned before—and the discursive struggle "[...] between those who believe that peace must be preserved, and those who believe that it must be attained." One way to deal with this dilemma is to take a step back, and incorporate the objectives and causes of antagonistic (violent) conflict (and their materialities) in the analysis.

In a historical analysis, Holsti (1996) pointed to the structural differences between violent collective conflicts over time. He used three categories—institutionalized war, total war, and wars of the third kind (or peoples' wars)—to describe war since 1648 (Holsti, 1996: 28). In the case of the highly codified institutionalized war, the objectives were political and often limited: "[...] a province, a crown, more defensible frontiers, a cut of colonial trade, or domination of particular waterways" (Holsti, 1996: 32). However, in the 20th century, total war transformed "[...] war as a contest between armed forces to a contest between nations" (Holsti, 1996: 35), with total victory (translated into unconditional surrender) as its main objective. And as Holsti (1996: 36) argued, war was

> "[…] total not only in its destructive capacity and deliberate targeting of civilians, but also in its purposes: the Nazis and Japanese turned their conquests into large slave labor and resource-exploitation zones. The victorious Allies reconstructed their conquests into duplicates of their own societies, the long-range consequences of which have been happy."

In wars of the third kind, the objectives change again; wars are "[…] fought to preserve or establish a community" (Holsti, 1996: 38), which has led to the dominance of intrastate conflict after 1945. The purpose of wars of the third kind "[…] is often to politicize the masses, to turn them into good revolutionaries and/or nationalists. Civilians not only become major targets of operations, but their transformation into a new type of individual becomes a major purpose of war" (Holsti, 1996: 39). In all three types of war, the political features prominently, even if the political objectives are structurally different, combining a wide variety of achieving material and discursive dominance. If "War is merely the continuation of policy by other means," as the Prussian general von Clausewitz (2007: 28) famously wrote, then agonism is the realization of these policies by other means but war, or the rejection of the policy objectives that lead to war (such as territorial gains or the self-control of a particular political community). The material is significant here, as the political demands that constitute these objectives are very much about the material; the negotiation about these demands is a material process of decision-making; and conflict togetherness, pluralization, and peaceful and non-violent interaction are also material processes.

Also, a more cause-driven perspective can be used to highlight the material nature of agonism. Ramsbotham, Miall, and Woodhouse (2011: 133), in their overview of the relevant literature on intrastate (violent) conflict, summarized these causes, which I have grouped in three clusters. These three clusters can be used to think about the prevention of violent conflict—as Ramsbotham, Miall, and Woodhouse (2011) did—but also (and relatedly) about the role of agonism (and its materiality). First, Ramsbotham, Miall, and Woodhouse (2011: 133) referred to a series of material inequalities, including poverty, displacement, and other social stratifications (e.g., related to ethnicity or religion), which can be labeled structural violence. When we then turn to agonism, we can revert to Eagleton's (2005) surprisingly simple phrase: "[…] the only solution to terror is justice" to argue that agonism, with its peaceful and non-violent interactions, concerns the reduction of material inequalities and injustices, within the knowledge that these material differences need the discursive to be articulated as inequality and injustice. A second cluster of causes of antagonism is related to the role of government, with the lack of global structures, authoritarian rule, human rights violations, and exclusionist policies as main categories. In the inverse, we can point to the importance of peace-enhancing policies, keeping Rasmussen's (2003: 4) short statement—"Peace is a policy, not a fact"—in mind. Agonism is then (also) about material democratic and peaceful governing practices, of a careful and proportional use of the state monopoly of violence (by police and the judiciary), and integrative policies, which do not deny conflict and difference, but which embed it within pluralist democratic practices. Finally, a third cluster of the causes of antagonism is more (but not exclusively) discursive, with polarized attitudes and weak communications[60] as main categories. Also, this absence of communication, or the presence of antagonistic communication, has a material dimension,[61] where these signifying machines can, for instance, give privileged access to particular actors and the discourses they entextualize (and not to others). In contrast, agonism requires the plurality of societal actors to have access to these communicational structures, enabling them to peacefully interact and democratically participate in them, and through these signifying machines, in society.

3.3 Community Media, Diversity, Dialogue, and Agonism

This long detour bring us back to the role community media can play in the support of agonism, through the generation of agonistic signifying practices that support agonistic discourses, but also through the creation of agonistic material practices. In the discussion on the potential role of community media in relation to conflict transformation, the starting point is their capacity to facilitate internal and external diversity, as this opens up their discursive and material structures for dialogues that support agonism, with its peaceful and non-violent interactions, conflicteous togetherness, and pluralization of the self. Platform 3 will develop these issues further, but a brief overview of the scarce literature on this matter will be discussed here.

As Fraser and Restrepo Estrada (2001: 18) remarked (in relation to community radio), "Community radio, through its openness to participation to all sectors and all people in a community/ies, creates a diversity of voices and opinions on the air." Community media are not homogeneous organizations serving a homogeneous community, but enable a diversity of people to produce media content that relates to a variety of societal groups and sub-communities, mixing minority and majority cultures, ethnicities, and languages, often in the same community media (Barlow, 1988; René & Antonius, 2009; Sussman & Estes, 2005). For instance, Santana and Carpentier (2010) showed the wide variety of activist, ethnic-linguistic, subcultural, and art communities that are being served by two Belgian community/alternative radio stations. Within the multiple communities approach, a considerable number of authors argue that community media facilitate a dialogue between these sub-communities or segments of society (Gaynor & O'Brien, 2011; Martin & Wilmore, 2010; Siemering, 2000).

Community media's ability to integrate a diversity of non-professional producers embedded in a diversity of (sub-)communities, which generates, in turn, a variety of voices to be heard (or read, or viewed), enabled through their identification with a participatory-democratic discourse, also ideally positions community media as facilitators of intercultural dialogue and tolerance. Here, the explicit commitment of community media towards democratic values (earlier labeled 'substantive participation'), which renders them different from open-access media, provides a protective environment for this diversity of voices. Internally, community media can act as physical meeting places for different social groups, and externally, as platforms for these different voices. As the Council of Europe (2009) recognized in its *Declaration of the Committee of Ministers on the Role of Community Media in Promoting Social Cohesion and Intercultural Dialogue*: "In today's radically changed media landscape, community media can play an important role, notably by promoting social cohesion, intercultural dialogue and tolerance, as well as by fostering community engagement and democratic participation at local and regional level."

Obviously, this capacity to stimulate intercultural dialogue is not to be taken for granted, as it very much depends on the embeddedness of the media organizational culture in a participatory-democratic discourse, and as it is, for instance, complicated by linguistic differences. Moreover, organizing dialogue within a context of diversity generates many thresholds and difficulties. One significant problem is generated by the risk of non-democratic voices and actors entering and damaging these realms devoted to democracy and participation. At the same time, an equal number of creative democratic practices have been developed to deal with these challenges. For instance, having to deal with many different languages inhibits dialogue, but a wide variety of techniques have been developed by organizations such as the Swiss radio school klipp+klang (2009), which has been experimenting with organizing multi-linguistic dialogues, in close collaboration with Swiss community radio stations such as the Zürich-based Radio Lora.

This capacity to foster diversity, intercultural dialogue, and tolerance has made community media privileged partners in peace-building, conflict transformation, and reconciliation projects. In contrast to the more general and widely recognized capacity to stimulate intercultural dialogue, there is much less (academic) research into the more specific role of community media to strengthen peace-building, conflict transformation, and reconciliation, although there are many particular projects,[62] mainly located in the global South. In one of the rare academic publications, Anheier and Raj Isar (2007: 323–324) suggested that community media can play a mediating role in conflicts. Pavarala (2015: 16) made a similar comment, pointing to "[…] evidence from different parts of the world that community media could play a potential peace-building role in conflict-prone or post-conflict societies."

Also, Rodríguez (2000: 147; 2011) attributed a central role to community media[63] in peace-building efforts and conflict transformation. In a ground-breaking research project in the Colombian Magdalena Medio region, researchers from four universities and a regional network of community radio stations joined forces and provided rare evidence for this central role of community media in a struggle for peace (Cadavid & Moreno Martínez, 2009; see also Rodríguez, 2011). One of Rodríguez's (2011: 255) key conclusions of her analysis of Colombian community media activities stresses the *performance* of peace-building: "Instead of transmitting messages about peacebuilding to audiences, Colombian citizens' media involve audiences in, and subject audiences to, the felt, embodied experience of peace."

The lack of attention from academic researchers[64] does not imply that no community media projects aimed at peace-building and conflict resolution have been organized (see, e.g., Brown & Buckley, 2011a). Different international institutions have been instrumental in supporting peace-building activities of community media, and especially the United Nations Educational, Scientific and Cultural Organization (UNESCO) (with its Community Media Program) has been at the forefront of these initiatives (*Mainstreaming the Culture of Peace*, UNESCO, 2002; *The United Nations System-Wide Special Initiative on Africa*, in Matoko & Boafo, 1998). In addition, AMARC has been actively promoting the capacity of community media to support peace-building, especially through its women's network(s). But not all initiatives have been sustainable; for instance, the UN peacekeeping radio stations have been critiqued for combining a lack of sustainability with a lack of local embeddedness (Orme, 2010).

Community media's capacity to support conflict transformation and agonistic practices often stands in stark contrast to the role mainstream media play in conflicts, in particular when their 'home' countries are involved, whether directly or indirectly. In the case of war, strong discursive alignments often (but not always) tend to occur, as has been frequently documented (e.g., Allan & Zelizer, 2004; Aulich, 1992; Hjarvard & Kristensen, 2014). Although this phenomenon is not the topic of this book, one illustration of the role of mainstream media, in this case British cinema during the Second World War, cannot be left out: "[…] of the most valuable tasks which the cinema could perform in wartime was to project an image of the national character and the national identity that would promote support for the war effort and attract the sympathy and support of oversees allies" (Richards, 1988: 43).

As most signifying machines, mainstream media organizations have a certain but varying degree of autonomy. They are also not outside dominant discourses (see Hall, 1973). Though many involved in mainstream media organizations like to believe that they are outside the operations of ideology—what Schlesinger (1987) has called the macro-myth of independence—ideology as such, and the workings of the discourse of war with its antagonistic logic, are difficult to escape, not least because, as Kellner (1992: 58) framed it, mainstream media organizations are "a crucial site of hegemony," which also implies that they are significant targets for the propaganda efforts of parties involved in violent conflicts. To use Stewart and Carruthers's (1996: 1) words: "Governments and their militaries have always considered it important how the wars and conflicts in which they have been engaged were reported and presented to the wider public."

At the same time, we should acknowledge that online media have offered opportunities for peace-building through their capacity to "diffuse latent or existing conflicts" (Singh, 2013: 239). Even if online media can easily be used to produce antagonistic signifying practices, the decentralized nature of online media offers substantial opportunities for the production and dissemination of a wide variety of signifying practices, including those agonistic signifying practices that counter hegemonic mainstream media. Also, mainstream media have the possibilities of identifying with counter-hegemonic discourses, including agonistic discourses that have the potential to question the taken-for-grantedness of antagonism. Moreover, within mainstream journalism, critical voices and reform projects do exist, with peace journalism as one of the most prominent examples (Galtung, 1998; Keeble, Tulloch, & Zollman, 2010; Lynch, 2008; Lynch & Galtung, 2010; Lynch & McGoldrick, 2005). Lynch and McGoldrick (2005: 5) have defined peace journalism in the following way: "Peace journalism is when editors and reports make choices—of what stories to report, and how to report them—that create opportunities for society at large to consider and value non-violent responses to conflict." A few years later, Lynch (2008: 3–4—emphasis in original) emphasized that it is "[…] an advocacy position vis-à-vis journalism itself, but *it is not trying to turn journalism into something else*." Despite the interest peace journalism has generated, it remains a minority position within the mainstream journalistic field, with many critics (see Lynch, 2008: 6ff, for a discussion). Peace journalism remains, nevertheless, an important movement towards mainstream media reform in relation to their often still problematic representations of collective violence.

Community media, with its participatory logic and aptitude towards diversity and dialogue, might be better placed to play an agonistic role in conflicts, although we need to be careful not to celebrate this (potential) capacity uncritically. In the next platform of this book, I will zoom in on a case study, whose analysis will be structured through the discursive-material knot (as discussed in Platform 1), and the participatory logics of community media (as discussed in this platform).

Notes

1. The media concept is used here in a more restrictive way than in Platform 1. It refers to the traditional media studies definition(s) of media as "organised technologies which make mass communication possible" (McQuail, 1994: 10), which is (are) then extended to include "semi-mass media" (Stempel, 1996: 101) and narrowcasters. To indicate this conceptual approach, the notion of media organization is used whenever possible.
2. These two labels refer to dominant usages of participation in these academic fields. This does not imply that this dominant use is exclusive, and that these fields are homogenous. The political studies approach towards participation will be abbreviated as the political approach, for reasons of brevity.
3. Interestingly, Carey (2009) did not use the concept of ritual participation in *Communication as Culture*. He did use "ritual of participation" (Carey, 2009: 177), which refers to a very different process, namely the emptying of the signifier participation as an elitist strategy. This use of the participation concept, mainly to be found in Chapter 7 of *Communication as Culture* ('*The History of the Future*,' co-authored with Quirk), is much more aligned with the political approach towards participation.
4. Miessen (2010: 54) described romantic participation as "[…] a model of participation [that] is not only concerned with local communities, cultural and social infrastructure, and ecology, empowerment of citizen vis-a-vis local politics; it also seems to have as one of its main goals the minimization of friction."
5. See http://www.lozano-hemmer.com/body_movies.php

6. One complication is that the concept of participation itself is part of these power struggles, which renders it highly contingent. The signification of participation is part of a "politics of definition" (Fierlbeck, 1998: 177), since its specific articulation shifts depending on the ideological framework that makes use of it.
7. Despite its importance, engagement will not have a central place in this book, in order not to complicate things too much.
8. AIP stands for Access—Interaction—Participation.
9. Talisse (2013: 142) argued that the democratic models that are described in this book as more maximalist participatory models also lean towards substantive democracy.
10. Arguably, the critique on the lack of substantive participation also drives, at least partially, books such as *Participation. The New Tyranny?* (Cooke & Kothari, 2001) and *The Nightmare of Participation* (Miessen, 2010), although the defense of the expert-creator model also plays a role.
11. Agency gains a different position here, as it becomes a nodal point in the construction of the subject position of the citizen.
12. As mentioned before, empowerment, with its multi-dimensionality (Kieffer, 2014: 9), is a broad concept (which renders it structurally different from participation). Here, I am referring only to one of its aspects, namely empowerment through the increase of power positions in decision-making processes.
13. The connection between the prod-user and participatory processes is not straightforward, but this is beyond the scope of this book.
14. This concept is also used in other settings; see, for instance, Centeno and Silva's (1998) edited volume that studies Latin American technocracy.
15. This has triggered debates about 'free labor' provided to cultural industries. Terranova (2004: 74), for instance, referred in this context to free labor as "Simultaneously voluntarily given and unwanted, enjoyed and exploited." For a discussion, see Hesmondhalgh (2010).
16. Mauss (1966) placed a strong emphasis on reciprocity—which tends to downplay altruism (see Kropotkin (1972) for an alternative perspective).
17. Marres's (2012: 67) citation is taken out of its context—in the original version it refers to Locke's defense of representative democracy.
18. The decision not to participate is in itself complex, and again part of the discursive-material knot, with a combination of materials and discourses (Leeuwis, 2013: 250).
19. Selecting an overarching label for participatory/community/alternative/civil society/rhizomatic media organizations poses an insoluble semantic problem. But, since in this strategy of combining the four different models, all become structurally incorporated, the question of the appropriate label seems relatively irrelevant. In this book, community media organization is chosen as the overarching label.
20. The object of this analysis—community media organizations—of course complicates an unequivocal society-centered approach. Instead, this type of approach should be interpreted as the radical societal contextualization of community media.
21. The argument that these four approaches and concepts provide the nodal points of the community media discourse that constructs the identities of the vast diversity of community media organizations in always-different ways has generated some confusion (see Hadl

& Dongwon, 2008: 97). This theoretical strategy has no ambition to discredit the labels that specific organizations prefer to use; in contrast, it aims to offer a framework to understand the discursive and material complexities of this field.

22. For a discussion of these policy initiatives at the European level, see Jiménez and Scifo (2010).
23. The World Association of Community Radio Broadcasters is usually referred to by its French acronym AMARC, or the *Association Mondiale des Radio Diffuseurs Communautaires*. The AMARC website is at: http://www.amarc.org
24. See also Van Vuuren (2008: 16–17) for a discussion of alternative representations of community, and the potential conflict between different groups that originates from contrasting articulations of community.
25. When Feenberg (2010: 80) wrote about the democratization of technology, he did not focus on community media, but was making a much more general point, pleading for "[…] broadly constituted technical alliances [that] would take into account destructive effects of technology on the natural environment as well on human beings." More in general, Feenberg (2010: 81) used a rather negative perspective on media.
26. Others use a less optimistic formulation. For instance, Fuchs and Sandoval (2015: 173) referred to "voluntary self-exploited labour." A few pages before, they wrote: "Their voices then tend to remain marginal, and their organisations tend to be based on unpaid and voluntary work of people who in addition to media activism must earn a living in the capitalist economy […]" (Fuchs & Sandoval, 2015: 168).
27. The proposed solution in this article was to refer to 'alternative mainstream media' to cover cases such as these.
28. The importance of their individuality does not imply that media professionals do not work in teams, and that teamwork is not an important component of their subject positions (De Smedt, 2015).
29. In defining civil society, Cohen and Arrato (1992: ix) explicitly included what they called the intimate sphere. The discussion about the exact nature of civil society, and the question of which spheres to include, is beyond the objectives of this book. Here, the intimate sphere is not seen as part of civil society.
30. For a brief genealogy of the concept, see Hintz (2009).
31. The full argument Keane (1998: xviii) used in favor of civil society is "[…] the impossibility, especially in the era of computerised networks of communication media, of nurturing 'freedom of communication' without a plurality of variously seized non-state communications media."
32. Sometimes the notion of 'uncivil society' is used, which I find a too problematic concept to use here. See Clifford (2011) for a critique.
33. Of course, undemocratic discourses can also become dislocated.
34. She used the concept of media citizenship differently than Hartley (1999: 157), who focused more on mainstream media.
35. This part is short to avoid repetition. The brevity of this discussion is not meant to indicate the lack of relevance of the material for this approach.
36. It still has to be acknowledged that "[…] spheres of commodified and non-commodified labour are not wholly separate and discrete" (Williams, 2014: 107).

37. Deleuze and Guattari's work is situated within the field of epistemology. Here I focus more on organizational structures that are seen as the sedimentation of the arbolic and/or rhizomatic ways of thinking.
38. Stage and Ingerslev (2015: 134) referred to "momentary equality," which is related to this discussion.
39. Also here, this discussion is brief to avoid repetition.
40. The images that Mitchell described are the virile and moral self and the alien intruder within the self-images on the one hand, and the black-top and puppet (enemy) leadership, the 'pro-us' (enemy) people and the unified enemy images on the other.
41. We should also not forget the very first lines of the United Nations Educational, Scientific and Cultural Organization (2014: 5) Constitution: "The Governments of the States Parties to this Constitution on behalf of their peoples declare: That since wars begin in the minds of men, it is in the minds of men that the defences of peace must be constructed."
42. Also, Žižek (2008: 1), in his "triumvirate" of subjective, systemic, and symbolic violence, discussed the importance of the violence that is "[…] embodied in language and its forms […]." Žižek (2008: 61) argued that language in itself has a violent dimension: "[…] there is some violent in the very symbolization of a thing, which equals its mortification."
43. At one point Mouffe (1993: 130—my emphasis) referred to symbolic violence in a way that seems to indicate a problematic hierarchy between symbolic and other forms of violence, when she wrote: "Where there is power, force and violence cannot be completely eliminated, even though these may *only* take the form of 'force of argument' or 'symbolic violence.'"
44. For a brief discussion on the relationship between pacifism and other religions (e.g., Jainism, Buddhism, Judaism, and Islam), see Ellwood and Alles (2007: 331).
45. See, for instance, Evangelista (1999) on the Pugwash movement. A concept related to 'academic activism' is 'academic diplomacy' (Wallenstein, 2009).
46. Realism is not to be conflated with *Realpolitik*. Unfortunately, this conflation seems to occur frequently in the field of conflict resolution.
47. Jackson (2008: 172) used constructivism referring to what is labeled constructionism in this book.
48. The use of the word 'only' indicates a preference for a particular answer to this question, which privileges the use of the conflict resolution concept.
49. Although Schmitt converted to Nazism, his theoretical work remains important. As Mouffe (1999a: 52) wrote: "Schmitt is an adversary from whom we can learn, because we can draw on his insights. Turning them against him, we should use them to formulate a better understanding of liberal democracy."
50. When discussing antagonism in connection to war in earlier work, I have labeled this the ideological model of war (Carpentier, 2008).
51. This is in line with, for instance, Haraway's (1991) analysis of the components of the dichotomy as interdependent.
52. Mueller (1973) used this metaphor to describe political support for U.S. presidents, but in my text, the "rallying round the flag" metaphor is used in a broader sense.
53. https://georgewbush-whitehouse.archives.gov/news/releases/2001/09/20010920-8.html

54. Their potential occurrence remains for Mouffe (2013a: 1) important, as this "[...] impedes the full totalization of society and forecloses the possibility of a society beyond division and power," but this analysis is made without any hint of celebration for the existence of antagonistic self-other relationships.
55. Deveaux (1999: 20) disagreed with this critique, and briefly mentioned (in a footnote) that "[...] the agonistic dimension of Arendt's account of action is often ignored in favor of 'communicative' and 'dialogical' interpretations [...]."
56. The articulation of agonism with a "shared set of rules" (Mouffe, 2005: 52) is problematic, as it suggests that antagonism (proper) is not structured by regulatory frameworks. For instance, even if the so-called *jus in bello* (as part of the law of war) is not always respected, it does exist and provides a shared regulatory framework for belligerent actors.
57. At least in the 20th-century version of this concept. Later, the logic of difference gains an alternative meaning, referring to the role of a particularity in constructing social reality. In Laclau's (2005: 78) words, the creation of chains of difference leads to the "[...] assertion of a particularity [...] whose only links to other particularities are of a differential nature ([...] no positive terms, only differences)."
58. This articulation of the (good) other-neighbor is not without alternatives, though. For instance, Painter (2012: 524) pointed out that the other-neighbor is more of an "unknown" in "highly urbanized societies [...]," and Žižek (2008: 59) (following Freud) labeled the other-neighbor "[...] a thing, a traumatic intruder, someone whose different way of life [...] disturbs us, throws the balance of our way of life off the rails, when it comes too close." In his inimitable style, Žižek (2008: 166—emphasis in original) wrote: "[...] a Neighbour is one who per definition *smells*."
59. See, for instance, Graham (2006) for a critical analysis of the construction of the city of Fallujah as a strategic target.
60. 'Weak communication' is a concept that hides too many complexities, as this problem not only concerns the lack of communication between societal actors, but also the use of what I prefer to call antagonistic communication, where enemies address each other as enemies, and what Ramsbotham confusingly called 'agonistic dialogue.' In a footnote, Ramsbotham, Miall, and Woodhouse (2011: 434–435) clarified the difference with Mouffe's use of the agonism concept.
61. See also the earlier discussion on the material components of community media.
62. These projects also generate reports, of course. See, for instance, Lykke Brorson (2016).
63. As mentioned before, Rodríguez called them citizens' media.
64. A few exceptions are listed in Rodríguez (2011: 20). See also Baú's (2014a, 2014b, 2015) work on participatory video. Some other research projects (e.g., Curtis, 2000) use the label 'local media,' but in practice analyze national media, and not so much community media, even though it is not always easy to discriminate between these types of media organizations.

PLATFORM 3

· 3 ·

THE CYPRUS CONFLICT

After the theoretical elaborations in the first two platforms, the ontology of the discursive-material knot, with its methodological translation into discourse-material analysis, will be used to analyze a particular case study. Of course, the second platform already paved the way for a case study analysis that focuses on participation, community media, and conflict transformation, as it developed the tertiary sensitizing concepts that will be used to support this case study analysis. It might not come as a surprise when the case study discussed in this platform analyzes a particular community media organization and its role in conflict transformation, or, in other words, in the transformation of antagonism into agonism.

Given the complex nature of the workings of the discursive-material knot, and its many layers, this case study zooms in on one particular community media organization, the Cyprus Community Media Centre (CCMC). This, rather automatically, also brings us to Cyprus,[1] one of the European countries characterized by a long-lasting conflict. Cyprus has been geographically and ethnically divided since 1974, when the Turkish Army invaded the north and occupied more than one third of the island, after decades of inter-communal collective violence between the two main communities on the island, Greek Cypriots and Turkish Cypriots.

Cyprus is a small island in the Eastern Mediterranean, with a surface area of 9,251 square kilometers and a population of about 1,15 million people,[2] but the country's political and historical complexity is the inverse of its size. When Lawrence Durrell published his book *Bitter Lemons* in 1957, in which he wrote about his 3-year stay in Cyprus (from 1953 to 1956), he wrote that "[…] the vagaries of fortune and the demons of ill luck dragged Cyprus into the stock market of world affairs" (Durrell, 2012: 100). Without subscribing to Durrell's explanation of Cyprus's ill luck and to his rather exclusive focus on the international dimension of the conflict, this sentence still contains a hint of the dramatic and intense nature of what is often termed the Cyprus Problem. Durrell's focus, and his omissions, also give a first idea of the difficulty of grasping the political complexity of the Cyprus Problem.

Dealing with this political complexity, through the gaze of the discursive-material knot, is also the challenge that this platform faces up to. Platform 3 aims to study how a participatory community media organization, CCMC, with its webradio, MYCYradio, intervenes in this long-lasting conflict, and how this organizational machine is attempting to contribute to the transformation of antagonism into agonism, through its participatory-democratic dynamics. The platform also analyzes how the discursive-material knot functions in social reality, or, in other words, how the discursive and the material interact in and through the practices of CCMC.

In order to provide understandable answers to these questions, another long detour is needed, which consists of a detailed description and analysis of the case study context. This chapter contains this contextual analysis, which is performed in two steps: In the first step, a factual overview of the history of the Cyprus Problem is provided. Even though each set of practices or events could be unpacked as an assemblage, and scrutinized in depth through a discursive-material analysis, this would take-up too much space and time. Instead, the choice was made to suspend the discursive-material analysis, and to re-analyze this basic and factual historical overview only in a second step, applying the lens of the discursive-material knot to bring out the key role of nationalism.[3] The textual analysis in part one is combined with my own photographic work (which, in Cyprus, focused on the memorializations of the Cyprus Problem), adding a visual-analytical component to this part.[4]

After the contextual analysis, the attention turns to CCMC itself in Chapter 4, and the case study. The first main part focuses on CCMC and MYCYradio's participatory dimension, while the second main part deals with their contribution to conflict transformation. The relationship between participation and agonism is further highlighted in the concluding reflections at the end of Chapter 4.

1 A Contextual Analysis of the Cyprus Problem

Any analysis of the Cyprus Problem, which is, given its long duration, necessarily historical, involves more than the traditional problems related to historical research. It would be naïve and arrogant, and in full contradiction with the constructionist paradigm used in this book, to assume that one particular historical analysis, academic or otherwise, can offer the final and ultimate interpretation of a specific set of practices and events from the past, even though this should not dissuade analysts from offering plausible attempts.

Zooming in on the history of a particular region of the world also produces the risk of decontextualization, with practices and events in other parts of the world, sometimes interconnected with that region, disappearing into the background. For instance, global and long-term processes such as the Cold War, the process of decolonization, the conflicts in the Middle-East, Africa, and Asia, and the economic crises, all involved a wide variety of discursive-material assemblages, and assemblages of assemblages, that all impacted on the Cyprus Problem. 1974, the year that the Turkish Army invaded Cyprus, was one of the years of dislocation and destruction in Cyprus, but many other dislocatory, and sometimes destructive, events took place in that very same year. 1974 was, for instance, also the year of the end of the OPEC oil embargo, the Carnation Revolution in Portugal, the dethroning of the Ethiopian emperor Haile Selassie, a Provisional IRA bombing campaign in the UK, and the resignation of the U.S. president Richard Nixon (following Watergate). The year before, the signing of the Paris Peace Accords implied the end of the U.S. involvement in Vietnam, and the Yom Kippur War raged in Israel and its neighboring countries. Not all these processes and events can be addressed here, but, to use another formulation, the myopia that writing a particular history produces should at least be acknowledged.

In the case of the Cyprus Problem, there are a number of particular issues that are added to the more traditional problems of historical analysis. Even though it is hard to escape the impression that Cyprus never managed to attract much more than superfluous international consideration, the number of publications on the Cyprus Problem, also written by non-Cypriots, is simply impressive. Dealing with the abundance of literature on the Cyprus Problem is both a luxury and a problem, especially when one aims to generate an overview of the entire period related to the Cyprus Problem that is respectful of historical non-linearity and complexity, whilst many practical restrictions worked against one consulting primary sources.

Moreover, the Cypriot Problem itself impacts on the historical signifying practices, including some of the academic ones, because these signifying practices are often highly politicized. This implies that navigating through the literature on the Cyprus Problem felt a bit like meandering through an intellectual minefield, where one can only hope to make it through unscarred. From a discursive-material perspective, it is, of course, no surprise that the (re) discursifications of practices and events—or of discourses—from the past are part of discursive struggles, but this obviously does not make the analyst's life any easier, in particular when the differences between the historical signifying practices in the north and south of Cyprus are quite radical, as Richmond (1999: 42) also ascertained:

> "It is important to note that the two communities in Cyprus, and their motherlands, have completely different perceptions of the history of the island; 'history' (i.e. the struggle for liberation) ended in 1974 for the Turkish Cypriots and began then for Greek Cypriots."

In particular, the nationalist interpretations of history tend to complicate the development of plausible academic-historical analyses. I (briefly) want to illustrate this problem by referring to two publications. The first example is Spryridakis's book (1974: 164), *A Brief History of Cyprus*, in which he wrote: "The Turks[5] made no intellectual or cultural contribution worth mentioning." On the next page, he concluded his chapter, '*The Role of the Archbishop of Cyprus as Ethnarch*,' as follows:

> "The Turkish rule of Cyprus ended in 1878. The scholar of the history of Cyprus [...] is forced to bypass 300 years of barrenness and desolation. The few oases flourishing in this vast desert of Turkish occupation are proofs of the undying and indomitable Hellenic faith in the human spirit." (Spryridakis, 1974: 165)

In the history chapter of the *North Cyprus Almanack*, an official publication of the TRNC[6] (1987), we find a different evaluation of the Ottoman period:

> "The Turks were greeted as liberators by the local population, who were treated with consideration in return. They abolished serfdom, recognized the supremacy of the Orthodox community over all other Christian dominations, and restored the

> Orthodox Archbishopric. Above all, the Cypriots were integrated into that remarkable institution known as the Millet system [...] which for centuries provided members of religious minorities within the Ottoman Empire with more freedom than was enjoyed by such groups anywhere in Europe."

The presence of these kinds of nationalist sentiments is, of course, understandable in the context of the Cypriot Problem, but it still produces a challenge for those who want to write a fair and balanced academic historical narration. At the same time, a thorough and careful literature review, based on the identification of reliable Cypriot and non-Cypriot authors, and on a continuous engagement with the unavoidable contradictions between Greek Cypriot and Greek, and Turkish Cypriot and Turkish (academic) narrations, remains possible, resulting in the historical analysis in the following two subparts.

2 A Brief Historical Overview of the Cyprus Problem

Cyprus is situated at a strategic location in the Mediterranean Sea, which has resulted in the island becoming a crossroads of a multitude of movements and currents. In all probability, Cyprus's first permanent inhabitants arrived from Anatolia and the Levant, with later populations also settling in from the Aegean (Karageorghis, 1982; Knapp, 2008, 2013; Steiner & Killebrew, 2014). As Hill (2010: 488–489) wrote:

> "Archaeological and anthropological research has shown that the primitive population of Cyprus was an offshoot from the regions of Asia Minor and North Syria and formed the bulk of the people of Cyprus as early as the Stone Age. In the earlier Bronze Age Cyprus received a further strong addition to its population from Asia Minor. The Greek, Phoenician and Egyptian strata were superimposed on this original foundation."

After a number of different kingdoms enjoyed an early stretch of independence, the island went through Assyrian, Persian, Hellenic, Roman, Byzantine, Lusignan, Venetian, Ottoman, and British periods (Mirbagheri, 2010: xxi–xxxi). All of these movements crystallized into two, currently separately living, populations—Greek Cypriots and Turkish Cypriots—along with a series of (religious) minorities such as Armenians, Maronites, and Latins,[7] as well as, amongst others, Brits, Turks, Greeks, Russians, and Filipinos. Despite the relevance of these earlier periods, my historical overview starts in 1570.

2.1 Cyprus in the Ottoman Empire

Cyprus became a part of the Ottoman Empire in 1571—a result of the Ottoman-Venetian War (Jennings, 1993: 5). The Ottoman Army landed on Cyprus on 1 July 1570, and turned against Nicosia first. The city fell on 9 September 1570 (Konstam, 2003: 10). Famagusta, the last city to hold out, fell into Ottoman hands on 4 September 1571 (Konstam, 2003: 10). During the Ottoman rule, a garrison with a nominal strength of about 4,000 soldiers (De Groot, 1954: 305; Hill, 2010: 10, 13) remained on the island, but it was (in particular in the later centuries) understaffed and underpaid, which led to "[…] all sorts of outrages" (Hill, 2010: 13). Also, in the years after the conquest, about 20,000 Ottomans either remained on the island after the army moved out, or were brought to Cyprus to settle (Hill, 2010: 21).

After Cyprus became part of the Ottoman Empire, the Greek-Orthodox Church was allowed to remain active on the island, in contrast to the Latin (Catholic) Church, which was banned. Hill (2010: 316) described how the Cypriot Greek-Orthodox bishops enjoyed "[…] very considerable power, as is apparent from the political history of the island, especially from the middle of the eighteenth century onwards to the catastrophe of 1821." They became responsible for the tribute payable by the island to the Ottoman regime. As the bishops could not collect taxes themselves, they delegated that responsibility to the Dragoman (Hill, 2010: 16–17), who was appointed by the bishops. The Ottoman regime relentlessly extracted taxes from the island, legally and illegally. A situation where the Ottoman officials were not sufficiently paid, "[…] left them a free hand to squeeze the population as dry as they possibly could" (Hill, 2010: 25). The economic oppression[8] caused several revolts, for instance, in 1764 (Hill, 2010: 80ff), 1804 (Hill, 2010: 107ff), and 1833 (Hill, 2010: 157ff).[9] As Panayiotou (2012: 73) wrote: "The class composition of these uprisings seems to have been to a large extent peasant, and the 'cause' seems to have been the rise of a new 'class' of tax collectors and traders in the broader context of the incorporation of the Ottoman Empire into the world economy."

The situation in Cyprus worsened in 1821, during the Greek War of Independence, aimed at gaining independence from the Ottoman Empire. It resulted in the creation of the Kingdom of Greece by virtue of the 1832 Treaty of Constantinople between Britain, France, and Russia on the one hand, and the Ottoman Empire on the other. At that stage, the Greek Kingdom only consisted of the most southern part of what is now mainland Greece (including the Peloponnese). As Rizopoulou-Egoumenidou (2010: 105) wrote, there was no direct Cypriot involvement in the Greek War of Independence, but there was still Cypriot support for Greek independence, for instance, through the delivery of supplies (Bryant, 2008: 410; Hill, 2010: 125; Karakasis, 2014: 16; Nevzat, 2005: 80; Rizopoulou-Egoumenidou, 2010: 105), and through the Cypriot involvement in the Greek 'Society of Friends' [*Filiki Eteria*], which had been preparing the Greek uprising (Michael, 2013: 57).

Even if the Cypriot involvement was limited (see also De Groot, 1954: 306), the consequences were more than severe for Cyprus. The Ottoman Governor, Küchkük Mehmed, asked and received reinforcements, and recommended "[…] the execution of all the leading Christians in the island, from the Archbishop downwards" (Hill, 2010: 125). Sultan Mahmud first hesitated, but then ordered the disarmament of the Christians, and later the execution of the 486 men "[…] who were wealthy and influential with the people, and had friends in Greece and Europe" (Hill, 2010: 128). On 9 July 1821, the executions started: Three leading laymen and three bishops were beheaded, and archbishop Kyprianos (and his archdeacon and secretary) were hanged. Hill (2010: 135) estimated that the killings went on for a month.

Figure 20. Mausoleum to the Cypriot national martyrs of 9 July 1821, Nicosia.
Source: Nico Carpentier.

This 1821 massacre "[…] marked the end of the elite of Cyprus and its lifestyle" (Rizopoulou-Egoumenidou, 2010: 106). In the decade to come, "Several hundreds […]" of Cypriots would fight "[…] as volunteers for the liberation of Greece" (Rizopoulou-Egoumenidou, 2010: 106), feeding the Cypriot desire for *enosis*, or unification with Greece.

2.2 The British Period

When the power of the Ottoman Empire receded, the island came under the control of the UK, first as a protectorate (between 1878 and 1914), as part of an agreement between the UK and Turkey to protect the latter against Russian expansion (Mallinson, 2005: 10). During the British rule, the relationship between Greek Cypriots and Turkish Cypriots aggravated, resulting in the first inter-communal clashes in May 1912. In a series of incidents, several Cypriots were killed, and about 150 were injured (Varnava, 2009: 189; see also Bryant, 2004: 91–92; Mirbagheri, 2010: xxviii).

At the start of the First World War, the island was then annexed by the UK (on 5 November 1914—Soulioti, 2006: 4), a state of affairs that was recognized by Turkey in the Lausanne Treaty of 1923. In 1925 Cyprus became a British crown colony (Markides, 2006: 32). These institutional changes did not undo the desire for *enosis* within a substantial part of the Greek Cypriots, even if Greece's political-military strength had been severely weakened, and the 'Megali idea' (the unification of all Greek-speaking territories) had been thoroughly frustrated, during the Greek-Turkish war of 1919–1922. This so-called 'Asia Minor Catastrophe' (from a Greek perspective) ended the millennia-old Greek presence in Asia Minor. It was immediately followed by the fall of the Ottoman Empire and the abolishment of the sultanate. The Republic of Turkey was established on 29 October 1923, with Mustafa Kemal Atatürk as its first president.

On Cyprus, nationalist sentiments and economic grievances (Faustmann, 2008b: 47–50; Richmond, 1998: 70; Soulioti, 2006: 17; Stefanidis, 1999: 1) triggered anti-British riots in October 1931. These so-called *Oktovriana* (October) riots again left several Cypriots dead, and British Government House was burned down. The British regime responded by deporting some of those involved in the riots, imprisoning others, dismantling the Legislative Council (Cyprus's consultative body—see Akgün, 2012), banning political parties, censoring the press, prohibiting the Greek flag being flown, and (a few years later, in 1937) restricting the autonomy of the Cypriot-Orthodox

Church (Bryant, 2004: 129; Calame & Charlesworth, 2011: 126; Soulioti, 2006: 17–18). Stefanidis (1999: 1) described this new political situation as "a bureaucratic autocracy," while Richter (2006) used the term "benevolent autocracy."

When the Second World War started, large numbers of Cypriots volunteered to fight in the British army, despite the tensions, and in many cases before Greece was attacked by Italy in October 1940 (and later by Germany in 1941), and obviously well before Turkey declared war against Germany in February 1945. Asmussen (2006: 167, 170) estimated the number of Cypriots engaged in armed combat to be between 30,000 and 35,000, while Calame and Charlesworth (2011: 126) wrote that "[…] approximately 37,000 Greek- and Turkish-speaking Cypriot volunteers served in several branches of the British armed forces during World War II." When discussing the motivation of these volunteers to join the British Army, Asmussen (2006: 172ff) pointed to the hope for *enosis*-as-reward that lived amongst many Greek Cypriots, combined with the need to assist 'motherland' Greece. On the Turkish Cypriot side, there were economic motivations, but also the feeling that only Greek Cypriots volunteering would bring the island closer to *enosis*.

In 1941 the strong grip of the British colonial power on Cyprus weakened, for internal and external reasons (Yiangou, 2012: 1). This was partially because of the Cypriot war efforts (Asmussen, 2006: 173), but also because of changes in the Mediterranean war theatre, and, in particular, the Nazi occupation of Greece in that year. The loosening of the grip, in turn, led to a revival of Cypriot political life. That very same year, the Progressive Working People's Party (AKEL)[10] and the Pancyprian Federation of Labor (PEO) were established (Adams, 1971: 22; Katsourides, 2014: 187–188; Stefanidis, 1999: 2), immediately gaining a strong position at the 1943 municipal elections. Also, the Turkish Cypriots become more organized, establishing the Cyprus Turkish Minority Association (KATAK) in 1943, with the breakaway Cyprus Turkish National People's Party[11] established by Fazil Küçük 1 year later (Soulioti, 2006: 49; Stefanidis, 1999: 3). The labor movement had already mobilized Cypriots earlier, at the start of the Second World War, responding with collective action to what Yiangou (2012: 35) called the "[…] intense economic dislocation […]" that the outbreak of war brought. These strikes were seen by government as "[…] the result of communist influence, but the growth of the restless labour movement was also clearly due to increasing unemployment" (Yiangou, 2012: 35). After the Second World War, AKEL consolidated its position in the 1947 municipal elections, which also forced the right to regroup and restructure itself, in alliance with the Church and its new archbishop, Michael Mouskos, or Makarios of Kyrenia (who would later become Cyprus's first president).

Figure 21. The statue of Makarios of Kyrenia in front of the archbishop's palace, Nicosia. Source: Nico Carpentier.

While after the Second World War the political situation in Cyprus (and even more so in Greece, because of the Greek Civil War) was tumultuous, something that "[…] owed more to the Left-Right division within the Greek Cypriot community than to nationalist passions" (Stefanidis, 1999: 3), Greek Cypriots still continued to rally for *enosis*. In December 1949 the Orthodox Church announced a plebiscite on the *enosis* question, much to the concern of the British colonial regime. When the votes were counted, at the end of January 1950, it turned out that 96.5% of the votes favored integration with Greece (Holland, 1993: 149).

In this period, Cyprus also became an item on the international agenda. After the Greek government forces (backed by the UK and the USA) had defeated the Greek Communists in the Greek Civil War at the end of 1949, the Greek government(s) could become more vocal in supporting Cypriot *enosis* (Stefanidis, 1999: 7), responding positively to Greek Cypriot (and popular Greek) pressure. As the UK dismissed Greek and Greek Cypriot calls for *enosis*, an internationalization strategy was developed, which also involved the USA, as both Greece and Turkey had joined the North Atlantic Treaty Organization (NATO) on 18 February 1952. The UK and USA had strongly insisted on these countries' NATO membership, as part of a strategy to "[…] establish their political influence and preponderance in the whole area of the Eastern Mediterranean and the Middle East" (Chourchoulis, 2014: 28). The stabilization of NATO's 'southern flank,' and the reduction of Greek-Turkish enmity, would remain a key USA policy for decades. But the Cypriot internationalization strategy also implied a strong commitment to the Non-Aligned Movement—Makarios was one of the participants at the Bandung Conference in 1955, and in 1961, the then established Republic of Cyprus would become one of the Non-Aligned Movement's founding countries at the Belgrade Conference (Anagnostopoulou, 2013: 258).

On 20 August 1954, Greece placed the Cyprus issue on the agenda of the United Nations General Assembly (Stefanidis, 1999: 74), but this diplomatic initiative failed to produce the desired outcome. Also, in that very same period, Turkey changed its policy and became more involved. Before, the official government line had been that there was no Cyprus issue, as Cyprus was a British colony (Özkan, 2015: 1, 12). Özkan (2015: 6—see also Baruh & Popescu, 2008: 80) confirmed this increased interest: "[…] from the early 1950s onwards, newspapers saw an upsurge in nationalist writings about Cyprus." And he continued: "Starting in 1954, the dream of annexing Cyprus became a national cause in Turkey" (Özkan, 2015: 7). That very same year, the Cyprus-is-Turkish Committee[12] was set up (Özkan, 2015: 7) and turned out to be highly successful, through a mixture of Turkish nationalism and virulent anti-communism. Later, the Turkish policy would come to focus on the partition (*taksim*) of the island.

2.3 The Independence War and the Independence of Cyprus

The pressure continued to build up, and in the mid-1950s, EOKA [*Ethniki Organosis Kyprion Agoniston*], led by the right-wing Georgios Grivas, who had been an officer in the Greek Army, politically supported by archbishop Makarios, launched a violent campaign against British rule, with the combined objectives of self-determination and *enosis*. EOKA officially announced the start of (what they called) the liberation struggle on 1 April 1955, with a series of bomb attacks. With a small group of between 250 and 300 guerrillas, and the support of an estimated 25,000 civilians (Demetriou, 2007), EOKA's leader Grivas had no intention to tackle the British head-on, but relied on sabotage and small-scale killings, combined with propaganda and strengthened by the passive resistance of the Greek Cypriot population.

Figure 22. Entrance of the EOKA struggle (1955–1959) commemoration site in Avgorou. Source: Nico Carpentier.

EOKA not only targeted the British, but also Greek Cypriots and the Cypriot police, which consisted of Turkish Cypriots to a relatively high degree (Faustmann, 2008b: 52–53; Sant Cassia, 2005: 19). After the anti-Greek pogrom in Istanbul, on 6 and 7 September 1955 (Papadakis, 2005: 20), which was directly related to the Cyprus Problem (Özkan, 2015: 8), Turkish Cypriots were more often targeted, which led to the establishment of Volkan, later integrated into the Turkish Resistance Organization (TMT). TMT in turn targeted Greek Cypriots, but also leftist Turkish Cypriots, and demanded *taksim* (Cockburn, 2004: 47–48).

The British field marshal John Harding, who became Governor of Cyprus on 3 October 1955, chose a military strategy, resulting in a situation described by Grivas (Grivas-Dighenis, 1964: 46) as follows: "Instead, the British flooded Cyprus with troops, so that one met a soldier at every step, with the only result that they offered plenty of targets and so sustained casualties." Grivas also used what Carruthers (1994: 228) called enforcement terror, where EOKA attacked Greek (and Turkish) Cypriots that were seen as ideological opponents and/or collaborators with the British. Furthermore, EOKA provoked

Figure 23. One of the Kokkinotrimithia detention camp barracks.
Source: Nico Carpentier.

the British into severe counter-measures, including the opening up of detention camps, and the use of torture (Cobain, 2012). The British regime also increased its reliance on Turkish Cypriots to man the police force, which further triggered inter-communal tensions and violence. The combination of this, as Corum (2008: 108) wrote, resulted in "[…] further alienating the Greek Cypriot population" and forced "[…] the whole Greek [Cypriot] community to support EOKA simply to provide some protection from the government forces and the Turk[ish Cypriot]s," despite the fact that "[…] many Greek[Cypriot]s had been reluctant to support EOKA's campaign of violence […]" (Corum, 2008: 111).

The EOKA strategy turned out to be effective, and on 9 March 1959, EOKA declared that it had reached its objectives, after the Zürich and London Agreements were concluded in February 1959, between Turkey, Greece, the UK, and the two Cypriot community leaders. Grivas left the island, but then heavily attacked Makarios in July 1959, for the concessions the latter had made, which "[…] sharply divided […]" "[…] the right wing of the Greek Cypriot community" (Faustmann, 2006: 416). Matters were made worse by the *Deniz* incident, when, on 18 October 1959, a British naval patrol found two cases of ammunition on board the Turkish ship *Deniz*, indicating that "[…] the Turkish Cypriots were arming themselves as a precaution against future troubles or a breakdown in the negotiations" (Faustmann, 2006: 416).

Nevertheless, Makarios was elected president on 13 December 1959, parliamentary elections were held in July and early August 1960, and Cyprus was declared an independent state on 16 August 1960, with its independence guaranteed by Greece, Turkey, and the UK (Faustmann, 2006: 417–418). The UK[13] retained control (through the Treaty of Establishment) over two bases on Cyprus, namely the Dhekelia and Akrotiri Sovereign Base Areas, and various communication facilities scattered over the island, the so-called "Retained Sites" (Constandinos, 2012: 28). The Treaty of Alliance allowed Greece and Turkey to each station a small military force (with a specified number of soldiers) on the island. Obviously, the independence of Cyprus meant that Greek Cypriot aim of *enosis* was not achieved, in part because of Turkish Cypriot and Turkish opposition. Their plea for *taksim* (division) was not realized either (Michael, 2011: 24). The Treaty of Guarantee explicitly forbade the union with any other country, or the island's secession.

The 1960 constitution created a complex governing structure with a strong protection of the Turkish Cypriots, which—as Hannay (2005: 4) remarked—"[…] could only ever have worked smoothly with a high degree of

Figure 24. Liberty statue in Nicosia.
Source: Nico Carpentier.

cooperation between the two sides; in the hands of people who were in no way motivated to try to make it work, it provided a recipe for deadlock and frustration." This constitution,[14] which is formally still in effect, defines the Greek Cypriot community and Turkish Cypriot community through a combination of origins, language, cultural traditions, and religion. The different powers are all constituted through a careful (and quantified) balance between Greek Cypriots and Turkish Cypriots. To give one instance: The president of the Republic of Cyprus is a Greek Cypriot,[15] and the vice-president Turkish Cypriot.[16]

2.4 The Return to Violence After Independence

After independence, tensions between the two communities did not disappear, despite these many constitutional safeguards. The multitude of rules aimed at protect the Turkish Cypriots were contested by many Greek Cypriots that favored a majoritarianist model (see later). This led to strong political disagreements, which ended in political deadlock (Mirbagheri, 2014: 18; Pericleous, 2009: 92ff; Safty, 2011: 83–84). Both Greek Cypriots and Turkish Cypriots had already developed plans to 'solve' the deadlock, with the Greek

Cypriot Akritas Plan being the most (in)famous (Mirbagheri, 2010: 7). At the end of November 1963, President Makarios proposed to change the Cypriot constitutional structure, with 13 amendments that mostly favored the Greek Cypriots, and that implied a shift in the direction of the majoritarianist model (Safty, 2011: 89).

New violence erupted on Bloody Christmas, in the night of 20 to 21 December 1963, triggered by an incident where an identity check by Greek Cypriot police went wrong (Calame & Charlesworth, 2011: 132; Dodd, 1993: 13). At the very end of 1963, representatives of Greek Cypriots, Turkish Cypriots, Greece, Turkey, and the British military forces—the latter had acted as a peacekeeping force before UNFICYP—agreed on a military border bifurcating Nicosia. Drafted on a map with a green pencil, on the early morning of 29 December 1963, this so-called Green Line would divide Nicosia until today (Calame & Charlesworth, 2011: 132–133). The rest of Cyprus would follow later.

The power-sharing structure completely collapsed when Turkish Cypriot politicians withdrew from the Cypriot governance structures early in the new year of 1964 (Safty, 2011: 94). When they attempted to return, the Greek

Figure 25. Paphos Gate fortifications in Nicosia.
Source: Nico Carpentier.

Cypriot (part of) government required them to accept the constitutional changes that Makarios had introduced, supported by a vote of confidence in the House of Representatives on 3 February 1964 (Safty, 2011: 94). The international community did not respond to the appeals of Turkish Cypriot politicians, claiming to not want to interfere in Cyprus's internal affairs (Yakinthou, 2009: 34).

This launched a phase in the conflict that is called the 'enclave period' (Morag, 2004), where most Turkish Cypriots withdrew into fortified enclaves scattered over the island. In an attempt to contain the conflict, a United Nations peacekeeping force, UNFICYP, was established in March 1964.[17] In the same month, Turkey threatened a military intervention (Nome, 2013: 62), and a few months later, on 4 June 1964, the Turkish cabinet decided to invade, only to back down under U.S. pressure (Nome, 2013: 55). In August 1964, the Greek Cypriot National Guard, led by Grivas, who had returned to Cyprus in June 1964, then attacked the Turkish Cypriot villages of Kokkina and Mansoura that were used by Turkish Cypriots (and Turkey) to land weapons and fighters (Bryant, 2012). Mansoura was evacuated by UNFICYP and is now one of the abandoned villages on the island, but Kokkina held out, with the support of the Turkish Air Force (Bryant, 2012). At a more general level, attempts to reach a negotiated settlement failed, complicated (amongst many other factors) by the coup d'état of the Greek junta on 21 April 1967 (Cockburn, 2004: 54–55; Richmond, 1998: 79–80), which made Makarios and his supporters more careful in their desire for *enosis* (Faustmann & Ker-Lindsay, 2008: 68).

Tensions further increased in the late 1960s, after an attack on the Turkish Cypriot village of Kofinou and the mixed village of Agios Theodhoros in November 1967, followed by a Turkish ultimatum toward Greece, which led to the withdrawal of Grivas and 7,000 Greek soldiers (Faustmann & Ker-Lindsay, 2008: 68). This was followed by the Turkish Cypriot proclamation of the Provisional Cyprus Turkish Administration on 28 December 1967 (Göktepe, 2005; Safty, 2011: 135) and the start of bi-communal talks in June 1968 (Faustmann & Ker-Lindsay, 2008: 68–69). These talks would later strand on Makarios' refusal to grant the Turkish Cypriots local autonomy. In the summer of 1968 the Greek Cypriot forces withdrew from around the enclaves, leaving the Turkish Cypriots free to leave, even though "[…] most of the Turkish Cypriot inhabitants continued to prefer the difficult conditions among their 'own' people rather than the potential to enjoy a higher-standard of living amongst the Greek Cypriots […]" (Morag, 2004: 601).

The Greek military junta contributed to the rising tensions within the Greek Cypriot community itself. Several right-wing organizations, including the National Front, were established. The latter "launched a series of terrorist activities against the Cyprus administration in late 1969 and 1970" (Uslu, 2003: 108). For instance, on 8 March 1970, Makarios survived an assassination attempt. The conflict received yet another impetus with the establishment of the Greek Cypriot paramilitary organization EOKA-B in 1971, led by Grivas, who had secretly returned to the island. In Greece, the leader of the junta, Georgios Papadopoulos, was replaced by (even more of a) hardliner Dimitrios Ioannides, in November 1973. The latter strongly supported EOKA-B, Grivas, and "[…] an enosis solution to the problem […]" (Faustmann & Ker-Lindsay, 2008: 69). In the meantime, EOKA-B was countered by paramilitary (or 'parastate') groups from the Left (AKEL and EDEK), and Makarios' own paramilitary unit, the Police Tactical Reserve Unit (Borowiec, 2000: 80; Henn, 2004: 173). When Makarios then "[…] publicly accused the Colonels in Athens of being in league with EOKA B […]" and "[…] demanded that the mainland officers (650) and half the National Guard of 10,000 be withdrawn" (Anthias & Ayres, 1983: 73), the Greek junta, who controlled the Cypriot National Guard through its Greek officers, staged a coup on 15 July 1974, which was quickly joined by EOKA-B.[18] President Makarios was replaced (for 8 days) by Nikos Sampson, who used the time to attempt to further purge the island of Greek Cypriot "[…] leftists and democrats […]" (Cockburn, 2004: 65–66), intensifying this (Greek Cypriot) civil war.

This coup led to the Turkish military invasion[19] on 20 July 1974, immediately followed by the collapse of the Greek military junta, and the coupist regime in Cyprus, on 23 July 1974. Initially, the Turkish forces only captured a small corridor in the north of Cyprus, but in a second phase of the invasion from 14 to 16 August 1974, they captured the entire northern part of the island. EOKA-B responded by massacring more than 200 Turkish Cypriots in the villages of Maratha, Santalaris, Aloda, and Tochni on 14 August 1974 (Copeaux, 2008: 263).

The total estimated number of Turkish Cypriots killed was 800 to 1,000 (Cockburn, 2004: 65). An estimated 3,000 Turkish soldiers were killed or wounded. On the Greek Cypriot side, around 5,500 to 6,000 people were killed during the invasion (Faustmann & Ker-Lindsay, 2008: 70; Jaques, 2007: 556). A substantial amount of bodies were never recovered. The exact number of the missing is contested, but in the 1980s and 1990s a figure of 1,619 missing Greek Cypriots circulated. In 2014, the Committee on Missing Persons in

Figure 26. The Grivas statue next to his grave in Limassol.
Source: Nico Carpentier.

Figure 27. Entrance of the House of the Missing in Pyrga, with Michalis Papadakis's statue. Source: Nico Carpentier.

Cyprus, which had been established by the UN in 1981, counted as many as 1,508 missing Greek Cypriots and 493 missing Turkish Cypriots.[20]

After Turkey gained control over the north of Cyprus, an estimated 160,000[21] to 200,000 Greek Cypriots (were) moved out (Cockburn, 2004: 65; Faustmann & Ker-Lindsay, 2008: 70; Gürel, Hatay, & Yakinthou, 2012: 8–10; Morag, 2004: 603; Sant Cassia, 2005: 22). Towns such as Famagusta, Kyrenia, and Morphou came under the control of the Turkish Army. Abandoned to slow decay, Varosha, the $3^1/_2$ -kilometer wide Greek Cypriot section of Famagusta, was transformed into a ghost town and became (and still is) no longer accessible. But also, from the south, between 40,000[22] and 50,000 Turkish Cypriots fled to the north (Tesser, 2013: 114). This effectively segregated the two communities, with only a few exceptions.[23] The ceasefire lines between the Cypriot National Guard and the Turkish Army became a fortified Buffer Zone, patrolled by UNFICYP, stretching out for more than 180 kilometers, from Kato Pyrgos[24] in the north-west of the island, to Paralimni[25] in the east of the island. The Buffer Zone (more or less) expands the Green Line that was established 11 years before, dividing the island in two parts (Calame & Charlesworth, 2011: 135), and it carried different names: "The Dead Zone [*Nekri Zoni*]—as Greek Cypriots called the dividing line—passed right through the walled city, cutting it in two. The line was known by various other names too: Green Line, line of shame, and Attila Line" (Papadakis, 2005: 46).

2.5 After 1974

On 13 February 1975, the Turkish Federated State of Cyprus was declared (Safty, 2011: 135), and Rauf Denktaş, who had headed the Turkish Cypriot Communal Chamber and was the Republic of Cyprus's second vice-president (Mirbagheri, 2010: 179), was elected as its first president (Isachenko, 2012: 44). This state was seen by Turkish Cypriots as "[…] one of the component States of the future Federal Republic of Cyprus" (Safty, 2011: 136). Changes not only took place at the institutional level, but also at the demographic level. Isachenko (2012: 73) pointed out that from 1974 onwards, a migration flow from the Turkish mainland to the North of Cyprus started, which was "[…] part of a policy aimed to reduce the labour shortage in the Turkish Cypriot economy, predominantly in the agricultural sector." Also, a considerable number of Turks migrated on their own initiative to the north of Cyprus (Hatay, 2005: 5). The estimates of the numbers of 'Turkish settlers' vary strongly. To give one number: Morag (2004: 603) suggested that 74,000 Turks moved to the north of the island, which structurally altered the demographics of the north. This was combined with the emigration of Turkish Cypriots (Isachenko, 2012: 73). Greek Cypriots, but also Turkish Cypriots (Hatay, 2005: 53), would often critique this situation (Isachenko, 2012: 74).

Simultaneously with the consolidation of the state's structures in the north, negotiations started. Richmond (1999: 52) described how the "[…] Greek Cypriot side immediately launched into a policy to start negotiations in order to regain some of what was lost," with a more nationalist tendency aiming at restoring a situation similar to 1960, while a more liberal fraction agreed to accommodate at least some of the Turkish Cypriot desires for security through autonomy. A first Good Offices[26] mission, initiated by UN Secretary-General Kurt Waldheim in April 1975, failed, but in 1977 a High Level Agreement between the two Cypriot leaders, Makarios and Denktaş, was reached. In this four-point agreement, it was stipulated that "[…] an independent, non-aligned, bi-communal Federal Republic" was sought for, even if "[…] many in the Greek Cypriot camp felt that this was a betrayal of the Republic of Cyprus and the state system more generally" (Richmond,

1999: 52). A few months later, on 3 August 1977, Makarios died of a heart attack. New attempts to further a solution, such as the 12-point proposal from November 1978, failed, even if there was another High Level Agreement in 1979 (Ker-Lindsay, 2009: 16–17).

On 15 November 1983, the Turkish Cypriots unilaterally declared independence, and established the Turkish Republic of Northern Cyprus (TRNC). Three days later, the UN Security Council passed a resolution in which it stated that the declaration of independence was in contradiction of the 1960 treaties, and declared the TRNC invalid. Resolution 541 also demanded that no other state recognize the TRNC (Isachenko, 2012: 47). Only Turkey recognized the TRNC.

Ker-Lindsay's (2009: 17–19) chapter on the peace talks in the 1980s and 1990s describes the considerable number of attempts in this period. After the TRNC declaration of independence, negotiations were resumed in 1985, this time between the new Republic of Cyprus president Spyros Kyprianou and Denktaş, but they failed. The UN '*Draft Framework Agreement*' from March 1986 was not accepted either. Nor was the '*Set of Ideas*,' proposed by the UN in June 1989. In July 1990, the Republic of Cyprus government applied to become a member of the European Union, which further complicated the negotiations. When, in 1992, UN Secretary General Boutros Boutros-Ghali took office, he tried to return to the '*Set of Ideas*,' but he too failed. In the 1990s, Denktaş moved further away from the federation-as-solution idea, and instead defended "[…] a loose confederation in which the two states would each be fully sovereign" (Ker-Lindsay, 2009: 19). This did not help to resolve the deadlock, and it continued throughout the 1990s.

Incidents regularly occurred in (or near) the Buffer Zone. One of the most serious incidents took place in 1996, in Deryneia (which is south of Famagusta), when on 11 August 1996, a group of "[…] motorcyclists trailing Greek flags tried to cross the buffer zone in the name of freedom, crying that they wanted to return to their homes" (Bryant, 2004: 217). Most of them were stopped by UN soldiers, but Tassos Isaak managed to get through and was beaten to death (Amnesty International, 1997: 36). On 14 August 1996, during the funeral procession along the Buffer Zone, Isaak's cousin, Solomos Solomou, slipped passed the UN soldiers, and started to climb a flag pole (presumably) in order to remove the Turkish flag. He was shot dead during the attempt. This was not the only casualty that year; the 1996 Amnesty International report (1997: 136) also mentions the killing of Petros Kakoulis, a Greek Cypriot, who was shot dead by Turkish Cypriot soldiers[27] when he, and his daughter's partner, were collecting snails. On 22 November 2005, the European Court of Human Rights found Turkey[28] guilty of human rights violations in the Kakoulli case,[29] and a similar ruling was made on 24 June 2008 in both the Isaak and the Solomou case,[30] awarding damages to the respective families.

Figure 28. The Isaak and Solomou memorial inside the EOKA struggle (1955–1959) commemoration site in Avgorou.
Source: Nico Carpentier.

The political negotiations were combined with a series of civil peace-building initiatives, but these had a very slow start (UNDP-ACT, 2013: 10). Broome and Anastasiou (2012: 310) did mention that "[…] intercommunal dialogue workshops had their beginnings in Cyprus in 1966, when John Burton and his colleagues in London offered a five-day workshop in 'controlled communication' […]," but they also added that "[…] only a few additional workshops were held during the subsequent 25 years." Fisher (2001) provided an overview of the first meetings in the 1960s, 1970s, and 1980s, which were often structured as problem-solving workshops[31] (Hill, 1982: 111) with elite actors (or so-called 'influentials'). Cypriot civil society, and within that the bi-community peace movement, only became "[…] vaguely noticeable in the early 1990s […]" (Anastasiou, 2008a: 15). It was supported by a new series of workshops and trainings (see Fisher, 2001: 320, for an overview), more aimed at a mixture of target groups. Broome (2005: 14) described the period between 1994 and the end of 1997, where "[…] bi-communal groups met regularly." He continued that in late 1997 "[…] at least one bi-communal group was meeting almost every day of the week, bringing together over 2000 individuals across the dividing line" (Broome, 2005: 14). There were also "[…] occasional visits by political party leaders to the other community" (Broome, 2005: 16). In addition, the first Buffer Zone concert took place in that year, with Sakis Rouvas and Baruk Kut performing. Performers and audience members were subjected to violent responses from both Greek Cypriot and Turkish Cypriot nationalist groups (Papallas, 2016: 38).

In 1998 the United Nations Development Program (UNDP) and the United States Agency for International Development (USAID) started their Bi-communal Development Program (BDP), which they claimed to be "[…] the first concerted effort by the international community to solicit and fund civil society initiatives that brought Greek Cypriots and Turkish Cypriots together to work on issues of common concern" (UNDP-ACT, 2013: 11). Also in 1998, the formal ascension negotiations between the EU and Cyprus[32] started, with the opening session on 31 March 1998 (Laulhé Shaelou, 2010: 49). The Turkish Cypriot and Turkish resistance was considerable, as the EU ascension was seen to be an *enosist* strategy "[…] through the backdoor of EU membership" (Bağcı, 1997, quoted in Isachenko, 2012: 77). Other arguments focused on the need to resolve the conflict first, to protect Turkish Cypriot cultural rights, and to have Turkey and Cyprus ascend together. The Turkish threat to integrate the TRNC more into Turkey never materialized, also because of the considerable opposition of Turkish Cypriots to this idea (Isachenko, 2012: 77).

The EU ascension negotiations put considerable pressure on the Turkish Cypriot position, aggravated by the decision of the European Court of Human Rights, on 10 May 2001, in which it held Turkey accountable for grave and continuing human rights violations in Cyprus (Loucaides, 2007: 107ff). In December 2001, Denktaş proposed new talks, an initiative that was labeled by Ker-Lindsay (2009: 19) as "[…] a delaying tactic aimed at trying to stop the EU from admitting Cyprus." The next year, the political constellation changed, with the Turkish AKP (the Justice and Development Party) coming to power after the November 2002 Turkish elections. On 14 March 2003, Recep Tayyip Erdoğan became Turkish prime minister. At that moment in time, AKP prioritized EU membership and accepted the reunification of Cyprus (Isachenko, 2012: 77–78). Two weeks after the Turkish elections (Ker-Lindsay, 2009: 20), the UN announced its new (and major) plan, which would be known by the name of the UN Secretary General, Kofi Annan. In this period, also, the political situation in the north of Cyprus changed, with large demonstrations in the North in support of reunification and EU membership in 2002 (Bahcheli, Bartmann, & Srebrnik, 2004: 178–179).

On 16 April 2003, the EU Accession Treaty was signed, allowing the Republic of Cyprus (which legally still included the areas under control of the Turkish Army) to become a member of the EU on 1 May 2004.[33] The Turkish Cypriot regime responded by announcing on 21 April 2003 (Hannay, 2005: 225; Hoffmeister, 2006: 162), only a few days after the signing of the Accession Treaty, the easing of the restrictions of free movement across the Green Line.[34] The opening of the Ledra Palace and Pergamos/Beyarmudu crossings (on 23 April 2003), which connected the north and the south of Cyprus, and a few days later the Agios Nikolaos-Strovilia/Akyar crossing (on 26 April 2003) (United Nations Security Council, 2003: 2), resulted in a major shift, as the almost complete separation of the two populations had suddenly ceased to exist. After the first three crossings were opened, several others followed,[35] and more crossings are expected to open.[36] Also, in 2004 (and relatedly), the UNDP Partnership for the Future (UNDP-PFF) became involved in the demining efforts, and in 2012 the UNDP-PFF reported that "[…] 27,000 land mines have been removed from the buffer zone."[37]

In parallel to these events, the Annan peace plan was developed, in five stages. The first version was presented on 11 November 2002. Annan II was published on 10 December 2002, and Annan III on 26 February 2003 (Hoffmeister, 2006: 115ff). No agreement could be reached. A few weeks later, as mentioned before, the EU signed the Accession Treaty. It took almost a year to finalize the Annan IV Plan, which was presented on 29 March 2004. The Annan Plan's final version, version V, was ready on 31 March 2004. This plan "[...] aimed to provide for a solution based on the principles of bizonality and bicommunality and the formation of a federal state, consisting of two constituent states, one predominantly Greek Cypriot (called 'the Greek Cypriot State') and the other predominantly Turkish Cypriot (called 'the Turkish Cypriot State')" (Platis, Orphanides, & Mullen, 2006: 1). On 24 April 2004, the Annan V Plan was rejected by referendum in the Greek Cypriot community (with more than 75% voting against it) and accepted in the Turkish Cypriot community (with almost 65% voting in favor) (Michael, 2011: 180). As it had to be accepted by both communities in order to be applied, Cyprus remained divided. On 1 May 2004, Cyprus still acceded the EU as a full member,[38] with a protocol that suspended the application of the European *acquis* in the areas that the Republic of Cyprus did not control (Hoffmeister, 2006: 129).

One significant outcome of the Annan plan was that the Turkish Cypriot leader Denktaş was sidelined (Michael, 2011: 184)—he had already announced in 2004 his intension not to stand as candidate for the 2005 TRNC presidential elections. Simultaneously, cooperation was strengthened on a number of levels, with the reinvigoration of the Committee of the Missing Persons (in 2004) as one important example. Loizides (2016: 157) wrote that "The CMP case demonstrates that conflict transformation is possible at least on humanitarian issues, despite the absence of an overall political settlement." Loizides (2016: 160) also pointed out that by May 2015, the CMP had exhumed more than a thousand remains, which makes the CMP "[...] the single most successful bicommunal project in the island." But the political negotiations also continued in the post-Annan phase. Direct negotiations were launched in 2008 between newly elected Republic of Cyprus president Demetris Christofias and TRNC president Mehmet Ali Talat, who had succeeded Denktaş in 2005 (Michael, 2011: 188). After the election of Derviş Eroğlu as president of the TRNC in 2010, the negotiations continued in the form of a series of tripartite meetings with the then UN Secretary General Ban Ki-moon, until the talks were suspended at the beginning of 2013.

During this period of negotiations, a series of other events brought both governments to collaborate. On 11 July 2011, the self-detonation of 98 containers of explosives at the Florakis Naval Base killed 13 people and severely damaged the Vasilikos power station, which provided 60% of the capacity of the Republic of Cyprus's Electricity Authority of Cyprus (2014: 77).[39] It took two years to repair the damage (Electricity Authority of Cyprus, 2014: 13).

The power shortage caused serious problems, and the Republic of Cyprus asked the TRNC for assistance, resulting in a collaboration between the two communities, negotiated by the chambers of commerce (UNDP-ACT, 2013: 17). When, on 17 July 2013, a tanker spilled more 100 tons of oil into the sea near the Karpasia peninsula,[40] the two chambers of commerce responded again. They "[…] brokered an agreement enabling the transfer of oil-absorbent booms from the Greek Cypriot Community to the site of the disaster" (UNDP-ACT, 2013: 18). It should immediately be added that collaboration turned out to be more difficult when the economic stakes were high. The 2011 discovery of a natural gas field (named Aphrodite)[41] in the country's maritime Exclusive Economic Zone has renewed tensions between Turkey, the TRNC, and the Republic of Cyprus. Turkey claimed a continental shelf "[…] delimited to the west of Cyprus by a median line between Turkey and Egypt" (Emerson, 2013: 170), and the TRNC claimed a series of research blocks in the Mediterranean that reached up to a few kilometers of the Aphrodite field. In contrast, the Republic of Cyprus has reaffirmed its plans to exploit the Aphrodite field.[42]

During the early 2010s, the civilian protest against the island's divide increased, with the actions of Occupy Buffer Zone (OBZ) as a prime example. From 15 October 2011 this activist group, consisting of Greek Cypriots and Turkish Cypriots (amongst others), and inspired by the global Occupy movement, launched weekly occupations of the Ledra/Lokmacı street crossing in Nicosia.[43] After a few weeks, the occupation became permanent, with a tent camp, and (later) squatted buildings. A police raid on 6 April 2012 closed the camp (Solera, 2014: 332) and ended the action. After a pause in the political negotiations in 2013, on 11 February 2014, the new Republic of Cyprus president Nicos Anastasiades and TRNC president Derviş Eroğlu agreed on a joint declaration, which triggered a government crisis in the south.[44] Then, in October 2014 Turkey sent a warship, the TCG Gelibolu, to monitor the sea drilling activities, and the talks were suspended again.[45] In May 2015, after the April 2015 election of Mustafa Akıncı as Turkish Cypriot president, the peace talks resumed, with, for instance, a Cyprus conference in Geneva on 12 January 2017 and a follow-up meeting in Mont Pèlerin on 18 and 19 January 2017. The peace talks are currently still ongoing.

The Republic of Cyprus was also deeply affected by an economic crisis in the 2010s, which had its worst impact in 2012 and 2013. The Republic of Cyprus, as a service-based economy, had strong economic growth in the 1990s and 2000s, although the Gross Domestic Product (GDP) (and its growth)

Figure 29. Buffer Zone sign with OBZ graffiti.
Source: Nico Carpentier.

showed considerable fluctuations. Zenios (2013: 6) wrote that since 1974 (and before the economic crisis struck the South "[…] the average GDP growth has been 4% and unemployment 3.5%." Also, the north had economic growth in 1990s and 2000s, but its GDP per capita was about half to three quarters of that of the Republic of Cyprus (see, e.g., Besim & Mullen, 2014: 88; State Planning Organization, 2015).[46] Moreover, the TRNC remained dependent on financial support from the Turkish government, and was restricted to Turkey as its main trade partner.

At the end of the 2010s, the south Cypriot economy started to contract,[47] which was severely aggravated by the banking crisis of 2012–2013. Christophorou, Axt, & Karadag (2014: 6) described how, in 2010, the debt and deficit levels exceeded the EU's Maastricht criteria, a situation that was worsened by the country's overexposure to Greek debts (Zenios, 2013: 18). Unable to rely on the international money markets because of the downgraded Cypriot credit ratings, and despite a series of government measures, the Republic of Cyprus government, then led by AKEL president Demetris Christofias, requested support from the European Stability Mechanism (ESM) on 25 June 2012.[48] The International Monetary Fund, the European Commission, and the European Central Bank agreed to provide support almost a year later (on 25 March 2013),[49] which was 3 weeks after the new DISY president Nicos Anastasiades was sworn in as president of the Republic of Cyprus. The Memorandum of Understanding (MoU) implied (among other measures) a so-called 'bail-in,' a financial model that ensures that "[…] shareholders and creditors will be carrying the losses rather than the taxpayers" (Schäfer, Schnabel, & Weder di Mauro, 2014: 3).[50] This bail-in (or 'hair-cut') was different for the Cyprus Popular Bank (or Laiki Bank) and the Bank of Cyprus. The Cyprus Popular Bank was split into a 'good' and a 'bad' bank, where the former, with all secured deposits,[51] was absorbed by the Bank of Cyprus. As the Association of Cyprus Banks (2013: 20) described it, the consequences for those involved in the Cyprus Popular Bank were most severe, as it "entailed the full contribution of equity shareholders, bond holders (subordinated and senior) and unsecured depositors." In the case of the Bank of Cyprus, "the resolution entailed the full contribution of equity shareholders, bond holders and the bail-in of up to 60% on unsecured deposits[[52]]" (Association of Cyprus Banks, 2013: 20). From 2015 onwards, there was again positive growth of the Republic of Cyprus's GDP, unemployment slowly decreased again, and on 31 March 2016, the Republic of Cyprus exited the 3-year Economic Adjustment Program.[53] Nevertheless, this economic dislocation severely affected the Greek Cypriot society, and its impact remains visible to this day.

3 Discourses and Materialities of the Cyprus Problem

The historical overview in the previous part can be revisited from the perspective of the discursive-material knot, to reflect further upon the construction of the Greek Cypriot and Turkish Cypriot enmity. What the preceding overview has already made abundantly clear is that nationalist discourses have been, and still are, a key driving force of the Cyprus Problem. For instance, Baruh and Popescu (2008: 80) wrote that "[...] there is no question that Cyprus is a contentious issue prone to focusing nationalistic discourses in both countries." A slightly more careful version that still points to nationalism as a significant discourse, can be found in Nevzat's (2005: 11) Introduction: "Nationalism, all agree, contributed to some extent at least to the conflict that wrought such havoc on the island during the twentieth century." These citations are indications of the importance of nationalism in Cyprus, but at the same time, the Cyprus Problem cannot be reduced to the workings of a particular discourse. Again, the discourse-material knot, deployed as an analytical strategy, offers a way to bypass this possible threat of reductionism, as it enables focusing on the nationalist assemblages, characterized by material presences (with their agencies), embedded in discursive struggles, and always affected by contingencies, at work at both the level of the discursive and the material. Even then, this part cannot (and definitely will not) claim to provide an all-encompassing analysis of the Cyprus Problem, given its complexity and intensity. Modesty is a very necessary attitude here.

3.1 On Nationalism—A Discursive-Material Re-Reading

As a starting point for this discursive-material (re-)analysis of the Cyprus Problem, it makes sense to first take a step back and briefly discuss the concept of nationalism, still from the perspective of the discursive-material knot, relying heavily on Billig's (1995) work on nationalism. When analyzing nationalism from the perspective of the discursive-material knot, we can argue that nationalism is one type of discourse about the self and the other, which interacts with meanings and materials in always particular ways. This particularity is generated through nationalism's connection with the signifier of the nation (the nodal point of the nationalist discourse, as De Cleen, 2012, argued), where "The term 'nation' carries two interrelated meanings. There is the 'nation' as the nation-state, and there is the 'nation' as the people living within the state. The linkage of the two meanings reflects the general ideology of nationalism" (Billig, 1995: 24). This articulation of the nation-as-people and the nation-(as-)state is at the very heart of the nationalist project.

Despite the specificity of the signifier nation, nationalism still uses an in-group and out-group logic, distinguishing between a self and one or more others. Billig (1995: 70) emphasized the centrality of the self in the following terms: "There is a case for saying that nationalism is, above all, an ideology of the first person plural," but he immediately added that nationalism "[…] is also an ideology of the third person. There can be no 'us' without a 'them'" (Billig, 1995: 78). But again, both self and other gain specific articulations in nationalist discourse. In the case of the self, the subject positions that are mobilized are the citizen on the one hand (linking subjects to the nation-state) and the member of the national community on the other (linking subjects to the people). The balance tends to be different, but both subject positions (or the interrelated concepts of state and community) are present. Weber's (1991: 176) definition of the nation is one illustration, when he wrote: "A nation is a community of sentiment which would adequately manifest itself in a state of its own; hence, a nation is a community which normally tends to produce a state of its own." We can find this combination also in Anderson's (2006: 6) book *Imagined Communities*, where he argued that the nation is both sovereign and a community. In the latter case, Anderson emphasized the notion of belonging that grounds community membership, as the nation is "[…] always conceived as a deep, horizontal comradeship." He added that "[…] it is this fraternity that makes it possible, over the past two centuries, for so many millions of people, not so much to kill, as willingly to die for such limited imaginings." When returning to Billig (1995: 73), we can see in the following example how the concept of nationality bridges the two subject positions:

> "If 'we' are to imagine 'ourselves' as unique, 'we' need a name to do so. […] 'we' must categorize 'ourselves' with a distinctive label, so that 'we' are 'French', or 'Belgian' or 'Turkish' (or 'Breton', or 'Flemish' or 'Kurdish'). The category not only categorizes 'us' in our particularity—demarcating 'us' as an 'us'—but the category is to be categorized (or proclaimed) as a national label in its universality. There is, in short, a universal code for the naming of particulars."

Also, the other becomes specific in the nationalist discourse, with the subject position of the foreigner acting as a constitutive outside of the self. Here, Billig referred to Kristeva's (1991) book *Strangers to Ourselves*, arguing that the other-foreigner is the subject (position) that does not belong to the state that defines the self, as the other-foreigner does not have that state's particular nationality. Kristeva (1991: 96) indeed wrote that "With the establishment of nation-states we come to the only modern, acceptable, and clear definition of foreignness: the foreigner is the one who does not belong to the state in which we are, the one who does not have the same nationality." But Kristeva also aimed to move away from the legalist articulation of the other-foreigner subject position, and offered a much richer discussion where the absence of belonging plays an important role. On the one hand, the other-foreigner is described in the following, rather depressing, terms: "Not belonging to any place, any time, any love. A lost origin, the impossibility to take root, a rummaging memory, the present in abeyance. The space of the foreigner is a moving train, a plane in flight, the very transition that precludes stopping" (Kristeva, 1991: 7–8). But on the other hand, Kristeva (1991: 7) also wrote that "The foreigner feels strengthened by the distance that detaches him from the others [...]. In the eyes of the foreigner those who are not foreign have no life at all: barely do they exist, haughty or mediocre, but out of the running and thus almost already cadaverized." Later, she added: "Always elsewhere, the foreigner belongs nowhere" (Kristeva, 1991: 10), again implying that the subject position is articulated outside the national community.

The other-foreigner in nationalist discourse can still take on different positions, as not all other-foreigners are articulated alike. As Billig (1995: 80) argued, by referring to McDonald's work: "If the imagining of foreignness is an integral part of the theoretical consciousness of nationalism, then foreignness is not an undifferentiated sense of 'Otherness' (McDonald, 1993). Obsessively fine distinctions can be made between different groups of foreigners." It is actually most helpful to cite Billig's (1995: 87) description of the diversity of otherness at length, as this illustrates the connection with Mouffe's antagonism (pure) and agonism discussion:

> "In consequence, there are infinite discursive possibilities for talking about 'us' and 'them': and, indeed, 'you'. 'We' are not confined to simple differentiating stereotypes, which downgrade the foreigner as the mysterious Other. Foreign nations are like 'ours', but never completely alike. 'We' can recognize 'ourselves' in 'them'; and, there again, 'we' can fail to recognize 'ourselves'. 'We' can become allies, 'they' becoming 'you'; and 'we' can become enemies. And 'we' can debate amongst 'ourselves' about

> the value of 'our' allies. 'We' can accuse 'them' of threatening 'our' particularity or of failing to act like proper, responsible nations like 'we' do. And 'we' can claim that 'they', in threatening 'us', threaten the idea of nationhood. In damning 'them', 'we' can claim to speak for 'all of us.'"

The last sentences of this quotation show the presence of the other-foreigner as enemy, which produces a type of nationalism that we can label antagonistic nationalism.[54] This type of nationalism identifies the other-foreigner as a radically different and inferior actor, which is a threat for the self. This then legitimates the use of violent strategies in order to destroy (or at least neutralize the threat originating from) this other-foreigner. Simultaneously, in antagonistic nationalisms, the self becomes articulated through a solidified chain of equivalence that homogenizes the self, also by defining enemies-within, which then need to become purged for the nationalist chain of equivalence, e.g., through the traitor signifier, which aligns the traitor with the other-foreigner-enemy. But, as the last Billig quotation illustrates, the other-foreigner can also be articulated differently; for instance, as other-foreigner-adversary or as other-foreigner-ally. Here, the other-foreigner needs to be dealt with through peaceful and non-violent actions, and both the self and the other-foreigner are accepted as part of the same symbolic space, even if they are still acknowledged as different. This conflictual togetherness is combined with a pluralization of the self, where the chain of equivalence of the self is combined with the logics of difference. This, then, brings us back to agonism; we can label this kind of nationalist discourse an agonistic nationalist discourse.

These different types of nationalism are still all part of an assemblage that also has a material component. Especially in the primordialist approaches of nationalism[55] (Özkirimli, 2010: 49ff), the material becomes amply visible, even if their essentialisms (leading to the naturalization of nationalism) are theoretically problematic, and irreconcilable with the discourse-material approach used in this book. But the primordialist argumentation brings out the role of the material very clearly. In the more socio-biological versions of primordialism, kinship and common descent are seen as the material backbone of nationalism, as van den Berghe (2001: 274) argued: "In simplest terms, the sociobiological view of these groups is that they are fundamentally defined by common descent and maintained by endogamy. Ethnicity, thus, is simply kinship writ large." Ethnic groups and 'races' are then seen as "[…] super-families of (distant) relatives, real or putative, who tend to intermarry, and who are knit together by vertical ties of descent reinforced by horizontal ties of marriage" (van den Berghe, 2001: 274). Writing from a more distant position, Connor (1978: 381) made a similar reference, but he added the important and often-used blood metaphor, referring to the material sharing of the 'same blood' to the analysis: "It is the intuitive conviction which can give to nations a psychological dimension approximating that of the extended family, i.e., a feeling of common blood lineage." Another material component is the homeland. As Özkirimli (2010: 51) wrote, nationalism sees "The nation [as] the sole depository of sovereignty and the only source of political power and legitimacy. This comes with a host of temporal and spatial claims—to a unique history and destiny, and a historic 'homeland.'" Or, to use Billig's (1995: 8) words: "Having a national identity also involves being situated physically, legally, socially, as well as emotionally: typically, it means being situated within a homeland, which itself is situated within the world of nations." A third material component of nationalism is the material dimensions of a set of cultural practices, where language, religion, and history are significant fields. For instance, Kristeva (1991: 178), in her discussion of Herder's work on the national genius (the '*Volksgeist*'), wrote: "[…] one nevertheless finds in Herder the first and most explicit expression of such an anchoring of culture in the genius of the language." Geertz (1993: 259) mentioned, in his discussion of primordial attachments in decolonized states, "[…] being born into a particular religious community, speaking a particular language, or even a dialect of a language, and following particular social practices." Özkirimli (2010: 51ff) also argued that history plays an important role in nationalist discourse, through the belief in the nation's continued existence (even if it is suppressed). Özkirimli (2010: 58) here referred to the perennialist version of primordialism, which is defined by Smith (1998: 159) in the following terms:

> "The perennialist readily accepts the modernity of nationalism as a political movement and ideology, but regards nations either as updated versions of immemorial ethnic communities, or as collective cultural identities that have existed, alongside ethnic communities, in all epochs of human history."

Özkirimli (2010: 52) provided us with an example of this perennialist logic, grounded in the idea that the nation has always been there, when he quoted the words of Adamantios Korais, who he described as "[…] the foremost figure of the Neohellenic Enlightenment […]":

> "In the middle of the last century, the Greeks constituted a miserable nation who suffered the most horrible oppression and experienced the nefarious effects of a long period of slavery. … Following these two developments [the opening of new channels for trade and the military defeat of the Ottomans] the Greeks. … raise their heads

> in proportion as their oppressors' arrogance abates. … This is the veritable period of Greek awakening. … For the first time the nation surveys the hideous spectacle of its ignorance and trembles in measuring with the eye the distance separating it from its ancestors' glory." (Korais, cited in Özkirimli, 2010: 52)

It is rather obvious that these cultural practices have a discursive component, but here it is particularly relevant to emphasize that cultural practices related to language, religion, and history also have material components, as they are performed in the present, even in the case of history, where the practices of memorialization are highly material. Finally, in discussing the material components of nationalism, we need to return to the nation-state, as also the nation-state apparatuses have strong material components. In his discussion of the nation-state, Billig referred to Giddens's (1985: 120, quoted in Billig, 1995: 20) definition of the nation-state as "[…] a set of institutional forms of governance maintaining an administrative monopoly over a territory with demarcated boundaries, its rule being sanctioned by law and direct control of the means of internal and external violence," which nicely illustrates this material dimension.

As an ideological project, nationalism is easy to integrate into the perspective of the discursive-material knot, at least when focusing on the discursive component. Within academia, the idea that nationalism is a discourse (or a construction, or a narrative, or a rhetoric) is widely accepted. For instance, Özkirimli (2010: 206) wrote, after discussing the many different theories on nationalism: "I treat nationalism as a 'discourse', a particular way of seeing and interpreting the world, a frame of reference that helps us make sense of and structure the reality that surrounds us." He continued this part with an overview of references to this perspective, with Hall as one of his sources. Hall (1996b: 613, cited in Özkirimli, 2010: 207) is quoted as saying that "[…] a national culture is a discourse—a way of constructing meanings which influences and organises both our actions and our conception of ourselves." Moreover, nationalist discourses are recognized to have been, over time, strong forces of interpellation that have driven millions to their deaths. To use Žižek's (1993: 202) words: "Nationalism […] presents a privileged domain of the eruption of enjoyment into the social field."

It was also Žižek (1993: 201) that offered a bridge from the discursive to the material component of nationalism, which is rare, as both components remain firmly segregated in most theories of nationalism. As mentioned before, primordialist theories do pay considerable attention to the material dimension of nationalism, but their irreconcilability with the discursive-culturalist approaches seems to hinder the combination of discursive and material components in theories of nationalism. One example that illustrates these difficulties is this quotation from Connor (1978: 389), when he attributed an ex-post role to the material in the following way:

> "Any nation, of course, has tangible characteristics and, once recognized, can therefore be described in tangible terms. The German nation can be described in terms of its numbers, its religious composition, its language, its location, and a number of other concrete factors. But none of these elements is, of necessity, essential to the German nation. The essence of the nation, as earlier noted, is a matter of self-awareness or self-consciousness."

Žižek (1993: 201), with his psychoanalytical approach, opens the door for looking at the nationalist interactions of the discursive-material when he wrote that "The element which holds together a given community cannot be reduced to the point of symbolic identification: the bond linking together its members always implies a shared relationship toward a Thing, toward Enjoyment incarnated." One of the other authors that thematizes the role of the material more, and brings together the rather dispersed reflections on materiality and nationalism—Kaygana (2012)—also commented on the scarcity of this kind of work:

> "Ideological and discourse-analytical approaches to everyday nationalism have been mainly interested the reproduction of the nation in the symbolic register—above all in political and media discourse, everyday talk and accompanying representations of the nation. Yet, nationalism in everyday life cannot be reduced to its representational aspects." (Kaygana, 2012: 91)

The material does play a significant role, also in relation to nationalism, as Edensor (2002: vii) formulated it: "[…] national identity is not only a matter of will and strategy, but is enmeshed in the embodied, material ways in which we live […]." Kaygana's (2012) overview touches upon the materiality of state apparatuses and the institutional basis of discourses of nationalism, in combination with the materiality of nationalist praxis and experience (see also Foucher, 2011: 100), where he referred extensively to Edensor's (2002) discussion on the temporal and spatial organization of the nation. Kaygana (2012: 96ff) also initiated an analysis on the role of material objects in nationalist discourse, after critiquing Billig's (1995) *Banal Nationalism*[56] for not paying enough attention to the material: "Whilst he also refers to material objects such as actual flags, Billig's main interest is in discursive 'flagging', with examples from politicians' speeches, mass media and academic discourse" (Kaygana, 2012: 87). In this part of the overview, Kaygana (2012) listed several types of material objects, including official state products (such as money and stamps), national cuisines, and nationally branded and commodified products. Edensor (2002: 108) paid a lot of attention to fashion, arguing that the "[…] most obvious material form in this regard, and that most closely associated with national identity, is clothing."

I would like to argue that these are examples of investment, where discourses provide meaning to material objects and these meanings enter (or are encoded) into the material. Coining is, for instance, the process where a coin die is used to strike an image on the metal, altering its form. Together with bank notes, with their images printed on paper, they become media that communicate elements of the "[…] 'national iconography', which encompasses state symbols, historical events and persona, the imagery of the dominant religion, etc." (Kaygana, 2012: 98). Moreover, their (relatively) unrestricted use is limited to particular geographies, with more complicated systems set up to deal with money moving outside these boundaries (e.g., exchange rates, exchange offices …). In the case of clothing, in particular, national or 'traditional' clothing, Edensor (2002: 108) pointed to the national(ist) meanings attributed to them: "In ceremonies, folk dancing, tourist displays and official engagements, clothing becomes an important marker of national identity." But this also implies that the textile is cut and combined in particular ways to produce the forms that are seen to emanate from the national identity.

At the same time, these materials also have agency, inviting particular meanings to be attributed to them. To give one example: Once a national dress has been produced, with its (more or less) characteristic form, it invites interpretation in particular ways. What Attfield (2000: 130) called their textility (not to be confused with textuality) affects the way clothes are produced, enabling particular forms to be created, and others not; particular types of material to be used, and others not. Textiles have an "[…] ability to withstand and adapt to changing conditions, and still manage to retain vestiges of their original form […]" (Attfield, 2000: 132). They also suffer from wear and tear, and—as Edensor (2002: 108) argued—they are inhabited, providing the bodies inside them with particular sensatory experiences, enabling these bodies to move in particular ways. Here, the material exercises its agency by offering, and sometimes imposing, particular "[…] ways of moving and feeling, sitting and fiddling […]" (Edensor, 2002: 108).

Also, the material and the discursive are embedded in the logic of contingency. Nationalist discourses change, as they are confronted with space and time. Even in primordialist approaches we can find references to contingency, as they refer to the 'awakening' of nationalist sentiments, or to the idea that "Particular nations may come and go [...]" (Özkirimli, 2010: 58). These discourses are also part of many different discursive struggles, with discourses defending and opposing the construction of national identities, and other discourses struggling over the specific articulations of national identities. One of the many historical examples is provided by Kane's (2000: 246) analysis of the Irish national identity during the Land War (1879–1882), where she retraced the "[...] discursive struggle between the various, and often conflicting, groups which constituted the core of the movement—tenant farmers, nationalists, and the Irish Catholic church." This mostly discursive struggle "[...] against landlords and British rule [...]," paralleled by a discursive struggle within the movement, eventually allowed that "[...] the Irish constructed new meanings, symbolic models, and shared understandings about themselves as a nation" (Kane, 2000: 246). Simultaneously, existing nationalist projects can also be unsettled (or strengthened) by new projects (such as the European Union), as De Cillia, Reisigl, and Wodak (1999: 150) remarked: "Apparently firmly established national and cultural identities have become contested political terrain and have been at the heart of new political struggles." These discursive struggles can also implicate the material, as is illustrated by the subcultural re-appropriation of style, which also implied a re-articulation of national identity. Edensor's (2002: 109) example deals with the re-articulation of Britishness: "Teddy boys recycled British Edwardian styles, and punks and Britpop bands have made ironic and celebratory use of older fashions." Contingency can also originate from the material, where events can dislocate nationalist discourses, or, in contrast, enable nationalist discourses to re/deconstruct older discourses. One example here is Norval's (1996: 51) analysis of the dislocatory force of a series of historical processes ("[...] the Depression, the great drought and the war") that co-determined the construction of "[...] an exclusivist Afrikaner nationalism [...]." If nationalism is (seen to be) located in particular materials, then these materials are not that easily tamed. Bodies, but also blood and genes, travel in uncontrollable ways, always undermining the homogeneity of ethnic groups and their gene pools. Özkirimli (2010: 58) referred here to Smith's (1995) critiques on the primordialist approaches, which can be used here as indicators of the agency of the material: "Intermarriages, migrations, external conquests and the importation of labour have made it very unlikely for many ethnic groups to preserve 'the cultural homogeneity and pure "essence" posited by most primordialists' ([Smith,] 1995: 33)." Cultural practices related to language, religion, and history, with their material dimensions, tend to be unstable, sometimes enhancing nationalism, but sometimes frustrating it. Objects invested with nationalist meanings can disappear or disintegrate, despite all conservation efforts, and new discoveries of objects considered significant can dislocate (or strengthen) nationalist discourses. Even territories produce their own contingencies, as geographies tend to change over time, not only by human intervention, but also sometimes as part of natural processes such as the changes in the course of a border river.[57]

3.2 Nationalisms in Cyprus

The Cyprus Problem can be defined and analyzed as a confrontation between two nationalisms on Cyprus, namely Greek Cypriot and Turkish Cypriot nationalism, which were forms of Greek nationalism and Turkish nationalism, respectively. This statement needs two immediate historical qualifications. First of all, these nationalisms developed asynchronously, with the Greek Cypriot nationalism being consolidated much earlier, acquiring a hegemonic position on the island, forcing those who did not identify with this ideological project into a weakened (discursive) position. Later, a Turkish Cypriot nationalism developed, partially in response to the Greek Cypriot nationalist project, but also partially fed by ideological changes in mainland Turkey. The second qualification is that these nationalisms were constructed. Nevzat (2005: 11) explained that the construction of Greek Cypriot nationalism was not an immediate event, but a long process:

> "It was not, however, a constant feature in this Mediterranean isle's history, nor did it emerge as an axis of tension in a sudden instant. Notwithstanding misconstrued appreciations of the nation as a virtually eternal entity, a fuller understanding of how and why rival Greek and Turkish national identities with conflicting political ideals evolved in Cyprus can only be acquired if the roots and evolutionary progression of these adversarial nationalisms are identified."

This ideological construction process took several decades, and was part of a discursive struggle for hegemony with other identity projects (see below). A crucial element in the successful construction of Greek Cypriot nationalism was Greek independence, which provided the nodal point for Greek Cypriot nationalism: Greekness, or, the subject position of the Greek. Anthias and

Ayres's (1983: 62) quotation below shows that the material creation of the Greek state, and its expansion, which took place over a long period of time, provided the Greek Cypriot (leadership) with a nation-state with which they could identify, and which they could call their 'motherland':

> "Since 1830, when Greece was freed from the Ottoman yoke, Greek-Cypriot leaders had wanted to become merged with the 'motherland'. Though not of itself chauvinist, the nationalist form that the desire for union [*enosis*] took was chauvinistic, romantic-idealist, thrived on the mythology of a glorious Hellenic past, and was aimed at the aggrandisement of the Hellenic world."

The exact starting point of this identity project may not be as clear as Anthias and Ayres (1983: 62) suggested. Brewer (2010: 139), for instance, placed the start of *enosis* later: "[…] the demand for union with Greece, *enosis*, […] began when the British took over the island in 1878 […]." The 1821 massacre in Cyprus, the Greek independence process, with its many stages (Koliopoulos & Veremis, 2010) and its expansionist ideology (the so-called 'Megali idea,' which captured the idea of bringing all Greek-speaking people into the Greek nation), would strongly feed the desire for *enosis*. This identity project was much supported by the Greek Orthodox Church of Cyprus, as Faustmann (2008b: 48) wrote:

> "The Orthodox community had gradually developed a Greek national identity based on ethic and cultural roots shared with the newly founded Greek state since the first half of the 19th century. Originally, this identity embraced by the small educated elite and the Church but it was soon passed on to the wider population. By the second half of the nineteenth century, Greek nationalism was clearly, 'engulfing the lower strata' […]."

Bryant (2004: 76) mentioned the role of Nikolaos Katalanos, a Greek immigrant, and a teacher, journalist, and politician, whose nationalist "[…] truths that he spoke resonated with Cypriots of the period, who recognized in his articulation of their culture a truth that was already being lived." She used the Katalanos example to warn against the reductionist focus on an "[…] intellectual class so often blamed for diffusing a homogenized, nationalist high culture" (Bryant, 2004: 75–76).

One example of the increasing role of nationalism is the struggle over the succession of archbishop Sofronios after his death in 1900. This decade-long struggle, between bishop of Kition, Kyrillos Papadopoulos, and bishop of Kyrenia, Kyrillos Vassiliou, "[…] resulted in the triumph of nationalist

Figure 30. The Nikolaos Katalanos statue in Nicosia.
Source: Nico Carpentier.

Figure 31. The Balkan War Dead memorial in Limassol.
Source: Nico Carpentier.

politics" (Bryant, 2004: 80). An equally important mobilizing set of events were the two Balkan Wars in 1912 and 1913 (Katsourides, 2014: 35), where about 1,500 Cypriot volunteers joined the war (Kolev & Koulouri, 2009: 92—see also Papapolyviou, 1997).

The Greek Cypriot self was thus constructed in alignment with Greece, and supported by claims about the material, in relation to a joint history, geography, language, religion, and culture. Anthias and Ayres (1983: 64) also pointed to the constitutive outside that was created to support the Greek subject position: "[…] it was an affirmation of 'Greekness', as opposed to 'Turkishness' or 'heathenism.'" This discursive construction of a new self (and its other) was not outside the material—it simply provided a new assemblage, which rearranged particular discourses (including subject positions) and materials, including some and excluding others. The new nationalist assemblage was discursively centered on Greekness, and thus aligned with the geography of the island, with its territory demarcated by the sea and its geographical position in the Eastern Mediterranean (close enough to the Greek 'motherland'), the material traces of the Aegean history (that are obviously present on the island), the many Greek-speaking bodies on the island, their religious practices structured by the Greek-Orthodox Church of Cyprus, and the strong presence of particular objects, in particular the Greek flag. Moreover, the institutional support for the Greek Cypriot nationalist project was extensive, and many organizational machines, with their material and signifying practices, mobilized to support the Greek Cypriot nationalist discourse: "All early Greek Cypriot newspapers, 'represented varying shades of Greek nationalism' [Katsiaounis, 1996: 95] [...] [and] the orthodox Cypriots imported teachers and textbooks from Greece which promoted the idea of union of Cyprus with Greece" (Faustmann, 2008b: 48). Constantinou and Papadakis (2002: 83) referred to "the historical studies" produced by Greek Cypriots "[...] proving their Greekness and continuity as a self-conscious actor who always resisted foreign domination [...]," as part of the discursive struggle with the British colonizer about the Greek (Cypriot) subject position. As mentioned before, this institutional support included the Greek Orthodox Church of Cyprus, as one of *enosis*'s fiercest proponents.

At the same time, the nationalist assemblage became engaged in a discursive struggle with a series of contending discourses, and had to deal with a number of potential dislocations, where the material threatened to disrupt the nationalist assemblage. This resulted in a series of successful exclusions and re-articulations countering these contingencies and preventing them from undermining the nationalist assemblage's discursive strength and hegemonic ambitions. One key exclusion was the possibility and/or desirability of non-nationalist Greek Cypriots as a part of the Greek Cypriot nationalist hegemonic project. Crucial here is how "[...] the different ways in which nationalism is naturalized [...]," which is "[...] central to understanding the ethnonationalist conflict that has divided the island," as Bryant (2004: 190) noted. This naturalization of nationalism was part (and the outcome) of a discursive struggle against Cypriotism, which privileged a national identity that also spanned the island but privileged a different assemblage, which consisted of Greek Cypriots, Turkish Cypriots, and other groups living in Cyprus, their combined organizational machines and cultural practices (with an emphasis on their similarities—see Doob, 1986: 391–392), and their histories of co-habitation. As Michael (2011: 40) remarked, Cypriotism was not a new phenomenon. Varnava (2009: 279) referred to the ecclesiastical conflict about the succession of archbishop Sofronios after his death in 1900 as a significant moment in the (pre-)history of Cypriotism, comparing the two competing bishops from the early 20th century with two Cypriot presidents:

> "Even the leaders of these two fractions—the nationalists and the Cypriotists—today, share the names of that did battle between 1900 and 1910; Tassos Papadopoulos, the Hellenist [and the fifth President of Cyprus], and George Vasilliou, the Cypriotist [and the third president of Cyprus], compare admirably to the volatile Kyrillos Papadopoulos [the bishop of Kition and later archbishop of Cyprus] and the stoic Kyrillos [Vassiliou] [the bishop of Kyrenia]."

More significantly, some of the Cypriot organizational machines, mostly located within the Cypriot Left, defended Cypriotism, witness the slogan that the Cypriot communist party (KKK) used "[…] from its inception […]": "[…] A united anti-British front of Greek and Turks" (Anthias & Ayres, 1983: 65). Katsourides (2014: 98) confirmed that the "Examination of the [KKK's] official Party newspaper reveals many articles promoting the need for a united front with the goal of independence (or autonomy) for Cyprus." After the October 1931 riots, also the British colonizer started to promote Cypriotism as "[…] an identity that would transcend cultural and linguistic affinities towards Greece and Turkey and pose no direct threat to British rule" (Morgan, 2010: 133). The Cypriotist position turned out to be untenable, and lost the discursive struggle for hegemony. Nationalism managed to claim the anti-colonialist position and integrate it into the nationalist chain of equivalence, as Anthias and Ayres (1983: 64) wrote:

> "As Crouzet [1973] has shown, […] both the right and left were drawn into the Enosis movement, for no group could denounce the form in which nationalism/anti-colonialism was articulated—since to be opposed to one was to oppose the other. It was the theoretical and necessary link established between these two analytically different positions that was responsible for this."

Other exclusions from the nationalist assemblage were the complexities that characterized the cultural practices from the Cypriot past and present, which potentially threatened to dislocate the nationalist assemblage and had to be re-articulated. The history of Cyprus is, as briefly sketched in the previous part, complex, which resulted in the nationalist project dividing the Cypriot history in periods with legitimate migrations (basically those who came from the Aegean), and illegitimate migrations, who were articulated as part of a process of occupation. In particular, the Ottoman period (but also earlier periods) became classified in the latter category, weakening the discursive positions of the populations that arrived in these 'illegitimate periods.' Also, the complexity of the island, caused by the presence of many different groups and beliefs, became simplified to enter the logic of the dichotomy.

Moreover, by privileging the national identity, other subject positions, in particular those related to class and gender,[58] had to be integrated into the nationalist chain of equivalence, but only in secondary positions, so that they could not threaten the main subject position of the Greek. This also implied that some of the earlier class-based revolts, which united Muslim and Orthodox peasants (Panayiotou, 2012), had to be (re)moved to the margins of historical narration. Anthias and Ayres (1983: 61) described these—what they called—"solidarity bonds" as follows:

> "There are other elements which appear to give some validity to the view that certain solidary bonds developed between Muslims and Christians, partly related to those families including both through the conversion process, but mainly structured by the common economic conditions of peasants. This is shown by a number of peasant revolts, under Christian or Muslim leaders, which included members from each faith."

The left-wing parties, in particular first KKK and later AKEL, did not manage to prioritize a class identity (Anthias & Ayres, 1983: 67), and eventually accepted the dominance of the national identity—as Anthias and Ayres (1983: 69) wrote about AKEL: "AKEL has always been extremely careful not to alienate popular nationalist feelings, justifying this theoretically by the need to maintain 'democratic' support." Still, these non-nationalist fractions of the Cypriot society continued to exist, producing counter-hegemonic signifying practices that could (potentially) disrupt the Greek Cypriot nationalist project.

Also, at a more everyday level, the dislocatory potential of the material had to be countered by the nationalist project. Here too, exclusions had to be organized, for instance, in relation to multi-linguistic practices. One should not forget that "[…] a large number of Turkish Cypriots spoke Greek until 1964 […]" (Soulioti, 2006: 4). The specificity of the Greek-Cypriot dialect matters as well, as it is "[…] relatively distinct from SG [Standard Greek]" (Themistocleous, 2015: 284), and has "[…] incorporated many Turkish words and was spoken by Christians and many Muslims […]" (Anthias & Ayres, 1983: 61). This material evidence of co-habitation and mutual influence, which rests uneasily with the Greek Cypriot nationalist discourse, was confirmed by Trudgill and Schreier (2006: 1886):

> "Lexical borrowings from Turkish are numerous (Pavlou 1993), reflecting the fact that the two communities coexisted rather peacefully for four centuries and that, prior to the Turkish occupation of the northern area, mixing and interaction between Greek and Turkish Cypriots was by no means exceptional."

Papadakis (2005: 12) described the proximity of Cypriot Greek to Turkish from a more personal perspective:

> "Speaking Turkish felt like a welcome liberation to my mouth. It often felt more comfortable than speaking Greek. In Cyprus, we mostly spoke the local Greek dialect. I now realized that it was full of sounds similar to the sounds of Turkish, ones that the Greeks from Greece had real trouble with […]."

When Greek Cypriot nationalism prevailed, it also hegemonized its definition of the Turkish Cypriots as other. The Turkish Cypriot subject position became articulated to refer to those who frustrated the Greek Cypriot desire for *enosis* and homogeneity, which sometimes resulted in their conflation with Turkey as the "eternal enemy" (Bryant, 2004: 224) of Greece and (Greek) Cyprus. The Turkish Cypriot other took a more complex position, with Turkish nationalism being developed significantly later than the Greek Cypriot nationalism (Markides, 2006: 27). In the earlier stages, at the end of the 19th century, Turkish Cypriots (or Muslim Cypriots, as they were labeled at the time) responded to the Hellenist nation-building process that threatened their position on the island, by (politically) mobilizing (Varnava, 2009: 183). This response consisted of "[…] inciting Cypriot Muslims against the Orthodox and Muslims they perceived ignoring it [the call for *enosis*]."

Nevzat (2005: 442) argued that "[…] the rise of Turkish nationalism on the island had become appreciable by the time of the October Revolt of 1931." The idea of Cyprus joining Greece—"[…] an arch-enemy of the Ottoman Empire—and, after 1923, Turkey […]" (Constantinou & Papadakis, 2002: 83)—did not particularly appeal to the large majority of the Turkish Cypriots. The community "[…] feared danger to its own existence […]," which was fed by examples of deportation, as, for instance, happened in Crete (Kizilyürek, 2006: 319). Moreover, the establishment of the Turkish state in 1923, on the ruins of the Ottoman Empire, provided the conditions for the development of Turkish Cypriot nationalism. Together with the state-building process, a particular Turkish nationalism was (further) developed, which paradoxically "[…] resulted in both a hostility towards and an imitation of Western ways [which] has accompanied the modernization process since the turn of the nineteenth century" (Kadıoğlu, 1998: 185). Its Kemalist version combined an emphasis on Turkishness (in contrast to Ottomanness), laicism, and republicanism, amongst others, as captured in the 'six arrows' idea (see Parla & Davison, 2004: 54ff for a discussion).

This Kemalist modernization project also had strong appeal in Cyprus (Akgün, Gürel, Hatay, & Tiryaki, 2005: 11), and supported the redefinition of Muslim Cypriots as Turks in the 1930s (Kizilyürek, 2005: 26), "[…] taking upon themselves an identity forged in the crucible of nationalism" (Bryant, 2007: 116). For instance, in Cyprus, the Arabic alphabet (for writing Turkish) was replaced by the Latin alphabet in 1928, the same year that it was replaced in Turkey (Kizilyürek, 2005: 25). Even if the modernization articulation was strong, the Turkish Cypriot nationalism "[…] was a nationalism that incorporated them [the Turkish Cypriots] into the larger Turkish nation and minimised their relationship to their island home" (Bryant, 2012: 188), using and developing the subject position of the Turk. This is nicely illustrated by Denktaş's much later statement: "The only true Cypriots are the wild donkeys of the Karpas peninsula" (cited by Güven-Lisaniler & Rodríguez, 2002: 183). Again, these nationalist discourses faced resistance. Here we can find a discursive struggle between Turkish Cypriot Kemalism, which had anti-colonial tendencies, and the traditionalist discourse, which was based on loyalty toward the British colonizer. Kizilyürek (2005: 25) described this struggle in the following terms:

> "This call on reform brought up a clash between the modernist and traditionalist elite groups, which, in fact, became a conflict about the power-distribution within the Turkish Cypriot community. On the one hand, there were the Kemalist modernists, who were aiming at a secular national education based on Turkish nationalism and on the other hand the traditionalist, who were loyal to traditional religious values and enjoyed the confidence of the colonial rule."

This discursive struggle, where the Kemalist discourse would eventually gain the upper hand, only slowly entered into the Turkish Cypriot community at large. After the Second World War and the Greek Civil War, Cyprus entered the international agenda, with both Greece and Turkey getting deeply involved in supporting 'their' respective communities in Cyprus. Lacher and Kaymak (2005: 151) described how, in the 1950s, Turkish Cypriot nationalism consolidated its hegemonic status in the Turkish Cypriot community, which translated into broad support for the Turkish and Turkish Cypriot demand for *taksim* (or partition) of Cyprus:

> "Among the Muslim population, by contrast, a similar turn towards an ethnonationalist identification as 'Turks' (which they had customarily been called by Greek Cypriots) was mostly a response to the (failed) 1954 attempt by Greece to gain sovereignty over the island, and the subsequent launch of the Greek Cypriot anti-colonial struggle organized by EOKA." (Kizilyürek, 2003: 222)

These two ideological projects, which eventually discursively (and later on materially) separated the Greek Cypriots and the Turkish Cypriots, were not disconnected from the Cypriot material structures. Even if Cyprus, with its mixed villages and towns,[59] was once characterized by "traditional coexistence" (Anthias & Ayres, 1983: 60), where "[…] if only occasionally, their relations had not been so thoroughly poisoned by the traditional enmity on the mainland, but had been semifriendly or even friendly" (Doob, 1986: 392), the level of material integration was nevertheless limited. This facilitated the othering process, initially of Turkish Cypriots, as part of Greek Cypriot nationalism, and later in a more reciprocal form.

Historically, even though the Ottoman millet system created a (limited) power base for the Orthodox Cypriots, the Ottoman rule still strengthened "[…] the Ottoman Muslims [who] were the colonial power and the Orthodox population was denied the freedom that its leaders, at least, desired" (Anthias & Ayres, 1983: 60). Later, under British rule, an ethnic categorization was implemented, also in material policies, and the Cypriot society evolved differently at the socio-economic level: "Under British colonialism, Greek-Cypriots developed commercially, whereas Turkish-Cypriots remained mainly peasants or administrators" (Anthias & Ayres, 1983: 72). Anthias and Ayres (1983: 63) also pointed to the different educational systems, in the following terms:

> "In education, Britain encouraged a rapid expansion of schools organised on religious lines (with separate schools for Muslims, Orthodox, Catholics, Armenians and Maronites), forcing the two main communities to become dependent for personnel and literature on mainland Greece and Turkey. This, in turn, exacerbated existing group differences and fostered national political elites concerned with protecting the political interests of their own communities."

At the more personal level, Greek Cypriot and Turkish Cypriot intermarriages remained rare, despite four centuries of coexistence (Polat, 2002: 106). In short, "The two populations had different religious beliefs and practices, their own language, largely separate familial and social life and a low degree of intermarriage" (Anthias & Ayres, 1983: 61).

Greek Cypriot nationalism and Turkish Cypriot Kemalism not only constructed each other as respective constitutive outsides, they also defined the British colonizer as the other-foreigner. At first, as Katsourides (2014: 36) remarked, "[…] Greek Cypriot nationalism was distinguished by its moderate approach towards the British. While demanding their freedom from the British Empire, Greek Cypriots were not anti-British." Even if the British were also frustrating the Greek Cypriot enjoyment of the Greek self by not ceding Cyprus to Greece, the Greek Cypriots choose, for a very long time (and with notable exceptions), to avoid violence, even though they continued their *enosis* campaign relentlessly. This situation was complicated by the articulation of the British as the best guarantee against *enosis* by one part of the Turkish Cypriot community, which resulted in the definition of the British colonizer as other-foreigner-ally, something that was gracefully accepted by the British. The British themselves were caught in an evenly complicated mixture of fascination for the Hellenic past of (Greek) Cyprus and their orientalist ideology of empire, which 'imposed' a civilizing mission upon the British. Morgan (2010: 126) described the position of Ronald Storrs, the British Governor between 1926 and 1932, as follows: "It would only be through a period of enlightened British government that Greek Cypriots could rediscover the values that underpinned their classical past—concepts of civic duty, public obligation, self-discipline and honour—from which they had been alienated for so many centuries." The complexity of this triangle between British, Greek Cypriot, and Turkish Cypriot subject positions is illustrated by the Cypriot war effort during the Second World War, where more than 30,000 Cypriots volunteered to fight in the British Army (Asmussen, 2006: 167, 170).

3.3 The Rise of Antagonistic Nationalism

In the mid-1950s, a major shift occurred, and Greek Cypriot nationalism evolved from a mostly agonistic nationalism to an antagonistic nationalism, when EOKA launched its guerilla war. As mentioned earlier, there had been acts of violence before, with the first inter-communal violence in 1912 (in relation to the Balkan Wars), and with the October riots of 1931 against the British, triggered by a mixture of economic and nationalist motives. But in 1955 the British became articulated as the other-foreigner-enemy that needed to be expelled from the island through the use of material force. This re-articulation affected all British inhabitants of Cyprus (civilians and military staff), but also Cypriots (and people with other nationalities) that were seen to 'collaborate' with the British regime. This process of othering, grounded in EOKA's anti-colonialist project, not only legitimated the guerrilla warfare of EOKA against the British enemy, but also the solidification of the Greek Cypriot chain of equivalence and the homogenization of the Greek Cypriot community in their fight against the British colonizer. The first and the last sentences of the oath of the EOKA youth organization illustrate, on the one hand, the construction of the British enemy, and on the other hand, the construction of the (potential) traitor as an enemy within, driven by the desire to purify the Greek Cypriot chain of equivalence:

> "I swear in the name of the Holy Trinity that: I shall work with all my power for the liberation of Cyprus from the British yoke sacrificing for this even my life [...] If I disobey my oath, I shall be worthy of every punishment as a traitor and may eternal contempt cover me." (EOKA Youth Organization oath, cited in Byford-Jones, 1959: 57)

In order to legitimate the particularity of guerrilla warfare, with its 'sneaky' nature, Grivas (1964: 43—see also Grivas-Dighenis, 1964: 68) placed a lot of emphasis on the selectivity and well-considered nature of the violent practices of EOKA, also here including 'traitors' in the list of targeted subjects:

> "The truth is that our form of war, in which a few hundred fell in four years, was more selective than most, and I speak as one who has seen battlefields covered with dead. We did not strike, like the bomber, at random. We shot only British servicemen who would have killed us if they could have fired first, and civilians who were traitors or intelligence agents. To shoot down your enemies in the street may be unprecedented, but I was looking for results, not precedents."

Quickly after the EOKA revolt was initiated, the other-enemy started to include Turkish Cypriots, triggered by the involvement of a considerable number of Turkish Cypriots in the British security forces, who were targeted by EOKA, and whose deaths were then reported by "[...] Turkish-Cypriot leaders and the press [...]," as "[...] Turks murdered by Greeks [...]" (Asmussen, 2011: 129). Moreover, the September 1955 riots in Istanbul targeting the Greek inhabitants of the city, and the formation of the Turkish Cypriot TMT to combat EOKA, were very material impulses that supported the inclusion of the 'Turks of Cyprus' in the articulation of the other-enemy. In his book *Guerrilla Warfare and EOKA's Struggle*, Grivas described how in 1957 he "[...] drew up plans for warding off Turkish [Cypriot] attacks in towns and villages [...]" (Grivas-Dighenis, 1964: 44). He continued:

> "About the middle of July 1958, after plenty of preparation, I launched a counter-offensive against the Turk[ish Cypriot]s, having received information that their morale was at a low ebb and that their activities were on the decrease rather than the contrary because of the strong and persistent resistance put up on our side which they had not expected." (Grivas-Dighenis, 1964: 45)

Furthermore, the nationalist desire for the homogenization of the self resulted in additional violence, with the left-right opposition playing a significant role in the EOKA period. More specifically, the right-wing and nationalist EOKA and TMT came to oppose the progressive members of Cypriot society. AKEL was viewed by EOKA as its opponent and also its members were, in some instances, effectively exposed to violence. TMT also killed left-wing opponents, with the execution in 1965 of two union members—the Turkish Cypriot Derviş Ali Kavazoğlu and the Greek Cypriot Kostas Misiaoulis, as emblematic examples. But as Nome (2013: 64) wrote, this strategy was used earlier: "During 1958, TMT was apparently responsible for a series of vandalism, shootings, killings and threats targeting Turkish-Cypriot leftists, which led hundreds of Turkish-Cypriot workers to withdraw from their ethnically mixed trade unions [...]." TMT also used the logic of the enemy-within, as exemplified by the signifier traitor in their oath:

> "I dedicate myself to resist against any attack from wherever it might come, which will threatens [sic] the lives, the freedoms, the properties and all that is sacred of the Turkish Cypriots. I will execute any duty given to me, even if it involves even my death. I will protect until the very end whatever I would see, hear, know or would be entrusted to me. I will not reveal anything to anybody. I know that revealing anything amounts to treachery the punishment of which is death. I swear in the name of honour, dignity and everything sacred that I will follow all the above."[60]

Figure 32. Damaged Kavazoğlu and Misiaoulis statues near Athienou.
Source: Nico Carpentier.

The end result of these struggles was that the left-wing connection between Greek Cypriots and Turkish Cypriots was cut:

> "In the ensuing conflict between the two communities, the activities of EOKA and TMT finally split the tenuous horizontal links between Greek- and Turkish-Cypriots, as the two military organisations took up a distinctly anti-communist position so that Turkish-Cypriot workers were forced to leave PEO and AKEL." (Anthias & Ayres, 1983: 69)

The 1955–1959 independence war was characterized by intense violence, leading to considerable material destruction and loss of life. The material destruction of the other-enemy, whether these were British, Turkish Cypriots, Greek Cypriots, or others,[61] continuously fed the processes of othering and the deep effects that supported these processes, and, in turn, legitimated more intense forms of violence. Morgan (2010: 248) described the intensity of these effects, from a British position, after EOKA killed Catherine Cutliffe, the wife of a British soldier:

> "The intensity of the hatred felt on both sides was unprecedented. After visiting Cutliffe's three bereaved children at their home Somerville wrote chillingly in her diary: 'Today's funny story. Royal Military Police (RMP) searching house of Greek doctor inform him two British women shot. "Good show" says doctor. "Say that again" say RMPs, he does—is taken to own clinic with fractured jaw and no teeth!'" (Morgan, 2010: 248, citing from the diary of Jean Somerville, the wife of a British battery commander)

The reprisals for the Cutliffe killing were widespread. Norton-Taylor (2012) described the violence used by British soldiers in the aftermath of the killing. As Cobain (2012) has also argued, the British used excessive force, and this material violence again supported the construction of the enemy-other:

> "A young British army officer recorded seeing 150 soldiers indiscriminately 'kicking Cypriots as they lay on the ground and beating them in the head, face, and body with rifle butts'. The officer described how he 'forcibly restrained several such groups of soldiers who had completely lost their heads. Many of them were screaming abuse and the whole area resembled a hysterical mob. … Several [Cypriots] appeared to be unconscious and bleeding profusely.'"

When EOKA announced its (initial) acceptance of the Zürich and London Agreements, and the Cypriot state was established in August 1960, the levels of material violence decreased drastically, and a brief period of pacification started. The foundation of the Cypriot state assemblage was a major rearticulation of the organizational machines that operated on Cyprus, with the withdrawal of the bulk of the British armed forces, and the replacement of the British colonial state apparatus by that of the Republic of Cyprus. Even if the material framework of the Republic of Cyprus was constructed, the identification with this new state was limited. One (very material) example was dislike of the new Cypriot flag, which was hardly used in the 1960s, as Papadakis (2005: 161—capital letters in original) explained: "Yellow was the main colour in the 1960 Republic of Cyprus flag, but this was despised as a symbol of defeat, the defeat of ENOSIS." Also, the idea of one Cypriot nation did not take root, something which is illustrated by Faustmann's (2006: 419) description of the independence celebrations: "The two communities celebrated separately, one celebrating the arrival of the Turkish [military] contingent, the other the return of the [EOKA] exiles. On the streets, mostly Greek and Turkish flags were used for decoration while hardly a Cypriot flag could be seen [...]." For a short while, the other-enemy became an other-adversary, even if, soon after independence, the political conflict erupted again, fed by mutual distrust (Uslu, 2003: 17). Reddaway (1986: 8) pointed out that the constitutional structure was unworkable, because "[...] it depended on a degree of goodwill from the leaders of both communities [...]," which was lacking. Moreover, "[...] it was deliberately wrecked either by the Greek Cypriots in the continuing pursuit of Enosis or by the Turkish Cypriots in the continuing pursuit of partition, or by both" (Reddaway, 1986: 8). Here, Greek Cypriot nationalism impacted on the prevailing democratic discourse. This articulation of nationalist and democratic discourses produced a particular, majoritanist perspective on democracy. Uslu (2003: 18—my emphasis) wrote:

> "It should be noted that the Greek majority had the upper hand in choosing its own way and the Turkish Cypriots could not do anything more than trying to protect their constitutional rights. [...] The present condition suited the interests of the Turkish community but irritated the Greek [Cypriot]s since they were extremely unhappy on not governing the island as they wished *in spite of their majority position*."

The majoritanist democratic articulation of democracy that Greek Cypriots were using led to a "[...] theorisation of Turkish-Cypriots *not* as a political representational group but as a 'minority' [...]" (Anthias & Ayres, 1983: 69—emphasis in original). This articulation of the other conflicted with the Turkish Cypriot desire for a degree of self-control (e.g., in the municipalities), but also fed the Greek Cypriot frustration with the Cypriot constitution, which was based on a consociational democratic model. This type of democratic model "[…] shares governmental decision making between political representatives of the disputant groups […]" (Yakinthou, 2009: 25), in order to prevent antagonistic conflict. The trigger for the collapse of the 1960 constitution was, not accidentally, Makarios's proposed constitutional reform, which would steer the Cypriot democratic model into the direction of a majoritarianist democratic model, removing some of the institutional safeguards that had been implemented to protect the Turkish Cypriot community.

In December 1963 Cyprus re-entered the domain of antagonistic nationalism, with the intense collective violence of 1963/1964 and 1967, and with yet another major restructuring of the Cypriot state assemblage, caused by Turkish Cypriot material withdrawal from the Cypriot state apparatus. Morag (2004: 601) argued that the 'enclave period' implied a de facto partition of the island. At the same time, this material rearrangement (and concentration) of Cypriot bodies on the island posed a continued frustration of the Greek Cypriot desire for a Greek Cyprus, as the Turkish Cypriot presence was still conflicting with the nationalist interpretation of the nation-state. Moreover, the forced relocation of Turkish Cypriot refugees deeply frustrated the possibility of Cypriot togetherness. According to Morag (2004: 601), in this era, the Turkish Cypriot community came to control "[…] about four percent of the territory of the island […]," with 39 enclaves dispersed all over Cyprus.[62] Many of mixed villages were abandoned by one of the communities.[63] This material segregation facilitated the construction of the other-enemy, as Morag (2004: 601) wrote:

> "The enclave period significantly contributed to the further deterioration of relations between the two national communities. Most Turkish Cypriots had no contact with Greek Cypriots and vice versa making it easier for each side to demonize the other. The congestion and tension within the Turkish Cypriot enclaves led to an externalization of tensions within the community and an exaggeration of national unity, with the authorities constantly reinforcing the belief that the Greek Cypriots were a serious threat."

But after 1967 the violence between Greek Cypriots and Turkish Cypriots paused, assisted by the official renouncement of *enosis* by Makarios in 1968, and the start of bi-communal talks. This did not imply the cessation of the violence on Cyprus, though. The establishment of the military junta in Greece in April 1967 had further dislocated *enosis*, and it strengthened the tensions within the Greek Cypriot community. The assassination attempt on Makarios in March

1970, unrelated to Turkish Cypriots or Turkey, made these intra-communal tensions very visible. When Grivas returned to Cyprus in September 1971 it further fed the conflict, with Makarios and Grivas fiercely opposing each other: The "[…] bloody clash between Grivas and Makarios' supporters dragged on until 1974" (Faustmann & Ker-Lindsay, 2008: 68). As a consequence, the subject position of the unified and homogenized Greek Cypriot self was shattered through the dislocation caused by the intra-communal violence within the Greek Cypriot community. Instead, two Greek Cypriot fractions, both nationalist, fought over the control over the Republic of Cyprus (while part of the Greek Left still tried to resist Greek Cypriot nationalism). Henn (2004: 172) described how Grivas first demanded Makarios' resignation for waging peace talks without *enosis* as objective. When this failed, EOKA-B resorted to violence, which reached a peak in 1973:

> "Attacks were made on police stations (some were destroyed and the weapons in them stolen), pro-government newspaper offices were bombed, cars were set alight and other acts of intimidation against government supporters and policemen."

The intra-communal violence within the Greek Cypriot community reached its peak with the failed 1974 coup d'état against Makarios by the Cypriot National Guard and the Greek junta, with the support of EOKA-B. Again, the internal division within the Greek Cypriot community became apparent and dislocated the nationalist discursive claim on homogeneity and unity. This attempt to yet again alter the Cypriot state assemblage failed, but soon after, the coup did result in the modification of two state assemblages—the Greek and the Cypriot, in a dramatic example of the logic of contingency. The coup immediately triggered the Turkish invasion in Cyprus, which eventually resulted in Turkey occupying the entire northern part of Cyprus (Faustmann & Ker-Lindsay, 2008: 68), including the north of Nicosia. This material reconfiguration of the island's geography and demography caused severe material destruction and harm, deeply dislocated hegemonic discourses related to safety and ownership, and, also, structurally altered the Republic of Cyprus state apparatus, as the latter lost control over more than one third of its territory. The Greek state assemblage was also transformed, as the Greek junta collapsed, three days after the Turkish military invasion, immediately followed by the collapse of the coupist regime in Cyprus (both on the same day). While the Turkish 'motherland' was seen to come to the rescue of the Turkish Cypriots, the Greek 'motherland' was unable to successfully assist the Greek Cypriots. One attempt to send a small group of reinforcements from

Figure 33. Victory monument in Famagusta (near Varosha).
Source: Nico Carpentier.

Crete to Nicosia airport ('Operation Niki') ended in disaster when Greek Cypriot air defense shot down one of the Greek troop-carrying planes.[64]

With the Turkish military invasion, the Turkish Cypriot and Turkish partition signifier, part of the nationalist discourse, became a material reality. An estimated 10,000 people were killed, with a substantial number of them not having their bodies recovered until decades later. The Buffer Zone, protected by the UN, replaced the 1974 front line and divided the island into two geographical entities, separated by a highly fortified and militarized frontier. In some cases, with Varosha as a well-known example, living spaces were transformed into ghost towns (and villages) because the material access to them was blocked. Large portions of the two populations became refugees, lost their homes, belongings (and family members), and fled to 'their' respective parts of Cyprus. As mentioned before, the numbers vary between 160,000 and 200,000 Greek Cypriots that were displaced and between 40,000 and 50,000 Turkish Cypriots that were displaced.

Behind each side of the Buffer Zone, the two communities would (further) develop their own state apparatuses, one as part of the internationally recognized Republic of Cyprus, and one as a de facto state, that would in 1983 become the Turkish Republic of Northern Cyprus (TRNC), only recognized by Turkey. These new assemblages would become responsible for the government of 'their' territories and their nations, with, in the case of the TRNC, considerable material support being provided by Turkey. This relationship of material dependency affected the power balance between the TRNC and Turkey, exemplified by the Turkish habit of referring to the TRNC as the 'babyland' ('*yavruvatan*') and to Turkey as the 'motherland' ('*anavatan*') (Canan-Sokullu, 2013: 113).

One additional particularity are the widespread ritualistic signifying practices that Greek Cypriots use to refer to the institutions of the TRNC. In order to avoid any possibility of suggesting that the Turkish Cypriot state structures are recognized, either quotation marks or the pseudo-prefix are used. This form of what Anastasiou (2007: 127) called "exclusionary language" is a modest type of symbolic violence, and part of the semantic war that continues to be waged today. In discussing some examples, Hannay (2005: 232) argued that the Turkish Cypriot community also tends to be selective when it comes to the choice of particular signifiers:

> "The TRNC was the 'pseudo state', its land 'the occupied territories', its people 'the Turkish Cypriot community', its politicians 'so-called ministers' and so on. In the north there were some equally egregious examples, the Turkish military intervention

Figure 34. Varosha seaside view.
Source: Nico Carpentier.

of 1974 being invariably referred to as 'the peace operation' and Greek Cypriot harassment referred to as 'genocide'. Turkish Cypriots were slightly less devoted to the textual exegesis of their visitors' statements than were the Greek Cypriots. [...] All this was translated by the politicians on both sides into highly vitriolic political discourse about the others."

After the military invasion of 1974, the Greek Cypriot articulation of the Turkish Cypriot subject position changed, as they became (co-)responsible[65] for the suffering of the Greek Cypriots, through the material destruction of Greek Cypriot lives and properties, through the 'hiding' of the missing Greek Cypriots, and through the appropriation of Greek Cypriot houses and businesses in the north (and, in particular, in Varosha). They remain articulated as a threat because of the "Turkish expansionism" (Bryant, 2004: 226). This articulation was sometimes combined with, and strengthened by, the articulation of Turkish Cypriot (economic) underdevelopment and primitiveness, linking up to orientalist discourses. From a Turkish Cypriot perspective, the Greek Cypriot other-enemy continued to be a threat to their security and their societal position. Bryant (2004: 224) wrote:

"Turkish Cypriot officialdom consistently describes their neighbours as 'fanatic' nationalists who still aim at uniting the island with Greece. When they do not so aim, they at least aim at destroying the hard-won freedoms of their Turkish Cypriot neighbours. In these portraits, Greek Cypriots ignore the 'realities' of the situation—the long-standing division of the island and the presence of the Turkish military—in their pursuit of an ethic ideal."

Bryant (2004: 226) continued a few pages further: "[...] many Turkish Cypriots interpret everything done by their Greek [Cypriot] neighbors as a move toward enosis, despite the fact that enosis died after 1974." In both cases, two subject positions merge: The self becomes the victim, through the violent practices of the other, but also "[...] of international conspiracies [...], victims of British colonial policy [...], victims of the 'mother countries,' [...] or victims of their own leaders" (Bryant, 2004: 187). This articulation of self and victim as part of the same chain of equivalence by both Greek Cypriots and Turkish Cypriots (with variations in some of the actual articulations, but not in the main structure) blocks the possibility for empathy with the other's suffering (something that Papadakis, 2006, called "ethnic autism"). It also inhibits that responsibility is taken for the violent practices perpetrated by the members of the self. Obviously, as Bryant (2004: 187—emphasis in original) remarked: "[...] Cypriots have certainly been victims, they have not *only* been victims," but this perpetratorship is erased. Ironically, the Greek Cypriot slogan 'I don't forget,' which became educational policy (Zembylas, Charalambous, & Charalambous, 2016: 61), focused on a very selective remembering driven by Greek Cypriot victimhood, which obscures Turkish Cypriot suffering. This articulation is supported by a series of affects, as Zembylas (2015: 190) described in relationship to the socialization of Greek-Cypriot children:

> "The 'us-versus-them' frame of reference is linked to a number of emotions: 'pride' for being Greek, feelings of obligations to struggle for the liberation of Cyprus; 'empathy' for refugees and the relatives of missing persons; and 'resentment' and 'bitterness' for being victims of injustice."

The logic of victimization, present in both the Greek Cypriot and Turkish Cypriot discursive positions, is also translated into the demands formulated by the two communities, which were summarized by Bryant (2004: 219) as demands for justice and respect: "[...] Greek Cypriots have demanded justice through those [popular] politics, while Turkish Cypriots have called for respect." The Turkish Cypriot demand for respect is articulated by, and grounded in the "[...] contingencies of daily life and the humiliations that Turkish Cypriots recall with vividness and feeling today" (Bryant, 2004: 229). Partially, some argue, this demand for respect can be traced back to "[...] their self-concept of lordliness and mastery [...]" (Volkan, 1979: 38), where—during the Ottoman rule—the Turkish Cypriot Community had a more privileged position. But, as Bryant (2004: 231—emphasis in original) argued, it is also articulated with the notion of toleration that also originated from the Ottoman Empire, where "[...] religious and juridical—as well as a certain amount of political—freedom was supposed to be granted to members of different *millets*, or religious communities, within the empire." From a Turkish Cypriot perspective, this discourse of respect was violated through the Greek Cypriot propagation of *enosis*, but even more through the material violence of Greek Cypriots, in particular the violence that was inflicted on Turkish Cypriots in 1963/1964 and 1967.

In the Greek Cypriot community, before 1974, the discourse of justice was articulated as a right to control the island as it had been 'Greek for 3000 years.' This right was "[...] absolute, framed in terms of universal justice" (Bryant, 2004: 237). The Ottoman rule became defined as an occupation, and its end as a liberation, both in relation to Greece and to Cyprus. *Enosis* was legitimated as a natural and just course for the future, also through the Greek struggle for independence and its long process of nation-building, with, for instance, the island of Crete on joining the Greek state only in 1913 (even though Cretan *enosis* had already been proclaimed in 1908). After 1974 the discourse of justice became rearticulated, referring to the need to end the injustice of the occupation of the north by the Turkish Army, and the return of the Greek Cypriot properties—confiscated in the north—to their Greek Cypriot owners. Also, the missing Greek Cypriots play an important discursive role here, as Turkey and the TRNC are accused of withholding information about missing Greek Cypriot soldiers and civilians who 'might still be alive.'

Between 1963 and 1974 around 2,000 Cypriots disappeared (as mentioned before), some three quarters of whom were Greek Cypriots. But whereas on the Turkish Cypriot side the death of the missing is accepted and the missing are viewed as martyrs, the Greek Cypriot missing—as Sant Cassia (2005) contended—were kept alive for decades by (artificially) feeding the hope of their return. An illustration of this process is the so-called Five of Tziaos: five Greek Cypriot soldiers who were captured by the Turkish Army, handed over to, and shot by, Turkish Cypriot irregular fighters. Photographs made by Turkish war reporter Ergin Konuksever fell into the hands of the Greek Cypriot Army when he was taken prisoner (together with another photographer, Adem Yavuz). However, the bulk of the photographs, including those of the executed soldiers, disappeared and the remaining photographs of the soldiers—then still alive—became one of the ultimate symbols of the missing. Later on, testimonies about the death of the five by the photographer, the Turkish Army commander, inhabitants of Tziaos, and Greek Cypriot soldiers, were ignored. It was only in 2009 when the CMP identified their found remains and returned these to the families, that their deaths were officially recognized (see Galatariotou, 2012: 257ff).

The Buffer Zone materially separated the belligerent parties, with the discursive constructions of the other-enemy also remaining firmly in place for a considerable amount of time. The cultural trauma[66] inflicted upon both communities after decades of discursive and material violence—even when both communities locate pain and blame in different eras—created a fertile soil for the discursive continuation of antagonistic nationalism. This antagonistic nationalist discourse articulated the Turk/Turkish Cypriot and the Greek/Greek Cypriot still as radically different, out for the destruction of the self, where Turkish Cypriots find evidence in the 1963/4 and 1967 events and where Greek Cypriot see 1974 as evidence. These Cypriot nationalist discourses are strongly supported by the signifying practices of key institutions, with their capacity to coordinate, synchronize, and harmonize different voices, even though, slowly but surely, the homogenization of the self becomes dislocated by material practices and contested by signifying practices, both providing evidence of internal plurality. Nevertheless, the homogenization of the self remained strongly protected by institutional actors, branding those who disagreed as traitors or as serving the enemy well into the 2000s. The Cypriot mainstream media play an important role in this process, as illustrated by Christophorou, Şahin, and Pavlou (2010: 7):

> "With the passage of time, intra- and inter-community polarisation appears to have deepened, with a blame-game directed by some not only against the 'other' side but also against those with different views as well. Any view diverging from the official line was sometimes seen as damaging and undermining the community's cause to the benefit of the 'enemies'; also, responsibility for unfavourable developments in one's own community was attributed to those with views different from the official view."

The material separation of the Buffer Zone has not been totally impregnable, as was also the case before the first crossing was opened in 2003. First of all, there are several villages within the Buffer Zone, with the mixed village of Pyla as the ultimate symbol of continued co-habitation. (Bi-)communal life in Pyla has not been easy, but at the same time, the local villagers have managed to keep the village mixed (and the door into the Buffer Zone open), despite severe outside pressures. Papadakis (1997: 366) described two incidents that show how localistic solidarities overruled antagonistic nationalism. The first incident took place in the early 1960s when (outside) Turkish Cypriot irregulars came to attack local Greek Cypriots, who were then protected by the local Turkish Cypriots. The second incident happened in 1974, immediately after the coup. Here, (outside) Greek Cypriot irregulars wanted to attack local Turkish Cypriots, but were stopped by local Greek Cypriots. The latter, also supporters of the coup, were engaged in rounding up the local Greek Cypriot communists, who were then questioned and released again. These events show the importance of localistic identifications,[67] and how localism can counter (antagonist) nationalism. Localism is grounded in the intimate connection between material practices, places (Pyla in this example), and a discursive structure that organizes belonging in relation to a community, even though, sometimes, localism becomes articulated as backward, primitive, and marginal (Herzfeld, 2003: 281; Nadel-Klein, 1991: 503) In our case, Pyla is a place of agonistic localism in the middle of the Buffer Zone, the material outcome of antagonistic nationalism.

The Buffer Zone also turned out to be less impregnable in more dramatic ways, with the militarized landscape having its own agency. Incursions into the Buffer Zones did happen, and were sometimes met with lethal violence. Some casualties were caused by landmines, which have their own deadly agency (see Human Rights Watch, 1999: 706). In other cases, people that entered the Buffer Zone were killed by (para-)military personal, as the deaths of Petros Kakoulis, Tassos Isaak, and Solomos Solomou sadly illustrate. The Isaak and Solomou killings in particular demonstrate the fierce struggle for the material space of the Buffer Zone, and how its entry is both possible and heavily policed (with deadly violence). At the same time, the Buffer Zone is a space overloaded with meaning, part of the discursive frameworks that give meaning to the self and the other as enemy, and that articulate this space as a space to be (re-)conquered and defended (see Papallas, 2016). It is highly significant, and deeply tragic, that Solomou died trying to remove the flag of an enemy, and that his killers killed him in order to protect the flag they identified with, a situation that is reminiscent of a century-old, but virtually disappeared, tradition of protecting the flag on the battlefield.[68]

Also other—less lethal—material and signifying practices were developed to overcome the divide. The negotiations between the representatives of the two states (not recognizing each other) consisted of material meetings (even though these representatives did not always share the same room). They started soon after 1974, as part of the UN Good Offices missions, and resulted, for instance, in two High Level Agreements in the 1970s, although they were severely criticized in Cyprus (see, e.g., Richmond, 1999: 52) from the respective dominant antagonistic nationalist positions. These endlessly ongoing negotiations, were, at times, purely ritualistic, aimed at avoiding the fact that the self and the international community blamed one community for an unwillingness to engage in a dialogue with the other-enemy. This rendered the negotiations strategic and more of a confirmation of antagonistic nationalism than a means of overcoming it, still triggering cycles of hope and anxiety. As Jarraud, Louise, and Filippou (2013: 45) wrote: "[…] attempts to find accommodation between the Greek Cypriot and Turkish Cypriot leadership have frustrated the peacemaking efforts of successive professional mediators and the division of Cyprus has become synonymous with intractability." At the more local level, collaboration remained possible, exemplified by the shared sewage treatment system in Nicosia, completed during "[…] a period of high political tensions between the two communities" (Calame & Charlesworth, 2011: 182). Here, political pragmatism, driven by the material scarcity of resources, overruled antagonistic nationalism: "[...] two sewage treatment networks were simply not affordable, and a cooperative scheme was necessary despite unfavorable political and diplomatic circumstances" (Calame & Charlesworth, 2011: 182), although one of the Turkish Cypriot civil engineers that Calame and Charlesworth quoted also added elements of agonism and humanism (even when still using the signifier Turk):

> "The Turkish people are using the treated water from the south in their farms to grow crops and make money to survive. The south side residents also benefit because their wastewater gets treated, which is important for health. Symbiosis. You don't have to talk about nationality. You just have to say, 'I'm a human being and I love my country. I love my environment.'" (Öznel, 2001, quoted in Calame & Charlesworth, 2011: 182)

The more formal, state-related initiatives to overcome the divide were complemented by civil society initiatives, which would eventually propagate an agonistic discourse of peace and reconciliation. Early peace activists, and the later-established bi-community peace movement, managed to overcome the material separation of the Buffer Zone, initially by meeting abroad or in Pyla. Jarraud, Louise, and Filippou (2013: 48) quoted an anonymous peace activist describing the material difficulties of organizing these meetings: "In the early days you needed to be brave to get involved as anyone from the other community was considered the enemy. There was no easy way of meeting and the authorities had to grant us permission to enter the UN buffer zone." Through later initiatives, from the mid-1990s onwards, "[...] thousands of Cypriots from across the island took part in bi-communal activities [...]" (Jarraud, Louise, & Filippou, 2013: 49; see also Broome, 2005: 12), again overcoming the material divide, but also weakening the hegemony of antagonistic nationalism. As Anastasiou (2008a: 15) wrote,

> "[...] by the year 2000, a bicommunal citizen peace movement [...] reached maturity as it developed a recognizable voice. Having joined efforts: [Greek Cypriot] and [Turkish Cypriot] citizens gradually introduced into the hitherto nationalist cultures of Cypriot ethnocentric politics, an alternative culture of peace and reconciliation as the indispensable foundation of civil society and multiethnic democracy."

Finally, it is also important to stress that discursive hegemony is never total. On Cyprus, one identity discourse contending with Greek and Turkish Cypriot nationalism, Cypriotism, never completely disappeared. In 1986, Doob (390) observed the continued presence of the Cypriotist ideology, or what he called "Cypriot patriotism":

> "Symptoms of Cypriot patriotism that transcended Turkish and Greek Cypriot patriotism and nationalism remained, even as persons on both sides could and would not forget their heritage as well as the economic and military assistance and encouragement received from the mother countries. They realized that they shared the same small island, in spite of the salient reality of their inability ever to cross the Green Line and of the existence of several new airports that were less efficient and more dangerous than the single one formerly serving the entire country. Without necessarily being unfriendly, Cypriots were curious concerning events and people on the other side."

Moreover, despite AKEL's sometimes ambiguous stance, this organizational machine can be seen as one of the long-term protectors of Cypriotism (Mavratsas, 1997; Papadakis, 1998), and one of the key actors in the post-1974 discursive struggle between Greek-Cypriot nationalism and Cypriotism.[69] Mavratsas (1997: 720) argued that in the first years after 1974 Greek Cypriot nationalism was weakened, "[…] precisely because nationalism was seen as at least partly responsible for the events of 1974 […]," which, for instance, led to the Greek Cypriot negotiators' acceptance of a federal solution (in the High Level Agreements of the late 1970s). Mavratsas (1997: 720) added that "Communist AKEL […] went beyond the discourse of the peaceful coexistence of the two communities and even talked about the 'brotherly' bonds between the Greek and the Turkish Cypriots." But writing at the end of the 1990s, Mavratsas (1997: 726) also argued that "Since the mid 1980s, Greek-Cypriot nationalist forces have returned to the forefront and to a considerable degree have again started to represent the political mainsteam [sic] of the Greek-Cypriot community […]." In the case of the Turkish Cypriot community, Loizides (2007: 180) wrote that "[…] Turkish Cypriots felt closely attached to Turkey immediately after 1974, in the following years, Cypriotism was on the rise, taking a politicized form." Cypriotism here implied an "emphasis on the differences between mainland Turks and Turkish Cypriots, paying particular attention to the cultural and linguistic similarities with Greek Cypriots" (Güven-Lisaniler & Rodríguez, 2002: 183). One specific element that strengthened Cypriotism in the north were tensions about the so-called Turkish 'settlers' in Cyprus. Navaro-Yashin (2012: 59) described this power struggle as follows:

> "Turkish-Cypriots employed their status, lifestyles, income levels, and claims to autochthony in their differentiation tactics vis-à-vis the settlers. In turn, some settlers (those who could) attempted to overcome their sociocultural marginalization in Cyprus by declaring their alliance with Turkey as its citizens, assuming a Turkish nationalist discourse, or voting for the right-wing parties of the trnc regime."

This power struggle generated difference, which was then—as Navaro-Yashin (2012: 55) wrote—played out by "[...] using terms that signify cultural difference and social class." In some cases, 'settlers' (who had sometimes 'settled' for a long time, and, for instance, included Kurdish people) even became "[...] conflated or confused [...]" with the Turkish soldiers (Navaro-Yashin, 2012: 55), using an other-foreigner articulation. As a consequence, the Turkish Cypriot nationalist homogeneity became dislocated, and a Cypriot identity—distinct from the Turkish one—was strengthened. We can find this discursive-political struggle, despite Denktaş long-lasting strong position in the TRNC, also at a more institutional level, where political and journalistic voices represented the Cypriotist ideology in the north of Cyprus. One example mentioned by Loizides (2007: 180) is the Communal Liberation Party [*Toplumcu Kurtuluş Partisi*—TKP] of Alpay Durduran, an opposition party established in 1976, which supported the establishment of a federal state (Kizilyürek, 2012).[70] In sum, and as Loizides (2007: 177) argued, at first the majority of the "[...] Turkish Cypriots saw the motherland troops as liberators," but then:

> "[...] these feelings waned in the following years, because of the resulting international isolation, Turkey's interference in Turkish Cypriot community affairs, economic stagnation, and the colonization of Cyprus by Turkish settlers (Lacher and Kaymak 2005). Ultimately, the new conditions led many Turkish Cypriots to reconsider their unconditional loyalty to the policies of the national center [...]."

3.4 The Annan Plan and the Continued Hegemony of Nationalism

Even if the dominant nationalisms were contested, these discourses managed to protect their hegemonic position for several decades. In 2001, Fisher (2001: 321–322) described the situation in Cyprus as follows:

> "Antagonism is expressed, but is not used as a springboard for reflexive reframing, invention or action planning. The parties are caught in self-defeating processes of antagonism, including blaming the other side, attributing negative qualities to them, and polarizing one's own side against them."

The Buffer Zone, with its guards and fortifications that cut through the island, remained the materialization of the antagonistic nationalist discourse, created out of the desire to separate Turkish Cypriots and Greek Cypriots. The guards, and their rules of engagement, still contain the threat of material violence, grounded in this nationalist logic. Secondly, and relatedly, the material inability of the refugees to return and reclaim their properties is another materialization of the antagonistic form of nationalism that continues to structure the island's geography, demography, and economy, until today. And finally, the existence of two clusters of state apparatuses, labeled as the Republic of Cyprus and the Turkish Republic of Northern Cyprus, are materializations of the antagonistic nationalist discourse. None of these three materializations have disappeared, but in 2003 the Buffer Zone's (almost) impregnable status changed significantly. Days after the Republic of Cyprus signed the EU Ascension Treaty, and under the pressure of the Turkish Cypriot 'This country is ours' platform, the TRNC regime announced the easing of the Green Line crossing restrictions. The opening of the first crossings in April 2003 allowed Cypriots to enter and pass through the Buffer Zone without being exposed to material violence. As Dikomitis (2012: 117) wrote, "The first border crossing was historic, life changing and also confusing for many Cypriots." Although some Cypriots were (and some still are) hesitant about crossing (see Dikomitis, 2012: 118ff) into the 'other' side, and the encounters did not always produce the desired outcomes (Scott, 2013: 127), the material permeability of the Buffer Zone has allowed for increased levels of contact between Greek Cypriots and Turkish Cypriots, also at an organizational (civil society) level.[71] Even more unexpected meeting places, such as casinos,[72] "[...] operate as a particular kind of bicommunal space, very different from those spaces promoted by international agencies [...]" functioning "[...] as places for the rediscovery and exercise of cultural intimacy" (Scott, 2013: 127). Most importantly, the other-enemy was no longer hidden behind the Buffer Zone, and was seen to share the same material space, which, in most cases,[73] allowed for the re-articulation of the subject position of the other, in a variety of ways, ranging from other-foreigner over other-ally to part of the self.

Also, material collaboration at the grassroots level was facilitated, as is exemplified by work of the relatives of the missing. Efthymiou[74] (2014) described how

> "[...] the relatives of the missing persons from both sides of the divide started crossing the dividing line in search of information for the fate of their relatives. The work of journalists working on the issue and spaces created by bi-communal activities provided the opportunities for relatives of the missing from both sides to meet and exchange experiences and information. Very soon these people identified with the pain of each other and remarkable friendships formed. [...] The victims of the massacres and atrocious crimes from both sides were coming together to challenge society to stop using their pain to enhance nationalism but face the realities of the

violent past and work so that no families in the future will again have to go through the same trauma."

This led in 2006 to the establishment of the "Bi-Communal Initiative of Relatives of Missing Persons, Victims of Massacres and Other Events 1963–1974" (later renamed "Together We Can"). Kovras (2012: 97) wrote about this initiative: "The 'open checkpoints' policy created an unprecedented opportunity for relatives of missing persons to build an effective organization structure, meet and exchange ideas regularly and organize collaborative events." The (early) activism of the relatives coincided with, and possibly contributed to, the re-activation of the Committee for the Missing Persons (CMP) in 2004 (Kovras, 2012: 89), after being dormant for almost 25 years. CMP has played (and still plays) a crucial role in the identification of the bodies of (a considerable part of) the missing, supporting closure for the families, even though it cannot raise "[…] issues of legal, moral or political accountability" (Kovras, 2012: 100).

In the same period, one more crucial event took place, which merits more attention, as it demonstrates the role of nationalism in Cyprus in this period. The Annan Plan—or its fifth version—was submitted to an island-wide referendum on 24 April 2004, in yet another failed attempt to change the Cypriot state assemblage(s). The Annan Plan period was a crucial moment in the contemporary history of Cyprus, because it showed the strength of the nationalist discourse in the 21st century, at least in the Greek Cypriot community, and its capacity to still mobilize large parts of the population. In the north, the Annan Plan demonstrated the relative weakness of nationalism and the contingency of its hegemony—in practice, it meant the political *fin-de-carrière* for Denktaş, and the coming of a new generation of more moderate political leaders. Still, the Annan Plan mobilizations also showed that there was no total consensus in either of the two communities, uncovering the lack of homogeneity. Moreover, the referendum, and the absence of inter-communal violence, illustrated how the antagonistic forms of nationalism remained at the discursive level.

Anastasiou's (2008b) analysis of the 'no' campaign for the Annan Plan referendum shows the role of institutionalized politics, mainstream media, and the Greek Orthodox Church of Cyprus in enhancing the Greek Cypriot nationalist discourse and consolidating its hegemony. In the case of the Orthodox Church, Anastasiou (2008b: 155) argued that this organization has been "Historically influenced by the rise of Hellenic nationalism during the nineteenth century […]," which led to the "[…] uncritical assimilation of impassioned ethnocentrism [...]." He illustrated this by citing the words of Bishop Pavlos of Kyrenia, who declared before the 2004 referendum took place that "[...] Those who say 'yes' will be party to this injustice, will lose their homeland and the kingdom of heaven! [...]" (Anastasiou, 2008b: 157). Also, many of the Greek Cypriot political parties identified with a nationalist discourse, including President Tassos Papadopoulos's DIKO party, the socialist party EDEK, the communist party AKEL,[75] and the Green Party. Anastasiou (2008b: 142) illustrated the workings of the nationalist discourse within the realm of institutionalized politics by analyzing Papadopoulos's crucial speech on 7 April 2004, which "[...] was tearful and impassioned." In this speech, the Greek Cypriot president (involved in the Annan Plan negotiations) called upon the Greek Cypriots to reject the Annan Plan. Anastasiou (2008b: 144) argued that Papadopoulos used two sets of signifying practices:

> "First, he tapped into the dormant nationalist memory and sentiments of the [Greek Cypriot] community, stirring, reactivating, and amplifying nationalism to the point of saturating the public debate and drowning out the pro-solution voices. Second, he reawakened the [Greek Cypriot's] sense of victimization and reintegrated it into the nationalist framework, thus re-associating the [Greek Cypriot's] sense of injustice with the typical reactionary culture of adversarial nationalism."

Also, the Turkish Cypriot sphere of institutionalized politics supported a nationalist discourse during the Annan Plan period. This support for a nationalist discourse was personified by Rauf Denktaş, at that time still president of the TRNC, even if his position was severely weakened after the 2002 protests and the 2003 parliamentary elections. Anastasiou (2008b: 122) referred here, for instance, to Denktaş's statement "[...] that the Annan Plan was nothing but a trap for the TCs [Turkish Cypriots]." He continued to argue that both Papadopoulos and Denktaş "[...] chose to opt for ethno-centric agendas and approaches that perpetuated the captivity of their people to the divisive and belligerent remnant of their nationalist past" (Anastasiou, 2008b: 162). But, in contrast to the sphere of institutionalized politics, popular support for the Turkish Cypriot nationalism "[...] had already been on the wane in the 1990s, even with a simultaneous hardening of the official position" (Tesser, 2013: 123).

The Greek Cypriot and Turkish Cypriot mainstream media often invoked a nationalist discourse (see, e.g., Anastasiou, 2002; Bailie & Azgin, 2008). Christophorou, Şahin, and Pavlou's (2010) research of both Greek Cypriot and Turkish Cypriot mainstream media included the year of 2002 (as one of their three research periods), where the Annan Plan had already taken a prominent position on the media agenda. The signifying practices of the Greek Cypriot dailies from 2002 were relatively consistent: "All the dailies, apart from Alithia, projected directly or indirectly that it was against the national interest to accept the Annan Plan" (Christophorou, Şahin, and Pavlou, 2010: 169). Simultaneously, these dailies constructed a distinction between the Turkish Cypriot people on the one hand, and the Turkish Cypriot leadership and Turkey on the other:

> "The dailies did not regard the Turkish Cypriot community as the 'other' or the enemy. The Turkish Cypriots were not seen as the foe of the Greek Cypriots, whose enemy /'other', was always Turkey and those who executed its orders such as its troops or the Turkish Cypriot leadership." (Christophorou, Şahin, & Pavlou, 2010: 171)

Moreover, the Greek Cypriot self was strengthened in the dailies' signifying practices: "[…] all the dailies portrayed the Greek Cypriots as those in the right and the victims of the conflict" (Christophorou, Şahin, & Pavlou, 2010: 171). There were a similar set of representations in the TRNC, although there was more diversity in the positions toward the Annan Plan. It should be noted that, more than is the case with the Greek Cypriot media, the Turkish Cypriot media "[…] relied heavily on articles originating from news agency dispatches and press releases," with nationalist discourses being a "[…] common feature of the Turkish Cypriot media, especially on issues related to the Cyprus Problem" (Christophorou, Şahin, & Pavlou, 2010: 177). Christophorou, Şahin, and Pavlou (2010: 177) mentioned here that all Turkish Cypriot dailies presented their "[…] arguments in terms of 'our' national interest," but they also pointed out that "[…] some media outlets represented the Annan Plan as being against the national interest, others represented it as the opposite […]." Still, the signifying practices employed "[…] the image of a homogenous nation, [and] also depicted the Turkish Cypriot side as united against the Greek Cypriots" (Christophorou, Şahin, & Pavlou, 2010: 177). A later example is Way's (2011a; 2011b) research on three Turkish Cypriot radio stations in 2010. Here too, Way (2011a: 29) pointed to diversity and contradictions: "[…] the TRNC news agency TAK […] produces stories that often contain mixed and confused ideological messages due to the requirement that it represents the pro-federation government positively alongside the strong influence of the civil service and Turkish military […]." But this diversity did not affect the nationalist bottom line: "[…] all events, including 'banal' events, are recontextualised in order to […] promote distinctive versions of national identity and national allegiance" (Way, 2011a: 29).

In the Annan Plan period, the signifying practices that entextualized nationalist discourses tended more toward antagonism, even though the calls for destruction remained at a discursive level. Anastasiou's (2008b: 162) summary of the negotiations leading up to the fifth Annan Plan (which was the version put to vote at the referendum) offers an indication of this kind of antagonism, where Papadopoulos (and the institutional actors backing him) aimed at the dismantlement of the TRNC, and Denktaş (again, with institutional support) opted for the dismantlement of the Republic of Cyprus:

> "The reality was that at the forefront of events were two adversarial nationalists with maximalist approaches to negotiations; the TC [Turkish Cypriot] leader was still attempting to 'negotiate' a secessionist solution and the GC [Greek Cypriot] leader was still pursuing a 'settlement' that resembled the unitary state of the pre-1974 era."

In addition, the antagonism was also translated in a series of violent attacks, and it is important here to quote Anastasiou's (2008b: 160–161—emphasis in original) description of these events at length, as this description demonstrates that these violent acts were intra-communal, and–as Anastasiou (2008b: 162) also emphasized—not inter-communal. In this stage of the conflict, the antagonistically defined other-enemy was purely situated within the self, both in the Greek Cypriot and in the Turkish Cypriot community, again leading to material destruction:

> "The head of the DISY party, the first to declare formally its support of the UN proposal, had a hand grenade thrown into his house. Alecos Constantinides, the chief editor of the center-right newspaper *Aletheia*, received anonymous calls 'threatening his life and expressing anger at the line the newspaper was following during the referenda.' [...] These events in the [Greek Cypriot] community paralleled phenomena in the [Turkish Cypriot] community during the run-up to the referenda. The most notable were the heavy beatings of pro-peace youths by the Grey Wolves, an extremist nationalist group rooted in Turkey's far-right nationalist past. Furthermore, [Turkish Cypriot] militants bombed the house of Mehmet Ali Talat, Republican Party leader and pro-peace 'prime minister' supporting the Annan Plan. Reactionary forces also bombed the offices of *Kibris*, a newspaper known for promoting peace with the [Greek Cypriots], supporting a negotiated settlement to reunify the Island, and criticizing the intransigent nationalism of the Denktash regime."

3.5 Post-Antagonist Nationalism in Cyprus?

With the title of her conclusion of *Imagining the Modern*, Bryant (2004: 249) raised the question of whether 2003 marked the start of Cyprus's evolution toward a "postnational" condition. She legitimated this question (and its possible positive answer) as follows: "Since the beginning of 2003, Cyprus has experienced tremendous change, much of it following upon the opening of the buffer zone and the opportunities for interchange that followed." The failure of the Annan Plan to reunite the island also triggered "[...] a revolution that has marginalized their [the Turkish Cypriot] long-time leaders [...]" (Bryant, 2004: 249), who in the past have provided significant support for the nationalist discourse, including its antagonistic version. Further support for this position can be found in the historical overview in the previous part of this book, which demonstrates the quasi-absence of material violence in the past two decades, but also shows how the hegemony of antagonistic nationalism weakened, and, again, illustrating the workings of contingency.

Even though it might be better, at least within the context of this book, to refer to a post-antagonistic nationalism (and not to a "postnational Cyprus," as Bryant did), there are still more arguments that can be mobilized to support Bryant's thesis. Contemporary signifying practices about the history of the Cyprus Problem, and about its possible solutions, continue to contain references to the enemy-other, but this enemy-other, in most cases, is situated in the past, even if the anxiety that the past might repeat itself has not disappeared ('Cyprus 2015' Initiative, 2011: 45). Still, the (possible) antagonistic nature of the contemporary other is articulated through the events from the past, and not so much through the more recent behavior of that other. One anonymous Turkish Cypriot stakeholder panel participant, cited in the 'Cyprus 2015' Initiative (2011: 92) report, formulated this concern as follows: "We have to accept our mistakes and understand each other's concerns. It's true that Greek Cypriots attempted to cleanse the island from Turkish Cypriots. They have to accept this and respect our security concerns." Another source of anxiety are so-called "extremists," as they are labeled in the 'Cyprus 2015' Initiative (2011: 98) report. This brings in another discursive logic, where the separation of normalcy and extremism shows the exceptionalism of antagonistic nationalism. This concern is formulated by another anonymous Turkish Cypriot stakeholder panel participant in the 'Cyprus 2015' Initiative (2011: 98) report:

> "'There are parties on each side whose interest lies with conflict and clashes in Cyprus' argued a Turkish Cypriot stakeholder. 'These people will try to make the new state of affairs collapse. We have to keep this in mind and do not let them escalate a minor event into a communal strife.'"

In addition, there is also a tendency, in particular in the Cypriotist discourse, to shift the responsibility (and with it, the subject position of the other-enemy) outside Cyprus. For instance, in Zembylas, Charalambous, and Charalambous' (2016: 9) list of characteristics of Cypriotism, "[…] proclaims Turkey as the aggressor […]" is mentioned. This implies a disarticulation of the Turkish Cypriot community from the other-enemy chain of equivalence, allowing it to become (at least) an other-adversary (or even a part of the self). There is a long history of disconnecting Turkish Cypriots from the Turkish enemy, where they sometimes—as Bryant (2004: 224) contended—become seen as victims of the Turkish state, which, in turn, strengthens the evilness and otherness of the Turkish enemy. One example is the missing, where, "The Greek Cypriots […] have long maintained […] that the main culprits are not the Turkish Cypriots but the Turkish army occupying half the island" (Sant Cassia, 2005: 23). Even if this articulation does not do justice to the complexity of the history of Cypriot antagonism, and is sometimes used to fragment and inferiorize the Turkish Cypriot other-enemy, this articulation still has the potential to support a more agonistic discourse. Similarly, the conspiracy theories that blame the USA (and, to a lesser extent, the UK) for the antagonisms on the island are, intentionally or not, part of a politics of blame, which removes responsibility (at least partially) from the Cypriot people and its organizational machines. One version of this conspiracy theory[76] is that "[…] both British passivity and a United States-led alliance actively colluding with Turkey in the invasion […]" paved "[…] the way for the de facto partition" (Trimikliniotis, 2012: 31). Even if their historical accuracy is highly debatable, these articulations of an enemy-other outside Cyprus (potentially) reconfigures the Cypriot other as non-enemy.

Also, the self has become more heterogeneous, both at the level of identifications with national identity discourses and at the level of political practice. Identifications with the different national(ist) discourses occur, and the merging of these identifications has become more intense, resulting in multiple subject positions. Vural and Rustemli's (2006) article on what they call "identify fluctuations" within the Turkish Cypriot community discusses the combination of Turkishness and Cypriotness, combined with Europeanness and being Moslim. They wrote:

> "As expected, ethno-national identity is the most frequent among the late adult and elderly generations, of whom most had experienced intercommunal conflicts and were trained as 'mujaheddins'. The adults who had little direct experience of the inter-communal struggles exhibited a preference for 'Cypriotness' over 'Turkishness'.

> The youngest generation showed a split between 'Turkishness' and 'Cypriotness.'" (Vural & Rustemli, 2006: 343)

Moslim and European identities are much less present than Turkishness and Cypriotness, but the point that needs to be made here is that Turkishness is no longer the dominant identification, or, in other words, the Turkish Cypriot nationalist subject position has lost its hegemonic position. Turkish Cypriot nationalism is now, much more than in past decades, part of an intra-communal discursive struggle. This, in turn, implies that *within* the particular communities, diversity and pluralism has increased. Also, generational differences play as significant role, as Vural and Rustemli's (2006: 343) above-rendered statement exemplifies. Webster's (2005) survey question about the preferred solution for the Cyprus Problem, shows, for instance, high support for the division with young Greek Cypriots (more than 40% of the 18–24 age group) and very low support with older Greek Cypriots (slightly more than 10% of the 55–65 age group). Another example is Faustmann's (2008a: 20–21) reference to two surveys in the Greek Cypriot community from 2006 and 2007, where, in the first survey, "[…] 54 per cent chose Cypriot as their identity, 8 per cent the category 'More Cypriot than Greek', 32 per cent 'Equally Cypriot as Greek', 2 per cent 'More Greek than Cypriot' and 3 per cent Greek" (Faustmann, 2008a: 20). The second survey produced the following outcomes:

> "Again, about half of the Greek Cypriots opted for a purely Cypriot identity. Out of the 800 people polled, 49 per cent identified themselves as Cypriots, 12 per cent as Cypriot Greek and a further 31 per cent as Greek Cypriot of whom about half have equal weight to being Greek and Cypriot. 7 per cent consider themselves Greeks of Cyprus and only 2 per cent as Greek." (Faustmann, 2008a: 21)

The following is an example from a qualitative study (Peristianis, 2006: 114) showing the workings of these multiple identities:

> "I feel [that I am] as much Greek as Cypriot. Greek as to ethnicity because we share with Greeks the same language, perceptions, civilization and religion; and Cypriot as regards citizenship, since I was born in Cyprus and I am a citizen of the Cyprus Republic, with all rights and duties that any citizen enjoys."

Also, the role of religious identities has become more complicated. Particularly in the Greek Cypriot case, the Orthodox Christian faith was a significant component of the Greek Cypriot nationalist chain of equivalence, with Greekness as its nodal point. Even though, as Roudometof (2009: 64—my translation) showed, an "overwhelming majority" of the Greek Cypriots still believe in God, but at the same time, the process of secularization has taken root in Cyprus: "[…] following the modernization of the Republic of Cyprus, the evolution of religiosity took the typical form of an intensification of the cleavage between a more conservative and religious wing, and a more secular wing […]" (Roudometof, 2009: 64—my translation). Again, this is an argument that supports the pluralization of the Cypriot society. In north Cyprus, because of the historical dominance of the Kemalist secular tradition, religion did not play a very significant role in the Turkish Cypriot nationalist chain of equivalence. Until today, the role of religion in north Cyprus has been fairly limited. In a 2009 article, based on data from 2006, Yeşilada (2009: 58) concluded that "[…] the Turkish Cypriots are some of the most secular Muslims in the world." Nevertheless, we can also find traces of an ongoing discursive struggle between different groups in the TRNC over the role of Islam in Turkish Cypriot society, with more traditional fractions and more secular fractions. Dayıoğlu and Hatay (2015: 159), for instance, referred to what they called the "public debates" over religious education for children, and the question of whether Qur'an summer courses could be organized by mosques (or only schools). Again, these struggles demonstrate the diversity of Turkish Cypriot society.[77]

A similar diversity of (overlapping) identifications, can be found in the 21st century political party landscape in Cyprus. Long established political parties in the south, such as DIKO and EDEK, still identify with a nationalist discourse, but the new Solidarity Movement, established in 2016 (incorporating the European Party—EVROKO), also takes a strong nationalist position, and so does the radical right-wing party ELAM. This explains Charalambous and Ioannou's (2015: 271) short summary: "[…] nationalism has neither been defeated nor limited to the margins […]." But other political parties, such as AKEL and DISY (with the latter providing the current president of the Republic of Cyprus, Nicos Anastasiades), are much less inclined to strongly defend nationalist positions, which produces more diversity within the sphere of institutionalized politics in the south. In the TRNC, we find a similar ideological diversity, with National Unity Party (UBP) and Democratic Party (DP) on the nationalist side of the political spectrum. DP is led by the son of former president Rauf Denktaş, Serdar. On the other side of the political spectrum (see Baruh & Popescu, 2008: 83), we find the social-democrats of the Republican Turkish Party (CTP) and the Communal Democracy Party (TDP), with the latter party currently providing the president of the TRNC,

Mustafa Akıncı. Again, important here is that, in both communities, this diversity has enabled different coalitions, for instance, bringing different government departments into the hands of different ministers.

One example is the attempted change of the Greek Cypriot educational policy after AKEL ascended to power, in 2008.[78] The new minister of Education and Culture, Andreas Demetriou, released a circular document that moved away from the 'I don't forget' policy, and instead formulated the following objective: "[…] the cultivation of peaceful coexistence, mutual respect and cooperation between Greek Cypriots and Turkish Cypriots, with the aim of getting rid of the occupation and re-unifying our country and our people" (cited in Zembylas, Charalambous, & Charalambous, 2016: 69). This Cyprio-tist strategy was not enforced, and "[…] with the governmental changeover in 2013, and the revival of the antagonistic discourse of 'I Don't Forget', the policy has been officially marginalized and implicitly rendered inactive" (Zembylas, Charalambous, & Charalambous, 2016: 72–73). Even if this attempt was unsuccessful, the example shows the discursive struggle between the different actors of the political landscape to materially control one of the key signifying machines (the educational system) that has been supportive of the antagonistic nationalist discourse.

Cypriot policies were not only affected by the internal heterogenization, but also links with the two 'motherlands,' which were, at moments, an intimate part of the hegemonic Greek Cypriot and Turkish Cypriot nationalist equivalential chains, became more complicated. After the fall of the junta, Greece became less involved in Cyprus (even if the connections were never severed). Greece's relationship with Turkey remained problematic until both countries were hit by successive earthquakes in 1999 and the caring responses intensified the already existent détente (Ker-Lindsay, 2007). But in the "post-kemalist" (Michael, 2011: 198) era of Turkey, tensions between Turkey, Greece, and the entire EU have increased again, for a variety of reasons, including the continuation of the Aegean dispute, the long and difficult Turkish ascension process into the EU, increasingly authoritarian rule in Turkey, and the Syrian Civil War (with its many refugees). In Cyprus, Turkey has kept a firm grip on the TRNC, both materially and discursively, although there have always been tensions. Isachenko (2012: 75–76), for instance, described the conflict that erupted when, in July 2000, Mustafa Akıncı (then-leader of TKP and deputy prime minister) raised the question whether it was still appropriate for a Turkish general to control the Turkish Cypriot police and fire brigades, which resulted in accusations of treason by the Turkish military.[79] These events fed into the 'This country is ours' platform. The very same Mustafa Akıncı said during his victory speech after the presidential elections that the relationship between Turkey and the TRNC would no longer be that of 'motherland' and 'babyland,' but would be based on an equal "relationship between brothers." When Akıncı repeated the same message on CNN Turk, Erdoğan responded as follows:

> "'Mr. President's ears should hear what comes out of his mouth. Working together even as brothers has its prerequisites. This country has paid a price for Northern Cyprus. We've sacrificed martyrs and we are continuing to pay a price. We spend about $1 billion for them annually', Erdogan said. 'Who is waging the battle for Northern Cyprus in the international arena? Can Mr. Akinci wage this battle on his own? [Turkey] will continue to see [the TRNC] just like a mother sees her baby.'"[80]

The ascension of Cyprus into the EU[81] added another significant state assemblage to the equation, further disrupting the structural 'Republic of Cyprus and Greece' versus 'TRNC and Turkey' dichotomy. The motivations for joining the EU were partially internal, as Michael (2011: 153) commented: "Greek Cypriot desire for accession to the EU was guided by broader strategic considerations." These considerations consisted of putting pressure on the Turkish Cypriot and Turkish political regime. To quote Michael (2011: 153) again: "Cyprus's efforts to join the EU had the potential both to exacerbate tensions between the Turkish Cypriots and Turkey and help resolve the conflict through some arrangement involving membership in return for a peace settlement." This strategy only worked partially, with the Annan Plan being rejected by the Greek Cypriot community. Some authors pointed to other problems. For instance, Ulusoy (2009: 397) wrote that "Especially as a result of the Republic of Cyprus and Turkey's membership applications [...] the EU has become a party to the conflict, not a catalyst for its solution."

Cyprus's connection with the EU also produced outcomes that can be considered more positive, as Cyprus moved symbolically closer to the other European countries in the EU, increasing its visibility, although Cyprus remained in a peripheral position. Still, the material consequences were considerable: As the entire island joined the EU (with the EU legislation suspended in the north), all Cypriots, also those living in the TRNC, became EU citizens, which offers possibilities for adding the identification with the European identity to the portfolio of possible identifications. EU citizenship also has material consequences, as it facilitates material movement through the possession of an EU passport. Moreover, some of the EU's material resources became available to Cyprus, again including the north.[82] For example, between 2007 and 2016 the EU has supported the Committee of the Missing Persons (CMP).[83] And thirdly, as Kyriakides (2014: 165) argued, "[…] the Court of Justice of the EU and the domestic courts of EU member states have been added to the architecture of the 'Cyprus Question,'" which produces more authoritative signifying practices that impact on, for instance, the ownership rights in relation to the Greek Cypriot properties in the north.[84]

Despite these changes in the Cypriot discursive and material spaces, and the changing international contexts, the material configuration of Cyprus has not changed drastically over time. The island remains divided by a militarized Buffer Zone, with all its material consequences, including the displaced Cypriots' inability to do more than visit their properties, and the TRNC's political and economic isolation (Talmon, 2001).[85] Also, the division of the Cypriot communicational spaces, with Cypriot mainstream media in most cases using either Turkish or Greek, does not facilitate inter-communal dialogue (Tringides, 2013: 42). Although there have been some material attempts to bridge the divide, for instance with the Florakis Naval Base and Karpasia oil disasters, the material-economic conflicts over the Aphrodite gas field exploitation have created a substantial number of new tensions. Also, the discursive environment has proved to be more rigid than the above-discussed changes might indicate, as the discursive divide between north and south, still grounded in what one could call post-antagonistic nationalist frameworks, continues to exist, and the many negotiations between Turkish Cypriot and Greek Cypriot political representatives (and international actors) have produced many signifying practices but no material peace agreement.

One important element in this analysis is the elite-driven nature of the politics of othering. Even if Cyprus, as a small island, is characterized by social proximity, this has not been translated in high levels of popular involvement, or, in other words, participation, in the quest for the agonization of the Cyprus Problem. Civil society, as a rhizome of organizational machines, could potentially play a significant role in facilitating this participation of ordinary Cypriots in conflict transformation. But Cypriot civil society, and, in particular, the bi-communal movement, has found it difficult to mobilize large numbers of Cypriots: "[…] while the public's participation in bi-communal activities has dropped, the depth of involvement of CSOs [Civil Society Organizations] which undertake such activities increased substantially […]" (CIVICUS, 2011: 17, quoted in Jarraud, Louise, & Filippou, 2013: 54). Despite some modest attempts (e.g., Interpeace's (2014) participatory polling project) this has left the development of negotiated signifying practices in the hands of the Cypriot (political) elites. Jarraud, Louise, and Filippou (2013: 56) confirmed the absence of a participatory approach, and organized a strong plea for this approach, in the following terms:

> "[…] almost every known form of conflict resolution has been attempted in Cyprus […]. One exception is the participatory approach, which could provide a voice to citizens and civil society at large, and thereby enable ownership by the wider public of the ongoing process for a political settlement married to the process of societal reconciliation. Though all parties involved agree that the peace process should be 'Cypriot-owned and Cypriot-led', a scenario where a wider cross-section of society can be part of the peacemaking project still needs to be designed and adopted."

Finally, the Cyprus Problem has continued to dominate Cypriot spaces for more decades than one can count, acting as a master signifier for the country and its inhabitants, an ultimate moment of self-referentiality that gives meaning to all. But also, the Cyprus Problem as master signifier became dislocated, again illustrating the logic of contingency. When, in 2012–2013, the economic crisis hit the south of Cyprus, it dislocated the centrality of the Cyprus Problem. Simultaneously, the economic crises also severely dislocated the articulation of the Greek Cypriot subject position as economically superior (in relation to the north). Although the Republic of Cyprus is slowly recovering from this economic crisis, and the dislocation of the centrality of the Cyprus Problem has been reduced again, the 2012–2013 economic crisis altered the Cypriot horizon, even when this alteration was only (semi-)temporary.

Notes

1. Throughout the text, English, and sometimes Greek, names, combined with a Latin spelling, are used for geographical entities. This was done mainly for the comfort of the author and the reader.
2. In 2014 the population in the south was 847,000 (Press and Information Office for the Statistical Service, 2015); in the north, a 2013 estimate suggests a number close to 295,000 (Encyclopaedia Britannica, 2014: 143).
3. As a consequence, this chapter's theoretization of nationalism will also feature as a tertiary sensitizing concept.
4. See http://nicocarpentier.net/icontroversies/ for a more detailed discussion.
5. Some authors use 'Turkish' for the Ottoman period. In this book 'Ottoman' is preferred.
6. TRNC refers here to the Turkish Republic of Northern Cyprus, the de facto state in north Cyprus. In the south of Cyprus, it is customary to add citation marks to TRNC, or to refer

to it as a 'pseudo-state.' The reader will have to forgive me for not indulging in this signifying practice, although this practice will be briefly analyzed further on in the book.

7. These three religious minorities are recognized in the Cypriot constitution of 1960. 'Latins' refers to Roman Catholics.
8. Later accounts reframed these revolts through an ethno-nationalist perspective—see Panayiotou (2012: 74) for a critique.
9. Mirbagheri (2010: xxvi) mentioned "[...] approximately 28 bloody uprisings [...]" between 1572 and 1668. Jennings (1993: 398) was nevertheless much more careful when he wrote: "In fact there is surprisingly little evidence of revolts in Cyprus at that time. [...] Almost all of the so-called revolts seem to be known through single sources."
10. The Communist Party of Cyprus (KKK) was established much earlier, with its first party congress organized on 14 August 1926 (Adams, 1971: 14). The party became illegal after the October 1931 riots. When AKEL was established, some of the key members of the Communist Party of Cyprus played a leading role.
11. Both parties merged in 1949 into the National Turkish Union Party of Cyprus (http://www.avrupaturkbirligi.eu/presidents.asp). In 1955 the name of this party was changed to the Cyprus-is-Turkish party (French, 2015: 253; Özkan, 2015: 7; Soulioti, 2006: 50).
12. As mentioned in an earlier footnote, in Cyprus, the National Turkish Union Party of Cyprus changed its name in Cyprus-is-Turkish in 1955.
13. The year after, in 1961, Cyprus joined the Commonwealth.
14. http://www.presidency.gov.cy/presidency/presidency.nsf/all/1003AEDD83EED9C7C225756F0023C6AD/$file/CY_Constitution.pdf
15. The constitution uses 'Greek' and 'Turk' when referring to people, and not 'Greek Cypriot' and 'Turkish Cypriot'.
16. Archbishop Makarios became the republic's first president, and Fazil Küçük its first vice-president.
17. This was based on the United Nations Security Council Resolution 186 which was passed on 4 March 1964.
18. By then, Grivas had died in his Limassol hide-out.
19. Different signifiers are used for this event: In practice, 'invasion' is juxtaposed with 'peace operation' (Mirbagheri, 2010: 83).
20. http://www.cmp-cyprus.org/. The numbers change over time, for a variety of reasons. In 2013, the Committee on Missing Persons in Cyprus counted 1,464 Greek Cypriot missing persons, and 494 Turkish Cypriot missing persons.
21. Dikomitis (2012: 10) referred to 142,000.
22. Faustmann and Ker-Lindsay (2008: 70) mentioned 45,000.
23. The mixed village of Pyla is the most well-known example (Papadakis, 1997; Papadakis, 2005: 207ff). Also, since the late 1970s there has been cooperation between north and south-Nicosia to process the city's sewage (Calame & Charlesworth, 2011: 121). Out of this collaboration grew the Nicosia Master Plan (UNDP-ACT, 2013: 20)—see http://www.nicosia.org.cy/en-GB/municipality/services/nmp/introduction/
24. Kato Pyrgos is on the Greek Cypriot side of the Buffer Zone. West of Kato Pyrgos is the Turkish Cypriot enclave of Kokkina, which was heavily fought over in the mid-1960s (see Bryant, 2012).

25. Famagusta (including the closed off district of Varosha) lies north of the Buffer Zone, on the Turkish Cypriot side. In the eastern part of the island, the Dhekelia Sovereign Base area interrupts the Buffer Zone.
26. The Office of the Special Advisor of the Secretary-General (OSASG) is also known as the UN Good Offices.
27. In the European Court of Human Rights case, a Turkish private was identified as the shooter (http://hudoc.echr.coe.int/eng?i=001-71208).
28. According to international law, Turkey (and not the TRNC) is considered to be responsible, as it de facto controls the northern part of Cyprus and its inhabitants are under its jurisdiction.
29. See http://hudoc.echr.coe.int/eng?i=001-71208
30. See http://hudoc.echr.coe.int/eng?i=001-87146 and http://hudoc.echr.coe.int/eng?i=001-87144
31. John Burton, Leonard Doob, and Herbert Kelman all contributed to the development of this method with their work on Cyprus (Hill, 1982).
32. This was together with five of the Central and Eastern European countries that would eventually also join the EU—this was called the '5+1 formula'—(Laulhé Shaelou, 2010: 49).
33. In June 2004, the Organization of Islamic Coorperation (OIC) also upgraded the Observer status of the 'Turkish Cypriot Community' to the 'Turkish Cypriot State' (Isachenko, 2012: 163), even though this change remained contested within the OIC. The current OIC description of the TRNC, which has observer status at the OIC, is 'Turkish Cypriot State' (see http://www.oic-oci.org/oicv3/page/?p_id=179&p_ref=60&lan=en), but at a 2014 New York OIC meeting, Egypt (supported by Iran and the United Arab Emirates) contested this formulation (see http://www.worldbulletin.net/haber/145743/egypts-sisi-demands-turkish-cypriots-removed-from-oic).
34. On 20 February 2003, the European Court of Human Rights also ruled in favor of plaintiff Ahmet Djavit An, who started a case against Turkey "[...] on account of the refusal by the Turkish and Turkish-Cypriot authorities to allow him to cross the 'green line' into southern Cyprus in order to participate in bi-communal meetings." See http://hudoc.echr.coe.int/eng?i=001-60953
35. The Agios Dometios/Metehan-Kermia crossing in 2003, the Astromeritis/Zodeia-Bostanci crossing in 2005, the Ledra street/Lokmacı crossing in the center of Nicosia in 2008, and the Limnitis-Kato Pyrgos/Yeşilırmak crossing in 2010. See: United Nations Security Council (2003), and Jacobson, Musyck, Orphanides, and Webster (2009). See also: http://www.eurasia.undp.org/content/rbec/en/home/ourwork/crisispreventionandrecovery/successstories/cyprus--bringing-down-barriers-to-peace.html
36. http://cyprus-mail.com/2016/02/18/demining-opens-way-for-lefka-and-dherynia-crossings/http://cyprus-mail.com/2016/08/03/road-contract-signals-progress-dherynia-crossing/
37. http://www.undp-pff.org/index.php?option=com_content&task=view&id=99&Itemid=142
38. This also implied that Cyprus withdrew from the Non-Aligned Movement (Kyriakides: 2014: 164). It is now registered as a guest country. See: http://www.csstc.org/v_ket1.

asp?info=15&mn=1. On 1 January 2008, the Republic of Cyprus also entered the Eurozone. See: http://ec.europa.eu/economy_finance/euro/countries/cyprus_en.htm

39. Later, the former defense minister, Costas Papacostas, and three others, would be convicted for manslaughter. See: http://cyprus-mail.com/2013/08/03/a-betrayal-of-those-who-died/
40. http://www.reuters.com/article/cyprus-spill-idUSL6N0FN1Z320130717
41. Other fields discovered in the region are Zohr (Egypt), Leviathan, and Tamar (Israel). See: http://in-cyprus.com/hope-yet-for-a-cyprus-gas-hub/
42. http://cyprus-mail.com/2015/11/24/aphrodite-gas-emain-on-track/
43. http://www.occupybufferzone.info/
44. http://cyprus-mail.com/2014/02/27/diko-decides-to-leave-coalition/
45. http://cyprus-mail.com/2014/10/20/turkish-survey-vessel-off-cape-greco/
46. See also http://data.worldbank.org/country/cyprus
47. Also, the north of Cyprus suffered from economic problems, although they were at a different scale, and Turkey played a significant role in restructuring the north Cypriot economy through a series of protocols, such as the '*2013–2015 Transition to a Sustainable Economy Program*' (Bozkurt, 2013).
48. http://www.esm.europa.eu/assistance/cyprus/
49. An earlier version was rejected by the Republic of Cyprus parliament on 19 March 2013.
50. The title of this working paper, '*Getting to Bail-in: Effects of Creditor Participation in European Bank Restructuring*' (Schäfer et al., 2014) uses participation in a way that could not be further away from its usage in this book.
51. The deposits below 100,000 Euros.
52. It is added that "[…] 37.5% [is] converted into shares with full voting rights and access to future dividend payments and a further 22.5% temporarily withheld to ensure the bank meets the terms of its recapitalization […]" (Association of Cyprus Banks, 2013: 20).
53. http://ec.europa.eu/economy_finance/eu/countries/cyprus_en.htm
54. Others have also used this concept; see, for instance, Kang (2012).
55. See Özkirimli (2010: 60ff) for a critique on these primordialist approaches.
56. In his defense, Billig (1995: 78) did pay attention to the material; for instance, when emphasizing that "[…] countries are materially established in this world […]."
57. One example is the changing course of the river Semliki, which altered the Uganda–DR Congo border. See: http://www.independent.co.uk/environment/changing-river-course-alters-uganda-dr-congo-border-1818532.html, http://www.theguardian.com/environment/2010/dec/07/climate-change-rerouting-semliki-river
    Another changing river border is the Rio Grande between the USA and Mexico. See: http://www.nytimes.com/1987/09/26/world/a-liquid-border-pays-no-heed-to-diplomacy.html
58. See Hadjipavlou (2010) for one example of an analysis of gender and the Cyprus Problem.
59. For instance, in the case of Limassol, the Ottoman census of 1831 counted 303 male Muslim Cypriots and 345 male Orthodox Cypriots. Later, the percentage of Turkish Cypriots decreased to about 20% to 25%, but until 1974 there was a considerably sized Turkish Cypriot community in Limassol. See http://www.prio-cyprus-displacement.net/default.asp?id=406
60. See: https://tr.wikisource.org/wiki/T%C3%BCrk_Mukavemet_Te%C5%9Fkilat%C4%B1_Yemini (in Turkish), http://www.cybc.com.cy/html/TMT%20ENGLISH.pdf (a rare

translation in English of the transcript of a CyBC television program, entitled '*TMT: With Blood and Fire*').

61. One instance is the killing of Bonici Mompalda, a Maltese shop manager, who was also a special constable.
62. Lytras and Psaltis (2011: 15) mentioned 42 Turkish Cypriot enclaves.
63. Lytras and Psaltis (2011: 17) referred to data collected by Patrick (1976) that indicated that in 1891 the number of mixed villages was 346. In 1960 the number had declined to 114, and in 1970 there were 48 mixed villages left. Lytras and Psaltis (2011: 17) remarked that not only "inter-communal frictions" but also urbanisation processes are responsible for this decrease. The number in the mid-1960s is likely to have been even lower, as "By 1971 [and according to Patrick's (1976) data], 2000 Turkish Cypriot refugees had returned to 19 mixed villages and to 5 Turkish Cypriot villages while 57 formerly mixed villages had become inhabited solely by Greek Cypriots" (Lytras & Psaltis, 2011: 18). Still, "[…] relations between the ethnic quarters of most mixed villages were characterised by 'outright hostility' […]" (Patrick, 1976: 8, quoted in Lytras & Psaltis, 2011: 17).
64. Also on the Turkish side, friendly fire—a dramatic example of human error, military tactics, and material agency—took its toll, as Turkish war planes sank the Turkish destroyer D-354 Kocatepe (http://www.worldnavalships.com/turkish_navy.htm), and damaged the D-353 Adatepe and the D-355 Tinaztepe.
65. Bryant (2004: 224) argued that sometimes Turkish Cypriots "[…] are portrayed as unwilling captives of Denktas and the Turkish military."
66. A cultural trauma is more than an aggregate of individual traumata (see Kansteiner, 2004: 209). It is a cultural phenomenon that "[…] appears in the aftermath of a particular type of social change" (Sztompka, 2000: 452).
67. Nadel-Klein (1991: 502) provided the following working definition of localism: "[…] the representation of group identity as defined primarily by a sense of commitment to a particular place and to a set of cultural practices that are self-consciously articulated and to some degree separated and directed away from the surrounding social world."
68. Gentles (2007: 94) described the military importance of the flag ('the colours'), referring to a quote from Captain Thomas Venn from 1672: "To lose one's 'colour' was regarded as a disgrace worse than death. 'Indeed, a greater act of cowardice cannot be found', declared Captain Thomas Venn, 'than the colours to be lost.'"
69. We should here bear Mavratsas's (1997: 723–724) words in mind: "[…] Cypriotist elements and orientations can be found in almost all political parties, and it should be clear that the reduction of the contest between nationalism and Cypriotism into a left-right opposition cannot be fully sustained and can only oversimplify the picture."
70. The Communal Liberation Party merged with the Peace and Democracy Movement into the Communal Democracy Party [*Toplumcu Demokrasi Partisi*—TDP], and the latter had Mustafa Akıncı elected as president of the TRNC in April 2015.
71. Witness the current set of civil society activities within the Ledra Palace crossing.
72. At that time, casinos were illegal in the Republic of Cyprus, but many casinos operated in the north. On 10 March 2016, the Republic of Cyprus parliament voted for a law allowing one integrated casino resort to be established, and on 4 November 2016

the Melco-Hard Rock consortium was invited to apply for a licence. See: http://cyprus-mail.com/2016/03/10/green-light-from-casino-from-parliament/http://cyprus-mail.com/2016/11/04/melco-hard-rock-casino-bid-gets-nod-approval/

73. There are still cases of violence against the other. For instance, on 17 May 2016, a Cyprus Mail news report referred to three Turkish Cypriots being attacked in their car in the southern part of Nicosia on 15 May 2016, by a group of Greek Cypriots, believed to be APOEL (soccer) fans. The damage to the car, which had a TRNC license plate, was estimated at 500 Euros. See: http://cyprus-mail.com/2016/05/17/police-investigate-claim-football-fans-attacked-turkish-cypriots/
74. Christos Efthymiou is, together with Sevgul Uludag, coordinator of Together We Can.
75. Anastasiou (2008b: 163ff) spent a lot of time analyzing the position of AKEL. AKEL's "[…] long-standing, interethnic rapprochement policy and ongoing contact and dialogue with the TCs [Turkish Cypriots]" (Anastasiou, 2008b: 163) made its decision to support the 'no' camp surprising, even though Anastasiou (2008b: 163) also argued that a strong push by a nationalist AKEL faction caused the party leadership to revise its original support to the Annan Plan, and eventually reject it. The internal AKEL struggle illustrates how organizational machines harmonize signifying practices.
76. For a more plausible analysis of the role of the USA in 1974, see Constandinos (2012). Stearns's (1992: 11) summary about the earlier stages of the conflict points to a similar argument, describing the USA initiatives as "[…] firefighting operations designed primarily to prevent general hostilities between Greece and Turkey or secure other short-term objectives."
77. These changes raise concerns in the south of Cyprus, as this online article shows: http://in-cyprus.com/religious-pressure-in-north/
78. Erhürman (2010: 274) described how in the period of the CTP government in the TRNC, the Turkish Cypriot history books were changed so that "[…] the past between Greek [Cypriots] and Turkish Cypriots was represented more positively than in the previous history textbook in order to prepare the ground for a possible reunification. Hence, the history textbooks are one of the most remarkable official mechanisms that show how narrations about the 'others' were articulated and constructed in changing power relations."
79. The Turkish Brigadier-General Ali Nihat Özeyranlı also requested the dismissal of some of the directors of the public service broadcaster BRT and the public news agency TAK, and had an editor of the Turkish Cypriot daily *Avrupa*, Şener Levent and three other journalists, arrested. See: http://www.economist.com/node/6632
80. http://www.al-monitor.com/pulse/originals/2015/04/turkey-greece-cypriot-baby-grow-up.html
81. Sometimes the rather awkward term of the 'Europeanization of Cyprus' is used to describe this process.
82. For instance, on 27 February 2006, the European Council (2006) approved the establishment of a 5-year aid program for the Turkish Cypriot community, consisting of 259 million Euros; after 2011, the assistance continued with a yearly allocated budget of 30 million Euros. See: http://ec.europa.eu/regional_policy/en/policy/themes/turkish-cypriot-community/http://ec.europa.eu/cyprus/turkish_cypriots/index_en.htm

83. This support amounted to 17,3 million Euros (European Commission, 2012: 26). See also http://www.cmp-cyprus.org/content/donors
84. Kyriakides (2014: 165) referred here to the Court of Justice's re-affirmation of property rights in the Apostolides cases.
85. Isachenko (2012: 157) added here that "[...] de jure isolated, informal states are nevertheless embedded in the network of international politics" and "[...] they find ways to escape isolation."

· 4 ·

CCMC AS A PARTICIPATORY AND AGONISTIC ASSEMBLAGE

In the last chapter, the attention is turned to the case study, which focuses on the Cyprus Community Media Centre (CCMC) and its community web radio station, MYCYradio. The previous two platforms have provided the theoretical and analytical toolkit for this case study's discursive-material analysis. In the first platform, the ontology of the discursive-material knot is developed, which feeds into all other platforms, either by structuring the theoretical re-readings or by providing analytical support through the generation of primary and secondary sensitizing concepts. And of course, the discursive-material knot is the ontological setting in which the CCMC assemblage exists, entangling a particular variety of discourses and materials. The second platform combines a set of theoretical frameworks that deal with participation, community media organizations, conflict, and conflict transformation. A discursive-material analysis of these theoretical (sub)fields has relevance in its own right, because it attempts to enrich (sub)fields that frequently place a strong emphasis on one of two components of the discursive-material knot, often without sufficiently theorizing their 'own' component and without discussing its entanglement with the other component. But the theoretical discussions in Platform 2 also support the analysis of CCMC's participatory and agonistic remit, as these theoretical re-readings provide the tertiary signifying concepts for this case study analysis. Finally, the third chapter of this book, which is part of the third platform, provides a discursive-material analyses of the Cyprus problem, and, in particular, of the role of the different nationalisms within this conflict. Apart from producing additional tertiary sensitizing concepts (in relation to nationalism), this chapter also touches upon the Cypriot context that is very necessary to make any sense out of the practices of the CCMC participatory assemblage in relation to the transformation of the Cypriot conflict.

The fourth and final chapter of this book reports on the discursive-material analysis of the CCMC's participatory and agonistic practices. First, CCMC and MYCYradio are introduced, followed by an elaboration of the methodological framework that will be used to analyze the CCMC case study. This part also describes in more detail the data that have been gathered. Then come the two main parts of Chapter 4. First, there is the discursive-material analysis of CCMC's and MYCYradio's participatory practices, from a production and a reception perspective. In the second main part, a similar analysis is performed on CCMC's and MYCYradio's agonistic practices. The interaction between these participatory and agonistic practices, and the ways in which they enhance each other (and not) is discussed in the conclusion of Chapter 4.

1 Introducing the CCMC and MYCYradio Case Study

CCMC was established in 2009 and is located in the UN-guarded Buffer Zone in Nicosia. Initially it was not a broadcasting organization, but centered on providing training, lending equipment to member organizations (that are part of the Cypriot civil society), creating productions for other organizations, staging public events, and offering media advice to members. Only in 2013 did CCMC's web radio station, MYCYradio, begin broadcasting, despite the fact that at present there is no explicit recognition of community media in either part of Cyprus.[1]

The starting point of CCMC's (pre-)history is 2005, when the United Nations Development Program (UNDP) and the United States Agency for International Development (USAID) launched the Action for Cooperation and Trust program (ACT) (UNDP-ACT, 2013: 11). The ACT program enabled UNDP to finance the establishment of the CCMC. In 2007, Seán Ó Siochrú, a consultant with a background in community media himself, was hired by UNDP. His assignment focused on the use of ICTs as a tool for strengthening and empowering civil society. In Ó Siochrú's report of 16 November 2007, he proposed the establishment of what he called a "multi-component community/NGO media initiative," with strong NGO ownership and capacity-building for NGOs through learning-by-doing (personal communication, Seán Ó Siochrú, 15 May 2016). The first CCMC staff members were hired in September 2009 (Interview CCMC staff member 3, January 2012), and the CCMC opened its doors in December 2009. UNDP-ACT (2013: 54) described CCMC in a 2013 report as "[…] one-stop-shop for inter-communal media collaboration and a resource for civil society-led advocacy."

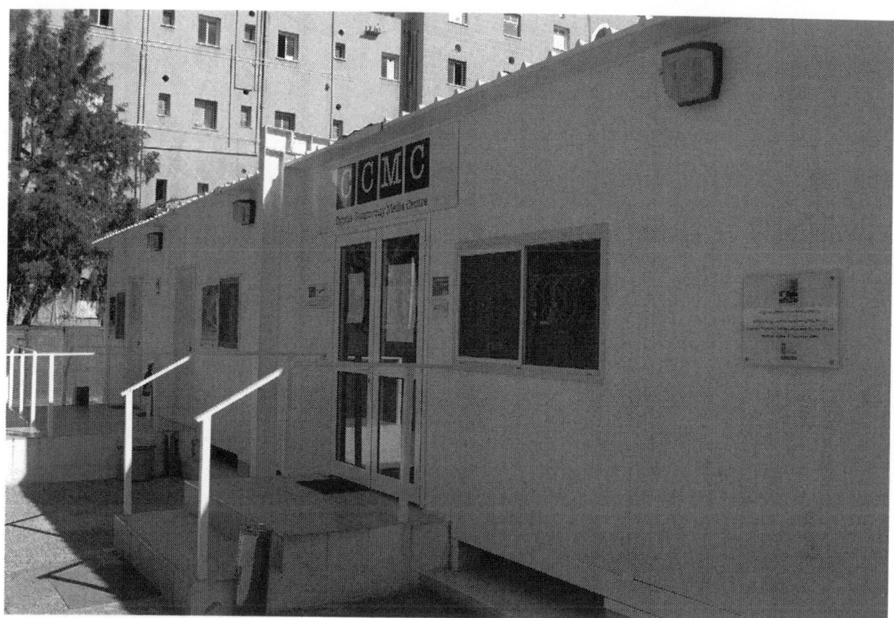

Figure 35. The CCMC building.
Source: Nico Carpentier.

In its *Foundation Charter*, the mission of CCMC (2009) is pithily summarized as "Empowering a media literate and active society," which shows its emphasis on community participation and empowerment. But the organization also aims to contribute to conflict transformation. Especially in the description of CCMC's 10 core values, the link to conflict transformation is made explicit. The first item on the list of core values is to "Unite people and communities through community media based on coexistence, dialogue, inclusion, reconciliation, and respect for diversity." In addition, the fifth core value emphasizes the inclusiveness of CCMC ("We value and respect the contributions of all people in society and aim to provide a forum for diversity, multiculturalism, and social inclusion through community media production based on creativity, dialogue, and innovation") and the ninth core value refers to CCMC's opposition toward "[...] all forms of discrimination based on concepts of race, ethnicity, class, gender, sexuality, creed, and/or religious belief and views."

UNDP-ACT supported CCMC within Phase II of ACT, from 2008 until 2011.[2] From 2012 to 2013, UNDP-ACT then provided financial support for CCMC's MultiCommMedia project.[3] At that stage, the structural collaboration between UNDP and CCMC ended, although CCMC was still involved in the UNDP-funded project Seeds for Democracy. In 2013 the European Commission Representation in Cyprus[4] provided CCMC with the funding which enabled the establishment of the community webcaster MYCYradio. This funding ended again in the middle of 2014. In the period after the UNDP funding, part of CCMC's income was generated by diverse and smaller projects (Interview MYCYradio producer 2, June 2016).

Similar to CCMC's charter, MYCYradio's (2013a) *Foundation Charter* also refers to inclusiveness, diversity, and participation: "MYCYradio aims to engage with and serve all communities living in Cyprus, by providing a platform for a diversity of voices to be heard. It aims to highlight cultural and linguistic diversity, encourage social integration thus promote a culture of active citizenship and participatory democracy." This diversity is also visible in the MYCYradio program schedule. For instance, in November 2013, at the time of the program analysis, MYCYradio had 32 programs, which used, apart from Greek, Turkish, and English, also Arabic, Cameroonian, French, Lingala, Persian, Sinhalese, Spanish, Swahili, and Tamil.[5] Despite the dominance of Greek and English (and, to some degree, Turkish),[6] we could still find a strong focus on linguistic minorities in the program schedule (MYCYradio, 2013b), where, for instance, the program *Al Jalia* was described as "[...] a bridge between Arabs themselves, the local society and other communities in Cyprus"; *Cypriots' Corner* "[...] invites you to find out about the true diversity of Cyprus, exploring the issues affecting minority groups in Cypriot society, and in particular the religious communities of Armenians, Maronites, and Latins," and *Rangarang* was seen as "[...] a platform where people can access information about the Iranian community in Cyprus." Also, issues related to other social groups, such as LGBTQA[7] and women's rights, featured in the program schedule, as the objective of the program *Kaleid 'Her' Scope* showed: "[...] 'giving a voice to voiceless women'—women for women, women to women, women about women!"

1.1 A Reflection on Discursive-Material Analysis (DMA)

In order to analyze the CCMC case study, a particular methodological framework is mobilized. In Platform 1, discourse-material analysis, the methodological framework that is used in this book, has already been touched upon, to explain the book's three-platform structure. In this part, I will develop this methodological framework further.

Discourse-material analysis is an analytical method that forms a methodological translation of discourse theory enriched by more materialist theoretical elements. As an analytical method, it is closely related to Glynos and Howarth's discourse analysis (2007), Carpentier and De Cleen's discourse-theoretical analysis (2007), Angermuller's poststructuralist discourse analysis (2014), and Marttila's post-foundational discourse analysis (2016), as all these approaches are grounded in a post-structuralist ontology and share a focus on discourse as representation (or ideology). Discourse-material analysis is also affiliated with other methodologies used in discourse studies, such as critical discourse analysis (Fairclough & Wodak, 1997; Van Dijk, 1995: 24; for a comparison between critical discourse analysis and discourse-theoretical analysis, see Carpentier & De Cleen, 2007). Finally, the reflections on new materialist methodologies (e.g., Fox & Alldred, 2015) are closely related to discourse-material analysis. To illustrate the latter, in their article entitled '*New Materialist Social Inquiry*,' Fox and Alldred (2015: 406; see also 2017: 169) presented the following list of characteristics for a new materialist research design, which clearly shows the affiliations with discourse-material analysis:

- "Attend not to individual bodies, subjects, experiences or sensations, but to assemblages of human and non-human, animate and inanimate, material and abstract, and the affective flows within these assemblages.
- Explore how affects draw the material and the cultural, and the 'micro', 'meso' and 'macro' into assembly together.
- Explore the movements of territorialisation and de-territorialisation, aggregation and disaggregation within the assemblages studied, and the consequent affect economies and micropolitics these movements reveal."

These methodologies can be labeled directive methodologies, as they direct their users to (primary) sensitizing concepts. In the case of discourse studies methodologies, this is the notion of discourse itself. Speaking more generally, this implies a combination of:

1. a priori (or internal) theoretical concepts, given through the (choice for the) directive methodology (e.g., discourse in discourse studies);
2. theoretical concepts external to the directive methodology;
3. reflections that are of a methodological-theoretical nature (e.g., about the ontology of research); and
4. methodological-procedural reflections (e.g., about the cyclical-iterative nature of research).

In other words, directive methodologies come with their 'own' (internal) theoretical concepts and frameworks, but also enable other (external) theoretical concepts and frameworks to be integrated. It is this dynamics of internal and external theoretical support that requires the integration and calibration of external theoretical concepts and frameworks in order to ensure the alignment of the external theoretical concepts and frameworks with the internal ones.

Conversely, non-directive qualitative methodologies, as advocated in the (traditional) grounded theory approaches, for instance (Glaser & Strauss, 1967), do not provide analysts with a priori (or internal) theoretical concepts that can act as anchorage points (through their sensitizing, non-definitive nature). This implies that non-directive (qualitative) methodologies only import theoretical positions that are external to the methodology into the analysis, or that these theoretical positions are expected to be generated by the analysis itself.

As already argued at the end of Platform 1, but worth repeating: The notion of the sensitizing concept provides the methodological bridge between the discourse-theoretical and materialist frameworks on the one hand, and the empirical research data to be analyzed on the other hand. Sensitizing concepts help analysts, as Ritzer (1992: 365) explained, in "[…] what to look for and where to look […]." These concepts are not intended to dominate and foreclose the analysis, but are kept in the back of the mind of the analyst and provide support when interpreting particular social realities and applying the categorization logics of qualitative analysis (Maso, 1989; Wester, 1987, 1995). Within discourse studies, it is (not surprisingly) the notion of discourse that features as primary sensitizing concept, whether we are dealing with discursive-material analysis, discourse-theoretical analysis, critical discourse analysis, or (linguistic) discourse analysis. Even if the signifier discourse is shared by all these different approaches, its meaning is not stable. The meaning of the notion discourse can vary strongly, depending on its position within the textual and contextual dimensions that were discussed earlier (see Figure 1). Moreover, in the case of discursive-material analysis, the material, and the interaction between the discursive and the material as captured by the metaphor of the knot, provide us with an additional primary sensitizing concept. When we visualize these discourse studies approaches, we can use a pyramidal model to signify the foundation provided by the basic principles of qualitative research, the family of discourse studies which shares the signifier discourse, and the different variations of the notion of discourse used by the different approaches in discourse studies (Figure 36—Model 1). Outside discourse studies, other, still directive, qualitative methodologies exist (Figure 36—Model 2). Also, the use of the non-directive qualitative methods (Figure 36—Model 3), and the use of quantitative methodologies (Figure 36—Model 4), which produce an entirely

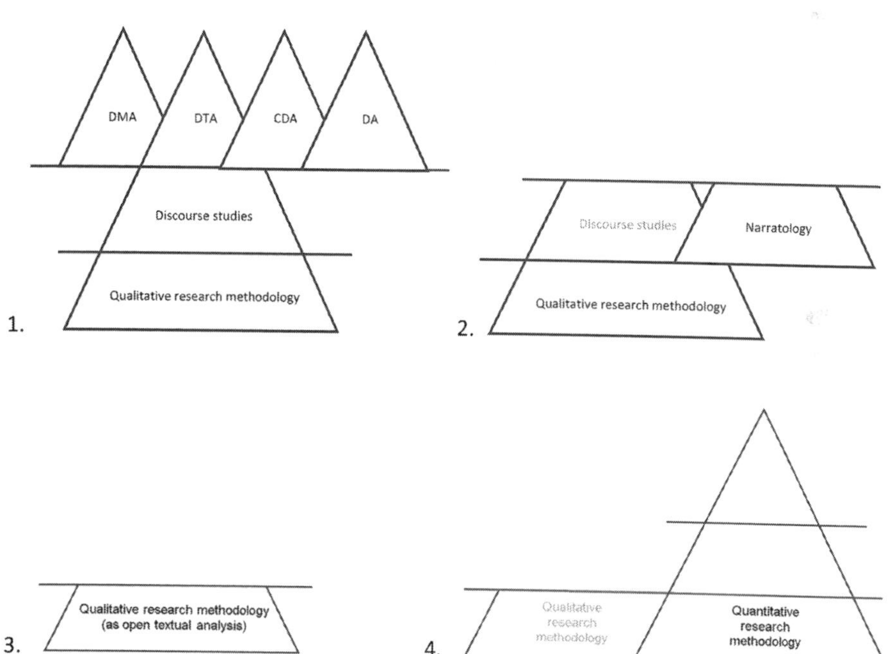

Figure 36. Primary sensitizing concepts in and outside discourse studies—four variations. Source: Adapted from Carpentier (2010: 262), with DMA = discursive-material analysis, DTA = discourse-theoretical analysis, CDA = critical discourse analysis, and DA = (linguistic) discourse analysis.

different set of pyramids, can be considered for research. In addition, multi-method and even multi-paradigm research projects remain possible, however difficult it may be to implement these in actual research practice and have them supported by discursive and materialist theories.

Within discourse studies, the specificity of a particular approach is not only defined by its definition of discourse (see Figure 37 for discourse-theoretical analysis), but also by the additional theoretical concepts that it mobilizes through its own theoretical groundings. In actual research practice, these theoretical concepts then serve as secondary sensitizing concepts. To use discourse-theoretical analysis as an example (Carpentier, 2010; Carpentier & De Cleen, 2007), discourse theory enables the production of a considerable list of secondary sensitizing concepts, which includes the concepts of articulation, nodal point, floating signifier, and subject position, but also contingency and overdetermination, chain of equivalence (and difference), antagonism, agonism, hegemony, and social imaginary.

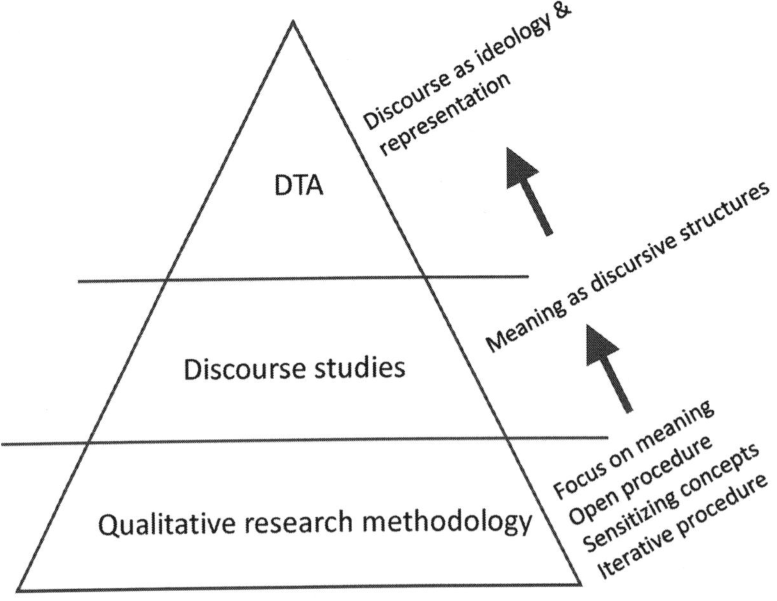

Figure 37. The specific articulation of discourse-theoretical analysis' primary sensitizing concept.
Source: Carpentier (2010: 261).

When shifting our attention to discourse-material analysis, the number of primary sensitizing concepts is increased, to also include the material and the discursive-material knot, together with the discursive. This implies that when analyzing particular social realities through discourse-material analysis, the analytical focus is not only placed on the identification of discourses, but also on the role of the material and how the discursive and the material interact. Secondly, with the increased attention for the role of the material (and materialist theoretical frameworks), the list of secondary sensitizing concepts is also expanded, with, for instance, the concepts of assemblage, dislocation, disruption, invitation, investment, and material (bodily and text-related) practices. Thirdly, the dimension of structure and agency is used to provide support to the analysis of the discursive-material knot, which produces additional secondary sensitizing concepts (which remain connected to the discursive-material dimension, as explained in Platform 1).

Figure 38 uses a pyramidal model to illustrate this combination of primary sensitizing concepts (at the top of the pyramid), with the secondary sensitizing concepts originating from discourse theory at the right-hand side of the pyramid, and the secondary sensitizing concepts that are derived from the materialist expansion of discourse theory on the left-hand side. At the very bottom of the pyramid, qualitative research principles and procedures continue to provide the foundation (Maso, 1989; Wester, 1987, 1995) for the entire methodological configuration.

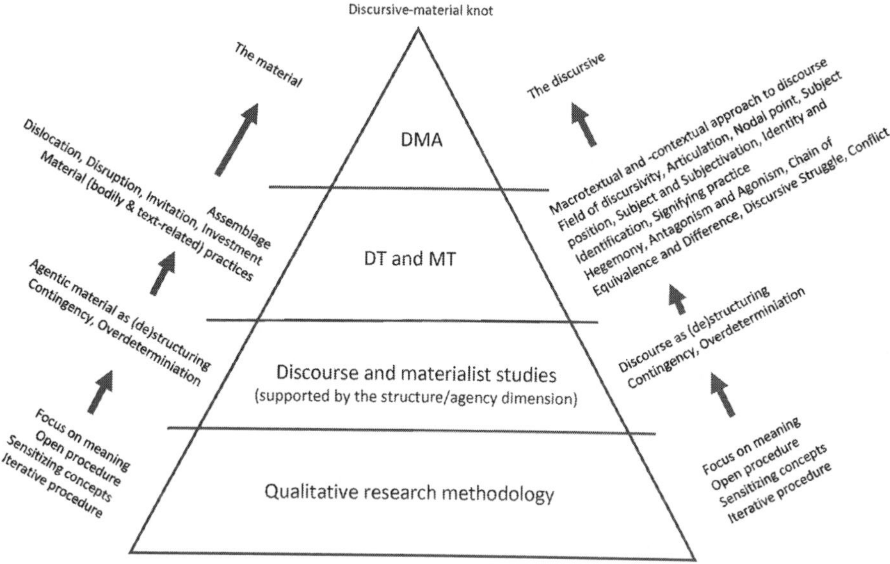

Figure 38. The primary and secondary sensitizing concepts of discourse-material analysis.

Even if the refusal of, for instance, Laclau and Mouffe to provide methodological guidelines[8] has not proven to be very helpful, their concern to protect the specificity of each research project is nevertheless something I deeply share. For this reason, discourse-material analysis (and discourse-theoretical analysis, for that matter) is grounded in a dynamics of sensitizing concepts internal to discourse and materialist theory, on the one hand, and sensitizing concepts external to discourse and materialist theory, but necessary for the theoretical grounding of the research project, on the other hand. The latter set of theoretical notions form the third layer of sensitizing concepts, and these are indeed very much specific to each research project. To avoid an ontological and paradigmatic schism between the internal and external sensitizing concepts, there is still a need to translate these external theoretical frameworks and bring them into the realm of discourse and materialist theory. This re-reading of existing theories consists of a discourse-material analysis of theoretical material not dissimilar to Derrida's deconstruction, even though he takes aim at theoretical-philosophical texts and does not focus so much on empirical research. The outcome of these re-readings are discursive-material versions of originally non-discursive-material theories, which are made consistent, or calibrated with the ontological-paradigmatic assumptions of discourse and materialist theories.

Guidance for this process of re-reading is provided by the primary and secondary sensitizing concepts of discourse-material analysis, which are then played out at the theoretical level. Key questions become what the dominant and non-dominant discursive articulations in a particular theoretical field are, what their nodal points and elements are, which subject positions feature in them, how this particular theoretical field constructs assemblages with these discourses and particular materials, how these theoretical frameworks enable agency of subjects and materials, and how the contingency of the social is (re-)present(ed) in these theoretical frameworks. In this book, Platform 2 is an illustration of the re-reading of three theoretical frameworks (related to participation, community media, and conflict (transformation)). An overview of the different types of sensitizing concepts, and how they can be classified as primary, secondary, and tertiary sensitizing concepts can be found in Figure 39, which also uses the discourse-theoretical distinction between nodal points and elements to differentiate between primary and secondary sensitizing concepts, and show the diversity within the cluster of tertiary concepts.[9]

After having constructed these different layers of sensitizing concepts, discourse-material analysis returns to the safe harbor of the procedures that

Level	Definition	Usages (in this book)
Primary sensitizing concepts	Theoretical nodal points internal to the methodology of discourse-material analysis (DMA)	The discursive, the material, the discursive-material knot
Secondary sensitizing concepts	Theoretical elements internal to the DMA-methodology	Articulation, nodal point, hegemony, antagonism, agonism, assemblage, agentic matter, invitation, investment, dislocation, disruption … (see Figure 38)
Tertiary sensitizing concepts	Theoretical nodal points external to the DMA-methodology	Participation (and interaction and access), community media (and community, alternativity, civil society and rhizome), conflict (transformation), nationalism …
	Theoretical elements external to the DMA-methodology	Power, leader, expert, citizen, owner, resources, community, audience, media infrastructure and proto-machines, violence, victim, perpetrator, other, friend, adversary, enemy (destruction), radical difference, homogenization of the self, peaceful and non-violent interaction, conflictual togetherness, pluralization of the self …

Figure 39. Sensitizing concepts: Levels, definitions, and usages.

have been developed within the more traditional approaches of qualitative analysis, for instance, when it comes to (theoretical) sampling, research design, coding, and saturation (see, e.g., Silverman, 2006). Nevertheless, in the context of this book's methodological discussion, it is important to stress the importance of coding procedures as interpretative processes that critically interrogate the social. Similar to sensitizing concepts, coding procedures form bridges between the (discursive-material) theoretical framework and the social reality that is being analyzed. These procedures play a protective role in disallowing sensitizing concepts to transform themselves into definitive concepts, and stifle the data (whether these are documents, observations …). It is through these coding procedures that sensitizing concepts can support the analyst in showing the rich diversity of the social. The combination of sensitizing concepts and coding procedures enables the analysts to produce academic signifying practices, justifiable and plausible, that still contain many analytical decisions. How the sensitizing concepts are exactly used, when a discursive entity is called a discourse, or a nodal point, or an element, or when a signifier is labeled as empty and/or floating, remain analytical choices that might be different in specific research projects. A similar question is when a material is labeled a material, and when it is called a proto-machine, and when an object. An analyst is perfectly entitled to make these choices, as long as they are explicitly and convincingly justified. Simultaneously, we should not forget that academic analyses are also indeed signifying practices, which attempt to, albeit temporary, fixate the social, but are ultimately doomed to fail in perfectly capturing this social reality in its entirety. Even if, from the point of view of an academic, these signifying practices might be the best and most plausible we have to capture social complexity.

1.2 About the CCMC Data

The discourse-material analysis, as it was discussed in the previous part, is used to analyze the CCMC/MYCYradio case study. Here, different clusters of data have been generated, looking at different components of CCMC's and MYCYradio's activities. Even if the main research stages overlap, it still makes sense to describe the data gathering and analysis in a chronological fashion. A first preparatory and exploratory stage consisted of small contextual historical research projects, intended to generate a sufficient degree of familiarization with the complex Cypriot history. One project focused on the Independence War, analyzing the ethical articulation of killing (Carpentier, 2014d). A second project, initially quite modest, focused on the representation of the Cypriot self through states and commemoration sites in the south of Cyprus (Carpentier, 2014e, 2016b). In addition to this more general historical research, two smaller research projects related to community media were organized, one focusing on CCMC (Carpentier & Doudaki, 2014) and one on the Limassol university radio station CUTradio (Carpentier, Doudaki, &

Christidis, 2015). Thirdly, a mapping was organized to create an overview of the relevant organizations on the island.

While the first stage was preparatory and exploratory, the second and third stages were the main research stages that this book reports on. The second stage focused on the content that community web radio station MYCYradio was producing, zooming in on three of its radio shows (and the production practices of producers and guests).[10] The third stage was a reception study, analyzing how a group of 74 people responded to a selection of fragments from the MYCYradio broadcasts that I had analyzed in the second stage. Both stages were supported by transversal ethnographic and participatory research phases that cut through the main research stages. The ethnographic phase was enabled by my research stay on Cyprus, from 1 October 2013, until 30 September 2014, supported by the Vrije Universiteit Brussel (VUB) and the Cyprus University of Technology (CUT). This research stay enabled a more general immersion in the cultural context of Cyprus, as well as facilitating participant observations and informal interviews at CCMC. After September 2014, several short-term stays enabled regular follow-up and deeper analyses.

In addition to the research project that this book reports on, which focuses on CCMC (and in particular MYCYradio), a large-scale research project, the Cypriot Community Media Research Program (CCMRP), started in September 2014. The CCMRP is funded by the FWO (the Research Foundation—Flanders) and consists of an island-wide study of community media in relation to conflict transformation. Currently, two PhD researchers, Christiana Voniati and Derya Yüksek, under my supervision (with Vaia Doudaki and Aysu Arsoy as their respective co-supervisors) work for the CCMRP. In particular, the first stage of the CCMRP, where two researchers, Christiana Voniati and Nicolas Defteras, mapped the Cypriot community media landscape, provided important contextual information for the CCMC research project that this book reports on. After my own CCMC research was completed, two of the CCMC staff members, Orestis Tringides and Hazal Yolga, were hired by the VUB as part-time researchers to support the two CCMRP PhD researchers.

1.2.1 The transversal ethnographic and participatory research phases

When returning to the CCMC research project, the two transversal phases need to be explained in more detail first. The transversal ethnographic phase, with its participant observations, tended, in some cases, toward what

Gold (1958) and Junker (1960) called observer as participant, with little active participation, while in other cases the role of participant as observer was chosen. In all cases, observations were overt. The observer as participant role was mostly used when I was present in the CCMC building, in the main meeting room, which connected the MYCYradio studio with the offices of the CCMC staff. The participant as observer role, in contrast, was used when project-based collaborations with CCMC were organized. More specifically, CCMC staff members and radio producers were involved, as project media partner,[11] in the organization of two editions of the '*Iconoclastic Controversies*' exhibition. This photographic exhibition communicated the outcomes of the earlier-mentioned project on the representation of the Greek Cypriot self through statues and commemoration sites, and provided some of the visual material included in this book.[12] Other NGOs were also involved in this project, namely the Association for Historical Dialogue and Research (AHDR), the Home for Cooperation (H4C), and the arts center NeMe.

In addition, the research project that this book reports on also used a more participatory research strategy (Bergold & Thomas, 2012; Fals-Borda & Rahman, 1991; Kindon, Pain, & Kesby, 2007; Mertens, 2008), as CCMC staff members and volunteers collaborated in the data-gathering for the two main research stages, in two particular moments. First of all, CCMC staff interviewed 17 radio show guests that appeared in the broadcasts I analyzed, and transcribed these interviews (Stage 2). Secondly, CCMC also collaborated with me in relation to the reception focus groups (Stage 3). This reception subproject was developed together with CCMC, and CCMC was (financially) compensated for the research time they invested. Within this subproject, CCMC was responsible for developing the participant selection strategy; inviting the focus group respondents; arranging for their informed consent; and collecting their permission forms (for both their participation and the academic use of the focus group material); organizing, hosting,[13] and moderating the focus groups; and making the recordings and transcribing them. In order to support the CCMC activities in this research collaboration, I trained some of the CCMC staff members, selected the fragments that were played during the focus groups, and produced the discussion topic list (in consultation with CCMC). I remained responsible for the analysis, although this component was also discussed with CCMC staff. This research procedure not only enabled me to circumvent the language problem (as I do not speak Greek or Turkish, and the use of three languages in the focus groups was preferable), but having CCMC as a research partner also facilitated the data collection, enriched the analysis, improved its quality, extended the opportunities for research feedback, and added another layer to the ethnographic dimension of this project. It also respected CCMC's own participatory logic better, reducing the power imbalance between the researcher and the researched. Even if no traces of a negative impact of this participatory research strategy could be noticed, there were a few strange situations created by CCMC researching itself, but they were handled well. In the interview fragment below, one of these strange situations becomes apparent: The CCMC interviewer asks a radio show guest how the guest had been invited to that broadcast—a question that had indeed been included in the interview topic list—only to receive the reply that the CCMC interviewer had personally invited the guest for that specific broadcast:

> "Interviewer: Section two. Can you briefly explain how you were contacted by the producer of the show?
>
> Guest 9: Via you. [laughing] You asked me to come here before my presentation here at the CCMC about my new book and I accepted." (Interview guest 9—*One Percent*, Spring, 2014)

1.2.2 The research project's two main stages in more detail

More detail can be added to the general discussion of the research project's procedure, and in particular its two main stages. In the case of Stage 2, the focus was placed on the production sphere and the content produced by MYCYradio. First of all, at the very beginning of the research project, a series of contextualizing formal interviews with MYCYradio coordinators and staff members were organized. On 30 January 2012, four staff members were interviewed at CCMC: Larry Fergeson (project manager), Michael Simopoulos (project coordinator), Sarah Malian, and Beran Djemal (outreach officers). Interviewers were Vaia Doudaki and myself. Three years later, on 7 January 2015, near the end of the data collection phase, Michael Simopoulos (at that stage the former ad interim project manager) was interviewed again, this time by myself only.

Secondly, 30 radio broadcasts of three MYCYradio shows were analyzed: the Turkish Cypriot *One Percent*, the Greek Cypriot *Downtown Choris Bakira*, and the mixed-community *Cyprus Oral History Project*. These three programs were selected in consultation with CCMC, in order to optimize the diversity of the analyzed media content. It is important to stress here that my analysis did not aim to be comparative at the level of programs or at the level of their reception by Greek Cypriots or Turkish Cypriots; diversity—also in relation to language and community affiliation—remained important, but exclusively in relation to the selection of programs and people.[14]

More specifically, the analysis centers on 10 episodes of each show, broadcast between September and November 2013. During this period, the Turkish Cypriot *One Percent*, produced by Doğukan Müezzinler, discussed the "[…] problems that the Turkish Cypriot community faces" (MYCYradio, 2013b), sometimes with a guest. In the interim, the MYCYradio program schedule changed, and *One Percent* was replaced by another program (*Cyprus 360*), which still involved Doğukan Müezzinler, at least until he left Cyprus. The program name of *One Percent* is explained as follows:

> "One percent was like an ironic title because we are as people of the radio and CCMC, Community media center and people who are pro-solution in Cyprus … because everything is being put in this perspective here, we have to keep that in mind. I consider [these people] as a smaller part of the general society, this is why we are trying to do things because it needs more effort for us, because we are in a way, we are not marginal, we are not talking about literally one percent but it's a smaller part. The big part of the both communities are more conservative. So I wanted to kind of make, in a way, fun of that, like, you know, we are small but it always starts from something small. So that's [where] one percent came from." (Interview MYCYradio *One Percent* producer, February 2014)

The Greek Cypriot *Downtown Choris Bakira*[15] focused on the urban realities of Nicosia's inner city. In the course of the research, this program had three producers—Orestis Tringides, Yiannis Ioannou, and Yiorgos Kakouris. The latter two producers subsequently left the radio station and the program was produced solely[16] by Orestis Tringides until September 2014, when it stopped. *Downtown Choris Bakira* re-started in June 2015, and ran until October 2015.

Finally, the *Cyprus Oral History Project* was grounded in Frederick University's *The Cyprus Oral History and Living Memory Project* (2011—see also Christodoulou, 2014), and was one of several Cypriot oral history projects (Briel, 2013). Its producer, Nicoletta Christodoulou, re-edited a selection of these interviews for the MYCYradio broadcasts. This program ran until July 2014.

The broadcasts of these three radio shows were transcribed, translated into English—from Greek or Turkish—when necessary,[17] and then analyzed. The analysis of the broadcasts is further contextualized by interviews with their five producers. A first wave of interviews took place in February 2014, with Orestis Tringides (10 February 2014), Nicoletta Christodoulou (10 February 2014), Doğukan Müezzinler (13 February 2014), and Yiorgos Kakouris and

Yiannis Ioannou (16 February 2016). Follow-up interviews were organized in the summer of 2014, with Yiannis Ioannou (9 June 2014), Yiorgos Kakouris and Orestis Tringides (19 June 2014), Nicoletta Christodoulou (26 June 2014) and Doğukan Müezzinler (2 July 2014).[18] Two final (e-mail) interviews with Orestis Tringides took place on 10 and 28 June 2016. All these interviews were conducted by myself. Moreover, 17 guests of the three radio shows were interviewed. In total, 28 guests from the 30 radio shows (analyzed in this project) were identified, and 17 of them could be traced and interviewed (see Figure 40). This last part of the research was performed in close collaboration with CCMC staff members (as explained before).

In all cases, given the possibly sensitive nature of some of their signifying practices, the names of the CCMC staff members, MYCYradio producers, and radio show guests are replaced by a code when their voices are cited (or paraphrased). This code combines their position (as staff member, producer, or guest) and one or two digits.

The analysis of programs and interviews was further complemented by an analysis of the web material related to these three shows. Afterwards, the five producers, together with the then CCMC ad interim manager, received a draft version of the production analysis.[19] Two producers, and the ad interim manager, provided additional feedback. One particular fragment was discussed extensively, which rightfully led to more emphasis on the playful nature of *Downtown Choris Bakira*, which has also been included in this book.

The second main part of the case study reports on the reception analysis[20] of these three radio shows. Between 24 April and 22 May 2014, ten focus group discussions were organized, again in close collaboration with CCMC (as explained above). In this reception study, 74 respondents took part, discussing a selection of fragments from the three MYCYradio shows (see Figure 41). For *One Percent* and *Cyprus Oral History Project*, there were five fragments, for *Downtown Choris Bakira* there were three. Because of time constraints, each focus group only discussed the material originating from one radio show.

As *Cyprus Oral History Project* contained both the voices of Greek Cypriots and Turkish Cypriots, two focus groups were in English, two in Greek, and two in Turkish. *Downtown Choris Bakira* had two focus groups discussing it in Greek; *One Percent* had two in Turkish. All Greek and Turkish discussions were translated in English. For each pair of focus groups, one included people that had listened more than once to MYCYradio, and one included respondents that had not (and often did not know the webradio station at all). In addition, a series of socio-demographic and ideological criteria were used to generate diversity. Figure 42 gives an overview of these 10 focus groups.

Name	Interview language	Interview date and location	Interviewer	Episode
Cyprus Oral History Project				
Guest 1	English	02/06/2014—H4C	Michael Simopoulos	09/09/2013
Guest 2	Greek	02/06/2014—Tseri (together with Guest 3)	Michael Simopoulos	16/09/2013
Guest 3	Greek	02/06/2014—Tseri (together with Guest 2)	Michael Simopoulos	30/09/2013
Guest 4	English	15/04/2014—CCMC	Hazal Yolga	14/10/2013
Guest 5	Greek	30/04/2014—CCMC/ Skype	Michael Simopoulos	11/11/2013
Guest 6	English	23/05/2014—CCMC/ Skype	Michael Simopoulos	18/11/2013
One Percent				
Guest 7	English	14/04/2014—H4C	Hazal Yolga	11/09/2013
Guest 8	English	15/04/2014—CCMC	Hazal Yolga	18/09/2013; 13/11/2013
Guest 9	English	17/04/2014—CCMC	Michael Simopoulos	18/09/2013
Guest 10(*)	English	15/04/2014—Kyrenia	Hazal Yolga	25/09/2013
Guest 11	English	08/04/2014—CCMC	Hazal Yolga	20/11/2013
Downtown Choris Bakira				
Guest 12	English (and some Greek)	16/04/2014—CCMC	Michael Simopoulos	12/09/2013
Guest 13	English	16/04/2014—Costa Cafe	Michael Simopoulos	03/10/2013
Guest 14	English	02/05/2014—INTOTO Studio	Michael Simopoulos	17/10/2013
Guest 15	English	15/04/2014—H4C	Michael Simopoulos	24/10/2013
Guest 16	English	14/04/2014—H4C	Michael Simopoulos	31/10/2013
Guest 17	English	14/04/2014—CCMC	Michael Simopoulos	07/11/2013

Figure 40. The 17 interviewed radio show guests.

(*) This interview was very brief, as the guest declined to answer most of the questions.

Fragment	Date broadcast	Summary	Relevant issues in fragment
		One Percent (in Turkish)	
1	18/09/2013	Host 3 talks with Guest 9 about his new book.	Bi-linguality, friendship, multi-perspective historical research, Cypriotness, critique on government, nationalism, and violence
2	18/09/2013		
3	27/11/2013	Monologue of Host 3 about community media and Cyprus.	Community media, political culture, critique on Cypriots (as passive), diversity
4	27/11/2013		
5	27/11/2013		
		Cyprus Oral History Project (in English)	
1	09/09/2013	Interview with Guest 1, who is introduced as a Turkish Cypriot.	Ordinary people, suffering and loss, collaboration and friendship, responsibility of the political system, and government critique
2	30/09/2013	Interview with Guest 3. She is Greek Cypriot and member of the Greek Maronite community of Cyprus.	Government responsibility, ordinary people, suffering and loss, kindness, bi-linguality
3	14/10/2013	Interview with Guest 4. She is a Turkish Cypriot.	Suffering and loss, fear, knowing the perpetrators
4	18/11/2013	Interview with Guest 6, who is a Greek Cypriot with American citizenship.	Negative portrayal of the other, lack of understanding, return to the homes (refugee), exclusive victimhood
5	18/11/2013		
		Downtown Choris Bakira (in Greek and English)	
1	12/09/2013	Interview of the three producers with Guest 12, who is a writer and professor of architecture.	Suffering and loss, Cypriot language, cultural critique, critique on the Church, Cypriot achievements
2	10/10/2013	One host (Host 3) interviews Guest 19[21] of the Turkish Municipality of Nicosia.	Bi-linguality, shared histories, diversity, collaboration and friendship, fear, stigmatization, and social pressure
3	31/10/2013	Host 4 and Host 5 are interviewing, Guest 16, an artist who is letting a diary circulate around the world, so that different artists can add their artwork to this diary.	Phone-in interaction, religious division, friendship and peace, the arts

Figure 41. Overview of the 13 fragments used in the focus group discussions.

FG code	Show	Language	Type of participants	# Participants	Date	Location	Moderator
FG1_EL	COHP	English	Listeners	8	24/04/2014	CCMC	Natalie Konyalian/Katherine Kotsireas
FG2_GL	DCB	Greek	Listeners	7	24/04/2014	CCMC	Michael Simopoulos/Natalie Konyalian
FG3_GL	COHP	Greek	Listeners	7	8/05/2014	CCMC	Michael Simopoulos/George Andriotis
FG4_TNL	1%	Turkish	Non-listeners	7	24/04/2014	CCMC	Hazal Yolga
FG5_TL	1%	Turkish	Listeners	6	06/05/2014	CCMC	Hazal Yolga
FG6_TL	COHP	Turkish	Listeners	6	07/05/2014	CCMC	Hazal Yolga
FG7_ENL	COHP	English	Non-listeners	10	21/05/2014	CCMC	Natalie Konyalian/Katherine Kotsireas
FG8_GNL	COHP	Greek	Non-listeners	8	21/05/2014	Urban Hive	George Andriotis/Michael Simopoulos
FG9_TNL	COHP	Turkish	Non-listeners	6	22/05/2014	CCMC	Hazal Yolga
FG10_GNL	DCB	Greek	Non-listeners	9	22/05/2014	Urban Hive	George Andriotis/Michael Simopoulos

Figure 42. Overview of the 10 focus groups.
COHP = *Cyprus Oral History Project*, DCB = *Downtown Choris Bakira*, 1%= *One Percent*.

Also in this case, the respondents' names have been anonymized when they are cited or paraphrased in this book. Their names have been replaced by a code, even if this impacts on the readability of this book. The first three characters of these codes refer to one of the 10 focus groups, the fourth character is respondent-specific. The first character after the underscore refers to the language of the focus group (Turkish, Greek, or English), and the second character to their listener status (Listener or Non-Listener). For instance, FG2C_GL refers to respondent C of Focus Group 2, which was a Greek language focus group with respondents that had listened to MYCYradio before.

The 74 respondents were identified in collaboration with CCMC, and then invited by CCMC. In order to achieve this aim, a search and selection strategy was developed, which combined a snowball method (initiated by the CCMC staff and volunteers), announcements in CCMC and MYCYradio (online) publications, advertisements in three newspapers, and calls for help to NGOs and municipalities. Diversity guaranteeing criteria were age, sex, community background, political position, and urban/rural residence.

The selection of the 74 respondents was indeed reasonably diverse, in particular in relation to criteria of age and sex, even though a majority of them were around 30 and higher educated (see Figure 43). 55 of them had a Cypriot nationality (and four more combined a Cypriot nationality with another one), eight respondents had another European nationality (including one Greek and three British citizens), and two respondents were U.S. citizens (the remaining five did not reply). Fifty-eight of them were born in Cyprus. Thirty-four respondents identified themselves as Greek Cypriots, and 24 as Turkish Cypriots. Generating more diversity on the basis of the urban/rural dimension did not work well: Many of the respondents (52) lived in

Year of birth		**Education**		**Sex**	
1940–49	4	Secondary education	6	Male	37
1950–59	2	Higher education	56	Female	36
1960–69	3	Other	11	No reply	1
1970–79	11	No reply	1		
1980–89	42				
1990 and later	11				
No reply	1				

Figure 43. Socio-demographics of the focus group respondents.

Nicosia or its suburbs, and another six mentioned two Cypriot residences, one of which is Nicosia.

When asked about their voting behavior at the last national elections, the diversity is considerable (see Figure 44). Still, it should be remarked that one third of the respondents (23 of them) did not vote, and another third (24) did not answer the question. Seven respondents said that they had voted for the conservative and Christian-democratic DISY, one for the nationalist EVROKO, and four for the communist AKEL. Three voted for the centrist-nationalist party DIKO, and one for the Ecological and Environmental Movement (KOP), a green party.[22] In the TRNC, four voted for the YKP, a socialist party not represented in the TRNC parliament, and one for the social-democrats of CTP. In the case of the respondents' professional activities, the diversity is even more considerable, and producing a good overview is hardly possible, although the low number of unemployed (three) is striking. Ten are students, and four did not reply. The other 57 respondents mentioned at least one profession (sometimes indicating it is on a freelance basis). The most frequently mentioned professions are: teacher (nine), NGO staff (six), engineer (five), entrepreneur (three), and consultant (three).

DISY (Democratic Rally)	7	Didn't vote	23
AKEL (Progressive Party of Working People)	4	Unclear/multiple	4
YKP (New Cyprus Party)	4	Outside Cyprus	3
DIKO (Democratic Party)	2	No reply	24
EVROKO (European Party)	1		
KOP (Ecological and Environmental Movement)	1		
CTP (Republican Turkish Party)	1		

Figure 44. Voting behavior of the focus group respondents.

The material collected in both main stages was then analyzed using discourse-material analysis. In all cases, saturation was established. The transversal participatory research phase, together with peer debriefings[23] and respondent feedback analysis,[24] provided ample assurance for the quality of the analytical-interpretative work, which is discussed in the next two parts, first focusing on participation, and then on conflict transformation. In reporting on these analyses, the strategy of thick description is used as much as possible.

2 CCMC, MYCYradio, and Participation

When analyzing the role of the community media webcaster MYCYradio within the Cypriot mediascape, the starting point is an inquiry into the participatory intensities of MYCYradio's production practices and the way these practices are contingently structured through the discursive-material knot. For analytical purposes, this part starts with an analysis of the discourse of participation in which MYCYradio is embedded, and how this discourse can be traced within the signifying practices of the producers and their guests in the MYCYradio broadcasts. This serves as the backbone of the production analysis, but is complemented with the signifying practices of the producers and the guests in the interviews, and on the social media pages affiliated with the programs. More specifically, the question about the articulation of the participatory identity of MYCYradio, as a counter-hegemonic initiative that engages with the hegemony of mainstream media, will drive this part of the analysis.

In a second phase, this construction of MYCYradio's identity, through the on-air signifying practices of the people that are affiliated with it, is then offered to MYCYradio's (potential) audience members. The reception study of the MYCYradio content—using 13 fragments from the programs—raises the question how MYCYradio listeners and non-listeners, Cypriot and non-Cypriot citizens, Turkish, English, and Greek-language speakers relate to the participatory identity of MYCYradio, communicated through these fragments. Here, in particular, discursive pluralism plays an important role, as not all (potential) audience members uncritically accept and identify with this discourse of participation (and the way the participatory identity of MYCYradio is articulated). What is of primary importance is the question whether and how these (potential) audience members *recognize* the articulation of MYCYradio's identity. At a second analytical level, the question becomes how they identify (as (potential) audience members) with this participatory identity.

In the third phase of the participatory analysis, the material will be brought into the equation, without disregarding the knotted nature of the relationship between the discursive and the material. This third phase of the analysis will thematize the material component of the discursive-material knot, guided by the distinction between access, interaction, and participation that was used in Platform 2. Analytically and methodologically, it is important to emphasize that also the signifying practices of producers, guests, and (potential) audience members are analyzed for traces of the role of the material, and that this third phase is not exclusively fed by the ethnography at CCMC. The textual material (in its wide diversity) and the ethnographic observations are used in all three phases of the analysis, although variations in the weight allocated to these different types of data do occur.

2.1 The Discourse of Participation and MYCYradio's Identity

In the first two phases of the analysis, the focus is on how the participatory identity of MYCYradio is constructed. This is done by focusing—in Phase 1—on the signifying practices of the producers and guests in the analyzed broadcasts and—in Phase 2—on the signifying practices of the (potential) audience members[25] in response to 13 carefully selected fragments. As mentioned before, these two core datasets are complemented by the analysis of the remainder of the data, including the participant observations.

2.1.1 Production and content analysis

The nodal point of MYCYradio's participatory identity is its alternativity, which is defined by articulating MYCYradio in contrast to mainstream media organizations, turning the latter into (agonist) constitutive outsides. As discussed before, community media practice relates to the four nodal points of the community media discourse in always particular ways, as there are still a multiplicity of identifications that can be used by these organizational machines to construct their identity, again bringing in contingency but also particular identificatory fixations. In the case of MYCYradio, the radio shows contain a series of elements that emphasize the difference between mainstream media and MYCYradio, and through this difference the identity of MYCYradio is defined. One illustration of this juxtaposition (but also its complexity) can be found in the interview with two MYCYradio producers who are also professional journalists: "So I have, we both I think, we both have a strong interest in community media, in alternative media. And I think the one reason is that we have been working in mainstream media. So we needed at some point to get out" (Interview MYCYradio producer 4, February 2014). Other elements are part of MYCYradio's participatory identity, but these are not so prominent that they merit the status of nodal point. Nevertheless, the signifier of the community is still very much part of MYCYradio's identity, and brings out its participatory dimension (slightly) more explicitly. Also, the civil society and rhizomatic elements play a role in MYCYradio's identity, although these two elements remain confined to the background.

Alternativity. The participation of volunteers, and their commitment to the community media broadcaster, is one way in which MYCYradio's identity is constructed as an alternative toward the mainstream media. As a CCMC staff member remarked in a 2012 interview: "People can participate and people should participate because [they] tend to be fed this dry crap media production" (Interview CCMC staff member 2, January 2012).

Actually, in the MYCYradio broadcasts, the producers rarely discuss their position; it is the materiality of their voices and their guests' voices (see later), structured by MYCYradio's program schedule, that makes them, and the participatory identity of the radio station, audible in the programs. Nevertheless, there are a few exceptions, where producers do talk about the (participatory) backstage of CCMC and MYCYradio. A particular *One Percent* broadcast (on 27 November 2013) discussed the expertise of the CCMC staff, articulated as friends and experts (without referring to a leader subject position), but also described the training of the volunteer producers to use the radio station's equipment:

> "Host: I think we have a core staff team of six people in the center. These are friends who have expertise in areas such as media communication, journalism etc. and everybody in here has the necessary theoretical and practical know-how for multimedia content production. For example, the colleagues in here taught us how to use this radio equipment. So the fact is that a large environment exists, where voice has been given to society, by having them learn new skills." (*One Percent*, broadcast 27 November 2013)

It is important to stress that in the programs, the producers, in their articulations of the identity of MYCYradio as alternative, ground its constitutive outside in an organizational reality. When referring to mainstream media, they are seen as organizations, with employees, that use distinct technologies (television, newspapers …) to produce media content. But MYCYradio is also seen as an organization, although of a different kind,[26] with a "[…] core staff team […]" and with many volunteers that together create an environment in which the enabling of participation, giving "[…] voice to society […]," is one of the main objectives (*One Percent*, broadcast 27 November 2013).

If we move away from the actual broadcasts, and shift to the interviews with CCMC staff members, MYCYradio producers, and radio show guests, the emphasis on community participation is much stronger. Already in the 2012 interviews, two CCMC staff members referred to the importance of a communication platform "[...] where it's very grassroots, where people [are] trying to provide a platform for voices to be heard" (Interview CCMC staff member 3, January 2012), and that is different from mainstream media: "[...] we have to help the people to raise their voices. The people who can't actually find space on mainstream media" (Interview CCMC staff member 4, January 2012). Or, as one of the MYCYradio producers formulated it, linking alternativity (as originality and outside the mainstream) to participation in the following way: Community media producers "[...] just want to be original and to reflect part of the communities that [are] usually unheard. [...] The way I understand community radio, community media, is [that it is about] about finding the unheard voice and amplifying it" (Interview MYCYradio producer 5, February 2014). Also, some of the radio show guests framed their experience as community participation, as this interview fragment shows: "Because, for the first time I was given the opportunity to express myself through something that was going to be listened to" (Interview guest 5—*Cyprus Oral History Project*, Spring, 2014). Other guests used a similar language: "Yes, she [the producer] was respectful and I felt myself heard" (Interview guest 4—*Cyprus Oral History Project*, Spring, 2014) and "I felt very empowered" (Interview guest 17—*Downtown Choris Bakira*, Spring, 2014).

Still, the representational position of the MYCYradio producers, and their articulation of the community member subject position, remains complicated. In some cases, the producers see themselves as representatives of one or more communities. Another (and interlinked) approach they are using is to refer to the (authentic) representation that they, as producers, are generating about the community/ies, as this citation illustrates: "[...] what I was trying to do, I was trying this representation of the community I think I am doing, to make it to be accessed by a wider audience" (Interview MYCYradio producer 4, June 2014). Yet another way of describing their representational position is by referring to their role of inviting guests from the community to speak to the community.

Despite the strong emphasis on the community media identity in the signifying practices of the different actors involved, in particular, the CCMC staff members created a series of nuances, which show the workings of contingency. In a 2012 interview, before MYCYradio was established, a CCMC staff member referred to CCMC as a hybrid community media organization: "[...] we are community media in a sense that we work with civil society and we're not for profit. But we're not quite the same community media as it is in other parts of the world" (Interview CCMC staff member 2, January 2012). Still, this CCMC staff member emphasized community ownership: "[...] one of the reasons behind CCMC being set up is specifically to fill the gap of not having an organization, a media organization that's contributed to and owned by, in a sense, by the two communities" (Interview CCMC staff member 2, January 2012). In a later interview, when the staff member was no longer involved in the CCMC, and reflected, in retrospect, upon the lack of involvement of the producers in the CCMC and MYCYradio management (see later), he also questioned the strength of the identification of the producers with the community media discourse:

> "Sometimes we take it for granted that people who come to CCMC to do whatever they are going to do understand what community media is, what its principles are. They get it, in a broader sense of the word. I don't think they grasp or fully appreciate the distinctive characteristics beyond it being an alternative or a different platform for people to express certain opinions." (Interview CCMC staff member 2, January 2015)

In addition to being a participatory organization, MYCYradio's identity is also defined in the broadcasts through a focus on its independence, again in contrast with mainstream media, which are represented as lacking this independence, for instance, because of their affiliation with the political system. In the following extract from *One Percent*, we find an exchange between the host and his guest, a university professor. Here, they not only emphasize the dependence of the mainstream media, but also articulate these mainstream media professionals as incapable of affecting the policies of their organization.

> "Guest: A big mission is for the media, but the media themselves are in distress. So if we talk about their role in politics, at least I think that unfortunately the media are not independent ...
> Host: They are not.
> Guest: ... No. So this is not a fourth power. This is a branch of some other powers, generally.
> Host: Yes.
> Guest: And it is manipulated. Of course, I absolve ... I generalize.
> Host: Of course, we always generalize.
> Guest: I absolve the employees, in general. Because there are employees working there and they are not determining the politics of that institution at all." (*One Percent*, broadcast 25 September 2013)

This powerlessness of mainstream media (professionals) then becomes juxtaposed with the alternative media (producers) of MYCYradio, who become directly and indirectly signified as empowered. Related critiques toward the mainstream media only strengthen this articulation, particularly when these critiques focus on the mainstream media's lack of honesty, truthfulness, respect, and freedom, which form the third articulation of MYCYradio's alternativity in the programs. The mainstream media's affiliations are seen to impede on their capacity to engage in truth-speaking, while MYCYradio is articulated as an alternative where people have the capacity and power to "[…] talk about things in all honesty" (*Downtown Choris Bakira*, broadcast 5 September 2013). Also, in the interviews with the MYCYradio producers, this comes up, for instance, when one of them says: "Yes, it's more free. You are the editor of your own show" (Interview MYCYradio producer 4, February 2014). In this articulatory logic, honesty sometimes becomes juxtaposed with politics, as the fragment below shows. Moreover, this fragment also illustrates the definition of mainstream media as lacking respect, not (always) treating their objects of attention in very humane ways.[27]

> "Host 1:[28] Here is your chance and our chance to talk about things in all honesty, without any politics, without those well-known and unknown [things] you hear in other shows, ok? And we'll talk even more without accusing anybody, we are not interested in intrigue, as I said […]." (*Downtown Choris Bakira*, broadcast 5 September 2013)

The emphasis on truthfulness is combined with a particular—alternative—ontology, which does not align well with factuality. Instead, the radio show producers often expressed their uncertainty about 'the' facts. As one of the producers formulated it: "I mean, I acknowledge my ignorance" (Interview MYCYradio producer 2, February 2014). We can find an example in one of the *One Percent* programs, which consists of a careful reference to soccer matches between Turkish and Greek Cypriot teams that took place in Limassol, a city on the south coast of Cyprus: "Even this year I think there were two football matches in Limassol. I'm not sure" (*One Percent*, broadcast 6 November 2013). This is combined with an emphasis on affect, exemplified by this quotation from one of the producer interviews: "So we have a very very serious moment and very quickly it goes to a totally absurd and ridiculous [one]. It is like right in the middle, we say, let's speak the language of how we feel" (Interview MYCYradio producer 2, June 2014). In contrast, at the more argumentative (and ideological) level, the producers used a more outspoken positionality. We can find an example in this blatant call to be critical, where the producer addresses the audience: "Don't form opinions without questioning the issue, without learning the realities and be careful for information pollution" (*One Percent*, broadcast 27 November 2013).

Fourthly, the radio shows also construct MYCYradio's alternativity by pointing to the social relevance of their content, which is focused on everyday life (in contrast to the mainstream media, who are articulated to be disconnected from, and disinterested in, the everyday). In *Downtown Choris Bakira*, a program that discusses issues related to the center of Nicosia, one of the producers said: "[…] we see that many things happen in the old city which the [mainstream] media don't cover." A few sentences later, he continued "[…] however, as I understand it, TV doesn't cover many things that are of interest to the public" (*Downtown Choris Bakira*, broadcast 3 October 2013).

Some of the ways in which MYCYradio is constructed as alternative are more form-related, where community media critique "canonical procedure," one of Downing's (2002: 323) concepts that I have mentioned before. In the case of the MYCYradio programs, we find a relaxed and self-relativizing way of presenting the programs, which produces an alternative version of the (media) expert subject position. When, for instance, in *One Percent*, tea is brought into the studio, the host tells his guest: "Let's have a little break if you want. After having some tea, we can continue to talk" (*One Percent*, broadcast 13 November 2013). Also in relation to technology, we can find this self-relativizing attitude where "[…] a phone [that] is ringing somewhere in the back" (*Downtown Choris Bakira*, broadcast 26 September 2013) is just mentioned, but not problematized. In general, mistakes were seen as natural, and not a violation of professionalism. Also, in the interviews with the guests,[29] the relaxed and self-relativizing atmosphere was often mentioned in a very appreciative way, as it made them feel free, relaxed, and at ease. One of the *One Percent* guests formulated this as follows:

> "[…] the producer made me feel relaxed and comfortable, and we prepared basically … And we talked about it before, and we talked about it after. So it felt really quite comfortable for me, and I didn't have any difficulties." (Interview guest 8—*One Percent*, Spring, 2014)

One of the *Downtown Choris Bakira* guests described her experience in similar terms: "We knew it was going to be relaxed and casual, so we didn't really have any inhibitions about what to talk or not. It was … we felt quite free" (Interview guest 13—*Downtown Choris Bakira*, Spring, 2014). Constitutive for the relaxed atmosphere is the format that is used, which is more conversational and dialogical. One variation of this is the emphasis with the guests on the lack of a pre-prepared structure, as this guest of *Downtown Choris Bakira* explained:

> "I think why I keep saying it was comfortable is because was because there wasn't really a structure—not structure, but there weren't fixed questions to what they were going to ask when I was there. It kind of ... they let the topic take us, they let the conversation do the show itself." (Interview guest 14—*Downtown Choris Bakira*, Spring, 2014)

Community, civil society, and rhizome. This emphasis on the participatory organization, as an alternative to the mainstream media, raises questions about the actors that participate, and in particular about the relationship between the broadcasters and the community/ies MYCYradio seek(s) to represent. The articulations of MYCYradio as an organization that serves the community/ies are not very dominant in the analyzed programs, and in many cases absent. Again, there are a few exceptions that can mostly be found in the *One Percent* broadcast of 27 November 2013. In this broadcast, the host points to the many languages that are used, and to the "[...] many different topics [that] are talked about [...]," resulting in a "[...] multicultural environment [...]," ranging "[...] from Greek to Turkish, from Arabic to other languages" (*One Percent*, broadcast 27 November 2013). Here we can see MYCYradio being defined through its connection to different linguistic-ethnic communities, but without specifying the exact nature of this connection.

At the same time, the host of *One Percent* emphasized the empowerment of the community/ies, by defining MYCYradio as a "platform" that can make the "[...] community's voice heard in order to strengthen civil society [...]" (*One Percent*, broadcast 27 November 2013). He explicitly mentioned the organizational nature of CCMC and MYCYradio, and the importance of the community controlling the media organization, referring to the articulation of the owner subject position as a collective. But again, when clarifying the nature of community control, he shifted back into the alternative media approach. MYCYradio becomes defined as being different from commercial and public media, thus implicitly black-boxing the community that MYCYradio is expected to serve.

> "Host: Now the Cyprus Community Media Centre, as indicated by its name, is actually a media organization made and controlled by the community for the community. So what does it mean 'controlled by the community'? It means a media approach which is not seeking profit like the commercial press, or that is not a public organization owned by the government. Therefore it is not facing political pressure. So this is the meaning of community media." (*One Percent*, broadcast 27 November 2013)

Articulating the relationship between MYCYradio, the radio show producers and the community/ies ran into other significatory difficulties, as the audience measurements, indicating very low audience ratings[30] and community disinterest, threatened to dislocate MYCYradio's participatory identity. When, in the case of *Downtown Choris Bakira*, the producers received word during the broadcast that they had 10 listeners, they first labeled the 10 "heroes," and then addressed them jokingly by using fictitious names, 'breathing life' into the abstract subject position of the audience. Finally, they called upon "[…] the community to embrace […]" them. In this last part, we can find an invitation toward the community to accept the producers as their symbolic representatives, showing the difficult relationship between those community members that can participate in and through the media organization on the one hand, and those community members that, in principle, can only interact with the content.

"Host 3: Guys, 10 persons are listening to us.
Host 1: Yes, yes, that's what [CCMC staff member] said.
Host 3: She's listening to us.
Host 1: No, it's not 10 persons that are listening to us, it's 10 heroes.
Host 2: 10 heroes.
Host 3: This is where we say 'good afternoon to our listeners, all 10 of you.' [in English]
Host 2: This thing exactly.
Host 1: So, in person, good afternoon Giota …
Host 3: Nikos, Theodore.
Host 2: Giorkis, Giannis.
Host 1: And Natalie, and possibly Christos.
Host 2: Michael.
Host 3: Guys, this is a show about the community. It is up to the community to embrace us. When we represent it, [the community] will talk about us [using] word of mouth [in English], share [in English] something, tell other friends, Kostas, Martha etc., 'You have to check it out.' [in English] In any case, it is up to you who are listening to us, guys." (*Downtown Choris Bakira*, broadcast 5 September 2013)

During the ethnography in the CCMC building, similar responses to the low audience numbers could be observed. In one case, two radio producers went into the CCMC staff office asking about the number of listeners to their show, which had just ended. The answer (which was also "10") visibly pleased them. Their satisfaction was not grounded in reference to a mass communicational model (which would have problematized these 'low' numbers), but in reference to an intrapersonal communicational model, which enabled them to think about these 10 listeners as 10 conversations they had. Another way these low audience numbers are dealt with is through the emphasis on the importance of the signifying practices, as one of the producers explained:

> "But I think my main motivation in hosting such a program was that I wanted the society or I wanted people who are members of the society who have something to say from a critical point of view to come up and find various platforms to speak. So regardless of what kind of audience we appeal to, we reach … I wanted to give the microphone to people to speak. Because it's very important for things to be discussed and for dialogue to happen in a society." (Interview MYCYradio producer 3, February 2014)

Moreover, also, the argument of the synergy, voices that amplify each other, is used by the same producer:

> "[…] somebody says something on their own Facebook page, you know, he gets like 10–15 people discussing it, somebody else does a radio program, somebody else writes an article in a newspaper or magazine and all of these. Although they are disconnected from each other. … In an aggregated way, they come and create the synergy. And I think that's what we are hoping for here." (Interview MYCYradio producer 3, February 2014)

Nevertheless, the producers do not entirely escape the problematization of the limited number of listeners, the dislocation it entails, and the contingency it brings. In one case, one of the MYCYradio producers mentioned the low audience ratings as one of the main reasons (apart from lack of time—see later) to quit the program. In the interview he started his answer by asking the following question: "So, what is the success? To have 20 people listening to you? That was one reason I got disappointed and stopped doing the show, beyond being very busy" (Interview MYCYradio producer 4, June 2014).

Interestingly, the guests of the broadcasts took a slightly different position, as their affective responses contained traces of a mass communicational model. In many cases, the guests explained during our interviews with them that they were stressed and nervous, at least at first. One *One Percent* guest explained that he was "A little stressed […]," because "[…] it was my first time in a radio station. So, it's kind of hard to talk to a big number of crowd which you don't see at the time" (Interview guest 7—*One Percent*, Spring, 2014). Also, one of *Downtown Choris Bakira* guests referred to the (at least potentially) large audience, when he explained that "I had to be careful. I mean this gets transmitted to all communities in Cyprus and of all political persuasions" (Interview guest 12—*Downtown Choris Bakira*, Spring, 2014). At the same time, the guests also expressed an awareness of the small audience numbers, where they used their own lack of prior knowledge about the radio station as indicator. For some, this was a reason to plead for more promotion: "[...] none of us know it [MYCYradio]. If you go to the center of. ... Because, here, I don't see many advertisements about it" (Interview guest 16—*Downtown Choris Bakira*, Spring, 2014). In one case, the guest did not know the radio station, or the program he was part of, but afterwards he became one of its audience members, as he explained: "I didn't know that the program existed before that, but I started listening to it on a weekly basis afterwards" (Interview guest 15—*Downtown Choris Bakira*, Spring, 2014).

In the broadcasts, the limited number of listeners becomes (partially) mediated through the emphasis on civil society as a replacement for community. Here we can see discursive repair at work. The citation that was already mentioned above—defining MYCYradio as a "platform" that can make the "[...] community's voice heard in order to strengthen civil society [...]" (*One Percent*, broadcast 27 November 2013)—is indicative of this shift from community to civil society, where the audience itself is seen as an "organised audience" (Reyes Matta, 1981; 1986). When asked, a CCMC staff member also made this connection explicit, using the following words: "We think those NGOs represent the community, yeah" (Interview CCMC staff member 1, January 2012).

In one broadcast, a guest even used the time allocated to him at the end of the broadcast to call on civil society organizations to participate in an EU grant proposal (*One Percent*, broadcast 11 September 2014), again indicating the importance of civil society, also, as a short-hand for Cypriot communities, and a way to escape from the dislocatory threat of audience/community disinterest. Simultaneously, this also shows the workings of the rhizome, where a variety of civil society organizations (and other social structures) meet within the radio station, turning it into a crossroads for civil society. Secondly, we also see a glimpse of the interconnection of Cypriot civil society with state actors, such as the EU (and, in the case of CCMC and MYCYradio, their funders: the European Commission Representation in Cyprus, and before, the United Nations Development Program (UNDP)).

2.1.2 The reception analysis of the three MYCYradio shows

When a selection of fragments is played for the focus group respondents, they react in different ways—radio broadcasts are no hypodermic needles, and individuals respond to the discourses that have been entextualized, in different ways. These participatory discourses are very much part of a discursive struggle in the Cypriot society, and in some cases the respondents identify with these participatory discourses, but in other cases they recognize these discourses without identifying with them. For an analysis of the radio programs, this is equally relevant information, even if the support for MYCYradio was clearly noticeable in the focus group discussions.

If we turn to the signifying practices of the respondents during the focus groups, then, we can see that also in the reception, alternativity is the nodal point of MYCYradio's identity, although different articulations, in comparison with the radio shows themselves, are used to construct this nodal point. Participation is hardly mentioned when discussing alternativity, as it is presupposed by the respondents. It is a signifier underlying all discussions, enabling the respondents to focus on the consequences this participatory setting has for the alternative identity of MYCYradio. It is only when the respondents shift to signifying practices that relate MYCYradio to the community that the signifier participation becomes more explicitly used.

Alternativity. One set of articulations simply refers to difference. For instance, one of the respondents stressed the uniqueness of a particular phone conversation, which was broadcast in *Downtown Choris Bakira:* "I have never heard such a phone intervention before, I've heard thousands, I'm 56 years old 'and counting' [in English], I never heard something like that before, if you're asking if it's something different" (FG2C_GL). FG1D_EL used a similar language to describe the *Cyprus Oral History Project* show: "There's no other program like that, it's amazing to give these voices ..." In some cases, the respondents grounded this uniqueness in a relation of difference with mainstream media in general, as way of thinking exemplified by FG4F_TNL: "[...] but the mainstream media don't do this kind of thing."

At the same time, respondents shied away from creating a dichotomy between community media and mainstream media, and they recognized the contingency of the mediascape. Repeatedly, they argued that mainstream media can also provide alternatives. In some cases, mainstream media are endowed with alternativity because they are outside the mainstream Cypriot public space, such as, for instance, online newspapers, English-language (Cypriot) newspapers, and Greek, Turkish, and British media organizations. In other cases, respondents referred to particular Cypriot media (where Astra, Channel 6, and the public broadcaster CyBC were mentioned), or to particular individuals, active in the mediasphere. Also other media were mentioned as alternative public spaces, with alternative cinema as one example. Further, social media's capacity as alternative was mentioned in the focus groups.

Apart from the more general articulation of these community media broadcasts as different, there were also a series of more specific articulations of alternativity. Three of these articulations are more focused on MYCYradio's content, by, firstly, emphasizing the diversity of this content, at the level of languages and formats used, voices and opinions to be heard. One example is the slightly poetic exchange about diversity at the end of Focus Group 9:

> "FG9D_TNL: Actually, we listened to four different voices. One of them was far removed from the peace language, one closer. There is not one voice, it's polyphonic. My first impression is this.
> FG9E_TNL: Yes, polyphonic.
> FG9C_TNL: yes …
> FG9E_TNL: I mean like … it's like having many flowers in the garden."

It is particularly here where the participatory identity of MYCYradio becomes a (bit) more explicit in the reception study. For instance, FG9B_TNL connected diversity with the control that the participants have, to produce and participate, but also to objectivity and pluralism, in the following way:

> "I mean, maybe the programs are formed around the ideas of people but as there are different personalities … even this can make the radio less one-sided, even objective. I don't know how much diversity there is in the participants, but having different people and different subjects, it forms an environment softer [laughing] than the other mediums."

Nevertheless, respondents also emphasized the difficulty in dealing with the diversity that these participatory practices generate. For instance, FG10D_GNL said:

> "It's easy to support participation, but, practically, I think it takes practice to accept that. And, to connect this to other things we said during this discussion, to accept the differentiation, to accept the other as another person, possibly. That is a very difficult thing to do, I think."

A second content-related articulation focused on the (social) relevance of the content produced by MYCYradio. For instance, FG3G_GL said: "[…] it also gives young people the opportunity to talk about issues that interest them, social [issues], and [issues related to the] sense of nature, and …" But the social relevance of MYCYradio's content was mostly argued through a critique on mainstream media, which are sometimes described as simply "rubbish" (FG3F_GL), outdated, not modern, trivial, and gossipy. FG7E_ENL's statement represents the last type of critique: "I often have the impression that Cyprus news, for example, is more like village gossip, you know?" Thirdly, MYCYradio's content was also articulated as objective, authentic, and truthful, which again pitches them against mainstream media. One example is the following statement about MYCYradio: "[…] it is one of the only objective things that you can listen to about what's happening to Cyprus from outside Cyprus" (FG1G_EL). Also, authenticity is used here: "[…] we have an authentic experience for people who are on the air and the audience" (FG2C_GL).

The alternativity of MYCYradio—also at the level of its objectivity, authenticity, and trustworthiness—is mostly articulated through a severe critique of mainstream media. Here, the condemning language that is used is quite strong, and the list of accusations launched at mainstream media has a considerable length—mainstream media are subjective, biased, distorted, one-sided, partisan, opportunistic, and untrustworthy. As one respondent put it, mainstream media, in collusion with the political system, are sources of misinformation: "[…] what is going on is terrible misinformation, that is, they are committing a crime, politicians are committing crimes on television, on the radio. The things they say are worthy of them being put in prison, I can't believe this thing" (FG2B_GL). Apart from disbelief, frustration was a sentiment that often came up in these discussions.

A series of other articulations defined MYCYradio more as alternative through its production practices and its politics. Still closely related to the previously discussed articulation is that MYCYradio is seen as responsible and sensitive, which again makes them an alternative to the mainstream media. When discussing the negativity of the mainstream media's coverage (after an initial positive response) of a Good Friday service organized in the Agios Georgios Exorinos church in Famagusta,[31] FG1B_EL said that "[…] this is where community radio and other responsible radios would come in and go: 'No' [against this negativity]." While mainstream media are portrayed as "clumsy" (FG6D_TL), MYCYradio is deemed sensitive, seen to take its social responsibility and play its social role.

Even more emphasis was placed on the alternativity of MYCYradio through its freedom and autonomy, which connects well to the more equal power balance that participation brings. This articulation is captured by FG6E_TL's statement: "[…] it's an open platform and everybody can reflect their opinions freely." MYCYradio was considered to be free *from* a wide range of constraints, including external interests, pressures, interferences, and censorship. This situation was, yet again, contrasted to mainstream media. For instance, FG9C_TNL said "It is free, everybody can say all they want, there isn't any censorship. On the other radios, as they are related with other things, they have some censorship restrictions." This autonomy also applies to the (subject position of the) community media producers, who were seen to function in more horizontal structures: "You play whatever you want, you understand?" (FG8C_GNL). In mainstream media, this autonomy was perceived as non-existent, as FG8A_GNL formulated it: "I believe they are the pawns of the radio station owners. If this or that station owner commands them to say … the radio station manager or owner: 'Say this thing', they will say it. There is no independence." In contrast, in the evaluations of MYCYradio's autonomy, two areas feature prominently, as MYCYradio was deemed to be free from both market (with the advertising, ratings, and profit motive it brings) and party politics.

In the focus groups, there was also emphasis on positive freedom, or the freedom to do particular things. This links up to the diversity and participation argumentation, where different groups were said to gain access to MYCYradio and to have their voices heard. These participants were free to express their ideas, which was considered to be beneficial, as FG6C_TL remarked: "The expression of the ideas, freely, can change [things] and can create confidence. People can feel the opportunity." In some comments, both types of freedom became interconnected: "I also like the fact that there is the choice of every producer adopting his/her own style, not following a directive to make the station more commercially successful and giving it a brand" (FG3B_GL).

Despite these rather positive evaluations, there were some critical voices in the focus groups that pointed to the limits of the freedoms of the MYCYradio producers, and of MYCYradio as a whole. Here we can see the contingency created by the tension between (institutionalized) politics and the political. MYCYradio remains "[…] intensely political without sticking to any particular political party" (FG2F_GL), and its affiliation to the "NGO world" may bring about certain perceptions that produce restrictions, as FG1C_EL argued: "I think that the difference between MYCYradio is that it doesn't have any political attachment to it. But at the same time, because it has this notion of being from the NGO world, people already put a political attachment to it." Moreover, MYCYradio still has to survive; as one of the respondents put it: "[…] it may also be an NGO, but it's still a business, isn't that so? OK, it's an organization [in Greek], an organization [in English]" (FG2E_GL).

Apart from its sensitivity and responsibility, and its freedom and autonomy, MYCYradio's identity was also articulated as alternative because of its production culture. MYCYradio producers were seen as relaxed, spontaneous, and casual; they improvise, enjoy themselves, and are not self-righteous. They are "[…] not professional radio people, they are people with guts" (FG2F_GL). Also this articulation of alternativity uses mainstream media as constitutive outside, where mainstream media producers are seen as not interested and bored, or heavy-handed.

At the same time, the respondents still articulated the subject position of the MYCYradio producers with quality work, even if the expert subject position sometimes becomes disarticulated from this community media producer subject position. MYCYradio is "[…] a nice establishment [in English] in which a nonprofessional may do something almost professional" (FG2F_GL). After all, "[…] there is no need to be Picasso to say that the milk is white. If it's white, it's white. There is no need for an expert" (FG5D_TL), and there is also "[…] a degree of amateurism, I think, [exhibited] by the [mainstream media] journalists, we have journalists who are uninformed and ignorant, they often don't even know how to talk properly or present" (FG10F_GNL). The same respondent, FG10F_GNL, expressed his appreciation for the spontaneous nature of the broadcasts, and the connection to quality, as follows:

> "I think it's more true … eh … it seems it's better that they are not professionals, it helps [the show] being more spontaneous, the show will be more spontaneous and lighter and encouraging and they will participate [in English] and get calls by people from the entire age spectrum."

The last articulation of alternativity is that MYCYradio is an actor of change, in contrast to mainstream media, which were represented as conservative protectors of the status-quo. As FG1C_EL said: "[…] the media here plays a very safe game in terms of keeping up the status quo." In contrast, MYCYradio was described as an organization with programs that attempt "[…] to bring the communities of Cyprus in a closer relationship to each other" (FG10A_GNL). In the same focus group, another respondent, FG10G_GNL, talked about one of MYCYradio's programs in the following terms: "Thus, in this dark room, so to speak, it let in a ray of light. Thus, it might have been a small thing, but it does make at least a small difference in its own way. So, I am not underestimating it."

The strong focus on the nodal point of alternativity, and the often positive evaluation of the alternative, does not imply the alternative is never problematized. Again, the community media discourse is not totally fixed, and different identifications are made, not always celebrating community media, and sometimes raising critical issues. One of the main concerns that the respondents expressed, was related to the survival of MYCYradio, and the consequences that particular survival strategies may have (see later). A second problem the respondents mentioned is MYCYradio's vulnerability in relation to the Cypriot political constellation. FG8D_GNL formulated this as follows: "[MYCYradio] will certainly contribute, it is a step toward democracy, but it can be expected that it will receive a lot of criticism by many extremists, which [CCMC] will have to address!" A third cluster of problematizations was related to the format and content of the MYCYradio programs, where we see a quality discourse (related to mainstream media production values) being used. In particular, the spontaneous and improvised production styles, often appreciated, did generate some critiques, where some argued for more structure in the scheduling and in the programs themselves. FG2F_GL said about one fragment: "But, man, this thing had no coherence, I am sorry but it had no coherence. It was a simply a rant, well …" FG8G_GNL complained about the monotonous nature of a fragment in the following terms: "[…] it was a monologue that became a bit monotonous and we got lost as a result. I'd prefer such a show to be in a question-and-answer format, as opposed to a monologue that touches on several different issues. I, specifically, let myself go at some points." Also, problems with the technical quality, and with missing content (e.g., news) were mentioned. Finally, MYCYradio's multilinguistic nature was problematized from an audience perspective: "The fact that [MYCYradio] is bi-lingual is nice, but it is better as an idea, and from a practical standpoint, it really is not very easy" (FG2E_GL).

Community, civil society, and rhizome. Apart from the nodal point of alternativity, the focus group respondents also mentioned a series of articulations that are connected to the serving the community approach, more than is mentioned in the radio shows themselves. Here, the emphasis on participation was more explicit, as the respondents stressed how MYCYradio gives voice to the community/ies in Cyprus. FG7D_ENL, for instance, said: "I think it's a fantastic opportunity for people to actually, to be given a voice, and that includes all communities in Cyprus." FG5D_TL even referred more explicitly to participation when saying: "The civil communities have more chance to have a place in it, in terms of organizing the program that they want and participating." Another variation is the following sentence from FG5D_TL: "[...] it tries to make heard the voice of all the communities living in the island as a part of the free community principle." In some cases, the connection between the people in the broadcasts and the community they represent is made clearer, with an explicit reference to 'us' (also linking it to the expert subject position): "The guests and the information comes from the community, they have some know-how, they have some experience [...] they are doing programs with jokes and this is so from us." This is also creating proximity, as exemplified by FG3F_GL: "[...] the few times I listened to [MYCYradio], it is closer to me. It's not some. ... It's not so impersonal."

The principle of offering voice to the community is also explicitly seen as part of a participatory-democratic logic, both internally and externally. The equalization of the power balances within MYCYradio was mentioned by FG6D_TL when she said: "[...] it is more about not to have the hierarchical structure in the radio." Again, in contrast to mainstream media ("[...] they don't let us to be involved"—FG9A_TNL), MYCYradio also enables participation of the community in media production, which led FG1G_EL to make the following statement:

> "[...] this is Cypriot democracy, it's participative democracy. Putting a cross on a piece of paper [a voting ballot] does not allow me to express my perspectives, my thoughts, my stories, my history. This medium does."

Nevertheless, the respondents also problematized the serving-the-community articulation of MYCYradio, even more than they used, or elaborated on, this articulation. One main concern was the (potentially) exclusionary nature of MYCYradio. This is related to the use of particular languages in the programs, such as English, in this quote: "[...] if it's only in English, again it might fall into the same bubble and attract the same audience" (FG1A_EL). Additionally, the exclusion of other communities (and the reduction of the signifier community to the two main communities of Cyprus) triggered concerns:

> "I mean, it makes me very uncomfortable to think that this is just bi-communal. Where it comes from? What is this two? I mean there are many things that we don't

see, minority groups, the immigrants. ... Those are very important. And the immigrants have to be treated the same as both sides." (FG4D_TNL)

Thirdly, the exclusions generated by the community media remit, with its focus on participation and conflict transformation, were critiqued, even if this triggered resistance from other focus group respondents and (in one case) a long discussion, which is only partially rendered here. In this focus group discussion, the discursive struggle over democracy itself, with its different positions and identifications, comes to the front:

"FG2F_GL: [...] the aim of democracy is to open the microphone to everybody, thus, theoretically, [the show] would become more democratic if you invited a person of far right wing ideology here to list, I don't know, the crimes committed by the Turkish authorities from 1950 until today, to say that a bi-zonal, bi-communal federation is unacceptable and violates human rights, to talk to you about the missing persons and do [all that], that would be democratic.

[...]

FG2C_GL: [...] I mean, we draw the line at some point, that is, I personally have a problem with [...], for instance, inviting an ELAM [a Greek Cypriot radical right-wing party] member to the studio, well ... I don't consider it democratic."

Another main concern was the inability of MYCYradio to reach its audience, and the limited impact MYCYradio has. This is partially related to a concern about exclusion, where MYCYradio was considered as "too much elitist" (FG4D_TL). In the same focus group, FG4F_TL expressed a similar concern: "I think that only people with the same opinion are listening to this program." The inability to reach its audience has a strong material dimension (see later), but it also connects to the experiences of the respondents, who mentioned, sometimes with surprise, that they did not know MYCYradio before they attended the focus group discussion: "I hadn't listened to this radio and I see myself as a peace-sided person. Maybe it didn't reach me, or I didn't listen" (FG9E_TNL). The perceived limited reach, problematized through a mass communication model, also feeds into the expectations toward a media organization, where a large reach is still deemed important (and articulated with effect). Its absence was problematized: "This is important in every community but I think CCMC reaches a very limited group. I mean, even if it's beneficial, it's very limited" (FG4F_TNL). This was again contrasted with mainstream media, who do have a large reach and attributed effect.

These kinds of analysis triggered discussions about the need for MYCYradio to expand, and to be promoted more. But other respondents nuanced this problematization, shied away from the mass communicational model, and argued against measuring the radio's success "[…] in terms of the number of the listeners […]" (FG2C_GL), after all, "[…] even if you influence one person, it's a gain" (FG2B_GL), one respondent argued. Or, as another respondent formulated it: "I think there is a saying, anyway, that says that if you think you are very small to change things, try sleeping in the same room with a mosquito" (FG10D_GNL).

Finally, there were only a few references to the civil society and rhizomatic articulations of community media. Most of these references relate to the connection of MYCYradio with the bi-communal movement, which was acknowledged, but also problematized. FG1C_EL argued for MYCYradio to "[…] become more accessible […]," so that "[…] it will move out of this sort of bicommunal, sort of buffer zone NGO world and be kind of more expansive." Also, FG1H_EL made a similar point when she said:

> "I think that not many people know it in Cyprus. Apart from this close community, let's say, of the NGO people, people who actually attend the usual events, multicultural, bi-communal events, peace development events, and are more likely to hear that this exists, the wider audience in Cyprus has no idea."

2.2 Material Participatory Practices

The signifying practices on MYCYradio, embedded in a discourse of participation that is mainly constructed through an identity construction of the community webcaster as alternative, are only (part of) one component of the discursive-material knot. Equally important is the material component of MYCYradio, and the ways participation is enacted, performed, and materially structured. MYCYradio is a particular assemblage that fixates meanings in evenly particular ways, but also integrates evenly particular materials, all within a context of contingency.

Before initiating this discussion, it is important to repeat that this analysis of the material component of the discursive-material knot is also based on the signifying practices of MYCYradio producers and guests (in the broadcasts and interviews), of CCMC staff in their interviews and on the CCMC and MYCYradio websites, and of respondents in the focus groups, in combination with the more ethnographic dimension of the analysis. These many different signifying practices were analyzed for traces of the material through the sensitizing concepts provided in the previous parts of this book, knowing that the analysis of the material can only be communicated through—in this case: academic—signifying practices. One cluster of sensitizing concepts, namely the three concepts of the AIP-model (access, interaction, and participation), will be used to structure the analysis in this part.

2.2.1 Access

When we focus on the access that MYCYradio provides, it is fairly easy to argue that MYCYradio is a production space where its producers can enter to produce the media content they wish to create, by themselves, or in interaction with others. Their bodies are again very much part of the assemblage. The producers can also invite others that do not have the status of MYCYradio producers—they are labelled 'guests'—to speak together, and have their voices broadcast. Even though they are not directly mandated by the many communities and civil societies on Cyprus, the producers and the guests often remain materially connected to these Cypriot communities and civil societies, and MYCYradio provides material access to the radio's proto-machines for these community members. Still, serendipity also plays a role, and not all guests are necessarily Cypriot. This very temporary entry into the community media assemblage is illustrated by Guest 18, who, in a *Downtown Choris Bakira* broadcast, called in from the Philippines, saying: "Yes, actually I was just listening, I have been listening from the start of the show and I heard [Guest 16] mention some of the angels [contributors to an arts project using a diary] and I decided to call. I could share with you a part of—a piece of the poem I wrote in the diary" (*Downtown Choris Bakira*, broadcast 31 October 2013).

Together, these people engage in a variety of bodily material practices, which are related to access. These practices range from entering the container building and the studio; operating the proto-machines in the studio, in particular the mixing board, the computer, and the microphones; speaking in the variety of languages that are used in MYCYradio, but also making coffee, and going outside to smoke, or to use the toilets (which are in separate container buildings). The openness of MYCYradio to non-professional media producers is also what makes it different from mainstream media practices, and what feeds the articulation of the radio station as alternative. At the same time, MYCYradio's access politics also show its rhizomatic nature and the permeability of categories that this entails, for instance, by incorporating producers into MYCYradio that also have a professional position in a mainstream newspaper, as one of the concerned producers himself explained: "I'm a journalist. I have been working in this newspaper for about four years where we start doing a political reporting and always been very interested in Cyprus Problem" (Interview MYCYradio producer 5, February 2014).

Access to MYCYradio[32] is not completely open, as it formally requires the endorsement of the CCMC Management Committee, but, in practice, this implies the endorsement of the CCMC staff, which grants candidates the status of MYCYradio producer and gives them permission to start a radio show. There are limitations to joining the assemblage: Candidates are, for instance, required to apply through the MYCYradio website[33] by filling out an application form and returning it to CCMC. Also, for guests, MYCYradio is not completely open, as an invite from an MYCYradio producer is required to gain access to the building. This access is then (at least to some degree) discreetly surveilled by the CCMC staff, who have their offices in the same container building. Also, the program schedule structures access to the radio station, as MYCYradio producers are allocated particular time slots, which enables organizing their presence and production work, but which also restricts it (even if exceptions—broadcasting at different moments—can always be negotiated). In one of the producer interviews, this structure, and its consequences, was briefly mentioned, in the following way: "So the shows here, the radio show, it's an hour. So then that means I have to make a selection which 50 minutes [of original material] to include" (Interview MYCYradio producer 1, February 2014). This reasonably rigid way of structuring time sometimes also makes it impossible for producers to be present in the studio at the time of the broadcast, as they have other commitments. As mentioned before, this very material consequence of the voluntary position of the involved radio producers is not considered a problem by them during the broadcasts; those who are already in the studio simply communicate their colleagues' late arrival or absence to the audience.[34] They display a relaxed attitude about absences, as it is considered normal that radio producers sometimes cannot make it to the live broadcast. Examples of statements in the broadcasts are: "[Host 2] had some business to attend to and he didn't come" (*Downtown Choris Bakira*, broadcast 24 October 2013), and "[Host 1] is in Amsterdam, so he's hopefully listening and I hope he regrets not being here with us" (*Downtown Choris Bakira*, broadcast 31 October 2013). Still, as we shall see later, the difficulties to reconcile, in the long run, voluntary work with (the need for) remunerated labor, are apparent.

MYCYradio, as a material architecture and a place, also plays a structuring role. MYCYradio is located in the Buffer Zone, next to Ledra Palace, a site that is invested with meaning. The Ledra Palace crossing, half of a wasteland with ruins that also has a strong NGO presence, and still a politically sensitive area, invites for diverse (and contradictory) meanings to be attributed to it (see Papallas, 2016: 28ff). But because of the geography of the Buffer Zone, it is not always easy to find MYCYradio. Here, the material is resisting human access, demonstrating its agency. As one of the staff members described it, making the CCMC (and MYCYradio) building more accessible has been an ongoing struggle:

> "And then next to that there is the world famous black gate, that's how we describe it to people on the phone: There's a black gate with a logo on it. But most people don't see the logo, because it's too low down, and more often than not, the door is kind of swung inwards open, so therefore they can't see it from the street. It's been the pain of our existence to try and put up a sign that sticks out into the road, but there is all these other parameters that come into play with the regards to health and safety that we still hadn't managed to navigate before I left." (Interview CCMC staff member 2, January 2015)

Given these material-spatial restrictions, constructing the MYCYradio studio was not easy: "Because if you are facing the UN car park, it couldn't go anywhere to the right because it would block the entry and exit of military vehicles" (Interview CCMC staff member 2, January 2015). Moreover, the entire container building housing both CCMC and MYCYradio looks very prefabricated and makeshift.

The CCMC building is the location that assembles the many objects that are used by the MYCYradio producers and CCMC staff members, and that provides access to them. All sorts of utilities (e.g., tables, office chairs, flipcharts, books, a fridge and water holder, air-conditioning, together with the electricity supply and internet connection) are combined with the proto-machines that are used for community media production. The latter are concentrated in one room, the studio. One of the MYCYradio producers described the studio's technological arrangement in these terms: "It has a DIY approach in the way it was built. But it's a professional studio. It's ok" (Interview MYCYradio producer 4, June 2014). He also added that "[…] it's designed for people […] that are not professional journalists" (Interview MYCYradio producer 4, June 2014).

Another part of the MYCYradio assemblage is the capital that is needed to keep the project running. Access to capital is not straightforward for CCMC, having to operate in a capitalist context. Originally, the material resources for CCMC came from an international donor, the UNDP, which also restricted CCMC's operations (see also below). At that time "[…] everything we make is signed off by UNDP, because they fund everything" (Interview CCMC staff member 3, January 2012). In the interviews with the CCMC staff members from that period, these restrictions, which came with the access to capital, are highlighted.

Another staff member gave a (rather painful) illustration of the material restrictions that the UNDP's donorship brought about when she mentioned that CCMC could not report on the Occupy Buffer Zone protests, a topic that was very much aligned with the remit of a community media organization committed to conflict transformation:

> "Yeah, yeah, well there's that movement in Cyprus [Occupy Buffer Zone] and because they're calling for, you know, Americans out Cyprus or UN or foreign negotiators. We're not able to touch on that subject either even though actually this is a spontaneous gathering of young people. Greek Cypriots and Turkish Cypriots living together in tents just outside, on the road. […] And it's all on the news, it's been in the news in Turkey, Greece, Al Jazeera, and we're not allowed to mention it or acknowledge it or talk about it." (Interview CCMC staff member 3, January 2012)

Still, the CCMC staff were careful to avoid the impression that CCMC is ungrateful for the support that UNDP provided, but they also positioned this material support as specific to the start-up phase, and still a threat to the organization's independence.

> "UNDP is great. I mean they are very. … They have done some amazing projects. But you know we need some more diversity of funding so we can be the best community center that we can be. Be more independent. You can't be a true community center unless you can have more independence. We can't have a single donor. It doesn't. I mean it's been great as a start-up, the motivation has been good all the way and we've had a lot of great support from UNDP." (Interview CCMC staff member 3, January 2012)

Later, CCMC and MYCYradio were no longer funded by UNDP, but a combination of funding agencies and projects contributed to the financial survival of CCMC and MYCYradio, even though this meant a strong reliance on project applications being approved to guarantee the organization's survival. More than before, this strategy brought about the uncertainties and contingencies common to community media organizations. This uncertainty, which already existed in the UNDP period, is exemplified by the words of one of the CCMC staff members: "I started here in June 2010 and my contract expires in a month" (Interview CCMC staff member 2, January 2012). Over time, all people employed by CCMC in the start-up phase, including the original project manager and the project coordinator, have left the organization, and the number of employed staff has been decreased, putting even more emphasis on voluntary labor than before. Sustainability then becomes even more of a problem, as was also discussed by some of the focus group respondents. FG8A_GNL put things simply: "The point is: can a station [like this] survive …" Especially when the suggested growth (e.g., by shifting to FM) is realized, there is—with these focus group respondents—the (perceived) need for more sponsorship, donor money or advertising, which then may transform MYCYradio in a "conventional radio" (FG3F_GL). Also, at least one staff member, in a 2015 interview, suggested the possibility of advertising as a way to decrease financial uncertainty, when he said that the CCMC Board

> "[…] can decide to think about maintaining the concept and the principles, but can start to generate revenue for itself and the station, by selling ads, based on some kind of model that it considers to be appropriate. […] I think if that revenue generation was to be successful, it would give people an added level of security that what they are doing actually it's not going to eventually fall flat on its face. And that there is some kind of business thinking going on into how to sustain the station beyond just hoping that the [EU] Commission is going to support us again. Which is not […]." (Interview CCMC staff member 2, January 2015)

Still, it should not be forgotten that MYCYradio is highly reliant on volunteers, who are donating their labor to the radio station, entering the community media organization together with the capital their labor represents. Again, this strongly relates to the alternativity of MYCYradio, as it is an alternative economic configuration driven by voluntarism and the economy of the gift. One of the producers briefly summarized his position as follows: "[…] the radio show was obviously a voluntary project" (Interview MYCYradio producer 3, February 2014). Also in the focus groups, the voluntary and non-remunerated nature of the radio work performed by the MYCYradio producers gets noticed, and is often appreciated.

The position of the volunteer, without employment contract and its obligations, produces freedom, as one of the producers remarked: "[…] because we are not doing it for money, we are not getting paid so we are not in a company. We don't get finance from anyone so we can do whatever we want" (Interview MYCYradio producer 2, February 2014). Although in some cases, other benefits are also acknowledged. For instance, one producer saw the ability to acquire skills as a form of compensation: "It was for free so they will train us for free" (Interview MYCYradio producer 2, February 2014). But in many cases, there is a material opportunity cost in a society structured by capitalist labor relations, which the producers are very much aware of, and which disrupts MYCYradio's functioning, as this producer's statement shows: "[…] because [it] is not paid, is not my job, I have to live, if I want it I could invest hours and hours but just don't" (Interview MYCYradio producer 2, February 2014). Or, in an even shorter version: "[…] you have to work for a living" (Interview MYCYradio producer 4, February 2014). This impacts on the material availability of time, which is problematized by all producers, as it impacts on the quality of their production work for MYCYradio. In one case, the requirements of producing a radio show, combined with the lack of available time, turned out to be very difficult to reconcile with a professional career, as producer 4's words show:

> "It needs dedication. If you want to do a project and you want to do it well, you have to respect the amount of time and effort, concentration. I think I wasn't ready for doing something like this, fully dedicated. Because at this time, when [the program] was taking place, I had several other priorities, that had to do with my personal life, my personal career, stuff like that." (Interview MYCYradio producer 4, June 2014)

The assemblage of these material elements, combined with the discursive elements discussed in the previous part, eventually results in the production of a series of broadcasts aimed at reaching an audience. Here too, the notion of access plays an important role, as this enables us to think about *how* the audience is reached (or, in other words, gains access to the broadcasts). Again, the materiality of proto-machines becomes involved, together with the audiences' agency, as the statements of the respondents in the focus groups demonstrate. They pointed to the combination of what they saw as 'old' and 'new' proto-machines, and sometimes expressed their appreciation. FG1G_EL formulated this as follows: "[…] it's technologically advanced because it's on the internet, but it's doing something quite traditional, on the internet." Also, the MYCYradio website (where all broadcasts are made available) was considered an asset, at least by some, as FG6B_TL said: "It's very practical in terms of clicking a link and reaching [the content] immediately." Although some also complained about the problems with the website interface (e.g., FG1A_EL), and internet connection (e.g., FG5F_TL), material agencies that frustrated their access. Also, problems with the sound quality are mentioned, although often quickly forgiven, as FG1A_EL's words show:

> "I mean, the same thing about editing or maybe the quality of the recording as well, that might have affected [me] negatively. But at the same time, the fact that it's not

someone's job, like paid job and it's someone's interest for like giving people the chance to voice their opinion and tell their stories is very positive."

Some of the other critiques tell us more about the (perceived) material audience practices and the particular ways of listening that disrupt the access to MYCYradio. One element that the respondents complained about was the requirement to be online all the time in order to have access to MYCYradio, which some respondents found unrealistic. Respondents also argued that newspapers have much more impact than radio, as one of them mentioned (referring to the situation in north Cyprus), "[...] because the primarily source of the Turkish Cypriot community talking Turkish is the newspapers" (FG6A_TL). Thirdly, the respondents pointed out that 'traditional' (terrestrial) radio broadcasting is also important to provide access to MYCYradio. One reason is that the material audience practices of the older generations are still geared toward terrestrial radio, as FG6A_TL's words illustrate: "I think it's good to be a webradio but except this, I think it has to turn back to classical radio in terms of reaching all the parts of the community. For example, elderly people are not used to the internet, at least [this applies to the] people around me." Another reason is the importance of listening to the radio in the car. Even if technical solutions exist that make it possible to listen to internet radio when driving, some respondents argued that the non-availability of MYCYradio on the airwaves reduces its (potential) audience because of these particular listening habits.

2.2.2 Interaction

When we move from the materiality of access to the materiality of interaction, the process of community media production itself offers a good starting point. Producers physically enter the radio studio to produce media content, and to become part of the radio's assemblage. Sometimes they do this in interaction with other producers of the program. Producer 4 described not only the affective relationship with his colleagues, but also the materiality of collaboration, sitting together at a meeting to discuss what the next episode will bring:

"Because with [producer 5] and [producer 2], beyond being people who collaborate in our radio show, we are friends, at some point we designed our show outside CCMC, so we had a meeting for a coffee or a drink to put down things and see what we are going to do next week, who are we going to visit, what will be the character of the show, the points of emphasis, stuff like that." (Interview MYCYradio producer 4, June 2014)

The broadcasts themselves consist of interactions between the producers (when there are several) and between the producer(s) and their guest(s). In this sense, radio enables audiences to witness very material conversations between producers and guests, where their voices meet and interact, with their bodies (often) together in the same (small) studio setting, also enabling eye-contact and other non-verbal communicational practices (which all have their material components).

The interactions also stretch beyond the confinements of the programs and the radio studio themselves, as the producers also interact with the CCMC staff members, sometimes during the programs, but almost always before and after the radio shows. These interactions are amicable, but also based on the provision of technical support, as one producer explained: "Yes, it's really fine, you know, we are friends with everybody here, they give us all the support that we need, even on the weekends, we can call them if we have any questions. So yes, we live perfectly in harmony" (Interview MYCYradio producer 3, February 2014).

Another set of interactions between those involved in MYCYradio is between the producers of different programs. Although not every producer is interacting with other producers, producers do exchange information (e.g., about guests) and visit each other's programs, as producer 2 explained: "So we share guests because we see what other people do. Also sometimes I invite or I am invited to other people's shows. Sometimes I go there uninvited" (Interview MYCYradio producer 2, June 2014). Another example of these interactions could be found in one of the *One Percent* broadcasts, where the producer had invited another MYCYradio producer to talk about his new show. He was introduced in the following way: "My first guest is [producer 6][[35]]. [Producer 6] is going to start to present a program in MYCYradio next week. We will talk with him about his program" (*One Percent*, broadcast 18 September 2013). In addition, the producers also collaborate in other projects and activities outside the radio station.

Proto-machines, such as production technologies, are an equally important part of the (material component of the) community media assemblage. They are concentrated in the MYCYradio studio, and enable the voices in the studio to be heard by the audiences outside, music and pre-recorded content to be played, and the balance between the difference audio sources to be regulated, through the interaction between producers and proto-machines. Even if the radio production technology is consciously kept simple (see also above), this small space, filled with proto-machines, can produce particular affects, namely anxieties:

> "[...] having seen people sitting in that seat, for the first time normally, I've seen people sweat, I've seen people get very nervous. ... It can be a very intimidating seat to be in. Probably because of the technology that surrounds you, even though if you think about it, and if you paid any attention to the training you've been through, be it more elaborate or more basic, you'll know that 95% of the time all you'll need to do is move up three faders, talk into the microphone in front of you—if you are a guest, to the side of you—and a computer [which] you know how to use anyway." (Interview CCMC staff member 2, January 2015)

The interactions between producers and technology are structured by particular skills, which are enhanced through the training provided by the CCMC staff. This training is brief, and mostly focused on using the proto-machines, as one producer explained: "It was quite easy, I think, we had an initial training of one hour or two hours and, then I had to learn by doing" (Interview MYCYradio producer 3, February 2014). When the problems turn out to be too difficult to solve for the producers and the proto-machines are too resistant, then the CCMC staff is called in to provide technical assistance, even though the producers are careful to not rely too much on them, as producer 2 explained:

> "First, we don't want to bother them too much because they are busy. Second, I [would like] them, when there is a technical problem to be ready [...] to come and fix it. Or at least show me how to. I would appreciate more proper radio training, because our training was how to use the equipment." (Interview MYCYradio producer 2, June 2014)

Both bodies and proto-machines are located within the architecture of the CCMC building and the small studio space. This has particular consequences in structuring the interactions that take place within this space, but the space also becomes part of the production assemblage and its many interactions. One rather annoying and disruptive consequence was only very briefly mentioned by one of the producers: "[...] it's getting too hot" (Interview MYCYradio producer 2, June 2014). The material form of the studio also has agency in privileging particular formats and genres, and dis-privileging and disrupting others, as one of the producer's words illustrate: "But at some point we had some students and it was very crowded, it was not working of course" (Interview MYCYradio producer 4, June 2014).

When asked about a less traditional setting, and the possibilities of a different spatial configuration that would involve the large CCMC meeting room next to the studio room, one of the CCMC staff members explained the choices that were made at the time when the radio studio was built, how mainstream media logics still intervened, but also his affecteous relationship with it:

> "I think the fact that we trusted for the configuration on a company that builds studios for mainstream media probably eliminated that option right from the very start. But I do remember around the same time that the studio started being built, we had a visit from a community radio […] activist in India, at Janakpur, and she described the radio production as happening on the floor. People sitting in a circle on the floor, on cushions and a mic being in the middle, and I remember thinking that would be cool but somehow it wouldn't work in a Cypriot setting. But that's something that would have been nice to experience in that space, for me, because I feel so comfortable in it." (Interview CCMC staff member 2, January 2015)

Importantly, the architecture of the studio, with its own agency, structures the practices of the producers. As is often the case in community radio studios, in contrast with mainstream radio studios, there are no separate rooms for technicians and presenters, which implies that the producers take on these different tasks themselves.

One of the MYCYradio producers was involved (as a child and as a teenager) in two mainstream radio shows, and during one of the interviews he compared the architecture of community and mainstream radio studios in the following terms:

> "It was fun. Of course there we didn't have to deal with the technical stuff because the studio was different. The technical part was separated, was behind the windows. We just had the microphones in front of us so we didn't have to worry about that." (Interview MYCYradio producer 3, February 2014)

The (material) interactions also move beyond CCMC and its building, touching upon other components (and structures) of Cypriot society. The rhizomatic network of CCMC (and MYCYradio) enables connecting with civil society, at the level of the programs and at the level of CCMC/MYCYradio as a whole. As one of the producers briefly formulated it: "We have extensive social circuits" (Interview MYCYradio producer 2, June 2014). And to use the words of one of the CCMC staff members, who made a similar point: "We've started to show that we're capable of building partnerships and building networks" (Interview CCMC staff member 2, January 2012). The (rhizomatic) network is mostly (but not exclusively) connected to civil society, in different ways, as explained by one of the producers:

> "There are two things are happening: It's a link between individuals and civil society, [the] society of citizens, and, on the other hand, it's just a network of individuals that

> are just interacting with the NGO sector. In a direct or indirect way." (Interview MYCYradio producer 4, June 2014)

Of course, many of the connections with NGOs originate from CCMC/MYCYradio's management structure, which incorporates a group of NGOs as members of CCMC. These NGOs and their representatives, often involved from the very beginning of CCMC, are privileged partners of CCMC, even though they sometimes have their own interests. CCMC/MYCYradio's civil society network also moves beyond Cyprus, mainly through CCMC's connection to the Community Media Forum Europe (CMFE), a European lobby organization for community media organizations, which held one of their meetings in Cyprus[36] (in collaboration with CCMC), and which currently includes a former CCMC staff member on its Board of Directors. Bringing several dozen community media activists to the CCMC, enabling interactions between them and CCMC staff, as well as with the member-NGO representatives, turned out to be important, as one of the staff members remarked in 2012: "I've learned a lot over the last few months especially with the CMFE conference and finding out that there's a whole world of people out there doing similar things" (Interview CCMC staff member 2, January 2012). These comments are echoed by the same staff member, three years later, in the following way:

> "I think this CMFE conference that we did, opened people's eyes as to what is out there and who else is like us, but not like us. But it never fully registered. The NGOs that are members of CCMC saw it primarily as an organization that could support their own projects and initiatives within Cyprus, for their own personal gain. I use gain in the institutional sense." (Interview CCMC staff member 2, January 2015)

Even if the focus of CCMC/MYCYradio's interactions is mostly geared toward civil society, there are also limited interactions with state and market actors that show the transgressive workings of the rhizome. Relations with market actors mostly involve the purchase of equipment and services that are not available through the gift economy. Talking about the period when the CCMC was established, one of the staff members referred to the purchases CCMC had to make then: "Basically that was a lot to set up the center: get a physical location, buy the equipment, buy all the office supplies, everything you needed to staff an organization" (Interview CCMC staff member 1, January 2012). Also, afterwards, the relations with market actors are partially related to the purchase of the required services (e.g., electricity, internet ...), although collaborations with mainstream broadcasters also exist. These collaborations with market and public media were more developed in the first phase of CCMC's existence, though. As one of the CCMC staff members said in 2012: "We try to work with both the mainstream media in both communities and try to find ways to make them collaborate with each other" (Interview CCMC staff member 4, January 2012). In the later phases, these collaborations still existed, but were less intensive. For instance, "CyBC2 radio played some [of MYCYradio's] news digests" and "We also did a 3-minute video for Euronews on STEM education" (Interview MYCYradio producer 2, June 2016).

Also, the rhizomatic interactions with the Cypriot regimes and their agencies are limited, but they do exist. It is important to mention here that MYCYradio is only using internet streaming, and not terrestrial or digital broadcasting, which exempts it from the need to apply for a broadcasting license, even if CCMC aspires to realize this option. Still, the difficulties related to this option are considerable; one of the staff members offered the following reflection about this: "[…] it's very interesting about how you would start up a terrestrial or digital broadcasting system in a conflict area where authorities don't recognize one another and systems are different. It's a really interesting case study. And I don't have the answers to how that will all work out" (Interview CCMC staff member 1, January 2012). But CCMC is still recognized as an NGO. Actually, its legal structure consists of two NGOs, one of which is recognized in the Republic of Cyprus, and one of which is recognized in the TRNC (Interview CCMC staff member 2, January 2012). When one of the staff members referred to this period of establishing the NGO(s), the narration about the time investment is combined with the word 'frustration': "Well, there's obviously the whole restructuring that I talked about before in becoming an NGO. That takes up a lot of time, physically. And mentally for staff. It stops them from taking this agenda forward. But, I'm frustrated" (Interview CCMC staff member 2, January 2012). In addition to the formal recognition of the two CCMC NGOs, little formal collaboration with government structures exists, although CCMC assisted the Municipality of Nicosia when it made its bid for the 2017 European Capital of Culture (Interview MYCYradio producer 2, June 2016).

As previously mentioned, CCMC/MYCYradio's interactions have mostly been organized through the support of international donors, who provided CCMC with the capital to establish and maintain CCMC and MYCYradio. In a first phase, this mainly concerned UNDP, whose bureaucratic procedures required permanent interactions between their representatives and CCMC staff. MYCYradio was established with the support of the European Commission Representation in Cyprus, but this support ended in the middle of 2014. Earlier, the strong influence of UNDP on the functioning of CCMC was already mentioned. Projects, and the contracts that enable them, also impose material requirements. For instance, all CCMC productions had to be "[…] signed off by UNDP, because they fund everything. You know, so little things that would sound innocuous. It's not that we've made anything dramatical or controversial but even little things get [screened]" (Interview CCMC staff member 3, January 2012). The UNDP's strong involvement not only impacted on the time investment of the staff and their activities, but also on the structure of the organization. While CCMC originally preferred to work more with (freelance) consultants, and not so much with (employed) staff members, this was frustrated by UNDP procedures: "We started off with this big roster of people that we thought we could make into this kind of team of community media people but the […] UNDP process of becoming a consultant is fairly tedious, lots of paperwork, renewals, so a lot of people ended up just dropping out […]." (Interview CCMC staff member 2, January 2012)

After the UNDP project ended, CCMC gained more independence, but (in particular after also the support of the European Commission Representation in Cyprus ended) became dependent on a diversity of smaller projects to have access to resources (Interview MYCYradio producer 2, June 2016). These smaller projects did open up new spaces for rhizomatic collaborations, though, as these projects are often with in collaboration with other NGOs (and universities). For instance, the Eco For Life (ECFOLI) project, a Media Education and Information Literacy project running from March 2015 to February 2017, has the following partners: Cooperativa de Formacao e Animacao Cultural (COFAC), with Lusofona University (Portugal), Forum de la Citoyenneté (Morocco), International Children's Film Festival of Cyprus (ICFFCY) (Cyprus), Partners for Sustainable Development (PSD) (Palestine) and Université Sorbonne Nouvelle (France).[37] Of course, the bureaucratic requirements that accompany such project work persist.

Another set of interactions takes place with the Cypriot communities (as a whole). As explained before, MYCYradio has individual producers that act as informal community representatives, and considers its connections to the Cypriot civil society as a shortcut to the communities it seeks to serve. The material link with the Cypriot civil society was discussed in the previous paragraphs, but as this connection does not become very visible in the broadcasts, it is, in particular, the MYCYradio producers, with their material presence within the MYCYradio broadcasts, that render the

Cypriot communities (and their diversity) visible, through the logics of representation. In some cases, this claim is made explicit, as illustrated by the very short, but very clear, statement from one of the *Downtown Choris Bakira* hosts: "[…] we are you" (*Downtown Choris Bakira*, broadcast 5 September 2013). This statement is part of a longer exchange that invites audience members to "Come close":

> "Host 1: […] We reach out to all of you. In this show, we do it for you. Ok, we also do it for fun—it's something we love to do and we devote our very soul to this endeavor, but we are you. Come close …
>
> Host 2: Don't go back, [don't] keep us in the dark." (*Downtown Choris Bakira*, broadcast 5 September 2013)

Formal representational mechanisms are missing, though, which opens up discussions about the representativeness of the producers that are materially present in the radio station, and how their presence should be legitimated. During one of the interviews with a CCMC staff member, these issues were raised in the following way:

> "The Iranian example is perfect. Because [producer 7], who is an Iranian broadcaster, is a Christian. What percentage of Iran his voice represents? I mean, there is definitely an Iranian Christian community in Cyprus. Probably a large percentage of the Iranians that are here are Christians for obvious reasons, but …" (Interview CCMC staff member 2, January 2015)

This problem is partially mediated at the level of MYCYradio's signifying practices through the selection of issues that are being addressed in the programs, and that are sometimes explicitly described as being relevant to the community. For instance, the following was said in the introduction of one of the *One Percent* broadcasts: "In the next hour, from 6:00 to 7:00 p.m., we will talk about the topics on the daily life of the Turkish Cypriot community" (*One Percent*, broadcast 11 September 2013). A similar statement was made in one of the *Downtown Choris Bakira* programs: "[…] this is a show about the community" (*Downtown Choris Bakira*, broadcast 5 September 2013). But there are also material solutions to the representational problems: The presence of other (informal) representatives of relevant communities in the broadcasts, earmarked as 'guests,' creates a material presence of the community (and of civil society). Sometimes these guests make use of signifying practices to explicitly label themselves as a part of the community, as was the case with Guest 11, who first explained that he knew "[…] the Turkish

Cypriot community [...]" "[...] very well and from nearby [...]," and then added, "As *I am a part of this community*, I also catch myself sometimes that this happens [defining themselves a victim]. Like, first you think positively and then you say, 'hmmm, can there be something behind this? What will happen? Let's see first ...'" (*One Percent*, broadcast 13 November 2013—my emphasis)

Nevertheless, the material infinitude of the community continues to frustrate and dislocate the logic of representation that legitimates the discursive connection between two materialities, which are the material presence of the producers in the studio, on the one hand, and the overlapping material structures that constitute a community, on the other. During an interview with one of the CCMC staff members, he expressed the impossibility of solving the problem in the following terms:

> "Do we represent the prison community, do we represent battered women? No. Are they part of the community? Yes. So I would think that, you know, you can't represent all segments of the community regardless of what you call the community, you know what I mean. So I don't know humanly any way possible to do that." (Interview CCMC staff member 1, January 2012)

Finally, the assemblage also consists of the material audience practices, even if these people are more at a distance. The access of these audience members was discussed earlier in this part, but the focus group discussions also provide insights into *how* these audience members *interact* with the content of MYCYradio's broadcasts. Here, I can refer to the two reception analyses that have been included in this book, knowing that these are only two tips of the iceberg of reception, as the wide diversity of topics broadcast on MYCYradio triggers an even more substantial diversity of receptions. Still, the two reception analyses, on the identity of MYCYradio as community media organization (see before), and on its contribution to conflict transformation (see later), offer a good perspective on how audiences (both the already-existing audiences and those especially created for the research project) interact with the content.

Still, it is important to argue that some audience members also interact with the producers themselves, bringing them closer to the radio's assemblage. This type of interaction is mostly mediated through the social media activities of the producers, at least for the two programs—*One Percent* and *Downtown Choris Bakira*—that use social media. In these two radio programs, we can find a more invitational strategy, where the openness of the programs is strongly emphasized. For instance, in *One Percent*, the producer of another MYCYradio program called *Gravity*, who is a guest in this *One Percent* broadcast, invited listeners to respond in the following way: "If you want to talk, or if you have some views on different topics, you can also send them to us, through the Facebook page or by mail. Yes, that's how it will be an open radio program" (*One Percent*, broadcast 18 September 2013). In the first broadcast of *Downtown Choris Bakira*, one of the hosts called on audience members to respond, using the following words: "If you think of something, there's Facebook, upload it, we've got Twitter, upload it, and we've also got an email [address]" (*Downtown Choris Bakira*, broadcast 5 September 2013). In another case, one of the producers of *Downtown Choris Bakira*, launched a call for new candidate-producers for radio shows on MYCYradio on his own Facebook page, again showing their invitational use of social media.

Despite the limited nature of these examples, social media use does enable some degree of interaction with audience members, as well as a very limited degree of participation in the broadcast, which is also highly dependent on the agency of these audience members. One example is *Downtown Choris Bakira*'s broadcast of 24 October 2013, on the Syrian Civil War, where a listener's message is mentioned in the broadcast. Even though they are reasonably rare, we can also find conversations between producers and audience members on the Facebook pages of *Downtown Choris Bakira* and its producers, where, for instance, audience members congratulate the producers, comment on pictures, or ask for technical advice. Obviously, their interventions are structured by the social media interfaces and require the mediation of the producers to have them enter the radio broadcasts. In one case, the producers posted a picture on the *Downtown Choris Bakira* Facebook page. This picture was sent to them by a listener, and portrayed the three producers as Teenage Mutant Ninja Turtles, labeling them the Green Zone Turtle Ninjas, something that was extensively discussed during the 5 September 2013 broadcast.

2.2.3 Participation

The third domain where the material features in the community media organization is participation. In this material component of the discursive-material analysis, we will distinguish between participation within the programs and participation within MYCYradio (and CCMC) as a community media organization. MYCYradio is an organizational machine, with particular hierarchies

Figure 45. Fan art on the *Downtown Choris Bakira* Facebook page.
Source: Nikos Malekos ©.

that structure the involvement of the different actors. Also, these hierarchies are structured through the discursive-material knot, with, for instance, the community media (participatory) identity interacting with the materialities of the radio station.

At the level of the programs, the decision-making process (and its material dimension) is fairly straightforward, as the producers have a high degree of freedom in deciding on the content of the program (within the program slot they have been allocated). The producers are the informal representatives of the community, and their participation in MYCYradio unlocks the Cypriot mediascape for ordinary people. It is this position that entitles them to exercise control over the broadcasts, or, as one of the producers put it: "You are the editor of your own show" (Interview MYCYradio producer 4, June 2014). Also, the CCMC staff is reluctant to interfere in the programs, and restricts its interventions to training and support. One of the producers described the relationship with the CCMC team as follows: "So we are completely left to do whatever we want basically. Of course, we are not taking advantage of that. But there is a mutual understanding" (Interview MYCYradio producer 3, February 2014). This strong power position of the producers is translated into a series of decision-making moments about the content of the program, the guests that are invited, and the music that is played, both before and during the program. Given the rather high levels of improvisation, many decisions are taken during the program itself, but preparatory meetings are (in some cases) organized.

The strong power position of the producers of course raises questions about the position of the other actors, and in particular the guests and the audience members. Also, the guests are constructed as the (informal) representatives of the community, and through this discursive logic the need arises to make them share in the decision-making process, even though they are often not involved in the preparatory stages of the program. This tension is resolved in a material way: During the broadcasts, they are often given ample speaking time. The guest's power position is further strengthened through the conversational style that is used, which has an equalizing effect in relation to the power positions of all present and impacts on the material turn-taking during the broadcasts. In one of the producer interviews, this is briefly summarized as follows: "[...] many times we want to give all the freedom to the speaker to say what's on their mind" (Interview MYCYradio producer 2, June 2014), although it is quickly added that this strategy impacts negatively on the structure of the broadcast. As mentioned before, the material absence of the audience members in the studio reduces their capacity to actively participate in the broadcasts. In the preparatory stages of the broadcasts, I never observed any audience involvement. The producers organize interactional opportunities for audience members, mainly through the program's social media initiatives, but these only very rarely allow audience members to become involved in the decision-making processes related to the programs.

The decision-making processes in relation to MYCYradio (and CCMC) as organization are more complicated, as MYCYradio has been struggling with its internal democratic-participatory processes. The power balance within MYCYradio (and CCMC) as organization is structured by the positions taken by three groups: the team, the board, and the producers. Even if "[...] the ultimate decision-making body is still the CCMC board" (Interview CCMC staff member 2, January 2015) the team takes a very strong power position within the organization.

In the MYCYradio *Foundation Charter* (2013a) the power relations between the different groups of MYCYradio are clearly regulated, with an MYCYradio Management Committee that has two MYCYradio broadcasters amongst its members (which, in addition to the MYCYradio broadcasters, consist of three members of the CCMC Governing Board, the MYCYradio Station Manager, and a representative of the European Commission Representation in Cyprus). Moreover, according to the MYCYradio *Foundation Charter*, MYCYradio also has a Program Committee, which consists of "[…] all the broadcasters participating in MYCYradio. The Committee acts in an advisory capacity for content broadcast on www.mycyradio.eu and elects two representatives that participate in the Management Committee" (MYCYradio, 2013a). In practice, the situation is different, and much less structured. One of the CCMC staff members described the actual situation as follows:

> "First of all, it's no exaggeration to say that MYCYRadio doesn't really have a structure. Or, the structure that's described on paper happens 75% when it actually happens, which is 50% of the year's total time. That is to say that the Management Committee that is described in the paperwork only comes together when there is a call for applications." (Interview CCMC staff member 2, January 2015)

Moreover, the formal representation of the producers in the Management Committee has also not been translated into practice, as the clear reply from one of the staff members shows: "Interviewer: Two representatives of the producers in the Management Committee. That was … CCMC staff member 2: Never happened" (Interview CCMC staff member 2, January 2015).

Also, the strong power position of the CCMC staff team is not captured in the MYCYradio *Foundation Charter* (2013a), even though in practice, the lack of implementation of the formal management structures left the CCMC staff in a very strong position, partially because of the vacuum left by the CCMC Board (and the producers). Even when the Board is still to some degree involved in the CCMC's decision-making process, in particular when it concerns strategic decision-making, and even if the Board became more active in more recent organizational reshuffles (where the functions of manager and coordinator were no longer filled in), the radio producers are hardly involved in the organizational management, as one of the staff members explained:

> "[In] the back of my mind, personally I was always aware that we weren't fulfilling the participatory element in the operational side of the station, beyond the production of programs. The reality was that there was too much to consider, from the technical point of view, the fulfilling of the requirements of whatever contract we had at the time […], that even though, it was in the back of my mind, it stayed in the back of my mind." (Interview CCMC staff member 2, January 2015)

This weak power position of the producers, including their involvement in the selection process of the new programs, was confirmed in the interviews with the producers:

> "We never had a meeting, many of us don't know each other. It's not there or if it's there, it's not happening. Or, in the best case, when there is a call for new shows, prospects come and there is a Board and there is a dialogue, all the shows are approved, then there is an iteration with the staff to agree on a format and give some guidelines on the themes, etc. etc." (Interview MYCYradio producer 2, June 2014)

The producers also rarely expressed an interest in a stronger involvement in the organizational management: when queried about potential interest from the producers, one of the staff members could only recall one instance: "There was one producer [...] who had expressed a desire to be more involved in the processes but was coming to a degree from a need to generate income" (Interview CCMC staff member 2, January 2015). Despite this more problematic division of power (at least from a maximalist participatory perspective), at the more informal level there are a number of corrective mechanisms that (to some degree) redress the power imbalance within the radio's assemblage. First of all, the producers remain committed to MYCYradio, and in some cases they do more than 'merely' producing their programs, as the following anecdote about promoting MYCYradio shows: "[...] we were something like 5–6 producers of shows volunteering, having the T-shirt of MYCYradio and EIMP [European Initiative for Media Pluralism]. We are starting [to become involved]" (Interview MYCYradio producer 2, June 2014). The producers also did express interest in the organization's well-being and also, from the perspective of the CCMC staff, some initiatives have been taken to involve the producers more:

> "[...] one of the things we did was to invite all the broadcasters to a social gathering, where we had kind of drinks and stuff and people. We had a big conversation with all of us, we wrote some ideas down on paper and it was decided that some kind of coordinating body with the broadcasters would be created, with meetings on a regular basis, that would just bring people closer to the station within the operational side of things." (Interview CCMC staff member 2, January 2015)

Again at the informal level, another link between the producers and the Board has been established. One of the producers was at the same time mandated by a member-NGO to have a seat on the Board, which enabled at least one person to contribute to the fulfillment of the statutory requirements. The concerned producer explained this himself as follows: "I'm sitting in the Board, so voluntary I give some my time to some [CCMC] projects as well" (Interview MYCYradio producer 2, February 2014). He continued:

"It is totally separated, I mean I'm just one voice in the Board and it is one opinion. And right now, I happen to be the youngest and the more free in terms that the other people, they have families, they have expenses, they have bills to pay, I have bills to pay too but because I don't have a family and I have very good girlfriend that allows me to do anything I like, allows me do ..." (Interview MYCYradio producer 2, February 2014)

3 CCMC, MYCYradio, and Conflict Transformation

The second main part of this discourse-material analysis focuses on CCMC and MYCYradio's contribution to conflict transformation. In this part, the emphasis will be placed on how the CCMC/MYCYradio assemblage supports the transformation of antagonism into agonism. CCMC and MYCYradio's practices are discursive and material interventions into the Cypriot political landscape, which counter the strong, sometimes dominant (post-)antagonistic discourses that still circulate on the island, and offer re-interpretations of the materials that invite interpretations that support these antagonistic discourses. MYCYradio's counter-hegemonic practices are themselves part of an assemblage, but these practices resist antagonistic discourses (and materials) that are partly the more encompassing meta-assemblage of the Cyprus Problem.

This part uses the same structure as the previous part. The study of the MYCYradio content (and its production sphere) comes first (Phase 1). Here, a series of re-articulations are discussed, where MYCYradio generates (and broadcasts) signifying practices that counter a (post-)antagonistic discourse, and (attempt to) transform it into a more agonistic discourse. In practice, this implies the use of an agonistic discourse, with its nodal points of peaceful and non-violent interaction, conflicteous togetherness, and pluralization of the self. These identifications with an agonistic discourse remain situated in the context of a still strong (post-)antagonistic discourse and of the frozen materiality of antagonism (as exemplified by the Buffer Zone). In this sense, MYCYradio, and its producers, engage themselves in a discursive-material struggle, trying to give more prominence to the agonistic discourse. Even within this objective, MYCYradio's broadcasts do not escape from the presence of (a limited number of) signifying practices that give oxygen to a more antagonistic discourse, showing MYCYradio's inability to escape from the signifying practices of antagonism.

In the second subpart, the reception study of MYCYradio's signifying practices is addressed (Phase 2), which shows us how the focus group recipients go to work with the signifying practices that MYCYradio offers. This implies that in this part, more than in the content and production study, the discursive-material struggle between a (post-)antagonistic discourse and an agonistic discourse becomes visible. Sometimes, respondents identify with the agonistic discourse that feeds MYCYradio's signifying practices, or even critique it for not being agonistic enough. In other cases, respondents recognize the agonistic discourse that MYCYradio, and its producers, identify with. But these respondents do not identify with the agonistic discourse themselves; they are closer to a (post-)antagonistic discourse. Even if the struggle between these different identifications (in connection to the antagonistic and the agonistic discourses) always remains civil, it is very much present during the focus group discussions.

Finally, the third subpart returns to the material component of MYCYradio (and CCMC) as agonistic assemblage (Phase 3). CCMC offers a space where peaceful and non-violent interactions can be performed, where the bodies that are labeled radically different—in a (post-)antagonistic discourse—can meet and collaborate, and where the plurality of the self becomes visible. At the same time, CCMC's location in the discursively and materially complex Buffer Zone is an invitation to rethink the Buffer Zone as a scar, and to re-signify this space as an area of agonistic possibility, while also, CCMC's rhizomatic civil society connections, as ways to overcome antagonism, are discussed.

3.1 MYCYradio's Agonistic Signifying Practices as Contribution to Conflict Transformation

The analysis of MYCYradio's signifying practices, and their reception, will focus on a series of re-articulations of the (post-)antagonistic discourse, which are connected with agonism's nodal points. But as these signifying practices are interventions, embedded in the logic of conflict transformation, the notion *re*-articulation is preferred here. In the case of the analysis of MYCYradio's signifying practices, four main re-articulations were identified, which were also present in the reception study. In the latter case, though, a fifth re-articulation was identified, which will be addressed later. In the third subpart, the material component will be added to the analysis, but first comes the analysis of MYCYradio's signifying practices.

3.1.1 Production and content

The analysis of MYCYradio's signifying practices will study the agonistic re-articulations that can be found in the broadcasts of the three programs,

One Percent, *Cyprus Oral History Project*, and *Downtown Choris Bakira*. This analysis is complemented by the analysis of the interviews with CCMC staff members, MYCYradio producers, and their invited guests. In this analysis, as mentioned, four main re-articulations are distinguished. These re-articulations are: The overcoming/decentering of the divide, the reconfiguration of time, the deconstruction of the homogeneous self, and the elaboration of the cost of the conflict.

Overcoming/decentering of the divide. While antagonistic discourses emphasize radical difference, agonistic discourses focus on conflictual togetherness. In a first set of re-articulations, the existence of a togetherness is emphasized, without ignoring differences and the conflicts this generates. These re-articulations, frequently present in the broadcasts, focus on showing that the divide is overcome, but also move away from considering the divide as the ultimate reference point. In the broadcasts, there is a wide variety of subtle signifying practices on how the separations and distinctions between Greek Cypriots and Turkish Cypriots—and sometimes between Greece and Turkey—are overcome or bypassed, representing togetherness in the process. Many of these signifying practices relate to contemporary everyday life in Cyprus and its many spheres, such as education, language, relations, the professional and culinary sphere, and sports. In a few cases, an explicit reference to a (united) Cypriot identity is made. Other accounts (see later) mention the ways that institutions overcome the divide, while yet others contain signifying practices that structurally decenter the divide. These re-articulations are often very implicit, and almost always made en passant.

One example, which demonstrates how the overcoming of the divide within the educational, professional, and linguistic spheres of the everyday is represented, occurred when a guest on *One Percent* initially described himself as someone who was born in Turkey ("My family is from the last Greeks that stayed in Istanbul"—*One Percent*, broadcast 18 September 2013), undertook his PhD in Athens, worked as a journalist for the (northern) Cypriot desk of a Greek newspaper, and—as an academic—wrote a book in Turkish about Cyprus. In discussing this book, the guest also referred to the other-friend articulation when he mentioned the possibility of having his book translated into Greek, for "[…] our Greek friends […]" (*One Percent*, broadcast 18 September 2013). Moreover, in other cases, the relational sphere is seen as a location where the divide is overcome, not in general, as in the previous example, but in more specific terms, when Turkish Cypriots refer to *their*

Greek Cypriot friends, and vice versa. By way of illustration: The following story was told, mostly in English, by a retired Greek Cypriot teacher in a *Cyprus Oral History Project* broadcast:

> "And I remember once my sister didn't have black shoes to go to the church and the … this Turkish [Cypriot] girl told her: Maroulla, να σου δώσω τα δικά μου είναι καινούργια [Greek in original—I'll give you mine, they are new]—her father was a doctor and they were rich. […] And I remember Maroulla telling her: no, I am not going to accept them. [The girl then replied:] I give them to you because you are my best friend." (*Cyprus Oral History Project*, broadcast 30 September 2013)

The overcoming of the divide is also grounded in other affects, such as empathy and remorse. In the above-mentioned *Cyprus Oral History Project* broadcast, the interviewee summarily captured these emphatic sentiments in the following way: "They suffered like we suffered" (*Cyprus Oral History Project*, 30 September 2013), which recognizes the suffering of the other, and not only focuses on the 'own' suffering (and the vilification of the other as perpetrator). Empathy can also be found in signifying practices concerning the visits by dislocated Cypriots to their original houses, as in the case of this retired Greek Cypriot civil servant:

> "The Turkish Cypriot woman came near me to hug me. Then she was afraid of seeing me, crying like this, she came and went […] The Turkish lady, I had nothing against her, it wasn't the Turkish lady's fault that she was inside. I truly didn't mind at all. I didn't have even the tiniest bit against her, so to speak. Because I said to myself, she had built her life for the second time too. Of course I didn't know this when I entered, [but] she had also lost a son in Istanbul." (*Cyprus Oral History Project*, broadcast 7 October 2013)

In some instances, empathy is explicitly grounded in a humanist stance, where the divide is overcome by emphasizing that all are human (and thus part of the self), as is the case in the following fragment:

> "[…] it's how you see your fellow human and the environment. You can't tell them apart. You must know to get in the other person's shoes. And Turkish Cypriots also have this problem, they are the same—we do not differ at all from the Turkish Cypriots […]. They sit, they eat, they drink. […] We are humans, we are not Greek Cypriots, Turkish Cypriots, Maronites, it's how you see your fellow human." (*Downtown Choris Bakira*, broadcast 12 September 2013)

At the same time, the humanity of all is sometimes protected by creating a distinction between extraordinary 'fanatics' and ordinary Cypriots, which is again used as a way to overcome the divide, as both sides are seen to be equal in 'having fanatics.' This construction comes with a risk, as it might be used to absolve those who call themselves 'ordinary.' In the *Cyprus Oral History Project* broadcast of 4 November 2013, the interviewee, a Turkish Cypriot biology teacher, used the other-neighbor articulation in combination with the fanatics signifier:

> "[...] we are Cypriots that couldn't find a way to protect ourselves, to protect our neighbors ... I mean ... against any [of the] fanatical movements."

But in yet another *Cyprus Oral History Project* broadcast, this dichotomy between fanaticism and normalcy is undermined, as the interviewee explained in detail how his "nationalistic feelings" led him to commit (minor) acts of vandalism as a child, and later, when he was a student, to consider planting a bomb in a factory. His entire radio interview is framed by his transformation from a Turkish Cypriot nationalist into a peace activist, despite the pressure from relatives, who were saying: "[...] how can you work with Greeks, to help the peace. With Greeks, when you know that they tried to kill your sister" (*Cyprus Oral History Project*, broadcast 23 September 2013).

Over and above that, the programs contain signifying practices about how the divide is materially overcome, by people moving into the 'other' space. Some of these crossings of the material divide are highly emotional, as the above-mentioned stories have shown in the visits of dislocated Cypriots to their original houses. The following is another story about an earlier visit:

> "We went to the village in 1975. When the people saw us arriving in the village, they were all surprised. About 100 people were crying, shouting. ... They shouted and said τα παιδιά του Ιωσήφ ήρθαν [Original in Greek—'Josephs' children came']." (*Cyprus Oral History Project*, broadcast 30 September 2013)

Years later, from 2003 onwards, when the border crossings were opened, moving across the divide became easier and more integrated into everyday life, as the following quotation shows:

> "We would talk about our most favorite places of both sides. On the other side, of course, we love Büyük Han [the Great Inn—a road side inn in Nicosia, built by the Ottomans in 1572] every Saturday around 11 o'clock. If anyone goes to Büyük Han, there is a long table there and I highly recommend everyone to go [...]." (*Downtown Choris Bakira*, broadcast 10 October 2013)

In addition, the space of the Buffer Zone, and in particular, the Ledra Palace crossing, plays an important role in materially overcoming the divide, because it is defined not as a zone "[...] with nothing in it [...]," but as a space that has structure and is inclusive: "People who love peace and want to discuss [their thoughts] with a lot of people from different places in Cyprus can come" (*Downtown Choris Bakira*, broadcast 19 September 2013), as one guest of the *Downtown Choris Bakira* program—a representative of the German-Cypriot Youth Exchange Program—remarked.

Not only references to the material overcoming of the divide, and to conflictual togetherness, can be found in programs, but also references to overcoming the divide through the identification with a Cypriot identity and culture, which at the same time does not privilege particular national identities over others. Sometimes these references are subtle, for instance, when a guest—an academic—constructed this Cypriot identity on the basis of the materiality of Cyprus's geography when he invited "[...] all the islanders [...]" (*One Percent*, broadcast 18 September 2013) to the presentation of his new book. However, in other cases, the articulation of a Cypriot identity is more explicit and celebratory. For instance, in a *Cyprus Oral History Project* broadcast, the interviewee, a Turkish Cypriot from Nicosia, said:

> "Because Cyprus is a very beautiful island, we love our island, our country. Both Greek Cypriots and Turkish Cypriots, we have common ways, we love kebab, souvlaki, we love ..." (*Cyprus Oral History Project*, broadcast 14 October 2013)

In the broadcasts, the climate, nature, food ("kebab and souvlaki"), history, architecture, and the Cypriot dialects (as linguistic variations of Greek and Turkish) are used to construct this Cypriot identity, which again supports togetherness.

The programs do not simply concentrate on the ways that the divide is overcome at the more everyday level, they also include references to how the divide is overcome in more institutionalized societal spheres. Here, we note that a multitude of societal fields are mentioned, including institutionalized politics. The producers point in these scenarios to the existing collaborations between north and south, for example, in relation to the sewage processing in Nicosia. One of the producers of *Downtown Choris Bakira* remarked that "Unification comes from the underground, my friend" (*Downtown Choris Bakira*, broadcast 19 September 2013). What is more, other fields feature in the programs: Civil society and activism, academia, medicine, sports, and, in particular, the arts are mentioned as institutionalized locations for overcoming the divide. In one of the *Downtown Choris Bakira* broadcasts, this was made explicit as follows: "But we are here—Artists are here to create a much better environment to bring the communities together" (*Downtown Choris Bakira*, broadcast 31 October 2013).

A variation of the overcoming of the divide articulation is its de-centering, where the status of the Cyprus Problem, as a master signifier that gives meaning to all Cypriot realities, is reworked. The centrality of the Cyprus Problem is sometimes jokingly undermined, as portrayed in a *Downtown Choris Bakira* broadcast, where one of the producers described a German Cypriot exchange program when questioning the significance of the Cyprus Problem and stating the need to see beyond it:

> "One year a group of German [visitors] came here and check[ed] us out, to see what is going on and to see what is going on with the stupid Cyprus Problem, and the society of course, beyond the Cyprus Problem […]." (*Downtown Choris Bakira*, broadcast 19 September 2013)

Statements are alluded to, pointing to the hybrid cultural origins of Cyprus, the complex mixture of internal and external explanations for the Cyprus Problem (e.g., colonialism and imperialism are mentioned), the many different ethnicities that live on the island, and the integration of Cyprus into Europe, and, in particular, the EU, can be seen as de-centering the Greek Cypriot/Turkish Cypriot dichotomy and the centrality of the Cyprus Problem. The strongest reformulation of this centrality comes from a guest in *Downtown Choris Bakira* who had recently returned from covering the Civil War in Syria. In a rather insensitive way, he questioned the severity of the 1974 Turkish invasion, by comparing it to the Syrian Civil War:

> "Look, we haven't actually had a war here. Here, Turkey invaded for 4–5 days and it was over. I mean, that is not war, but a cakewalk and—on the one hand, people got killed, but on the other hand, you cannot compare the magnitude [of that conflict] with [what is going on in] Syria." (*Downtown Choris Bakira*, broadcast 24 October 2013)

In the interviews with the guests, another form of the de-centering of the divide came up, as several guests expressed their satisfaction that the Cyprus Problem was not the central topic of the broadcast they were involved in. A *One Percent* guest argued this position as follows: The Cyprus Problem "[…] wasn't discussed directly specifically. Because I think this rhetoric of the division, it doesn't add much to reconciliation process. It normalizes it a bit" (Interview guest 11—*One percent*, Spring, 2014). Another guest explained this as follows: "The fact that we don't discuss it [the Cyprus Problem], for me is helping resolve the matter. As soon as we, you know, discard the labels that we have for ourselves, the sooner we'll just be ourselves and be together and be just people and …" (Interview guest 13—*Downtown Choris Bakira*, Spring, 2014). But especially the following comment from one of the guests, at the very end of the interview, where she spontaneously mentioned her satisfaction that the Cyprus Problem was not explicitly discussed, is illustrative of the decentering mechanism:

> "Guest 17: Can I say something by the way?
> Interviewer: Yes, sure.
> Guest 17: I was happy that the Cyprus Problem was not mentioned.
> Interviewer: Ok. Why is that?
> Guest 17: Because usually the Cyprus Problem … overlaps? … no, covers?
> Interviewer: Yes: Covers.
> Guest 17: Yes … covers all other important issues. I was happy that they did not bring it in the conversation." (Interview guest 17—*Downtown Choris Bakira*, Spring, 2014)

This position can also be found in the interviews with the CCMC staff members, for instance, when the CCMC coordinator said that "CCMC doesn't, doesn't [emphasize] and shouldn't do conflict resolution" (Interview CCMC staff member 2, January 2012). When asked to explain, his reply contained the following summarizing statement: "[…] personally I don't think that being so vocal about conflict resolution or reconciliation works, especially here. It's been proven that it doesn't work. On the other. … It works in the opposite way" (Interview CCMC staff member 2, January 2012). He then continued by critiquing the conflict resolution projects that tend to be too explicit:

> "But we tend to go a little bit beyond that and we, well it's a horrible way to say, but we tend to vomit reconciliation on people. It's just too much. If you just turn it down, you know maybe use a different term for it. It's a … or, cultural dialogue to communal relations. It doesn't have to be so overt." (Interview CCMC staff member 2, January 2012)

The reconfiguration of time. In the second re-articulation, time is reconfigured. Here, the main re-articulation still relates to conflictual togetherness, but locates it in a different period, arguing that conflictual togetherness has existed in the past, and will be possible in the future. In one variation, there is sometimes a nostalgic return to the pre-conflict past, which then becomes represented as an idyllic era of co-habitation and peace. This can mostly be found in the

Cyprus Oral History Project broadcasts, where interviewees talk about the 1960s and 1970s. For instance, a Turkish Cypriot pharmacist talked about visiting a "beautiful children's garden" in the Greek Cypriot part of Nicosia, and then, "[…] after coming back to Nicosia—our side […]," always being offered an ice cream in a Ledra street shop by her father (*Cyprus Oral History Project*, broadcast 9 September 2013).

In some stories, the conflict is already more present, but it is described how, before the actual (complete) division of the island, Turkish Cypriots and Greek Cypriots would defend each other, using articulations of togetherness, localism, and the other-neighbor:

> "I know some villages that I really admire for protecting each other. [These villagers said:] 'Those Turkish Cypriot villages are neighbors and they cannot touch them unless you kill us.'" (*Cyprus Oral History Project*, broadcast 4 November 2013)

In the second variation of this time-based re-articulation, the focus is placed on the future, which includes explicit discussions about the solutions for the Cyprus Problem, and the requirements for their implementation. This variation contributes to the agonistic re-articulation through the communication of the implicit belief that solutions can be realized, creating future togetherness, and that a future without the Cyprus Problem can be imagined. Some of the strategies that are discussed are highly individual, such as the need to raise one's child with a high degree of autonomy, so that she/he is not dependent on anybody.

Other strategies are more encompassing. Sometimes, more institutional-political solutions are mentioned, such as the establishment of a federation with the two communities, the island's demilitarization, or the provision of guarantees since:

> "[…] we want the rest of our lives to be secure somehow, at least for the elements we cannot control. It [is] the same for both sides." (*Cyprus Oral History Project*, broadcast 11 November 2013)

Similarly, small scale political solutions such as establishing a bazaar in the Buffer Zone are discussed. Not surprisingly, different, and sometimes contradictory, positions are defended when discussing these institutional-political solutions, again showing that the (present and future) togetherness is conflictual. For example, in dealing with the problem of returning the lost properties, some defended a compensation model, while others simply said:

> "[…] we want our houses, we want the places in which we were born and grew up, and let the Turk[i]s[h] [Cypriots] have their own houses back." (*Cyprus Oral History Project*, broadcast 11 November 2013)

In a few other cases, the solution is placed in more (politico-)culturally oriented solutions, such as the need for a "moral rebirth" (*Downtown Choris Bakira*, broadcast 12 September 2013); for Cypriots "[…] to be more questioning as a community […]" (*One Percent*, broadcast 25 September 2013) or to "[…] focus on more local or smaller things. To experience this, we can start to manage ourselves in neighborhood-wide [schemes]" (*One Percent*, broadcast 20 November 2013). Here, we find a strong emphasis on the argument for Cypriots to take control themselves: "I think it is up to Cypriots to come together and to work together to have a big future—a better future for all of us" (*Cyprus Oral History Project*, broadcast 14 October 2013).

A variation of this type of re-articulation can be found in the references to a post-conflict Cyprus, which attempt to imagine the country—and in particular the still-divided capital city of Nicosia—after the conflict has been resolved, where both national (e.g., the urban development of Limassol) and international examples (e.g., Berlin) are used to show the potentially bright future of Cyprus and Nicosia.

The deconstruction of the self. The third re-articulation of antagonism into agonism deconstructs the subject position of the self, a process that is based on processes of anti-homogenization and pluralization. In the antagonistic discourse, the self becomes glorified and homogenized—as the self is seen as united in its courageous battle against the enemy. Deconstructions of the self in the MYCYradio broadcasts firstly consist of critiques or rediculizations of particular components of the self (such as the 'own' political system, the army, the church, the media …), or of the entire 'own' culture and ideology, where the passive and uncritical nature of Cypriot society, the "victim psychology" (*One Percent*, 20 November 2013), is shown. Cyprus's consumerist and intolerant characteristics are frequently mentioned, and its nationalism is critiqued. As one of the MYCYradio producers said: "We didn't make a program about nationalism but there was a tendency to make fun of it. In any way we can, it just comes out actually" (Interview MYCYradio producer 5, February 2014).

The critiques on the 'own' institutional-political system are especially severe. Although nuances are sometimes made, politicians are described as both impotent and power-hungry, incompetent, corrupt, and unethical. Furthermore, they are described as playing games and being involved in intrigues. They serve private interests, and their actions lack transparency; their policies are repeatedly critiqued for being nonsensical. Moreover, they 'brain-wash' and 'manipulate' people, pitching them against each other. One of the guests in *One Percent* captured it quite clearly: "Yes, the politics is dirty; yes, it's degenerated" (*One Percent*, broadcast 13 September 2013). Also, the 'own' allies (mostly Turkey in the Turkish Cypriot program) and the 'own' historical leaders are not spared.

Different other 'own' institutions are also critiqued, sometimes in a more serious tone, sometimes jokingly. The position of the 'own' military and police is put into question by linking the paramilitary forces of the 1960s and 1970s to fanaticism and terrorism. In one example, the heroism of ordinary people (in this case: in the Syrian Civil War) is celebrated, and (later) juxtaposed to militarism:

> "I met a 15-year-old [...] who literally crawled on the ground for 45 meters in order to retrieve a woman who had been shot and who nobody could get close to." (*Downtown Choris Bakira*, broadcast 24 October 2013)

But the critique affects present-day military and police forces as well, where the police are linked to police brutality, and the competence of the army is questioned. In *Downtown Choris Bakira*, especially, the Greek Cypriot Army is—rather playfully—ridiculed; something that is triggered by one of the producer's absences because of his duties as an army reservist. Here, irony is frequently used, with the others addressing that particular producer as 'General' and the producer himself stating: "I'm ready for war!" (*Downtown Choris Bakira*, broadcast 24 October 2013). When interviewed, one of the producers described this part of the broadcast as follows:

> "Yeah, he called us and said 'I am in a [un]disclosed location' like it was in Area 51. And it was somewhere in the Starbucks of Nicosia, because this is how the reserve works. You do nothing. You go there and spend 24 or 48 hours of your life doing nothing." (Interview MYCYradio producer 4, June 2014)

The same discursive logic applies to the 'own' media and religious institutions, where the former's lack of independence (in relation to both politics and the market), quality, relevance, and respect, and the latter's business and political interests, are critiqued. As a pun based on the word βρωμάριος—a wordplay that combines βρώμα (which means 'bad smell') with Makarios (the first president of the Republic of Cyprus)—in the *Downtown Choris Bakira* broadcast of 17 October 2013, shows that these critiques that desacralize the key figure of contemporary Cypriot politics are sometimes communicated through humor.

The homogeneity of the self is also sometimes re-articulated through the emphasis on internal diversity such as the (often suppressed) left-right divide or the distinction between 'fanatics' and ordinary people. This emphasis on the internal divide is partially contemporary—"Of course, immediately, the press, or rather the public in general, is split" (*One Percent*, broadcast 6 November 2013)—and partially historical, as is illustrated by the story of a Greek Cypriot interviewee in the *Cyprus Oral History Project*, in relation to how she took shelter in a coffee shop when trying to get home during the 1974 coup:

> "We went there, we tried to be aware for the people of EOKA [B] because that coffee shop belonged to the AKEL. There the Greek soldiers were shooting at us [...]. Because EOKA [B] was the extreme right and AKEL the extreme left. So at that time the coup was against AKEL as well. That's why the soldiers were shooting [...]. They didn't have the intention to shoot everybody, at least I think that they wanted to frighten us. I remember, I had [to] hide under the table." (*Cyprus Oral History Project*, broadcast 21 October 2013)

The elaboration of the cost of the conflict. Finally, the fourth re-articulation consists of signifying practices that offer a straightforward narration of the cost of the conflict and the division. In doing so, they express the undesirability of the destruction that accompanies the antagonistic model. The signifying practices on the conflict, especially in the *Cyprus Oral History Project* program, are very detailed memorializations of the fear, pain, and destruction that characterized the intra-communal violence in the 1960s and the Turkish invasion in 1974. More than attributing blame, these memorializations demonstrate the suffering caused by war, which, ironically, unifies Greek Cypriots and Turkish Cypriots, without privileging the suffering of one side—the latter is a frequently occurring process that Papadakis (2006) called "ethnic autism." For instance, in the *Cyprus Oral History Project* broadcast of 7 October 2013, a Greek Cypriot refugee, whose husband is still missing, said the following about her status as refugee:

> "But still, it troubles me very much. I mean, not only the fact that I'll never go back to my house, but the future of our country, what our children will inherit, where our children and our grandchildren are going to live."

In the *Cyprus Oral History Project* broadcast of 14 October 2013, one week later than the previous citation, a Turkish Cypriot refugee told her story:

> "In 74 we became a refugee once again, for the second time. [...] Because we had to move again, in this stage to a Greek Cypriot home. And it was [a] very bad experience, again, because ... since we lived this situation in 63 we knew how it feels to leave your family, leave your house and go away."

At this juncture, it is important to add that the programs show that the trauma has not disappeared, but is still part of the everyday lived experience, and it also concerns everyday routines:

> "Look, the fact that you go to the supermarket and you buy 1 kg. of cucumbers, 1 kg. of tomatoes and 15 cans, that is not something that happens in countries that have not suffered war. This is a small issue and it sounds really funny, but this thing is essentially the refugee's syndrome." (*Downtown Choris Bakira*, broadcast 31 October 2013)

The interviews with the guests of the three programs, and in particular the *Cyprus Oral History Project*, also show the impact of the trauma through the difficulties the guests report talking about their war experiences in the interviews. Guest 5, for instance, said: "It left us with many wounds, both to us as a family and to me as an individual. And whenever I think of them, the same emotions come to me" (Interview guest 5—*Cyprus Oral History Project*, Spring, 2014). In one case, the guest reported relief after the interview: "I was feeling relieved, to tell you the truth. Maybe by saying these things I made my sadness get out of me. Until now it hurts just the way it hurt us at the beginning" (Interview guest 3—*Cyprus Oral History Project*, Spring, 2014).

In the actual broadcasts, these signifying practices about the impact of war, past and present, are complemented by references to the cost of the divide, which, for instance, draw attention to the political-economic isolation of the north, the political instability and uncertainty generated by the divide, and the lack of access to property and—for a long time—to people. In a *Downtown Choris Bakira* broadcast (31 October 2013), it was explained that the divide not only impacts on material access, but also has a discursive dimension:

> "[...] you always tend to hit a wall which has been erected, not only as a result of the special political circumstances that are in effect now—that [Nicosia] is a divided city—but also due to conceptions about what this or that person will say, etc."

In addition, we find discussions on the everyday consequences of the divide as well. A typical example is the impossibility of taking a pet for a walk to the other side, or of providing medical assistance:

> "[…] for many years no one could find practical ways to get an ambulance [English in original] across [the Green Line] in cases of a medical emergency." (*Downtown Choris Bakira*, broadcast 31 October 2013)

These re-articulations are not without internal tensions and contradictions, which limit the programs' capacity to support agonism. The Cyprus Problem is very much part of a discursive struggle, and it is no coincidence that the broadcasts contain identifications with other, more antagonistic, articulations of the Cyprus Problem. One significant limit consists of the different interpretations linked to the signifying practices on the cost of the conflict and the divide, as these narrations could potentially serve an antagonistic discourse and its emphasis on radical difference, particularly when only the suffering of the 'own' side is emphasized. Although in many cases this is compensated for by expressions of empathy by the same person in the same broadcast, and by other persons in other broadcasts, we can, in some cases, find more self-centered narrations that only articulate the self as victim, and the other as perpetrator, or at least as uncivil and uncaring. The following cynical statement of a Greek Cypriot retired civil servant shows the presence and strength of these kinds of signifying practices:

> "Ok, so what did we learn? You simply find out how the strong prevail and [what] the fate of the weak [is]. I mean, we are weak, we have right on our side but we are still doomed by the strong. I believe this is a principle that applies to all peoples. You just realize what this world is and how it works." (*Cyprus Oral History Project*, broadcast 7 October 2013)

A second set of signifying practices in the broadcasts, supporting an antagonistic discourse, are related to the normalization of violence and militarism, fed by nationalism. For instance, the violent 1974 National Guard coup, initiated by the Greek junta, is downplayed by one Greek Cypriot interviewee[38] as the actions of "[…] a political party [that] tried to change the government […]," which is something that "[…] happens every day in every country" (*Cyprus Oral History Project*, broadcast 18 November 2013). Likewise, the denial by the same interviewee of the existence of pre-1974 violence, which disproportionally affected Turkish Cypriots, is an example of these signifying practices that show the identification with an antagonistic discourse:

> "This is 1974, I am happy, I have anything I looked for, I live in a nice town, and enjoy the beauty of the town, I was enjoying my vacations, my family and it was not a country where it was anarchy or dictatorship. We lived in a democracy and everything was peaceful." (*Cyprus Oral History Project*, broadcast 18 November 2013)

Thirdly, within the island-wide Cypriot identity discourse, we can also ascertain traces of new constitutive outsides that still counter the logic of pluralization, and might form (or become) new other-enemies. One new constitutive outside is the foreign immigrant. The latter not only includes the Turkish 'settlers' in the north, but also (and mainly) immigrants from other regions of the world that are subjected to negative, sometimes racist, judgments. In one *Cyprus Oral History Project* broadcast, the Turkish Cypriot interviewee, a pharmacist, talked about 'unregistered' immigrants in the following way:

> "Most [...] are very poor people, and illiterate, and coming here just to work. So they are not living in [...] good conditions. They destroyed everything. They are not clean." (*Cyprus Oral History Project*, broadcast 9 September 2013)

One other constitutive outside that is mentioned in the broadcasts—mostly in the program *One Percent*—are gay people, but these discriminations are fiercely dismissed by all who are present in the studio, and the negative consequences of these discriminations are highlighted, making these references much less problematic and antagonistic. Nevertheless, it remains important to reiterate that the presence of these three sets of signifying practices weaken the programs' agonistic capacities, even when they rarely occur and when their existence within Cypriot society at large cannot be denied.

3.1.2 The reception of the three radio shows

In the reception of the three radio shows, the four re-articulations that were discussed in the production part are also acknowledged and recognized, although there are many variations and contestations. Here, we see the discursive struggle about the Cyprus Problem in the Cypriot society, the different discourses that circulate there, and the multiplicity of identifications these discourses generate. For instance, in the discussions that are related to one particular re-articulation, namely, the deconstruction of the homogeneous self, we find *more* emphasis on Cypriot diversity and pluralization. Respondents frequently argued for the rejection of the juxtaposition of Greek Cypriot and Turkish Cypriot communities (which is said to lead to their homogenization), and in favor of the acknowledgement of the existence of other communities (apart from the Greek Cypriot and Turkish Cypriot communities). In addition, a fifth re-articulation comes to the fore in the reception of the radio shows. This re-articulation is a celebration of ordinariness, where the everyday life experiences and common sense of ordinary people that are given a voice in the radio shows are seen as an important instrument to counter the nationalist signifying practices of political and mainstream (elite) actors.

While these five re-articulations of antagonism into agonism are recognized by the respondents, and the respondents sometimes identify with these re-articulations, in other cases the respondents remain skeptical toward the social relevance of these re-articulations, or toward their efficacy. More fundamentally, in a few cases, the respondents' signifying practices refer to the rejection of MYCYradio's capacity to contribute to conflict transformation altogether. One version of this rejection occurs when respondents use a third actor perspective, saying that others will (or might) reject MYCYradio, as illustrated in this statement: "[...] the things I hear from people when I mention the station is, 'oh yeah, it's the bi-communal hippies,' or 'yeah, that's just the peace lovers,' or 'that's just an extremist group of the civilians' [...]" (FG1B-EL). Another version, already mentioned in the discussion about MYCYradio's identity, is the radio station's confinement to the NGO world, connected to the NGO presence in the Buffer Zone.

In a few cases, the actual content discussed in the focus groups becomes discredited, not because of issues with the quality of the radio shows (see earlier), but because of the perceived irrelevance or naiveté of the content. In one case, a broadcast with a phone-in from the Philippines, with a strong pacifist-humanist undertone, was met with irony and sarcasm:

> "FG10I_GNL: Ok, the girl, of course, let us not digress, she meant that we are all one world and all of us [are] people.
> FG10H_GNL: We are all under the same god. Regardless of whether ... regardless of whether he is called Allah, Christ, or Buddha, whatever [in English].
> FG10G_GNL: And, to conclude, make love not war [in English]
> [Laughter and applause]."

A last structural critique transcends the focus on MYCYradio, and questions the capacity of media in general to contribute to conflict transformation. In the example below, the formulated critique was quickly resisted, as one of the other respondents immediately replied by saying: "Even it's not enough, it's important" (FG6C_TL). This critique went as follows:

> "The media whose progress is of course effective and necessary. I mean, to realize the other side's pain, to mention the friendship, to encourage and to have a critical view on the politicians are, of course, very valuable but it is fancifulness to think that it will establish peace. The solution of the problem is not so easy." (FG6D_TL)

Overcoming/decentering of the divide. The first re-articulation of the antagonistic discourse that the respondents related to, and often identified with, is the capacity of MYCYradio to overcome the divide between the Turkish Cypriot and Greek Cypriot communities, and to communicate (conflicteous) togetherness. FG2A_GL's formulation summarized this re-articulation in a succinct way, when describing MYCYradio as follows: "Yes, and it's quite diverse [in English], and it builds bridges, which is very useful. It also has a social role to fulfil, and it does fulfil it." Of course, given the diversity of focus group respondents (including their diverse political stances), this bridging role is not always accepted, even if the re-articulation's existence in the radio shows is recognized. For instance, in one of the *Downtown Choris Bakira* broadcasts (10 October 2013) a reference is made to the maps of Nicosia, which often only have the street names of the 'own' part of Nicosia, and an argument is developed to have maps of the entire city (symbolically bridging the divide). One of the focus group respondents then rejected the desirability of this overcoming of the divide. His argument was that this type of map would imply a recognition of the TRNC, "the false state," which is (for him) politically unacceptable:

> "All our struggles now, from 1974 until today, the greatest … one of the greatest [of our] struggles has been the recognition of the false state. The non-recognition of the false state. Why, then, should the CTO [Cyprus Tourism Organization] include something about the [other side], if they want, let CTO put in their booklet [in English] something like, look, in 1974 the coup was staged, two invasions took place, eh … 300,000, 200,000 people were driven from their homes because of the war and came to the southern part of Cyprus, ehm … let them put that in, why not, but why should we put anything about the false state in the CTO booklet [in English]?" (FG10H_GNL)

In the focus group discussions, several ways of overcoming the divide were touched upon, even though not many of the everyday life transgressions of the divide, subtly but prominently present in the broadcasts, were mentioned in the focus groups. The first way of overcoming the divide was related to communication and dialogue, where respondents emphasized the radio's capacity to bridge the divide by organizing dialogue. As FG10B_GNL said, in a more general manner: "I believe the most important step is to, to start a conversation, so to speak. And to become equal to the other so you can talk to them and to first look at the commonalities [between you]. That is, to engage in self-criticism and say, ok man, I don't belong to the Aryan race."

The following is an example more focused on MYCYradio: "[…] if you're living in the Greek Cypriot community, hearing what a Turkish Cypriot thinks is important to Greek Cypriots. I mean, that was even like, you know, putting it out there, bringing these ideas into contact with the listener" (FG1E_EL). Even if some mainstream media are accredited for having similar (bridging) projects, it is particularly MYCYradio that is seen to be able to overcome the divisions that are generated by the stereotypes about the other that circulate on Cyprus, also through the mainstream media.

This dialogue is not only direct; also talking about the self, the other, and the relations between the two enables countering the silence about the more agonistic positions—as FG2E_GL remarked: people "[…] may not say it out loud because they are afraid people will snub them, or they are even afraid of themselves, but they leave [this stuff] inside themselves." MYCYradio's approach is then seen as a broader evolution, as described by FG1B_EL:

> "[…] people breaking the silence and the taboos. Ten years ago a Greek Cypriot talking about the coup was a taboo, now it's a given. Even the right-wingers are talking about the coup or condemning it. That was unthinkable ten years ago. A Greek Cypriot talking about Turkish Cypriot victims—unthinkable ten years ago, it's happening now."

Nevertheless, critical voices argued that MYCYradio's programs do not take this far enough, because of the exclusive focus on Greek Cypriot and Turkish Cypriot communities (in the fragments), without the homogeneity being explicitly questioned (see later). A similar critique is that the individual shows are mono-communal and do not allow for dialogue between (representatives of) the different communities. The critique on the lack of (sufficient) pluralization is illustrated by this statement:

> "To contribute to both sides' democracy, the people have to come together, discuss, for example, as we said for a while, both sides could come together and do some work together in small groups maybe in company of a group therapist. It could be watched or it could be on the radio." (FG9E_TNL)

The second way the bridging re-articulation is played out is through a variety of affects. In particular, empathy, mentioned in the broadcasts as a bridging mechanism, is strongly present in the focus groups. "Standing in the other's shoes" is often used as a metaphor in this context. The acknowledgement of mutual suffering is one element of bridging through empathy, as FG7E_ENL explained:

> "[...] here [in the Greek Cypriot community] the general story goes that only the Greek Cypriots have suffered and it [the fragment] clearly shows that, of course, the Turkish Cypriots have suffered, so it's important to listen to the other side as well and to acknowledge that both sides have suffered, which doesn't happen often."

A mere acknowledgement of the other's suffering is still deemed insufficient by some, as the affectious dimension of empathy—feeling the pain of the other—is important: "[...] empathizing with the other, without pretending superiority to any pain" (FG6D_TL). This empathy is grounded in the recognition of the other as human, after all, as FG7C_ENL argued: "[...] as human beings on this planet we all roughly lead the same lives." In some cases, the respondents expressed this empathy in response to the interviewees they have been listening to:

> "I felt her agony, the fact that a Turkish Cypriot village was surrounded by Greek Cypriots during a time of war, or even before the invasion, during the time period in which EOKA B [was active]. I felt her agony, I felt her fear, and people faced similar fear and agony in Greek Cypriot villages as well." (FG8G_GNL)

Again, we can find critical comments in the focus groups, when respondents do not identify with the agonistic discourse and its nodal points. Here, the argument of overload is used: "I think it's important that these stories are being told but again, if it's too much and too often I think there's a danger of people just switching off" (FG7E_ENL). Stronger critiques are grounded in the rejection of the empathy that is offered in the radio shows, as, for instance, FG10F_GNL's claim on exclusive victimhood exemplifies:

> "At the end of the day, we feel victimized, we are the victims in this case because it wasn't us who decided to invade, nor was it us who drove them away, nor was it us who slaughtered them, they came here to invade, I mean, at the end of the day, we feel that we are the victims, they are making us feel guilty through the way this logic is presented."

Other affects (than empathy) are also referred to as bridging mechanisms. In a few (rare) cases, the importance of the broadcasts in countering fear are mentioned, as, for instance, in FG6E_TL's intervention, who sees the MYCYradio broadcasts as ways to counter the fear for the other captured in questions such as "[...] what are you going to do on the other side if they stab you?" (FG6E_TL)). But apart from empathy, also friendship, and the acknowledgement of the possibility of the other-friend, play a significant role. Even though the limits of what (the representation of) friendship can do are mentioned, the bridging capacity of friendship is still recognized, witness the following exchange:

> "FG9F_TNL: We are a generation who grew up with the hate and marginalization speeches. To listen to that is very important [in order] to live with the people of the other side. Our feeling of trust is collapsed. It's important to feel the trust again.
>
> FG9D_TNL: Yes. With taking into consideration that we are a community who is not used to listen or read, to hear this kind of speech while listening to a radio is important.
>
> FG9C_TNL: A generation lives this friendship …"

Also, here, the broadcasts trigger personal narrations about friendship and similarity, such as in the following citation: "I have a Turkish friend. The number of common elements you can find between us is unbelievable" (FG10H_GNL).

Apart from the communicational and dialogical bridge that MYCYradio itself forms, and the bridging affects that create togetherness in its broadcasts, there are two other mechanisms that overcome the divide featured in the broadcasts. First, there is the construction of a Cypriot identity, which overcomes, or complements, the Greek Cypriot or Turkish Cypriot identity. One respondent, FG2D_GL, for instance, said:

> "[…] Now, if, along with this country, a Cypriot identity is being developed, in the sense that [people] feel more Cypriot than Greek Cypriot or Turkish Cypriot, because of MYCYradio and the connections that are created, I think it isn't bad at all, that is, one might not say that MYCYradio is an attempt by the modern Cypriots to develop something."

Secondly, also, the bridging capacities of different institutions are recognized. As one of the MYCYradio programs has a clear historical dimension, history (and historical research) is mentioned in this context: "[…] it's useful to have a common informative medium about common history" (FG5B_TL). Also, academia in general, and the arts, are mentioned here: "Art has this transcendent dimension, it transcends many things, many of the petty human things that tend to keep us apart" (FG2C_GL).

Apart from overcoming or bridging the divide, the decentering of the divide is also seen as part of this re-articulation. The MYCYradio programs are acknowledged for their capacity to move Cypriots beyond the Cyprus Problem, provoking statements that Cyprus is not "[…] the center of the earth"

(FG2F_GL), as FG7D_ENL also said: "[…] part of the problem, I think, is the fact that Cypriots think that Cyprus is the center of the earth. You know what? We are a dot on the map. And on big maps, we are not even there." The main discursive location of this process of decentering the Cyprus Problem is, however, the deconstruction of the ethnic-national identity, undermining the centrality on which the Cyprus Problem is built, which will be addressed in one of the next parts.

The reconfiguration of time. The focus group respondents also recognized a second re-articulation, which has been labeled the reconfiguration of time. This re-articulation can be divided into two components that both include a more agonistic dimension: The presence of a communality in the past, and the development of a common future. In relation to the past, a number of respondents emphasized the importance of the past for the present, in more general terms. For instance, FG9F_TNL said:

> "It's important to establish the memory. For example I'm not so sure but I think George Orwell said: 'If you control today, you can control the past. If you control the past, you can control the future.' I mean, it has to establish a different, alternative memory in here and this would be the determiner of the future. That's why it's important. Our memory is formed with the speeches told or written by specific groups. It's important to create a new memory."

Narrating the histories of conflict is deemed important because—as FG8B_GNL argued—the truth about the crimes needs to be told: "From the point at which they started killing each other, those are crimes, and even beyond friendships, these must also be brought to light!" In the focus groups, three types of historical signifying practices were mentioned. In focus group 3, there was a brief reference to the importance of the histories of bi-communal pacifism, and the meetings organized in Pyla or Ledra Palace. Secondly, also, the common history of suffering, as a mechanism for agonism, was touched upon, for instance by FG7E_ENL, when she referred to a fragment of the *Cyprus Oral History Project* in which a Turkish Cypriot talked about her fears caused by the threatening presence of Greek Cypriot soldiers in her village in 1974. It is a quotation from the focus group discussions that is worth repeating:

> "I think it's a very powerful account and […] it shows … I mean … here [in the Greek Cypriot community] the general story goes that only the Greek Cypriots have

> suffered and it clearly shows that, of course, the Turkish Cypriots have suffered, so it's important to listen to the other side as well and to acknowledge that both sides have suffered, which doesn't happen often."

But the historical dimension that is frequently referred to is the history of co-habitation. In focus group 6 there was the following exchange that illustrates the importance attributed to these signifying practices:

> "FG6C_TL: Two communities lived separately for years and they believed all the things told. […] It's good to share moments when they were living together.
> FG6A_TL: It's necessary to establish a common ground for the future.
> FG6B_TL: This is evidence of its possibility. It can be something like that in the future because people had already lived together before."

The knowledge of each other's language is seen as one important element of this co-habitation. FG7C_ENL added the following personal experience of bi-lingualism to the discussion about the fragments:

> "Especially the fact that people speak both languages, whether Greek Cypriot or Turkish Cypriot. I personally know Turkish Cypriots that speak fluent [Greek] Cypriot, as fluent as any [Greek] Cypriot on this side. I grew up in a village that was a mixed village of Greek Cypriots and Turkish Cypriots which is 15 minutes from Nicosia but nobody on this side likes to acknowledge the fact that it existed."

The respondents do raise two types of comments to the historical signifying practices about co-habitation. The first argument is that the history of co-habitation should not be restricted to the two main communities, as FG7C_ENL also explained:

> "Cyprus has always been a mixing pot of a whole lot of nationalities, religions, different kinds of people. It's never been this whole perceived Hellenic nation throughout the past two, three thousand years of this country's history. It's been everything and anything except one certain nationality, one certain culture."

And secondly, the histories of co-habitation should not be uncritically celebrated, ignoring the difficulties that occurred in these pasts. This is where conflicteous togetherness becomes explicit, although also, references to the co-occurrence of antagonism and agonism are made. FG7D_ENL formulated this as follows:

> "I mean, my father spoke Turkish for example. When I went to London to study, I met a Turkish Cypriot who saw, on the day his grandchild was born, or rather he asked God for enough days so that he could teach his grandchild Greek. Those are very good examples, and we have plenty. We need to offer them, we need people to know, but we should also be realistic to what we had earlier rather than present an ideal world on which of course you cannot build."

The focus groups also contained discussions about a common future for Cyprus. As was the case in the radio shows, some solutions are situated at a highly individual level. FG5A_TL's statement is an example of this type of argumentation: "If a person starts to interrogate himself, I can say that this is good step." For the respondents, this also implies personal closure in relation to the misfortunes the interviewees talked about. Moreover, in the same focus group, FG5F_TL argued that personal change can result in collective change: "[…] we can develop personnel initiatives, then have people who think the same joining them, and we can turn it into a communal initiative and we can solve communal problems."

In other cases, the common future of Cyprus is linked to institutional change. Much less than was the case in the broadcasts, political solutions featured in the focus group discussions. The institutional reforms (allowing for an agonistic Cyprus) that were mentioned are mostly related to the educational and the media sphere. For instance, in response to one of the more antagonistic fragments, FG6F_TL said: "These people can get educated," to which FG6E_TL responded: "With socializing …" In other cases, solutions are more specific, such as, for instance, the implementation of bi-lingual education: "[…] people need to at least be offered the option of learning Turkish in schools over here […]" (FG7C_ENL). Critiques on the Cypriot media also feature prominently, nicely captured by FG9E_TNL's words: "[…] I mean, if the media can't help and rescue us, we have to rescue the media first and then it can be." Here too, we find more specific suggestions, such as, for instance, the creation of island-wide media or the inclusion of journalists of different communities in one media organization.

Finally, as was the case in the broadcasts, the respondents mentioned different examples of reconciliation and conflict transformation. In some cases, the role of citizens as driving forces of change in regions and countries such as Northern Ireland and South Africa was emphasized, while the peaceful relations between the linguistic communities in Belgium were also mentioned, in combination with a reference to the Alsace, and Franco-German relations:

> "Alsace changed hands six times between 1870 and 1945. That is, an entire people were sometimes part of Germany, sometimes part of France. We, Cyprus, aren't the only [such case], we are not the only country in which there was ethnic conflict [in English]. There were also countries much bigger than us that were wounded, that suffered invasions, that suffered anomalies, rapes, calamities [...]." (FG10D_GNL)

The deconstruction of the self. A third main re-articulation deconstructs one of the basic categories of the antagonistic model, the self, providing support for the logic of pluralization. Even if the subject position of the enemy sometimes features in the focus group discussions, for instance, when respondents argued that both sides had (and have) "fanatics" (FG7C_ENL), which implies also that each community was (and is) politically diverse, it is mainly the homogeneous self that becomes target of these deconstructions. In the focus groups, the (need for this) re-articulation itself is sometimes thematized, through the signifier of self-criticism.

One example of the plea for self-criticism (and thus, for the deconstruction of the self) is this discussion in focus group 10, which simultaneously critiques the MYCYradio broadcast for not being critical enough, and for resembling too much a "coffee house conversation" (FG10D_GNL):

> "FG10D_GNL: Regarding this particular issue, it's that ... yes, I completely agree, criticism and self-criticism should happen, but not ...
>
> FG10I_GNL: Not of this type.
>
> FG10D_GNL: Not the 'coffee house conversation' type. It was a little bit of a coffee house conversation for me, both in the way [it went on] and in its approach, of course I don't know if this is what they want to get out of the show, but for me the way he presented [the issue] was very superficial and quite ... and I agree with [FG10I_GNL] that it was not a critique worthy of someone sitting down to listen to and pay much attention to it."

In the same focus group, one respondent also formulated a limit to the self-critique, as it cannot force people to move outside (what is perceived to be) their national identity, again showing a different identification, here with culture, as part of the discursive struggle that characterizes the Cyprus Problem:

> "We cannot reduce culture to 'ah, the Cypriot' and 'the Cypriot.' That is, I met, I don't know how many, other peoples and I cannot say that we are ... how to say it, the gorillas in this whole affair, or anything like it [laughter]. It's simply that, ok,

self-criticism is very good, yes, but, on the other hand, not [if] we expect our children to necessarily act as people from another culture. It's …" (FG10A_GNL)

In the responses to the fragments, respondents recognized different deconstructions of the self (focused on different components). In a first series of deconstructions, the goodness and wisdom of the self were undermined, with statements such as: "We can't get anything right. Until now, we have a problem with the state perception and the choice of leader" (FG4C_TNL), and "Cyprus has grown a bit too big for its boots as far as a lot of things are concerned. And everybody as we said, very early on, people are concerned with the money but they've lost sight of everything else" (FG7C_ENL). Other statements were more in relation to the Cyprus Problem: "One side tries to hide what their own people did, and the other side tries to demonstrate in any way that their own people were victimized" (FG8F_GNL). In particular, the lack of responsibility for the 'own' crimes is a reoccurring topic: "We need this kind of things. We need to confront [ourselves] with our own crimes, wounds and pains" (FG4B_TNL), although these crimes are sometimes (in a very protective move) disconnected from the self: "[…] we can, with such testimonies, show that in 1963 we didn't do [these things], the 100–200 followers of Denktaş did, and the 500 followers of the guerrilla leaders of this side. They did it, it wasn't us!" (FG8B_GNL). In the same focus group, FG8C_GNL explicitly addressed the difficulties of coming to terms with the idea that some of the perpetrators of violence belonged to their own community: "It's going to be more difficult to admit that not you personally, but your people, those you represent, those among which you belong anyway, also did bad things. It's difficult to say that."

A second type of deconstruction of the self that are recognized in the programs, and often shared by the respondents, undermine particular social institutions, where in particular the 'own' state and government are fiercely critiqued. After listening to a fragment from the *Cyprus Oral History Project* about peaceful co-habitation and the humanity of the other, FG1H_EL responded in the following way, placing the responsibility for the Cyprus Problem with the governments:

"And you will find what she said about, 'it's not the people, you know, we're ok with the people, it's not their fault, we're all similar, we're all the same, it's the governments.' You know, this is a stereotype, I mean, it has developed into being a stereotype statement in Cyprus, perhaps from both sides, yet it's so true."

Also the critiques on the educational system are echoed in the focus groups, recognizing that the 'own' schooling system has supported an antagonistic discourse, as, for instance, FG4D_TNL denounced, in the following terms:

> "You have the right to know the reality. I want to know what happened exactly. Differences, or manipulative [representations], or something that positions someone as an enemy. … You can understand that the only reason is the 9-year old school books, which are totally bullshit. Completely different things are mentioned [there]."

Other social institutions, linked to the 'own' community, were also critiqued. The 'own' civil society is deemed to be too disconnected from the people, as FG4F_TNL explained: "I mean civil organizations have to be inside the community, not disconnected." Also, the critiques on the Orthodox Church are recognized and shared:

> "I certainly agree with the criticism when it comes to the negative roles the official Orthodox Church has assumed. I mean, it has assumed more of a political than a spiritual role, and from the entire spectrum of political views they have mostly chosen an extreme right-wing view that is not Christian to begin with." (FG2C_GL)

Finally, also the critiques of the mainstream media (which were discussed in the previous part on the identity of MYCYradio) undermine the homogenous self through the deconstruction of its institutions. To take only one focus group as example: In focus group 2, the 'own' mainstream media are labeled "toxic" (FG2B_GL), "counterproductive" (FG2A_GL and FG2D_GL), "[…] the expression of our problem and the division of the country" (FG2C_GL), and they are said to "[…] cause enormous damage when it comes to the image they paint for anyone who supports the other side" (FG2C_GL). Even if some improvement in the past years is acknowledged, the negative representation of the other by the 'own' mainstream media is critiqued, in combination with the mainstream media's tendency to stereotype those who defend bi-communalism, as this exchange illustrates:

> "FG7E_ENL: Yes, you hear hardly any voices that talk about bi-communal activities, the bi-communal spirit. On the contrary, I think these people are often portrayed as nutcases or as utopians …
>
> FG7C_ENL: Free-thinking hippies …
>
> FG7D_ENL: Traitors …
>
> FG7E_ENL: Traitors, exactly, yes. They are not taken seriously and they are belittled very often. And you hardly hear any voices that don't

agree with the mainstream opinion as it's perpetrated by most of the parties as well, so …"

The third type of deconstruction of the self that is recognized is explicitly targeted against the homogeneity of the self, and rejects the homogeneity of the Turkish Cypriot and Greek Cypriot community, their dichotomous relationship, but also the reduction of Cypriots to these two communities. In these focus group discussions, the MYCYradio programs (and, more specifically, the fragments that were played in the focus groups) were critiqued for not going far enough in the deconstruction of community homogeneity, for not recognizing the Cypriot diversity more, and for not being pluralized enough. Respondent FG5F_TL verbalized the rejection of homogeneity, but also formulated an uneasiness with the use of the categories of Greek Cypriot and Turkish Cypriot:

> "I feel uncomfortable in here. I don't think that the communities are homogeneous. When you talk about […] the Turkish Cypriot community, I have a problem with that. Basically, I have an understanding of hybridity. I never felt a Turkish Cypriot. My language is Cypriot Turkish but I can't define myself as a Turkish Cypriot. At the same time, it's a mistake to perceive Cypriot Greeks and [Greeks] as wholes. From the moment that you put [these identities] into a mould, the mistake starts."

There is also a negative version of the recognition of diversity and heterogeneity, which problematizes the lack of homogeneity and calls upon the creation of more consensus within the 'own' community, even if—in this exchange—it is formulated as a route toward conflict transformation:

> "FG10G_GNL: How could we then work things out with the Turkish Cypriots, when one side wields Greek flags and the other side wields […] Cypriot ones. We can't be friends amongst ourselves, how can we be friends with the Turkish Cypriots?
> FG10H_GNL: [FG10G_GNL] …
> FG10G_GNL: Therefore, we need to get things settled in our own 'house' [term used figuratively], we need to work things out amongst ourselves and then let us say that we will try and work things out …
> FG10H_GNL: No, the main point …
> FG10G_GNL: That our people waved Greek flags and the others Cypriot ones, or that a team was playing abroad, in Europe, and because it is was associated with a particular political party, all the flags were Greek as if Greece played and there wasn't even a single Cypriot flag, man."

Next to the rejection of homogeneity (as a principle or a practice), we can also find the emphasis on the multi-community nature of Cyprus. For instance, the presence of a Maronite guest in one of the broadcasts was seen as an important counterweight for the reduction of Cyprus to a bi-communal country:[39] "It's very interesting that, the woman was Maronite, huh? I have been meaning to actually comment on the fact that Cyprus is not, has never been, for a long time, for many centuries, bi-communal only. And I think it's very important for us to realize that" (FG7D_ENL). FG7D_ENL continued to stress the importance of having the constitutionally recognized Cypriot minorities (e.g., the Maronites) but also the Roma, represented in the broadcasts: "I think it's very important for MYCYradio to include them [these minorities], as well as, of course, the new minorities and the new communities in both parts of the country. So in that respect, it's very important that her community or her minority status to be stated and promoted [...]." In some other cases, the argument for a multi-communal approach is more general, and formulated as a critique toward MYCYradio, as illustrated by FG5B_TL's intervention:

> "FG5B_TL: I became irritated.
> Moderator: To what? [laughs]
> FG5B_TL: Again Turkish Cypriot, again Greek Cypriot. I mean in that period, the people in the city or in the village were the same? Or the people in a mixed village or in a Turkish village were the same? Those who migrated or not? The women, men? The children? The disabled people? I don't know, it was the same for the sex worker living then? For transgenders or homosexuals living at that time? Did they have the same point of view? No. We are always talking about that dichotomy, everything is about that and we just give importance to the thoughts of these two communities. The second [point] is: We are acting like the communities are homogenous in itself. ... Yes, it was a good step to try to understand each other, to show both points of view together. [...] This was very important but after the opening of the doors [the border crossings] and the [bi-communal activities], it started to be insufficient. It has to be interrogated who are Turkish Cypriots or Greek Cypriots ... and other communities."

The elaboration of the cost of the conflict and the divide. The focus group respondents recognized a fourth re-articulation, which focuses on showing the costs related to antagonistic conflict. When asked to describe the contents of a fragment, one of the respondents, FG1G_EL, said that "It's describing the war," but immediately added the following evaluation: "I think there's a lack of discourse about what the war was like." Some of the focus groups also showed the lack of knowledge or the disputed histories in relation to events that are featured in the broadcasts, but they too emphasized the importance of these signifying practices, also as learning experiences, illustrated by this exchange from focus group 8:

"FG8B_GNL:	A very vivid description of what exactly happened back then [...] Lefka was an enclosed area which was always self-managed and autonomous, it was always autonomous. And these assaults took place. She refers to the assaults by ...
FG8G_GNL:	By the army!
FG8B_GNL:	Essentially they were assaults by EOKA B, by the coup instigators. That is the truth. It's quite characteristic. ... You will hear similar stories from Limassol. It was also the same case there. Where they would put them in [...] the stadium, the cinemas, the mosques ... I think it's very ...
FG8G_GNL:	Crucial. It's very crucial.
FG8B_GNL:	The events she's describing, we 'over here' either took no notice of them ...
FG8G_GNL:	I don't think we had the opportunity to take notice of them ...
FG8B_GNL:	We didn't take notice of them and neither could we imagine them, because we could only see the parachutes dropping in the north. [...]
FG8D_GNL:	Besides, war is never mutual caresses. It is mutual killings."

In some cases, the respondents referred to the societal impact that these signifying practices might have, in support of an agonistic discourse. One of respondent's comments refers to the importance of showing the cost of war: "Because out of this experience, I think if you hear how horrible war is, you can appreciate people who say: No war again, at no cost, any war [...]" (FG7E_ENL). Although references to the cost of the divide were rarer, respondents did refer to these parts of the broadcasts, and also argued that they might have impact, as is illustrated by FG2B_GL's response to a fragment with a personalized narration:

> "And it's these little elements that he highlighted, I think, and it's very positive, and this chit chat [in English], for example, at some point the girl started to say 'I can't have a Turkish Cypriot friend', 'I can't have a Turkish Cypriot boyfriend' [in English], 'I can't go to that side because I will be stigmatized', these are small considerations entertained by everybody and they hit a nerve ..."

Nevertheless, sometimes the respondents objected and argued that representing the cost of war might not serve an agonistic discourse. The respondents, for instance, argued for the need to show restraint in broadcasting these signifying practices, partially because they might jeopardize reconciliation, as FG6C_TL said: "The aim is to establish a peaceful understanding. Of course bad things happened. It must be used in a specific rate in terms of telling how bad war is. Without entering too much in detail. I mean, as long as it is insisted on, it can't support a peaceful environment." Other respondents were also concerned by the consequences for the audiences' interest if they are exposed too frequently: "You don't want young people to be bored and switch off, you want them to learn so that we all learn together from history and not repeat the same mistakes" (FG7D_ENL). Here, the way that MYCYradio deals with the cost of war was contrasted to mainstream media, as FG1E_EL's words, talking about the mainstream media coverage of the Cyprus Problem, show: "I think it just perpetuates the pain, the suffering, the ideas we have about the other side, so it just keeps the situation as it was 20 years ago."

The importance of restraint, and the dangers related to signifying practices that support an antagonistic discourse, are illustrated by the responses in the focus groups to a fragment from the *Cyprus Oral History Project*, where an (internal) refugee, who later emigrated, strongly identified with the antagonistic representation of the other.[40] In the six focus groups that got to listen to this fragment, most focus group respondents responded negatively. Across the different focus groups, the exclusive focus on the interviewee's own victimhood was considered "one-sided and selfish" (FG6F_TL), a narration of "his truth," which "[…] doesn't help the reconciliation process" (FG1D_EL), "racist" (FG7D_ENL), "simplistic" (FG8A_GNL), and his way of talking renders him an "outsider" (FG8C_GNL). FG8D_GNL labeled the interviewee "[…] a man who went abroad at a young age and the fact that he and his family were driven off their home remained inside him like a festering wound."

More in general, the interviewee's words were seen as representative for 'the refugees'. FG8C_GNL, for instance, said: "The fact that this is the view of the [typical] refugee is very accurate, though! That is, only from refugees will you hear 'they took our house and it's abandoned' […]." A few sentences later, FG8B_GNL said: "What I register is the pattern we repeat as refugee organizations, as occupied municipalities/communities, this entire culture that has been developed." Also, FG1D_EL referred to the weight that the refugee voice has in Cypriot culture: "I think this is the main voice that we hear, in our community, in the Greek Cypriot community, and probably there are voices [like this] in the Turkish Cypriot community." Even so, the respondents express their disagreement with his point of view, even when they respected his pain and anger:

"What I don't like is when he's talking about the people living in the homes of the refugees, which are actually refugees themselves. … I don't know if he's actually talking about immigrants from Turkey, the settlers, but even then these people no matter who they are, they cannot be … the way he's accusing people of taking his home is …" (FG7H_ENL)

The responses to this antagonistic voice became particularly visible in two focus groups. In the first focus group, comprising Greek-speaking non-listeners, one respondent immediately reacted after the fragment ended and the moderator opened up the floor for responses:

"Moderator: So … This gentleman poses a lot of questions.
FG8C_GNL: A correct question, however! Correct viewpoint, good view, shall we say. … Yes, they came, there was a war, they killed us, they did [this and that] to us. In the 40 years that passed since then, what did they do with all they looted?"

After a brief discussion about the interviewee's refugee status, FG8B_GNL mentioned his (partial) disagreement with the interviewee, arguing that the interviewee's words are representative of refugee voices: "He is saying what refugees keep saying, that they [the occupants of the houses] didn't repair them. Yes, some old derelict houses that couldn't be repaired weren't repaired! But they repaired them so that northbound refugees would live in them. It is clearly the viewpoint of the [typical] Greek Cypriot refugee." After that, another respondent, FG8G_GNL, pointed to the conflation of Turkish Cypriots and Turks: "At some points, the terms 'Turkish Cypriot' and 'Turk' are still synonymous. And this man did the same. He says 'they,' meaning the Turks. He has no other point of view. […] And there's probably lots of people like him." It is after this discussion that FG8C_GNL, who first expressed his agreement with the interviewee, nuanced his position and made his realization explicit, demonstrating the discursive lure of the antagonistic discourse and the possibility of overcoming it:

"The fact that this is the view of the [typical] refugee is very accurate, though! That is, only from refugees will you hear 'they took our house and it's abandoned'. … I mean, I hadn't realized it, I'm just expressing a realization of my own right now."

Later, FG8C_GNL explicitly pointed to the dangers of these kinds of statements, arguing that those who identify with an antagonistic discourse will find support in it. He also linked the statement to the way the educational system has been emphasizing the antagonistic discourse:

> "Still, he truly is a victim, but I also don't feel that he wants to fanaticize people. Of course, a person who already is a fanatic would take this excerpt and say 'what have these people done to this man, they ruined him, the Turks are to blame again', all the usual stuff they teach us at school."

Also, the discussion in focus group 9 shows the consequences of this antagonistic voice, but in a very different way, as this fragment brings out a very defensive response from the Turkish-speaking non-listeners:

> "Moderator: Okay … Let's ask the next question … he told us that he didn't understand the situation: They came in 74, they confiscated the house and nobody explained anything and 'I didn't understand why.' 'I haven't understood for 36 years what happened in 74,' [he said]. Could you understand him? Is it something that we can feel sympathy for?
>
> FG9E_TNL: Turkish Cypriots can have the same feeling …
>
> FG9C_TNL: Finally, it was necessary that he immigrated.
>
> FG9E_TNL: Somebody told them to go and they did. If I went to his home, it was not me telling him to get out. I am also in inconvenient situation, because to move someone out of his house means that another one also moves out of his own house."

Despite the many discussions and concerns the fragment provoked, respondents still agreed that the interviewee was entitled to speak out, even if they deemed his statements not constructive. As FG6C_TL, for instance, said: "I don't say that he mustn't talk but this kind of speeches doesn't contribute to the peace." Moreover, several respondents argued that one also has to take seriously what he is saying: "But you have to listen to these voices too. I mean these people are also part of the process so you have to be aware that this argumentation, this thinking, exists" (FG7E_ENL). Finally, there is also empathy for his feelings, as illustrated by FG1E_EL:

> "[…] he's talking from a wounded position; he's hurt, the wounds stayed and he just still doesn't understand. He's still asking, 'Why did you do this then? Why did this happen?' And somehow I feel a little sad for him or a little sorry for him […]."

The ordinary as site of agonism. The fifth re-articulation, which sees the ordinary as a site of agonism, is specific for the reception study. Although the ordinary does feature in the production study, it does not have the same weight, and is not so much linked to conflict transformation. But in the reception study, the respondents expressed particular appreciation for the voices of ordinary people, which they connected to authenticity, sincerity, reality, and community. Arguably, behind this appreciation, we can find the idea that the plurality of experiences, which dislocates the still strong antagonistic discourse, is better communicated by ordinary people—some would say the multitude—and not by the Cypriot elites that are critiqued for supporting (and for still trying to hegemonize) the antagonistic model. For instance, in one of the Turkish Cypriot focus groups, FG9C_TNL said: "[…] we are listening to the real people's personal experiences, maybe they generalize a bit but I think it's important to hear something alternative." Another example is the following brief exchange about one of the fragments, which they compared to the one fragment they had listened to before:

> "FG6E_TNL: It is much more from the community.
> FG6D_TNL: More sincere. She told about real pains, real experiences. It was very sincere talk and not in political way.
> FG6B_TNL: The main idea was the same in both conversations but this aligns much more with the individual experience. It covers it. It's much more effective."

FG1G_EL added more components to the way the subject position of the ordinary is appreciated, through the emphasis on comprehensibility and proximity, connecting identification and disagreement. This citation from the first focus group shows the strength that originates from the attribution of signifying practices with ordinary people, a subject position the respondents themselves also claimed:

> "What I liked is that it sounds like a member of the general population speaking, telling, sharing a story which they totally understand and where you can see the influence of different people on that person. And that it is a genuine perspective that someone has, but I don't agree with everything that she's saying or the linkages that she's making, so that makes it very interesting."

The respondents argued that the signifying practices of ordinary people, conveying an agonistic discourse, get their strength from the fact that there are communicated *by* ordinary people. This interpretation was illustrated by FG1G_EL when he said:

> "So I think these stories are really powerful in terms of not allowing people to over-intellectualize it, not allowing people to, 'well I'm an academic so I can talk about it because I've been studying it for 40 years' or 'I've been in politics all my life dear.' It's our issue […]."

The above citation also shows that ordinary people are defined as different from societal elites, just as the intervention of FG8G_GNL, comparing mainstream media to community media, illustrates: "We listen to shady politicians, corrupted individuals, bullies, and we don't listen to people who have an opinion, who have intellectual richness and culture. ... We don't listen to [such] people. Unfortunately, voices like that aren't heard." FG9B_TNL also referred to a pluralism argument when saying: "[...] it's important to hear something from the mouth of the people but not the same ones, we have already heard them a lot. Therefore it needs to be different people's experiences."

Even if the respondents validated the ordinary people subject position, they did not celebrate it univocally. FG7E_ENL mentioned that ordinary people are not always well-protected, and making public statements might be harmful for them: "I can see how this can be really taken just the wrong way by certain media." Also, FG7I_ENL pointed to the risk of manipulation when she said that: "It's authentic but it's also something that is a more powerful tool if you want to manipulate with it." In particular one fragment repeatedly provoked protests from the respondents. In this fragment, a former member of parliament[41] is positioned as ordinary person, which is then rejected by the respondents. The following excerpt from focus group 6 shows this rejection, putting even the moderator on the defensive:

"FG6D_TL:	Ordinary person? She was not an MP in the past?
Moderator:	Yes, she was, but she is chosen as an ordinary person in the interview.
FG6D_TL:	It is good to interview an ordinary person and to give information about the Cyprus Problem. Because everybody, even when their points of view are different, can put themselves in her place. But I don't think that she is an ordinary person. The political opinion of an ex-MP is certain.
FG6A_TL:	I agree, but these types of conversation can be beneficial.
FG6B_TL:	It was a very political speech, there wasn't any personal content."

3.2 Material Agonistic Practices

CCMC, as an assemblage, enables the performance of a series of material agonistic practices, within the organizational machine itself, as it is part of a rhizomatic (civil society) network, and as it distributes its signifying practices to the 'outside world.' Within CCMC we can find a wide variety of peaceful and non-violent interactions between producers, guests, and CCMC staff members, who are (seen as) affiliated to a diversity of communities and social groups, including Greek Cypriots and Turkish Cypriots. Equally important are the peaceful and non-violent interactions between CCMC members and other actors, mostly located within Cypriot civil society, even though there are also interactions with actors outside civil society and outside Cyprus. CCMC's transmissions do not contain the sounds of violence and destruction, even if the producers' signifying practices refer to this violence, also in its materiality. But the material traces of antagonistic interactions, with their affect-ridden expressions of embodied enmity, are absent from all interactions that the representatives of CCMC are involved in, whether this is within the studio and the CCMC building, the meeting spaces where encounters with civil society representatives take place, or the MYCYradio broadcasts. Also, as the following interview excerpt from 2012 illustrates, societal groups that are hostile to bi-communal organizations (such as CCMC) have not engaged with CCMC:

> "[…] there is nothing stopping us at the moment. No one. No one has raised their head to say: 'Hey, you're traitors because you do intercommunal work.' We haven't had that. Which has happened in the past […]. We've haven't had those attacks." (Interview CCMC staff member 2, January 2012)

This does not imply that there are no conflicts and differences of opinion, externally or internally. Within CCMC itself, conflicts do occur, but they are mostly resolved through internal dialogue. The CCMC staff has struggled with severe power imbalances within the team and with inter-personal conflicts, and these tensions were worsened by several financial crises. Conflicts between staff and producers also occurred; these were mostly related to the frustration caused by the weak internal power position of the radio producers, but also by problems caused by the proto-machines (e.g., when objects broke down) (Interview MYCYradio producer 2, June 2016). One of the producers, also involved in the CCMC management, formulated their agonistic conflict management procedures as follows:

> "[…] it is important to say we found a lot of workarounds and with the patience, persistence and collaboration of the producers, we found a lot of solutions. We fought a few times and I told them 'don't expect everything from CCMC and staff—you should take over and take [the] initiative. It is your thing and we can't and shouldn't run after you […] for every little thing.'" (Interview MYCYradio producer 2, June 2016)

The nodal point of alternativity in MYCYradio's identity illustrates how central conflict is to CCMC, as this organizational machine defined itself as structurally different from mainstream media organizations. This difference was also performed through material practices, in relation to, for instance, the bodies that can access CCMC and produce radio shows, the specificity of the production practices, and the specificity of their decision-making practices. But simultaneously, CCMC has collaborated with mainstream media organizations at an organizational level but has also, at a more individual level, welcomed journalists working for mainstream media organizations (more specifically the newspaper, *Politis*) to become MYCYradio producers.

The same argument can be formulated about the agonistic-conflictual nature of the relationships with international donors, Cypriot governmental regimes, and Cypriot political parties, where a critical stance is combined with certain degrees of material interaction (for instance, the donor-relation with UNDP, and CCMC's double recognition as NGO by the Republic of Cyprus and the TRNC). This does not mean that conflict is absent. It is very much present, but mediated through democratic (and non-violent) procedures. When one CCMC staff member was asked about the possibility of organizations with a more antagonistic stance becoming a member of CCMC, there is some relief in the acknowledgement that that situation has not occurred yet. By referring to the example of ELAM, a Greek Cypriot radical right-wing nationalist political party, the CCMC staff member explained that the CCMC *Charter* would legitimate a decision not to collaborate with ELAM:

> "Luckily, we haven't come across it yet. We haven't had [the radical right-wing party] ELAM or someone come and say: We want to be a member [of CCMC]; we want to make a video, help us. Because they would have to read our charter. And we would review their constitution. We would ask other members of the community: Are these people representing themselves correct, you know, the way they are and the community would say: No, they're not. And their constitution would say: no, they're not. And so we would say: I am sorry, you can't belong [to CCMC]. Just like probably we couldn't belong to their organization. You know, because I wouldn't agree with their constitution." (Interview CCMC staff member 1, January 2012)

The agonistic material practices of CCMC are located in a container building, next to the (former) Ledra Palace Hotel, which towers over it. The Ledra Palace Hotel used to be one of the most glamorous hotels in Cyprus, and has a particular architecture: "Cypriots speaking of the Hotel often describe it as built in a 'modern oriental' style within a 'colonial architecture' frame because of the arches" (Demetriou, 2015: 185). Nowadays, this "[…] quintessential building in the Cypriot UN-controlled Buffer Zone […]" (Demetriou, 2015: 183) serves as the headquarters of the British UN Roulement Regiment, which is responsible for patrolling sector 2 of the Buffer Zone. Its history, as both a 'neutral' place where negotiators met and as a militarized location (Demetriou, 2015: 195) remains very much visible as the building is marked by bullet holes. It is this history, as Demetriou (2015: 184) wrote, that landed the building on the local authorities' list of monuments in the 1990s. As a military base, it is surrounded by barbed wire, walls, and all sorts of other fortifications. The CCMC building is adjacent to the Ledra Palace Hotel, with a view from the former's windows on the UN parking lot, and behind it, one of the destroyed houses in the Buffer Zone.

Figure 46. The CCMC room with a view.
Source: Nico Carpentier.

Both the back entry of the Ledra Palace Hotel and the main entry of the CCMC, with its "world famous black gate" (Interview CCMC staff member 2, January 2015) next to it, have to be accessed from the main road of the border crossing, connecting the part controlled by the Republic of Cyprus, in the south, and the part controlled by the TRNC, in the north. On both sides, there are guarded checkpoints, with a strong presence of national symbols and colors. One of the CCMC staff members, when asked to describe the southern checkpoint, referred to the large pictures of (Greek Cypriot) 'national heroes' that one sees there:

> "When you first walk across the speed bump—I think that's where the entry to the buffer zone starts—you see these placards, these images and texts of describing

> the incidents of 1996 when two Greek Cypriots were killed in protest riots within the buffer zone on the eastern side of Cyprus." (Interview CCMC staff member 2, January 2015)

Together with the abundance of flags, Greek and Cypriot in the south, Turkish and TRNC in the north, the southern entry is specific, as it is half-blocked by two 2-meter high concrete slabs that force visitors to zig-zag around them. They are painted in blue and white, the Greek colors, but, as one interviewee remarked: "[…] these big concrete slabs were at one point painted in blue and white, [but they] have since faded quite a bit […]" (Interview CCMC staff member 2, January 2015). Combined with the destroyed buildings, the barbed wire, the concrete fortifications, the UN observation posts, and the many national symbols, some buildings have been renovated to house some of NGOs active on the island. The contrast is considerable, as exemplified by one of the CCMC staff member's description:

> "To the left there is a building that looks like … what was the fairytale with that building made of candy? … Hansel and Gretel? … So the Goethe Institute to the left is so colorful and so neat and so … you always want to reach out and touch it and feel … I look at it and that's the image that comes into my head when I see it, I don't think I want to bite it [laughing]." (Interview CCMC staff member 2, January 2015)

This ambiguous materiality invites for different readings of the Buffer Zone. The material destruction, so visible in the Buffer Zone, can be interpreted as a reminder of the evilness of the enemy, who is to be blamed for the destruction, or as a reminder of the cost and senselessness of war and antagonistic nationalism. Still, its liveliness, with the terrace and bar of the Home for Cooperation and the NGO staff members and volunteers that work there, with the Cypriots and tourists passing by, contrasts strongly with the label of the Dead Zone that is sometimes given to the Buffer Zone, as Papadakis (2005: 46) explained. The reclaiming of this inaccessible material space—a Buffer Zone that could, for decades, hardly be entered by civilians—by entering it, can, in itself, be seen as an act of resistance against the antagonistic discourse, as one of the interviewees explained:

> "That gets me thinking about how we describe that space. That it is inaccessible. To some. Or that it can be seen as inaccessible. Yes, it can. But part of the great thing about it. … Part of the great thing about the first time you gain access to it, is that it then no longer is as inaccessible as you thought it was. So actually getting there, achieving the goal of arriving at CCMC is … […] you have gone some way to

breaking down some of the distance that one has." (Interview CCMC staff member 2, January 2015)

Using this space to produce radio shows with content that contributes to a more agonistic discourse also produces particular affects. One of the guests of the MYCYradio broadcasts explicitly mentioned this experience, and pointed to the positive emotions it provokes:

> "For personal reasons mainly. It was time for the presentation of my book and, as I said, it is a historical place to have a radio presentation here in the Buffer Zone. For me, it feels very different and special." (Interview guest 9—*One Percent*, Spring, 2014)

The Buffer Zone still has its own agency, and entering it is not always straightforward. Finding the CCMC (with its small black gate) is not always that easy, as one of the CCMC staff members explained:

> "If you consider it [CCMC's location] within the context of the Buffer Zone, and not in the context of Nicosia or Cyprus in general, the location is completely and utterly disabling. As my first experience of trying to get there would demonstrate to me, because I had to call two or three times to find out where it is, and I had been on the receiving end of phone calls asking where it is, where to park, why is the police hustling me, why are you not in the Home for Cooperation …" (Interview CCMC staff member 2, January 2015)

The activities within the CCMC building also disrupt the idea of radical difference and distance in a material way. The CCMC is a very material location, where different people, affiliated to different communities, have access to, interact and participate. Through these peaceful and non-violent material interactions (and participations) they undermine (and dislocate) the idea of the other-enemy who should not be trusted and can only be destroyed. In contrast, these material practices invite an agonistic discourse that articulates these others as other-adversaries (or other-allies, or even other-friends) with whom collaboration is possible. Moreover, the sharing of the material space, working together within CCMC's remit, and the shared entitlement to speak in, and about, Cyprus, also counters the idea of the other-foreigner or the other-enemy who is denied this entitlement. This togetherness is partially linked to the bodies of producers and staff members being situated in the same space, working together on the production of radio programs (or other content), but also collaborating in the management of the radio station, even if this is limited. This interaction and participation, of people connected to different communities is also mentioned in the interviews as a significant contribution to agonism:

> "I think the physical presence is important, especially in our case. And I lean towards the understanding of community media being not only a ... being on the airwaves or being on TV but also being a space where people come to co-produce or discuss about how to do productions." (Interview CCMC staff member 2, January 2012)

The same staff member, in the 2012 interview, also emphasized that the material nature of the inter-communal collaboration might be more important than signifying practices that explicitly communicate agonism:

> "[...] you don't necessarily need to be so vocal about the reconciliation what you do because of the nature of the work that you do. You open up a space for training [people] from all communities; you're open to people coming here to work from wherever they come from. The location is ideal because people can come from both sides and not have the problem of crossing." (Interview CCMC staff member 2, January 2012)

As MYCYradio is a webradio station, this interaction and participation is also made visible (or better, audible) through the broadcasts, materially crossing the divide. But even when there are broadcasts with representatives of 'only' one community, then these voices are still carried to the 'other' side, allowing members of one of the communities to hear the other's voices. As respondent FG1E_EL said: "[what is] interesting was hearing, let's say if you're living in the Greek Cypriot community, hearing what a Turkish Cypriot thinks is important to Greek Cypriots." Language plays an important role in this communicational process, as the material use of a particular language can impede or facilitate understanding. In 2012, before MYCYradio was established, one of the staff members stressed the need for multi-language programming, when saying:

> "I would like to see a station, probably a radio station or a web radio that can accommodate programming in both languages exclusively. Not necessarily everything being in two languages but maybe mirror programs that would more or less talk about the same thing or even more than two languages, it doesn't have to be just Greek and Turkish, it can be Armenian or Maronite." (Interview CCMC staff member 2, January 2012)

At the same time, already in 2012, the CCMC staff members acknowledged the problems that language use would create, and where the ideal solution turned out to be outside the reach of MYCYradio, even if the use of, for instance, English, produces—at least partial—solutions.

> "It's almost impossible to do it. Now we have the technologies that we can broadcast at the same time but again you fall into this language trap [...]. If you're speaking

> one language the other community can't understand that. So then do you just speak English, which then alienates a lot of people? Even though English has a high percentage of use on the island." (Interview CCMC staff member 1, January 2012)

Other solutions consist of the use of multiple languages within one program, or to look at the linguistic plurality at the level of the radio station (and not at the level of the individual programs). But what is particularly appreciated in the reception focus groups is the situation where a Turkish Cypriot speaks Greek (and the other way around, although this is not mentioned in the focus group discussions). What we see here is not so much the focus on the content of the intervention, but on the material language use as a contribution to agonistic relations, grounded in additional material practices, such as language acquisition (with its investment in material resources, time and energy):

> "[…] the fact that we have a Turkish Cypriot woman who speaks Greek, I'd say, putting myself in the position of a Greek Cypriot audience, the most interesting bit was that they spoke Greek. […] because I believe that these people have gone through the trouble of learning the other [community's] language, and when the other person listens to them speaking his language, their contribution to the creation of a coexistence culture is huge." (Respondent FG2C_GL)

Of course, these collaborations do not imply that a full consensus exists within the walls of CCMC, within its broadcasts, or within the reception of these broadcasts. As the reception analysis (that was discussed earlier) frequently shows: Not all respondents completely identified with the agonistic discourse that can be found in the signifying practices of the producers, or, conversely, they claimed that the signifying practices of the producers are not sufficiently embedded within an agonistic discourse. Even in some of the MYCYradio programs, in particular the *Cyprus Oral History Project*, antagonistic signifying practices are present, for instance, when interviewees talked about the cost of the conflict and focused on the self, which connects to the representation of the other as perpetrator. Nevertheless, CCMC brings together these different voices, within an overarching framework of agonistic discourse, and also materially rearticulates the other-enemy and other-foreigner, at least as other-adversary and sometimes as other-ally, other-neighbor, other-friend, or part of the self.

CCMC's conflictual togetherness not only concerns bodies working together, but is also related to the material sharing of places, proto-machines, and capitals. The members of the organization not only have access to these resources, without differences in access being legitimated through community affiliation, but these resources also become part of the participatory assemblage, where they facilitate and enable the joint production of radio programs. Because of their material specificities they also structure these collaborations. Moreover, they become objects of conflict, which requires the implementation of agonistic conflict management strategies, and they are part of the participatory decision-making structures (even if these are not radical-maximalist in CCMC). These different materials, and the participatory practices in relation to these materials, contribute to the shift from a hierarchization between communities and other-enemies, toward a structural balance between the different (representatives of the) multitude of communities, where the logics of inferiorization and superiorization do not apply. Finally, the material nature of the organizational machine, and the rigidity it produces, also has a protective dimension over time, avoiding that this assemblage evaporates, as would most likely happen if it would have been 'only' a project, without organizational backbone, as one of the CCMC staff members explained:

> "[…] again I go back to the presence issue, having an organization that specializes or is known to be working … to be helping people to do this kind of work is hugely important because everything that was attempted in the same field before, whether it be seed funding for working together, whether it's workshops or a discussion room, whatever. … It was always short term. The 6 months project or the 12 month project, x number of people participated; nothing happened. You know, you created some relationships in the room but then you never followed it up. So the idea is that this center at this point can become a reference point for people like this so we do get people calling up even just for basic information saying: Oh, I heard this in the press or the other community. Can you verify or can someone put me in touch who can. But, these are the very small things. But probably they may not have happened, if we were not here." (Interview CCMC staff member 2, January 2012)

Also, the last component of the agonistic model, pluralization, is anchored in the material logics of CCMC. MYCYradio's program schedule, with the diversification of radio producers that is almost imposed by this schedule, moves away from the community-based homogenous self, in a variety of ways. The preference for representatives that are affiliated with a multitude of communities shows the complex construction of the self, and its multi-layered composition. These bodies enter the radio station and its program schedule materially, showing the complexity of the self. This multiplicity of voices is further enhanced by MYCYradio's focus on ordinary people, even if they are often part of civil society and different social movements, as this implies a shift away from the strong dominance of elite voices in the Cypriot public spaces, in particular concerning political and media elites. This multiplicity transgresses the 'mere' presence of a diversity of bodies within the CCMC building, or within the MYCYradio broadcasts, but also, for instance, concerns the variety of material language use, the variety of material formats that are used to structure the signifying practices in the programs, the variety of ways MYCYradio's proto-machines and spaces are used to generate content, and the variety of decision-making practices in its management.

To some extent, CCMC's organizational network also enables pluralization. As an organization, CCMC links up to different NGOs and has created strong connections with the European community media movement through its collaboration with the Community Media Forum Europe. There are limits to the reach of this network, as several respondents in the focus group discussions have mentioned, referring to the (too) firm embeddedness of CCMC in the bi-community movement, and its difficulties of moving outside this sphere of Cypriot society. To repeat the words of one of the focus group respondents: FG1C_EL pleaded for MYCYradio to "[…] become more accessible […]," so that "[…] it will move out of this sort of bicommunal, sort of Buffer Zone NGO world and be kind of more expansive." Nevertheless, the "Buffer Zone NGO world" is not homogenous and conflict-free, but characterized by internal differences and conflicts. Also, the international dimension of CCMC's network connects Cyprus more to the European realities and contributes to the decentering of the Cypriot nationalist logics and its exclusive focus on the Cyprus Problem, and thus on the Cypriot self. Finally, and this is a slightly ironical last point, also the *absence* of nationalist, right-wing groups in CCMC, who shy away from playing a role in the bi-communal movement, signifies ideological diversity and a pluralist Cypriot self.

4 A Concluding Reflection on the Articulation of Participation and Agonism

> "But [CCMC] could be one small outlet where energy is channeled. You know, and the theory is that if then that energy is channeled and the messages are compelling enough, that people see a different message than [the one] they have heard, then perhaps they'll be able to relate, perhaps, there will be this space for forgiveness created, I mean, this is all conflict resolution theory as well. And perhaps over time humanity will prevail. The good side of humanity [can] prevail, people could …"
>
> —Interview CCMC Staff Member 1 (January 2012)

The question that remains to be answered is how the participatory dimension of community media organizations is articulated with their agonism-enhancing dimension. The previous parts of Chapter 4 discussed these two dimensions separately—a necessity because of their complexity—but in this conclusion, the question about the interconnection (or articulation) of participation and agonism in the community media assemblage is addressed. Also in this concluding reflection, the discursive-material knot provides the ontological backbone of the analysis, which implies that attention is paid to the workings of the discursive and the material, in entangled interaction and within the context of contingency, to discuss how participation and agonism feature together in the community media assemblage.

Before initiating a more detailed discussion, a number of preliminary remarks need to be made. First of all, the articulation between participation and agonism is not a necessity. The theoretical approach of the discursive-material knot, and, in particular, its grounding in contingency, shows that articulations are political processes, and not pre-given realities. Nevertheless, assemblages (operating within the discursive-material knot) have the capacity to fixate social reality, creating sedimentations that can, in turn, privilege particular articulations. In this particular case, the participatory component of the community media assemblage also privileges agonism, in a variety of ways that will be discussed. Still, this does not mean that this articulation is bound to occur, or that once it has been established, it will continue to occur for eternity. Identifications with the discourses of participation and agonism are necessarily always particular, and community media organizations translate both these discourses, and their articulation, in always-unique community media practices. Secondly, these community media practices are always embedded in particular contexts, which include, to mention but a few, the configurations of nation-states, regions, and localities; community and group affiliations; capitalist economies, geographies, and territories; and a multitude of identity discourses. Many of these are assemblages (or meta-assemblages—assemblages of assemblages) in their own right, but it is mainly important here to stress the context-dependency of the articulation of participation and agonism. One illustration of this context-dependency can be found in the notion of alternativity, one of the nodal points of the community media discourse. Alternativity is a highly relational concept, which implies that the articulation of this nodal point very much depends on how mainstream media are organized and function within an evenly particular public space. The unavoidable context-specificity of the Cypriot case study thus needs to be emphasized, even though, arguably, many of the articulatory mechanisms that connect participation and agonism are more structural, and stand a good chance of being applicable to other contexts. But some other mechanisms are very much part of the Cypriot configuration, and might not be too easy to transpose to these other contexts. This, of course, does not detract from the importance of these more localized mechanisms for the Cypriot case study itself. But in this concluding reflection, a more general and abstract analysis of the articulation of participation and agonism—within a context of *collective* violence—is offered, which remains anchored in the theoretical and empirical research project this book reports on. The third and final general comment is that in order to discuss these articulatory mechanisms and answer the question how community media's participatory dimension strengthens its capacity for agonism, and its capacity for transforming antagonism into agonism, the four nodal points of the community media discourse will be used as an overarching structure.

The community service nodal point strongly focuses on the participation of the community, a logic that is embedded in a participatory-democratic discourse. Through this embeddedness, the community service nodal point is supported by a number of discursive elements, of which inclusivity, equality, and diversity are of particular importance here, as all three elements work in agonism's favor. The element of inclusivity is especially important because of the particular signification it receives in the community media discourse. In this community media discourse, inclusivity becomes articulated with both quasi-universality and with the hegemony of democracy. In practice, this implies the maximization of inclusivity, to allow as many community members (and other community actors) as possible to participate in the community media organizational machine. This does not mean, though, that this universality is total, and that all community actors are to be involved, without any restriction. Even though the chain of equivalence of the community media self is extensive and fluid, a constitutive outside remains, which are those community actors that do not accept the basic democratic principles, which is sometimes referred to as the hegemony of democracy. As Mouffe (2005: 31) wrote about agonistic democracy, more in general: "Consensus is needed on the institutions constitutive of democracy and on the 'ethico-political' values informing the political association"; community media's articulation of inclusivity is defined by, and restricted to, this consensus. Nevertheless, the emphasis on the maximization of inclusivity strengthens an agonistic discourse, as it can—or at least has the potential to—undermine, soften, or even overcome the construction of the enemy-other.

Also, equality and diversity are elements of the community media discourse that support agonism. The articulation of equality plays a significant role in avoiding the logics of superiorization and inferiorization, which are part of the antagonistic discourse and sustain the radical difference between the self and the other-enemy. The notion of diversity strengthens multiplicity and pluralism, which produce contestations of the homogeneous self—a nodal point of the antagonistic discourse. In other words, diversity enables transgressing the frontiers of the self and bringing together people that represent different communities, with their different cultural practices, into the community media assemblage. This includes the other-adversary, the other-ally, the other-neighbor, and the other-friend. As a consequence, two (or more) chains of equivalence that each structure a different self come to co-exist in the same symbolic (and material) space, which stimulates their re-articulation and possible integration, through the creation of chains of difference. Moreover, diversity also enables a strong presence and visibility of the internal diversity of the self, again working against the homogenization of the self (which is, as repeatedly mentioned, a nodal point of the antagonistic discourse). Through the emphasis on internal diversity, the solidification of the chain of equivalence is countered, which again serves agonism, this time through the strengthening of pluralism, where the solidified chain of equivalence is replaced by combinations of chains of equivalence and difference.

The elements of inclusivity, equality, and diversity also structure the material practices of community media, as they are closely related to the material welcome that community media extend, to enter these organizational machines, and to interact and participate in them. Through the emphasis on inclusivity, the bodies of community media members can gain access and become part of the community media assemblage. Strengthened by the logic of diversity, these people can be affiliated to a multiplicity of communities and groups, and can identify with a variety of discourses and subject positions, supported *and* demarcated by a participatory-democratic discourse. The logic of equality then structures their interactions and their participation, and simultaneously prevents that differences, originating from this diversity of identifications, privilege particular communities, groups, or people. This also enables community media members, who are defined in an 'outside world' as each other's other-enemies by hegemonic antagonistic discourses, to interact and participate in the community media assemblage. The togetherness that these collaborations create, facilitated through the material presence of diverse bodies who voluntarily enter these places and work with each other, donating their labor, renders these community media assemblages places of agonism.

This is further strengthened by the discursive visibility that is achieved through these community media organizations, when they are broadcasting (or publishing, or webcasting, …) this togetherness. Participation *through* community media assemblages enables agonistic signifying practices, at least potentially, to be heard; but in some cases, the mere fact that an agonistic discourse becomes entextualized—translated into signifying and material practices—is already a significant contribution to agonism. Especially when antagonism has achieved a strong hegemonic position, the possibility of being confronted with the existence of agonistic signifying practices, to stumble upon these counter-hegemonic practices, matters. Additionally, the fact that particular community members publicly take a position and communicate how they identify with an agonistic discourse, with their voices and their collaborations with the other clearly audible or visible, also matters in this scenario. Of course, in situations where the (post-)antagonistic discourse's hegemony is less strong, agonistic practices, produced thanks to the participation of community members in community media organizations, can enter the public spaces and, in so doing, strengthen the position of the agonistic discourse in its discursive struggle. Again, it is the combination of signifying and material practices that matters, which, for instance, includes the sharing of the same material space, the material interaction of collaboration, and the material use of different languages (where a community member is, for instance, heard or seen whilst engaging in a conversation using the 'other's' language).

As argued before, the link between participation and agonism is not necessary and to be taken for granted. This also implies that the community service nodal point can be articulated in particular ways, or can be dislocated, so that the articulation of participation and agonism is disrupted. If the articulations of the community, and the subject position of the community member, are defined in more exclusive ways, and diversity thus becomes restricted by this articulation, then the enemy-other will remain an enemy-other, firmly positioned as the constitutive outside of the chain of equivalence of the self. This exclusionary process can, in some cases, be enforced by the contexts in which community media assemblages are functioning. For instance, when interaction with the enemy-other is defined as treason by the legal assemblage of the nation-state in which the community media organization is located, this will strongly impact on this community media organization's agonistic capacity. Relatedly, the interpellatory lure of hegemonic antagonism is strong, especially when all state apparatuses, other institutions, and large parts of the population are aligned with this hegemonic project. Community media organizations are not always able (or willing) to escape from this lure. Moreover, there are also material processes that can dislocate the articulation of participation and agonism (and the discourses of participation and agonism themselves). In some cases, as already hinted at in this paragraph, the other-enemy simply might not have access to the community media organizational machine, because of closed frontiers or front lines. Also, the practices of community members can be dislocatory, as they might not be willing or able to participate in (and through) the community media organization, or to become its audience. Community members can also reject the representative link between the community media organization and 'their' community. These material practices can then be discursified, de-legitimating the community media organization, questioning its social relevance (e.g., by reverting to a mass communication model to critique small audience numbers) or undermining the agonistic discourse itself.

The second nodal point, alternativity, also produces opportunities for the articulation of participation and agonism. Firstly, the alternative articulations of a series of subject positions and identities play a role in the strengthening of agonism through community media's participatory practices. The focus on the diverse community, especially when it is articulated with localism, offers a potential counter-weight (and alternative) for the more traditional units of antagonism, such as the nation, as materialized in nation-states (with its armies). Community media's focus on the participation of ordinary people and its more critical position toward societal elites, as part of its self-definition as alternative, also opens up spaces for agonism, in a number of ways. Ordinary voices are often articulated with authenticity (see Carpentier & Resmann, 2011; Scannell, 2001; Thornborrow, 2001), which renders them powerful vehicles of agonism when they become aligned with an agonistic community media assemblage. The signifying practices of ordinary people also tend to include a more affectious dimension, which opens up spaces for the expression of empathy and care for the other, and for the expression of the pain, suffering, and trauma of both self and other. While the former counters the articulation of the other as a radically different, distant, and inferior other, often seen as perpetrators, the latter shows the human and material cost of antagonism. The validation of ordinary people also produces, and is strengthened by, the alternative articulations that the subject positions of the leader, expert, and owner gain in participatory assemblages. Community media's focus on democratic leadership, collective and/or community ownership, and community-situated knowledge not only serves a participatory agenda, but also supports the pluralization and de-hierarchization of society, which again has the capacity to support agonism. Finally, the identity of being a media organization plays a role here, as community media's shift away from a large-scale mass communicational model to a more small-scale media conversational model provides space for more extended agonistic dialogues within diverse communities.

The nodal point of alternativity also impacts on the community media organization's signifying practices, as these assemblages lean more toward the production and distribution of counter-hegemonic signifying practices, which—in situations of hegemonic antagonism, or in cases of elite-driven post-antagonism—almost automatically implies a preference for agonistic signifying practices. Community media provide spaces for internal diversity, critique, and deconstruction, in combination with the deployment of humor as an agonistic strategy, which is facilitated by the self-relativizing articulation of the community media producer subject position. The counter-hegemonic alternativity of community media also implies that these critiques are aimed at the self, which counters the glorification and homogenization of the self, and serves its pluralization. The use of alternative media formats, shifting away from dominant media formats characterized by brevity and speed, and giving community media producers and their guests time to express themselves, to pay attention to nuance and complexity, is yet another way that diversity and plurality is supported.

The strengthening of the articulation between participation and agonism through alternativity has also a material component. As participatory alternative assemblages, community media rely on alternative ways of funding their activities, which increases their autonomy in relation to market and state. This often coincides with the independence from elites that are entrenched in antagonistic positions. Internally, community media's reliance on volunteers also avoids remunerations (or the threat of its withdrawal) being used to enforce compliance within internal policies that are not accepted by these volunteers. Their participation on a voluntary basis, and the difficulties related to attuning them to imposed streamlining guidelines, enhances diversity, again contributing to the pluralization of society. The internal participatory-democratic, horizontally organized decision-making practices, as alternative toward mainstream verticality, facilitates inclusivity and equality, which, in turn strengthens conflicteous togetherness. When it comes to community media's distributional capacities, agonistic dialogues, in particular within a (post-)antagonistic hegemonic context, might be better served by limited visibility produced by the small-scale media conversational model. Finally, even though this is fairly specific for CCMC, this community media organization's preference to include alternative spaces into their assemblage opens up the use of space and place for agonistic purposes. More specifically, the CCMC building, located in the Buffer Zone, enables the re-signification of this space, tilting it away from its meaning as material reminder of the destructivity of the other-enemy.

Yet again, alternativity can also work against the articulation of participation and agonism. We should shy away from a celebration of ordinary people as a necessarily privileged site of agonism, as ordinary people can just as well identify with an antagonistic discourse, and become enthusiastically engaged in war. Ordinary people can also identify with new chains of equivalence that overcome old divides between self and other-enemies, but simultaneously create new and evenly solidified chains of equivalence that construct new constitutive outsides and new other-enemies. Even if, in a scenario where they support an antagonistic discourse, these people might not exactly queue to enter an agonistic community media assemblage, in some cases they do enter, as the analysis of the MYCYradio broadcasts also shows. This then raises poignant questions about how to deal with these antagonistic incursions, as this puts community media's affinity with inclusivity, quasi-universality, and diversity to the test, even if the hegemony of democracy does provide a litmus test to allow or disallow these signifying practices. This problem does not only relate to ordinary people as community media producers, but also to ordinary people as audience members. Community media organizational machines are obviously no hypodermic needles, and a multitude of identifications and dis-identifications with their signifying and material practices remain possible, which, in turn, can strengthen or weaken their agonistic capacities. This problem is (again potentially) increased by community media's frequent use of alternative formats, the instances where technical problems arise (e.g., the required access to internet, or problems with technical quality) and the cases where the audience's preferences for mainstream media's quality definitions (see Carpentier, 2011: 324ff, for an example) still dominate the reception. Multiplications of alternativities can render community media signifying practices a bit difficult to receive, to process, and to comprehend, even for audience members that share the community media's agonistic discursive positions.

Thirdly, the nodal points of civil society and rhizome (which will be discussed together) enable us to consider the relationship between participation and agonism. When it comes to the subject positions and identities that are part of the community media assemblage, in particular the articulation of the citizen subject position plays an important role. Community media enable ordinary people to enact their citizenship in particular ways, privileging multi-layered forms of citizenship, where localist, civic, ethnic, national(ist), international class, gender, and many other identifications and affiliations are combined at the individual and the organizational levels, also translating them into material practices. This pluralism-enhancing set of identifications counters and disrupts the solidified chain of equivalence that feeds an antagonistic discourse. In other words, the shift away from essentialism and from the arbolic structures (of the state), and the contingency and fluidity that this generates, together with the promise of the deterritorialization of state (and market) assemblages, works against the construction of enemies, with its dichotomizations, homogenizations, and solidifications.

Also, the civil society and rhizome nodal points have material components. Community media assemblages are civil society organizations, which gain stability and autonomy through their material organizational structure, place-based operations, and earmarked capitals (which are under its own control). This investment in an agonistic production center also has a protective dimension, toward an outside world which might not support its existence, and internally, within the walls of its premises, facilitating the agonistic practices of the community media members. As a fairly stable discursive and material place of peace (in the case of CCMC, even protected by the UN peace keepers next-door), it can continue to perform and communicate peace-related signifying practices to the outside world, but also practice peaceful and non-violent interaction through its internal agonistic conflict resolution procedures. This performance of peaceful and non-violent interaction is embedded in a rhizomatic civil society network, and not restricted to the community media organizational machine itself. Other different-but-like-minded civil society organizations (and sometimes elements of the state and market assemblages) turn community media into crossroads of agonistic activism, simultaneously protected by the always-present levels of elusiveness and fluidity.

Finally, it is important to stress here again that the articulation of participation and agonism is not to be taken for granted. The logic of deterritorialization is one of the most difficult to translate into social practice, and when community media organizations move too close to the arbolic assemblages there is a risk of community media being harmed or incorporated (or both). Also, conflicts within civil society are not necessarily resolved in agonistic ways; examples of conflicts escalating into antagonistic practices have indeed been documented in the world of community media (see, e.g., Dunaway, 2005). This means that participatory rhizomes remain vulnerable, and the incorporation of community media assemblages into the state apparatuses or market assemblages (sometimes closely connected to these state apparatuses) might neutralize their agonistic capacity, or even transform them into communication channels of antagonism. These slippages are not always part of a master plan, but can occur, for instance, simply because of contractual obligations resulting from national subsidies or international donorships. Finally, the material sedimentation of community media organizations in particular locations, with organizational structures that still need to be recognized by states, remain highly vulnerable to war machines that can very easily destroy what is deemed to be part of the enemy-within.

In 2003, when an earlier version of the analysis of the community media discourse, with its four nodal points, was published, there was already a strong plea to combine what was then labeled as the "[…] four theoretical approaches […]," in order "[…] to capture both the diversity and specificity of these community media and to show their importance" (Carpentier, Lie, & Servaes, 2003: 51). The analysis of the participatory-agonistic role of community media assemblages in this book confirms and strengthens this need, because it allows "[…] for a complementary emphasis on different aspects of the identity of community media […]" (Carpentier, Lie, & Servaes, 2003: 51). Without integrating the perspectives offered by the nodal points of community service, alternativity, civil society, and rhizome of the community media discourse, it is impossible to analyze the role community media assemblages play in the articulation of participation and agonism. Even more so, in order for participatory community media assemblages to play an agonistic role, the agonistic elements linked to each of the four nodal points need to be co-present. For instance, without a participatory-democratic discourse that brings inclusivity, equality, and diversity into the community media assemblage, media organizations established and run by ordinary people can very rapidly develop into another *Radio Télévision Libre des Milles Collines*, with its terrifying role in the Rwandan genocide (see, e.g., Chrétien, 1995).

Moreover, the discursive-material knot has proven to be a vital theoretical-ontological instrument for analyzing the role of the community media assemblage, in particular in the case of CCMC/MYCYradio. The importance of this community media organization, in relation to participation and agonism, is related to much more than what can be found in its broadcasts. Arguably, its material existence, as a container building in the Cypriot Buffer Zone, where peaceful and non-violent interactions are performed as sets of embodied practices, where the other-enemy becomes a human being to work with, in an atmosphere of conflicteous togetherness, and where the self becomes pluralized, is just as important, even if we should not remain blind to the many problems that haunt community media assemblages such as CCMC/MYCYradio, and will continue to do so. Speaking more generally, understanding social reality by studying the discursive *and* the material, *and* their knotted interaction, without privileging one component over the other, seems to offer a good route to do justice to the social's complexity, even though, of course, more focused approaches (focusing on the discursive, or the material) still remain valid and relevant. Still, theoretically developing and analytically deploying the discursive-material knot has proven to be—at least for me—a most enriching research experience.

Notes

1. Neither the internationally recognized Cyprus Radio and Television Authority (CyRTA), nor the Higher Broadcasting Authority in north Cyprus, have made legislative provisions for analog or digital frequencies to be made available to community media organizations.
2. http://www.cy.undp.org/content/cyprus/en/home/ourwork/actionforcooperationandtrust/successstories/a-buzz-in-the-buffer-zone.html
3. http://www.cy.undp.org/content/dam/cyprus/docs/ACT%20Publications/factsheet_ccmc_2013_Final.pdf
4. http://ec.europa.eu/cyprus/news/speeches/archives/20130424_en.htm
5. These are the labels that are used for these languages on the MYCYradio website. In some cases (e.g., Cameroonian), the label is not entirely clear, but it is rendered here as it is used on the website.
6. Twelve programs use Greek, half of them in combination with English. Eleven other programs also use English as exclusive language, or in combination with other languages (two programs use Spanish, French, and Cameroonian in combination with English). Three programs use Turkish, five programs another language, and one program plays non-stop music.
7. CCMC's involvement in Lesbian, Gay, Bisexual, Transgender, Queer/Questioning, and Asexual/Ally (LGBTQA) issues is also exemplified by its video series on the occasion of the 2012 International Day Against Homophobia, Biphobia and Transphobia (IDAHOBIT). See https://cypruscommunitymediacentre.wordpress.com/2012/05/10/video-countdown-to-idahobit-begins/
8. Phillips and Jørgensen (2002: 8) wrote that Laclau and Mouffe are "[…] short on specific methodical guidelines and illustrative examples."
9. Technically, one could create a fourth level, to distinguish between the external sensitizing concepts, as nodal points and as elements, but this would take us too far. Methodologically, it is mainly important to distinguish between primary/secondary and tertiary sensitizing concepts, as this drives the analysis.

10. This also implies that other MYCYradio shows, and the material produced by CCMC outside MYCYradio, were not analyzed.
11. Also in relation to this photographic project, CCMC was paid to cover for its work.
12. The '*Iconoclastic Controversies*' project website, reporting on this subproject, can be found here: http://nicocarpentier.net/icontroversies/
13. Two out of 10 focus groups were organized in another place, to reduce the ideological bias that the CCMC as a location might generate for the focus group discussions.
14. Even if this was not a comparative research project, I remained attentive for the possibility of structural differences between the Cypriot communities—these did not occur.
15. As the producers explained, the name combines three languages: "MYCYradio producer 5: The name [...] is, like triple: Downtown in English, χωρίς in Greek, Bakira is a Turkish word. [...] MYCYradio producer 4: Which means being broke downtown" (Interview two *Downtown Choris Bakira* MYCYradio producers, February 2014).
16. A few of the last episodes had Nikos Malekos as a co-host.
17. Most of the *Cyprus Oral History Project* broadcasts were in English (although there were three Greek broadcasts), all *One Percent* broadcasts were in Turkish, and most *Downtown Choris Bakira* broadcasts were in Greek (one was in English, and two combined Greek and English). Greek and Turkish broadcasts were translated into English. All quotations in this article are reproduced in English, and only special cases of (multi-)language use are indicated.
18. During these interviews, I provided a summary of the findings of the content and production analysis. All five producers expressed their agreement with the analysis.
19. This version was later published as a journal article (Carpentier, 2014a).
20. See Staiger (2005) for a methodological discussion.
21. Some guests could not be interviewed for the research project—this applies to Guest 18 and Guest 19.
22. In the meanwhile, several of these parties have changed their names, or have merged with other parties.
23. An important component of the peer-debriefings were a series of conference presentations and publications. Of particular importance were the two publications that were directly related to this project (Carpentier, 2014a; 2015a), one of which was published in a Cypriot academic journal (the *Cyprus Review*).
24. Apart from the feedback mentioned earlier on particular parts of the analysis, Hazal Yolga and Orestis Tringides provided feedback on a draft version of Chapter 4 in July 2016.
25. A shorter version of the analysis of the producers' signifying practices, of their social media use, and a very brief analysis of the reception, has been published before, as part of a peer debriefing strategy (Carpentier, 2014a; 2015a).
26. Nevertheless, the first interviews with the CCMC staff members, before MYCYradio was established, produced an important nuance, as CCMC then also regularly worked with mainstream media. Later, this decreased (Interview MYCYradio producer 2, June 2016).
27. This is very much in contrast with how the guests of the three MYCYradio programs talked about their experiences. For instance, Guest 5 talked about her interviewer in the following terms: "[...] she was patient. She was listening carefully the things that I was narrating. It was as if she was living it" (Interview guest 5—*Cyprus Oral History Project*, Spring, 2014).

28. When there are several hosts in one radio show, 'host' is combined with a number to refer to a particular host.
29. In one interview with a MYCYradio producer, talking about the guests, we find a trace of the identity of ordinary people, through the emphasis on the guests being unknown (in contrast to the guests that commercial media tend to invite): "[…] usually the commercial radio stations, they rely on people that are doing something that is already known and they are already known people so it attracts listeners. For me, it could be someone that did something interesting but no people know about it" (Interview MYCYradio producer 2, February 2014).
30. The small number of listeners also shows on the related Facebook pages. Postings rarely received more than 10 likes, and only very few comments. On 15 February 2014, the total number of likes of the *Downtown Choris Bakira* Facebook page was 347. On 22 May 2014, it had increased to 435. *One Percent*, on the same day, had 33 likes.
31. This Famagusta Good Friday service was held on 18 April 2014, in the presence of both Greek Orthodox and Islamic clerics. It was the first Good Friday service in that church since 1957. See http://cyprus-mail.com/2014/04/17/famagusta-good-friday-service-a-grand-event-despite-changes-to-route/

    On 28 July 2014, 1,000 pilgrims from the north could visit, for the first time in many years, the Hala Sultan Tekke, a Muslim shrine on the west bank of the Larnaca Salt Lake (Dayıoğlu & Hatay, 2015: 158).
32. MYCYradio's access to the airwaves is not open, as there is no legal framework specifically allowing for community media.
33. http://mycyradio.eu/get-involved/apply-for-a-show/
34. Some producers also pre-record their programs.
35. This producer has not been interviewed—but also here, a code is used.
36. This meeting took place from 17 to 19 November 2011.
37. See: http://www.cypruscommunitymedia.org/index.php?option=com_content&view=article&id=610 &Itemid=144&lang=tr
38. In our own interview with this guest, he said that it was "[…] not a fanatic interview […]" but only addressed questions such as "[…] 'why?' and 'what they did to us?'" (Interview guest 5—*Cyprus Oral History Project*, Spring, 2014)
39. In one case, one of the respondents defined the Maronite guest as a potential enemy-within. Even if this positioning still shows internal heterogeneity, this statement is very much aligned with the antagonistic discourse: "That girl is Maronite, for starters. And there is a percentage of Maronites, I'm not referring to this particular girl of course—who sympathize with Turkey and would rather live among the Turks. And if that girl theoretically belongs to that category of Maronites, then what she is saying is a lie and [an example of] populism. That is, 'I am saying all this to convince you that Greek Cypriots harassed the Turkish Cypriots.' And vice versa!" (FG8D_GNL)
40. Also, another fragment, where a Turkish Cypriot talked about the 'own' suffering, provoked negative reactions, with one Turkish Cypriot respondent saying that the fragment was "one-sided" (FG9C_TNL).
41. This was confirmed in the interview with Guest 1—*Cyprus Oral History Project*, Spring, 2014.

REFERENCES

Abu-Nimer, Mohammed (2012). *Dialogue, Conflict Resolution, and Change: Arab-Jewish Encounters in Israel.* New York: SUNY Press.

Adams, Thomas W. (1971). *AKEL. The Communist Party of Cyprus*. Stanford: Hoover Institution Press.

Airaghi, Giulia Federica (2014). *The Political Dimension of Consumption: The Case of Online Barter*. PhD thesis. Milan: Università Cattolica del Sacro Cuore, http://tesionline.unicatt.it/handle/10280/2480, accessed 7 June 2016.

Akgün, Mensur, Gürel, Ayla, Hatay, Mete, Tiryaki, Sylvia (2005). *Quo Vadis Cyprus?* Istanbul: Tesev.

Akgün, Sibel (2012). "The Manner of Implementation of Britain's Colonial Administration Policy in Cyprus: The Legislative Council," *TODAIE's Review of Public Administration*, 6(4): 99–128.

Albert, Michael (1997). "What Makes Alternative Media Alternative?" *Z Magazine*, October, http://subsol.c3.hu/subsol_2/contributors3/alberttext.html, accessed 7 June 2016.

Albert, Stuart, Whetten, David A. (1985). "Organizational Identity," *Research in Organizational Behavior*, 7: 263–295.

Allan, Stuart, Zelizer, Barbie (eds.) (2004). *Reporting War. Journalism in Wartime*. London: Routledge.

Allen, Danielle, Bailey, Moya, Carpentier, Nico, Fenton, Natalie, Jenkins, Henry, Lothian, Alexis, Qui, Jack, Schaefer, Mirko Tobias, Srinivasan, Ramesh (2014). "Participations: Dialogues on the Participatory Promise of Contemporary Culture and Politics. Part 3:

Politics," *International Journal of Communication*, 8 (Forum): 1129–1151, http://ijoc.org/index.php/ijoc/article/view/2787/1124, accessed 7 June 2016.

Althusser, Louis (1982). "Contradiction and Overdetermination," *For Marx*. London: Verso, pp. 87–128.

AMARC-Europe (1994). *One Europe—Many Voices. Democracy and Access to Communication.* Conference report AMARC-Europe Pan-European conference of community radio broadcasters, Ljubljana, Slovenia, 15–18 September 1994. Sheffield: AMARC.

Amnesty International (1997). *Amnesty International Report 1997*. London: Amnesty International Publications.

Anagnostopoulou, Sia (2013). "Makarios III, 1950–77: Creating the Ethnarchic State," Andrekos Varnava and Michalis N. Michael (eds.) *The Archbishops of Cyprus in the Modern Age: The Changing Role of the Archbishop-Ethnarch, Their Identities and Politics*. Newcastle upon Tyne: Cambridge Scholars Publishing, pp. 240–292.

Anastasiou, Harry (2002). "Communication Across Conflict Lines: The Case of Ethnically Divided Cyprus," *Journal of Peace Research*, 39(5): 581–596.

Anastasiou, Harry (2008a). *The Broken Olive Branch. Nationalism, Ethnic Conflict, and the Quest for Peace in Cyprus. Volume 1: The Impasse of Ethnonationalism*. Syracuse: Syracuse University Press.

Anastasiou, Harry (2008b). *The Broken Olive Branch. Nationalism, Ethnic Conflict, and the Quest for Peace in Cyprus. Volume 2: Nationalism Versus Europeanization*. Syracuse: Syracuse University Press.

Anastasiou, Maria (2007). *The Institutionalization of Protracted Ethnic Conflicts. A Discourse Analysis of "the Cyprus Problem."* Unpublished PhD thesis. Columbia: University of South Carolina.

Anderson, Benedict (2006). *Imagined Communities: Reflections on the Origin and Spread of Nationalism*. London: Verso.

Anderson, Heather (2015). "Prisoners' Radio. Connecting Communities Through Alternative Discourses," Chris Atton (ed.) *The Routledge Companion to Alternative and Community Media*. London and New York: Routledge, pp. 426–436.

Angermuller, Johannes (2014). *Poststructuralist Discourse Analysis. Subjectivity in Enunciative Pragmatics*. Houndmills: Palgrave Macmillan.

Anheier, Helmut, Raj Isar, Yudhishthir (eds.) (2007). *Conflicts and Tensions*. London: Sage.

Anthias, Floya, Ayres, Ron (1983). "Ethnicity and Class in Cyprus," *Race & Class*, XXV(1): 59–76.

Archer, Margaret S. (1988). *Culture and Agency. The Place of Culture in Social Theory*. Cambridge: Cambridge University Press.

Arendt, Hannah (1998). *The Human Condition*, second edition. Chicago and London: University of Chicago Press.

Arnstein, Sherry R. (1969). "A Ladder of Citizen Participation." *Journal of the American Institute of Planners*, 35(4): 216–224.

Ashcraft, Karen Lee, Kuhn, Timothy R., Cooren, François (2009). "Constitutional amendments: 'Materializing' Organizational Communication," *Academy of Management Annals*, 3: 1–64.

Ashcroft, Bill, Griffiths, Gareth, Tiffin, Helen (2000). *Post-Colonial Studies: The Key Concepts*. Oxford: Psychology Press.

Askins, Kye, Pain, Rachel (2011). "Contact Zones: Participation, Materiality, and the Messiness of Interaction," *Environment and Planning D: Society and Space*, 29: 803–821.

Asmussen, Jan (2006). "'Dark-Skinned Cypriots Will Not Be Accepted! Cypriots in the British Army (1939–1945)," Hubert Faustman and Nicos Peristianis (eds.) *Britain in Cyprus. Colonialism and Post-Colonialism 1878–2006*. Mannheim and Möhnsee: Bibliopolis, pp. 167–185.

Asmussen, Jan (2011). "Conspiracy Theory and Cypriot History: The Comfort of Commonly Perceived Enemies," *The Cyprus Review*, 23(2): 127–145.

Association of Cyprus Banks (2013). *Annual Report 2012–2013*. Nicosia: Association of Cyprus Banks.

Attfield, Judith (2000). *Wild Things: The Material Cultures of Everyday Life*. Oxford: Berg.

Atton, Chris (2002). *Alternative Media*. London: Sage.

Atton, Chris (2015). "Introduction. Problems and Positions in Alternative and Community Media," Chris Atton (ed.) *The Routledge Companion to Alternative and Community Media*. London and New York: Routledge, pp. 1–18.

Atton, Chris (ed.) (2015). *The Routledge Companion to Alternative and Community Media*. London and New York: Routledge.

Atton, Chris, Hamilton, James F. (2008). *Alternative Journalism*. London: Sage.

Aulich, James (1992). *Framing the Falklands War: Nationhood, Culture and Identity*. Milton Keynes: Open University Press.

Avruch, Kevin (1998). *Culture and Conflict Resolution*. Washington: United States Institute of Peace Press.

Babe, Robert E. (2010). *Cultural Studies and Political Economy: Toward a New Integration*. Lanham: Lexington.

Bacharach, Walter Zwi (2002). "Antisemitism and Racism in Nazi Ideology," Michael Berenbaum (ed.) *The Holocaust and History: The Known, the Unknown, the Disputed, and the Reexamined*. Bloomington: Indiana University Press, pp. 64–74.

Bachrach, Peter, Baratz, Morton S. (1970). *Power and Poverty. Theory and Practice*. New York: Oxford University Press.

Bağcı, Hüseyin (1997). "Cyprus: Ascension to the European Union—A Turkish View," Hans-Jürgen Axt and Hansjörg Brey (eds.) *Cyprus and the European Union: New Chances for Solving an Old Conflict?* München: Südosteuropa Gesellschaft, pp. 159–169.

Bahcheli, Tozun, Bartmann, Barry, Srebrnik, Henry (2004). *De Facto States: The Quest for Sovereignty*. London: Routledge.

Bailey, Olga, Cammaerts, Bart, Carpentier, Nico (2007). *Understanding Alternative Media*. Maidenhead: Open University Press/McGraw Hill.

Bailie, Mashoed, Azgin, Bekir (2008). "A Barricade, a Bridge and a Wall: Cypriot Journalism and the Mediation of Conflict in Cyprus," *Cyprus Review*, 20(1): 57–92.

Bain, Read (1937). "Technology and State Government," *American Sociological Review*, 2(6): 860–874.

Baker, Mona, Blaagaard, Bolette B. (2016). "Receptualizing Citizen Media. A Preliminary Charting of a Complex Domain," Mona Baker and Bolette B. Blaagaard (eds.) *Citizen Media and Public Spaces*. London: Routledge, pp. 1–22.

Barad, Karen (2007). *Meeting the Universe Halfway: Quantum Physics and the Entanglement of Matter and Meaning*. Durham and London: Duke University Press.

Barad, Karen, (with Dolphijn, Rick, van der Tuin, Iris) (2012). "An Interview With Karen Barad," *New Materialism: Interviews and Cartographies*. Ann Arbor: Open Humanities Press, pp. 48–70.

Barker, Chris (2004). *The Sage Dictionary of Cultural Studies*. London: Sage.

Barker, Chris (2011). *Cultural Studies: Theory and Practice*. London: Sage.

Barker, Colin, Johnson, Alan, Lavalette, Michael (2001). "Leadership Matters: An Introduction," Colin Barker, Alan Johnson, and Michael Lavalette (eds.) *Leadership and Social Movements*. Manchester: Manchester University Press, pp. 1–23.

Barker, John, Tucker, Richard N. (1990). *The Interactive Learning Revolution: Multimedia in Education and Training*. London: Kogan Page.

Barlow, William (1988). "Community Radio in the US: The Struggle for a Democratic Medium," *Media, Culture and Society*, 10(1): 81–105.

Barnard-Wills, David (2013). *Surveillance and Identity: Discourse, Subjectivity and the State*. Farnham: Ashgate.

Barrett, Gene (2015). "Deconstructing Community," *Sociologia Ruralis*, 55(2): 182–204.

Barry, Andrew (1998). "On Interactivity: Consumers, Citizens and Culture," Sharon Macdonald (ed.) *The Politics of Display. Museums, Science, Culture*. London and New York: Routledge, pp. 85–102.

Barry, Andrew (2001). *Political Machines: Governing a Technological Society*. New York: Athlone.

Barthes, Roland (1973). *Mythologies*. London: Granada.

Barthes, Roland (1975). *The Pleasure of the Text*. New York: Farrar, Straus & Giroux.

Baruh, Lemi, Popescu, Mihaela (2008). "Guiding Metaphors of Nationalism: The Cyprus Issue and the Construction of Turkish National Identity in Online Discussions," *Discourse & Communication*, 2(1): 79–96.

Basar, Shumon (2006). "The Professional Amateur," Markus Miessen and Shumon Basar (eds.) *Did Someone Say Participate? An Atlas of Spatial Practice*. Cambridge: MIT Press, pp. 30–34.

Bass, Bernard M., Bass, Ruth (2008). *The Bass Handbook of Leadership: Theory, Research, and Managerial Applications*. New York: Simon & Schuster.

Battersby, Christine (2013). *The Phenomenal Woman: Feminist Metaphysics and the Patterns of Identity*. London: Routledge.

Baú, Valentina (2014a). "Communities and Media in the Aftermath of Conflict: Participatory Productions for Reconciliation and Peace," Helen Ware, Bert Jenkins, Marty Branagan, and D. B. Subedi (eds.) *Cultivating Peace: Contexts, Practices and Multidimensional Models*. Newcastle upon Tyne: Cambridge Scholars Publishing, pp. 266–282.

Baú, Valentina (2014b). "Telling Stories of War Through the Screen. Participatory Video Approaches and Practice for Peace in Conflict-Affected Contexts," *Conflict & Communication Online*, 13(1), http://www.cco.regener-online.de/2014_1/pdf/baú.pdf, accessed 6 June 2016.

Baú, Valentina (2015). "Building Peace Through Social Change Communication: Participatory Video in Conflict-Affected Communities," *Community Development Journal*, 50(1): 121–137.

Bauman, Richard, Briggs, Charles L. (1990). "Poetics and Performance as Critical Perspectives on Language and Social Life," *Annual Review of Anthropology*, 19: 59–88.

Beck, Ulrich (1996). "Risk Society and the Provident State," Scott Lash, Bronislaw Szerszynski, and Brian Wynne (eds.) *Risk, Environment and Modernity: Towards a New Ecology*. London: Sage, pp. 27–43.

Benasayag, Miguel, Sztulwark, Diego (2002). *Du Contre-Pouvoir/On Counter-Power*. Paris: La Découverte & Syros.

Benkler, Yochai (2006). *The Wealth of Networks: How Social Production Transforms Markets and Freedom*. New Haven: Yale University Press.

Bennett, Jane (2010). *Vibrant Matter. A Political Ecology of Things*. Durham and London: Duke University Press.

Bennett, Tony (2002). "Home and Everyday Life," Tony Bennett and Diane Watson (eds.) *Understanding Everyday Life*. Oxford: Blackwell, pp. 1–50.

Bennett, Tony, Watson, Diane (2002). "Introduction," Tony Bennett and Diane Watson (eds.) *Understanding Everyday Life*. Oxford: Blackwell, pp. i–xxiv.

Ben-Shaul, Nitzan S. (2008). *Hyper-Narrative Interactive Cinema: Problems and Solutions*. Amsterdam: Rodopi.

Berger, Peter L., Luckmann, Thomas (1966). *The Social Construction of Reality: A Treatise in the Sociology of Knowledge*. Harmondsworth: Penguin Books.

Bergold, Jarg, Thomas, Stefan (2012). "Participatory Research Methods: A Methodological Approach in Motion," *Forum: Qualitative Social Research*, 13(1), http://www.qualitative-research.net/index.php/fqs/article/view/1801/3334, accessed 11 June 2016.

Bergson, Henri (2004). *Matter and Memory*, fifth edition. Mineola: Dover.

Berrigan, Frances J. (1979). *Community Communications. The Role of Community Media in Development*. Paris: United Nations Educational, Scientific and Cultural Organization.

Besim, Mustafa, Mullen, Fiona (2014). "Cyprus in the Global Financial Crisis. How Lack of Banking Sophistication Proved an Advantage," Susannah Verney, Anna Bosco, and Marina Costa Lobo (eds.) *Southern Europe and the Financial Earthquake: Coping With the First Phase of the International Crisis*. London: Routledge, pp. 87–101.

Beurier, Joëlle (2004). "Death and Material Culture: The Case of Pictures During the First World War," Nicholas J. Saunders (ed.) *Matters of Conflict. Material Culture, Memory and the First World War*. London and New York: Routledge, pp. 109–122.

Bey, Hakim (1985). *T.A.Z.: The Temporary Autonomous Zone, Ontological Anarchy, Poetic Terrorism*. Brooklyn: Autonomedia.

Biglieri, Paula, Perelló, Gloria (2011). "The Names of the Real in Laclau's Theory: Antagonism, Dislocation, and Heterogeneity," *Filozofski vestnik*, XXXII (2): 47–64.

Billig, Michael (1995). *Banal Nationalism*. London: Sage.

Black, Jonathan (2004). "Thanks for the Memory: War Memorials, Spectatorship and the Trajectories of Commemoration 1919–2001," Nicholas J. Saunders (ed.) *Matters of Conflict*.

Material Culture, Memory and the First World War. London and New York: Routledge, pp. 134–148.

Blackman, Lisa (2008). *The Body: The Key Concepts*. Oxford and New York: Berg.

Blackman, Lisa (2012). *Immaterial Bodies: Affect, Embodiment, Mediation*. London: Sage.

Bloomfield, David (2003). "Reconciliation: An Introduction," David Bloomfield, Teresa Barnes, and Luc Huyse (eds.) *Reconciliation After Violent Conflict. A Handbook*. Stockholm: International Institute for Democracy and Electoral Assistance, pp. 10–18.

Blumer, Herbert (1969). *Symbolic Interactionism: Perspective and Method*. Englewood Cliffs: Prentice Hall.

Bogaerts, Jo, Carpentier, Nico (2012). "The Postmodern Challenge to Journalism: Strategies for Constructing a Trustworthy Identity," Chris Peters and Marcel Broersma (eds.) *Rethinking Journalism. Trust and Participation in a Transformed News Landscape*. London: Routledge, pp. 60–71.

Bogue, Ronald (2013). *Deleuze on Literature*. London: Routledge.

Borowiec, Andrew (2000). *Cyprus: A Troubled Island*. Westport: Praeger/Greenwood.

Boulding, Elsie (1990). *Building a Global Civic Culture: Education for an Interdependent World*. Syracuse: Syracuse University Press.

Bourdieu, Pierre (1998). *Masculine Domination*. Trans. Richard Nice. Stanford: Stanford University Press.

Bourdieu, Pierre (2000). *Pascalian Meditations*. Stanford: Stanford University Press.

Bourdieu, Pierre, Wacquant, Loïc J. D. (1992). *An Invitation to Reflexive Sociology*. Chicago: University of Chicago Press.

Bourke, Joanna (1999). *An Intimate History of Killing. Face-to-Face Killing in Twentieth-Century Warfare*. London: Granta Books.

Bozkurt, Umut (2013). "Cyprus: Divided by History, United by Austerity," *openDemocracy*, http://www.opendemocracy.net/umut-bozkurt/cyprus-divided-by-history-united-by-austerity, accessed 27 June 2016.

Braddock, Chris (2009). *Performing Contagious Bodies: Ritual Participation in Contemporary Art*. Basingstoke: Palgrave Macmillan.

Breen, Keith (2009). "Agonism, Antagonism and the Necessity of Care," Andrew Schaap (ed.) *Law and Agonistic Politics*. Farnham: Ashgate, pp. 133–146.

Brett, Judith (2006). "The Contours of the Everyday: Writing 'Ordinary People's Politics,'" *The Monthly* (September), http://www.themonthly.com.au/issue/2006/september/1193117308/judith-brett/contours-everyday, accessed 18 June 2013.

Brewer, David (2010). *Greece. The Hidden Centuries. Turkish Rule From the Fall of Constantinople to Greek Independence*. London: I. B. Tauris.

Briel, Holger (2013). "The Uses of Oral History in Cyprus: Ethics, Memory and Identity," *Language and Intercultural Communication*, 13(1): 27–43.

Brock, Peter (1972). *Pacifism in Europe to 1914*. Princeton: Princeton University Press.

Broome, Benjamin J. (2005). *Building Bridges Across the Green Line. A Guide to Intercultural Communication in Cyprus*. Nicosia: United Nations Development Programme.

Broome, Benjamin, Anastasiou, Harry (2012). "Communication Across the Divide in the Cyprus Conflict," Dan Landis and Rosita D. Albert (eds.) *Handbook of Ethnic Conflict: International Perspectives*. New York: Springer, pp. 293–326.

Brown, Rosamond, Buckley, Steve (2011a). "Colombia: AREDMAG—Defending Media in the Face of Conflict," Steve Buckley (ed.) *Community Media: A Good Practice Handbook*. Paris: United Nations Educational, Scientific and Cultural Organization, pp. 43–44.

Brown, Rosamond, Buckley, Steve (2011b). "El Salvador: ARPAS—A Frequency That Enabled a Network," Steve Buckley (ed.) *Community Media: A Good Practice Handbook*. Paris: United Nations Educational, Scientific and Cultural Organization, pp. 19–20.

Browne, Donald R. (2012). "What Is 'Community' in Community Radio? A Consideration of the Meaning, Nature and Importance of a Concept," Janey Gordon (ed.) *Community Radio in the Twenty-First Century*. Oxford: Peter Lang, pp. 153–173.

Bruns, Axel (2008). *Blogs, Wikipedia, Second Life, and Beyond—From Production to Produsage*. New York: Peter Lang.

Bryant, Rebecca (2004). *Imagining the Modern. The Cultures of Nationalism in Cyprus*. London and New York: I. B. Tauris.

Bryant, Rebecca (2007). "Disciplining Ethnicity and Citizenship in Colonial Cyprus," Veronique Benei (ed.) *Manufacturing Citizenship: Education and Nationalism in Europe, South Asia and China*. London: Routledge, pp. 104–125.

Bryant, Rebecca (2008). "Writing the Catastrophe: Nostalgia and its Histories in Cyprus," *Journal of Modern Greek Studies*, 26(2): 399–422.

Bryant, Rebecca (2012). "The Fractures of a Struggle? Remembering and Forgetting Erenköy," Rebecca Bryant and Yiannis Papadakis (eds.) *Cyprus and the Politics of Memory. History, Community and Conflict*. London: I. B. Tauris, pp. 168–194.

Buckingham, David (1987). *Public Secrets: EastEnders and its Audience*. London: British Film Institute.

Bunge, Mario A. (1977). *Treatise on Basic Philosophy: Volume 3: Ontology I: The Furniture of the World*. Berlin: Springer.

Burckhardt, Jacob (1964). *Force and Freedom: Reflections on History*. New York: Pantheon.

Burr, Vivien (2003). *Social Constructionism*. London: Routledge.

Butler, Judith (1988). "Performative Acts and Gender Constitution: An Essay in Phenomenology and Feminist Theory," *Theatre Journal*, 40(4): 519–531.

Butler, Judith (1990). *Gender Trouble. Feminism and the Subversion of Identity*. London: Routledge.

Butler, Judith (1993). *Bodies That Matter. On the Discursive Limits of "Sex."* New York, London: Routledge.

Butler, Judith (1997). *Excitable Speech. A Politics of the Performative*. New York: Routledge.

Byford-Jones, Wilfred (1959). *Grivas and the Story of EOKA*. London: Robert Hale.

Byrne, Sean, Senehi, Jessica (2008). "Conflict Analysis and Resolution as a Multidiscipline: A Work in Progress," Dennis J. D. Sandole, Sean Byrne, Ingrid Sandole-Staroste, and Jessica Senehi (eds.) *Handbook of Conflict Analysis and Resolution*. London: Routledge, pp. 1–17.

Cadavid, Amparo, Moreno Martínez, Óscar (2009). "Evaluación Cualitativa de Radio Audiencias por la Paz en el Magdalena Medio Colombiano" [Qualitative Assessment of Radio Audiences for Peace in the Magdalena Medio Region of Colombia], *Signo y Pensamiento*, 54(28): 276–299.

Caiani, Manuela, Parenti, Linda (2013). *European and American Extreme Right Groups and the Internet*. Farnham: Ashgate.

Calame, Jon, Charlesworth, Esther (2011). *Divided Cities: Belfast, Beirut, Jerusalem, Mostar, and Nicosia*. Philadelphia: University of Pennsylvania Press.

Canan-Sokullu, Ebru (2013). *Debating Security in Turkey: Challenges and Changes in the Twenty-First Century*. Boulder: Rowman & Littlefield.

Carden-Coyne, Ana (2014). "Men in Pain. Silence, Stories and Soldiers' Bodies," Paul Cornish and Nicholas J. Saunders (eds.) *Bodies in Conflict: Corporeality, Materiality, and Transformation*. London and New York: Routledge, pp. 53–65.

Carey, James W. (2009). *Communication as Culture. Essays on Media and Society*, revised edition. New York: Routledge.

Carlbaum, Sara (2011). "Reforming Education. Gendered Constructions of Future Workers," Annika Egan Sjölander and Jenny Gunnarsson Payne (eds.) *Tracking Discourses: Politics, Identity and Social Change*. Lund: Nordic Academic Press, pp. 79–111.

Carpentier, Nico (2001). "Managing audience participation," *European Journal of Communication*, 16(2): 209–232.

Carpentier, Nico (2005). "Identity, Contingency and Rigidity. The (Counter-)Hegemonic Constructions of the Identity of the Media Professional," *Journalism*, 6(2): 199–219.

Carpentier, Nico (2007). "The On-Line Community Media Database RadioSwap as a Translocal Tool to Broaden the Communicative Rhizome," *Observatorio (OBS*)*, http://obs.obercom.pt/index.php/obs/article/view/44, accessed 7 June 2016.

Carpentier, Nico (2008). "Dichotomised Discourses of War. The Construction of the Self and the Enemy in the 2003 Iraqi War," Nico Carpentier and Erik Spinoy (eds.) *Discourse Theory and Cultural Analysis. Media, Arts and Literature*. Cresskill: Hampton Press, pp. 29–54.

Carpentier, Nico (2010). "Deploying Discourse Theory. An introduction to Discourse Theory and Discourse Theoretical Analysis," Nico Carpentier, Ilija Tomanić Trivundža, Pille Pruulmann-Vengerfeldt, Ebba Sundin, Tobias Olsson, Richard Kilborn, Hannu Nieminen, and Bart Cammaerts (eds.) *Media and Communication Studies Intersections and Interventions. The Intellectual Work of ECREA's 2010 European Media and Communication Doctoral Summer School*. Tartu: Tartu University Press, pp. 251–265.

Carpentier, Nico (2011). *Media and Participation. A Site of Ideological-Democratic Struggle*. Bristol: Intellect.

Carpentier, Nico (2012). "Discursive Structures in the Network Society. A Theoretical Case Study on the Role of Immaterial Structures in Media Organisations," *Javnost—The Public*, 19(4): 25–40.

Carpentier, Nico (2013a). "The Identity Constructions of Media Professionals. Coping With Modernist Articulations of the Media Professional as Author and the Recognition of Difference," Stefan Mertens (ed.) *Perspectieven op Internationale Journalistiek* [Perspectives on International Journalism]. Gent: Academia Press, pp. 5–18.

Carpentier, Nico (2013b). "The Participatory Organization: Alternative Models for Organizational Structure and Leadership," Tobias Olsson (ed.) *Producing the Internet: Critical Perspectives of Social Media*. Göteborg: Nordicom, pp. 63–82.

Carpentier, Nico (2014a). "The Cypriot Web Radio MYCYradio as a Participatory Mélange. Overcoming Dichotomies in the Era of Web 2.0," *Sociologia e Politiche Sociali*, 17(2): 91–108.

Carpentier, Nico (2014b). "Reality Television's Construction of Ordinary People: Class-Based and Nonelitist Articulations of Ordinary People and Their Discursive Affordances," Laurie Ouellette (ed.) *A Companion to Reality Television*. Chichester: John Wiley and Sons, pp. 345–366.

Carpentier, Nico (2014c). "'Fuck the Clowns From Grease!!' Fantasies of Participation and Agency in the YouTube Comments on a Cypriot Problem Documentary," *Information, Communication & Society*, 17(8): 1001–1016.

Carpentier, Nico (2014d). "Ethics, Killing and Dying. The Discursive Struggle Between Ethics of War and Peace Models in the Cypriot Independence War of 1955–1959," Leen Van Brussel and Nico Carpentier (eds.) *The Social Construction of Death: Interdisciplinary Perspectives*. New York: Palgrave Macmillan, pp. 161–184.

Carpentier, Nico (2014e). "Beeldenstrijd in Cyprus. Het Problematische Herdenken van een Conflictueus Verleden" [Iconoclastic Controversies in Cyprus. The Problematic Re-Thinking of a Conflicteous Past], *nY*, 24: 129–168.

Carpentier, Nico (2014f). "Facing the Death of the Author. Cultural Professional's Identity Work and the Fantasies of Control," Pille Runnel and Pille Pruulmann-Vengerfeldt (eds.) *Democratising the Museum. Reflections on Participatory Technologies*. Frankfurt am Main: Peter Lang, pp. 111–130.

Carpentier, Nico (2015a). "Articulating Participation and Agonism. A Case Study on the Agonistic Re-Articulations of the Cyprus Problem in the Broadcasts of the Community Broadcaster MYCYradio," *The Cyprus Review*, 27(1): 129–153.

Carpentier, Nico (2015b). "Differentiating Between Access, Interaction and Participation," *Conjunctions*, 2(2): 7–28.

Carpentier, Nico (2016a). "Beyond the Ladder of Participation: An Analytical Toolkit for the Critical Analysis of Participatory Media Processes," *Javnost—The Public*, 23(1): 70–88.

Carpentier, Nico (2016b). "The Trinity of Decidedness, Undecidedness and Undecidability. A Post-Structuralist Exploration of the Meaning of the Decision in the Political," Leif Kramp, Nico Carpentier, Andreas Hepp, Richard Kilborn, Risto Kunelius, Hannu Nieminen, Tobias Olsson, Simone Tosoni, Ilija Tomanić Trivundža, and Pille Pruulmann-Vengerfeldt (eds.) *Politics, Civil Society and Participation: Media and Communications in a Transforming Environment*. Bremen: edition lumière, pp. 87–103.

Carpentier, Nico (2016c). "Power as Participation's Master Signifier," Darin Barney, Gabriella Coleman, Christine Ross, Jonathan Sterne, and Tamar Tembeck (eds.) *The Participatory Condition in the Digital Age*. Minneapolis: University of Minnesota Press, pp. 3–21.

Carpentier, Nico, Dahlgren, Peter, Pasquali, Francesca (2014). "The Democratic (Media) Revolution: A Parallel History of Political and Media Participation," Nico Carpentier, Kim Schrøder, and Lawrie Hallett (eds.) *Audience Transformations: Shifting Audience Positions in Late Modernity*. London: Routledge, pp. 123–141.

Carpentier, Nico, De Cleen, Benjamin (2007). "Bringing Discourse Theory Into Media Studies," *Journal of Language and Politics*, 6(2): 267–295.

Carpentier, Nico, Doudaki, Vaia (2014). "Community Media for Reconciliation. A Cypriot Case Study," *Communication, Culture and Critique*, 7(4): 415–434.

Carpentier, Nico, Doudaki, Vaia, Christidis, Yiannis (2015). "Technological Struggles in Community Media," Chris Atton (ed.) *The Routledge Companion to Alternative and Community Media*. New York: Routledge, pp. 483–493.

Carpentier, Nico, Lie, Rico, Servaes, Jan (2003). "Community Media—Muting the Democratic Media Discourse?" *Continuum*, 17(1): 51–68.

Carpentier, Nico, Resmann, Nick (2011). "The 'Ordinary' on Commercial Radio and TV. A Reception Analysis of the Subject Position of Ordinary People in the Participatory Programmes Recht van Antwoord and Zwart of Wit," *Communication Review*, 14(1): 1–23.

Carpentier, Nico, Spinoy, Erik (eds.) (2008). *Discourse Theory and Cultural Analysis. Media, Arts and Literature*. Cresskill: Hampton Press.

Carpentier, Nico, Van Brussel, Leen (2012). "On the Contingency of Death. A Discourse-Theoretical Perspective on the Construction of Death," *Critical Discourse Studies*, 9(2): 99–115.

Carpignano, Paolo, Anderson, Robin, Aronowitz, Stanley, Difazio, William (1990). "Chatter in the Age of Electronic Reproduction: Talk Show and the 'Public Mind,'" *Social Text*, 25/26: 33–55.

Carruthers, Susan Lisa (1994). *Propaganda, Publicity and Political Violence: The Presentation of Terrorism in Britain 1944–60*. Leeds: University Of Leeds, Institute of Communications Studies, http://etheses.whiterose.ac.uk/524/1/uk_bl_ethos_223442.pdf, accessed 1 January 2014.

Castells, Manuel (2010a). *The Rise of the Network Society*, second edition. Oxford: Blackwell Publishers.

Castells, Manuel (2010b). *The Power of Identity*, second edition. Oxford: Blackwell Publishers.

Castree, Noel (1995). "The Nature of Produced Nature: Materiality and Knowledge Construction in Marxism," *Antipode*, 27: 12–48.

Centeno, Miguel A., Silva, Patricio (1998). *The Politics of Expertise in Latin America*. Basingstoke: Palgrave Macmillan.

Chacko, Priya (2012). *Indian Foreign Policy: The Politics of Postcolonial Identity from 1947 to 2004*. London: Routledge.

Chandler, Daniel (2004). *Semiotics: The Basics*. New York: Routledge.

Charalambous, Giorgos, Ioannou, Gregoris (2015). "No Bridge Over Troubled Waters: The Cypriot Left in Government, 2008–2013," *Capital & Class*, 39(2): 265–286.

Charmaz, Kathy (2003). "Grounded Theory: Objectivist and Constructivist Methods," Norman K. Denzin and Yvonna S. Lincoln (eds.) *Strategies for Qualitative Inquiry*, second edition. Thousand Oaks: Sage, pp. 249–291.

Chatzipanagiotidou, Evropi (2012). "The 'Leftovers' of History. Reconsidering the 'Unofficial' History of the Left in Cyprus and the Cypriot Diaspora," Rebecca Bryant and Yiannis Papadakis (eds.) *Cyprus and the Politics of Memory. History, Community and Conflict*. London: I. B. Tauris, pp. 94–117.

Chidgey, Red, Gunnarsson Payne, Jenny, Zobl, Elke (2009). "Rumours From Around the Bloc," *Feminist Media Studies*, 9(4): 477–491.

Chourchoulis, Dionysios (2014). *The Southern Flank of NATO, 1951–1959: Military Strategy or Political Stabilization*. Lanham: Lexington.

Chrétien, Jean-Pierre (ed.) (1995). *Rwanda: Les Médias du Genocide* [Rwanda: Media of Genocide]. Paris: Karthala.

Christodoulou, Nicoletta (2014). "Oral History and Living Memory in Cyprus: Performance and Curricular Considerations," *Transnational Curriculum Inquiry*, 11(1): 30–43, http://ojs.library.ubc.ca/index.php/tci, accessed 7 June 2016.

Christophorou, Christophoros, Axt, Heinz-Jürgen, Karadag, Roy (2014). *2014 Cyprus Report*. Gütersloh: Bertelsmann Stiftung.

Christophorou, Christophoros, Şahin, Sanem, Pavlou, Synthia (2010). *Media Narratives, Politics and the Cyprus Problem*. Report 1. Oslo: Peace Research Institute Oslo (PRIO).

Clark, David B. (1973). "The Concept of Community: A Re-Examination," *Sociological Review*, 21: 397–417.

Clifford, Bob (2011). "Civil and Uncivil Society," Michael Edwards (ed.) *The Oxford Handbook of Civil Society*. Oxford: Oxford University Press, pp. 209–219.

Cobain, Ian (2012). *Cruel Britannia: A Secret History of Torture*. London: Portobello Books.

Cockburn, Cynthia (2004). *The Line: Women, Partition and the Gender Order in Cyprus*. London: Zed Books.

Cockerham, William C. (2003). "The Military Institution," Larry T. Reynolds and Nancy J. Herman-Kinney (eds.) *Handbook of Symbolic Interactionism*. Walnut Creek: Rowman Altamira, pp. 491–510.

Cohen, Anthony P. (1989). *The Symbolic Construction of Community*. London: Routledge.

Cohen, Jean L., Arato, Andrew (1992). *Civil Society and Political Theory*. London: MIT Press.

Collins, Harry, Evans, Robert (2007). *Rethinking Expertise*. Chicago and London: The University of Chicago Press.

Colman, Felicity (2014). *Film Theory: Creating a Cinematic Grammar*. New York: Columbia University Press.

Committee on Missing Persons in Cyprus (2013). *Quick Statistics: February 2013*. Nicosia: Committee on Missing Persons in Cyprus. http://www.cmp-cyprus.org/, accessed 21 July 2013.

Connolly, William E. (1995). *The Ethos of Pluralization*. Minneapolis: University of Minnesota Press.

Connor, Walker (1978). "A Nation Is a Nation, Is a State, Is an Ethnic Group Is a …," *Ethnic and Racial Studies*, 1(4): 377–400.

Constandinos, Andreas (2012). *The Cyprus Crisis. Examining the Role of the British and American Governments During 1974*. Plymouth: University of Plymouth Press.

Constantinou, Costas M., Papadakis, Yiannis (2002). "The Cypriot State(s) in Situ. Cross-Ethnic Contact and the Discourse of Recognition," Thomas Diez (ed.) *The European Union and the Cyprus Conflict: Modern Conflict, Postmodern Union*. Manchester: Manchester University Press, pp. 73–97.

Cooke, Bill, Kothari, Uma (eds.) (2001). *Participation. The New Tyranny?* London: Zed Books.

Cooper, Joel (2007). *Cognitive Dissonance: Fifty Years of a Classic Theory*. London: Sage.

Cooren, François, Brummans, Boris H. J. M., Charrieras, Damien (2008). "The Coproduction of Organizational Presence: A Study of Médecins Sans Frontières in Action," *Human Relations*, 61(10): 1339–1370.

Copeaux, Étienne (2008). "Politique et Toponymie au Nord de Chypre," Gilles de Rapper and Pierre Sintès (with Kira Kaurinkauski) (eds.) *Nommer et Classer dans les Balkans*. Athens: École Française d'Athènes, pp. 257–268.

Cornwall, Andrea (2008). "Unpacking 'Participation': Models, Meanings and Practices," *Community Development Journal*, 43: 269–283.

Cornwall, Andrea, Coelho, Vera Schattan P. (2007). "Spaces for Change? The Politics of Citizen Participation in New Democratic Arenas," Andrea Cornwall and Vera Schattan P. Coelho (eds.) *Spaces for Change? The Politics of Citizen Participation in New Democratic Arenas*. London: Zed Books, pp. 1–29.

Corum, James S. (2008). *Bad Strategies: How Major Powers Fail in Counterinsurgency*. Minneapolis: Zenith Imprint.

Couldry, Nick (2003). *Media Rituals. A Critical Approach*. London: Routledge.

Couldry, Nick (2012). *Media, Society, World: Social Theory and Digital Media Practice*. Cambridge: Polity Press.

Council of Europe (2009). *Declaration of the Committee of Ministers on the Role of Community Media in Promoting Social Cohesion and Intercultural Dialogue*. https://wcd.coe.int/ViewDoc.jsp?id=1409919, accessed 30 June 2012.

Council of the European Union (2006). *Council Regulation (EC) No 389/2006 of 27 February 2006 Establishing an Instrument of Financial Support for Encouraging the Economic Development of the Turkish Cypriot Community and Amending Council Regulation (EC) No 2667/2000 on the European Agency for Reconstruction*. Brussels: European Council. http://eur-lex.europa.eu/legal-content/EN/TXT/?uri=CELEX:32006R0389, accessed 6 June 2016.

Coyer, Kate (2011). "Community Media in a Globalized World: The Relevance and Resilience of Local Radio," Robin Mansell and Marc Raboy (eds.) *The Handbook of Global Media and Communication Policy*. Oxford: Blackwell, pp. 166–179.

Coyer, Kate, Dowmunt, Tony, Fountain, Alan (2007). *The Alternative Media Handbook*. London: Routledge.

Cresswell, Tim (1996). *In Place/Out of Place: Geography, Ideology, and Transgression*. Minneapolis: University of Minnesota Press.

Crouzet, François (1973). *Le Conflit de Chypre 1946–1959* [The Conflict of Cyprus 1946–1959]. Bruxelles: Établissements Émile Bruylant.

Cummings, Thomas, Worley, Christopher (2014). *Organization Development and Change*, tenth edition. Stamford: Cengage Learning.

Curl, John (2009). *For All The People: Uncovering the Hidden History of Cooperation, Cooperative Movements, and Communalism in America*. Oakland: PM Press.

Curtis, Devon E. A. (2000). "Broadcasting Peace: An Analysis of Local Media Post-Conflict Peacebuilding Projects in Rwanda and Bosnia," *Canadian Journal of Development Studies/Revue Canadienne d'Etudes du Développement*, 21(1): 141–166.

Cyprus Community Media Centre (CCMC) (2009). *Foundation Charter*, http://www.cypruscommunitymedia.org/images/stories/CCMCFoundationCharter.pdf, accessed 1 May 2014.

The Cyprus Oral History and Living Memory Project (2011). *The Frederick Research Centre*, http://www.Frederick. ac.cy/research/oralhistory/, accessed 1 May 2014.

Cyprus 2015 Initiative (2011). *Solving the Cyprus Problem: Hopes and Fears. Interpeace/Cyprus 2015 Initiative*, http://www.interpeace.org/resource/solving-the-cyprus-problem-hopes-and-fears/, accessed 6 June 2016.

Dahl, Robert A. (1969). "The Concept of Power," Roderick Bell, David V. Edwards, and R. Harrison Wagner (eds.) *Political Power: A Reader in Theory and Research*. New York: The Free Press, pp. 79–93.

Dahlgren, Peter (2000). "The Internet and the Democratization of Civic Culture," *Political Communication*, 17(4): 335–340.

Dahlgren, Peter (2009). *Media and Political Engagement*. New York: Cambridge University Press.

Dahlgren, Peter (2013). *The Political Web*. Basingstoke: Palgrave Macmillan.

Dakroury, Aliaa (2009). *Communication and Human Rights*. Dubuque: Kendall/Hunt Publishing.

Dalle, Matthieu (2006). "Les Radios Libres, Utopie 'Deleuzoguattarienne'" [Free Radios, the "Deleuzoguattarian" Utopia], *French Cultural Studies*, 17(1): 55–72.

D'Arcy, Jean (1969). "Direct Broadcasting Satellites and the Right to Communicate," *European Broadcasting Union Review*, 118: 14–18.

Davies, William (2012). "Ways of Owning: Towards an Economic Sociology of Privatisation," *Poetics*, 40: 167–184.

Dayan, Daniel, Katz, Elihu (2009). *Media Events: The Live Broadcasting of History*. Cambridge: Harvard University Press.

Dayıoğlu, Ali, Hatay, Mete (2015). "Cyprus," Oliver Scharbrodt, Samim Akgönül, Ahmet Alibašic, Jørgen Nielsen, and Egdunas Racius (eds.) *Yearbook of Muslims in Europe*, volume 7. Leiden: Brill, pp. 157–173.

de Certeau, Michel (1984). *The Practice of Everyday Life*. Trans. Steven Rendall. Berkeley: University of California Press.

De Cillia, Rudolf, Reisigl, Martin, Wodak, Ruth (1999). "Discursive Construction of National Identities," *Discourse & Society*, 10(2): 149–173.

De Cleen, Benjamin (2008). "Downloading as Piracy: Discourse and the Political Economy of the Recording Industry," Nico Carpentier and Erik Spinoy (eds.) *Discourse Theory and Cultural Analysis. Media, Arts and Literature*. Cresskill: Hampton Press, pp. 245–265.

De Cleen, Benjamin (2012). *The Rhetoric of the Flemish Populist Radical Right Party Vlaams Blok/Belang in a Context of Discursive Struggle: A Discourse-Theoretical Analysis*. Unpublished PhD thesis. Brussels: Vrije Universiteit Brussel.

DeFilippis, James (2004). *Unmaking Goliath: Community Control in the Face of Global Capital*. London: Routledge.

De Groot, Alexander H. (1954). "Kubros," Hamilton Alexander Rosskeen Gibb (ed.) *The Encyclopaedia of Islam*. Leiden: Brill, pp. 301–309.

De Jaegher, Hanne, Di Paolo, Ezequiel (2007). "Participatory Sense-Making. An Enactive Approach to Social Cognition," *Phenomenology and the Cognitive Sciences*, 6(4): 485–507.

DeLanda, Manuel (1996). *The Geology of Morals. A Neo-Materialist Interpretation*, http://www.t0.or.at/delanda/geology.htm, accessed 7 June 2016.

DeLanda, Manuel (2006). *A New Philosophy of Society. Assemblage Theory and Social Complexity.* London and New York: Continuum.

Delaney, Tim, Madigan, Tim (2009). *The Sociology of Sports: An Introduction.* Jefferson: McFarland.

Delanty, Gerard, Wodak, Ruth, Jones, Paul (2008). *Identity, Belonging and Migration.* Oxford: Oxford University Press.

Deleuze, Gilles (1993). *The Fold. Leibniz and the Baroque.* London: Athlone Press.

Deleuze, Gilles, Guattari, Félix (1984). *Anti-Oedipus. Capitalism and Schizophrenia.* London: Athlone Press.

Deleuze, Gilles, Guattari, Félix (1987). *A Thousand Plateaus. Capitalism and Schizophrenia.* Minneapolis: University of Minnesota Press.

Demetriou, Chares (2007). "Political Violence and Legitimation: The Episode of Colonial Cyprus," *Qualitative Sociology*, 30: 171–193.

Demetriou, Olga (2015). "Grand Ruins: Ledra Palace Hotel and the Rendering of 'Conflict' as Heritage in Cyprus," Marie Louise Stig Sørensen and Dacia Viejo-Rose (eds.) *War and Cultural Heritage. Biographies of Place.* Cambridge: Cambridge University Press, pp. 183–207.

Demmers, Jolle (2012). *Theories of Violent Conflict: An Introduction.* London: Routledge.

Der Derian, James (2001). *Virtuous War: Mapping the Military-Industrial-Media-Entertainment Network.* New York: Basic Books.

Derrida, Jacques (1988). "Signature Event Context," Jacques Derrida (ed.) *Limited Inc.* Evanston: Northwestern University Press, pp. 1–23.

Derrida, Jacques (1998). *Of Grammatology.* Baltimore: JHU Press.

Derrida, Jacques (2005). *The Politics of Friendship.* London: Verso.

Descartes, René (1985). "The Passions of the Soul", *The Philosophical Works of Descartes*, Volume 1. Trans. John Cottingham, Robert Stoothoff, and Dugald Murdoch. Cambridge: Cambridge University Press, pp. 328–404.

De Smedt, Eva (2015). *The Construction of a Media Professional Identity in Political Television Talk.* Unpublished PhD thesis. Brussel: VUB.

De Sola Pool, Ithiel (1983). *Technologies of Freedom.* Cambridge: Harvard University Press.

Deutsch, Morton (1991). "Subjective Features of Conflict Resolution. Psychological, Social and Cultural Influences," Raimo Väyrynen (ed.) *New Directions in Conflict Theory: Conflict Resolution and Conflict Transformation.* London: Sage, pp. 26–56.

Deuze, Mark (2005). "What is Journalism? Professional Identity and Ideology of Journalists Reconsidered," *Journalism*, 6(4): 442–464.

Deveaux, Monique (1999). "Agonism and Pluralism," *Philosophy & Social Criticism*, 25(4): 1–22.

Dikomitis, Lisa (2012). *Cyprus and its Places of Desire. Cultures of Displacement Among Greek and Turkish Cypriot Refugees.* London: I. B. Tauris.

Dittmar, Norbert (1976). *Sociolinguistics. A Critical Survey of Theory and Application.* London: Edward Arnold.

Dodd, Clement (1993). "Cyprus: A Historical Introduction," Clement H. Dodd (ed.) *The Political, Social, and Economic Development of Northern Cyprus.* Huntingdon: Eothen Press, pp. 1–14.

Dolphijn, Rick, van der Tuin, Iris (2012). *New Materialism: Interviews and Cartographies.* Ann Arbor: Open Humanities Press.

Donley-Reid, Linda W. (1990). "A Structuring Structure. The Swahili House," Susan Kent (ed.) *Domestic Architecture and the Use of Space. An Interdisciplinary Cross-Cultural Study*. Cambridge: Cambridge University Press, pp. 114–126.

Doob, Leonard W. (1986). "Cypriot Patriotism and Nationalism," *Journal of Conflict Resolution*, 30(2): 383–396.

Dourish, Paul (2001). *Where the Action Is*. Cambridge: MIT Press.

Dourish, Paul, Mazmanian, Melissa (2013). "Media as Material. Information Representations as Material Foundations for Organizational Practice," Paul R. Carlile, Davide Nicolini, Ann Langley, and Haridimos Tsoukas (eds.) *How Matter Matters: Objects, Artifacts, and Materiality in Organization Studies*. Oxford: Oxford University Press, pp. 92–118.

Dovey, Kim (2013). "Assembling Architecture," Helene Frichot and Stephen Loo (eds.) *Deleuze and Architecture*. Edinburgh: Edinburgh University Press, pp. 131–148.

Downing, John (with Tamara V. Ford, Geneve Gil and Laura Stein) (2001). *Radical Media. Rebellious Communication and Social Movements*. London: Sage.

Downing, John (2002). "Radical Media Projects and the Crisis of Public Media," Robin Mansell, Rohan Samarajiva, and Amy Mahan (eds.) *Networking Knowledge for Information Societies: Institutions and Interventions*. Delft: Delft University Press, pp. 320–327.

Du Gay, Paul, Hall, Stuart, Janes, Linda, Mackay, Hugh, Negus, Keith (1997). *Doing Cultural Studies. The Story of the Sony Walkman*. Milton Keynes: Open University Press.

Dunaway, David K. (2005). "Pacifica Radio and Community Broadcasting," *Journal of Radio & Audio Media*, 12(2): 240–255.

Durkheim, Émile (1991). *Professional Ethics and Civic Morals*, second edition. London: Routledge.

Durrell, Lawrence (2012). *Bitter Lemons*. New York: Open Road Integrated Media.

Eagleton, Terry (2005). "The Roots of Terror," *Red Pepper*, September 2005, http://www.redpepper.org.uk/The-roots-of-terror/, accessed 7 June 2016.

Eckstein, Susan (2001). "Community as Gift-Giving: Collectivistic Roots of Volunteerism," *American Sociological Review*, 66(6): 829–851.

Edensor, Tim (2002). *National Identity, Popular Culture and Everyday Life*. Oxford: Berg.

Edward, Mark (2008). "A (Brief) Critique of LacLau and Mouffe's Discourse Analysis," Struggleswithphilosophy.wordpress, https://struggleswithphilosophy.wordpress.com/2008/09/11/a-brief-critique-of-laclau-and-mouffes-discourse-analysis/, accessed 7 June 2016.

Efthymiou, Christos (2014). "Reflections on Bi-Communal Relations in Cyprus," *openDemocracy*, https://www.opendemocracy.net/can-europe-make-it/christos-efthymiou/reflections-on-bicommunal-relations-in-cyprus, accessed 5 June 2016.

Electricity Authority of Cyprus (2014). *Annual Report 2013*. Lefkosia: Author.

Elleström, Lars (2010). "The Modalities of Media: A Model for Understanding Intermedial Relations," Lars Elleström (ed.) *Media Borders, Multimodality and Intermediality*. New York: Springer, pp. 11–48.

Ellul, Jacques (1973). *Propaganda: The Formation of Men's Attitudes*. New York: Vintage.

Ellwood, Robert S., Alles, Gregory D. (2007). *The Encyclopedia of World Religions*. New York: Infobase Publishing.

Emerson, Michael (2013). "Fishing for Gas and More in Cypriot Waters," *Insight Turkey*, 15(1): 165–181.

Encyclopaedia Britannica (2014). *Britannica Book of the Year 2014*. Chicago: Author.

Erhürman, Heycan (2010). *Articulations of Memory in Northern Cyprus: Between Turkishness, Europeanness and Cypriotness*. Unpublished doctoral thesis. Westminster: University of Westminster.

Errejón, Íñigo, Mouffe, Chantal (2016). *Podemos. In the Name of the People*. London: Lawrence & Wishart.

Etzioni, Amitai (1961). *Complex Organisations*. New York: Holt, Rinehart and Winston.

Etzioni, Amitai (1964). *Modern Organizations*. Englewood Cliffs: Prentice Hall.

Etzioni, Amitai (1991). "The Socio-Economics of Property," *Journal of Social Behavior and Personality*, 6(6): 465–468.

European Commission (2012). *Closer to the European Union. EU Assistance to the Turkish Cypriot Community*. Brussels: Author.

European Parliament (2008). *Resolution of 25 September 2008 on Community Media in Europe* (2008/2011(INI)). http://www.europarl.europa.eu/sides/getDoc.do?type=TA&reference=P6-TA-2008-0456&language=EN, accessed 30 June 2012.

Evangelista, Matthew (1999). *Unarmed Forces: The Transnational Movement to End the Cold War*. Ithaca: Cornell University Press.

Fairbairn, Jean (2009a). "What Is it We Want to Sustain? Defining Community Media," Jean Fairbairn (ed.) *Community Media Sustainability Guide*. Arcata: Internews Network, pp. 7–11.

Fairbairn, Jean (2009b). "Business Models, Plans and Community Media," Jean Fairbairn (ed.) *Community Media Sustainability Guide*. Arcata: Internews Network, pp. 30–31.

Fairchild, Charles (2001). *Community Radio and Public Culture: Being an Examination of Media Access and Equity in the Nations of North America*. Cresskill: Hampton Press.

Fairclough, Norman, Wodak, Ruth (1997). "Critical Discourse Analysis," Teun Van Dijk (ed.) *Discourse as Social Interaction*. London: Sage, pp. 258–294.

Fairhurst, Gail T., Putnam, Linda L. (2004). "Organizations as Discursive Constructions," *Communication Theory*, 14: 5–26.

Fairhurst, Gail T., Putnam, Linda L. (2013). "Organizational Discourse Analysis," Linda L. Putnam and Dennis K. Mumby (eds.) *The Sage Handbook of Organizational Communication: Advances in Theory, Research, and Methods*. London: Sage, pp. 271–295.

Fals-Borda, Orlando, Rahman, Muhammad Anisur (1991). *Action and Knowledge. Breaking the Monopoly with Participative Action Research*. New York: Intermediate Technology/Apex.

Fararo, Thomas J., Skvoretz, John (2002). "Theoretical Integration and Generative Structuralism," Joseph Berger and Morris Zelditch, Jr. (eds.) *New Directions in Contemporary Sociological Theory*. Boulder: Rowman & Littlefield, pp. 295–316.

Farman, Jason (2013). *Mobile Interface Theory: Embodied Space and Locative Media*. New York and London: Routledge.

Faustmann, Hubert (2006). "Independence Postponed: Cyprus 1959–1960," Hubert Faustman and Nicos Peristianis (eds.) *Britain in Cyprus. Colonialism and Post-Colonialism 1878–2006*. Mannheim and Möhnsee: Bibliopolis, pp. 413–429.

Faustmann, Hubert (2008a). "Aspects of Political Culture in Cyprus," James Ker-Lindsay and Hubert Faustmann (eds.) *The Government and Politics of Cyprus*. New York: Peter Lang, pp. 17–44.

Faustmann, Hubert (2008b). "The Colonial Legacy of Division," James Ker-Lindsay and Hubert Faustmann (eds.) *The Government and Politics of Cyprus*. New York: Peter Lang, pp. 45–62.

Faustmann, Hubert, Ker-Lindsay, James (2008). "The Origins and Development of the Cyprus Issue," James Ker-Lindsay and Hubert Faustmann (eds.) *The Government and Politics of Cyprus*. New York: Peter Lang, pp. 63–82.

Featherstone, David (2011). "On Assemblage and Articulation," *Area*, 43(2): 139–142.

Feenberg, Andrew (2010). *Between Reason and Experience: Essays in Technology and Modernity*. Cambridge: MIT Press.

Festinger, Leon (1957). *A Theory of Cognitive Dissonance*. California: Stanford University Press.

Fierlbeck, Katherine (1998). *Globalizing Democracy. Power, Legitimacy and the Interpretation of Democratic Ideas*. Manchester: Manchester University Press.

Fischer, Frank (2009). *Democracy and Expertise. Reorienting Policy Inquiry*. Oxford: Oxford University Press.

Fisher, Desmond, Harms, Leroy S. (eds.) (1982). *The Right to Communicate. A New Human Right*. Dublin: Boole Press Limited.

Fisher, Kelly, Robbins, Christine Reiser (2015). "Embodied Leadership: Moving From Leader Competencies to Leaderful Practices," *Leadership*, 11(3): 281–299.

Fisher, Ronald J. (2001). "Cyprus: The Failure of Mediation and the Escalation of an Identity-Based Conflict to an Adversarial Impasse," *Journal of Peace Research*, 38(3): 307–326.

Foley, Michael W., Edwards, Bob (1996). "The Paradox of Civil Society," *Journal of Democracy*, 7(3): 38–52.

Forde, Susan (2011). *Challenging the News. The Journalism of Alternative and Community Media*. Basingstoke: Palgrave Macmillan.

Forde, Susan, Foxwell, Kerrie, Meadows, Michael (2009). *Developing Dialogues. Indigenous and Ethnic Community Broadcasting in Australia*. Bristol: Intellect.

Foucault, Michel (1972). *The Archaeology of Knowledge*. Trans. Alan Sheridan. New York: Pantheon.

Foucault, Michel (1977). *Discipline and Punish. The Birth of the Prison*. London: Tavistock.

Foucault, Michel (1978). *History of Sexuality, Part 1. An Introduction*. New York: Pantheon.

Foucher, Vincent (2011). "On the Matter (and Materiality) of the Nation: Interpreting Casamance's Unresolved Separatist Struggle," *Studies in Ethnicity and Nationalism*, 11(1): 82–103.

Fox, Nick J., Alldred, Pam (2015). "New Materialist Social Inquiry: Designs, Methods and the Research-Assemblage," *International Journal of Social Research Methodology*, 18(4): 399–414.

Fox, Nick J., Alldred, Pam (2017). *Sociology and the New Materialism: Theory, Research, Action*. London: Sage.

Fox O'Mahony, Lorna, O'Mahony, David, Hickey, Robin (2014). *Moral Rhetoric and the Criminalisation of Squatting: Vulnerable Demons?* London: Routledge.

Foxwell-Norton, Kerrie (2015). "Community and Alternative Media. Twenty-First-Century Environmental Issues," Chris Atton (ed.) *The Routledge Companion to Alternative and Community Media*. London: Routledge, pp. 389–399.

Fraser, Colin, Restrepo Estrada, Sonia (2001). *Community Radio Handbook*. Paris: United Nations Educational, Scientific and Cultural Organization.

Fraser, Nancy (1997). *Justice Interruptus*. New York: Routledge.

Freeman, Jo (1971–1973). "The Tyranny of Structurelessness" (Online Version Based on Three Previous Versions), http://www.jofreeman.com/joreen/tyranny.htm, accessed 7 June 2016.

French, David (2015). *Fighting EOKA. The British Counter-Insurgency Campaign on Cyprus, 1955–1959*. Oxford: Oxford University Press.

Fuchs, Christian (2013). *Social Media: A Critical Introduction*. London: Sage.

Fuchs, Christian, Sandoval, Marisol (2015). "The Political Economy of Capitalist and Alternative Social Media," Chris Atton (ed.) *The Routledge Companion to Alternative and Community Media*. London: Routledge, pp. 165–175.

Furby, Lita (1978). "Possession in Humans: An Exploratory Study of its Meaning and Motivation," *Social Behavior and Personality*, 6: 49–65.

Fuss, Diana (1989). *Essentially Speaking. Feminism, Nature & Difference*. London: Routledge.

Galatariotou, Catia (2012). "Truth, Memory and the Cypriot Journey Towards a New Past," Rebecca Bryant and Yiannis Papadakis (eds.) *Cyprus and the Politics of Memory: History, Community and Conflict*. London: I. B. Tauris, pp. 242–263.

Galtung, Johan (1965). "Institutionalized Conflict Resolution: A Theoretical Paradigm," *Journal of Peace Research*, 2(4): 348–397.

Galtung, Johan (1969). "Violence, Peace and Peace Research," *Journal of Peace Research*, 6(3): 167–191.

Galtung, Johan (1998). *The Peace Journalism Option*. Taplow: Conflict & Peace Forums.

Galtung, Johan (2009). *Theories of Conflict. Definitions, Dimensions, Negations, Formations*. Oslo: Transcend.

Gamble, Christopher N., Hanan, Joshua S. (2016). "Figures of Entanglement: Special Issue Introduction," *Review of Communication*, 16(4): 265–280.

Gardner, Andrew (2004). *Agency Uncovered: Archaeological Perspectives On Social Agency, Power and Being Human*. London: Routledge.

Garnham, Nicholas (1995). "Political Economy and Cultural Studies: Reconciliation or Divorce?" *Critical Studies in Mass Communication*, 12(1): 62–71.

Garton, Alison (1995). *Social Interaction and the Development of Language and Cognition*. Hove: Psychology Press.

Gastil, John (1994). "A Definition and Illustration of Democratic Leadership," *Human Relations*, 47(8): 953–975.

Gaventa, John (2004). "Towards Participatory Governance: Assessing the Transformative Abilities," Samuel Hickey and Giles Mohan (eds.) *Participation—From Tyranny to Transformation?: Exploring New Approaches to Participation in Development*. London: Zed Books, pp. 25–41.

Gaynor, Niamh, O'Brien, Anne (2011). "Because it All Begins With Talk: Community Radio as a Vital Element in Community Development," *Community Development Journal*, 47(3): 436–447.

Gee, James Paul (1990). *Social Linguistics and Literacies. Ideology in Discourses, Critical Perspectives on Literacy and Education*. Bristol: Falmer Press.

Geertz, Clifford (1993). *The Interpretation of Cultures: Selected Essays*, second edition. London: Fontana.

Geisler, Cheryl (2013). *Academic Literacy and the Nature of Expertise: Reading, Writing, and Knowing in Academic Philosophy*. London and New York: Routledge.

Genosko, Gary (2002). *Félix Guattari. An Aberrant Introduction*. London and New York: Continuum.

Gentles, Ian (2007). "The Iconography of Revolution: England 1642–1649," Ian Gentles, John Morrill, and Blair Worden (eds.) *Soldiers, Writers and Statesmen of the English Revolution*. Cambridge: Cambridge University Press, pp. 91–113.

Geras, Norman (1987). "Post-Marxism?," *New Left Review*, 163: 40–82.

Geras, Norman (1990). *Discourses of Extremity*. London: Verso.

Gibson, James J. (1979). *The Ecological Approach to Visual Perception*. New York: Psychology Press.

Giddens, Anthony (1976). *New Rules of Sociological Method: A Positive Critique of Interpretative Sociologies*. London: Basic Books.

Giddens, Anthony (1979). *Central Problems in Social Theory: Action, Structure and Contradiction in Social Analysis*. London: Macmillan Press.

Giddens, Anthony (1984). *The Constitution of Society. Outline of the Theory of Structuration*. Cambridge: Polity Press.

Giddens, Anthony (1985). *The Nation-State and Violence*. Cambridge: Polity Press.

Giddens, Anthony (1994). *Beyond Left and Right: The Future of Radical Politics*. Cambridge: Polity Press.

Giddens, Anthony (1998). *Conversations with Anthony Giddens. Making Sense of Modernity*. Interviewer Christopher Pierson. Cambridge: Polity Press.

Giddens, Anthony (2006). *Sociology*, fifth edition. Cambridge: Polity Press.

Girard, Bruce (ed.) (1992). *A Passion for Radio*. Montreal: Black Rose Books.

Girard, Bruce (2008). "Community Radio, New Technologies and Policy. Enough Watching. It's Time for Doing," *Fighting Poverty. Utilizing Community Media in a Digital Age*. Montreal, Berne and Paris: AMARC, SDC and UNESCO, pp. 61–65.

Giroux, Henry A. (2007). *University in Chains: Confronting the Military-Industrial-Academic Complex*. Boulder: Paradigm Publishers.

Gist, Noel P. (1950). "Social Interaction and Social Process," Seba Eldridge (ed.) *Fundamentals of Sociology; A Situational Analysis*. New York: Thomas Y. Crowell Company, pp. 361–380.

Glaser, Barney G., Strauss, Anselm L. (1967). *The Discovery of Grounded Theory. Strategies for Qualitative Research*. Chicago: Aldine.

Glynos, Jason, Howarth, David (2007). *Logics of Critical Explanation in Social and Political Theory*. London and New York: Routledge.

Göktepe, Cihat (2005). "The Cyprus Crisis of 1967 and Its Effects on Turkey's Foreign Relations," *Middle Eastern Studies*, 41(3): 431–444.

Gold, Raymond L. (1958). "Roles in Sociological Field Observation," *Social Forces*, 36(3): 217–223.

Gordon, Janey (2015). "The Economic Tensions Faced by Community Radio Broadcasters," Chris Atton (ed.) *The Routledge Companion to Alternative and Community Media*. London: Routledge, pp. 247–257.

Gosden, Chris (1999). *Anthropology & Archaeology. A Changing Relationship*. London: Routledge.

Graham, Stephen (2006). "Remember Fallujah: Demonising Place, Constructing Atrocity," Markus Miessen and Shumon Basar (eds.) *Did Someone Say Participate? An Atlas of Spatial Practice*. Cambridge: MIT Press, pp. 202–216.

Gramsci, Antonio (1999). *The Antonio Gramsci Reader. Selected Writings 1916–1935*. London: Lawrence and Wishart.

Green, Kathryn E., Lund, Jens Friis (2015). "The Politics of Expertise in Participatory Forestry: A Case From Tanzania," *Forest Policy and Economics*, 60: 27–34.

Grindstaff, Laura (2002). *The Money Shot: Trash, Class, and the Making of TV Talk Shows*. Chicago: University of Chicago Press.

Grivas, Georgios (1964). *The Memoirs of General Grivas*. New York: Praeger.

Grivas-Dighenis, George, General (1964). *Guerrilla Warfare and EOKA's Struggle: A Politico-Military Study*. London: Longmans.

Grosz, Elizabeth A. (1994). *Volatile Bodies: Toward a Corporeal Feminism*. Sydney: Allen & Unwin.

Guattari, Félix (1972). "Machine et Structure" [Machine and Structure], *Change*, 12 September: 54–55.

Guattari, Félix (1993). "Machinic Heterogenesis," Verena Andermatt Conley (ed.) *Rethinking Technologies*. Minneapolis: University of Minnesota Press, pp. 13–27.

Gunder, Michael, Hillier, Jean (2009). *Planning in Ten Words or Less: A Lacanian Entanglement with Spatial Planning*. Burlington: Ashgate.

Gürel, Ayla, Hatay, Mete, Yakinthou, Christalla (2012). *An Overview of Events and Perceptions. Displacement in Cyprus - Consequences of Civil and Military Strife*, 5. Oslo: Peace Research Institute Oslo (PRIO).

Güven-Lisaniler, Fatma, Rodríguez, Leopoldo (2002). "The Social and Economic Impact of EU Membership on Northern Cyprus," Thomas Diez (ed.) *The European Union and the Cyprus Conflict: Modern Conflict, Postmodern Union*. Manchester: Manchester University Press, pp. 181–202.

Hadjipavlou, Maria (2010). *Women and Change in Cyprus. Feminisms and Gender in Conflict*. London: I. B. Tauris.

Hadl, Gabriele, Dongwon, Jo (2008). "New Approaches to Our Media: General Challenges and the Korean Case," Mojca Pajnik and John D. H. Downing (eds.) *Alternative Media and the Politics of Resistance. Perspectives and Challenges*. Ljubljana: Peace Institute, pp. 81–109.

Hadland, Adrian, Thorne, Karen (2004). *The People's Voice: The Development and Current State of the South African Small Media Sector*. Cape Town: HSRC Press.

Haeckel, Stephan H. (1998). "About the Nature and Future of Interactive Marketing," *Journal of Interactive Marketing*, 12(1): 63–71.

Hájek, Roman, Carpentier, Nico (2015). "Alternative Mainstream Media in the Czech Republic: Beyond the Dichotomy of Alternative and Mainstream Media," *Continuum: Journal of Media & Cultural Studies*, 29(3): 365–382.

Hall, Stuart (1973). "The Determination of News Photographs," Stanley Cohen and Jock Young (eds.) *The Manufacture of News: Social Problems, Deviance, and the Mass Media*. London: Constable, pp. 176–190.

Hall, Stuart (1981). "Notes on Deconstructing 'The Popular,'" Raphael Samuel (ed.) *People's History and Socialist Theory*. London: Routledge and Kegan Paul, pp. 227–240.

Hall, Stuart (1996a). "On Postmodernism and Articulation," David Morley and Kuan-Hsing Chen (eds.) *Stuart Hall. Critical Dialogues in Cultural Studies*. London: Routledge, pp. 131–150.

Hall, Stuart (1996b). "The Question of Cultural Identity," Stuart Hall, David Held, Don Hubert, and Kenneth Thompson (eds.) *Modernity: An Introduction to Modern Societies*. Oxford: Blackwell, pp. 595–634.

Hall, Stuart (1997a). "The Work of Representation," Stuart Hall (ed.) *Representation. Cultural Representations and Signifying Practices*. London: Sage, pp. 13–64.

Hall, Stuart (1997b). "Culture and Power," *Radical Philosophy*, 86: 24–41, https://www.radicalphilosophy.com/interview/stuart-hall-culture-and-power, accessed 7 June 2016.

Halleck, DeeDee (2002). *Hand-Held Visions: The Impossible Possibilities of Community Media*. New York: Fordham University Press.

Hammer, Michael, Champy, James (1993). *Reengineering the Corporation: A Manifesto for Business Revolution*. New York: Harper Business.

Hanlon, Gerard (2010). "Knowledge, Risk and Beck: Misconceptions of Expertise and Risk," *Critical Perspectives on Accounting*, 21(3): 211–220.

Hannay, David (2005). *Cyprus. The Search for a Solution*. London: I. B. Tauris.

Haraway, Donna J. (1988). "Situated Knowledges: The Science Question in Feminism and the Privilege of Partial Perspective," *Feminist Studies*, 14(3): 575–599.

Haraway, Donna J. (1991). *Simians, Cyborgs and Women. The Reinvention of Nature*. New York: Routledge.

Harcup, Tony (2013). *Alternative Journalism, Alternative Voices*. London and New York: Routledge.

Harcup, Tony (2015). "Listening to the Voiceless. The Practices and Ethics of Alternative Journalism," Chris Atton (ed.) *The Routledge Companion to Alternative and Community Media*. London: Routledge, pp. 313–323.

Hardy, Cynthia, Thomas, Robyn (2015). "Discourse in a Material World," *Journal of Management Studies*, 52(5): 680–696.

Harle, Vilho (2000). *The Enemy With a Thousand Faces: The Tradition of the Other in Western Political Thought and History*. Westport: Praeger.

Hartley, John (1994). "Mass Society/Mass Society Theory," Tim O'Sullivan, John Hartley, Danny Saunders, Martin Montgomery, and John Fiske (eds.) *Key Concepts in Communication and Cultural Studies*. London: Routledge, pp. 173–174.

Hartley, John (1999). *Uses of Television*. London and New York: Routledge.

Hatay, Mete (2005). *Beyond Numbers: An Inquiry Into the Political Integration of the Turkish "Settlers" in Northern Cyprus*, report 4/2005. Oslo: Peace Research Institute Oslo (PRIO).

Hatch, Mary Jo (1997). *Organisation Theory. Modern, Symbolic, and Postmodern Perspectives*. Oxford: Oxford University Press.

Haymes, Tom (2008). "The Three-E Strategy for Overcoming Resistance to Technological Change," *Educause Quarterly*, 4: 67–69.

Heidegger, Martin (1996). *Being and Time*. Trans. Joan Stambaugh. Albany: State University of New York Press.

Hein, Hilde (1990). *The Exploratorium: The Museum as Laboratory*. Washington: Smithsonian Institution Press.

Held, David (1996). *Models of Democracy*, second edition. Cambridge and Stanford: Polity Press and Stanford University Press.

Henn, Francis (2004). *A Business of Some Heat: The United Nations Force in Cyprus Before and During the 1974 Turkish Invasion*. Barnsley: Pen & Sword.

Herda-Rapp, Ann (1998). "The Power of Informal Leadership: Women Leaders in the Civil Rights Movement," *Sociological Focus*, 31(4): 341–355.

Heritage, John (1984). *Garfinkel and Ethnomethodology*. Englewood Cliffs: Prentice-Hall.

Hermes, Joke (1998). "Cultural Citizenship and Popular Culture," Kees Brants, Joke Hermes, and Liesbeth Van Zoonen (eds.) *The Media in Question. Popular Cultures and Public Interests*. London: Sage, pp. 157–168.

Herzfeld, Michael (2003). "Localism and the Logic of Nationalistic Folklore: Cretan Reflections," *Comparative Studies in Society and History*, 45(2): 281–310.

Hesmondhalgh, David (2010). "User-Generated Content, Free Labour and the Cultural Industries," *Ephemera: Theory & Politics in Organization*, 10(3/4): 267–284.

Hewson, Chris (2005). *Local and Community Television in the United Kingdom: A New Beginning? A Policy Review*. Lincoln: University of Lincoln.

Hill, Barbara J. (1982). "An Analysis of Conflict Resolution Techniques. From Problem-Solving Workshops to Theory," *Journal of Conflict Resolution*, 26(1): 109–138.

Hill, George (2010). *A History of Cyprus. Volume 4: The Ottoman Province. The British Colony, 1571–1948*. Cambridge: Cambridge University Press.

Hintz, Arne (2007). "Civil Media at the WSIS: A New Actor in Global Communication Governance?," Bart Cammaerts and Nico Carpentier (eds.) *Reclaiming the Media. Communication Rights and Democratic Media Roles*. Bristol, UK & Portland, USA: Intellect, pp. 243–264.

Hintz, Arne (2009). *Civil Society Media and Global Governance*. Münster: LIT.

Hjarvard, Stig, Kristensen, Nete Nørgaard (2014). "When Media of a Small Nation Argue for War," *Media, War & Conflict*, 7(1): 51–69.

Hoffman, Donna, Novak, Thomas (1996). "Marketing in Hypermedia Computer-Mediated Environments: Conceptual Foundations," *Journal of Marketing*, 60: 58–60.

Hoffmeister, Frank (2006). *Legal Aspects of the Cyprus Problem: Annan Plan and EU Accession*. Leiden and Boston: Martinus Nijhoff Publishers.

Holland, Robert (1993). "Never, Never Land: British Colonial Policy and the Roots of Violence in Cyprus, 1950–54," *The Journal of Imperial and Commonwealth History*, 21(3): 148–176.

Holland, Robert (1998). *Britain and the Revolt in Cyprus, 1954–1959*. Oxford: Oxford University Press.

Holsti, Kalevi J. (1996). *The State, War, and the State of War*. Cambridge: Cambridge University Press.

Horton, John, Kraftl, Peter (2014). *Cultural Geographies. An Introduction*. London: Routledge.

House, Robert J., Hanges, Paul J., Javidan, Mansour, Dorfman, Peter W., Gupta, Vipin (2004). *Culture, Leadership, and Organizations. The GLOBE Study of 62 Societies*. London: Sage.

Howard, Michael (2001). *The Invention of Peace. Reflections on War and International Order.* Hatton Garden: Profile Books.

Howarth, David (1998). "Discourse Theory and Political Analysis," Elinor Scarbrough and Eric Tanenbaum (eds.) *Research Strategies in the Social Sciences*. Oxford: Oxford University Press, pp. 268–293.

Howarth, David (2000). *Discourse*. Buckingham, Philadelphia: Open University Press.

Howarth, David (2012). "Hegemony, Political Subjectivity, and Radical Democracy," Simon Critchley and Oliver Marchart (eds.) *Laclau: A Critical Reader*. London: Routledge, pp. 256–276.

Howarth, David, Stavrakakis, Yannis (2000). "Introducing Discourse Theory and Political Analysis," David Howarth, Aletta J. Norval, and Yannis Stavrakakis (eds.) *Discourse Theory and Political Analysis*. Manchester: Manchester University Press, pp. 1–23.

Howley, Kevin (2005). *Community Media. People, Places, and Communication Technologies*. Cambridge: Cambridge University Press.

Howley, Kevin (2010). "Civil Society and the Public Sphere," Kevin Howley (ed.) *Understanding Community Media*. London: Sage, pp. 71–77.

Huesca, Robert (2008). "Youth-Produced Radio and its Impacts. From Personal Empowerment to Political Action," Nico Carpentier and Benjamin De Cleen (eds.) *Participation and Media Production. Critical Reflections on Content Creation*. Newcastle upon Tyne: Cambridge Scholars Publishers, pp. 97–111.

Human Rights Watch (1999). *Landmine Monitor Report 1999: Toward a Mine-Free World*. New York: Author.

Hume-Cook, Geoffrey, Curtis, Thomas, Potaka, Joyce, Tangaroa Wagner, Adrian, Woods, Kirsty, Kindon, Sara (2007). "Uniting People With Place Through Participatory Video: A Ngaati Hauiti Journey," Sara Kindon, Rachel Pain, and Mike Kesby (eds.) *Participatory Action Research: Connecting People, Participation and Place*. London: Routledge, pp. 160–169.

Hunter, Ian, Laursen, John Christian, Nederman, Cary J. (2013). "Introduction," Ian Hunter, John Christian Laursen, and Cary J. Nederman (eds.) *Heresy in Transition: Transforming Ideas of Heresy in Medieval and Early Modern Europe*. Aldershot: Ashgate, pp. 1–8.

Iannello, Kathleen P. (1992). *Decisions Without Hierarchy: Feminist Interventions in Organization Theory and Practice*. New York: Routledge.

Ingold, Tim (2007). "Materials Against Materiality," *Archaeological Dialogues*, 14(1): 1–16.

Interpeace (2014). *An Innovation to Engage People in Peace Processes: Reflections From Cyprus*, http://3n589z370e6o2eata9wahfl4.wpengine.netdna-cdn.com/wp-content/uploads/2015/01/2015_01_06_PiP_Cyprus_Participatory_Polling.pdf

Isachenko, Daria (2012). *The Making of Informal States: Statebuilding in Northern Cyprus and Transdniestria*. Basingstoke: Palgrave Macmillan.

Iser, Wolfgang (1978). *The Act of Reading: A Theory of Aesthetic Response*. Baltimore and London: The Johns Hopkins University Press.

Israel, Paul (1992). *From Machine Shop to Industrial Laboratory: Telegraphy and the Changing Context of American Invention, 1830–1920*. Baltimore: Johns Hopkins University Press.

Jabri, Vivienne (1996). *Discourses on Violence: Conflict Analysis Reconsidered*. Manchester: Manchester University Press.

Jackson, Richard (2008). "Constructivism and Conflict Resolution," Jacob Bercovitch, Victor Kremenyuk, and Ira William Zartman (eds.) *The Sage Handbook of Conflict Resolution*. London: Sage, pp. 172–189.

Jacobson, David, Musyck, Bernard, Orphanides, Stelios, Webster, Craig (2009). *The Opening of Ledra Street/Lockmaci Crossing in April 2008: Reactions From Citizens and Shopkeepers*. Oslo: International Peace Research Institute, Oslo (PRIO).

Jacobson, Thomas L. (1998). "Discourse Ethics and the Right to Communicate," *Gazette*, 60(5): 395–413.

Jacobsson, Bengt, Pierre, Jon, Sundström, Göran (2015). *Governing the Embedded State: The Organizational Dimension of Governance*. Oxford: Oxford University Press.

James, William (1984). "The Moral Equivalent of War," Bruce Wilshire (ed.) *William James: The Essential Writings*. Albany: State University of New York Press, pp. 349–361.

Jankowski, Nick (1994). "International perspectives on community radio", AMARC-Europe (ed.) *One Europe – Many Voices. Democracy and Access to Communication*. Conference report AMARC-Europe Pan-European conference of community radio broadcasters, Ljubljana, Slovenia, 15–18 September 1994. Sheffield: AMARC, pp. 2–3.

Jankowski, Nick, Prehn, Ole (2002). *Community Media in the Information Age: Perspectives and Prospects*. Cresskill: Hampton Press.

Jaques, Tony (2007). *Dictionary of Battles and Sieges: F–O*. Westport: Greenwood Publishing Group.

Jarraud, Nicolas, Louise, Christopher, Filippou, Giorgos (2013). "The Cypriot Civil Society Movement: A Legitimate Player in the Peace Process?" *Journal of Peacebuilding & Development*, 8(1): 45–59.

Jencks, Charles A. (1977). *The New Paradigm in Architecture: The Language of Post-Modernism*. London: Academy Editions.

Jenkins, Henry (1992). *Textual Poachers. Television Fans & Participatory Culture*. New York & London: Routledge.

Jenkins, Henry, Carpentier, Nico (2013). "Theorizing Participatory Intensities: A Conversation About Participation and Politics," *Convergence*, 19(3): 265–286.

Jenning, Venus Easwaran (with Weidemann, Victoria) (2015). *Background Paper. Community Radio Sustainability: Policies and Funding*. Paris: United Nations Educational, Scientific and Cultural Organisation. http://www.unesco.org/new/fileadmin/MULTIMEDIA/HQ/CI/CI/pdf/Events/cms_sept15_background_paper_en.pdf, accessed 7 June 2016.

Jennings, Jeremy (1999). "Anarchism," Roger Eatwell and Anthony Wright (eds.) *Contemporary Political Ideologies*. London, New York: Pinter, pp. 131–151.

Jennings, Ronald C. (1993). *Christians and Muslims in Ottoman Cyprus and the Mediterranean World, 1571–1640*. New York: New York University Press.

Jensen, Olaf, Szejnmann, Claus-Christian W. (2008). "Preface," Olaf Jensen and Claus-Christian W. Szejnmann (eds.) *Ordinary People as Mass Murderers; Perpetrators in Comparative Perspectives*. Basingstoke: Palgrave Macmillan, pp. xi–xii.

Jiménez, Núria Reguero, Scifo, Salvatore (2010). "Community Media in the Context of European Media Policies," *Telematics and Informatics*, 27(2): 131–140.

Johnson, Mark (1987). *The Body in the Mind*. Chicago: University of Chicago Press.

Jones, Robyn L., Armour, Kathleen M., Potrac, Paul (2003). "Constructing Expert Knowledge: A Case Study of a Top-Level Professional Soccer Coach," *Sport, Education and Society*, 8(2): 213–229.

Joseph, Jonathan (2003). *Hegemony: A Realist Analysis*. London and New York: Routledge.

Junker, Buford H. (1960). *Field Work: An Introduction to the Social Sciences*. Chicago: University of Chicago Press.

Juran, Joseph M. (2003). *Juran on Leadership for Quality*. New York: Simon & Schuster.

Kadıoğlu, Ayşe (1998). "The Paradox of Turkish Nationalism and the Construction of Official Identity," Sylvia Kedourie (ed.) *Turkey: Identity, Democracy, Politics*. London: Frank Cass, pp. 177–193.

Kafka, Ben (2012). "The Administration of Things: A Genealogy," *West 86th: A Journal of Decorative Arts, Design History and Material Culture*, http://www.west86th.bgc.bard.edu/articles/the-administration-of-things.html, accessed 7 June 2016.

Kane, Anne (2000). "Narratives of Nationalism: Constructing Irish National Identity During the Land War, 1879–82," *National Identities*, 2(3): 245–264.

Kaner, Sam (2014). *Facilitator's Guide to Participatory Decision-Making*. Chichester: John Wiley and Sons.

Kang, Jin Woong (2012). "The Disciplinary Politics of Antagonistic Nationalism in Militarized South and North Korea," *Nations and Nationalism*, 18(4): 684–700.

Kansteiner, Wulf (2004). "Genealogy of a Category Mistake. A Critical Intellectual History of the Cultural Trauma Metaphor," *Rethinking History*, 8(2): 193–221.

Kant, Immanuel (1991). "On the Common Saying: 'This May Be True in Theory, but it Does Not Apply in Practice,'" Hans S. Reiss (ed.) *Kant: Political Writings*. Cambridge: Cambridge University Press, pp. 61–92.

Kant, Immanuel (2003). *To Perpetual Peace: A Philosophical Sketch*. Indianapolis and Cambridge: Hackett Publishing.

Karageorghis, Vassos (1982). *Cyprus. From the Stone Age to the Romans*. London: Thames & Hudson.

Karakasis, Vasileios P. (2014). *The Historical Background: From Antiquity to the Berlin Congress (1878)*. Report No. 6. Athens: Bridging Europe, http://www.bridgingeurope.net/uploads/8/1/7/1/8171506/bref_cyprus_report_no.6_vp.karakasis.pdf, accessed 4 February 2016.

Katsiaounis, Rolandos (1996). *Labour, Society and Politics in Cyprus During the Second Half of the Nineteenth Century*. Nicosia: Cyprus Research Center.

Katsourides, Yiannos (2014). *History of the Communist Party in Cyprus: Colonialism, Class and the Cypriot Left*. London: I. B. Tauris.

Kaup, Brent Z. (2008). "Negotiating Through Nature: The Resistant Materiality and Materiality of Resistance in Bolivia's Natural Gas Sector," *Geoforum*, 39: 1734–1742.

Kaygana, Harun (2012). *Material Objects and Everyday Nationalism in Design: The Electric Turkish Coffee Maker, Its Design and Consumption*. Unpublished PhD Thesis: University of Brighton.

Keane, John (1998). *Democracy and Civil Society*. London: University of Westminster Press.

Keeble, Richard, Tulloch, John, Zollman, Florian (eds.) (2010). *Peace Journalism, War and Conflict Resolution*. New York: Peter Lang.

Keen, Sam (1986). *Faces of the Enemy*. New York: Harper & Row.

Kellner, Douglas (1992). *The Persian Gulf TV War*. Boulder: Westview Press.

Kendall, Gavin, Wickham, Gary (1999). *Using Foucault's Methods*. London: Sage.

Kenix, Linda Jean (2011). *Alternative and Mainstream Media. The Converging Spectrum*. London: Bloomsbury.

Ker-Lindsay, James (2007). *Crisis and Conciliation: A Year of Rapprochement Between Greece and Turkey*. London: I. B. Tauris.

Ker-Lindsay, James (2009). "A History of Cyprus Peace Proposals," Andrekos Varnava and Hubert Faustmann (eds.) *Reunifying Cyprus: The Annan Plan and Beyond*. London: I. B. Tauris, pp. 11–22.

Kieffer, Charles H. (2014). "Citizen Empowerment: A Developmental Perspective," Robert E. Hess (ed.) *Studies in Empowerment: Steps Toward Understanding and Action*. London and New York: Routledge, pp. 9–35.

Kindon, Sara, Pain, Rachel, Kesby, Mike (eds.) (2007). *Participatory Action Research Approaches and Methods. Connecting People, Participation and Place*. London: Routledge.

King, Brayden G., Felin, Teppo, Whetten, David A. (2010). "Finding the Organization in Organizational Theory: A Meta-Theory of the Organization as a Social Actor," *Organization Science*, 21(1): 290–305.

King, Gretchen (2015). "Hearing Community Radio Listeners: A Storytelling Approach for Community Media Audience Research," *Participations*, 12(2): 121–146.

King, Preston, Smith, Graham M. (2013). "Introduction," Preston King and Graham M. Smith (eds.) *Friendship in Politics: Theorizing Amity in and Between States*. London: Routledge, pp. 1–7.

Kirby, Vicki (2006). *Judith Butler. Live Theory*. London and New York: Continuum.

Kittler, Friedrich A. (1990). *Discourse Networks, 1800/1900*. Trans. Michael Metteer (with Chris Cullens). Stanford: Stanford University Press.

Kizilyürek, Niyazi (2003). *Milliyetcilik Kiskacinda Kibris* [Cyprus in the Stranglehold of Nationalism]. Istanbul: Iletisim Yayinlari.

Kizilyürek, Niyazi (2005). "Modernity, Nationalism, and the Emergence of the Ethnic Conflict in Cyprus," Giampiero Bellingeri and Matthias Kappler (eds.) *Cipro Oggi*. Bologna: Casa editrice il Ponte, pp. 13–32.

Kizilyürek, Niyazi (2006). "The Turkish Cypriots From an Ottoman-Muslim Community to a National Community," Hubert Faustman and Nicos Peristianis (eds.) *Britain in Cyprus. Colonialism and Post-Colonialism 1878–2006*. Mannheim and Möhnsee: Bibliopolis, pp. 315–325.

Kizilyürek, Niyazi (2012). "Turkish-Cypriot Left. A Historical Overview," Nicos Trimikliniotis and Umut Bozkurt (eds.) *Beyond a Divided Cyprus: A State and Society in Transformation*. Basingstoke: Palgrave Macmillan, pp. 169–184.

Klepp, Ingun Grimstad, Bjerck, Mari (2014). "A Methodological Approach to the Materiality of Clothing: Wardrobe Studies," *International Journal of Social Research Methodology*, 17(4): 373–386.

klipp+klang (2009). *Integration durch Freie Radios. Die Bedeutung von mehr- und fremdsprachigen Sendungen für die Integration von Migrantinnen und Migranten.* [Integration Through Free Radio Stations. The Importance of Multi- and Foreign Language Broadcasts for the Integration of Female and Male Migrants]. Zürich: klipp & klang radiokurse, http://www.klippklang.ch, accessed 13 October 2012.

Knapp, A. Bernard (2008). *Prehistoric and Protohistoric Cyprus. Identity, Insularity, and Connectivity.* Oxford: Oxford University Press.

Knapp, A. Bernard (2013). *The Archaeology of Cyprus. From the Earliest Prehistory Through the Bronze Age.* Cambridge: Cambridge University Press.

Knapp, A. Bernard, Meskell, Lynn (1997). "Bodies of Evidence on Prehistoric Cyprus," *Cambridge Archaeological Journal*, 7(2): 183–204.

Knorr Cetina, Karin (2001). "Objectual Practice," Theodore R. Schatzki, Karin Knorr Cetina, and Eike von Savigny (eds.) *The Practice Turn in Contemporary Theory.* London and New York: Routledge, pp. 184–197.

Kolev, Valery, Koulouri, Christina (2009). *The Balkan Wars. Workbook 3.* Thessaloniki: Center for Democracy and Reconciliation in Southeast Europe (CDRSEE).

Koliopoulos, John S., Veremis, Thanos M. (2010). *Modern Greece. A History Since 1821.* Malden: Wiley-Blackwell.

Konstam, Angus (2003). *Lepanto 1571: The Greatest Naval Battle of the Renaissance.* Oxford: Osprey.

Kopytoff, Igor (1986). "The Cultural Biography of Things: Commoditization as Process," Arjun Appadurai (ed.) *The Social Life of Things. Commodities in Cultural Perspective.* Cambridge: Cambridge University Press, pp. 64–91.

Kovras, Iosif (2012). "De-Linkage Processes and Grassroots Movements in Transitional Justice," *Cooperation and Conflict*, 47(1): 88–105.

Kriesberg, Louis (2007). "The Conflict Resolution Field: Origins, Growth and Differentiation," I. William Zartman (ed.) *Peacemaking in International Conflict: Methods and Techniques.* Washington: United States Institute of Peace Press, pp. 25–60.

Kristeva, Julia (1991). *Strangers to Ourselves.* Hemel Hempstead: Harvester/Wheatsheaf.

Kropotkin, Peter (1972). *Mutual Aid: A Factor of Evolution.* New York: New York University.

Kyriakides, Klearchos A. (2014). "The Rule of Law," James Ker-Lindsay (ed.) *Resolving Cyprus: New Approaches to Conflict Resolution.* London: I. B. Tauris, pp. 158–169.

Lacan, Jacques (1977). "Desire and the Interpretation of Desire in 'Hamlet,'" *Yale French Studies*, 55/56: 11–52.

Lacan, Jacques (1979). *The Four Fundamental Concepts of Psycho-Analysis*, Jacques-Alain Miller (ed.). Trans. A. Sheridan. London: Penguin.

Lacan, Jacques (1994). *Le Séminaire de Jacques Lacan 1956–1957. Livre IV, La Relation d'Objet* [The Seminar of Jacques Lacan 1956–1957. Book IV, the Object Relation]. Paris: Éd. du Seuil.

Lacan, Jacques (1998). "The Split Between the Eye and the Gaze," *The Four Fundamental Concepts of Psychoanalysis. The Seminar of Jacques Lacan. Book XI*, Jacques-Alain Miller (ed.). New York, London: Norton, pp. 67–78.

Lacan, Jacques (1999). *The Seminar of Jacques Lacan. Book XX, On Feminine Sexuality: The Limits of Love and Knowledge: Encore 1972–1972*, Jacques-Alain Miller (ed.), Trans. with notes by Bruce Fink. New York: Norton.

Lachapelle, Paul (2008). "A Sense of Ownership in Community Development: Understanding the Potential for Participation in Community Planning Efforts," *Community Development: Journal of the Community Development Society*, 39(2): 52–59.

Lacher, Hannes, Kaymak, Erol (2005). "Transforming Identities: Beyond the Politics of Non-Settlement in North Cyprus," *Mediterranean Politics*, 10(2): 147–166.

Laclau, Ernesto (1977). *Politics and Ideology in Marxist Theory: Capitalism, Fascism, Populism*. London: New Left Books.

Laclau, Ernesto (1988). "Metaphor and Social Antagonisms," Cary Nelson and Lawrence Grossberg (eds.) *Marxism and the Interpretation of Culture*. Urbana: University of Illinois, pp. 249–257.

Laclau, Ernesto (1990a). "New Reflections on the Revolution of Our Time," Ernesto Laclau (ed.) *New Reflections on the Revolution of Our Time*. London: Verso, pp. 3–85.

Laclau, Ernesto (1990b). "Theory, Democracy and Socialism," Ernesto Laclau (ed.) *New Reflections on the Revolution of Our Time*. London: Verso, pp. 197–245.

Laclau, Ernesto (ed.) (1990c). *New Reflections on the Revolution of Our Time*. London: Verso.

Laclau, Ernesto (1996). *Emancipation(s)*. London: Verso.

Laclau, Ernesto (2000a). "Constructing Universality," Judith Butler, Ernesto Laclau, and Slavoj Žižek (eds.) *Contingency, Hegemony, Universality: Contemporary Dialogues on the Left*. London: Verso, pp. 281–307.

Laclau, Ernesto (2000b). "Identity and Hegemony: The Role of Universality in the Constitution of Political Logics," Judith Butler, Ernesto Laclau, and Slavoj Žižek (eds.) *Contingency, Hegemony, Universality: Contemporary Dialogues on the Left*. London: Verso, pp. 44–89.

Laclau, Ernesto (2005). *On Populist Reason*. London: Verso.

Laclau, Ernesto (2014). *The Rhetorical Foundations of Society*. London: Verso.

Laclau, Ernesto, Mouffe, Chantal (1985). *Hegemony and Socialist Strategy: Towards a Radical Democratic Politics*. London: Verso.

Laclau, Ernesto, Mouffe, Chantal (1990). "Post-Marxism Without Apologies," Ernesto Laclau (ed.) *New Reflections on the Revolution of Our Time*. London: Verso, pp. 97–132.

Lammers, Cornelis J. (1987). *Organisaties Vergelijkenderwijs. Ontwikkeling en Relevantie van het Sociologisch Denken over Organisaties* [Organizations in Comparison. Development and Relevance of Sociological Thought on Organizations]. Utrecht: Het Spectrum.

Landström, Catharina, Whatmore, Sarah J., Lane, Stuart N., Odoni, Nicholas A., Ward, Neil, Bradley, Susan (2011). "Coproducing Flood Risk Knowledge: Redistributing Expertise in Critical 'Participatory Modelling,'" *Environment and Planning A*, 43: 1617–1633.

Latour, Bruno (1991). "Technology is Society Made Durable," John Law (ed.) *A Sociology of Monsters. Essays on Power, Technology and Domination*. London: Routledge, pp. 103–131.

Latour, Bruno (2005). *Reassembling the Social. An Introduction to Actor-Network-Theory*. Oxford: Oxford University Press.

Laulhé Shaelou, Stéphanie (2010). *The EU and Cyprus: Principles and Strategies of Full Integration*. Leiden and Boston: Martinus Nijhoff Publishers.

Law, John (1991). "Introduction: Monsters, Machines and Sociotechnical Relations," John Law (ed.) *A Sociology of Monsters: Essays on Power, Technology and Domination*. London: Routledge, pp. 1–23.

Lederach, John Paul (2003). *The Little Book of Conflict Transformation*. Intercourse: Good Books.

Lee, Jae-Shin (2000). "Interactivity: A New Approach," paper presented at the 2000 Convention of the Association for Education in Journalism and Mass Communication, Phoenix, Arizona.

Leeuwis, Cees (2013). *Communication for Rural Innovation: Rethinking Agricultural Extension*. Chichester: John Wiley & Sons.

Lefebvre, Henri (1991). *The Production of Space*. Oxford: Blackwell.

Lemke, Jay L. (1990). *Talking Science: Language, Learning and Values*. Norwood: Ablex Publishing.

Lepik, Krista (2013). *Governmentality and Cultural Participation in Estonian Public Knowledge Institutions*. Unpublished PhD thesis. Tartu: University of Tartu Press, http://dspace.utlib.ee/dspace/bitstream/handle/10062/32240/lepik_krista_2.pdf?sequence=4, accessed 7 June 2016.

Leunissen, Jef (1986). "'Community' en 'Community Development' bij de Australische Aborigines" ['Community' and 'Community Development' With the Australian Aborigines"], Martin Van Bakel, Ad Borsboom, and Hans Dagmar (eds.), *Traditie in Verandering: Nederlandse Bijdragen aan Antropologisch onderzoek in Oceanië* [Tradition in Change: Dutch Contributions to Antropological Research in Oceania]. Leiden: DSWO Press, pp. 57–82.

Levinas, Emmanuel (1978). *Otherwise Than Being or Beyond Essence*. Trans. Alphonso Lingis. Dordrecht: Kluwer Academic Publishers.

Lewin, Kurt, Lippitt, Ronald (1938). "An Experimental Approach to the Study of Autocracy and Democracy: A Preliminary Note," *Sociometry*, 1: 292–300.

Lewin, Kurt, Lippitt, Ronald, White, Ralph K. (1939). "Patterns of Aggressive Behavior in Experimentally Created 'Social Climates,'" *Journal of Social Psychology*, 939(10): 271–279.

Lewis, Herbert S. (1974). *Leaders and Followers: Some Anthropological Perspectives*. Module in Anthropology no. 50. Reading: Addison-Wesley.

Lewis, Peter (1993). "Alternative Media in a Contemporary Social and Theoretical Context," Peter Lewis (ed.) *Alternative Media. Linking Global and Local*. Paris: United States Educational, Scientific and Cultural Organization, pp. 15–20.

Lewis, Peter (2015). "Community Media Policy," Chris Atton (ed.) *The Routledge Companion to Alternative and Community Media*. London: Routledge, pp. 179–188.

Lezaun, Javier (2007). "A Market of Opinions: The Political Epistemology of Focus Groups," *The Sociological Review*, 55: 130–151.

Lieu, Judith (2015). *Marcion and the Making of a Heretic*. Cambridge: Cambridge University Press.

Lievrouw, Leah A. (2011). *Alternative and Activist New Media*. Cambridge: Polity Press.

Lindberg, Aron, Lyytinen, Kalle (2013). "Towards a Theory of Affordance Ecologies," François-Xavier de Vaujany and Nathalie Mitiv (eds.) *Materiality and Space. Organizations, Artefacts and Practices*. Basingstoke: Palgrave Macmillan, pp. 41–61.

Lindlof, Thomas R. (1988). "Media Audiences as Interpretative Communities," *Communication Yearbook*, 11: 81–107.

Loizides, Neophytos G. (2007). "Ethnic Nationalism and Adaptation in Cyprus," *International Studies Perspectives*, 8: 172–189.

Loizides, Neophytos (2016). *Designing Peace: Cyprus and Institutional Innovations in Divided Societies*. Philadelphia: University of Pennsylvania Press.

Lomsky-Feder, Edna, Ben-Ari, Eyal (2011). "Trauma, Therapy and Responsibility: Psychology and War in Contemporary Israel," Aparna Rao, Michael Bollig, and Monika Bock (eds.) *The Practice of War: Production, Reproduction and Communication of Armed Violence*. New York: Berghahn Books, pp. 111–131.

Loucaides, Loukis G. (2007). *The European Convention on Human Rights: Collected Essays*. Leiden: Martinus Nijhoff.

Love, Serena (2013). "Architecture as Material Culture: Building Form and Materiality in the Pre-Pottery Neolithic of Anatolia and Levant," *Journal of Anthropological Archaeology*, 32: 746–758.

Luke, Harry Charles (1921). *Cyprus Under the Turks*. Oxford: Oxford University Press.

Lukes, Steven (1974). *Power: A Radical View*. Basingstoke: Palgrave Macmillan.

Lury, Celia (2011). *Consumer Culture*. Cambridge: Polity Press.

Lykke Brorson, Semine (2016). *Broadcasting Peace. A Case Study on Education for Peace, Participation and Skills Development through Radio and Community Dialogue*. Kampala: United Nations Children's Fund.

Lynch, Jake (2008). *Debates in Peace Journalism*. Sydney: Sydney University Press.

Lynch, Jake, Galtung, Johan (2010). *Reporting Conflict: New Directions in Peace Journalism*. Brisbane: Queensland University Press.

Lynch, Jake, McGoldrick, Annabel (2005). *Peace Journalism*. Stroud: Hawthorn Press.

Lyotard, Jean-Francois (1984). *The Postmodern Condition. A Report on Knowledge*. Manchester: Manchester University Press.

Lytras, Eleni, Psaltis, Charis (2011). *Formerly Mixed Villages in Cyprus: Representations of the Past, Present and Future*. Nicosia: The Association for Historical Dialogue and Research.

MacBride Commission (1980). *Many Voices, One World. Towards a New More Just and More Efficient World Information and Communication Order*. Report by the International Commission for the Study of Communication Problems. Paris and London: United Nations Educational, Scientific and Cultural Organization & Kogan Page.

Macdougall, David (1975). "Beyond Observational Cinema," Paul Hockings (ed.) *Principles of Visual Anthropology*. The Hague: Mouton, pp. 109–124.

Mackenzie, Adrian (2002). *Transductions. Bodies and Machines at Speed*. London and New York: Continuum.

Macpherson, C. B. (1966). *The Real World of Democracy*. Oxford: Oxford University Press.

Macpherson, C. B. (1973). *Democratic Theory: Essays in Retrieval*. Oxford: Clarendon Press.

Macpherson, C. B. (1977). *The Life and Times of Liberal Democracy*. Oxford: Oxford University Press.

Mallinson, William (2005). *Cyprus. A Modern History*. London: I. B. Tauris.

Manca, Luigi (1989). "Journalism, Advocacy, and a Communication Model for Democracy," Marc Raboy and Peter Bruck (eds.) *Communication For and Against Democracy*. Montréal and New York: Black Rose Books, pp. 163–173.

Mansfield, Nick (2008). *Theorizing War. From Hobbes to Badiou*. Basingstoke: Palgrave Macmillan.

Marchart, Oliver (2007). *Post-Foundational Political Thought: Political Difference in Nancy, Lefort, Badiou and Laclau*. Edinburgh: Edinburgh University Press.

Markides, Diana (2006). "Cyprus 1878–1925: Ambiguities and Uncertainties," Hubert Faustman and Nicos Peristianis (eds.) *Britain in Cyprus. Colonialism and Post-Colonialism 1878–2006*. Mannheim and Möhnsee: Bibliopolis, pp. 19–33.

Marres, Noortje (2012). *Material Participation. Technology, the Environment and Everyday Publics*. Basingstoke: Palgrave Macmillan.

Marshall, Thomas H. (1992). "Citizenship and Social Class," Thomas H. Marshall and Tom B. Bottomore (eds.) *Citizenship and Social Class*. London: Pluto Press, pp. 1–51.

Marttila, Tomas (2016). *Post-Foundational Discourse Analysis. From Political Difference to Empirical Research*. Basingstoke: Palgrave Macmillan.

Martin, Joanne (2002). *Organisational Culture. Mapping the Terrain*. Thousand Oaks: Sage.

Martin, John W. (2007). "Preface," John W. Martin (ed.) *The Concise Encyclopedia of the Structure of Materials*. Oxford: Elsevier, p. vii.

Martin, Kirsty, Wilmore, Michael (2010). "Local Voices on Community Radio: A Study of 'Our Lumbini' in Nepal," *Development in Practice*, 20(7): 866–878.

Martin, Roderick (2013). *Constructing Capitalisms: Transforming Business Systems in Central and Eastern Europe*. Oxford: Oxford University Press.

Martin-Barbero, Jesus (1993). *Communication, Culture and Hegemony. From the Media to Mediations*. Newbury Park: Sage.

Masciulli, Joseph, Molchanov, Mikhail A., Knight, W. Andy (2013). "Political Leadership in Context," Joseph Masciulli, Mikhail A. Molchanov, and W. Andy Knight (eds.) *The Ashgate Research Companion to Political Leadership*. Aldershot: Ashgate, pp. 3–27.

Maso, Ilja (1989). *Kwalitatief Onderzoek* [Qualitative Research]. Amsterdam: Boom.

Massey, Doreen (2005). *For Space*. Los Angeles: Sage.

Matoko, Firmin, Boafo, Kwame (eds.) (1998). *The United Nations System-Wide Special Initiative on Africa: Component 1c, Peace Building, Conflict Resolution and National Reconciliation: Communications for Peace Building. Conceptual Framework and Strategy*. Paris: United Nations Educational, Scientific and Cultural Organization.

Mattelart, Armand, Piemme, Jean-Marie (1983). "New Technologies, Decentralization and Public Service," Armand Mattelart and Seth Siegelaub (eds.) *Communication and Class Struggle. 2. Liberation, Socialism*. New York/Bagnolet: International General/IMMRC, pp. 413–418.

Mauss, Marcel (1966). *The Gift: Forms and Functions of Exchange in Archaic Societies*. London: Cohen & West, https://archive.org/details/giftformsfunctio00maus, accessed 7 June 2016.

Mavratsas, Caesar V. (1997). "The Ideological Contest Between Greek-Cypriot Nationalism and Cypriotism 1974–1995: Politics, Social Memory and Identity," *Ethnic and Racial Studies*, 20(4): 717–737.

McDonald, Maryon (1993). "The Construction of Difference: An Anthropological Approach to Stereotypes," Sharon Macdonald (ed.) *Inside European Identities: Ethnography in Western Europe*. Oxford: Berg, pp. 219–236.

McKinnon, Katharine (2007). "Postdevelopment, Professionalism, and the Politics of Participation," *Annals of the Association of American Geographers*, 97(4): 772–785.

McLuhan, Marshall (1964). *Understanding Media: The Extensions of Man*. New York: McGraw-Hill.

McQuail, Denis (1994). *Mass Communication Theory. An Introduction*. London: Sage.

Meadows, Michael, Forde, Susan, Ewart, Jacqui, Foxwell, Kerrie (2007). *Community Media Matters. An Audience Study of the Australian Community Broadcasting Sector*. Brisbane: Griffith University.

Mehta, Uday Singh (1999). *Liberalism and Empire: A Study in Nineteenth-Century British Liberal Thought*. Chicago: University of Chicago Press.

Melucci, Alberto (1989). *Nomads of the Present: Social Movements and Individual Needs in Contemporary Society*. Philadelphia: Temple University Press.

Merleau-Ponty, Maurice (1988). *In Praise of Philosophy and Other Essays*. Evanston: Northwestern University Press.

Merleau-Ponty, Maurice (2005). *Phenomenology of Perception*. London, New York: Routledge.

Merrill, Francis E., Eldredge, H. Wentworth (1957). *Society and Culture: An Introduction to Sociology*. Englewood Cliffs: Prentice-Hall.

Mertens, Donna M. (2008). *Transformative Research and Evaluation*. New York: Guilford Press.

Miall, Hugh, Ramsbotham, Oliver, Woodhouse, Tom (2005). *Contemporary Conflict Resolution. The Prevention Management and Transformation of Deadly Conflicts*. Cambridge: Polity Press.

Michael, Michalis N. (2013). "Kyprianos, 1810–21: An Orthodox Cleric 'Administering Politics' in an Ottoman Island," Andrekos Varnava and Michalis N. Michael (eds.) *The Archbishops of Cyprus in the Modern Age: The Changing Role of the Archbishop-Ethnarch, Their Identities and Politics*. Newcastle upon Tyne: Cambridge Scholars Publishing, pp. 41–68.

Michael, Michalis Stavrou (2011). *Resolving the Cyprus Conflict*. Basingstoke: Palgrave Macmillan.

Miessen, Markus (2010). *The Nightmare of Participation*. Berlin: Sternberg.

Miller, Toby (2011). "Cultural Citizenship," *Matrizes*, 4(2): 57–74.

Mirbagheri, Farid (2010). *Historical Dictionary of Cyprus*. Lanham: Scarecrow Press.

Mirbagheri, Farid (2014). *Cyprus and International Peacemaking 1964–1986*. London: Routledge.

Mitchell, C. R. (1981). *The Structure of International Conflict*. Basingstoke: Macmillan.

Mol, Annemarie (2002). *The Body Multiple: Ontology in Medical Practice*. Durham: Duke University Press.

Montuori, Alfonso, Purser, Ronald E. (1995). "Deconstructing the Lone Genius Myth: Toward a Contextual View of Creativity," *Journal of Humanistic Psychology*, 35(3): 69–112.

Morag, Nadav (2004). "Cyprus and the Clash of Greek and Turkish Nationalisms," *Nationalism and Ethnic Politics*, 10(4): 595–624.

Morgan, Tabitha (2010). *Sweet and Bitter Island: A History of the British in Cyprus*. London: I. B. Tauris.

Morozov, Evgeny (2011). *The Net Delusion: How Not to Liberate the World*. London: Allen Lane.

Morton, Lois W., Bitto, Ella A., Oakland, Mary J., Sand, Mary (2008). "Accessing Food Resources: Rural and Urban Patterns of Giving and Getting Food," *Agriculture & Human Values*, 25(1): 107–119.

Mouffe, Chantal (1988). "Radical Democracy: Modern or Postmodern," Andrew Ross (ed.) *Universal Abandon? The Politics of Postmodernism*. Minneapolis: University of Minnesota Press, pp. 31–45.

Mouffe, Chantal (1992a). "Citizenship and Political Identity," *October*, 61: 28–32.

Mouffe, Chantal (1992b). "Democratic Citizenship and the Political Community," Chantal Mouffe (ed.) *Dimensions of Radical Democracy*. London: Verso, pp. 225–239.

Mouffe, Chantal (1993). "Politics and the Limits of Liberalism," Chantal Mouffe (ed.) *The Return of the Political*. London: Verso, pp. 135–154.

Mouffe, Chantal (1996). "Deconstruction, Pragmatism and the Politics of Democracy," Chantal Mouffe (ed.) *Deconstruction and Pragmatism*. Simon Critchley, Jacques Derrida, Ernesto Laclau, and Richard Rorty. London and New York: Routledge, pp. 1–12.

Mouffe, Chantal (1997). *The Return of the Political*. London: Verso.

Mouffe, Chantal (1999a). "Carl Schmitt and the Paradox of Liberal Democracy," Chantal Mouffe (ed.) *The Challenge of Carl Schmitt*. London: Verso, pp. 38–53.

Mouffe, Chantal (1999b). "Deliberative Democracy or Agonistic Pluralism?" *Social Research*, 66(3): 745–758.

Mouffe, Chantal (2000). *The Democratic Paradox*. London: Verso.

Mouffe, Chantal (2005). *On the Political*. London: Routledge.

Mouffe, Chantal (2013a). *Agonistics. Thinking the World Politically*. London: Verso.

Mouffe, Chantal (2013b). "Politics and Passions. The Stakes of Democracy," James Martin (ed.) *Chantal Mouffe. Hegemony, Radical Democracy and the Political*. London: Routledge, pp. 181–190.

Moyo, Last (2014). "Converging Technologies, Converging Spaces, Converging Practices. The Shaping of Digital Cultures and Practices of Radio," Hayes Mawindi Mabweazara and Okoth Fred (eds.) *Online Journalism in Africa: Trends, Practices and Emerging Cultures*. London: Routledge, pp. 49–64.

Mueller, John E. (1973). *War, Presidents and Public Opinion*. New York: John Wiley & Sons.

Müller, Martin (2012). "Opening the Black Box of the Organization. Socio-Material Practices of Geopolitical Ordering," *Political Geography*, 31: 379–388.

Müller, Martin (2015). "Assemblages and Actor-Networks: Rethinking Socio-Material Power, Politics and Space," *Geography Compass*, 9(1): 27–41.

Mumby, Dennis K. (1988). *Communication and Power in Organizations: Discourse, Ideology and Domination*. Norwood: Ablex.

MYCYradio (2013a). *MYCYradio Foundation Charter*, http://mycyradio.eu/the-charter/, accessed 1 May 2014.

MYCYradio (2013b). *MYCYradio. Meet our Broadcasters*, http://mycyradio.eu/who-we-are/broadcasters/, accessed 12 November 2013.

Myers, Mary (2011). *Voices From Villages: Community Radio in the Developing World*. Washington: Center for International Media Assistance.

Nadel-Klein, Jane (1991). "Reweaving the Fringe: Localism, Tradition, and Representation in British Ethnography," *American Ethnologist*, 18(3): 500–517.

Navaro-Yashin, Yael (2012). *The Make-Believe Space. Affective Geography in a Postwar Polity*. Durham and London: Duke University Press.

Neeson, Jeanette M. (1996). *Commoners: Common Right, Enclosure and Social Change in England, 1700–1820*. Cambridge: Cambridge University Press.

Neil, Andrew (1996). *Full Disclosure*. London: Macmillan.

Nevzat, Altay (2005). *Nationalism Amongst the Turks of Cyprus: The First Wave*. Unpublished PhD thesis. Oulu: University of Oulu.

Newman, Oscar (1980). *Community of Interest*. Garden City: Anchor Press/Doubleday.

Nome, Martin Austvoll (2013). "When Do Commitment Problems Not Cause War? Turkey and Cyprus, 1964 versus 1974," *International Area Studies Review*, 16(1): 50–73.

Norman, Donald A. (1988). *The Design of Everyday Things*. New York: Basic Books.

Norton-Taylor, Richard (2012). "Documents Released by the National Archives Describe Incidents of Abuse by British Forces Against Opponents of Colonial Rule," *The Guardian*, 27 July 2012, http://www.theguardian.com/uk/2012/jul/27/brutality-british-forces-1950s-cyprus, accessed 1 January 2014.

Norval, Aletta J. (1996). *Deconstructing Apartheid Discourse*. London: Verso.

O'Connor, Alan (2004). *Community Radio in Bolivia—The Miners' Radio Stations*. Lewiston: The Edwin Mellen Press.

Offe, Claus (2006). "Political Institutions and Social Power. Conceptual Explorations," Ian Shapiro, Stephen Skowronek, and Daniel Galvin (eds.) *Rethinking Political Institutions: The Art of the State*. New York: NYU Press, pp. 9–31.

Ogdon, Bethany (2006). "The Psycho-Economy of Reality Television in the 'Tabloid Decade,'" David S. Escoffery (ed.) *How Real Is Reality TV? Essays on Representation and Truth*. Jefferson: McFarland, pp. 26–41.

Oi-Wan, Lam, Iam-Chong, Ip (2009). *Info Rhizome. Report on Independent Media in the Chinese-Speaking World (2008/2009)*. Hong Kong: Hong Kong In-Media.

Oksala, Johanna (2012). *Foucault, Politics, and Violence*. Evanston: Northwestern University Press.

Orme, Bill (2010). *Broadcasting in UN Blue: The Unexamined Past and Uncertain Future of Peacekeeping Radio*. Washington: Center for International Media Assistance.

Orr, David W. (1979). "U.S. Energy Policy and the Political Economy of Participation," *The Journal of Politics*, 41: 1027–1056.

Ortner, Sherry B. (1984). "Theory in Anthropology Since the Sixties," *Comparative Studies in Society and History*, 26(1): 126–166.

Osborne, Thomas, Rose, Nikolas (1999). "Do the Social Sciences Create Phenomena?: The Example of Public Opinion Research," *The British Journal of Sociology*, 50(3): 367–396.

Özkan, Behlül (2015). "Making Cyprus a National Cause in Turkey's Foreign Policy, 1948–1965," *Southeast European and Black Sea Studies*, 15(4): 541–562.

Özkirimli, Umut (2010). *Theories of Nationalism. A Critical Introduction*, second edition. Basingstoke: Palgrave Macmillan.

Padovani, Claudia, Calabrese, Andrew (eds.) (2014). *Communication Rights and Social Justice. Historical Accounts of Transnational Mobilizations*. Basingstoke: Palgrave Macmillan.

Painter, Joe (2012). "The Politics of the Neighbor," *Environment and Planning D: Society and Space*, 30: 515–533.

Pajnik, Mojca (2015). "Changing Citizenship, Practising (Alternative) Politics," Chris Atton (ed.) *The Routledge Companion to Alternative and Community Media*. London: Routledge, pp. 113–122.

Panayiotou, Andreas (2012). "Hegemony, Permissible Public Discourse and Lower Class Political Culture," Rebecca Bryant and Yiannis Papadakis (eds.) *Cyprus and the Politics of Memory: History, Community and Conflict*. London: I. B. Tauris, pp. 71–93.

Papadakis, Yiannis (1997). "Pyla: A Mixed Borderline Village Under UN Supervision in Cyprus," *International Journal on Minority and Human Rights*, 4: 353–372.

Papadakis, Yiannis (1998). "Greek Cypriot Narratives of History and Collective Identity: Nationalism as a Contested Process," *American Ethnologist*, 25(2): 149–165.

Papadakis, Yiannis (2005). *Echoes From the Dead Zone. Across the Cyprus Divide*. London and New York: I. B. Tauris.

Papadakis, Yiannis (2006). "Toward an Anthropology of Ethnic Autism," Yiannis Papadakis, Nicos Peristianis, and Gisela Welz (eds.) *Divided Cyprus: Modernity, History, and an Island in Conflict*. Bloomington: Indiana University Press, pp. 66–83.

Papallas, Andreas (2016). *Urban Rapprochement Tactics. Stitching Divided Nicosia*. Unpublished MPhil thesis. Cambridge: University of Cambridge.

Papapolyviou, Petros (1997). *Η Κύπρος και οι Βαλκανικοί Πόλεμοι. Συμβολή στην Ιστορία του Κυπριακού Εθελοντισμού* [Cyprus and the Balkan Wars. Contribution to the History of Cypriot Volunteering]. Nicosia: Cyprus Research Center.

Parla, Taha, Davison, Andrew (2004). *Corporatist Ideology in Kemalist Turkey: Progress or Order?* Syracuse: Syracuse University Press.

Pateman, Carole (1970). *Participation and Democratic Theory*. Cambridge: Cambridge University Press.

Patrick, Richard A. (1976). *Political Geography and the Cyprus Conflict, 1963–1971*. Ontario: Department of Geography, University of Waterloo.

Pavarala, Vinod (2015). "Community Radio 'Under Progress.' Resuming a Paused Revolution," *Economic & Political Weekly*, L(51): 14–17.

Pavlou, Pavlos (1993). "The Semantic Adaptation of Turkish Loanwords in the Greek Cypriotic Dialect," Irene Philippaki-Warburton, Katerina Nicolaidis, and Maria Sifianou (eds.) *Themes in Greek Linguistics: Papers From the First International Conference on Greek Linguistics, Reading, September 1993*. Amsterdam: John Benjamins, pp. 443–448.

Pels, Dick (1998). *Property and Power in Social Theory. A Study in Intellectual Rivalry*. London: Routledge.

Pericleous, Chrysostomos (2009). *Cyprus Referendum: A Divided Island and the Challenge of the Annan Plan*. London: I. B. Tauris.

Peristianis, Nicos (2006). "Cypriot Nationalism, Dual Identity, and Politics," Yiannis Papadakis, Nicos Peristianis, and Gisela Welz (eds.) *Divided Cyprus: Modernity, History, and an Island in Conflict*. Bloomington: Indiana University Press, pp. 100–120.

Pettinger, Lynne (2006). "On the Materiality of Service Work," *The Sociological Review*, 54(1): 48–65.

Pettit, Jethro, Salazar, Juan Francisco, Dagron, Alfonso Gumucio (2009). "Citizens' Media and Communication," *Development in Practice*, 19(4&5): 443–452.

Philips, Louise, Jørgensen, Marianne W. (2002). *Discourse Analysis as Theory and Method.* London: Sage.

Pick, Daniel (1993). *War Machine. The Rationalisation of Slaughter in the Modern Age*. New Haven and London: Yale University Press.

Platis, Stelios, Orphanides, Stelios, Mullen, Fiona (2006). *The Property Regime in a Cyprus Settlement. A Reassessment of the Solution Proposed Under the Annan Plan, Given the Performance of the Property Markets in Cyprus, 2003–2006*. Oslo: International Peace Research Institute (PRIO).

Plato (2000). *Timaeus*. Trans. Donald J. Zeyl. Indianapolis: Hackett Publishing.

Polat, Necati (2002). "Self-Determination, Violence, Modernity. The Case of the Turkish Cypriots," Thomas Diez (ed.) *The European Union and the Cyprus Conflict: Modern Conflict, Postmodern Union*. Manchester: Manchester University Press, pp. 98–116.

Pondy, Louis R. (1967). "Organisational Conflict: Concepts and Models," *Administrative Science Quarterly*, 12: 296–320.

Prehn, Ole (1991). "From Small Scale Utopism to Large Scale Pragmatism," Nick Jankowski, Ole Prehn, and Jan Stappers (eds.) *The People's Voice. Local Radio and Television in Europe*. London, Paris, Rome: John Libbey, pp. 247–268.

Press and Information Office for the Statistical Service (2015). *Cyprus in Figures*, 2015 edition. Nicosia: Press and Information Office.

Proudhon, Pierre-Joseph (2008). *What Is Property? An Inquiry Into the Principle of Right and of Government*. Fairford: Echo Library.

Pullen, Alison, Vachhani, Sheena (2013). "The Materiality of Leadership," *Leadership*, 9(3): 315–319.

Putnam, Robert D. (1993). *Making Democracy Work: Civic Traditions in Modern Italy*. Princeton: Princeton University Press.

Putnam, Robert D. (1995). "Bowling Alone: America's Declining Social Capital," *Journal of Democracy*, 6: 65–78.

Quinney, Richard (1975). "Who is the Victim?" Joe Hudson and Burt Galaway (eds.) *Considering the Victim. Readings in Restitution and Victim Compensation*. Springfield: Charles C. Thomas, pp. 189–197.

Rafaeli, Anat (1997). "What is an Organization? Who are the Members?" Cary L. Cooper and Susan E. Jackson (eds.) *Creating Tomorrow's Organizations. A Handbook for Future Research in Organizational Research*. New York: Wiley, pp. 121–139.

Rahman, Momin, Witz, Anne (2003). "What Really Matters? The Elusive Quality of the Material in Feminist Thought," *Feminist Theory*, 4(3): 243–261.

Ramakrishnan, Nagarajan (2007). *CR: A User's Guide to the Technology. A Guide to the Technology and Technical Parameters of Community Radio in India*. Paris: United Nations Educational, Scientific and Cultural Organization.

Ramsbotham, Oliver, Miall, Hugh, Woodhouse, Tom (2011). *Contemporary Conflict Resolution*, third edition. Oxford: Polity Press.

Rappaport, Julian (1987). "Terms of Empowerment/Exemplars of Prevention: Toward a Theory for Community Psychology," *American Journal of Community Psychology*, 15: 121–144.

Rasmussen, Mikkel Vedby (2003). "Introduction: A Time for Peace," Mikkel Vedby Rasmussen (ed.) *The West, Civil Society and the Construction of Peace*. Basingstoke: Palgrave Macmillan, pp. 1–15.

Raunig, Gerald (2007). *Art and Revolution. Transversal Activism in the Long Twentieth Century*. Los Angeles: Semiotext(e).

Rawls, John (2009). *A Theory of Justice*. Harvard: Harvard University Press.

Real, Michael R. (1996). *Exploring Media Culture: A Guide*. Thousand Oaks: Sage.

Reddaway, John (1986). *The British Connection With Cyprus Since Independence*. Oxford: University Printing House.

René, Marie-France, Antonius, Rachad (2009). "La Diversité Vue Par un Journal Communautaire Maghrébin à Montréal" [Diversity Seen By a Maghreb Community Journal in Montreal], *Global Media Journal—Canadian Edition*, 2(2): 91–111.

Renna, Thomas (1980). "Peace Education: An Historical Overview," *Peace & Change*, 6(1–2): 61–65.

Renner, Karl (1949). *The Institutions of Private Law and Their Social Functions*. London: Routledge.

Rennie, Ellie (2006). *Community Media: A Global Introduction*. Boulder: Rowman & Littlefield.

Rennie, Ellie (2011). "Community Media and the Third Sector," John D. H. Downing (ed.) *Encyclopedia of Social Movement Media*. Thousand Oaks: Sage, pp. 115–121.

Reyes Matta, Fernando (1981). "A Model for Democratic Communication," *Development Dialogue*, 2: 79–97.

Reyes Matta, Fernando (1986). "Alternative Communication, Solidarity and Development in the Face of Transnational Expansion," Rita Atwood and Emile G. McAnany (eds.) *Communication and Latin American Society. Trends in Critical Research, 1960–1985*. Madison: University of Wisconsin press, pp. 190–214.

Reznick, Jeffrey S. (2004). "Prostheses and Propaganda. Materiality and the Human Body in the Great War," Nicholas J. Saunders (ed.) *Matters of Conflict. Material Culture, Memory and the First World War*. London and New York: Routledge, pp. 51–61.

Rheingold, Howard (1993). *The Virtual Community. Homesteading on the Electronic Frontier*. Reading: Addison-Wesley.

Rhodes, R. A. W. (2000). "A Guide to the Esrc's Whitehall Programme, 1994–1999," *Public Administration*, 78(2): 251–282.

Richards, Jeffrey (1988). "National Identity in British Wartime Films," Philip M. Taylor (ed.) *Britain and the Cinema in the Second World War*. London: Macmillan, pp. 42–61.

Richmond, Oliver P. (1998). *Mediating in Cyprus: The Cypriot Communities and the United Nations*. London: Routledge.

Richmond, Oliver P. (1999). "Ethno-Nationalism, Sovereignty and Negotiating Positions in the Cyprus Conflict: Obstacles to a Settlement," *Middle Eastern Studies*, 35(3): 42–63.

Richter, Heinz A. (2006). "Benevolent Autocracy 1931–1945," Hubert Faustman and Nicos Peristianis (eds.) *Britain in Cyprus. Colonialism and Post-Colonialism 1878–2006*. Mannheim and Möhnsee: Bibliopolis, pp. 133–149.

Ritzer, George (1992). *Sociological Theory*. New York: McGraw-Hill.

Rizopoulou-Egoumenidou, Euphrosyne (2010). "Lifestyle and Social Behaviour of the Elite of Cyprus, c. 1775–1821," *Folk Life*, 48(2): 87–111.

Robertson, Toni (1997). "Cooperative Work and Lived Cognition: A Taxonomy of Embodied Actions," Proceedings of the Fifth European Conference on Computer-Supported Cooperative Work, Lancaster, UK, September 7–11, 1997. Dordrecht: Kluwer Academic Publishers, pp. 205–220.

Rock, Frances (2005). "'I've Picked Something up From a Colleague.' Language, Sharing and Communities of Practice in an Institutional Setting," David Barton and Karin Tusting (eds.) *Beyond Communities of Practice: Language Power and Social Context*. Cambridge: Cambridge University Press, pp. 77–104.

Rodríguez, Clemencia (2000). "Civil Society and Citizens' Media: Peace Architects for the New Millennium," Karin Wilkins (ed.) *Redeveloping Communication for Social Change: Theory, Practice, Power*. Boulder: Rowman & Littlefield, pp. 147–160.

Rodríguez, Clemencia (2001). *Fissures in the Mediascape: An International Study of Citizens' Media*. Cresskill: Hampton Press.

Rodríguez, Clemencia (2011). *Citizens' Media Against Armed Conflict. Disrupting Violence in Colombia*. Minneapolis: University of Minnesota Press.

Rodwell, Christine M. (1996). "An Analysis of the Concept of Empowerment," *Journal of Advanced Nursing*, 23: 305–313.

Roemer, Michael K. (2007). "Ritual Participation and Social Support in a Major Japanese Festival," *Journal for the Scientific Study of Religion*, 46(2): 185–200.

Roudometof, Victor (2009). "Le Christianisme Orthodoxe au Sein de la République de Chypre: Développement Institutionnel et Attitudes Religieuses" [Orthodox Christianity in the Republic of Cyprus: Institutional Development and Religious Attitudes], *Social Compass*, 56(1): 60–68.

Rouse, Joseph (2001). "Two Concepts of Practices," Theodore R. Schatzki, Karin Knorr Cetina, and Eike von Savigny (eds.) *The Practice Turn in Contemporary Theory*. London and New York: Routledge, pp. 198–208.

Ruming, Kristian (2009). "Following the Actors: Mobilising an Actor-Network Theory Methodology in Geography," *Australian Geographer*, 40(4): 451–469.

Safty, Adel (2011). *The Cyprus Question: Diplomacy and International Law*. Bloomington: iUniverse.

Sahlins, Marshall (1972). *Stone Age Economics*. Chicago: Aldine-Atherton.

Sahlins, Marshall (1976). *Culture and Practical Reason*. Chicago: Chicago University Press.

Said, Edward (1994). *Representations of the Intellectual. The 1993 Reith Lectures*. New York: Vintage Books.

Said, Edward (2003). *Orientalism*. London: Penguin.

Sakolsky, Ron (1998). "Introduction: Rhizomatic Radio and the Great Stampede," Ron Sakolsky and Stephen Dunifer (eds.) *Seizing the Airwaves. A Free Radio Handbook*. Oakland: AK Press, pp. 7–13.

Salerno, Melisa A., Zarankin, Andrés (2014). "Discussing the Spaces of Memory in Buenos Aires: Official Narratives and the Challenges of Site Management," Alfredo González-Ruibal and Gabriel Moshenska (eds.) *Ethics and the Archaeology of Violence*. New York: Springer, pp. 89–112.

Sandoval, Marisol, Fuchs, Christian (2010). "Towards a Critical Theory of Alternative Media," *Telematics and Informatics*, 27(2): 141–150.

Sant Cassia, Paul (2005). *Bodies of Evidence: Burial, Memory and the Recovery of Missing Persons in Cyprus*. New York: Berghahn Books.

Santana, Maaike, Carpentier, Nico (2010). "Mapping the Rhizome. Organizational and Informational Networks of Two Brussels Alternative Radio Stations," *Telematics and Informatics*, 27(2): 162–174.

Sayyid, Bobby, Zac, Lilian (1998). "Political Analysis in a World Without Foundations," Elinor Scarbrough and Eric Tanenbaum (eds.) *Research Strategies in the Social Sciences*. Oxford: Oxford University Press, pp. 249–267.

Scannell, Paddy (2001). "Authenticity and Experience," *Discourse Studies*, 3: 443–457.

Schäfer, Alexander, Schnabel, Isabel, Weder di Mauro, Beatrice (2014). *Getting to Bail-In: Effects of Creditor Participation in European Bank Restructuring*. Working Paper 08/2014. Wiesbaden: German Council of Economic Experts.

Schatzki, Theodore R. (2001). "Practice Mind-Ed Orders," Theodore R. Schatzki, Karin Knorr Cetina, and Eike von Savigny (eds.) *The Practice Turn in Contemporary Theory*. London and New York: Routledge, pp. 50–63.

Schein, Edgar (1985). *Organisational Culture and Leadership*. San Francisco: Jossey-Bass.

Schellenberg, James A. (1996). *Conflict Resolution: Theory, Research, and Practice*. New York: SUNY Press.

Schlesinger, Philip (1987). *Putting "Reality" Together*. London: Methuen.

Schmitt, Carl (1996). *The Concept of the Political*. Chicago: University of Chicago Press.

Schmitt, Carl (2004). *The Theory of the Partisan. A Commentary/Remark on the Concept of the Political*. Trans. Alfred C. Goodson. East Lansing: Michigan State University Press.

Schou, Jannick (2016). "Ernesto Laclau and Critical Media Studies: Marxism, Capitalism, and Critique," *tripleC*, 14(1): 292–311.

Schumpeter, Joseph (1976). *Capitalism, Socialism and Democracy*. London: Allen & Unwin.

Schwanecke, Christine (2015). "Filmic Modes in Literature," Gabriele Rippl (ed.) *Handbook of Intermediality: Literature—Image—Sound—Music*. Berlin and New York: Walter de Gruyter, pp. 268–286.

Scott, Julie (2013). "'Properly Playing.' Casinos, Blackjack and Cultural Intimacy in Cyprus," Rebecca Cassidy, Andrea Pisac, and Claire Loussouarn (eds.) *Qualitative Research in Gambling: Exploring the Production and Consumption of Risk*. London: Routledge, pp. 125–139.

Scott, Richard W. (1992). *Organizations. Rational, Natural and Open Systems*. Englewood Cliffs: Prentice Hall.

Seigworth, Gregory J., Gregg, Melissa (2010). "An Inventory of Shimmers," Melissa Gregg and Gregory J. Seigworth (eds.) *The Affect Theory Reader*. Durham: Duke University Press, pp. 1–25.

Selznick, Philip (1957). *Leadership in Administration. A Sociological Interpretation*. New York: Harper & Row.

Sénécal, Michel (1991). "The Alternative in Search of its Identity," Nancy Thede and Alain Ambrosi (eds.) *Video the Changing World*. Montreal: Black Rose Books, pp. 209–218.

Servaes, Jan (1998). "Human Rights, Participatory Communication and Cultural Freedom in a Global Perspective," *Journal of International Communication*, 5(1–2): 122–133.

Servaes, Jan (1999). *Communication for Development. One World, Multiple Cultures*. Cresskill: Hampton Press.

Sewell, William (1992). "A Theory of Structure: Duality, Agency, and Transformation," *American Journal of Sociology*, 98(1): 1–29.

Shapiro, Ian (1996). *Democracy's Place*. Ithaca: Cornell University Press.

Sharma, Rajendra Kumar (1996). *Fundamentals of Sociology*. New Delhi: Atlantic Publishers & Dist.

Shildrick, Margrit (with Price, Janet) (1999). "Openings on the Body," Janet Price and Margrit Shildrick (eds.) *Feminist Theory and the Body. A Reader*. New York: Routledge, pp. 1–14.

Shilling, Chris (1993). *The Body and Social Theory*. London: Sage.

Siehl, Caren, Martin, Joanne (1984). "The Role of Symbolic Management. How Can Managers Effectively Transmit Organisational Culture?" James G. Hunt, Dian-Marie Husking, Chester A. Schriesheim, and Rosemary Steward (eds.) *Leaders and Managers. International Perspectives on Managerial Behaviour and Leadership*. New York: Pergamon Press, pp. 227–239.

Siemering, William (2000). "Radio, Democracy and Development: Evolving Models of Community Radio," *Journal of Radio Studies*, 7(2): 373–378.

Sihlongonyane, Mfaniseni Fana (2015). "Empty Signifiers of Transformation in Participatory Planning and the Marginalization of Black People in South Africa," *Planning Practice & Research*, 30(1): 83–100.

Silverman, David (2006). *Interpreting Qualitative Data: Methods for Analysing Talk, Text and Interaction*, third edition. London: Sage.

Singh, J. P. (2013). "Media and Peacebuilding," Craig Zelizer (ed.) *Integrated Peacebuilding. Innovative Approaches to Transforming Conflict*. Boulder: Westview Press, pp. 225–247.

Skeggs, Beverly, Wood, Helen (2011). "Introduction: Real Class," Beverly Skeggs and Helen Wood (eds.) *Reality Television and Class*. London: Palgrave Macmillan, pp. 1–29.

Slomp, Gabriella (2013). "Carl Schmitt on Friendship: Polemics and Diagnostics," Preston King and Graham M. Smith (eds.) *Friendship in Politics: Theorizing Amity in and Between States*. London: Routledge, pp. 83–97.

Smith, Anna Marie (1999). *Laclau and Mouffe: The Radical Democratic Imaginary*. London, New York: Routledge.

Smith, Anthony D. (1995). *Nations and Nationalism in a Global Era*. Cambridge: Polity Press.

Smith, Anthony D. (1998). *Nationalism and Modernism: A Critical Survey of Recent Theories of Nations and Nationalism*. London: Routledge.

Smith, Harry (2005). "Place Identity and Participation," Cliff Hague and Paul Jenkins (eds.) *Place Identity, Participation and Planning*. London and New York: Routledge, pp. 32–45.

Soegaard, Mads (2015). "Affordances," Mads Soegaard and Rikke Friis Dam (eds.) *The Glossary of Human Computer Interaction*. Aarhus: Interaction Design Foundation, https://www.interaction-design.org/literature/book/the-glossary-of-human-computer-interaction/affordances, accessed 7 June 2016.

Solera, Gianluca (2014). "Revolutionary Contagion: Social Movements Around the Mediterranean," Larbi Sadiki (ed.) *Routledge Handbook of the Arab Spring: Rethinking Democratization*. London: Routledge, pp. 331–340.

Sophocleous, Andreas (2008). *Mass Media in Cyprus*. Nicosia: Nicocles Publishing House (In Greek).

Soteri-Proctor, Andri (2011). *Little Big Societies: Micro-Mapping of Organisations Operating Below the Radar*. Working Paper 71. Birmingham: University of Birmingham.

Soulioti, Stella (2006). *Fettered Independence. Cyprus, 1878–1964. Volume One: The Narrative*. Minnesota: University of Minnesota.

Spivak, Gayatri Chakravorty (1985). "The Rani of Sirmur: An Essay in Reading the Archives," *History and Theory*, 24(3): 247–272.

Spivak, Gayatri Chakravorty (1988). "Can the Subaltern Speak?" Cary Nelson and Lawrence Grossberg (eds.) *Marxism and the Interpretation of Culture*. Urbana and Chicago: University of Illinois Press, pp. 271–313.

Spryridakis, Constantinos (1974). *A Brief History of Cyprus*. Nicosia: Zavallis Press.

Stage, Carsten, Ingerslev, Karen (2015). "Participation as Assemblage: Introducing Assemblage as a Framework for Analysing Participatory Processes and Outcomes," *Conjunctions: Transdisciplinary Journal of Cultural Participation*, 2(2): 117–136.

Staiger, Janet (2005). *Media Reception Studies*. New York: New York University Press.

Stam, Robert (2005). *New Vocabularies in Film Semiotics*. New York: Routledge.

Starr, Amory (2005). *Global Revolt: A Guide to the Movements Against Globalization*. London and New York: Zed Books.

State Planning Organization (2015). *Ekonomik ve Sosyal Göstergeler/Economic and Social Indicators 2014*. Nicosia: Author.

Stearns, Monteagle (1992). *Entangled Allies: U.S. Policy Toward Greece, Turkey, and Cyprus*. New York: Council on Foreign Relations.

Stefanidis, Ioannis D. (1999). *Isle of Discord. Nationalism, Imperialism and the Making of the Cyprus Problem*. New York: New York University Press.

Steiner, Margreet L., Killebrew, Ann E. (eds.) (2014). *The Archaeology of the Levant. C. 8000–332 BCE*. Oxford: Oxford University Press.

Stempel, Tom (1996). *Storytellers to the Nation: A History of American Television Writing*. Syracuse: Syracuse University Press.

Sternberg, Robert J. (2000). *Practical Intelligence in Everyday Life*. Cambridge: Cambridge University Press.

Stewart, Ian, Carruthers, Susan L. (1996). "Introduction," Ian Stewart and Susan L. Carruthers (eds.) *War, Culture and the Media. Representations of the Military in 20th Century Britain*. Trowbridge: Flicks Books, pp. 1–4.

Stiegler, Bernard (1998). *Technics and Time, 1. The Fault of Epimetheus*. Stanford: Stanford University Press.

Stinchcombe, Arthur L. (1967). "Formal Organizations," Neil J. Smelser (ed.) *Sociology. An Introduction*. New York: Wiley, pp. 151–202.

Strobl, Rainer (2004). "Constructing the Victim: Theoretical Reflections and Empirical Examples," *International Review of Victimology*, 11: 295–311.

Sussman, Gerald, Estes, J. R. (2005). "KBOO Community Radio: Organizing Portland's Disorderly Possibilities," *Journal of Radio Studies*, 12(2): 223–239.

Svare, Helge (2006). *Body and Practice in Kant*. Dordrecht: Springer Science, Business Media.

Syvertsen, Trine (2001). "Ordinary People in Extraordinary Circumstances: A Study of Participants in Television Dating Games," *Media, Culture & Society*, 23(3): 319–337.

Sztompka, Piotr (2000). "Cultural Trauma. The Other Face of Social Change," *European Journal of Social Theory*, 3: 449–466.

Szuprowicz, Bohdan O. (1995). *Multimedia Networking*. New York: McGraw-Hill.

Tabing, Louie (2002). *How to Do Community Radio. A Primer for Community Radio Operators*. New Delhi: United Nations Educational, Scientific and Cultural Organization.

Talisse, Robert B. (2013). *A Pragmatist Philosophy of Democracy*. London and New York: Routledge.

Talmon, Stefan (2001). "The Cyprus Question Before the European Court of Justice," *European Journal of International Law*, 4: 727–750.

Terranova, Tiziana (2004). *Network Culture: Politics for the Information Age*. London: Pluto Press.

Tesser, Lynn (2013). *Ethnic Cleansing and the European Union: An Interdisciplinary Approach to Security, Memory and Ethnography*. Basingstoke: Palgrave Macmillan.

Themistocleous, Christiana (2015). "Digital Code-Switching Between Cypriot and Standard Greek: Performance and Identity Play Online," *International Journal of Bilingualism*, 19(3): 282–297.

Thomas, Katie Lloyd (2007). "Introduction. Architecture and Material Practices," Katie Lloyd Thomas (ed.) *Material Matters: Architecture and Material Practice*. New York: Routledge, pp. 2–12.

Thornborrow, Joanna (2001). "Authenticating Talk: Building Public Identities in Audience Participation Broadcasting," *Discourse Studies*, 3: 459–479.

Thumim, Nancy (2006). "Mediated Self-Representations: 'Ordinary People' in 'Communities,'" *Critical Studies*, 28: 225–274.

Toffler, Alvin (1980). *The Third Wave*. New York: Bantam Books.

Tönnies, Ferdinand (1963). *Community and Society*. London: Harper & Row.

Torfing, Jacob (1999). *New Theories of Discourse. Laclau, Mouffe and Žižek*. Oxford: Blackwell.

Tridish, Pete (2007). "Starting a Community Radio Station," Kate Coyer, Tony Dowmunt, and Alan Fountain (eds.) *The Alternative Media Handbook*. London: Routledge, pp. 273–274.

Trimikliniotis, Nicos (2012). "The Cyprus Problem and the Imperial Games in the Hydrocarbon Era: From a 'Place of Arms' to an Energy Player?" Nicos Trimikliniotis and Umut Bozkurt (eds.) *Beyond a Divided Cyprus: A State and Society in Transformation*. Basingstoke: Palgrave Macmillan, pp. 23–46.

Tringides, Orestis (2013). "The Role of Mass Media in the Settlement of the Cyprus Problem," Mensur Akgün (ed.) *Managing Intractable Conflicts: Lessons from Moldova and Cyprus*. Istanbul: GPoT, pp. 39–48.

TRNC (1987). *North Cyprus Almanack*. London: Rustem & Brother.

Trudgill, Peter, Schreier, Daniel (2006). "Greece and Cyprus/Griechenland und Zypern," Ulrich Ammon, Norbert Dittmar, Klaus J. Mattheier, and Peter Trudgill (eds.) *Sociolinguistics/*

Soziolinguistik: An International Handbook of the Science of Language and Society/Ein internationales Handbuch zur Wissenschaft von Sprache und Gesellschaft, second completely revised and extended edition, Volume 3. Berlin: Walter de Gruyter, pp. 1881–1888.

Tuan, Yi-Fu (1977). *Space and Place. The Perspective of Experience*. Minneapolis: University of Minnesota Press.

Tuchman, Gaye (1978). "The Symbolic Annihilation of Women by the Mass Media," Gaye Tuchman, Arlene Kaplan Daniels, and James Benet (eds.) *Hearth and Home. Images of Women in the Mass Media*. New York: Oxford University Press, pp. 3–38.

Tulloss, Janice K. (1995). "Citizen Participation in Boston's Development Policy: The Political Economy of Participation," *Urban Affairs Review*, 30(4): 514–535.

Turner, Graeme (2005). *British Cultural Studies*. London: Routledge.

Turner, Graeme (2010). *Ordinary People and the Media: The Demotic Turn*. Thousand Oaks: Sage.

Ulusoy, Kivanç (2009). "Europeanization and Political Change: The Case of Cyprus," *Turkish Studies*, 10(3): 393–408.

United Nations Development Programme—Action for Cooperation and Trust in Cyprus (2013). *Citizen Peacemaking in Cyprus. The Story of Co-Operation and Trust Across the Green Line*. Nicosia: Author.

United Nations Educational, Scientific and Cultural Organization (2002). *Mainstreaming the Culture of Peace*. Paris: Author.

United Nations Educational, Scientific and Cultural Organization (2014). *Basic Texts*, 2014 edition. Paris: Author.

United Nations Security Council (1964). *186 (1964). Resolution of 4 March 1964* [on the establishment of the UN Peace-Keeping Force in Cyprus (UNFICYP)]. New York: United Nations.

United Nations Security Council (2003). *Report of the Secretary-General on the United Nations Operation in Cyprus (for the Period From 16 November 2002 to 20 May 2003)*. New York: United Nations Security Council, http://www.un.org/Depts/DPKO/Missions/unficyp/N0337258, accessed 7 June 2016.

Uslu, Nasuh (2003). *The Cyprus Question as an Issue of Turkish Foreign Policy and Turkish-American Relations, 1959–2003*. New York: Nova.

Van Brussel, Leen (2015). *Constructing the Good Death. Representations of the Medicalised Death in Belgian Print Media and Their Audience Receptions: A Discourse-Theoretical Analysis*. Unpublished PhD thesis. Brussels: VUB.

Van Creveld, Martin (1991). *The Transformation of War*. New York: The Free Press.

van den Berghe, Pierre (2001). "Sociobiological Theory of Nationalism," Athena S. Leoussi (ed.) *Encyclopedia of Nationalism*. New Brunswick: Transaction, pp. 273–279.

Van den Hoonaard, Will C. (1997). *Working With Sensitizing Concepts. Analytical Field Research*. Thousand Oaks: Sage.

Vander Stichle, Alexander, Laermans, Rudi (2006). "Cultural Participation in Flanders. Testing the Culture Omnivore Thesis With Population Data," *Poetics*, 34: 45–56.

Van Dijk, Teun A. (1995). "Aims of Critical Discourse Analysis," *Japanese Discourse*, 1: 17–27.

Van Dijk, Teun A. (1997). *Discourse as Structure and Process*. London: Sage.

Van Dijk, Teun A. (1998). *Ideology: A Multidisciplinary Approach*. London: Sage.

Van Dyne, Linn, Pierce, Jon L. (2004). "Psychological Ownership and Feelings of Possession: Three Field Studies Predicting Employee Attitudes and Organizational Citizenship Behavior," *Journal of Organizational Behavior*, 25: 439–459.

Van Vuuren, Kitty (2008). *Participation in Australian Community Broadcasting. A Comparison of Rural, Regional and Remote Radio*. Saarbrücken: VDM.

Varela, Francisco J., Thompson, Evan, Rosen, Eleanor (1991). *The Embodied Mind*. Cambridge: MIT Press.

Varnava, Andrekos (2009). *British Imperialism in Cyprus, 1878–1915*. Manchester: Manchester University Press.

Väyrynen, Raimo (1991). "To Settle or to Transform? Perspectives on the Resolution of National and International Conflicts," Raimo Väyrynen (ed.) *New Directions in Conflict Theory: Conflict Resolution and Conflict Transformation*. London: Sage, pp. 1–25.

Vellinga, Marcel (2007). "Anthropology and the Materiality of Architecture," *American Ethnologist*, 33: 756–766.

Vitt, Lois A. (2010). "Class," George Ritzer and Michael Ryan (eds.) *The Concise Encyclopedia of Sociology*. Oxford: Oxford University Press, pp. 65–66.

Volkan, Vamik (1979). *Cyprus—War and Adaption*. Charlottesville: University of Virginia Press.

Volti, Rudi (2006). *Society and Technological Change*, fifth edition. New York: Worth.

von Clausewitz, Carl (2007). *On War*. Trans. Michael Howard and Peter Paret. Oxford: Oxford University Press.

Vujnovic, Marina, Singer, Jane, Paulussen, Steve, Heinonen, Ari, Reich, Zvi, Quandt, Thorsten, Hermida, Alfred, Domingo, David (2010). "Exploring the Political-Economic Factors of Participatory Journalism: Views of Online Journalists in 10 Countries," *Journalism Practice*, 4(3): 285–296.

Vural, Yücel, Rustemli, Ahmet (2006). "Identity Fluctuations in the Turkish Cypriot Community," *Mediterranean Politics*, 11(3): 329–348.

Wallensteen, Peter (1991). "The Resolution and Transformation of International Conflicts: A Structural Perspective," Raimo Väyrynen (ed.) *New Directions in Conflict Theory: Conflict Resolution and Conflict Transformation*. London: Sage, pp. 129–152.

Wallensteen, Peter (2009). "The Strengths and Limits of Academic Diplomacy: The Case of Bougainville," Karin Aggestam and Magnus Jerneck (eds.) *Diplomacy in Theory and Practice*. Malmö: Liber, pp. 258–281.

Wallensteen, Peter (2012). *Understanding Conflict Resolution*, third edition. Los Angeles: Sage.

Waller, James (2007). *Becoming Evil: How Ordinary People Commit Genocide and Mass Killing*, second edition. Oxford: Oxford University Press.

Waller, James (2008). "The Ordinariness of Extraordinary Evil: The Making of Perpetrators of Genocide and Mass Killing," Olaf Jensen and Claus-Christian W. Szejnmann (eds.) *Ordinary People as Mass Murderers Perpetrators in Comparative Perspectives*. Basingstoke: Palgrave Macmillan, pp. 145–164.

Walsh, David F. (1998). "Structure/Agency," Chris Jenks (ed.) *Core Sociological Dichotomies*. London: Sage, pp. 8–33.

Waltz, Mitzi (2005). *Alternative and Activist Media*. Edinburgh: Edinburgh University Press.

Walzer, Michael (1992). "The Civil Society Argument," Chantal Mouffe (ed.) *Dimensions of Radical Democracy: Pluralism, Citizenship, Community*. London: Verso, pp. 89–107.

Walzer, Michael (1998). "The Idea of Civil Society. A Path to Social Reconstruction," Eugene J. Doinne Jr. (ed.) *Community Works: The Revival of Civil Society in America*. Washington: Brookings Institution Press, pp. 124–143.

Warburton, Jeni (2006). "Volunteering in Later Life: Is it Good for Your Health?" *Voluntary Action*, 8: 3–15.

Wasko, Janet, Mosco, Vincent (eds.) (1992). *Democratic Communications in the Information Age*. Toronto & Norwood: Garamond Press & Ablex.

Way, Lyndon C. S. (2011a). "The Local News Media Impeding Solutions to the Cyprus Conflict: Competing Discourses of Nationalism in Turkish Cypriot Radio News," *Social Semiotics*, 21(1): 15–31.

Way, Lyndon C. S. (2011b). "The Undemocratic Role of Turkish Cypriot Radio News in the Cyprus Conflict," *Critical Approaches to Discourse Analysis Across Disciplines*, 5(1): 45–61.

Weber, Max (1947). *The Theory of Social and Economic Organization*. New York: Free Press.

Weber, Max (1991). *From Max Weber: Essays in Sociology*. New York: Psychology Press.

Webster, Craig (2005). "Division or Unification in Cyprus? The Role of Demographics, Attitudes and Party Inclination on Greek Cypriot Preferences for a Solution to the Cyprus Problem," *Ethnopolitics*, 4(3): 299–309.

Wegerich, Kai, Warner, Jeroen (2004). *The Politics of Water: A Survey*. London: Routledge.

Wenger, Etienne (1999). *Communities of Practice: Learning, Meaning and Identity*. Cambridge: Cambridge University Press.

Wenman, Mark Anthony (2003). "Laclau or Mouffe? Splitting the Difference," *Philosophy Social Criticism*, 29(5): 581–606.

Wester, Fred (1987). *Strategieën Voor Kwalitatief Onderzoek* [Strategies for Qualitative Research]. Muiderberg: Couthinho.

Wester, Fred (1995). "Inhoudsanalyse als Kwalitatief-Interpreterende Werkwijze" [Content Analysis as a Qualitative-Interpretative Method], Harry Hüttner, Karsten Renckstorf, and Fred Wester (eds.) *Onderzoekstypen in de Communicatiewetenschap* [Research Types in Communication Science]. Houten/Diegem: Bohn Stafleur Van Loghum, pp. 624–649.

White, Ralph K., Lippitt, Ronald (1960). *Autocracy and Democracy: An Experimental Inquiry*. New York: Harper & Brothers.

Williams, Bernard (1996). "Toleration: An Impossible Virtue?" David Heyd (ed.) *Toleration. An Elusive Virtue*. Princeton: Princeton University Press, pp. 18–27.

Williams, Colin C. (2014). "Non-Commodified Labour," Martin Parker, George Cheney, Valérie Fournier, and Chris Land (eds.) *The Routledge Companion to Alternative Organization*. London: Routledge, pp. 103–119.

Williams, Raymond (1977). *Marxism and Literature*. Oxford: Oxford University Press.

Williams, Raymond (1981). *Keywords: A Vocabulary of Culture and Society*. London: Flamingo.

Wilpert, Bernhard (1991). "Property, Ownership, and Participation: On the Growing Contradictions Between Legal and Psychological Concepts," Raymond Russell and Veljko Rus (eds.) *International Handbook of Participation in Organizations (2), Ownership and Participation*. Oxford: Oxford University Press, pp. 149–164.

Wilson, Ross J. (2012). *Landscapes of the Western Front: Materiality During the Great War*. London and New York: Routledge.

Wodak, Ruth (2013). "Recontextualization and the Transformation of Meanings: A Critical Discourse Analysis of Decision Making in EU Meetings About Employment Policies," Srikant Sarangi and Malcolm Coulthard (eds.) *Discourse and Social Life*. London: Routledge, pp. 185–206.

Wodiczko, Krzysztof (2012). *The Abolition of War*. London: Black Dog.

Woodward, Rachel (2011). *Military Geographies*. Chichester: John Wiley & Sons.

World Health Organization (2002). *World Report on Violence and Health: Summary*. Geneva: World Health Organization.

Wray, Stefan (1998). *Rhizomes, Nomads, and Resistant Internet Use*, http://www.thing.net/~rdom/ecd/RhizNom.html, accessed 7 June 2016.

Yakinthou, Christalla (2009). "Consociational Democracy and Cyprus: The House that Annan Built?" Andrekos Varnava and Hubert Faustmann (eds.) *Reunifying Cyprus. The Annan Plan and Beyond*. London: I. B. Tauris, pp. 25–39.

Yeşilada, Birol (2009). "Islam and the Turkish Cypriots," *Social Compass*, 56(1): 49–59.

Yiangou, Anastasia (2012). *Cyprus in World War II: Politics and Conflict in the Eastern Mediterranean*. London: I. B. Tauris.

Yiannopoulou, Effie (2012). "Globality, the Totalitarian Mass and National Belonging," Ruth Parkin-Gounelas (ed.) *The Psychology and Politics of the Collective: Groups, Crowds, and Mass Identifications*. London: Routledge, pp. 121–135.

Ytreberg, Espen (2004). "Formatting Participation Within Broadcast Media Production," *Media, Culture & Society*, 26(5): 677–692.

Zembylas, Michalinos (2015). *Emotion and Traumatic Conflict: Reclaiming Healing in Education*. Oxford: Oxford University Press.

Zembylas, Michalinos, Charalambous, Constadina, Charalambous, Panayiota (2016). *Peace Education in a Conflict-Affected Society*. Cambridge: Cambridge University Press.

Zenios, Stavros A. (2013). "The Cyprus Debt: Perfect Crisis and a Way Forward," *Cyprus Economic Policy Review*, 7(1): 3–45.

Zertal, Idith (1998). *From Catastrophe to Power: Holocaust Survivors and the Emergence of Israel*. Berkeley: University of California Press.

Žižek, Slavoj (1993). *Tarrying With the Negative: Kant, Hegel, and the Critique of Ideology*. Durham and London: Duke University Press.

Žižek, Slavoj (1995). *The Sublime Object of Ideology*. London: Verso.

Žižek, Slavoj (2008). *Violence. Six Sideways Reflections*. New York: Picador.

Žižek, Slavoj (2014). *Event: A Philosophical Journey Through a Concept*. New York: Melville House.

INDEX

A

B

C

D

E

H

K

L

M

N

O

P

Q

R

S

T

U